10/23

TED SHACKLEY

AND THE

CIA'S

CRUSADES

David Corn

BLOND GHOST

Simon & Schuster

New York London Toronto

Sydney Tokyo Singapore

SIMON & SCHUSTER
Rockefeller Center
1230 Avenue of the Americas
New York, New York 10020

Designed by Karolina Harris
Manufactured in the United States of America

1   3   5   7   9   10   8   6   4   2

Library of Congress Cataloging-in-Publication Data
Corn, David.
Blond Ghost : Ted Shackley and the CIA's crusades / David Corn.
p.   cm.
Includes bibliographical references (p.   ) and index.
1. Shackley, Ted, 1927–   .   2. Spies—United States—Biography.   3. Intelligence service—
United States.   4. United States. Central Intelligence Agency—Biography.   I. Title.
E839.8.S53C67   1994
327.12′73′092—dc20
[B]   94-21932   CIP
ISBN 0-671-69525-8

For my parents

CONTENTS

Every thing secret degenerates . . .
nothing is safe that does not show
how it can bear discussion and publicity.

—LORD ACTON

NOTE TO THE READER

THE term "denied area" is used by intelligence professionals to describe a region that exists beyond the range of the normal powers of observation. It is unfriendly and closely guarded territory, where an outsider cannot move freely, cannot readily learn what is happening. It is, in the lingo of the spy, hard to penetrate.

For journalists, historians, and the American public, the Central Intelligence Agency is a denied area. Since it was established in 1947, the CIA has conducted practically all of its business in secret. This is especially true for the clandestine service of the Agency, which has been responsible for both espionage (the collection of intelligence related to foreigners and their governments) and covert actions, including coups, assassination efforts, drug experiments, election-rigging, political bribes, and propaganda campaigns. All this work is highly classified, and the names of American intelligence officers who carry out these activities are largely unknown. In the rare instances when covert projects and officers do come to the public's attention, only slices of the full story are disclosed.

This book covers a particular patch of this denied area: the career of a single officer of the clandestine service, Theodore G. Shackley. He spent twenty-eight years in the Agency, serving on the front lines of the Cold War and rising through the Directorate of Plans, the official and euphemistic name for the clandestine service for much of that period. (Today it is called the Directorate of Operations.) His career embodies both elements of the cloak-and-dagger business: he ran espionage operations, recruiting agents and trying to infiltrate the Soviet bloc, and he managed large paramilitary covert actions—or, perhaps more accurately, small secret wars.

Ted Shackley, like most CIA people, was no James Bond. He was a manager and, in that sense, a representative of a certain breed of intelligence officer, an intellcrat. He made decisions and participated in actions with life-and-death consequences, but usually from behind a desk. For many CIA employees during the Cold War, the real drama in the intelligence business did not come from face-to-face confrontations with an armed KGB officer. It was found in the office—in headquarters or a base overseas—where a U.S. government employee decided which foreign national would be enticed to become a spy, how to handle a defector, where to land a sabotage team, what village or area should be targeted for bombing. Shackley was a government bureaucrat who did all this.

He was an organization man, a spy in a gray flannel suit. Through decades of the Cold War, Shackley took orders that came from the White House and the CIA's top command and turned them into reality. People like Shackley were the heart and soul of the Agency, the ones who saluted sharply and made concrete the abstractions of the Cold War, the people who guaranteed that the dirty work got done. The history of Ted Shackley is that of both the Cold War writ small and the CIA. His career provides a window to the murky clandestine world and all the dilemmas that exist within it: the clash between democracy and secrecy, the conflict between espionage and covert action, the relationship of deceitful means to geopolitical ends. By examining Shackley's career, one can obtain a rare view of what life was truly like within the Company during that era and evaluate the CIA's actions in the tense years of the Cold War.

Because Shackley spent most of his adult life enshrouded by mystery, this is not a typical biography. As is true of some of the better spies, he was not a colorful man. Moving up through the ranks of the CIA, Shackley did not leave behind a series of striking anecdotes. His association with several controversial, sometimes scandalous episodes can be found in the scanty public record of the Agency's history, but his fingerprints are often blurred. In many instances, the effects of his actions and decisions can be discerned more readily than the specifics of the actions themselves.

Shackley can best be described and measured by what he wrought. Those agents and officers following his orders were extensions of Shackley. By examining their deeds and the consequences, one can acquire insights into the elusive, secretive Ted Shackley and his covert community.

Shackley declined to cooperate fully in the writing of this book. After two years of refusing to meet with me, he finally consented to a one-time-only interview. But I interviewed more than 250 persons for this book. Over 100 of them were former CIA officers, each of whom once signed a secrecy oath pledging not to reveal Agency information. Some spoke on the record, but many discussed Shackley and their own CIA pasts only on the condition they not be quoted by name. It is unfortunate whenever any statement in a book is not directly attributed to a fully identified source, but employing unnamed sources is the only way one can write thoroughly about the CIA. Whenever possible, I have tried to note the position held by an unnamed source, so the reader can better evaluate the information the source provided. Others interviewed for this book included former U.S. government officials who worked with Shackley, foreign officials who came into contact with him, government investigators who probed his activities, and friends and relatives of his. And tens of thousands of documents—congressional reports, U.S. government materials released under the Freedom of Information Act, court records, State Department cables, Agency memoranda—were reviewed. These include scores of memos and cables written by Shackley. There is not an expansive public paper trail specifically on Shackley, but some of his actions are documented in records that have seeped out of the covert world.

Composing a coherent portrait of the CIA's clandestine service through the career of one of its most prominent officials is like creating a mosaic. One can collect a great many pieces, place them together, and a picture emerges. But both the author and the reader must keep in mind that there are pieces missing—and that we know neither how many they are nor what stories they hold.

CHAPTER ONE

A SUBSTANTIAL MYSTERY

TED SHACKLEY was furious. Sitting in a Capitol Hill conference room on the hot and humid morning of September 15, 1987, he stared at the young, upstart lawyers across the table from him. The atmosphere was tense. Shackley let his exasperation show. What did these busybodies want of him? They had slapped him with five subpoenas listing the names of dozens of individuals and businesses. Shackley had turned over all the information that he possessed regarding these names. And now the congressional investigators had a long list of official questions for him. They also had a host of unofficial questions, for the man before them had spent nearly thirty years in the dark world of the Central Intelligence Agency and was one of that elite group of civil servants to reach the highest echelons of the Agency. At the table was someone who had recruited spies and sent them behind the Iron Curtain, who had directed covert wars around the globe, who had plotted worldwide political intrigue, who knew some of the most precious secrets of the United States. In Miami, in Laos, and in Vietnam, he had directed the Agency's most controversial affairs. And when the secrets finally began to spill, his name was linked to the seamiest aspects of intelligence: collusion with drug-runners, the netherworld of rogue arms dealers, and assassinations.

Shackley's life was a tale of the CIA and the Cold War. He represented that clandestine portion of the American government that rarely is exposed to public view. Moreover, Shackley was, to his own chagrin, one of the few CIA officers to obtain a status approaching public notoriety. Observers of this secret world knew him by reputation: a secretive, ruthless, ambitious, dedicated, powerful Company man. Along the way, he even had picked up a melodramatic nickname, one he could not stand: the Blond Ghost.

In the eight years since his retirement from the CIA in 1979, Shackley had been a target of government lawyers, prosecutors, and journalists curious about his role in intelligence-related scandals. He was also one of twenty-nine persons named as defendants in a much-publicized lawsuit filed by the Christic Institute, a liberal, public-interest legal group that alleged Shackley and others masterminded a global conspiracy involving drug-trafficking, gunrunning, and political assassinations. Now the Iran-Contra scandal was forcing Shackley, who preferred to keep the details of his life private, into the harsh glare of public scrutiny. He had devoted nearly three decades to serving his country, to fighting the Cold War. After all that, he simply asked to be left alone so he could pursue in private his post-Agency career as a businessman, one who put his government experience to lucrative use by, among other things, collecting intelligence for international corporations, including a mysterious oil venture. But the desire for anonymity would go unsatisfied.

A few minutes earlier, Shackley had arrived with his own lawyer at the Hart Senate Office Building. A square-jawed man with light hair, a pale complexion, and a solid build, Shackley, sixty years old, wore a dark business suit and glasses. He looked like a corporate executive, perhaps on his way to lobby a senator.

Shackley's destination, the ninth floor, was a tightly secured portion of the building. Only one set of elevators reached that floor. Once out of the elevator, visitors passed armed guards. The walls surrounding the ninth floor were reinforced to render them impenetrable to eavesdropping devices that might be deployed by enemies of the United States.

In this suite of guarded offices, the mood was frenetic. Dozens of Senate staffers and lawyers were hurriedly conducting an investigation of the Iran-Contra affair. The scandal was composed of two overlapping secret operations: the White House–approved arms deal with Iran designed, in part, to free American hostages held in the Middle East, and the covert network run by Colonel Oliver North that, in defiance of Congress, was supplying weapons to the Contra rebels fighting the Marxist Sandinista government of Nicaragua. The two projects shared much of the same cast, and $3.8 million of the profits raised by the Iran initiative had been diverted to the Contras.

Committees in the Senate and House of Representatives had been trying to unravel the various aspects of the Iran-Contra affair for nine months. Since May, the committees had staged televised public hearings. As the investigators probed, the public watched Oliver North, retired Major General Richard Secord, financier Albert Hakim, Attorney General Edwin Meese III, White House chief of staff Donald Regan, Secretary of Defense Caspar Weinberger, Secretary of State George Shultz, and twenty-one other individuals appear before the panels. Now, with the final report due to be completed within a month or so, lawyers for the committees were bringing in Shackley for an official deposition.

Shackley and his lawyer were escorted into a small conference room adjacent to the reception area of the ninth-floor headquarters. Four attorneys from the Senate and House committees were waiting, led by Cameron Holmes. The thirty-eight-year-old Holmes had studied economics and law at Harvard. As a prosecutor in the Arizona attorney general's office, he pioneered methods of investigating financially complex criminal enterprises and helped draft one of the nation's first anti-money-laundering laws. Holmes was brought in to the investigation to make sense of the intricate finances of the Iran-Contra network. He and his colleagues were intrigued by Shackley.

The Iran-Contra scandal cast the former intelligence officer in a curious cameo role. Congressional investigators traced part of the origins of the Iran initiative to a November 1984 meeting in Hamburg between Shackley and Manucher Ghorbanifar, a wheeling-dealing Iranian entrepreneur who had been a CIA informant and possibly an asset for the Shah of Iran's intelligence service and for Israeli intelligence. Ghorbanifar told his American visitor that for a price he could arrange the release of the three American hostages then held in Lebanon—among them CIA official William Buckley. He also suggested that if the United States supplied antitank TOW missiles to Iran, then in the midst of a fierce war with Iraq, Tehran could in return provide captured Soviet military equipment. Upon his return to the United States, Shackley wrote a memorandum about these conversations and delivered it to the State Department, which said it had no interest in the proposed deals. But several months later, Michael Ledeen, a National Security Council consultant, self-styled terrorism expert and sometime business associate of Shackley, asked Shackley to determine if the Ghorbanifar channel was still open. Ledeen was eager to start a joint U.S.-Israeli initiative to improve relations between the ayatollahs of Iran and the West. Shackley confirmed that Ghorbanifar was still available and passed that information to Ledeen. The first weapons shipment, ninety-six TOW missiles, occurred a little over two months later, on August 20, 1985. As far as Shackley was concerned, he was not involved. He had only forwarded, as a mere courtesy, some information he had come across accidentally.

Holmes and the other lawyers were not so sure. After all, Shackley was a close friend and past business partner of key Iran-Contra players, including Secord, Hakim, and Thomas Clines, a CIA-officer-turned-arms-dealer. A few years earlier Shackley had been caught up in a scandal with the same figures, when they were revealed to be associates of Edwin Wilson, a rogue ex-CIA officer caught peddling high-tech explosives and training to Libyan dictator Moammar Qaddafi. Was Shackley's presence in the Iran-Contra affair just a coincidence? Or had the master operator covered his tracks? The congressional investigators were looking for some answers, some clues that might explain more than Shackley's claim that it was all a chance occurrence. Some even hoped they might penetrate the veil of secrecy that surrounded Shackley's CIA career and his post-Agency activities.

Shackley, though, was not going to be much help. Before submitting to the lawyers' questions, he insisted on making a statement. His manner was polite but cool. He declared his belief that the committees had no cause to be bothering him: "The questions, from my point of view, are, 'Why are you doing this? And what do you want?' These are not rhetorical questions born out of frustration and anger. The issue is one of fairness." He complained that the subpoenas had forced him to spend two hundred and fifteen hours searching his files: "Why is my business being put in jeopardy, and why am I being harassed?" Ever suspicious after a life in the shadows, Shackley suggested he was the victim of some unforeseen plotting. He went on: "I'm trying to understand what this assault is on me, for what reason? And, Mr. Holmes, I would be specifically interested in hearing your response to those questions, so I can understand why you called me down here." Holmes declined to answer other than to remind Shackley that the committees had a legitimate interest in facts contained in Shackley's memory and files. Shackley was not satisfied: "What does that mean? What are you saying, that you are not going to answer my question?"

Holmes and Shackley tangled a bit more before the questioning began. The deposition was a grueling affair, lasting two days and producing a 476-page transcript. "It was quite unpleasant," said Timothy Woodcock, one of the investigating lawyers.

With two boxes of documents at his side, Holmes asked Shackley question after question regarding a host of subjects. The other lawyers jumped in with their own queries. The investigators covered Shackley's relationships with the main operators of the scandal, several of whom he had worked with while in the CIA. They delved into his Agency past and grilled him about his recent business activities. He was quizzed about his professional and personal contacts with Edwin Wilson.

Shackley avidly stuck to his position that he possessed no relevant knowledge about the Iran-Contra controversy beyond his own innocuous trip to Hamburg: "I had a meeting. I reported it. Bang! Finished!" He reluctantly described some of his business deals, providing a very narrow view of the secretive international oil trade. At one point he grudgingly explained a 1985 proposed arrangement whereby Iran would sell crude oil to a Portuguese company and use the cash to buy weapons from another Portuguese firm. Shackley's client, an independent oil company, would have bought the refined oil from the Portuguese oil business, but the deal fell through. He obligingly answered theoretical questions about aspects of the intelligence business, such as "plausible deniability"—when an intelligence service conducts activity so it cannot be tied to government leaders. He reminisced about his days as a young CIA case officer in Berlin in the 1950s, where opportunities for espionage were plenty. Most of this was of little use to Holmes and his colleagues.

"Shackley was a consummate deponent," Holmes recalled. "He can be evasive and combative without being evasive and combative." His answers to questions were usually short, to the point, rarely expansive. "You could tell this had come from years of training," Woodcock said. Another of the lawyers noted that Shackley was "not volunteering anything. It was fascinating to watch." After hours and hours of questioning, Holmes said, he "did not get the feeling—as I sometimes do in my business—that I now know what this person knows about the events I am investigating."

Holmes and the others were not sure whether to suspect Shackley of hiding his own operational involvement in the Iran initiative and the Contra support network, but they thought he certainly was being stingy in providing information about these matters. How could someone of his background and with his contacts not have picked up any hints of these two covert actions? In his line of work as an international consultant, it certainly would have been useful to know about such enterprises. The lawyers did not accept his claims of ignorance. Maybe Shackley told them all he knew, but Holmes and his colleagues assumed it more likely that they had been aced by a very experienced intelligence veteran. "The whole thing was oddly coincidental," Woodcock said. "I had a sense that we had not gotten a full account [from Shackley]. It was very frustrating." Nor were they able to pry too far into Shackley's Agency past and ask him about the hundreds of secrets he carried. And since the committees were rushing to complete their investigation—dropping and ignoring leads at every turn—no more time would be devoted to exploring Shackley and his activities.

When the former intelligence official left the ninth floor at the end of the two-day deposition, Holmes shook his head and said to himself, "Shackley remains a substantial mystery."

CHAPTER TWO

ORIGINS

EVEN to colleagues within the Central Intelligence Agency, Ted Shackley seemed mysterious. Over the years, vague stories circulated, sometimes in whispers, about his origins. Many who watched Shackley rise through the ranks of their secret world wondered about the man's past.

CIA people are more attuned than most government employees to the lineage of their fellow workers. This is not surprising. In its younger days, the Agency developed the reputation for being an enclave of the scions of the Ivy League and the eastern establishment. A large number of early CIA people, especially in the higher posts, were products of prestigious breeding, hailing from elite schools and blueblood circles. Though the pedigree diluted as the Agency grew rapidly in the 1950s, the culture of the CIA still encouraged many officers to nurse a preoccupation with the social history of their peers. Snobbery aside, an intelligence officer's fascination with the background of his comrades is natural. Intelligence professionals must read others well, whether they are in a foreign country courting agents or behind a desk in headquarters evaluating the actions and personality of a world leader. Good intelligence officers hunger for any bit of information available. And those attracted to the intelligence field tend to be competitive and, thus, maintain an intense interest in their colleagues. "This is a very tough business," explained an Agency veteran of twenty-five years. "We're assessing each other all the time."

Ask a good many CIA people about Ted Shackley, and they note there was something odd about his childhood. They concede that they do not know the full story but that he was—and here there is often a dramatic pause—an orphan. Such was the word on Shackley among people who toiled beside, beneath, or above him. Armchair analysts in the Agency speculated that Shackley had adopted the insular CIA as a surrogate family. "Some of our pop psychologists attributed his unfortunate approach to the world to his mistreatment in an orphanage," said Bill White, an analyst who once served under Shackley.

The gossip was not accurate. Theodore G. Shackley, Jr., was no orphan. But he did experience an untraditional childhood, due to his mother, a strong immigrant woman determined to be seen as a full American.

On September 4, 1925, Lena Anna Sadova married a salesman in Hartford, Connecticut. To the registrar she gave her age as twenty-one, but she was closer to seventeen. Sadova also declared she was born in Brattleboro, Vermont. Actually, she had been born in Poland and had immigrated with her family to the United States in 1913. Sadova did not want anyone to know she was not a native-born American. Her husband, Theodore George Shackley, indeed twenty-one years old on their wedding day, was a first-generation American. His father, George William Shackley, born in 1876 in Sheffield, England, came to the United States when he was two years old and grew up to become a polisher at a Smith and Wesson factory.

Shortly after Lena Anna and Theodore wed, they moved to Springfield, Massachusetts, where Theodore found work as a house painter. On July 16, 1927, Lena Anna—who had changed her name to the more American-sounding Eleanor—gave birth to Theodore George Shackley, Jr.

The marriage between Theodore and Eleanor was not a good one. Theodore was a drinker, whose alcoholism would drive him to an early death. Often Ellie, toting her son, searched for her absentee husband in various taverns, sometimes finding him collapsed in his own vomit and waste. One of her son's earliest memories was accompanying his mother as she looked for his drunken father.

Eleanor Shackley, a strong-willed woman, could not bear to stay with her husband. Two and a half years after Ted was born, on a December evening in 1929, she took her son and ran away. For months, she had saved nickels and pennies from the food budget. With this money she purchased a train ticket and headed toward the home of her sister, who lived in Queens, New York. Years afterward when she told the tale of her flight to another family member, Eleanor explained her decision to flee by remarking that Theodore Shackley, Sr., "wasn't the greatest husband" and that he had been "a little abusive."

Ellie Sadova Shackley, short, pretty, blonde, personable, industrious, and the owner of an engaging smile, went to work as a hostess at the New Yorker, one of Manhattan's better hotels. At some point, Ellie sent Ted to live with an older Polish woman, and he attended grammar school outside the city in Morganville, a small New Jersey suburb. As an adult, Ted Shackley would not identify this older woman to his immediate family. But when his wife and daughter discovered old family letters, they drew an obvious conclusion: the older Polish woman was Ellie's mother. Shackley would neither confirm nor deny their guess. He only acknowledged that the woman had been a family friend. Shackley's family wondered if Ellie had kept the woman's identity a secret from her son.

Whoever this woman was, she taught him Polish. (His knowledge of Polish would later ease his way into a career in intelligence.) Shackley's guardian also gave him what became one of his most prized possessions, a small Polish Bible. As a youth, Shackley was an altar boy and hoped to become a priest.

One day on the job at the hotel, Ellie met Justin Manning, a purchasing agent for the New Haven Railroad. Six feet tall, the trim fifty-year-old Manning sported a mustache and dark hair. His first marriage had ended in divorce, and his two sons lived with their mother. In the course of his subsequent visits to the New Yorker, Manning and Ellie fell in love. On November 5, 1937, Ellie's husband filed for divorce, charging she had "utterly deserted" him eight years earlier. Over a year later, a judge granted Theodore Shackley, Sr., the divorce.

Justin Manning was lucky with investments and in the early 1940s retired from the railroad and moved to West Palm Beach, Florida. Ellie and Ted joined him there. Justin and Ellie did not marry at first; rather they lived together, an unconventional arrangement for the times. They finally wed, and Manning, no sentimentalist, noted at the end of a letter to a son, "Incidentally, Ellie and I got married."

Ellie took to Florida living. She developed a good tan and embraced golf. Asked if she practiced a particular religion, a family friend replied, "She was an avid golf player." Many evenings she spent at the driving range. When she was out on the course, she often was winning another tournament. To other members of the Manning family, she talked little of her past.

The Manning household was well furnished, but not lavish. Justin

Manning's portfolio was strong enough for him to keep a vacation home in New Hampshire, but he was not generous. And he and young Ted, now of high-school age, did not develop a close relationship. Ted was Ellie's responsibility, and Manning, a strict, stern fellow, did not show his wife's son much affection. Shackley had become a hot-tempered young man, with a know-it-all manner. The stepfather and stepson often clashed.

Shackley worked at a funeral parlor that was owned by one of West Palm Beach's most prominent and well-off citizens, Napoleon Washington Mizell. "That caused a lot of hilarity," recalled classmate Loyal Gould, "Ted Shackley working with the stiffs." With white wavy hair and a dramatic presence, "Uncle Mo" Mizell looked like a colonel in the Rebel army. He was the number-one booster for Palm Beach Central High's football and baseball teams, and he owned one of the nicest homes in town. Perched on a slight rise, the house had a sun deck from where one could gaze out, over the rooftops of the other houses, at the Atlantic Ocean. When the atmosphere at Shackley's home became too much for Shackley to bear, he went to live at the house known as "Uncle Mo's castle."

To most of Shackley's schoolmates, it was unclear why Shackley could be found residing in the "castle." They figured that Mizell was doing another one of his good turns for a player; Shackley was a tackle on the football team. One thing was for certain: you didn't ask Shackley about it. "He was the toughest and meanest kid," recalled Ed Eissey, a running back for whom Shackley fiercely blocked. "He didn't take any nonsense. He wasn't a bully. If he liked you, he was very loyal. But you knew not to cross him." Some schoolmates kept their distance from Shackley, fearful of getting on his wrong side. Eissey witnessed bare-fist fights in which Shackley pounded an opponent: "It was usually one of the big heroes from another school who said something disparaging about our high school or our football team. Ted would get into these real brawls, and he would win overwhelmingly."

Shackley was now almost six feet tall. He possessed a sturdy, muscular build. He had grown into a handsome young man, with blond hair and a striking face with sharp features. His chin was strong; his eyes intense.

Shackley's best friend was Norman Hamer. In their senior year, Hamer was president of the student government and the quarterback of the football team. The pair were leaders of an exclusive high-school fraternity. Together they planned their futures. To Hamer, Shackley confided that he looked forward to a life in government service, possibly a political career. "I had to remind him," Hamer said, "that he had to tone himself down a bit. You can't pursue politics if you're going to punch people in the nose."

At school, Shackley was considered one of the brightest, ready and able to speak up in any classroom discussion. As a good-looking scholar-athlete, he was popular with the girls. He dated a few, but one especially caught his fancy, Elizabeth Ann Brown, who wanted to be a teacher. Everyone called her Betts.

Shackley and his friends attended high-school dances or gathered at The Hut, the local drive-in, to down burgers and Cokes. The usual talk was of girls, sports, and school. "But it was always interesting to me," Eissey noted, "how Ted had a great deal of knowledge about what was going on in the world outside of West Palm Beach. He really had an interest in politics and international affairs." Hamer, too, was struck by his friend's preoccupation with global matters and his ability to intelligently discuss such subjects: "At that age he could talk about most anything. He was able to talk with the grown-ups."

It was a time of war. Shackley was a high-school senior in 1945, the last year of the Second World War. For years, Palm Beach County had been one big military base. The Coast Guard was stationed at the inlets. Horseback patrols kept watch along the beaches. Servicemen were everywhere. The big hotels in Palm Beach were transformed into hospitals for those injured on the African front. Britain's Royal Air Force operated a training base in nearby Boca Raton. Lights were blacked out at night. Local volunteers joined the war effort, collecting scrap metal or spotting enemy aircraft.

Even in this atmosphere of widespread concern, Shackley stood out for his obsession with war developments. To his friends, he was a super-patriot. "He was always talking about what a great country we lived in," Eissey recalled. "He was like John Wayne. 'Just let me at 'em.' He really wanted to serve." Shackley may have inherited his drive from his mother, but friends did not understand the origin of his patriotic fervor. Ted Brown, Jr., a Shackley friend and brother of Betts Brown, thought Shackley might have picked it up from his natural father, with whom he spent a summer or two in Springfield. But maybe the explanation was simple. "Ted was," Brown observed, "an all-out sort of fellow."

Shackley missed his chance to be John Wayne. His high-school graduation was in June 1945. The Allies had triumphed in Europe the month before. The war in the Pacific ended with the U.S. nuclear attacks on Hiroshima and Nagasaki on August 6 and 9. Shackley did not enlist in the Army until October 25.

The war was over, the nation was demobilizing, and the United States was grappling with defining its role in the postwar world. There was a rush to return to normalcy. But the war had yielded a new set of issues the United States would have to address. In Washington, policymakers would deal with these abstractions of national security. On the ground in the war-scarred areas of Europe, Shackley and other Americans would confront the harsh realities of the burgeoning Cold War.

Shackley's Army enlistment application was routine. But one item made his personnel file of particular interest to some military official: Shackley reported that he spoke, read, and wrote Polish. Young men with the right language skills were in demand by a U.S. military that now had peacetime, global responsibilities—and, even more so, by U.S. intelligence.

On April 13, 1946, eighteen-year-old private first-class Theodore Shackley reported for duty at the 970th Detachment of the Counter Intelligence Corps in occupied Germany. The U.S. Army had placed Shackley on the pathway toward his career as a spook.

At the end of the Second World War, the Third Reich was literally buried beneath four hundred million cubic feet of rubble. Millions of Germans lived in bombed-out buildings and in makeshift shelters. Ten million refugees searched frantically for housing and food. The social fabric of Germany barely existed. The country's industrial and agricultural infrastructure was devastated. The Allied nations—the United States, Britain, France, and the Soviet Union—had split the conquered nation into four administrative zones. Berlin, surrounded by the Soviet-controlled section of Germany, was also sliced into four sectors. The divided country and city were fast turning into a central battlefield of the Cold War, a playing field for geopoliticians, military commanders, and spies.

The main U.S. force in Germany was now a constabulary. Much of the German population was apprehensive. Germans feared famine and disease. Theft was on the rise. Anonymous propaganda claimed German food was being diverted to American soldiers. In this uncertain climate, the U.S. Army's Counter Intelligence Corps was responsible for protecting the American occupiers and their secrets—and for conducting early programs of the Cold War.

The CIC was created by the Army in the summer of 1941 to catch spies, saboteurs, and subversive agents and to prevent U.S. military secrets from falling into the wrong hands. In the postwar period, the Counter Intelligence Corps had much to handle. In broad terms, "counterintelligence" refers to efforts to protect a government and military from foreign intelligence operations and to destroy the effectiveness of threatening intelligence services. The enemies were many in Germany: Nazis on the loose, neo-Nazis with plots for the future, other Germans critical of the Western occupation, and communists and agents of the Soviet Union, a partner in a cracking alliance.

The primary CIC task was to apprehend the former Nazis at large. The service investigated acts and threats of subversion and sabotage. The Corps spied on the German Communist Party. It countered Soviet espionage efforts in the U.S. zone of occupation. For example, on July 22, 1946, top-secret raids by the CIC picked up 407 suspected Soviet agents. CIC agents screened repatriated German citizens and thousands of displaced persons.

During the war years, the CIC had earned a solid reputation for its derring-do. "The CIC has more adventure stories buried in its secret files than a month's output of blood and thunder comic books," *The New York Herald-Tribune* exclaimed at the war's end. But the Corps Shackley entered was deteriorating. Many of its best men had headed back to the States. The new crop of CIC agents landed in Germany without any proper training. An official CIC history was unrelenting in its low estimate of the 970th Detachment in the postwar years. Agents in the field—"young, inexperienced boys"—could "not at all measure up to the standards of quality either desired or previously obtainable."

Shackley was young and green. But his ability to speak Polish was a valuable asset. He was made a clerk-general, a post usually reserved for administrative work. But he was not relegated to paper-pushing. Inexperienced as he might have been, Shackley was sent into the wreckage of Berlin as a low-level CIC operator.

There are no indications that Shackley had a special tenure in the CIC. He did not come to the notice of those who ran the CIC in Germany. But Shackley was selected to attend the European Theater Intelligence School in Oberammergau, located in southern Germany. Strict quotas permitted only a few CIC officials to enter the school. At Oberammergau, Shackley went through a basic eight-week course. Newcomers to intelligence were taught methods of questioning people. There were courses in counterespionage and countersubversion. Shackley and his classmates learned how to conduct surveillance.

CIC training introduced Shackley to the fundamental act of spying: recruiting an agent. That means finding a person with access to information (usually a native of the targeted nation or a member of a worrisome organization) and convincing that individual, via persuasion, payment, or blackmail, to betray his or her government or institution and assume the danger of passing secrets to another power. Shackley found himself captivated by intelligence work.

After the courses in Oberammergau, he was ordered to the bombed-out and divided city of Berlin. He worked in displaced persons camps and put his Polish skills to use interviewing refugees, looking for war criminals, past Gestapo agents, and subversive Poles. Shackley did more than question DPs. He trundled through the rubble-strewn streets of

Berlin in search of persons on the automatic arrest lists, as well as those the United States government much desired: former Nazi scientists. Under Operation Paperclip—previously code-named Operation Flypaper and, before that, Operation Mesa—young CIC men in Berlin were dispatched to run down leads on the whereabouts of German scientists, to check out last-known addresses. Shackley was not aware of the policy debates in Washington, where government officials tussled over which former Nazis qualified for special treatment. His assignment usually was straightforward: go knock on the door of a residence and see if you can uncover any information about where a targeted German—and the subject could be a former intelligence officer, not just a scientist—might be found.* If Shackley's gumshoe work succeeded, ex-Nazis would be relocated to the United States, where they could escape their pasts and contribute to the Cold War needs of their new patron.

After spending ten months overseas, two of them in training at the intelligence school, Shackley in February of 1947 left the defeated country and headed home. An Army official wrote in Shackley's personnel file, *"Recommended for further military training."*

His tour in Germany had exposed Shackley to both the world of spies and the early days of the Cold War. That short spell whetted his appetite. Once back in the United States, Shackley soon was telling friends that he was contemplating a career in the military, perhaps in intelligence. William Klee, who met Shackley shortly after his CIC stint, vividly recalled—even four decades after the fact—the story that Shackley told about his CIC days. As Klee remembered it, Shackley said he had parachuted behind enemy lines into some sort of a camp with the impossible mission of identifying prominent Gestapo and SS personnel. Klee, unaware Shackley had not seen wartime service, was impressed by the self-glorifying tale. An acquaintance from high-school days, Loyal Gould, heard through the grapevine that Shackley had engaged in gutsy actions behind enemy lines. And after Shackley became an attention-getting figure within the CIA, the hallway gossip held that he personally helped Nazis escape Germany. Another rumor was that Shackley tried to snatch up Polish agents for his own spy network.

It is improbable the young clerk managed such daring projects during his brief stay with the Corps. Still, his CIC days would come to be part of the Shackley mystique.

---

* The most notorious instance of this CIC activity began in early 1947, when Corps agents recruited Klaus Barbie, the Lyon Gestapo chief who had deported Jews to death camps and tortured and killed resistance fighters. The Americans desired Barbie's help in espionage endeavors aimed at the Soviet Union. CIC officers hid Barbie from French investigators and spirited him out of Europe.

. . .

By the time Shackley had returned to the United States, the Cold War was not yet entrenched but was well under way. In the time since their joint victory over Nazi Germany, Washington and Moscow had clashed over the future of Germany, politics in central Europe, war reparations, and other matters. Hardliners in the U.S. government—who warned that the Soviet Union was an expansionistic, threatening country, with a foreign policy driven by extreme ideological imperatives—had triumphed in winning control of U.S. policy. Secretary of War Robert Patterson declared that the Soviets actually desired war with the United States. Clark Clifford, a top adviser to President Harry Truman, urged that public opinion be aroused regarding the Soviet threat. Truman established the Temporary Commission on Employee Loyalty, a forerunner of government programs to root out communists and so-called subversives. In January 1947, via a fraudulent election, the communists in Poland won an overwhelming majority in the parliament. A crisis in Greece was brewing. Out of it would come the Truman Doctrine, which committed the United States to a global crusade against the Soviets.

Shackley left military service on February 22, 1947. Four days later, President Truman sent legislation to Congress to establish an organization to help prosecute the Cold War for the United States: the Central Intelligence Agency.

Five years earlier, World War II had given birth to the Office of Strategic Services, which produced propaganda, collected information, churned out intelligence reports, conducted sabotage, and waged guerrilla warfare. The OSS became distinguished for its loose and freewheeling ways and for employing the best and the brightest of the 1940s. Among its ranks were Paul Mellon, the banker, his brother-in-law David Bruce, some of the Morgans, and William Vanderbilt. The joke was that OSS really stood for "Oh So Social." It established the basic structure of modern American intelligence organization: espionage—the quiet gathering of information—would be housed under the same roof as noisy paramilitary activity and controversial covert political and psychological operations, the so-called dirty tricks of the spy trade.

Toward the war's end, William Donovan, a successful Wall Street attorney who founded the OSS, tried to convince President Franklin Delano Roosevelt and then Truman that the OSS ought to be transformed into an ongoing civilian central intelligence service. Truman, though, abolished the OSS in September of 1945 and spread its responsibilities to other government agencies, including the newly created and bureaucratically weak Central Intelligence Group.

The second director of the CIG, Lieutenant General Hoyt S. Vandenberg, was determined to turn his unit into the paramount intelligence agency. He proposed establishing an independent central intelligence organization, headed by a powerful Director of Central Intelligence. Truman ultimately agreed and included Vandenberg's idea in the National Security Act he sent Congress in February 1947.

The notion that the United States should have a peacetime, civilian, centralized intelligence service, which it had not possessed previously, was not universally accepted. Some in Congress worried aloud that this new intelligence agency might become the President's own secret police. In appearances before congressional committees, Vandenberg pressed hard. The oceans had shrunk, he told the legislators. Europe and Asia were as close as Canada and Mexico. The United States must know the intentions and capabilities of other nations if it was to be forewarned against aggression, especially in this new era of atomic warfare. Those who found something un-American about espionage, he said, should realize that not all intelligence was sinister. Congress approved the National Security Act, and on July 20, 1947, President Truman signed into existence the Central Intelligence Agency.

The CIA was assigned five general tasks: to advise the newly created National Security Council; to recommend how to coordinate the intelligence activities of other agencies; to correlate, evaluate, and disseminate intelligence; to carry out "service of common concern"; and "to perform such other functions and duties related to intelligence affecting the national security as the NSC will from time to time direct." Its fifth task, expressed in a catchall phrase, would be used in later years to justify a host of CIA actions, including the most infamous ones that, once revealed, would cause scandal and controversy. But the Agency had been created without a great deal of fuss. America, the new global power, had its first peacetime, centralized spy service.

The summer of 1947, Ted Shackley was readying for college. Before he and Norman Hamer had joined the military after high school, the two friends vowed to attend the same school. Shackley had applied to Princeton and was accepted. But Hamer was not. Shackley honored his promise to his best friend, and both enrolled at the less-prestigious University of Maryland. It was not Ivy League, nor did it enjoy much of a reputation for academic excellence. But the school, located a few miles beyond the district line of Washington, D.C., boasted geography in its favor. Shackley and Hamer believed that Maryland offered them at least one future career option: government work.

The Maryland campus overflowed with former servicemen, like Shackley, taking advantage of the GI bill. Many were older men toughened by military life overseas. Students lived in military barracks left over from the war. Life there was boisterous. Poker games were frequent. Students stayed up all night, drinking, gambling, and cutting loose. Pep rallies and football games spilled over into riots. The 1950 yearbook observed that the departing class was composed of an "unusual group, a group characterized by a lack of restraint oddly combined with a serious desire to study."

Shackley entered the University of Maryland in September of 1947 and thrived. His major was history. He attended courses in European history, studied German, and earned mostly As. At Maryland, he continued to impress his peers. "This was a strong-willed person," said Dean Steliotes, who lived next to Shackley in the Phi Delta Theta fraternity. "You got the idea he knew where he was going. And he wasn't going to let anyone stand in his way." That was quite clear to William Bruce Catton, the son of the famous Civil War historian and a fellow member with Shackley in Phi Alpha Theta, the campus honorary historical society. "He was an operator," Catton observed. "You could tell he liked to run things. You could even see that with the historical society. . . . He was a little bit cocksure and self-confident. I wouldn't want to play cards with him if I didn't have a new deck."

Shackley was good-looking and knew it, a guy who would walk into a fraternity party, smooth his hair back, look around, and seem to say, well, which one of you girls will be lucky tonight? "He was," Catton observed, "a gung-ho type who wanted to make things happen, to be where the action was. And his ego didn't hurt any." Ambitious—that was the consensus among his fraternity mates.

Shackley struck some schoolmates as aloof, a touch arrogant. But others observed in him a spark of leadership, if for no more reason than Shackley believed so thoroughly in his own powers. He continued to display a keen interest in world events and shared the conservative politics of the day. He served in the ROTC.

In his junior year, Shackley offered himself as a candidate for student government president. Fred Stone, Shackley's opponent and a much-liked cheerleader, built, the school newspaper reported, "the most powerful political machine the campus has seen in a long time." Stone played up the fact that he served three and a half years with the infantry in the Pacific—an experience Shackley tried to match by stretching the truth. In a statement that ran in the school newspaper the day before the election, Shackley claimed that he had been in Army counterintelligence during the war, when actually he was a peacetime soldier.

Shackley's platform challenged the established order. He urged revising the student government constitution to remove the special interest vote of fraternities. "We wish to see a more democratic set-up in the

Student Government," Shackley declared. Shackley, a Greek himself, was running against the powerful fraternities. But he was not a natural maverick. "I don't know how much he meant it," his closest friend, Norman Hamer, recalled. "That was a platform he decided might be useful."

Shackley's strategy failed. He collected 1,021 votes; Stone pulled 1,562. And Stone's slate swept every position contested. "It was the first time in the history of the University," the college paper reported, "that an election was so one-sided."

The summer before his senior year, Shackley married Betts Brown, his high-school sweetheart. Even though they had been apart for most of the previous five years, the couple had maintained their relationship. During that time, Betts had become a public school teacher in Florida. The wedding occurred at the First Presbyterian Church in West Palm Beach. Betts and Shackley exchanged vows by a candlelit altar. The local newspaper account of the wedding listed the impressive academic honors Shackley had earned at college and repeated the white lie that he had spent a year in Germany during the war.

Shackley cut short his senior year. He had enough credits to graduate early and did so in January of 1951. To the students leaving at that time, the editors of the campus paper, troubled by affairs of the day, issued somber parting words:

> It isn't a pretty picture for either the graduating senior or the under-graduate.
> We can only hope for a favorable solution; one that would be brought about more quickly if Uncle Joe [Stalin] and his ward bosses would crawl back into their paleolithic caves.
> For the veterans among the graduating class the word "future" may be a little hard to stomach. They entered the University four or more years ago thinking, or at least fervently hoping, that victory in the war meant "peace in our times."
> They find themselves leaving at a time when the future of the world is no more certain than it was when a maniac named Adolph [sic] Hitler first started his ravings.

It was an appropriate farewell for Ted Shackley.

CHAPTER THREE

GERMANY: SPYING

I

USUALLY it was at night when Lucien Conein escorted an agent—
"the body"—to the German-Czechoslovak border. In a U.S. Army jeep,
Conein and the agent drove through the hills of the Bohemian Forest.
Then Conein pulled over at a secluded point. The two got out and
tramped through the woods, with Conein guiding his charge to an isolated point where the agent—most often a Czechoslovak refugee recruited, trained, and paid by the CIA—could slip over the border,
literally crossing the Iron Curtain on a mission for the United States.

Conein never stayed with the agent all the way. At a spot about a
kilometer from where the agent was to enter the East, Conein pointed
and issued directions: head that way, then go three kilometers, and keep
the stream on your left. He shook hands with a man he knew little about
—not even his real name—and said good-bye. Both Conein the CIA
man and the agent knew the rule: once you're in, you're on your own.
The agent trudged off into the darkness, and Conein sat, waited, and
listened for gunshots. He typically gave it an hour. No noise was good
news. If all he heard was the sounds of the night, he headed back to his
home and a shot of cognac. Alone, he lifted the glass and offered a toast:
"Well, another one's gone."

Thirty-two years of age, Conein was already an experienced intelligence hand. During the war, he served with the Jedburghs, a daring
multinational band directed by the OSS and the British Special Opera-

tions Executive. Conein jumped into France in 1944 and fought with the Corsican Brotherhood, an underworld organization allied with the resistance. He made drops into China and Indochina. A tall dark-haired swashbuckler, Conein's tough-guy appearance was enhanced by two missing fingertips on his right hand, the result not of a mysterious covert operation but an automobile mishap. In the years after the war, Conein stayed with American intelligence and became first-generation Agency. In 1951, the CIA chief of espionage for Germany, Gordon Stewart, sent Conein to establish an Agency base in Nuremberg in the south of West Germany. About seventy-five miles from the Czech border, it became one of the many CIA launches for infiltrating into the Soviet bloc agents who could gather information for Washington policymakers now prosecuting a full-blown Cold War.

Conein, a major in the Army, opened shop in the large building where Nazi war criminals had been tried. The modest Agency base included two small offices and a secretary. As Conein saw it, he was merely a covert escort service. "They'd send me a body," he said, "and I'd get it across." When Conein took the body to the point of departure, he was the last American to wish the East European good luck. During the drive back to Nuremberg, he sometimes wondered what the hell he was doing wasting his time on such piddling operations. The morning after, Lou Conein returned to the small CIA base to start planning the next operation, and as he entered the office, he might grunt a good morning at the young, gung-ho Agency officer sent to work alongside him: Ted Shackley.

After graduating early from the University of Maryland, Shackley planned to go to law school. He was not certain what he wanted to do after that, but his time in the Counter Intelligence Corps had prompted him to consider returning to intelligence. War got in the way. In May of 1951, Shackley, a member of the Army Reserve, was called up for the Korean War. The notice arrived shortly after Shackley learned his father, only forty-seven years old, had died of acute alcoholism and heart failure.

Shackley reported for duty and was detailed to the Military Police Corps in South Charleston, West Virginia, with the rank of second lieutenant. At slightly more than six feet tall and weighing 195 pounds, he possessed the right physique for the job. But the military police is not the best place for an ambitious young man, and Shackley did not remain an MP long.

Three months into his service, he was ordered to a Pentagon office. A clerk pulled his file and told him to go to a Washington address. Shackley proceeded to an office in one of the temporary buildings thrown up around the reflecting pool near the Lincoln Memorial during the Second World War. When he entered the building, he encountered a host of stares. Something was wrong. You're wearing a uniform, one person said, you're not supposed to come in here in a uniform. "I don't even know where the hell I am," Shackley replied. "Tell me where I am." He was in the unmarked and supposedly secret headquarters of the four-year-old and little-known Central Intelligence Agency.

Shackley never learned who had spotted him as a potential Agency man. The CIA, expanding at a quick pace, needed new officers. Its personnel increased sixfold in its first six years, spurred on by the Korean War and the new foreign policy objectives of a government committed to confronting communism around the globe. The CIA was requisitioning the military for recruits, and Second Lieutenant Shackley fit the profile: an honors student, an ROTC leader, a CIC veteran, a patriot with overseas experience, who now spoke both Polish and German. His military file was forwarded to the Agency, and the CIA wanted him.

Shackley was inducted into a secret community. He was subjected to a security check and "fluttered"—that is, submitted to the standard and grueling polygraph examination all newcomers faced. A young group of people filled the ranks of this bright, new organization. "There was a sense of being chosen," said Donald "Jamie" Jameson, who also joined the Agency in 1951 and later became a close associate of Shackley's. A disproportionate number of those selected had come from the better schools or were members of the eastern establishment—but not Shackley, whose promise to a friend had prevented him from attending Princeton.

The fresh officers were instructed in the basics. Shackley and about twenty other young men took courses in how to recruit and run agents, how to communicate clandestinely with them, how to arrange a rendezvous, how to service dead-drops, how to plant bugs, set up safe houses and shake tails, how to write reports, how to process the chemicals used in secret writing, how to work miniature spy cameras.

Students exercised their newfound skills by role-playing recruitments. They conducted surveillance all around Washington. In local hotels, they practiced agent meetings. In one exercise, Shackley and his classmates had to surveil a restaurant where a KGB officer was meeting an agent—both played by Agency personnel. The novices' mission was to identify the spies and secretly photograph the exchange.

The newcomers were schooled in the psychology of spying so they could spot agents and exploit personal problems and political doubts. The young intelligence officers were introduced to communist theory and practice. They had to know the methods of their enemy. In his class,

Shackley was a standout. He scored perfect or near-perfect grades across the board. He worked harder than anyone else.

Members of the secret society Shackley had joined learned how to live the double life. Such training carried perils, as William Colby, a future Director of Central Intelligence, later noted:

> Considering the importance and all-consuming nature of the work I was doing at the Agency; considering the missionary zeal, sense of elitism and marvelous camaraderie among my colleagues there . . . one can see how easy it would have been for me to drop out of [the outside] world and immerse myself exclusively in the cloak-and-dagger life. And some of my colleagues at the Agency did just that. So-cially as well as professionally they cliqued together, forming a sealed fraternity. They ate together at their own special favorite restaurants; they partied almost only among themselves; their families drifted to each other, so their defenses did not always have to be up. In this way they increasingly separated themselves from the ordinary world and developed a rather skewed view of that world. Their own dedicated double life became the proper norm, and they looked down on the life of the rest of the citizenry. And out of this grew . . . an inbred, distorted, elitist view of intelligence that held it to be above the normal processes of society, with its own rationale and justification, beyond the restraints of the Constitution, which applied to everything and everyone else.

Michael Burke, who in 1951 oversaw all covert actions in the East launched from Germany, calculated that the sacrifices of the secret life were surpassed by the rewards: "The price of anonymity was probably offset by an air of romance and mystery that cloaked the profession, by an elixir of glamour that curled up from their secret papers, by danger vicariously shared with agents operating on hostile ground, by the pos-session of a secret—a host of secrets—that set [intelligence officers] apart, placed them among an elite few."

Inside the collection of rat-infested temporary buildings that com-posed CIA headquarters, the atmosphere was hectic, exciting. A war was on in Korea—and a battle ensued between Moscow and Washington. "There was this feeling that we were spreading the American message," one CIA novice said. "We all had the missionary complex. The Agency was involved in important things, having to do with the very security and defense of the country." Few among the young recruits doubted the conventional wisdom that the communist threat was real and dangerous. They were to be a secret line of defense in the Cold War.

Shackley remained in Washington for eight months. His life was shrouded in secrecy. He could not discuss much about his new job with his friends or family, even Betts. When he saw his closest friend, Norman Hamer, Shackley did not disclose many details but he let his enthusiasm show. "He wanted to go right to the top of the CIA," Hamer said. "He was dedicated, totally dedicated to the CIA." Both Shackley and Betts were delighted when Shackley heard that the Agency was sending him overseas, back to Germany.

Since 1947, the CIA had grown in both size and influence, and it had resolved a fundamental question: did the Agency exist to coordinate and collect information for government policymakers or to promote, through clandestine means, U.S. interests abroad? The answer: it was expected to do both.

On September 18, 1947, "Wild Bill" Donovan, the onetime OSS chief and godfather of the Agency, sent a note to Rear Admiral Roscoe Hillenkoetter, the first head of the CIA, urging him to run propaganda and covert political activities. Hillenkoetter was doubtful. The Agency already had enough to do with its espionage responsibilities. Hillenkoetter asked the Agency's legal counsel, Lawrence Houston, to determine if the law would permit the CIA to assume such duties. As Houston read the National Security Act, it did not grant the CIA the authority to engage in subversion and sabotage. Congress had not meant to supply the Agency with broad operational powers.

President Truman's advisers in the National Security Council rendered a more liberal interpretation. The time was urgent. The communists looked awfully strong in the upcoming Italian elections. Truman's men saw the CIA as a hidden weapon to be unleashed against the Reds. On December 17, 1947, the National Security Council assigned the Agency the task of conducting covert psychological operations.

This was precisely what Hillenkoetter hoped to avoid. Covert actions and espionage clash. Black propaganda—say, planting a false report in a newspaper about financial improprieties within a leftist political party —depends for success upon publicity; clandestine intelligence is supposed to escape attention. The Admiral also questioned the use of guerrilla tactics and resistance movements. Associating espionage with the more confrontational covert activity, he thought, was likely to ruin the former. He acknowledged these more visible endeavors had a place in the campaign against the Soviet Union, but said they should be run by the armed services. Nevertheless, the Truman advisers had decided: the CIA was to be an agency of secret warriors.

The Agency's new covert operations group began modestly. It acquired a radio transmitter for broadcasting into the Soviet bloc, set up a secret propaganda printing plant in Germany, and assembled a fleet of balloons to drop propaganda into Eastern Europe. But the cold warriors held greater ambitions for the young intelligence service. In the spring of 1948, the United States government was gripped by near hysteria, with several key policymakers and the public at large frightened by a cable sent by General Lucius Clay, the commander in chief of the European Command. Clay reported, "I have felt a subtle change in Soviet attitude which I cannot define but which now gives me a feeling that it [war] may come with dramatic suddenness."* Though subsequent intelligence estimates concluded the Soviet Union was unlikely to attack, U.S. officials demanded more drastic measures than piping propaganda into Eastern Europe.

The result was the creation of a unit that could run covert political action, wage sabotage, assist anticommunist guerrillas, and directly intervene in the electoral processes of foreign governments. Eventually named the Office of Policy Coordination, the organization was housed in the CIA. Its operations were to be executed in such a fashion that if the world learned of them, the United States government could disclaim any responsibility.

The OPC was let loose and frantically moved to slip $1 million in secret funds to pro-American, noncommunist political parties in Italy. In the April 1948 elections, the U.S.-favored Christian Democrats won almost half the vote. The success in Italy emboldened those in the United States government who embraced secret meddling as the way to handle thorny problems of international affairs. Italy put the Agency on a course that would bring the CIA much controversy and would change the lives of thousands of people in the dozens of countries where the Agency saw fit to interfere.

Under the leadership of Frank Wisner, a wealthy Mississippian, Wall Street lawyer, and OSS operative, the OPC grew into what the imaginative Wisner dubbed "the mighty Wurlitzer," a grand instrument that could play different tunes—mount operations, rig elections, control newspapers, sway opinion. The OPC in 1949 joined with its British cousins in an ill-fated paramilitary operation to overthrow the communist regime of Enver Hoxha in Albania. After the outbreak of war in Korea, the OPC waged paramilitary operations there. In 1949, OPC's total personnel strength was 302; in 1952 it was 2,800, who were helped by an additional 3,100 contract employees overseas. During these years,

---

* Clay's cable was inconsistent with his previously expressed view that the true challenge from the East was political not military. Years later, Clay explained he wrote the alarmist cable assuming it would be used only in private sessions with Congress, which was then reluctant to restore the draft as the military wanted. The cable was leaked to the media.

its budget ballooned from $4.7 million to $82 million. It was a high-flying era. "A friend of mine said, all you needed to get a project going was to assemble three emigrés in a telephone booth, claim they were a committee," Jamie Jameson recalled, "and you could get one hundred thousand dollars for that."

Within the CIA, a rivalry developed between the Office of Special Operations (the espionage division) and the OPC. The two units competed for funds in Washington and for assets in the field overseas. There was also a matter of style. OSO employees regarded themselves as hard-headed intelligence purists, professionals who engaged in the arduous, low-profile task of clandestine collection. OPC's high-risk, attention-grabbing operations were a threat to the maintenance of OSO security, its budget, and perhaps even its silent, long-term objectives in espionage and counterespionage.

Actually, the line between espionage and certain types of covert action —such as political operations—could sometimes blur. It is not a large step to go from recruiting (and paying) a foreign government official to pass along the minutes of a Cabinet meeting, to suggesting to this agent that he or she initiate a policy position. But at the heart of the distinction between these two forms of clandestine work is the difference in intention: the practitioner of espionage seeks to understand the world; the covert action operator seeks to change it.

In August of 1952, the OSO and OPC merged into the Directorate of Plans, known internally as the DDP, which accounted for three quarters of the service's budget and 60 percent of its personnel. The DDP was separate from the Directorate of Intelligence (the DDI), the so-called open side of the house, which produced intelligence analysis for government policymakers. By this time, within the DDP the covert action outfit had overtaken the secret collection department in budget and staff. The CIA was devoting more energy to managing secret warfare against an enemy it knew little about than to discovering secrets about the world beyond its borders.

Gordon Stewart, chief of espionage for the German station, was a familiar Agency type, the genteel scholar-spy. A son of a Baptist minister, he studied history at the University of Chicago and joined the research department of the OSS in 1943. He then was transferred to the espionage section and stationed in Germany. After the war, Stewart became head of the Agency's Office of Special Operations in Germany, one of the CIA's most vital stations. His fellow CIA officers dubbed him "the Bishop," a moniker that poked fun at Stewart's all-too-proper bearing. No one dared even tell an off-color joke in his presence.

Germany was the center for Agency operations against the East. In 1948, after the communists won power in Czechoslovakia, the Czech station made a hurried exit to Germany and relocated to a big house on the Main River, near Frankfurt. The CIA base in Munich targeted the Soviet Union. Agency-trained Ukrainians parachuted into their homeland hoping to contact what exiles claimed was a burgeoning resistance. But the Agency failed to hook up with any resistance there.

For Stewart, his first years as a spy brought into sharp focus the ethics of espionage. "The collector risks little," he observed afterward. A CIA officer serving abroad is usually protected by international law, if he or she is operating under diplomatic or military cover. The agent recruited has no such protection. The agent breaks the laws of his or her own country, risking loss of liberty and sometimes life. Some Agency people thought the Ukraine operations had gone too far in jeopardizing others. Stewart saw it as a close call, but felt no unease. The need to be informed on conditions in the Soviet Union justified the program.

The intelligence business is full of moral quandaries. Stewart oversaw the Agency's embrace of former Nazi intelligence officers. After the war, the CIA helped General Reinhard Gehlen, who had directed German military intelligence on the Soviets, pull together an intelligence outfit that used wartime files to produce information on Soviet forces in East Germany and the Soviet Union. Several Agency officers were upset by the CIA's close collaboration with Gehlen and his subordinates. Their objections did not affect policy. There was a Cold War to wage, and Gehlen's top-notch service was one of the best tools the Agency had. Stewart and the brass saw no choice other than to enlist former Nazis. Covert battles demanded such ugliness.

In 1952 Stewart sent Shackley to the small base in Nuremberg, once the spiritual capital of Nazism. Stewart hoped Nuremberg could become a staging ground for operations into Czechoslovakia and Poland. The Agency-subsidized Gehlen outfit boasted many agents in East Germany, Czechoslovakia, and Poland. But the CIA, Stewart believed, ought to have its own assets, if only to confirm the material it received from Gehlen.

The Agency planted spotters in refugee camps and processing centers to find promising candidates. It was tough to convince a person who had fled a country to turn around and head back as a spy. "But money talks," Stewart said, "and some people were quite desperate." Exploiting an agent, Stewart recalled, "is the central aspect of clandestine operations. You persuade someone else to do something that is hardly in his interest as an individual."

On his first Agency assignment, Shackley was to be a purist, to be part of the OSO collection mechanism. He was to run agents. His primary target was his mother's birthplace, Poland. Situated between the Soviet

Union and East Germany, Poland was a top Agency priority. U.S. intelligence gathering in Eastern Europe was dominated by the assumption that a Soviet attack on Western Europe was not long in coming. Early warning was the goal. When the CIA was founded in 1947, Secretary of State George C. Marshall reportedly said, "I don't care what the CIA does. All I want from them is twenty-four hours' notice of a Soviet attack." Troops, weapons, supplies sent to Soviet forces in East Germany would pass through Poland. The Agency, pressed by the military, searched for high-level Polish sources, who could supply information about the policy and plans concocted in Warsaw and Moscow, and "little agents" (as Stewart called them), who could report train, truck, and troop movements that would precede an attack.

But Polish operations were a source of frustration and bewilderment. Most Agency intelligence on Poland came by way of its Berlin base. Poles who escaped their land and reached the American sector of Berlin were questioned by U.S. military intelligence. Some were recruited by the Agency, trained, and dispatched to Poland as intelligence-gathering agents. Agents who went back usually disappeared. The stymied chief of Polish operations in Berlin begged Stewart to be shifted to East German operations.

Stewart, pessimistic about Shackley's prospects in Nuremberg, posted him there on the assumption that the Agency should not rely entirely on the Berlin operations. And small bases like this made good training grounds, where young intelligence officers could try their hand at operations and obtain experience. Shackley impressed Stewart as a driven newcomer, a skilled linguist, a person who thought he had all the answers, precisely the sort to be given the hard task of running agents into Poland.

When Shackley arrived in Nuremberg, Lou Conein fixed him up with an office and a secretary. Like Conein, Shackley and Betts resided in a requisitioned house in a nice part of town. The CIA men did not have to pay for their rent, electricity, or telephone service—just food and drink. Booze was cheap. To Shackley, that did not matter; the son of an alcoholic, he was not much of a drinker.

Cross-border operations were not becoming any easier. In 1951, the Czechoslovak government began burning and dynamiting churches, schools, farmhouses, and whole villages to create a no-man's-land along its two-hundred-mile border with Bavaria. The next year, the government initiated a registration campaign for its citizens throughout the country. Warsaw did the same and ordered its twenty-six million citizens photographed, identified, and classified. The totalitarians of Warsaw and Prague regularly cited U.S. spy operations against their countries as justification for their repressive initiatives.

Spy trials in the East were much in the news. Some were obviously pure political propaganda. But U.S. intelligence operatives, recruiting, training, and dispatching refugees, knew that many accused agents— some of whom were caught crossing the border carrying a radio transmitter, maps, poison, counterfeit money, and false identity cards—were accurately charged. On November 27, 1951, Rudolf Slansky, the deputy premier of Czechoslovakia, was arrested, imprisoned, and charged with espionage. Observers in the West tended to dismiss the allegation as a trumped-up charge that served a political purpose. But Slansky had been approached by a Czechoslovak asset of the CIA who hoped to recruit him as a spy or a defector. A CIA case officer had procured a fake set of documents for Slansky to use in an escape from Czechoslovakia. Slansky was executed.

Shackley embraced his position as an intelligence officer with passion. He compensated for his lack of experience with diligence. Conein often found Shackley at his desk late in the evening. For the most part, the two went their separate ways. Conein was a hell-raiser. Shackley was calm and cool, a detailist, who plotted the most minute specifics of an operation. The pair shared an occasional drink at the officers' club and lunched together maybe once a month, but they did not collaborate. The guiding principle was need-to-know, a sacred rule of secret services. There was no reason for these two officers to be aware of the other's activity.

Shackley went about developing operations, and he needed his own bodies. The most lucrative source of potential agents was nearby Camp Valka, a large refugee camp for Eastern Europeans. Over 20,000 persons passed through the facility between 1950 and 1953. Some were stuck there for years, living in grim conditions—poor food and little security —within barracks surrounded by a concrete wall topped with barbed wire. The ideal prospect was a refugee who had access to the government of one of the East bloc nations. His cousin might work for a ministry, or a schoolmate for a munitions plant. Maybe a friend lived near a military airfield.

The Soviet bloc countries knew what the Agency was doing in Camp Valka. A Czechoslovak media report called the site a "recruiting center of criminals, spies, and saboteurs" to be sent to "our Republic to murder enthusiastic builders of our new and happy life." The security services of the East planted their own operatives in the camp and hoped that their refugee-agents would be recruited by Western intelligence. A camp director estimated that 10 percent of the refugees were communist agents.

Shackley mined the camp for trustworthy refugees who could return to Poland as CIA spies. He forwarded the names of potential Polish agents to the Polish desk, which vetted them to ascertain they were not being used by someone else or known security risks. He then wrote an operations report proposing a mission. "With a shrewd and reliable person like Ted, unless something came up in the name checks, we tended to say, sure, give it a whirl, see what you could do," Stewart recalled.

Every six or so weeks, Conein and Shackley visited Frankfurt for a staff meeting at the CIA's Germany station, which was set up in the former headquarters of the I. G. Farben corporation. For Conein, a diehard cynic, these gatherings were "dog-and-pony shows." Everybody would tell the brass what great jobs they were doing. "It was all lies," Conein said. "You had to look good." Shackley was a cool customer at these meetings. "He would not show his feelings," Conein observed, "but he was always worried about his image."

Perhaps he worried that his diligent activity was not producing many results. Like his colleagues, Shackley had little luck in developing productive agents in Poland. On this front, the CIA remained blocked. "All intelligence operations are frustrating," recalled another young case officer assigned to the Polish target. "You put so much in and score so seldom. If you need immediate gratification, you have to choose another line of work. We didn't have great successes. We were right out of the universities. We knew little about clandestine operations. We were not as smart as we thought we were."

Shackley's failure in Nuremberg—in general, if not in detail—was well known to the enemy. The regimes in both Poland and Czechoslovakia trumpeted their victories over the spies of Washington and disclosed details of espionage plots they smashed. In one instance in 1952, the Polish press agency broadcast reports of a trial of five alleged U.S. agents. Each had been recruited in West Germany or West Berlin—one in Camp Valka. The Czechoslovaks released a slim volume that detailed numerous espionage plots they thwarted. In one case, two sixteen-year-old boys in the camp accepted a pitch from an American intelligence officer. They were sent to Czechoslovakia, bolstered with forged documents, weapons, and money. One boy was to gather copies of identity cards and applications for residence permits. The other was to obtain the plans of airports and collect information on military garrisons. Both, the Czechoslovak government said, were caught and confessed.

The Agency's operations against Poland and Czechoslovakia resulted in numerous "losses"—the delicate term intelligence officers employ when an agent is killed or arrested. Were they worth it? "In retrospect, I wish we had never done any of that," said one of Shackley's colleagues in Germany who ran agents into Eastern Europe. "People got killed or had their legs blown off or worse. And for what? There was no war to prepare for." Gordon Stewart's impression was that Shackley's Nuremberg base and other efforts aimed at Poland and Czechoslovakia produced "no steady intelligence."*

"No claim can be made for a significant return on the heavy investment in these cross-border operations," Harry Rositzke, a top CIA officer in Germany, declared decades later. ". . . They were started at the insistence of understandably apprehensive military commanders, and they developed their own momentum in the atmosphere of an audacious undertaking against great obstacles. The hard work in documenting and training an agent, the excitement of his successful dispatch, the tension in awaiting his return, the despair at his loss—these often contrived to cloud case officers' judgments on the value of the intelligence their agents were producing." But Rositzke grasped a silver lining: "the first generation of CIA operations officers was learning its trade by doing, by developing know-how, both in what to do and what not to do."

This education did not come cheap. At the time, Jan Nowak, a prominent emigré who ran the Polish desk at the Agency-supported Radio Free Europe, was upset by the Agency's use of his fellow exiles. "This was one of the darkest aspects of the CIA, recruiting poor Poles and sending hundreds back," said Nowak, a secret courier for the Polish underground in the Second World War. "There were almost 100 percent losses. It was all very ruthless and senseless."

In the fall of 1990, while reflecting back on those days, Stewart admitted that, in the large sense, "Nowak has got it right." Sitting on a plush couch in the living room of his home in well-to-do northwest Washington, D.C., Stewart, with a slight trace of regret, concluded that operations against Eastern Europe were "dismally unsuccessful."

In the spring of 1953, First Lieutenant Theodore Shackley faced a life-defining decision. His military discharge date was looming. On August 1, 1953, Shackley would be out of the Army and free to leave the Agency and pursue the legal studies he had deferred. As he recruited spies to penetrate the Iron Curtain, Shackley pondered his future. Should he leave the cloak-and-dagger world and return to the United States to study law? Choosing was not so wrenching. He had thrown himself into the world of intelligence. The work was challenging, exciting, and seemingly important. He was part of the secret elite on the front lines of the Cold War. He fit well into this community. Shackley decided to stay with the CIA.

---

* Both Lou Conein and Gordon Stewart estimated that Shackley had worked on about a dozen operations during his stint in Nuremberg.

II

In Washington, the Agency continued to develop its standing as the clandestine action arm of the executive branch. The new director, Allen Dulles, the pipe-smoking, blue-blooded OSS veteran, was a covert action enthusiast and firm advocate of the anticommunist rollback policy of the new Eisenhower administration, in which his brother, John Foster Dulles, served as Secretary of State. Washington policymakers regarded the Agency as a major weapon they could deploy against the communists. But after the dismal failures of the Albanian and Ukrainian schemes, the more thoughtful cold warriors realized their best game was not played on the territory of the East. The Agency, no longer expected by the White House to overturn the communist regimes of the Soviet bloc, was unleashed in other theaters. In 1953, the Agency helped to overthrow Premier Mohammed Mossadegh in Iran and restore the Shah. The following year, it choreographed the coup against President Jacobo Arbenz Guzman of Guatemala. Both of these targets leaned to the left, and the actions against them were pulled off with little bother and loss of blood.

By the Agency's standards, both operations were tremendous successes. But they bred bitter fruit. The regime of the Shah was terribly repressive and eventually would be overthrown by a fundamentalist, anti-America Islamic revolution in 1979. Postcoup Guatemala experienced years of government corruption, civil strife, increasing poverty, and death squads. Yet at the time the lesson gathered was that the CIA could do the job.

Shackley could take pride in knowing he was part of an organization that official Washington viewed as a young, vital institution that served the highest national purpose. Its top man, Dulles, was fascinated by the operational aspects of intelligence, rather than the bureaucratic task of coordinating the intelligence community. The clandestine service, as some called the Directorate of Plans (or DDP), held a preeminent position in Dulles's CIA, and the Director pored over plans with desk officers. The DDP was growing faster than the rest of the Agency. Between 1953 and 1961, two thousand people would enter its ranks.

Yet the endeavors of all the Shackleys—in some instances at the expense of lives—were not being put to good use. One government task force issued a harsh finding in 1954: "It appears that the clandestine collection of raw intelligence from the U.S.S.R. has been overshadowed by the concentration of the DCI and others of an inordinate amount of their time and efforts on the performance of the Agency's cold war functions." A panel convened by President Eisenhower acknowledged the problems the secret intelligence collectors had experienced in piercing the Iron Curtain. "Most borders are made physically secure by elaborate systems of fencing, lights, mines, etc., backed by constant surveillance," it reported. "Once across borders—by parachute, or by other means—escape from detection is extremely difficult because of constant checks on personnel activities and personal documentation. The information we have obtained by this method of acquisition has been negligible and the cost in effort, dollars and human lives prohibitive."

This study group, chaired by General James Doolittle, the well-known World War II aviator, had a most important message for the President: "It is now clear that we are facing an implacable enemy whose avowed objective is world domination by whatever means and at whatever cost. There are no rules in such a game. Hitherto acceptable norms of human conduct do not apply. If the United States is to survive, longstanding American concepts of 'fair play' must be reconsidered. We must develop effective espionage and counterespionage services and must learn to subvert, sabotage and destroy our enemies by more clever, more sophisticated and more effective methods than those used against us. It may become necessary that the American people be made acquainted with, understand and support this fundamentally repugnant philosophy." For the CIA, the ends justified the means.

Ted Shackley, twenty-seven years old, was a junior case officer whose first tour had taken place in a backwater outpost. But in his fourth year in the CIA, Shackley joined the ranks of the select few. He received what for a spy was the assignment of a lifetime—a posting to Berlin.

In 1955 the occupied city was the center of the universe for intelligence officers, an island behind enemy lines. It was where West met East, where the CIA was belly-to-belly with the KGB. "Berlin had so many intelligence officers, agents and goons in it that they must have made up a measurable percentage of the population," wrote David Chavchavadze, a CIA case officer there.

To the imaginative copywriters of *Time* magazine, the city was "an Alfred Hitchcock dream of subterfuge and suspicions. In back streets, darkly mysterious houses lurk behind high wire fences suggestive of darker and more mysterious doings within. Newsmen recently counted twenty-seven separate agencies of Western intelligence known to be at work in Berlin. Their operatives—some fashionably clothed in the gray flannel of New York's Madison Avenue, some with armpit holsters bulging under blue serge—report to different headquarters, and rarely know what their colleagues are up to." Persons could freely travel between the Soviet-controlled sector and the parts of the city supervised by the West. No wall yet divided the city. Intelligence officers had ready access to agents and potential recruits. The city was a doorway to East Germany, other satellite countries, and the Soviet Union. An intelligence officer could actually meet the other side in Berlin. At diplomatic receptions and other affairs, an Agency official might encounter the spies of the Soviet bloc services. In the cafés, hotels, and nightclubs along the neon-lit Kurfürstendamm, freelancers of all stripes peddled information —it might even be accurate—sometimes selling the same material to different buyers.

The city had an edge. There was a tacit understanding between Western and Soviet intelligence organizations. They would not kill or kidnap each other's staff people. But the agents enlisted by the competing services enjoyed no such protection. Between 1945 and 1961, the police of West Berlin tallied 229 actual kidnappings and 328 attempts attributed to communist security forces.* It was not uncommon for a CIA asset to be grabbed off the street, pushed into a taxi, and driven to the Eastern sector of the city.

When Shackley arrived in Berlin, the devastation of war was still evident. Buildings were battle-scarred. Monuments and statues were in pieces. The city's grand trees had been cut down by Berliners desperate for firewood. Thousands of refugees from the East poured into West Berlin every month. But in the Western zone, life was lively. The economy of West Berlin, a city of 2,250,000 people, was rebounding, with extensive construction and reconstruction under way. West Berlin was still an island, but the Soviets had not issued any threatening noises recently.

Within the Soviet sector, the war seemed closer in time. Bombed-out areas looked much as they did the day the war ended. Political slogans replaced advertising signs. *"One Patriot Can Do Much,"* exclaimed one poster. *"Millions of Patriots Can Create Unconquerable Strength."* Shop windows displayed portraits of Soviet leaders. Compared with its bustling neighbor, the Eastern sector was grim. A pair of travel writers observed that East Berlin cast "an impression of apathy and tight-lipped silence."

The Agency in West Berlin conducted its operations out of the old German Luftwaffe headquarters. The Berlin base, where 40 to 50 case officers and about 150 other employees worked, was a three-story building that ran for about a third of a city block. It was located in a large American compound surrounded by a stone wall in the Dahlem neighborhood, a suburban part of town known as the "Golden Ghetto." Fine housing for the Americans was nearby. The entrance to the compound

---

* No such figures are available regarding Western kidnappings of agents of the East.

was guarded by a high metal fence and soldiers. To the world at large, Shackley was another analyst for the U.S. Army, the cover frequently assigned CIA officers in Berlin.

Every officer the Agency assigned to Berlin was someone to watch. But Shackley immediately demonstrated to his peers that he warranted close attention. Before Shackley's arrival, Walter Potocki, a Polish-American who had handled Czechoslovak operations for nearly three years, was told that he could expect a promotion to head the group of six or so officers working on Czechoslovakia. But Potocki took home leave before the promotion came through. He returned to an unpleasant shock. Shackley had become head of both Polish and Czechoslovakian operations, which were now combined into one satellite branch.* The message was clear to base officers. Shackley was a comer.

William Harvey, head of the Berlin base and already a CIA legend, had not only personally selected Shackley for this tour but had become taken with the young officer—which would mean much for Shackley in the years ahead. Harvey was an unlikely Agency star. No pipe-smoking sophisticate, he was a heavyset fellow with bulging eyes and a low, rumbling froglike voice. His manner was more that of a cop than a spy. He was brusque and demanding. His subordinates nicknamed him the Pear and Tweedledum, comments on his portly dimensions. He instilled intense loyalty within his men and women. Harvey was the quintessential intelligence officer, a man with a fertile operational mind and prodigious memory, who always saw the pitfalls of any scheme and who could suggest five better ways of running an operation. And though not everyone knew it yet, Harvey had been the first in the Agency to become wise to the Soviet Union's most famous penetration agent, Harold "Kim" Philby.

Born in 1915, Harvey grew up in Danville, Indiana. He attended Indiana University Law School and opened a one-man law practice in Kentucky. But Harvey, a blunt fellow with no talent for small talk, lacked the requisite social skills to drum up business. In December of 1940 he joined the Federal Bureau of Investigation, and by 1945 he was one of three agents† in Washington assigned to the Soviet Union, which was technically an ally. Harvey was hunting Soviet spies before it was fashionable. But nearly two years of labor failed to produce a single prosecutable case of espionage. He became discouraged.

On the night of July 11, 1947, Bill Harvey did not return home from a

---

*Technically, other Soviet bloc nations, including Hungary and Romania, fell under this designation. But the satellites that earned the most attention of the Berlin base were Poland and Czechoslovakia. East Germany was part of the German branch.

† Unlike the CIA, the FBI calls its own field officers "agents."

party. The next morning his wife Elizabeth notified the Bureau he was missing. Harvey showed up at his home later that morning, claiming his car had broken down and he had pulled over and gone to sleep. Harvey had violated the regulation that an agent be on two-hour call at all times. FBI Director J. Edgar Hoover ordered him transferred to Indianapolis. Harvey declined the reassignment and resigned.

Harvey found a home in the other civilian organization in town worried about Soviet spies, a new outfit called the Central Intelligence Agency. He was placed in charge of its counterintelligence unit, Staff C. The match was not an easy one. The Agency was animated by the camaraderie and spirit of the establishment; the FBI was middle America. But Harvey had years of experience in the counterespionage field that few, if any, in the CIA could equal. Eventually he would prove himself sharper than the Agency's most renowned counterintelligence expert.

On the weekend of May 25, 1951, two officials of the British embassy in Washington, Guy Burgess and Donald Maclean, disappeared. Burgess was a former British intelligence officer; Maclean was the subject of an American-British spy hunt. Both were linked to Kim Philby, the British intelligence representative in Washington. James Jesus Angleton, the Agency's premier counterintelligence officer, concluded that his good friend Philby was not involved in any untoward intrigue. Harvey, reviewing the Burgess-Maclean case and another episode that involved Philby, wrote a memo declaring Philby a Soviet agent. The CIA notified London that Philby was no longer welcome in Washington.*

Angleton, although fooled by Philby, was appointed by Dulles to head an enlarged counterintelligence division and went on to become the infamous, notoriously paranoiac counterintelligence czar of the Agency. Harvey was named chief of the Berlin base.

In the rough-and-tough espionage capital of the world, Harvey thrived. But he buckled under the restraints of the ever-expanding bureaucracy. When a young officer visited the Berlin base to conduct an inventory of special technical equipment (such as listening devices and weapons), Harvey refused to sign for the items consigned to the base. Sitting behind his elevated desk, on which he kept a huge Dickensian ledger used for recording all matters large and small, he shouted down at the young officer, "I wouldn't give my signature to the president of the goddamn country." When Germans rioted in East Berlin in June of 1953, an excited Harvey asked headquarters for permission to dispense weapons to protesters. John Bross, chief of the East European division,

---

* An inquiry in London produced inconclusive results. Philby resigned and later became a Middle East correspondent for two British publications. In 1963, he disappeared from Beirut and followed his old friends Burgess and Maclean to Moscow.

cabled back: do everything you can to express sympathy but do not supply guns. Later that day, a disappointed Harvey huffed, "I've been up to my ass in midgets all day."

The cloak-and-dagger atmosphere of Berlin justified one of his quirks, a passionate attachment to guns. Like a local sheriff, Harvey always had pistols at his side, often a weapon on each hip, sometimes in shoulder holsters. During meetings, he paced about his office holding a gun. Harvey challenged his subordinates to shooting contests. One officer upon arriving at the base headed first to the lavatory. As he sat in the john, another fellow entered the next stall. A clatter erupted as a gun hit the floor and slid into the newcomer's stall. Five stubby fingers followed, pawing for the weapon. The new man kicked the gun back toward its owner. The hand and gun disappeared and a low rumbling "thank you" resounded. The officer, bewildered by this introduction to base life, was amused when he was shortly ushered into the base chief's office and the same growling voice issued a "hello." Life in Berlin for a CIA officer may have posed risk, but Harvey overplayed the drama. "If you ever know as many secrets as I do," he grumbled, "then you'll know why I carry a gun."

Bill Harvey latched on to Shackley. The junior officer quickly established himself as one of the most diligent people in Harvey's command. Officers were on the job six or seven days a week. Agent meetings were usually scheduled at night. Officers might put in thirty-six straight hours on a pressing operation. And Shackley toiled longer than the rest. "Shackley was very single-minded, purposeful, and uncomplicated in his thought processes," recalled Thomas Polgar, chief of plans for the Eastern Europe division. Shackley excelled in paperwork and briefings. "He was," Polgar added, "a real delight to have as a subordinate."

Harvey and Shackley shared several traits. Both had little time for tact and subtleties. Both hailed from the nonestablishment side of the tracks. But there was at least one difference between them. Until he settled down with his second wife, Clara Grace, Harvey liked to drink with his boys. Berlin was a nighttime city; bars and clubs flourished after dark. Most officers were hardy pub crawlers. Shackley stayed off the circuit.

For a spy so devoted to the job, Berlin was paradise. Speaking years later, Shackley waxed nostalgic about those days: "In Berlin there were thousands of people flowing across the border daily, so there was a lot of opportunity to get exposure and experience in pursuing programs, because there was just this vast array of people coming out there, which was a potential pool within which to work. . . . In the earlier days, the guy had trouble deciding which of the ten good things he was going to pursue in the course of a day." His satellite operations in Berlin had a host of targets. Czech and Polish diplomats and military officials were nearby. One favorite pool of potential assets was the group of captains that piloted ships on the Elbe, which snakes from Czechoslovakia through eastern Germany and into Hamburg. Shackley dispatched a subordinate to Hamburg to recruit a Polish maritime official overseeing a ship purchase. For days, the case officer wined and dined the Pole. But when he made his pitch, the Pole refused to consider spying for the West. He was too afraid. "It took a lot of practice and courage," recalled the case officer, "to look somebody in the eye and say how would you like to be a traitor to your country and risk your life and that of your family. I taught myself to do it."

Shackley and his case officers pursued Germans who worked in Polish or Czechoslovak missions, maybe as drivers or janitors, who had access to documents or conversations. They chased after Westerners who conducted business in or with Czechoslovakia and Poland. "If you got a guy who could provide you with a railroad timetable for these countries," Polgar said, "that was a rare item in those days."

Down-and-out refugees remained a perennial target. At the Marienfelde Reception Center in Berlin, refugees from the East were processed and debriefed. Bright prospects were passed to the Agency. If they checked out, they were invited by one of Shackley's pseudonymous officers to return to their homeland to gather intelligence or establish an espionage network. Finding refugees willing to return was hard. "We were very lucky to get one out of twenty we approached," said a case officer who worked with Shackley. "Having just risked their necks to get across the border, they were not eager to go back."

Shackley and a subordinate recruited West German engineers and technicians who regularly traveled to factories in Poland to assist in the economic rebuilding there. German firms ordered employees not to cooperate with American intelligence for fear of losing business. But Shackley and the other case officer dangled money in front of potential recruits and found volunteers eager to report what they observed of their industrial surroundings in Poland. "This was the most productive program we had going," said the case officer. "And still the intelligence was all on such a pathetically low level."

In the United States the public knew little about the CIA and even less about the specific work done by secret public servants like Ted Shackley. But Warsaw and Prague routinely hailed their defeats of U.S. intelligence. In May of 1956, Prague publicized the arrest of ten members of an espionage network that sought information about its military airports and military industry facilities. The operation was managed by "an American spy center" in West Berlin, which directed the network via radio and agents that crossed into Czechoslovakia from West Germany. In 1957, the Czechoslovak security forces captured Adolf Gemler, a dentist, and claimed he earlier had fled to West Berlin, been recruited by U.S. intelligence, and returned to Czechoslovakia to deliver espionage equipment to other assets. In a highly celebrated case, Vladimir Vesely, a radio and television commentator, was arrested, tried, and sentenced to twenty-five years for spying for the CIA. Within the Agency, Vesely had been regarded as one of its best recruits. In another episode detailed by Prague, an escaped Czechoslovak bank robber was recruited in West Berlin by the CIA. His assignment was to ferry money, secret inks, and code pads to agents already in Czechoslovakia and to locate a Czechoslovak safecracker he could recruit and bring to West Germany. The safe man would then be trained and dispatched to Czechoslovakia to pilfer documents from offices and factories. Czechoslovak authorities nabbed the bank robber before he could complete his mission.

In the 1950s, such accounts of American spy activity were dismissed in the West as communist propaganda. In retrospect, many have the ring of truth. In 1990, a retired Agency officer involved in East European activities in the 1950s reviewed a long list of Poles and Czechoslovaks arrested by their governments for being CIA agents. "Most of these were ours," he said.

Gossip comes naturally to members of the intelligence community, people who spend their lives looking for single bits of information that reveal important secrets. Rumors about Shackley began to spread. A case officer in another German base heard stories about the fierce softball games organized by Shackley, who browbeat his fellow officers into playing. One ugly tale circulated that Shackley publicly slugged an agent who screwed up a task.

One episode, known to only a few officers, raised the question of whether Shackley's ego hampered his effectiveness as an intelligence officer. Two case officers, who were transferred from the Berlin base by Bill Harvey, accused Shackley of being a fabricator. Their father confessor was another base chief in Germany, who picked up the pair. The two—one was Gus Hathaway, who would go on to a long, distinguished Agency career—told the base chief that Shackley was generating reams of reports based on material from one Polish agent. But Hathaway and the other case officer did not think the agent actually said what Shackley reported.

"I stewed about this for a long time," the base chief recalled. "A snowstorm of reports came out of this agent, and these guys said Shackley was making them up." The base chief was deeply troubled by the allegation. As he put it, "I can't think of any higher crime for an intelligence officer. If you can't have integrity, you may as well not have an intelligence agency."

The base chief realized that if he raised a flap he would be in a losing game. Shackley would deny he had rigged the intelligence to make himself look good. Harvey would make a stink and remind all that he had booted the two accusers from the prestigious Berlin post. The base chief, who did not speak Polish, was in no position to conduct an independent evaluation. He considered broaching the subject with John Bross, the head of the Eastern Europe division, but decided not to, reasoning it would only place Bross in the same no-win situation. Ultimately, the base chief did nothing. But he decided to keep a close watch on Shackley. He knew that an intelligence service attracts ambitious individuals, trains them to be duplicitous, assigns them tasks that are not amenable to thorough and intrusive oversight, and so must rely upon their personal integrity. To question the integrity of an officer was to question the most crucial aspect of the system.*

April 24, 1956, was a good day to be in the CIA, particularly if you were in Berlin, and especially if you had been privileged enough to work on "the Tunnel." On that day, several East Berlin newspapers reported that the Soviets had discovered that U.S. operatives had dug a tunnel into East Berlin and tapped into major communications cables of the Soviet bloc. Berliners in the Western zone reacted by congratulating any American they encountered. The CIA, it seemed, had succeeded in conducting one of the most daring espionage operations of the Cold War. The Agency's accomplishments were unknown to most Americans. Its coup-choreography in Iran and Guatemala was a highly guarded secret. Here was a fine introduction. "Frankly, we didn't know that American intelligence agents were that smart," ran a commentary in *The Boston Post.* "In fact, we were beginning to think that what the Central Intelligence Agency needed was a few lessons on the fundamentals of espionage from some defected Russian agent. But now we take it all back."

Shackley was one of a fortunate few. Most case officers in the base were kept in the dark. Need-to-know dictated who was let in on this highly sensitive project. Shackley's role in the project was not major. He handled liaison with British intelligence. But at least he was part of Bill

---

* For decades, Shackley and Hathaway maintained a feud that became well known within the Agency. Many officers were aware it stemmed from their days in Berlin; few knew of its origin.

Harvey's pet project, and his work on the Tunnel would become an integral part of his reputation.

For the Soviets, Berlin was the hub of their communications system. If a Soviet military officer in Poland telephoned Moscow, the call transited Berlin. The digging had begun in the summer of 1954, and on February 25, 1955, "Harvey's Hole"—1,476 feet long and 78 inches in diameter— was done. British operatives installed the taps, and the tape recorders were turned on.

For a year, the Tunnel produced mountains of intelligence. Agency listeners learned about Soviet troop movements and the personalities of the Soviet command in the East. The Tunnel operation revealed that railroad tracks in East Germany were in terrible disrepair—a comforting fact to those who worried about a Soviet military move against the West. It produced plenty of gossip, including conversations between a top Soviet military commander and his mistress. The price tag for the project was between $25 million and $30 million, and perhaps the most vital achievement of the Tunnel was what it did not show. It picked up no information to substantiate the fear that the Soviets planned an assault on Western Europe.

But there was a problem no one in the CIA knew of at the time—and it was located in the part of the operation that reportedly concerned Shackley, the British end. One of the British intelligence officers involved in the initial discussions about the project, a man named George Blake, was a Soviet agent. The KGB was informed of the Tunnel before a single spade struck the ground. But the Soviets did not try to stop it. To do so would have jeopardized Blake, one of their best assets.

Not until Blake was revealed as a Soviet mole in 1961 did U.S. and British intelligence realize Moscow had been aware of the Tunnel from the start. For decades afterward, CIA people speculated about the degree to which Blake had compromised the Tunnel. Perhaps the KGB had not shared its inside information about the Tunnel with comrades in the military. Perhaps military and intelligence officials were warned not to use the tapped channels for their most sensitive conversations. Perhaps the KGB took the opportunity to whisper disinformation into the taps of the competition. No matter how the Soviets had played it, the general consensus among Agency veterans held that most of the product was bona fide.

The Tunnel demonstrated that intelligence victories might not be what they seem. But at the time of its discovery, anyone with a hand in the operation could expect it to be a career booster. Harvey's reputation was further enhanced. Even after the Agency learned of Blake's betrayal, its officials still marveled at the skill, imagination, and boldness the project represented. To the artisans of intelligence, execution mattered as much as results. The Tunnel would be a factor in deciding Harvey's next assignments. That meant the Tunnel would also shape the career of Ted Shackley.

Shackley left the spy capital of Berlin in the fall of 1958. His years there had been hard work, but he had not much to show for it. One case officer who toiled alongside Shackley claimed that many of the satellite branch operations were rolled up by the East's security forces, "either because of their stupidity, or because they were penetrated by the opposition, or due to George Blake." Not only had Blake revealed the Tunnel to his Soviet colleagues, he supplied the KGB with the identity of MI-6 agents—maybe, by his count, five hundred. Blake did not see documents that named the agents run by Shackley and the Berlin base. But he did read intelligence reports that indicated where the Agency had been able to establish agents. By passing such information to his Soviet contacts, Blake provided the intelligence services of the East with leads for their spycatchers.

Failures and roll-ups aside, among his bosses, Shackley developed a solid reputation. "He thought of himself as pretty good," a fellow case officer remarked, "and most people accepted that view." He had not pulled in any spectacular catches, but he possessed strong management skills, could write a decent report and be counted on to get a job done. In Washington, Tom Polgar evaluated operations of the Berlin base and Shackley's branch. "I had a sense," he recalled, "they were very impressive, energetic and enthusiastic. They were trying very hard to push a big rock up the hill. You couldn't fault the effort. We had no better people."

Alex Shatton, a Polish desk officer, was less polite: "Polish intelligence was a disaster. I was convinced that half the agents we were recruiting were reporting to the UB" (the Polish security service). Moreover, much of the satellite branch's operation was geared toward gathering information that would be useful should war come. Since war never arrived, the intelligence obtained meant little. "None of us had any great stroke of luck," said a case officer who worked for Shackley. "No case was terribly good."

An intelligence officer needed to cultivate a certain amount of obliviousness regarding the difficulties of the trade. Once when Juliusz Katz-Suchy, a prominent Polish statesman, was sitting in a train at a railway station, Shackley approached the outside of the car and held up a note in Polish. Mr. Ambassador, it read, do you wish to defect? Katz-Suchy turned away from the young American. It was not a brilliant plan, but it was an attempt. The United States had sent Shackley and his colleagues to Berlin to be the eyes and ears of Washington's cold warriors. They had to do something.

That was how the game was played in the early days of Cold War espionage. The ultimate value of the intelligence produced was not the sole criterion for judging performance. How one went about the nearly impossible task of penetrating the Iron Curtain counted for much. Did an officer show grit, nerve, persistence, and dedication? Shackley did, and the hard-to-please Bill Harvey thought so highly of Shackley that CIA people referred to the young officer as "the son of Pear."

Shackley never hid his ambition. During his tour in Berlin, he clearly demonstrated he expected to ascend through the ranks. The Agency was populated by many young men eager to get ahead, but some saw Shackley as a step or two beyond in this category. He began to prompt two distinct sets of reactions from his fellow spooks. Friends saw his ambition as a natural quality for an intelligent, determined, capable man. Detractors claimed it was self-centered, an essential component of an arrogant, not-quite-trustworthy man obsessed with his own advancement. These conflicting views of Shackley would follow him throughout his entire career in the CIA. The two sides might agree on the basics: he was bright, a compulsive worker, an able manager. But after that, he was either an upright Agency man or a bastard you had to keep your eye on; a demanding boss who did not suffer fools or an intimidating s.o.b. who looked out only for himself; a decisive leader who could grasp the essence of an issue or a fellow completely immune to the subtleties of life. One time two Agency men entered into an angry argument about Shackley and turned to a nearby CIA officer for his opinion. When the third man reported he had no strong feelings on the subject, they both jumped on him. What's the matter with you? they exclaimed. We're talking about Ted Shackley.

III

Shackley was in Washington for a short time before headquarters ordered him to Japan. What was supposed to be a six-week assignment turned into a difficult three and a half months. A senior Polish military intelligence officer in Japan had approached the United States to defect. The CIA yearned for such defectors. But the Agency does not accept turncoats at their word. Shackley flew to the U.S. air base on Okinawa, where the Pole was being held. His task was one of the toughest jobs a CIA officer can face: to evaluate a would-be defector, to determine if he is the real thing, to handle him so that he comes over smoothly.

Several officers in headquarters suspected the Pole was a fake, that he was posing as a defector for a devilish purpose, possibly to plant bad information on the CIA or to discover what the CIA knew of Polish operations. After arriving in Okinawa, Shackley joined Ed Juchniewicz, a CIA case officer based in Tokyo, in interrogating the Pole. They spent months with him and concluded that he was a bona fide defector. But messages whizzed back and forth, as officers in Washington continued to question the Pole's desire to defect.

The Pole did not help his own case. During his sessions with Shackley and Juchniewicz, he refused to discuss certain portions of his past. There were discrepancies in his cover story. He also was reluctant to talk about his wife, who was a Polish spy still stationed in Paris. Shackley and Juchniewicz pressed him: come clean all the way, or we cannot accept you as a defector. They believed that the Pole was holding back either to protect his wife or to save information for later bartering. But the two case officers could not take him in unless he was entirely forthcoming.

Assessing the Pole became moot. In the midst of the security review, the Pole bolted. Shackley and Juchniewicz had failed to hold on to him. The Pole rushed back to his intelligence service. But his return was not rewarded. Several years later, Juchniewicz was posted to Poland. One day there he came across a story in a military newspaper noting that the Pole had been tried and executed.

After his return from Japan, Shackley took over the Czech desk of the Eastern Europe division. In the clandestine service, an intelligence officer had two career choices. He or she could stay a field operative, running agents and actions, or take the other path, up the management pyramid—from case officer, to desk officer, to base or station chief, to division head and maybe beyond. This trail turned officers into intelligence managers, intellcrats.

Desk officers monitor cable traffic from the field, check names of proposed assets, clear operations, provide support, evaluate reports. Headquarters peers over the shoulders of field officers every step of the way, firing off cables to case officers full of questions and suggestions about their prospective operations and agents. The officers in the field often grumble about being second-guessed by the bureaucrats; the desk officer might worry that a field person had become so entranced with an operation that his or her judgment was clouded.

Shackley's time on the desk put him in direct and daily contact with the high officials of the division. It also revealed where his real talent as a CIA employee lay. He was a born administrator. "Ted was a superior manager," his friend Jamie Jameson observed. "And a managerial ability is in contrast to the case officer style. A good case officer is someone who could deal beautifully with a complicated individual and a particular situation. The most distinguishing parts of Shackley's career would come from managing others, not being a case officer." Shackley was not a spymaster in the Allen Dulles mold. He was an organization man.

Penetrating Czechoslovakia remained a daunting task. But the HUMINT (spy jargon for human intelligence) business was changing. Cross-border operations were down. The Agency was relying more upon a new type of asset, the walk-in. By the late 1950s the Iron Curtain was not as tightly drawn as it had been after Stalin's crackdown on Eastern Europe in the late 1940s and early 1950s. Soviet bloc countries were increasing their diplomatic and trade presence overseas. More Czechoslovak officials now came into contact with the West, and Western business people traveled to Czechoslovakia. All this led to more opportunity for the espionage officers of the CIA.

This evolution in espionage made life easier for the officers in the field and those on the desk. No longer did they have to fret as much about dangerous border-crossings. Now, as the Czechoslovak regime bolstered its foreign legations, the Agency received unsolicited offers from Czechoslovak officials willing to spy for the Americans.

Usually someone showed up unexpectedly at a U.S. embassy or contacted a U.S. official. The fellow would claim to be a Czech intelligence officer, note that he had misused a couple of thousand dollars of official funds, and explain that his accounts were to be audited next week. The offer was clear: for a few thousand dollars he would supply information. A few walk-ins were propelled by higher motives; they rebelled against the totalitarian state they served. Most betrayed their nation for material gain. "Money was the great motivator," a desk officer said. "We'd wait for the knock on the door. A lot came. This was a cleaner way to do things. There were less flaps, no bodies on the borders."

Agency officials still pursued recruitments—all of which had to be approved by Shackley. But the best cases that crossed Shackley's desk were the walk-ins. And of all the walk-ins, the most valuable was a Czechoslovak intelligence officer with a penchant for drinking and gambling, who was posted in Vienna. He had money problems and one day approached the U.S. embassy and offered his services for a fee.

The Czech passed along bits and pieces on the Czechoslovak service. It was not spectacular material. But one day he produced a fine item of gossip: his boss in the STB (the Czechoslovak acronym for State Secret Security) was in a happy mood after a trip to England to meet an agent connected to the West German Parliament and the Social Democrats. With that lead, Shackley and his branch set out to find the West German spy.

It proved an easy task. One of Shackley's deputies pored over German newspapers and quickly discovered that a small parliamentary group from Bonn had been in England during the days in question. The desk man looked up the official biographies of the Social Democrats and produced an obvious suspect: Alfred Frenzel, a member of the West German Bundestag and a Sudeten (Czechoslovak) German, who served on the Bundestag's Defense Committee. The Agency informed German intelligence about Frenzel, and the West German authorities initiated their own inquiry. Eventually the Germans spotted him exchanging identical briefcases with a Czech operative. A year after receiving the tip, the West Germans arrested Frenzel in the Bundestag on October 28, 1960. They seized three Czechoslovak agents as part of a ring that serviced Frenzel.

The Czech desk's uncovering of Frenzel produced other wins for the West in the war of spies. His arrest caused the STB to instruct operatives in the West to stand down. Following this order, a Czech agent in Switzerland buried his secret radio transmitter in a spot where refuse from a shooting range was dumped. A Swiss citizen looking for brass cartridges later unearthed the radio and notified the authorities. The Swiss found a fingerprint on the radio that led them to its owner and allowed them to roll up a network of several persons. Years later, the CIA's Czech desk learned that the Czechoslovak service feared that the Frenzel arrest and the Swiss roll-up indicated it was badly penetrated and that the service had suspended most espionage activity for a year.

Frenzel went on trial on April 24, 1961. He admitted he had turned over secret documents on West German military programs and collected about $70,000 from the Czechoslovaks. The Federal Supreme Court of West Germany sentenced the sixty-one-year-old Frenzel to fifteen years at hard labor.

After the Frenzel affair, the Czech desk heard that when German intelligence presented a budget request, the Bundestag replied that the figure was too low and asked the service to resubmit a higher number. To anyone who worked in an intelligence bureaucracy, that was a sign of a truly successful operation.

The Frenzel case was a classic spy-versus-spy affair. It was rewarding for Shackley's desk officers to bag a Czechoslovak agent. But the desk's prime mission was to collect positive intelligence—information about developments within the target. The priority remained the Czechoslovak military. "If we could get a diagram of an airfield, that would be pretty hot stuff," said one desk officer. The desk maintained contact with about twenty assets who produced material on Czechoslovakia. Yet the Czechoslovak officials the Agency managed to recruit had few important secrets to share. "We had this guy in Cairo who could tell us a little about Czech-Egyptian trade," said a desk officer. "It was interesting, but it didn't affect the Cold War very much." Most cases fizzled out. A Czechoslovak official recruited at a trade fair would never be heard from. One case in twenty-five, a desk officer estimated, produced any material at all.

While many in the Directorate of Plans were obsessed with covert action, Shackley's desk encountered few chances to engage in undercover skulduggery. It was difficult enough to find out what was happening within Czechoslovakia, let alone change what was occurring within this denied area. The Agency supported Czechoslovak exile publications. But most exile groups were ineffectual, penetrated, or too busy warring with political rivals to get anything done. The best Shackley and his officers could do was to attack the communists of Prague with research. The Czech desk ran a name trace on a communist leader of Slovakia and found that he had been imprisoned by the Germans during the war but was set free after only a year. The short sentence seemed odd. To a suspicious mind, it suggested he had collaborated. The Czech desk floated the information about the short sentence in a Vienna newspaper via a journalist asset. The plan succeeded—or seemed to. Shortly after the Agency planted the story, the communist leader was removed from his post. Shackley's Czech desk claimed his departure a victory. "Such operations were pinpricks, I suppose," said a desk officer involved in this scheme. "But they showed we were doing something."

Shackley had become one of the intellcrats—the increasing number of CIA officials who managed the endeavors of others. He sat in his office—one officer recalled Shackley kept the room poorly illuminated —read cables, dealt with turf battles, coordinated plans with other desks and divisions. His decisions affected the lives of foreign citizens he did not know. He pushed paper, and operations proceeded or halted. And he was doing well within the CIA labyrinth. When Dean Almy, who had been a training classmate, stopped by, Shackley told him that the U.S. ambassador to Czechoslovakia was on his way over. Almy was impressed. He had been in the business as long as Shackley and had yet to have an ambassador pay a call on him.

After a short time at the Czech desk, Shackley was bumped to a higher administrative post, one that evaluated operations from an administrator's vantage. His concerns were no longer the nuts and bolts of specific operations. He focused on larger matters. Where were division resources being spent? Was the budget adequate? This assignment moved him further from late-night agent meetings, dead-drops, secret radios, and erratic agents. Within the Agency this was the path to power.

Throughout the 1950s, the CIA was expanding and extending its reach into matters that would decades later spark controversy and scandal. In its mission to do ideological battle, overseas it was supporting journalists, trade unions, publications, and political organizations deemed sufficiently anticommunist. In 1953, the Agency began a secret mail-opening program and initiated a group of projects known as MKULTRA, which sought ways to control human behavior through drugs and other means. The Agency achieved a notable espionage feat in 1956 when it obtained a full text of Nikita Khrushchev's behind-closed-doors denunciation of Stalin. And it was pioneering another type of espionage: high-tech spying. In 1955, the Agency deployed a fleet of twenty-two U-2 high-flying, reconnaissance aircraft.

The top brass remained enamored of the notion of unleashing secret warfare against communists and those sympathetic to Marxists. In 1957, the Agency assisted rebel Indonesian army colonels who opposed the government of President Sukarno, who allowed communists into his cabinet. At a secret site in Colorado, the Agency trained troops of the Dalai Lama, the exiled leader of Chinese-occupied Tibet. Throughout the 1950s, the CIA dropped agent teams into China to collect intelligence and seek out anticommunist resistance. In Costa Rica in the mid-1950s, a halfhearted CIA campaign sought to unseat President José Figueres, a moderate socialist, who left office in 1958.

Not everyone in the Company appreciated the continued drift toward political meddling and covert action. Espionage purists were put off by the interventionist activities of their colleagues. "I did not care for the whole covert action business," said Richard Kovich, a Soviet branch case officer. "It had a bad effect on what we did and on what the United States government did." But such sentiments did not rule. The Agency was heading toward more and grander covert actions, and Shackley, a good soldier, would be there to carry them out.

On April 28, 1960, Betts Shackley entered the county courthouse in West Palm Beach and lied. When her attorney asked where her husband was employed, Betts, sworn to tell the truth, reported that Shackley worked for the U.S. State Department. Even as she sought a divorce from Shackley, she would not blow her husband's cover.

Two months earlier, Betts had filed papers to end her marriage. Ever since returning from Berlin in 1958, she and Shackley had lived apart. Her divorce petition claimed that in Germany Shackley had told her he no longer loved her and would not provide a home for her. She went back to West Palm Beach alone. Betts had made several trips to Washington to attempt a reconciliation but was rebuffed each time. Shackley refused her pleas that they consult a marriage counselor. She told the court the whole travail had brought her serious mental and physical anguish.

The Shackley marriage had fared poorly in Berlin. The two arrived seemingly happy. But they were posted to an environment hard on couples. The clandestine profession imposes isolation. Such a situation was, CIA officer Michael Burke observed, "more trying for wives who shared little of substance of their husbands' work, and thus bore the limitations without the involvement, the penalty without the reward of achievement." In Berlin, a case officer assumed his house was bugged, his phone tapped, and the domestic help was an asset for the other side. "You certainly didn't bring your work home and talk about it," one said. Some officers bent the rules, but Shackley took security precautions quite seriously. "He was very, very secret about what he did," said Ted Brown, Jr., his high-school friend and Betts's brother. "He never said what he did to anyone, including his wife."

The lifestyle of a CIA man tested a good marriage and exacerbated the problems of a shaky one. Most agent meetings occurred at night. Husbands were off at all hours, and they were forbidden from fully explaining their travels. Spying provided cover for any husband who wanted to run around. Divorce became common within the clandestine service before it did in American society at large.* A loose pattern developed among divorced CIA men; many subsequently married a woman in the business. They were nearest at hand, but they also understood the limitations of a life ruled by secrecy. And that was what Shackley would do.

In Berlin, Shackley fell in love with Hazel Burson, a tall, striking woman, with long black hair and sharp features that reflected her Native American lineage. She was a strong-willed woman—a good match for Shackley. Inconveniently, she was married to another base officer, James Burson. As had Betts Shackley, Hazel had followed her husband to Berlin. But she was not an outsider to the covert world of the Agency. She was employed in the base in an administrative post.† A few times she was asked to help out on operations. Once she was outfitted with a purse that contained a hidden camera and told to take pictures of certain sites in East Germany. But mostly she was a secretary at the base. On one

---

* No figures are publicly available regarding divorce in the Agency, but anecdotal evidence indicates it was widespread. There were other prices to pay for being an undercover patriot. Many Agency veterans share the impression that members of their profession suffered a disproportionate rate of heart attacks and alcoholism.

† In the mid-1950s, there was one woman case officer in the Berlin base, another worked in a supervisory position, and all the other women were either report writers or secretaries.

occasion she was assigned to Shackley's office as a temporary. Afterward, Shackley instructed a clerical supervisor not to send Hazel to him anymore and explained: "She's dangerous."

Shackley did not stay away from Hazel Burson. The two began an affair. Whether or not Betts—or James Burson—knew of it, others in the base cultivated their own suspicions about the pair. "When people become indiscreet and use official facilities like safe houses, you become aware of it," one case officer noted. To some of his less-charitable colleagues, the episode revealed one more facet of Shackley's persona: when he saw something he wanted, he took it. Don't mess with her, one CIA man told Richard Dane, a new arrival in Berlin caught staring at Hazel, she's married to Burson, but she belongs to Shackley. Within the Company there was gossip that Shackley had arranged a temporary assignment out of Berlin for Burson to clear the way for his pursuit of Hazel.

The breakup of her marriage was painful for Betts Shackley. Her brother, Ted Brown, Jr., told the Florida court that when he and his wife, Ann, visited the couple in Germany in 1957, Shackley made it plain that he no longer loved Betts. He constantly sniped at her. Ann Brown noted that Shackley harshly berated Betts about household matters. Betts told the judge her marital problems landed her in the Army hospital in Berlin.

Shackley declined to appear at the divorce hearing. He and Betts had earlier agreed on a settlement. Betts received all the household items, a 1959 Volkswagen, the interest in two Florida properties they had held, and a fifteen-hundred-dollar payment from Shackley in lieu of alimony. A court-appointed special master found that Betts had suffered "extreme cruelty," and the divorce was granted in May of 1960.

Two months later, Hazel and James Burson divorced. Ted Shackley and Hazel Tindol Burson were free to enter into their own intra-Agency marriage.

On the evening of November 17, 1961, a solemn Willy Brandt, the mayor of West Berlin, appeared before a large, anxious crowd in his city. That afternoon an American military cargo plane on its way to Berlin had crashed in the Berlin corridor—the airspace over East Germany reserved for flights from the West. A French fighter aircraft accompanying the cargo aircraft had failed to return to its base. The last radio message from the French pilot reported that an East German fighter had buzzed his aircraft and the military transport. Two hours later the Soviet Union released a startling charge: an Allied plane had strafed an East

German airbase, killing seven persons, and had been shot down. A state of "undeclared war" had descended upon central Europe, according to Moscow. The East German government announced it would no longer allow the West to transport any military equipment to Berlin and that all flights into Berlin must be subject to East German inspection.

As Brandt proclaimed to his fellow West Berliners that a moment of reckoning was at hand, a group of U.S. officials convened in Camp David, the presidential retreat. The secret gathering included John McNaughton from the Department of Defense, David Henry from the Department of State, Carl Kaysen and Henry Kissinger from the White House, and Ted Shackley from the CIA. Their task was to figure out how the United States should respond to the dramatic events unfolding in Germany.

This select assembly at Camp David were among the few to be aware of the situation, for the crisis had not occurred. It was merely the product of the imagination of Thomas Schelling, a strategy theorist for the Rand Corporation. He had devised this scenario to allow the U.S. government to "play" a crisis—with these officials assuming the roles of both U.S. and Soviet decision-makers—to gain insight into the dynamics of Cold War tensions. Schelling's Berlin crisis was reduced to a seven-page memo, distributed to the government representatives when they landed at Camp David on Friday evening, September 8, 1961, for the weekend.

The prospect of a Berlin crisis similar to Schelling's scenario was not farfetched. The Berlin Wall had been erected less than four weeks earlier.* Schelling, the author of *The Strategy of Conflict,* had designed the Berlin game to stress uncertainty. He also was curious to see what role nuclear weapons might play in a confrontation. In July of 1961, he had authored a paper that suggested what calculations U.S. policymakers should make before launching a limited nuclear strike. In only the way a theorist can, he argued that if nuclear weapons must be used, they should be employed for symbolic purposes rather than for military utility. "Destroying the target," he observed, "is incidental to the message the [nuclear] detonation conveys to the Soviet leadership."

The mood was intense that Friday evening, as Shackley and some of the best and brightest of the U.S. government lifted off in helicopters from the pads outside the Pentagon and flew to the presidential retreat. "We kept thinking we might be overtaken by real events," said Alan Ferguson, an economist who assisted Schelling at Rand. Right away, eleven officials from the White House, the State Department, the Penta-

---

* The Agency had failed to detect any sign that the Soviets and East Germans were planning such a bold move. "How come we didn't know anything about this?" President John Kennedy complained when told about the barricade's appearance.

gon, and Rand were divided into two squads. The Red Team, predictably, represented the Soviet leadership; the Blue Team was the United States. Kaysen and Henry were now Soviets; Kissinger and McNaughton were running the U.S. government. They picked up the scenario where it left off and called the shots as the crisis proceeded. A control team, led by Schelling, monitored the two sides and dictated the procession of events.

Shackley was not among those who wrestled with the heavy decisions. His role was modest but vital. He was on the control team to provide a reality check. If the Blue Team decided to stage some kind of incident in Berlin—say, knock out a civilian radio transmitter in East Berlin—Schelling wanted someone on his squad who could say whether that could be done. Schelling had asked for a knowledgeable CIA officer with field experience in Berlin matters. The Agency produced Shackley.

The decision game finished without a true climax when the weekend ended. Though military maneuvering never ceased, both Red and Blue teams appeared more interested in negotiation than confrontation. This development came as a surprise to Schelling and his associates. "To those of us on the control team, it became a cliché that it's terribly, terribly hard to get a war started," Schelling recalled.

Shackley, a junior intelligence officer, had been fortunate to see how the other half, the policymakers, live. These men were the ones who rendered the decisions that sent Shackley and hundreds of his Agency comrades into action. Those granted access to this secret exercise could find in it some reason for optimism in a tense world. Shackley, though, drew no such conclusion. The event had been too artificial for him to apply to reality. No matter how much they pretended, they were playing a game, not making the hard choices that one day might need to be reached.

One aspect of the exercise particularly discouraged Schelling and his associates. Neither side, it turned out, accurately read the moves of the other. At a postgame meeting, members of both teams were stunned to learn what their foes had been thinking and trying to achieve. During the exercise, one team would embark on an action believing it sent a clear message to the enemy. But the postmortem showed that the enemy almost never interpreted the move as expected. This was a disturbing conclusion for the geopolitical theorists. It also could be worrisome for a Cold War foot-soldier—an intelligence officer—called on to participate in those high-risk actions designed by higher-ups to send signals.

A postgame memorandum observed that the weekend at Camp David disclosed an additional lesson: a "small sign of boldness is a sign of weakness. . . . It may be better to do nothing and be *thought* cautious."

As Shackley was to witness firsthand, this lesson would be utterly lost upon those U.S. officials who dictated policy on the newest Cold War confrontations, in Cuba and Southeast Asia, officials who would be relying on Shackley to do their dirty work.

CHAPTER FOUR

MIAMI: COWBOYS, GUNS, AND SPIES

I

ON April 21, 1962, Bill Harvey, the gruff, gun-toting CIA man, was in Miami. He had not come to Florida to relax. The Agency's not-too-covert war against communism had shifted to a new locale. Forget Europe, the Reds were now in Cuba, less than one hundred miles away, truly in the backyard. Harvey, no longer in charge of the Berlin base, had been entrusted with perhaps the most sensitive assignment in the Agency. He was to arrange the assassination of Fidel Castro, the Marxist leader of Cuba, whose demise was an obsession of the Kennedy administration.

Harvey arrived in Florida carrying four poison pills concocted by the chemists of the CIA. As part of the scheme, Harvey was to provide $5,000 worth of explosives, detonators, rifles, handguns, and boat radar to a leader of Cuban exiles in Miami. In return, this exile would smuggle the death pills into Cuba. Harvey ordered the Agency's Miami station— code-named JMWAVE—to procure the equipment. The man in charge of rounding up the lethal goods was the officer Harvey had handpicked to head the JMWAVE station and serve as the field commander for the crusade against the communists of Cuba, Ted Shackley.

Harvey and Shackley drove an arms-filled U-Haul truck through the wet streets of Miami to a drive-in restaurant parking lot. Harvey passed the keys to a mob-linked hoodlum named John Rosselli, who was supposed to transfer the weapons to Cuban exiles. Fearing a double-cross, Harvey and Shackley kept the parking lot under surveillance until the

Cubans arrived as planned and drove the truck away. The CIA, as part of an unholy trinity that included the Mafia and right-wing Cuban expatriates, was a step closer to murder. A short time later, the Cubans returned the truck empty, and Harvey and Shackley brought it back to the rental office. Then, for the spymaster and his young associate, it was on to more official U.S. government business.

The parking-lot rendezvous was but one episode in a long series of underhanded anti-Castro actions waged by the Agency following the triumph of Castro's revolution in early 1959. After he and his comrades marched into Havana, Castro quickly showed he would not be deferential to the superpower to the north. His forces staged a large number of public executions, mainly of ex-military officials. The new government seized the property of U.S. businesses that had flourished during the corrupt tenure of dictator Fulgencio Batista. In April, Castro came to Washington and met with Vice President Richard Nixon, who then recommended to Eisenhower that the United States quash the revolution. Castro had yet to publicly embrace communism, but communists held important posts in his government.

After a year of watching, Eisenhower told the Agency to act. The CIA began to teach would-be resistance fighters in Miami paramilitary skills, such as how to use exploding bullets, silencer-equipped machine guns, homemade explosives, and napalm. The Agency found plenty of volunteers. Following the revolution, thousands of Cubans had fled Cuba and settled in Miami. The city turned part Latino. A Little Havana neighborhood grew with more and more refugees. Many of these Cubans refused to consider their move to Florida a permanent relocation. They gathered in restaurants, bars, hotel lobbies, and residences to plot revenge that would lead to their return home.

In taverns and diners along the highways of Florida, pseudonymous American intelligence officers met with angry and vengeful expatriates. The mysterious Americans pitched political strategies. They came looking for recruits for secret missions. They dispensed cash. They encouraged and blessed the ongoing intrigue.

In Washington, the exiles' unseen accomplices searched for a shortcut. Starting in March of 1960, Agency officials—bureaucrats following the wishes of their ultimate commander, the President—plotted fanciful schemes against Castro. The brainstorming was extreme. One imaginative CIA thinker proposed spraying Castro's broadcasting studio with a hallucinogenic chemical. The geniuses of the Technical Services Division (TSD) produced a box of cigars treated with a substance that would lead a smoker to become temporarily disoriented. The hope was that

Castro could be induced to light up before a speech. Another plan called for exposing Castro to a compound that would cause his beard to fall out. Nothing came of all this.

The higher-ups of the Directorate of Plans sought a more permanent solution. In the summer of 1960, the craftsmen of TSD contaminated a box of Castro's favorite cigars with a lethal toxin. But the cigars never made it to Castro. That same summer, the CIA enlisted members of organized crime (Rosselli, Salvatore Giancana, and Santos Trafficante) and Robert Maheu, a private investigator and occasional CIA operative, in a conspiracy to spike Castro's food with poison. This plan went bust when Castro stopped visiting the Havana restaurant where he was to be poisoned. The CIA-Mafia conspiracy was put on hold. But the top men of the Agency had something bigger in mind.

Deputy Director for Plans Richard Bissell, regarded a sure bet as a future director, proposed a paramilitary invasion of Cuba. Dulles embraced the idea, and first Eisenhower and then President John Kennedy approved. The CIA was now in the secret-war business. The news flowed through the chatty exile community of Miami: a liberation army was forming. Those interested could visit a storefront in Miami, fill out an application, and wait until contacted. By March of 1961, Cubans throughout Miami talked hopefully about the coming invasion and the impending fall of Castro.

On April 17, 1961, thirteen hundred or so anti-Castro Cubans—all trained, armed, managed, and assured by the Agency—landed on Cuban beaches at the Bay of Pigs. Within days, Castro forces captured almost twelve hundred of the invaders and killed about one hundred in a pathetically lopsided battle. The event, so early in the Kennedy administration, was an utter disaster. For years afterward, participants and partisans argued about who was at fault. Kennedy loyalists maintained the new President had been pressured, perhaps even bamboozled, by overly optimistic and enthusiastic CIA men, that he was told the assault would trigger a popular uprising against Castro. CIA advocates cried that Kennedy, too worried about keeping the United States' obvious hand hidden, faltered by not providing enough air cover for the men on the ground and doomed them to a military rout. The operation, though, was such a flop that there was enough blame for anyone involved who had not tried to halt the folly. The misjudgments, errors, and foul-ups that comprised the Bay of Pigs invasion prompted one historian to label it a "perfect failure."

Kennedy, the Agency, and the exiles were humiliated before the world. Their embarrassment was Castro's victory. Privately the President vowed "to splinter" the Agency into "a thousand pieces and scatter it to the winds." Bissell and Allen Dulles were marked. They would be granted a respectable period of time before they had to clear their desks and depart from the Agency.* But the Kennedy brothers, particularly Robert, the Attorney General, would soon be back knocking on the Agency's door, demanding something be done about Castro.

The defeat did not alter the administration's view toward Cuba. A Kennedy-commissioned review of the Bay of Pigs debacle concluded that "there can be no long-term living with Castro as a neighbor." Castro was, the secret report proclaimed, "a real menace capable of eventually overthrowing the elected governments" of other Latin American nations. The study observed that operations such as the Bay of Pigs "are a form of Cold War action in which the country must be prepared to engage" and that the United States was locked in a "life and death struggle which we may be losing, and will lose unless we change our ways and marshal our resources with an intensity associated in the past only with times of war."

Professional intelligence analysts saw it differently. The CIA and the State Department released a joint paper on Cuba noting that the "survival of the Castro regime would probably not in itself pose a direct threat to the immediate security of the U.S." The report cast a pessimistic assessment of any campaign to uproot Castro. Still, the analysts wrote, if Washington left Cuba alone, Latin American regimes would interpret that as "evidence of weakness." Their message: Castro was not a danger to the United States, his ability to spread revolution was limited, there was little hope of toppling him, but something had to be done to preserve the image of the United States.

Only weeks after the Bay of Pigs, Robert Kennedy was anxious to revive the anti-Castro campaign. "The Cuba matter is being allowed to slide," the younger Kennedy complained in a June 1 memorandum. But he knew why: "Mostly because nobody really has the answer to Castro." In July of 1961, the Special Group, the National Security Council committee that reviewed covert actions, agreed that U.S. policy should be to stir opposition to Castro and, as one NSC memo put it, "help bring about a regime acceptable to the U.S." This was a task for the CIA.

But in the months following the Bay of Pigs, the atmosphere at the JMWAVE station in Miami was desultory. The debacle had sucked the life out of the post and cost the Agency many agents on the island. Slowly, the Miami station returned to life. Espionage operations were mounted. Paramilitary activity resumed, with an occasional, not very significant raid. Yet no overall strategy ruled the station's actions.

By the fall of 1961, the Kennedys were impatient with the lack of

---

* Days after the debacle, Dulles, speaking about large-scale covert actions, ruefully noted, "I would like to get out of this business. It is going to ruin the Agency."

progress and turned to two non-Agency men to design a new covert action program to rid the President of Castro. Assigned to the task were Richard Goodwin, a presidential aide, and Brigadier General Edward Lansdale. A silver-tongued, sharp-looking but gangly adman, Lansdale had joined the OSS during the war and had become a counterinsurgency expert. On loan to the CIA from the Air Force in the early 1950s, he advised Ramon Magsaysay, the U.S.-supported Philippine leader, on how to overcome the communist-backed Hukbalahap rebels. There he displayed his taste for the unconventional. In one episode, his operatives spread rumors in villages about the existence of a local vampire. Then Filipino army teams snatched a Huk in the middle of the night, punched two holes in his throat, hung him upside down, and returned the bloodless corpse to a spot where fellow Huks would discover it—all part of an attempt to stir fear of the darkness among the rebels. After ensuring Magsaysay's victory, Lansdale moved to Vietnam as a senior CIA officer. He was an imaginative, crafty fellow who never lost the Madison Avenue spirit. He believed one could win a war with the right PR. The Kennedys were taken with this results-getter and problem-solver. Collaborating with Bobby Kennedy, Lansdale and Goodwin drafted a blueprint for trouncing Castro.

The analysts of the CIA, the State Department, and the military's intelligence services, if consulted, might have told Bobby Kennedy not to waste his time—and might have said the same to those who would do the spying, fighting, and dying for the Americans. On November 28, 1961, the Agency submitted to President Kennedy an intelligence estimate that belittled the potential of any anti-Castro campaign. Castro's regime "still commands substantial popular support," the estimate said. The analysts observed that increasing aid to the internal resistance might boost the amount of anti-Castro activity, but they concluded "it is highly improbable that an extensive popular uprising ... could be fomented." Castro's death, they added, probably would result in a significant increase in the strength of the Communist Party.

The pessimistic CIA estimate did not slow the White House or Lansdale. Two days after its release, President Kennedy created an interagency team to devise a plan of action on Cuba. Progress was to be monitored by an expanded version of the Special Group—which included the new CIA director John McCone (a Republican businessman who had formerly chaired the Atomic Energy Commission), national security adviser McGeorge Bundy, U. Alexis Johnson of the Department of State, Roswell Gilpatric of the Defense Department, and General Lyman Lemnitzer of the Joint Chiefs of Staff, General Maxwell Taylor, and Robert Kennedy. Secretary of State Dean Rusk and Secretary of Defense Robert McNamara were to attend meetings of the Special Group

(Augmented). Lansdale was named chief of operations. The man the Agency selected to run its portion of the Cuban program—its Task Force W—was Bill Harvey.

In January of 1962, Lansdale, working in his Pentagon office, put the finishing touches on his master plan to overthrow Castro and committed it to a nine-page memorandum. His ambitious design covered everything: political intrigue, economic warfare, psychological operations, and paramilitary action. "The climactic moment of revolt," Lansdale predicted, "will come from an angry reaction of the people," who would rise up against Castro and appeal to Washington for military help. The entire U.S. operation against Cuba was code-named Operation Mongoose.

In his memo, Lansdale complained that the CIA so far had failed to produce the "necessary political agents" in Cuba to guide a popular movement. He gave the Agency three weeks to complete an evaluation of eight to ten possible candidates. The Agency also had two weeks to devise plans for establishing an anti-Castro underground in twenty locales in Cuba. He expected the CIA in less than a month to submit a schedule for sabotage actions inside Cuba.

Copies of the Lansdale memorandum were circulated to the Kennedys and the highest levels of the U.S. government. The next day the interagency group on Cuba met with Bobby Kennedy. The President's brother told the participants that they must apply the maximum effort to win the secret battle against Cuba. There would be no acceptable excuses. In a postmeeting memorandum to the members, Lansdale wrote, "We have all the men, money, material, and spiritual assets of this most powerful nation on earth. It is our job to put the American genius to work on this project, quickly and effectively."

Within a month of the initial Mongoose meetings, Lansdale composed a detailed, top-secret plan of action that presented a week-by-week schedule of events that would inexorably lead to an overthrow of the Castro government in precisely the first two weeks of October of 1962. Lansdale confessed little was known of the "real situation" inside Cuba but, nevertheless, maintained anti-Castro sentiment was strong enough to support a resistance program.

He mapped out all the specifics. Before March was over, the Agency was to have three agents in Cuba to report on potential resistance and to convince would-be partisans that the United States was ready to supply them with weapons, ammunition, and equipment. In April the CIA would establish five more agents. That month the Agency would set up a clandestine radio transmitter inside Cuba to broadcast news, slogans, and music of the resistance. By June, another twelve CIA agents would be settled on the island. Then three "resistance teams" would be infiltrated into different areas. Guerrilla bases and a leadership headquarters would be established. In July five more resistance teams would arrive. The next month, the resistance would stage a general work slowdown throughout the country; paramilitary preparations would continue. In September, the underground would expand "to every locality in Cuba." A general strike kicked off October. Finally, there came combat. The resistance, according to Lansdale, would need only two weeks to gain control of a large piece of Cuban territory and organize a provisional military government.

The plan was absurd. It envisioned nothing but success for each phase. The Special Group (Augmented) discussed the proposal and requested that Lansdale submit a more modest one that focused on intelligence collection. It took Lansdale a day to come up with an intelligence collection plan "upon which to base the decision to undertake actions to cause the overthrow of Castro." Lansdale set the goal of placing between thirty-three and seventy assets in Cuba by the end of July.

The Special Group (Augmented) permitted the CIA to conduct covert actions, as long as they were not designed specifically to inspire a rebellion in Cuba. That left a lot of wiggle room. The Kennedy advisers desired Castro out of power, but they were not willing to commit to an all-out effort. And the group approved Lansdale's highly optimistic plan to dispatch to Cuba two teams of agents every two weeks through the middle of May, at which point the program would send off four teams every other week.

Lansdale set preposterous quotas for the Agency: 105 agents recruited and 50 trained by March 31; another 50 chosen and 35 more trained by the end of May. Two months after that, the Agency was expected to have found an additional 100 agents and to have prepared 70 more for infiltration. All told, within half a year, the CIA was to recruit 255 Cuban spies—an astonishingly unrealistic number.

In the basement of the Agency's new headquarters in Langley, Virginia, a suburban community a few miles from Washington, the men and women of Task Force W directed the nerve center for the undeclared war against Cuba. A sense of elitism was present. They were all toiling on an operation that everyone knew was dear to the President. The Cuban show was where the action was. Harvey was pleased to be in charge. Bodies were scooped from all over the world to fill personnel slots in the task force. Few came with any expertise in the area.

The front line of the campaign was the secret JMWAVE station in Miami. At the start of 1962, the station was in disarray. Station funds were unaccounted. A boat or two was missing. Harvey needed his own man in Miami, someone who could impose order on the chaos, and he chose Ted Shackley.

Bumping the JMWAVE chief out of his post and replacing him with a young, brash officer would have triggered a bureaucratic uproar. Harvey did the next best thing. In early 1962 he installed Shackley as a deputy to the station chief and told him to straighten out the mess in Miami. (Shackley came to town with his new wife, the former Hazel Burson.) Within a short time, the chief of station went on too public a drinking binge, and he was removed. Harvey slid his man from the deputy position to the top spot. For the thirty-four-year-old, ever self-confident Shackley, it was a career-making move.

II

Shackley presided over a clandestine empire, the largest CIA post outside of headquarters. JMWAVE was a collection of unimpressive refurbished wooden office buildings and warehouses secluded on a heavily wooded 1,571-acre tract. The site was a onetime Navy blimp base that the University of Miami was leasing from the government. Not even the president of the university knew the true identity of his ostensible tenant, a firm called Zenith Technological Enterprises. Access was restricted; gray-uniformed guards patrolled the perimeter. Phony sales charts and business licenses hung on the wall. Shackley's own office was spartan, not-too-large, and furnished with a drab government-issued desk and chairs.

Shackley's station was run as a foreign post; everyone overlooked the fact that the Agency, which was not supposed to engage in domestic operations, was managing an expansive in-country operation. His officers set up front companies—boat shops, gun stores, travel companies, real estate firms, and detective agencies—to provide services to the station and cover for employees. More than one hundred vehicles were leased to JMWAVE. CIA warehouses stocked armaments of varied makes and types and all necessary supplies, including caskets. Medical personnel, psychologists, and polygraph experts were assigned to JMWAVE. Its holdings included dozens of pieces of real estate, from small apartments to palatial residences, used as safe houses. Operational sites were scattered throughout the region. There were training camps on various keys off the coast and in the swampy Everglades; one was disguised as a private hunting club.

Shackley's station possessed a few airplanes and developed its own small navy that included a mother ship, supply ships, speedboats, and small rubber landing craft—vessels used to ferry agents to and from Cuba and to deliver weapons and equipment to Cuban allies in the secret war. A small naval base was set up behind a luxurious home in Coral Gables.

Shackley supervised hundreds of Americans, several dozen of whom were case officers handling Cuban agents, assets, and operatives. Contract employees provided special services—for example, boat-piloting training. And at Shackley's command were hundreds, if not thousands, of Cuban exiles who were paid assets—men and women whom Shackley generally never met.

Shackley and his officers were to nurture, support, and control the Cuban exiles. Political action experts guided lush U.S. subsidies to the favored of the exile community. The foreign intelligence (FI) staff of JMWAVE, often relying on exiles, sought to gather information on what was happening in Cuba: within the military, within the economy, within society at large, and, with little success, within the small ruling group Castro headed. Overseeing FI was Warren Frank, a somber Nebraskan, who previously served as deputy to Shackley on the Czechoslovakia desk. A training division prepared exile volunteers for runs to the island. Other JMWAVE sections maintained security, directed counterintelligence, handled communications. The annual budget for the Cuban show would come to surpass $50 million, with Shackley's station claiming much of that.

As the lord of JMWAVE, Shackley had to manage the two disparate sides of the Directorate of Plans: the boom-and-bang of paramilitary activity, and the stealthy collection of intelligence. Shackley was a classicist; his first decade as an officer had been in espionage. But he was not one of those CIA officers who passionately cast themselves into one camp or the other. To be successful in the Agency he had to handle both.

The paramilitary gang considered themselves swashbucklers, comrades-in-arms with the rugged and daring Cuban exiles, bold enough to take matters right to Castro. The station's PM officers, about a dozen or so, ran their own separate shops and kept far away from JMWAVE headquarters. They commanded platoons of willing exiles and operated out of various safe houses, which Shackley occasionally visited. They were not desk jockeys, and they disdained the Agency paper pushers.

The most prominent CIA cowboy in Miami was William (Rip) Robertson. A tall Texan, fiftyish, slouched and usually dressed in wrinkled clothes, Robertson was a longtime Agency PM man. He had helped organize the Bay of Pigs attack. At the start of that assault, when reluctant exiles refused to leave their ship and hit the beach, Robertson urged them on with the shout, "Get off, you bastards. It's your fucking war!" Since the summer of 1961, Robertson's band of CIA-backed exiles had kept alive the war against Castro. To pump up his boys, Robertson once offered Ramon Orozco, an Agency commando, fifty dollars if he brought back an ear from a raid. Orozco returned with two. Robertson paid him the hundred.

Grayston Lynch, another of Shackley's PM officers, had been the top American at the Bay of Pigs. Lynch, a round, balding, wide-necked Texan, had served with the Special Forces in Laos. For Shackley's JMWAVE, he ran his own outfit of exile raiders.

One of the PM experts at Shackley's station, Bob Wall, a broad and tall officer who had joined the Agency in 1947 and served in Malaya in the early 1950s, developed a specialty of infiltrating into Cuba small teams that searched for islanders who opposed Castro in order to try to organize a resistance. Wall's principal agent in Miami, a Cuban, sifted through the community of exiles looking for leads on Cubans his teams should contact. Perhaps somebody in Miami had recently heard from a disenchanted cousin in a certain province. If that person checked out, one of Wall's teams would find him, encourage him to join or start a resistance movement, and promise him guns and money.

In both espionage and paramilitary operations, the Americans ran the show. Cuban exiles were their foot-soldiers. The pay for Cuban agents was low, about $200 a month. Some case officers fell for their agents, believing too much in their powers and reports. But among many Agency people, there existed a disdain for their allies in anticommunism: Cubans were too hot-blooded to get the job done, they were not completely trustworthy, and—the ultimate sin in the world of spies—they could not keep a secret. "To a Cuban a secret is something you tell only one hundred people," quipped Justin Gleichauf, chief of the CIA's small field office in downtown Miami. "The Agency and administration were naive in dealing with Cubans. They thought they were dealing with some breed of Europeans where self-discipline is part of the character. The Cubans had no self-discipline." Such sentiments were widely shared. "A Cuban," a Task Force W official snarled, "is someone who can't keep his mouth shut."

The exile scene in Miami was a near free-for-all. "Every Cuban, it seemed, had his own political party and strike force," Gleichauf recalled. Weapons were everywhere. Felix Rodriguez, an agent of the station, managed a mini-armory of the equipment JMWAVE provided him, including recoilless rifles and bazookas. One time he and a few friends were pulled over by a sheriff's deputy on a highway. The deputy noticed that the rear of the stationwagon contained a 57-mm recoilless and some ammo, shells that were about two feet long. The Cubans told him they were duck-hunting.

Shackley's was a heady task. The Cuban show was a pet project of the President, whose youth, vigor, and energy Shackley admired. Shackley considered himself a doer, much as Kennedy seemed to be. To friends and colleagues, he did not come across as a strident ideological Cold Warrior. Certainly he was an anticommunist, and he definitely was no liberal. But more than a politically motivated zealot, he was passionately goal-oriented. His natural intelligence seemed best suited to practical matters, how to achieve the mission at hand, not vexing abstractions of political philosophy. He was neither a flamboyant personality nor a person prone to great bouts of self-reflection. "He was an executive more than anything else," said Jamie Jameson. He was precisely the sort of man—a salute-and-get-the-job-done type—the policymakers at the top needed to wage their secret crusades.

Shackley inspired strong first impressions. When he assumed control of JMWAVE, some station personnel wanted out, including Thomas Clines, a case officer. Clines had joined the Agency in the late 1940s and became a courier. Through much of the 1950s, he worked for the technical division, which included overseas jobs, such as bugging foreign embassies. In the spring of 1960, he was deployed to Panama to train Cuban exiles for what he believed was a program to build slowly a resistance force inside Cuba. No one told him about the pending Bay of Pigs operation. His agents on the island, also left in the dark, were caught unawares by the security crackdown triggered by the invasion. After that massive screw-up, Clines asked to be transferred from the Cuban program. He was persuaded to stay as a case officer in Miami. Someone had to meet the Cuban agents who escaped capture and returned. Clines, an affable, burly man, was a natural schmoozer. He made a perfect greeter.* But Clines wished he were elsewhere.

Clines did not have high hopes for the new station chief. When Shackley took over, he called the JMWAVE staff together. There would be, Shackley declared, tighter management of the boom-and-bang. There would be more emphasis on intelligence collection. This was not an informal getting-to-know-you session. This was Shackley laying down the law. If you don't want to go along with this, he added, you can transfer out of here. Clines decided to accept Shackley's offer. But that night, over a bottle of scotch, Rocky Farnsworth, chief of covert operations for the station and Clines's supervisor, said that he himself would not last long at JMWAVE under Shackley. Farnsworth was not interested in espionage. He wanted to hit Castro. Since he would soon be gone,

---

* In this capacity, Clines first encountered Rafael "Chi Chi" Quintero, who would become a lifelong friend and a player in later controversies. Quintero, according to Clines, infiltrated into Cuba prior to the invasion and was apprehended by Cuban security at the time of the Bay of Pigs. In jail, Quintero, who assumed he would be executed, answered a call for another prisoner who was asleep. His jailers removed him from the cell, handed him the other man's clothes, and told him to be on his way.

Farnsworth told Clines, it was important, for continuity's sake, that Clines remain. Clines would have to find a way to live with Shackley.

The new JMWAVE chief's priority was an intelligence program that could produce the information needed for planning the end of Castro's revolution. Espionage was his field of expertise. But Shackley's tenure in Miami as chief of spies did not start well. In April of 1962, his station tried to infiltrate two agent teams into Cuba and exfiltrate another. It failed on all three. Life on the ground was not as easy and neat as Lansdale's carefully composed schedules. Bill Harvey hopped a flight to Miami to check on the situation.

Harvey personally watched over Shackley's shoulders as the station initiated a new series of infiltrations. It was on this trip that Harvey, who earlier had been ordered to develop an in-house CIA capacity for assassinating foreign leaders, enlisted Shackley for the drop-off of weapons to mobster John Rosselli as part of the effort to kill Castro. Decades afterward, Shackley asserted he knew "virtually nothing of the substance" of Harvey's relationship with Rosselli and that he never met the gangster—not even when he accompanied Harvey to the parking lot. His boss simply had asked him to obtain a shopping list of weapons. "We had no need to know," Shackley explained, speaking for his entire station. He was not even curious, he insisted. Washington was running a number of its own operations and occasionally called upon his station to do a task related to some undisclosed scheme. Straight-and-true Company officers did not ask why. They respected the cherished principle of compartmentation: only those who need to know are told the details. Shackley honored this sacrosanct rule better than anyone else—especially on matters concerning his boss. Unless you were a fool, you did not ask questions of Bill Harvey.

After Harvey returned from his visit to Miami, he notified the overseers of Operation Mongoose that Shackley had succeeded in infiltrating three agent teams into Cuba and that seventy-two actual or potential reporting sources were in place. (The public record does not indicate how he defined "potential.") Lansdale then reported to the Special Group (Augmented) that with Shackley managing JMWAVE, the "CIA now has largely solved its difficult organizational and personnel staffing problems. . . . CIA is now moving ahead with the intelligence collection needed to construct appropriate political, psychological and resistance operations to win our goal." Brimming with optimism, the general declared the Agency was ready to move into a fuller operational phase, which would include paramilitary training on an "intensive scale."

Not all went smoothly for Shackley. In early May, a JMWAVE boat attempting to land one of his agent teams was spotted by a Cuban patrol. The CIA men fired on the Cubans and escaped. Havana announced that the Agency operatives killed three Cuban sailors and wounded five others. Shackley whipped off a report to headquarters: the incident was not his fault or that of any of his officers. The patrol merely had stumbled upon Shackley's boat. And days later, Shackley's station succeeded in sneaking a three-man team into Oriente province. This raised to four the number of teams Shackley had prowling through Cuba.

An enthusiastic Lansdale drew up another of his schedules for Operation Mongoose. In the next month he wanted the U.S. Information Agency to create musical and visual symbols to express anti-Castro sentiments (including "a hand symbol as easy to do as 'V for Victory'") and the Pentagon to induct and train Cuban-Americans "for possible future military action inside Cuba." Shackley's JMWAVE was to produce Cuban defectors; to ready a "voice of Cuba" radio transmitter; to help the USIA devise the right music and symbols; to step up the infiltration of its agent teams; to train exiles in guerrilla skills; and to plan one major sabotage operation. The sabotage, Lansdale explained, should demonstrate that there is popular resistance to Castro. Lansdale, sitting in his Pentagon office, sincerely believed that a few Americans with a few good ideas—Shackley among them—and a well-organized plan could spark a revolution in another land.

Operation Mongoose was not proceeding in lockstep with Lansdale's schedule, but Shackley was trying to develop as many reporting sources inside Cuba as he could. During the first week of June, he heard from the team he had dispatched to Oriente province. Cuban security forces were on its trail. Three weeks later, JMWAVE picked up a report that the Cubans had found and destroyed a CIA team in Oriente. Nevertheless, Lansdale was delighted that Shackley recently had managed to hide a cache of arms and ammunition within Cuba.

Lansdale inspected the JMWAVE station at the end of June. After being briefed by Shackley, a sharp briefer able to put his programs in the best light possible, the general returned to Washington favorably impressed with the Miami chief and his crew. "I was pleased to note," Lansdale wrote, "that CIA has built a team which has a number of people experienced in operations into Communist-controlled areas (Europe and Asia), whose know-how strengthens the operations of people with Latin American experience. . . . Overall, this is a splendid effort by CIA within present guidelines. On intelligence-collection, the magnitude of the special emphasis given the operation is indicated by the presence of 45 agents now in the Habana area alone (a rather remarkable accomplishment in a Communist capital where there is no official U.S. presence). In addition, there are agents and teams in the provinces; efforts are being made to complete the provincial coverage at an early date, since there are some areas insufficiently covered now." Lansdale was also happy to announce that the CIA had begun broadcasting its "Voice of Cuba."

On July 11, 1962, Shackley sent Harvey a long cable describing an operation being run in Cuba by a JMWAVE agent. The agent had built a network of dozens of collaborators—mostly women—who fed him information, often through an intermediary. His crew included a high-ranking Cuban army officer, the widow of a banker, and a secretary. Shackley paid the agent $500 a month, and JMWAVE heard from the agent every few weeks via secret writing—notes written in a form of invisible ink and mailed to cover addresses.

Much of Shackley's cable was devoted to examining whether the CIA had to worry about the agent's true loyalties or security. Was it possible he was a double agent or that his operation might be known to or compromised by Cuban intelligence? The man appeared trustworthy. But, Shackley noted, "at least ten persons with varying degrees of knowledge of his clandestine operations have been held temporarily or permanently by" Cuban intelligence. Any of these might have squealed. Shackley expected this project to yield high-priority intelligence, yet he had to acknowledge its success might be imaginary. His memo revealed a constant in his trade: certainty was a rare commodity.

Shackley's station did not suffer for a lack of volunteer spies. "There was no shortage of leads," an FI man recalled. "We had lots of offers— send me a radio, I know how to run it." Several Havana doctors were recruited through relatives in Miami, and they provided information on officials who were patients. By early autumn of 1962, Shackley had about six covert radio agents in Cuba. His espionage officers were particularly pleased with one asset in Havana who sent out clandestine radio reports; they secretly brought him to Miami for three days of debriefing. While this Cuban was in Miami, the station received a coded radio message from this same agent. How could he be in two places at once? Oh, don't worry, the ace agent replied, that's my brother-in-law transmitting. Another typical Cuban lapse in security, the CIA men sighed.

The station exploited friendly diplomats in Havana, especially those in the West German and British embassies. Agency technicians developed containers that looked like stones. Inside Shackley's officers placed a message, a cipher pad, secret writing supplies, or a radio crystal for an agent. The stones were shipped to Cuba in diplomatic pouches and then placed at sites suitable for agent pickups.

All together, a senior JMWAVE espionage officer estimated, Shackley had about forty reliable agents throughout Cuba that he could call upon —a more modest estimate than the chief of JMWAVE had provided to Lansdale.

Shackley did achieve a minor coup. His station was running the sister of Fidel Castro. In early 1960, Juana Castro turned against her brother. Upset about the growing influence of communists, she developed contacts with the underground. Shackley's station communicated with her through an intermediary in a Havana embassy. She eventually agreed to receive an Agency representative. In August of 1962, Shackley dispatched Warren Frank to Mexico City to rendezvous with her. The Agency wanted one of its own to size her up and give her a pat on the back.

Frank met Juana Castro at an Agency safe house. Juana Castro no longer knew much about what was happening within her brother's government. Nevertheless, she was the sister of AMTHUG—the CIA cryptonym for Castro—and told some interesting tales, even if only gossip. She shared unflattering stories about the young, self-centered Fidel. She pinned the blame for his conversion to Marxism-Leninism on Che Guevara (AMQUACK, in CIA communications) but insisted that Castro possessed a strong independent streak and predicted he would not become a pro-Moscow hack. She offered no insight on significant matters, such as Castro's talks with the Soviet Union and his future plans.

Fidel's sister supplied the Agency samples of her handwriting, which were passed to an in-house handwriting expert. (The graphologist later pronounced Juana Castro stable.) Frank purchased several hundred Cuban cigars from her as an easy way to help her out financially without placing her on the CIA payroll. He sent some of the cigars to headquarters, and JMWAVE officers subsequently heard that President Kennedy himself had distributed them in the White House. The Agency always liked to have a case it could trot out before the President, and this one made Shackley and the station look good, even if Juana Castro produced little first-class intelligence.*

III

On paper in Washington, Operation Mongoose was relegated to an intense intelligence collection program, one that might lead to an operation to overthrow Castro. Despite the wishes of the Kennedy brothers to see Castro ousted, the national security bureaucracy was not yet officially committed to a specific program to force out the Cuban leader. Still, Shackley in Miami was overseeing paramilitary and sabotage operations. Agency assets targeted bridges and production plants in Cuba—more for show than any strategic purpose. Harvey complained about the "tight controls exercised" by Washington and the need to provide "excruciat-

---

* In June of 1964, Juana Castro left Cuba for good and embarked on a propaganda tour of South America organized covertly by Shackley's station and CIA headquarters. For years afterward, Langley paid her $16,800 annually and supported a foundation she created.

ing details" to his supervisors. He and others griped about the plans they had to write for every proposed action. "It went down to such things as the gradients on the beach, and the composition of the sand on the beach in many cases," said Samuel Halpern, Harvey's assistant. To Harvey, the Special Group (Augmented) was pussyfooting with Castro. Then there were Lansdale's ridiculous schedules. But lost upon Harvey were what the men at the White House considered the finer points of foreign policy. For them, lurking always in the background was the desire not to rile the Soviets too much.

Personality conflicts in Washington hindered the campaign against Castro. Harvey and Lansdale could not stand one another. More serious was the enmity between Harvey and the Cuban show's true overseer, Bobby Kennedy. JMWAVE and Task Force W officers picked up a steady stream of stories about battles between Harvey and Kennedy. In one encounter, an impatient Kennedy supposedly demanded to know why Shackley had not yet infiltrated a team into Cuba. Harvey responded by explaining that the team members had to be trained. I'll take them out to my estate and train them, Kennedy said. What will you teach them, sir? Harvey shot back. Babysitting? Harvey routinely referred to Kennedy as "that fucker." He criticized the Kennedy brothers as "fags" who did not have the guts to take on Castro. Halpern learned of one White House meeting when his boss offered the observation that those in attendance wouldn't be in this goddamn pickle if the Kennedy brothers had displayed balls in earlier days.

Bobby Kennedy, the overeager godfather of Operation Mongoose, frequently asked Richard Helms, Deputy Director for Plans, for details on JMWAVE missions. He cultivated his own links with Cuban exiles. Several were guests at his family estate. Members of a JMWAVE commando group directed by Grayston Lynch regularly talked on the telephone to Bobby. "I'd come into the safe house in the morning," Lynch recalled, "and they would say, Bobby says this, Bobby says that." Kennedy routinely called Harvey and officers further down the line to find out what was happening, to offer assistance or to cheer them on.

In Shackley's station, there was real fear that Bobby Kennedy was too close to the exiles. Shackley sent into Cuba an agent who had met Kennedy in Washington. The agent's mission was to evaluate resistance groups on the island. For a spy, the operative had a bad habit. He went to church every morning. One day Cuban security was waiting there for him; a girlfriend had fingered him. Shackley received reports the agent was undergoing torture. Station officers feared he might tell the Cubans of his encounter with the President's brother. Any public statement along such lines would embarrass the White House. That was precisely the type of "noise" Shackley and his subordinates were paid to prevent.

The agent was tried and executed, and when the Miami station received a report on the trial, its officers let out a collective sigh. Their man had not talked.

Kennedy passion did not translate easily into policy. Throughout the summer of 1962, as Phase I of Operation Mongoose (the intelligence-collection period) drew to a close, the policymakers reviewed what Shackley and the CIA had achieved and what was next for the Cuban show. Lansdale wanted the White House to endorse a step-by-step plan toward a counterrevolution. The national security bureaucracy was split. In a memorandum to Lansdale, Robert Hurwitch, a senior State Department aide, summed up Foggy Bottom's view: "The policies and actions which the United States might feasibly adopt and undertake against Cuba (short of the employment of military force) will at best probably have only marginal effect on Cuba." The State Department favored a strategy of harassing Castro with covert actions and seeing what happened. But Brigadier General Benjamin T. Harris, the military's representative for Operation Mongoose, urged devising a plan to overthrow Castro, one that might demand the use of his armed forces.

In Lansdale's own evaluation of Operation Mongoose, he praised Shackley for organizing a major intelligence effort. JMWAVE had infiltrated eleven Agency teams into Cuba. But nineteen maritime missions were aborted. (Lansdale did not report that these numbers were much lower than his earlier schedules anticipated.) The general highlighted the accomplishments of a JMWAVE unit in Pinar del Rio province in western Cuba. The team, Lansdale claimed, attracted recruits and was resupplied with arms and equipment by Shackley's station. Lansdale reported that this team's "potential" participants numbered two hundred and fifty—"a sizable guerrilla force." If equally large rebel groups could be developed in other Cuban provinces, he noted wishfully, a revolt was within reach.

But Shackley's operations elsewhere were not as effective. "The effort in more remote provincial areas of Cuba, where guerrilla resistance was expected to be spotted, recruited and organized, was short of the hoped-for goal," Lansdale wrote. Yet he remained wedded to an October revolution. A revolt could be triggered with the right nudges. "Our own U.S. assets in organization, personnel, and equipment are sufficient to liberate Cuba, given the decision to do so," he proclaimed. Lansdale, without hard facts, was convinced that enough Cubans were ready to take up arms against Castro.

As Lansdale was trying to convince the White House to unleash Shackley's station, Agency analysts issued yet another pessimistic estimate on

Cuba. "The Cuban ground forces are well able to intimidate the general population and to suppress any popular insurrection likely to develop in present circumstances," the report concluded. Lansdale was operating in another world.

In Miami, Justin Gleichauf, the chief of the Agency's downtown field office, did not need the DDI eggheads to tell him that Operation Mongoose was destined to fail. "It's a good thing they didn't ask me any questions," he said. "I would have told them to forget it—all these Cubans with their half-baked schemes." His colleague Ted Shackley, though, did not share such misgivings. It was not in his nature. "He did what he was supposed to do," Gleichauf remarked. "I doubt he ever said anything [against the program]. He was supposed to go out—and charge."

Under Shackley's command, JMWAVE spun at a crisis pace. People were always trotting about with clipboards and papers. Lunch breaks were short; business moved at the chief's intense velocity. Washington, from the Kennedys to the Special Group to Harvey, was pushing hard for results. Harvey visited the station and delivered the message that the Kennedy men expected regular hits against Castro. It was not necessary to kill a lot of people, but those at the top wanted plenty of boom-and-bang.* Shackley transferred the pressure to the staff of JMWAVE. He was "very demanding in a cold, cold, calm, deliberate way," said CIA officer Jamie Jameson. An officer challenged him at his own peril. He was an intimidating figure. Lynch was astounded by Shackley's ability to absorb, retain, and recall information. When Lynch handed him a proposal for a raid, Shackley read it so fast it seemed he was, at best, skimming. But then, days or weeks later, Shackley quoted whole passages. Lynch drew a useful conclusion: "You didn't try to bullshit him."

Shackley always advertised that he was in control. He insisted on approving every single expenditure made by any JMWAVE employee. He would be at his desk until midnight reading financial reports. His fastidiousness caused unpopular delays in reimbursements. FI chief Warren Frank became a minor hero of the station staff when he persuaded Shackley to allow him to sign off on expenditures up to $300.

Shackley visited headquarters periodically to brief Agency personnel on all he was accomplishing in Miami. He had developed a reputation as a sharp briefer. He could distill information and present it in the crisp fashion busy bureaucrats appreciated. He displayed charts illustrating

---

* Harvey visits had their special moments. On one trip to the station, Harvey, looking for a way out of a building, confronted a door that was boarded with a two-by-four. "I don't have time for this fucking door," he growled, reeled back, and kicked it open.

the reporting sources his station recruited and their productivity. It was clear, said one Task Force W official who attended the briefings, that Shackley embellished such reports. "There was always a healthy skepticism among the senior people about Ted and other station chiefs who would come in and tell us what a great show they were running," this officer recalled. "No station chief ever came back and said, we're fucked up." But some of his colleagues and peers suspected Shackley was particularly adept at presenting positive information about his programs.

Shackley kept a tight rein on the PM squad. He demanded to be informed of all the details of a mission. He ordered the station's cowboys to submit detailed operational plans. Case officers dreaded the time when they had to brief Shackley on a proposed action. Rocky Farnsworth, chief of covert operations, resented the intrusions of Shackley, who had no experience in this field. After a short time of wrangling with Shackley over specifics of various missions, Farnsworth dropped an ultimatum: if you don't quit interfering, I'm out of here. Shackley responded, you're out now. He replaced Farnsworth with Dave Morales, a large, mean-talking veteran of the CIA's coup in Guatemala. Morales was devoutly loyal to Shackley. "He would do anything, even work with the Mafia," Tom Clines recalled. Morales hated communists, and years later bragged to an Agency colleague how he had once in South America parachuted out of an airplane with men he suspected of being communists. Before they all leaped, the story went, Morales sabotaged the parachute packs of the Reds. He had the pleasure of waving good-bye to them, as they plummeted to death.

A nearly impossible job for Shackley was counterintelligence (CI). There were hundreds of Castro agents milling about Miami. "The exile community was penetrated to the fullest degree," said Al Tarabochia, an officer in the Dade County sheriff's intelligence unit. Shackley was desperate to improve CI. He introduced tougher psychological and polygraph tests for potential agents. He demanded that the reports of agents be double-checked. If an agent said he visited a certain town during an infiltration, Shackley wanted someone to be able to tell him that the agent showed up there. No longer were weapons and supplies personally delivered to a resistance group on the island. If JMWAVE had to ferry arms to Cuba, one of Grayston Lynch's team went in, cached the munitions and left. Then the station notified the recipients where they could find the materiel. This lessened the threat of ambush. Shackley ordered station case officers not to use assets affiliated with the exile groups. As much as possible, he wanted unilateral agents, people who answered only to the Agency. Despite all these efforts, Havana remained well aware of JMWAVE and its activities.

"Always be forward-leaning"—that was a Shackley pet phrase. He urged his counterintelligence crew to look to that day when U.S. forces would invade Cuba. Shackley's CI division compiled massive files on Cubans it believed were communists, connected to Cuban intelligence, or troublesome for other reasons. Such persons were to be apprehended come an invasion. Managing information on thousands of Cubans was a nightmare, so the Agency in 1962 sent Peter Dyke, a data processing expert, to Miami to ease the pain.

Dyke's task was to tailor Langley's main data system to accommodate Shackley's gargantuan needs. The station's CI staff officers insisted on indexing every single name they came across, even if the information was incomplete or sketchy. For instance, if they suspected a Cuban named Gonzalez—whose first name they did not possess, whose age they could only roughly guess, and of whom they knew little else—was possibly a communist, they wanted to be able to place that person on their list. Dyke protested to Shackley. This would lead to indiscriminate indexing. These names could turn into innocent people being arrested. Shackley's response, Dyke recalled, was, mind your own business and do it: "He didn't give a damn." The episode convinced Dyke that Shackley had "total contempt for any of the human values involved in the work we were engaged in."

Since Shackley's station confronted a denied area, the potential for nonviolent covert action was low. His officers and Agency researchers plowed through the background of prominent Cuban officials, looking for any speck that could be exploited. In one instance, CIA excavators discovered that a senior military comandante had been arrested once in California. Shackley's station arranged for an anonymous letter to be sent to the Cuban embassy in Mexico City, and sometime after that the comandante was removed from his post.*

JMWAVE tried to engage in all the standard dirty tricks. Shackley's

---

* In 1963, the CIA used an asset to sell to Cuban intelligence fake papers that indicated that the Cuban vice minister of defense was a CIA agent. The project was part of an Agency campaign to strain relations between Moscow and the Castro government, in which old-line Communist Party members and newer revolutionaries were often at odds. The vice minister was part of the pro-Moscow group, and as a result of the CIA activity he was arrested in 1964 and charged with treason. The vice minister, his wife, and another high government official were jailed. In 1978, a congressional committee asked about this operation, but the CIA would only share a sketchy account with the investigators. "The story would make dramatic headlines," one CIA memo noted, "if it became publicly known. . . . The fact that several persons were deprived of their freedom as a result of the operation would attract further attention."

maritime unit delivered propaganda material to the island. JMWAVE-controlled front organizations supplied anti-Castro radio programming to Florida radio stations. The Agency operated its own covert radio station, based on tiny Swann Island in the middle of the Caribbean. In Miami, Shackley's men oversaw the various political groups, funding some, keeping others in line, as much as they could. The station tracked the infighting as exile organizations proliferated, split, and merged. It even had an exile agent reporting on the internal deliberations of the Association of Cuban Dentists in Exile. At one point, the CIA reported to the FBI that it had recorded the existence of at least 371 exile groups. Shackley assigned the hearty Clines the task of handling relations with the major political groups. Shackley wanted to know what they were planning and demanded his station be able to influence their deliberations.

At his desk at JMWAVE, Shackley was far removed from the bickering and hand-wringing of Washington. But he knew that the policy elite had not made up its collective mind. The instructions to his station changed often. He proposed operations, and the response he received, or lack thereof, indicated indecision was present in the highest regions of government. "Ted wanted to do things," recalled Mickey Kappes, a young PM officer in Miami. "The commitment to sabotage went up and went down. It was tough to figure out what was going on."

In Washington, Lansdale was pushing the policymakers of the Kennedy administration to egg on the more extreme Cubans, some of whom were staging raids against Cuba without aid from Shackley. He urged approval of what was called "stepped-up Course B"—a plan of increased pressure but no direct military intervention. Lansdale envisioned overflights for agent infiltrations, resupply and leaflet drops, submarine transportation of agents to and from the island, intensified psychological actions, and major sabotage raids. On August 10, the Special Group (Augmented) turned him down.

But at an August 21, 1962, meeting of the Special Group (Augmented), McNamara declared it time to take every possible aggressive step in the fields of intelligence, sabotage, and guerrilla action. McCone observed that all this could be done but that, to date, Shackley's efforts with the agent teams had been disappointing. Future sabotage missions, he predicted, were more likely to fail than to succeed. Nevertheless, on August 23, Kennedy finally ordered that the stepped-up Course B "be developed with all possible speed."

On August 30, Kennedy's advisers approved a proposal for Shackley's station to blow up the Matahambre copper mine in Pinar del Rio province. The ore from this facility was hauled to the port of Santa Lucia by a cable-car system. CIA planners dreamed of knocking out the giant cable towers. But Matahambre had been an elusive target for JMWAVE. In late 1961, a CIA team made it only halfway to Cuba before the boat engine went bad and the radio battery died. A subsequent try ended when a team encountered a Cuban patrol and retreated.

Shackley's station composed a list of additional sabotage targets that included refineries and nickel plants. Lansdale suggested it destroy Cuban "crops by fire, chemicals, and weeds." It seemed Shackley was about to be the front-line manager of a serious secret war.

IV

On September 19, 1962, the analysts of the CIA released a report on Cuba that contained what would become one of the most infamous lines in the history of modern intelligence: "The establishment on Cuban soil of Soviet nuclear striking forces which could be used against the U.S. would be incompatible with Soviet policy as we presently estimate it." Dozens of Soviet ships had arrived in Cuba with military and construction supplies. But, the analysts argued, setting up offensive missile bases "would run counter to current Soviet policy."

The national estimate was considered by Miami station officers a slap in the face. For months, Shackley's station had received information from agents reporting on the presence of missiles and other major weapons in Cuba. By the count of Warren Frank, JMWAVE's foreign intelligence chief, the Agency had collected about 200 "solid leads." But in headquarters the desk men of the Directorate of Intelligence pooh-poohed the reports, many of which did not pan out. Missiles observed by Shackley's agents routinely proved to be torpedoes, fuel tanks, industrial pipes, mooring buoys, or short-range defensive missiles. "We certainly had no reluctance to discover and report the presence of Soviet offensive missiles," Russell Jack Smith, a senior DDI officer, asserted in his memoirs, "but we could not find decisive evidence. Report after report turned out to be demonstrably false, the work of Cuban exiles who hoped for a U.S. intervention in Cuba, or uselessly ambiguous."

But come the summer of 1962 McCone had a hunch that the Soviets indeed were placing offensive missiles in Cuba. His premonition did not affect the bureaucracy. As far as the JMWAVE crowd could tell, stubborn analysts remained reluctant to accept reports indicating they might be wrong. One headquarters officer insisted the station only forward missile reports originating with non-Cuban assets; Cubans were too emotional. That irritated Warren Frank. How could headquarters expect his shop to collect intelligence by only using diplomats and other foreign nationals who happened to be in Cuba? Should he ask allied diplomats to drive through the countryside in search of missiles?

The analysts were right to worry about the station's assets. Shackley's Cuban agents were motivated by a desire to see Castro go. Many longed for U.S. intervention and realized that Kennedy might be more likely to unleash his power if Castro could be portrayed as profoundly menacing. Reports from Cuban sources had to be evaluated with this in mind. Tom Clines ran an agent in Cuba who sent back secret-writing letters claiming he had seen missiles. But Clines was uneasy about this guy. When the agent was in a CIA training camp, he read a lot of science fiction. He also belonged to a political group that longed for a U.S. invasion of Cuba. "I wondered if he was trying to get us into a war," Clines said. When Shackley asked Clines to judge his agent's report, Clines had to share his reservations about the man.

Shackley's officers were frustrated that their agents were being dismissed by the analysts. "It got to be a morale thing for us," one JMWAVE espionage officer said. "Why waste the time, if the guys in Washington do not believe us?" Shackley felt the reporting was being ignored, but he stayed clear of the fight between field and headquarters. He read all the reports and believed the signs indicated there were offensive missiles. But Shackley was disappointed he could not unearth conclusive evidence. "I can't get my teeth into it," he complained to Clines. "I've got to prove this." His officers and their agents kept looking.

Outside the administration, Republicans and conservative Democrats jeered at the notion that the Soviets were shipping only defensive weapons to Cuba and clamored for Kennedy to take care of Castro. With the missile controversy brewing, on October 4, the key men of Operation Mongoose gathered for a meeting chaired by Bobby Kennedy. The Attorney General and the President were upset with the lack of progress in the sabotage program. Shackley's station had infiltrated a few agents and cached some weapons on the island, but it had not produced any big knockout blows. His operatives had not yet hit the Matahambre copper mines, the Attorney General griped. The lack of forward motion, McCone argued, was due to "hesitancy" in administration circles. Kennedy and McCone quarreled over this, but the disagreement finally gave way to a decision to develop more sabotage proposals. The missing ingredient in the Cuban policy remained absent: what was the point of such activity? Was it merely spiteful harassment or the road to revolution? No one could say.

As the policy shuffle in Washington continued, one of Shackley's teams departed for another try at the Matahambre mine. The men were ferried to Cuba by one of JMWAVE's best boat captains, Rolando Martinez, and landed on October 19. The team split up to set the plastic explosive charges on the cable-car towers. But the commandos were spotted by Cuban forces; they retreated before accomplishing the mission. Only six of the eight saboteurs returned to the boat.

For the next two nights, Shackley's raiders stayed close to shore, hoping to locate their missing comrades. On the third night, while listening to the radio, they heard President Kennedy tell the world that the United States had discovered offensive missiles in Cuba and had imposed a naval blockade. The failed commandos were excited and heartened. The team, minus two, returned to Florida, believing that the decisive moment was at hand.*

On October 14, a U-2 had flown over western Cuba and returned with photographs of a ballistic missile launch site under construction in San Cristobal. For the next several days the President and his advisers, in secrecy, debated how to react. The site, once completed, would be able to hurl nuclear weapons on to the mainland of America. On the evening of October 22, President Kennedy disclosed that the United States possessed "unmistakable evidence" that the Soviet Union was establishing offensive, nuclear-capable missiles in Cuba, and he announced a U.S. naval blockade aimed to prevent further shipments of offensive military equipment to Cuba. Soviet ships were soon heading toward U.S. forces.

All those missile sightings claimed by JMWAVE assets now seemed justified. But they were not. On October 18, Harvey had sent the Director a three-page memo that summarized the best of the reports Shackley's station and other CIA components had collected regarding the Cuban missiles. The list contained "all we have been able to dredge up," Harvey wrote. The intelligence was not impressive. The most reliable dispatch came from a source on the island who on September 12 saw a convoy of twenty Soviet-driven trucks pulling canvas-covered trailers

---

* Weeks later, Cuba disclosed that it had captured the two missing agents. Havana newspapers reported one of the captured, Miguel Angel Orozco, admitted that there were twenty Agency "operators" inside Cuba collecting information, that an embassy in Havana was using its diplomatic pouches to help the Agency, that his team had its headquarters in a safe house south of Miami near the Monkey Jungle tourist attraction, and that an Agency man named Bob Wall was running the show. (Rip Robertson was Orozco's case officer and had allowed the Cuban to sit in his safe-house office and overhear his phone conversations with Wall.) The CIA refused to comment. The Cubans claimed Orozco shared the plans for two other CIA projects. One called for exile Cubans disguised as Castro troops to attack a site in Nicaragua. The other involved the installation of an anti-Castro provisional government on an island off the coast of Cuba. After Orozco's capture, Castro launched a radio serial about the CIA campaign against Cuba. Two characters were named Robertson and Wall.

heading west toward Ciudad Libertad. The source drew sketches of the load; the drawings resembled the surface-to-surface SS-4 Shyster missile, a medium-range ballistic missile. Other reports, the Harvey memo noted, had been less definitive—mostly sightings of short-range missiles.

For some reason, Harvey did not include on his list two reports that in hindsight looked solid. The Agency had received a secret-writing report on September 15 from a JMWAVE agent in Havana who claimed that Soviet soldiers were guarding a large area near the city of San Cristobal in Pinar del Rio and that sensitive missile work was proceeding there. And six days earlier, Castro's personal pilot had told an Agency asset that Cuba possessed "many mobile ramps for intermediate-range rockets."

Even if these two reports were espionage prizes, it was not Shackley's intelligence program that uncovered the missile mystery. The first source Harvey mentioned, the one who witnessed the convoy and provided the most convincing intelligence, was no secret agent. He was a refugee. Six days after observing the missile-bearing trucks, he left Cuba. At the Opa-Locka refugee reception center in Florida, this middle-aged accountant told an interrogator about the missiles he had observed. His information was sent to Agency headquarters immediately. This was the first time a missile of offensive dimensions actually had been seen by a credible source. A second refugee report, received at Opa-Locka on September 27, dovetailed with the accountant's observations. The Opa-Locka reports—valuable intelligence—were nothing for which Shackley's station could take credit.

An ongoing program of U-2 surveillance overflights was already in progress. Between October 1 and 3, Agency analysts, primarily on the basis of the two refugee reports, prepared a target card for San Cristobal. On October 3, a decision was made to photograph that region of western Cuba. Some evidence indicates that the flight was scheduled also because a Defense Intelligence Agency analyst, who had examined previously taken photographs, believed a nuclear missile base might be under construction there. On October 14, a U-2 passed over the San Cristobal site and captured photographs that proved the Soviets and Cubans were building such a base.

Years after the crisis, several Agency veterans of the Cuban show maintained that the September 15 secret-writing report from the JMWAVE agent in Havana had been a true tip-off, that Shackley's station had discovered Moscow's precious secret. But neither this report nor the one reporting the remark of Castro's pilot played a role in the decision to send the U-2 over San Cristobal. Perhaps they were dismissed by the analysts or lost in the shuffle. In any event, it was intelligence that looked brilliant after the fact, not intelligence that affected the course of the episode. A postcrisis analysis determined that no threatening missiles were shipped to Cuba before September 8. That meant the hundreds of missile sightings reported by JMWAVE's agents prior to then had been errors, concoctions, or observations of defensive weapons. For all his effort, Shackley had failed to acquire high-level Cuban agents, sources close enough to Castro to pick up definitive notice of the Cuban leader's brash missile plans.

This had frustrated Shackley's bosses in Washington. In the midst of the crisis, Bobby Kennedy asked what was wrong with U.S. intelligence? After the crisis ended, Roswell Gilpatric, the undersecretary of defense, complained, "I never was satisfied with what we got—intelligence—out of Cuba, as such, leaving aside [electronic intelligence] and leaving aside aerial reconnaissance. The inability of our intelligence mechanisms to penetrate in any way, shape, or form into this island . . . always frustrated and alarmed me. I just didn't see how it could be we couldn't get more out of that. We knew more about Soviet Russia than we did about what was going on in Cuba."

But once the missiles were discovered, anyone in Shackley's station, including its chief, who wanted to gloat could do so. Few people knew the source of the intelligence that had led to the detection of the missiles. Without providing details to prove his case, Shackley, three decades afterward, asserted that the station played "a crucial role in determining that the deployment of offensive missiles was the end objective of both Khrushchev and Castro." His agents had been right in instinct, if not in fact. But facts, not suspicions, are what count in intelligence. Shackley and his colleagues were fortunate that in this case the two coincided.

In Miami, Cuban exiles and some CIA officers hoped that the ultimate reckoning had arrived. Throughout the nation and the world, people looked on as the two superpowers moved toward armed, possibly nuclear, confrontation. The U.S. military mobilized hundreds of thousands of troops. In the frantic Miami station, Shackley and his troops prepared for war. Shackley ordered his case officers to locate exile agents willing to parachute into Cuba in advance of a U.S. invasion. Bob Wall, on Shackley's orders, flew to Fort Bragg to discuss invasion plans with the head of Special Forces. Wall reported that he had a resistance in the western end of Cuba organized and ready to go. Shackley dispatched officers to brief U.S. military pilots on what to expect if they were shot down or forced to land in Cuba. Those officers returned to JMWAVE convinced that the balloon was about to go up. Justin Gleichauf was ordered to procure 6,000 roadmaps of Cuba. JMWAVE employees joked about who would be named chief of station in Havana. Maybe Shackley would get that plum.

In the middle of the crisis, Bobby Kennedy told McCone to halt all Agency operations against Cuba. But Shackley, acting on Harvey's behalf, had ordered men to Cuba. Shackley's PM specialists, Robertson and Lynch, were to use submarines to infiltrate Cuba with teams of exiles, join up with existing guerrillas, send back intelligence that the U.S. military might need, and secure areas where U.S. Special Forces could land. Lansdale and the Joint Chiefs of Staff had signed off on this plan concocted by Harvey. Yet when Bobby Kennedy learned of it, he was angered. At a White House meeting, the Attorney General commanded Harvey to cease all such activity. Harvey responded that some of his teams were beyond recall. Kennedy stormed out of the room. Later that day, McCone remarked, "Harvey has destroyed himself today. His usefulness has ended."

At the time Shackley's officers received the stand-down order, Robertson was aboard an airplane heading toward the U.S. naval base in Guantanamo. Lynch and a band of Cuban commandos were at the Homestead military base in Florida, preparing to rendezvous two days later with Robertson in the Cuban mountains.

On October 24, Soviet ships heading toward the U.S. naval blockade slowed or changed their course. Kennedy and Khrushchev in private and public communications maneuvered for diplomatic advantage and an end to the crisis. A U-2 was shot down over Cuba. The first U.S. Minuteman intercontinental nuclear missile went on alert.

Then on October 28, Khrushchev announced the Soviets would crate and return the missiles to the Soviet Union. In previous days, Kennedy and Khrushchev had hammered out a deal. The Soviets would pull out the missiles for a Kennedy pledge not to invade Cuba and to remove Jupiter missiles from Turkey. (The latter action was already in the works.) Other issues were to be resolved, but the crisis was over. A furious Castro publicly accused Khrushchev of lacking *cojones*. The Cuban leader was not content with the ephemeral noninvasion pledge, and rightfully so, for the Kennedy crusade against Cuba—managed by Shackley—would continue, noninvasion pledge or not.

What had Khrushchev been thinking? That question engaged much of the U.S. public, administration officials, and intelligence analysts and was to become a focus of much historical inquiry in the decades ahead. Back in 1962, public consideration of Khrushchev's motives did not include speculation that the activities of several hundred secret U.S. employees in Miami—Shackley and his people—might have been a factor in Soviet and Cuban thinking. From their end of the table, Soviet and Cuban leaders peering at the American covert program did not see the delays and problems that hindered anti-Castro activity. They observed a Kennedy commitment to undoing Castro, one that did not stop short of the use of force. "In the spring of 1962, we in Moscow were absolutely convinced that a second Bay of Pigs was at hand," recalled Sergo Mikoyan, the son of Anastas Mikoyan, a senior Soviet official involved in Cuban policy. Khrushchev later claimed he chivalrously deployed the missiles to protect an ally. Present as well was probably a desire on his part to obtain, in one bold gambit, a strategic gain against his geopolitical rival.

No fan of the Kennedy administration would want its president saddled with the responsibility of having, even if only partially, provoked the Soviets into a disproportionate response. "The secret war against Castro was . . . *not* the cause of the Soviet attempt to make Cuba a nuclear missile base," declared Kennedy aide and historian Arthur Schlesinger, providing his own emphasis. But it is not preposterous that the actions of Shackley and his compatriots influenced Soviet and Cuban leaders when they considered the brazen action of setting up nuclear missile bases. A postcrisis Agency study that analyzed Khrushchev's motives concluded that while he had been looking for a dramatic move against the West, he believed that the creation of a Soviet missile base in Cuba would forestall U.S. attempts to destroy the Castro regime. Robert McNamara conceded in 1989 that "if I had been in Moscow or Havana at that time, I would have believed the Americans were preparing an invasion."

The missile crisis was the end of Operation Mongoose. On October 30, 1962, the Special Group (Augmented) told Lansdale to cease all sabotage and paramilitary operations during the coming negotiations with Cuba. Two days before that, Robert Kennedy had notified the FBI he did not want any "crackpot" individuals or organizations going to Cuba at this sensitive time. FBI headquarters, reacting to Bobby Kennedy's newfound skittishness, ordered its Miami office to pursue any information on freelance exile scheming.

The more fervent anti-Castro exiles were downhearted by the nonviolent resolution of the crisis. To achieve peace with the Soviets, Kennedy seemed to have sold out their cause. Kennedy's no-invasion pledge, one prominent exile wrote, delivered "a soul-shattering blow." The curtain began to fall. The FBI and other U.S. agencies started to restrict the paramilitary activities of exile groups operating outside the control of Shackley's station. On October 31, Customs agents arrested ten Cubans aboard a thirty-five-foot yacht heading for open sea. The vessel was loaded with arms and ammunition. The feds then rounded up a band of American freelance mercenaries who trained anti-Castro Cubans. "U.S. Nabs Anti-Castro Fighters—Why?" read a mournful *Miami Herald* headline.

Bitterness set in among the exiles. "We were cut off after the Cuban Missile Crisis and we were betrayed," recalled Frank Sturgis, an independent anti-Castro activist scheming apart from the CIA. For the exile community, Operation Mongoose had been one big disappointment. The Agency, Sturgis said, "kept putting the idea in the minds of the exiles that we were going to overthrow Castro only in order to get intelligence information. I didn't like that. They were using the Cubans." Irate Miami Cubans badmouthed the CIA and charged, of all things, that Shackley's officers possessed loose lips and that the CIA was penetrated by Castro's intelligence service. Most anti-Castro crusaders, a *Miami Herald* columnist noted, "now make it a major objective to steer clear of the CIA."

A discredited Bill Harvey realized that Operation Mongoose was virtually over. In a draft memo to McCone, he wrote that the no-invasion promise "will preclude any meaningful CIA action on a phased basis to provoke a revolt inside Cuba, since . . . such a revolt if provoked would be totally destroyed by Cuban counteraction in a matter of hours or, at the most, a few days unless supported by a major United States military commitment." Kennedy's pledge to Khrushchev, Harvey noted, also prevented the United States from invading Cuba on the "pretext of a contrived provocation such as an attack" on the U.S. Navy base at Guantanamo. The resolution of the crisis, he went on, had damaged the morale of anti-Castro exiles and rendered it more difficult for the CIA to recruit agents. With Kennedy having assured the continued existence of the Castro regime, sabotage raids were now largely counterproductive, especially since they would mean little and get in the way of intelligence operations. Finally, Harvey predicted—rightly, as it would turn out—that "Higher Authority" would continue to press the CIA for a "maximum effort," with the goal the overthrow of Castro. "This," Harvey declared, "is an unrealistic objective."

On December 29, 1962, the President stood before a crowd of 40,000 at the Orange Bowl in Miami and accepted the flag of Brigade 2506—the Bay of Pigs force. His administration had succeeded in its attempt to free the captured exiles. After months of negotiations, Castro let them go, but only in return for $53 million in medical supplies and food. The President told the crowd of brigade members, relatives, and friends, "I can assure you that this flag will be returned to this brigade in a free Havana." The crowd chanted, "Guerra, guerra"—war, war.

Shackley, who did not dare attend the public rally, was more cynical.

It was obvious that the President's rhetoric soared above policy intentions. To the man in charge of the secret *guerra,* Kennedy's speech was
nothing but "a magnificent public relations gesture."

V

"There is well nigh universal agreement that Mongoose is at a dead
end." McGeorge Bundy delivered that message to President Kennedy
four days into the new year. And Bundy did what bureaucrats do when
policy does not produce the desired results; he began a reorganization.
Bobby Kennedy blamed Harvey. "We'd been working with him for a
year—and no accomplishments," he later said. His criticism indicted
Shackley and his troops in Miami. But the problem was as much with
the mission as the performance. "Mongoose was poorly conceived and
wretchedly executed," judged Arthur Schlesinger. "It deserved greatly to
fail. It was Robert Kennedy's most conspicuous folly." Lansdale, decades
afterward, told his biographer he wished he had never become involved
in the Cuba show.

Operation Mongoose was terminated. Lansdale cleared out his desk
in the Pentagon. Harvey was booted off the Cuban beat. He pulled the
plug on his assassination plot with John Rosselli, which had sputtered
along but not come close to fruition. But this was not the end of the
Cuban business for Shackley and JMWAVE. Another interagency group
on Cuba was established. The Kennedys had not given up.*

Harvey was replaced by Desmond FitzGerald, the handsome and deb-
onair chief of the Far East Division. FitzGerald, once married to the
prominent and liberal socialite Marietta Tree, was ensconced in the
Georgetown set. The well-bred FitzGerald, a personal friend of the Kennedys, took a shine to Shackley—a good thing for the young officer,
since, with Harvey excommunicated, Shackley lacked a mentor. FitzGerald would propel Shackley's career forward, setting him on a trajectory
toward the highest regions of the CIA.†

* In 1976, Rosselli's body was found in an oil drum floating in Biscayne Bay near
Miami. He had recently testified in secrecy to a Senate committee about the CIA-
mob alliance to knock off Castro, and he had shared his story with columnist Jack
Anderson.

† Harvey was shipped off to Rome as station chief. There his well-known drinking
problem worsened. Station officers who resented their new uncultured boss forwarded to Washington all the negative gossip. Stories circulated in Langley about
the time one of Harvey's guns went off in his office. Harvey was brought home
and dumped in a unit that developed countermeasures to electronic surveillance.
Alcoholism continued to impair his performance, and Harvey resigned. After an
unsuccessful stint at practicing law in Washington, he returned to Indiana and obtained a job as a law editor for Bobbs-Merrill. He died in 1976, following a heart
attack.

Task Force W was transformed into a new CIA organizational designation—the Special Affairs Staff. High-level oversight of Cuban operations diminished. The stand-down issued during the crisis was lifted, and Shackley informed his PM officers that the White House and the Agency were anxious to prosecute the vendetta against Castro.

Shackley's station resumed its boom-and-bang operations. But these raids, recalled Sam Halpern, now an assistant to FitzGerald, were "nothing more than pinpricks." Some officers in the Cuban show, as did Harvey, doubted the Agency could overthrow Castro. FitzGerald, though, was a believer. (The enthusiastic FitzGerald asked an assistant to see if an exploding seashell could be rigged and deposited in an area where Castro went skin diving; the Technical Services Division concluded the idea was impractical.) His operational hopes were out of line with the intelligence—such as a State Department study that stated that anti-Castro groups within Cuba "seem to be even less coordinated and less capable of instigating revolt than before."

As JMWAVE's fight against Castro continued, so did Shackley's less noisy espionage program. Castro's immediate circle remained an elusive target. After the missile crisis, returns from JMWAVE deteriorated. Enhanced Cuban security rendered agent recruitment more difficult. Many reporting assets in Cuba faded in productivity; many fled the island. The Cuban government routinely announced captures of CIA teams, declining to recognize the distinction between Agency-sanctioned operatives and freelancers. Those convicted of being CIA agents were sentenced to long prison terms and, in some cases, death.

In Miami the feds chased after anti-Castro weekend warriors not affiliated with Shackley's station, often pursuing them in high-speed boat chases throughout the waterways of southern Florida. But the CIA had its favorite exiles, upon whom it lavished much support—and the most prominent recipient of CIA largess was Manuel Artime, a Bay of Pigs veteran who led the Movement to Recover the Revolution (MRR). In early 1963, Artime set up four bases in Costa Rica and Nicaragua, in preparation for another exile military campaign against Castro. As much as there was a plan, it called for MRR to carry out scores of acts of sabotage with the goals of harassing Castro, hindering shipping, provoking resistance inside Cuba, and perhaps assassinating the man. That spring, Artime and Rafael Quintero, a onetime CIA operative and now Artime's deputy, were telling other expatriates that Bobby Kennedy and the President were behind their program.

Despite the President's no-invasion pledge, the game was not over. The Kennedys—and the CIA—were willing to help those Cubans who played by their rules. If Artime's army kept its operations outside the United States, Washington would provide all the necessary funds and ensure that Nicaragua and Costa Rica were hospitable. With its headquarters in Miami, the Artime project recruited several hundred men for its paramilitary force. Payroll cost ran more than $50,000 a month. The CIA trained Artime's men, as Artime pulled together a small navy, obtained several planes, and collected over 200 tons of American-made arms. The CIA budget for Artime's war would come to total $7 million.

Shackley was none too pleased with this new spin-off. Washington, not JMWAVE, was in control of this enterprise. "He couldn't stand it," recalled Clines, the JMWAVE liaison to Artime's operation. "He hated the idea that the Cubans had gotten to the Kennedys and convinced them that they could operate on their own." In theory, the MRR was supposed to run a stand-alone endeavor. But as long as CIA money was floating the damn enterprise, Shackley figured, it ought to be directed better—and by him.*

JMWAVE operatives ferried barges full of arms and equipment to points off the Nicaraguan coast where they left them for Artime's army. Clines passed to Quintero and Felix Rodriguez, the project's communications chief, JMWAVE intelligence useful for planning raids. The Artime operation was loosely run and, predictably, became an open secret in Miami. To Shackley and other Agency professionals, the Artime sideshow represented the indulgence of Bobby Kennedy. Shackley's objections aside, it rolled on, toward what would be a great embarrassment and murder.

Shackley's station also cheered on a competing clan of expatriates led by a man whom Artime followers hated as much as Castro: Manuel Ray Rivero, a Batista opponent who had joined the revolutionary government and then became disenchanted with Castro. Ray left his government job and organized in Cuba the Revolutionary Movement of the People (MRP), which opposed Castro but pressed a democratic left agenda. He then departed Cuba and attempted to establish MRP in

---

* When Artime visited Washington, the CIA put him up in a Maryland safehouse loaded with electronic bugs that secretly recorded all his conversations. CIA officers also worried about a girlfriend of Artime. An investigation conducted by Shackley's counterintelligence shop found that she was bisexual, had been a mistress to Batista in Cuba and a Venezuelan dictator, and had posed for pornography. All this troubled Langley, but CIA officers concluded there was little they could do about Artime's love life. They did fear that a CIA employee might leak the information to harm Artime's reputation. As one CIA report noted, "There are a number of persons currently in [the Special Affairs Staff] who have very strong unfavorable opinions about" Artime. This memo observed that resentful "personnel at JMWAVE possessed certain ill feelings" toward Artime's operation, since it could do what JMWAVE was no longer permitted to do: conduct sabotage.

Miami. When he asked the Miami station for help—specifically $50,000 —the CIA said no. One Agency official noted in a memo that Ray was so far "left in his thinking that he would be as dangerous to U.S. interests as Castro."

In April of 1962, Ray organized a new group, the Cuban Revolutionary Junta, known as JURE for its Spanish acronym. JURE proved to be of use to Shackley and the station. It provided the CIA information on people in Cuba who might be recruited by the Agency or enticed to defect. But Ray's leftist politics still troubled JMWAVE officers. Consequently, his organization received a smaller share of Agency funds and stroking than Artime's MRR. Ray and his comrades resented this and thought rightfully that Shackley was toying with them to exploit their contacts in Cuba. Shackley instructed Clines to convince JURE otherwise, so the Agency could string it along.

In June of 1963, the Agency finally agreed to support fully JURE operations. In a deal similar to the one with Artime, the CIA offered financial aid and advice to JURE, as long as its actions against Castro were mounted from beyond U.S. territory. It would take time for Ray's force to become operational, but like Artime's outfit, the CIA-backed JURE was rushing toward ignominy.

The Artime and Ray organizations were primed by Shackley and his station, but the Agency's own analysts continued to be pessimistic about a home-grown, Cubans-only policy. In April of 1963, Sherman Kent, the chairman of the Office of National Estimates, penned a memo to McCone predicting developments in Cuba in the coming year. "No serious challenge to [Castro's] power and control seems likely to emerge for some time," Kent concluded. A report prepared by the Joint Chiefs of Staff acknowledged that a spontaneous, widespread revolt was not likely to happen soon. The Pentagon chiefs noted that clandestine intelligence collection in Cuba is "extremely slow and limited"—a slap at Shackley and his station. They complained that Washington would not be able to appraise any revolt until it had already succeeded or failed.

Two years after the defeat at the Bay of Pigs, Kennedy's advisers— Shackley's bosses—were without a coherent policy. But the top Kennedy men definitely wanted Shackley to keep harassing Cuba, and they were disappointed. During the first months of 1963, Shackley's massive station had not conducted any major sabotage raids against Cuba. At a May 28 gathering of White House aides, Bundy pressed for steps to squeeze the Cuban economy, to subvert the Cuban armed forces, and to encourage military leaders to topple Castro. An exasperated Bobby Kennedy fumed that "the U.S. must do something against Castro, even though we do not believe our actions would bring him down."*

In the course of attempting to mount one substantial operation, Shackley was conned. On April 18, William Pawley, a prominent Miami businessman and former ambassador, called Shackley and asked the JMWAVE chief to drop by his office. (Shackley had met Pawley in the summer of 1962, and since then the businessman had done assorted favors for the station.) When Shackley saw Pawley later that day, Pawley explained that Jay Sourwine, counsel of the Senate internal security subcommittee, had requested Pawley's participation in a daring scheme to bring to the United States four Soviet military defectors in Cuba. The Russians would be hurried to Washington and handed over to the committee, where they would spill secrets about the continuing Soviet military presence in Cuba. (The disclosure of such information might well embarrass the administration.) Pawley asked Shackley for advice on managing this operation.

Sensing a grand opportunity—four Soviet defectors were a prize—Shackley told Pawley this could not be accomplished legally without CIA involvement. And Shackley wanted the Agency to be the first to debrief the Soviets. With Shackley watching, Pawley called Sourwine and received his permission to bring the CIA into the project.

Pawley informed Shackley that a key figure in the plan was John Martino, a Cuban-American in contact with the resistance fighters in Cuba who supposedly held the Soviets. Shackley noted that Martino was a lowlife whose previous leads never panned out. (Martino also carried mob connections.) But neither man saw a reason not to proceed with the plan, under which Pawley was to use his yacht to exfiltrate the Soviets.

Pawley and Cuban exiles spent weeks working out the details. The former ambassador was surprised when he learned that Martino had arranged to bring a *Life* photographer on the mission. Shackley tried to persuade Pawley to cut *Life* out of the picture. But Martino was adamant; *Life* was putting up $15,000 for the expedition. The best Pawley could do was to negotiate with *Life* an agreement under which certain information would be censored from its account.

---

* The younger Kennedy had not lost any of his zest for the campaign against the man who had humiliated his brother in 1961. Bobby Kennedy still was in touch with exiles in the field. When Clines in Miami had trouble requisitioning a boat for a mission, his Cubans crowded a pay phone and rang the President's brother. "We got the boat," Clines recalled, "and Shackley was pissed at me."

Shackley concluded the odds were one in a thousand that this project would come off. But he committed to the operation several officers, including PM specialists Rip Robertson and Mickey Kappes. When Shackley found out in early June that a flamboyant exile leader named Eddie Bayo was involved in the plotting, he had more cause for worry. "Headquarters will recall fiasco which resulted from previous WAVE involvement with [Bayo] during Sept/Oct 62," Shackley cabled Langley, without further explanation. "Have advised Pawley [Bayo] unsavory type who exaggerates, etc. Pawley inclined discount past record and believes this long shot which worth playing." And Shackley went along.

On June 5, Pawley's yacht, the *Flying Tiger II,* left Miami with Kappes for an uninhabited island. Three days later, a CIA flying boat Shackley had leased to Pawley landed with Pawley, Robertson, a *Life* photographer, and the ten Cubans who would pick up the Soviets. Meanwhile a JMWAVE ship ferried to this spot the boat the Cubans would use and a collection of arms and ammunition.

The Cubans boarded the *Flying Tiger II,* which was towing the smaller vessel, and headed toward a launching point off the coast of Cuba. Under cover of the night, ten exiles crowded into the twenty-two-foot-long boat. The Cubans said they would return in two days with the Soviets.

They never came back. Shackley tried to determine what had gone wrong. His men who trained and accompanied the Cubans reported that Bayo and the Cubans had not seemed interested in the CIA preparations to retrieve them and the Soviets from Cuba. A few weeks later, Shackley received a report from an agent who noted that five of the ten missing Cubans, including Bayo, had been involved in planning an invasion of Cuba through a dissident wing of Artime's MRR. Now Shackley realized what had occurred. The Cubans had invented the story of the Soviet defectors to trick Pawley, *Life,* and a Senate subcommittee into supporting a freelance strike against Cuba. And they had lucked out by snaring Shackley and his station.

Shackley had covered his rear by telling headquarters not to expect much from this mission. But once he knew he had been snookered, he did his best to squeeze some good out of the humiliation. In a cable to Des FitzGerald, he listed all the fringe benefits of the operation: Pawley, who previously assailed Kennedy's lack of commitment to overthrowing Castro, had gained confidence in Shackley's station; *Life* had learned of the difficulties in clandestine paramilitary operations and would be less likely to knock the Agency in the future; the Senate subcommittee members had seen that the CIA was willing to take a risk for a worthy cause; ten armed men had been infiltrated into Cuba, and they might be irritating Castro; and valuable experience had been obtained.*

Shackley had to put up with other harebrained projects. A few months earlier, headquarters had sent him a proposal for an operation to foment opposition to Castro within Cuba's military, with the ultimate goal of encouraging a coup. The plan had an odd origin. It was hatched by Nestor Moreno and George Volsky, both Cuban exiles who distrusted the CIA. Tad Szulc, a *New York Times* reporter friendly with Volsky, brought it to the State Department and the White House. Foggy Bottom and the White House welcomed the proposal, which called for infiltrating exile operatives into Cuba to organize a network of anti-Castro military officers. They passed it to the CIA, which decided Shackley's station should handle the project. JMWAVE began screening and training agents for this endeavor, but Shackley wanted none of it. He fired back a cable declaring that the operation should be terminated. With Szulc and the others involved, security was already lousy, and this program would compete with other JMWAVE attempts to penetrate the Cuban military. It was clear this was going to be another adventure Shackley could not dominate and control. He recommended that the Agency hand the exiles cash so they could try this on their own. "This operation has a very high 'flap potential,'" he declared. Headquarters initially agreed, but then, probably due to White House pressure, instructed Shackley to continue supporting the program.

Slowly the operation, known as AMTRUNK, proceeded. But it was hindered by an assortment of problems. One key agent, José Rabel, a Cuban army defector in Miami who screened leads for AMTRUNK, continually pressed JMWAVE to help him retrieve his wife and children from Cuba. He became more upset as this went undone. Shackley had to visit Rabel and tell him there was little the station could do and he would have to be patient. When Moreno, the AMTRUNK leader, started talking about organizing an army in exile and establishing a military resistance on the island, Shackley was introduced to him so he could dampen the exile's ambitions. Let's stick to the current plan, he diplomatically advised, and we'll see what we can do next.

Over the next two years, Moreno and Volsky's operatives, with the help of Shackley's station, managed several infiltrations into Cuba and enlisted a few military officers. But the operation never achieved much

---

* After the infiltration, one unconfirmed report indicated the Bayo band was waging raids in Oriente province. But the station could dig up no definitive information on what became of the Cubans. Since JMWAVE had not received word of the Cubans' return to Miami or their capture or death in Cuba, the prevailing—and optimistic—assumption was that they were fighting Castro somewhere in Cuba.

—except for the arrests in Cuba of unfortunate AMTRUNK recruits. Shackley's instincts were right. The Agency should have stayed clear. But it was not his call. Shackley could not pick and choose which clandestine acts he conducted for the anticommunists of Washington.*

On June 19, 1963, the President decided it was time for Shackley to attempt riskier projects, and he approved a program of major sabotage, with the goal of encouraging resistance within Cuba. (Five days earlier, the Agency issued an intelligence estimate that stated, "It is unlikely that internal political opposition or economic difficulties will cause the regime to collapse.") Des FitzGerald compiled a list of targets for Shackley's station: electric power installations, petroleum refineries and storage facilities, railroad tracks and highways, and factories. The first of this new series of attacks was scheduled for mid-July.

FitzGerald was excited. He traveled to Shackley's station. In front of the senior officers of JMWAVE, he declared that the aim was to wage one major act of sabotage every month. At station briefings during the summer, Shackley continued to pass along the full-steam-ahead orders. JMWAVE, the chief asserted, was going to produce more and better hit-and-run raids. Infiltrations and intelligence-gathering missions were to be intensified. The station was to rev up its covert battle with Castro.

Soon Shackley had success to report to Washington. One group of Shackley raiders pulled off two daring sabotage raids. On August 31, this team hit an oil facility in Casildo Harbor. But at the time of the assault, the harbor was under an air defense alert. Shortly after Shackley's saboteurs opened fire with an 81-mm mortar and a 75-mm recoilless rifle, they came under attack. The JMWAVE commandos inflicted damage on the site and hastily fled. Then on September 30, the same band assaulted a large sawmill on the coast of Oriente province. The CIA men encountered no Cuban forces, and the mill, a main producer of railroad ties,

---

* Several Cuban military men recruited during AMTRUNK were arrested in 1965 and 1966, and the program was terminated. "In retrospect," a CIA review noted, "the activity appears to have been insecure and doomed to failure from its inception." Agency officials wondered if the operation was, from the beginning, an ingenious plan by the Cubans to learn the identities of disloyal Cuban military officers and to tie up JMWAVE resources in a phony operation. They even suspected that Volsky and the Polish-born Tad Szulc were communist agents. Szulc's journalism—he had written critically of the Agency—had prompted Langley to question his loyalty. Shackley's station and other CIA components repeatedly conducted analyses of Szulc's and Volsky's pasts, looking for evidence that they were enemy operatives. But, as one CIA report noted, "Suspicions about [Szulc's] motives or possible connections with foreign intelligence services have never been proven."

was destroyed. Weeks later, after a hurricane destroyed many railroad tracks in Cuba, Castro in a speech bemoaned the loss of the vital sawmill. Shackley and his officers could claim a sabotage mission that actually hurt the Cuban economy.

With the clandestine war on Cuba entering a new phase, Shackley decided to inspect some of his troops—but in secrecy. At Jewfish Creek on Key Largo, Shackley and a subordinate met Bradley Ayers, an Air Force captain on loan to JMWAVE, who was training would-be saboteurs. The three men drove to a campsite near Dynamite Pier. Shackley, with his usual obsession for operational security, did not want to be seen by Ayers's Cuban trainees. Ayers had ordered all of them away from the base. He and the two station men ate a Cuban meal alone. Ayers then escorted Shackley and the other CIA man to a concealed location on the coast. From there, they watched Ayers's trainees paddle ashore in rubber boats and move through the wooded area. His men conducted the exercise without a hitch. But afterward Shackley had nothing to say about what he witnessed. Whatever Shackley felt, as he stood in the mangroves and watched, he did not share.

Shackley's sabotage endeavors—even many of the details—were no secret to Castro, or anyone who bothered to listen to him. The accusations the Cuban leader regularly hurled at the aggressive imperialists of the north contained much accurate information on what Shackley was engineering. On October 30, 1963, Castro charged that the Agency was using a 150-foot-long ship called the *Rex* in operations against Cuba and that the vessel was berthed in Palm Beach. In the same three-hour speech, he accused the CIA of landing weapons and infiltrators in Cuba and murdering Cuban workers. Journalists found the ship. If any reporter had been able to climb aboard and peer underneath the over-turned fifty-five-gallon drums on the deck, he or she would have spotted gun turrets.

Shackley's station had been caught red-handed. It recently had used the *Rex* to ferry raiders close to the Cuban shore. The commandos were supposed to meet two comrades infiltrated the previous week; instead they were ambushed by Cuban security. Cuban forces unleashed a barrage of gunfire. The agents escaped and raced back toward where the *Rex* had been, but the mother ship was gone. Its captain was obeying a sacrosanct rule of Shackley's station: do not get caught. The fleeing commandos found a merchant ship that took them aboard.

The Cubans went looking for Shackley's *Rex,* but instead found the *J. Louis.* Mistaking it for the Agency vessel, Cuban fighter aircraft strafed the American-owned ship. Days afterward, the U.S. State Department, citing this Cuban aggression, rejected Castro's call for an end to the economic embargo Kennedy had imposed against Cuba. Two weeks later, Cuba executed thirteen Cubans accused of spying for the CIA. Following the episode, Shackley wired headquarters: the *Rex* and the *Leda,* another CIA ship, "would undergo at earliest opportunity [a] paper sale from current corporations to cut-out corporations to new corporations who would re-register vessels under different flag, change names, change home port, change port of call, repaint, and make whatever modifications possible in superstructure silhouette." Then the vessels would take to the seas again.

In the fall of 1963, Shackley had a lot to track. His own officers were planning attacks. Artime's forces were building up. And the CIA-backed JURE of Manuel Ray decided it was ready to launch its first raid. It selected a Havana power plant to knock out. Ray asked JMWAVE to cache on an island the high explosives his men needed. Shackley okayed the request. The Agency hid the explosives for Ray's raiders, but the JURE boat never showed up. Ray claimed the JURE vessel ran low on gas. The Agency's client was off to a poor start.

As Shackley-managed raids continued and Castro's denunciations reverberated, far in the background Kennedy and Castro took slight moves toward accommodation. In early September, Carlos Lechuga, the Cuban ambassador to the United Nations, discreetly mentioned to William Attwood, the U.S. ambassador to Guinea, that Castro was interested in exploratory talks with his American enemy. The following month, Kennedy informed Jean Daniel, a French journalist on his way to see Castro, that he could live with a socialist Cuba, but not one ruled by a Soviet lackey. See me when you get back from Cuba, Kennedy told Daniel.

The CIA was not in synch with these peace feelers. In the fall of 1963, one of its top assets within Cuba, a revolutionary war hero and government official named Rolando Cubela, delivered his handlers an ultimatum—help me kill Castro or I will leave the island. The CIA was back in the assassination business. (Cubela, code-named AMLASH, had been recruited in June of 1962 after a JMWAVE asset told Shackley's station that Cubela was looking to defect on an upcoming trip to Helsinki. A CIA man met him there and convinced him to return to Cuba as a spy.) Cubela, an erratic fellow who drank excessively and who had recently considered suicide, now demanded military supplies and an audience with Bobby Kennedy.

Des FitzGerald, posing as a personal representative of Bobby Kennedy, saw Cubela in Paris on October 29. He promised Cubela that the United States would support a rebellion against Castro. On November 22, 1963, FitzGerald and case officer Nestor Sanchez again rendezvoused with Cubela in Paris. The CIA men pledged that Shackley's station would deliver Cubela weapons, including high-powered rifles that could be used to kill Castro. (Afterward, Langley cabled Shackley and told him to prepare a cache of hand grenades, guns, ammunition, and plastic explosive for AMLASH.) The two CIA men presented Cubela with a ballpoint pen rigged to contain poison. Surely, Cubela protested, the Agency could come up with something better. He refused to take the pen with him to Cuba.

A CIA internal report, referring to the AMLASH case, later observed, "It is likely that at the very moment President Kennedy was shot, a CIA officer was meeting with a Cuban agent . . . and giving him an assassination device for use against Castro."

In Cuba, Castro on November 22 was lunching with Jean Daniel, the French journalist, when he learned Kennedy had been shot dead. "This is bad news," he responded. Later in the day, he asked Daniel, "What authority does [Lyndon Johnson] exercise over the CIA?"

The day after Kennedy's death, Langley ordered Shackley to activate JMWAVE's propaganda assets. The CIA wanted to make certain that media reports on the tragedy observed that Kennedy's "last major address to [a Latin American] audience concentrat[ed] on Cuban freedom." Headquarters also cabled Shackley, "Postpone [sabotage] ops indefinitely. Rescheduling will depend upon consultations with appropriate officials"—the new President and his advisers.

VI

Shackley's commander, whose covert warriors had tried all sorts of crazy ways to kill Castro, died in a Dallas hospital, and the man accused of shooting him was obsessed with Cuba. In the months prior to the assassination, Lee Harvey Oswald, an enigmatic former Marine who had defected to the Soviet Union and then returned to the United States, was a highly visible representative in New Orleans of the pro-Castro Fair Play for Cuba Committee. In later years, evidence emerged indicating Oswald may have associated with anti-Castro partisans. John Kennedy's demise then might trace back to Cuba—and the efforts of Shackley and hundreds of others. Perhaps Oswald was motivated to kill the President by Washington's anti-Cuba campaign. (Much of it was secret and unknown to Oswald, but Castro did rail publicly about the attacks mounted against him and his country.) It could be that the Cuban leader was paying back Kennedy for the CIA attempts to kill him. It was conceivable that vengeful, extreme Cuban exiles had plotted the murder in retaliation for Kennedy's no-invasion pledge, the Bay of Pigs mess, and the crackdown on freelance anti-Castro activists. Yet the FBI made no special investigation of possible Cuban government or exile involvement in the murder of the President. Nor did the CIA. The Agency even neglected to inform the Warren Commission about its numerous attempts to assassinate Castro.

CIA operations against Castro and its relationship with assorted exiles offered leads federal investigators ought to have followed. Two lawyers for the Warren Commission, appointed by President Lyndon Johnson to investigate the assassination, speculated at the time that Oswald, despite his appearance as a Castro sympathizer, was truly an agent of Cuban exiles and part of a plot to pin blame for the assassination on Castro.

After the assassination, some of Shackley's officers collected rumor related to the slaying. Within Miami's exile community, speculation flew that Castro had authored Kennedy's death. One source in Cuba claimed that Castro was "extremely concerned" that the U.S. investigation into the assassination would reveal Kennedy's death was plotted in Cuba by Chinese communists and Cuban sympathizers. Shackley forwarded this information to the Secret Service and the FBI. But station intelligence also vaguely pointed toward the exiles. A JMWAVE agent reported hearing secondhand that a prominent exile leader had remarked on November 21 that "something big would happen soon that would advance the Cuban cause." In a cable to headquarters, Shackley noted, "This remark when taken out of context is impossible to evaluate."

One JMWAVE case officer called his agents in Miami and radioed those in Cuba to ask if they knew anything regarding the assassination. He requested his assets supply him with information on any Cuban exiles who had disappeared from Miami before or after November 22, who had asked for assistance in obtaining sizable amounts of funds or weapons, or who might have been capable of orchestrating the murder in order to precipitate war between the United States and Cuba.

This officer recognized the possibility of a connection between JMWAVE activity and Kennedy's end. But Shackley's station did not unearth any significant information in this regard. Its effort, however, was modest. Shackley believed that since the CIA did not have primary responsibility for probing Oswald and the assassination, his station only had to collect information "in a passive way" from existing sources.

Shackley and the CIA should have been more curious. "The conspiratorial atmosphere of violence which developed over the course of three years of CIA and exile group operations," a Senate committee later observed, "should have led CIA investigators to ask whether Lee Harvey Oswald and Jack Ruby [Oswald's assassin], who were known to have at least touched the fringes of the Cuban community, were influenced by that atmosphere." In 1979, the House Select Committee on Assassinations judged Shackley harshly, without naming him. His station, its report declared, ought to have debriefed thoroughly all its sources to determine if there were any links between Oswald and Havana, and it should have swept fully its contacts to see if any anti-Castro partisans possessed knowledge pertaining to the murder of the President.*

In the weeks after the tragedy, JMWAVE sabotage operations remained on hold, but Shackley's station whirred. When a cache of weapons linked to Cuba was uncovered in Venezuela in early December, Shackley urged the station's media friends to play up the story and push the theme that this proved there could be no coexistence with Castro. JMWAVE stage-managed anti-Castro demonstrations at Cuban consulates throughout Latin America.

At the same time, Shackley had to fret about several operatives. A Western diplomat who had supplied information to the Agency and used the diplomatic pouch to smuggle radio equipment into Cuba for a CIA agent was out of Cuba and complaining about the CIA's use of him. This man, Shackley cabled the Director, "is no mental giant." He explained that the Miami station "has made frequent and repeated use [of] virtually all Western embassy pouch facilities to transmit equipment and supplies to inside agents." He dismissed the diplomat's remarks.

More worrisome was a blown operation being publicized in a Havana courtroom. Donald Lippert, a Canadian pilot, had been arrested with copilot William Milne at Havana International Airport on October 24 after customs inspectors found explosives among their food cargo. Cuban security also apprehended Maria Magdalena Volta, Lippert's Cuban aunt. The Cubans accused the trio of being CIA operatives. The Cubans were right about Lippert and Volta. Lippert had smuggled into Cuba arms and sabotage equipment destined for a CIA-backed team code-named AMSHATTER, which picked up the contraband from Volta. Lippert confessed after his arrest but claimed Milne was innocent.

Shackley was not one to miss an opportunity. In a cable to headquar-

---

* The House select committee concluded neither the Cuban government nor anti-Castro exile organizations "as groups" played a role in the murder, but it carefully noted that the available evidence "does not preclude the possibility that individual members [of anti-Castro organizations] may have been involved." In 1991, Shackley rejected the possibility of an anti-Castro conspiracy. "My view," he said dispassionately, "was that there was no evidence to suggest Oswald had acted because he had ties to both sides of Cuba's political spectrum—that is, the pro-Castro and the anti-Castro. [He] seemed to be . . . moving about in that milieu to get cover, whatever he was doing. My initial suspicions were that Oswald was either crazy or acting as an agent of a foreign power. . . . As more information became available you had to look at the question of whether it was the Soviet Union. You also had to consider if that foreign power was Cuba. The priority issues in my mind were to examine these two [theories]. Unfortunately, neither of those could be pursued because Oswald was killed, and we're all left with kind of an enigma as to what really happened, who was really behind it. I certainly don't have any authoritative view as to what the bottom line is on that."

ters, he observed that the pending "show trial" of Lippert was designed to bolster the Cuban government's recent seizure of food and clothing parcels mailed to Cuba. Even though Lippert was guilty, Shackley proposed that the Agency wage a "psych campaign designed [to] expose [the] purpose [of the] mock trial as [a] smokescreen for continued Cuban violations [of] international conventions and human rights."

One aspect of the Lippert affair puzzled Shackley. In publicizing Lippert's arrest, the Cubans had not mentioned the AMSHATTER team that collected the arms Lippert had smuggled. Shackley assumed that the Cubans now controlled AMSHATTER and that the silence indicated Cuban intelligence intended to run AMSHATTER members as double-agents against JMWAVE. The CIA was talking to Canadian officials about the Lippert case, but Shackley pushed for the Agency to keep the Canadians uninformed about the tie between Lippert and AMSHATTER. If the Canadians were aware of the connection, he thought, they might somehow use it in Lippert and Milne's defense. "This would be tantamount," Shackley wrote Washington, "[to] telling [the Cubans] we know [the] team [is] controlled, possibly resulting [in the] execution of the team." In late November, as Shackley safeguarded the AMSHATTER secret, a military tribunal found Milne innocent, but sentenced Volta to nine years. Lippert, the CIA pilot, was sentenced to thirty years.

Shackley also was weighing what to do about another problem agent in Cuba—a woman whom Shackley believed was known to the Cubans and likely to be apprehended soon. But the woman, whose arrest probably would lead to the capture of other agents, refused to leave Cuba because her mother was ill. In a cable to headquarters, Shackley sounded as positive as he could: "It [is] WAVE opinion this is not time [to] await developments with stoicism but it is time [to] influence developments via sound action. Thus despite [her] initial refusal to leave Cuba [we] propose [we] continue attempts [to] exfil[trate] her although this problem [is] currently complicated by [the] fact we have no direct contact with [her] and do not know where she [is] located."

Shackley was concerned with more than the woman's safety. He wanted to recruit one of her best contacts—an employee in the insurance office of the Finance Ministry who was close to Che Guevara and who collaborated with Cuban intelligence. He asked headquarters to devise a scheme by which this man would be invited to London to discuss Cuban insurance matters. There a JMWAVE officer would make a pitch.

Nothing happened immediately with the woman in hiding or the insurance man, but Shackley soon collected another catch: a Cuban intelligence defector. Stationed in East Germany, Jorge Alfonso Medina Bringuer, a captain in Cuban military intelligence, had written his mother in New Orleans asking her to meet him in West Berlin. Luckily for the CIA, the mother was in touch with a JMWAVE case officer. In mid-December, the case officer accompanied the mother to Germany. When son and mother met at the Berlin Hilton, the case officer tried to recruit Bringuer and convince him to remain with Cuban intelligence. Shackley had authorized the officer to offer the Cuban $1,000 and a monthly payment of $500. If Bringuer stayed in place for two years, he would receive a bonus of at least $5,000 from JMWAVE and help in resettling. Bringuer elected to defect and earned a smaller reward: a sum of $1,000 and the promise of $400 a month and living expenses for six months. Bringuer was flown to Miami and installed in a JMWAVE safe house. In a cable to Langley, Shackley declared this operation a "job well done."

But intelligence out of Cuba remained a disappointment. The station had almost no coverage at all in Camaguey and Oriente provinces. Shackley's intelligence sources sent JMWAVE a host of tidbits, but much information came through an unreliable chain of hearsay. A military officer reported to Miami on a conversation he had with a former government official, who disclosed the contents of a talk he had with a senior military commander. This commander had speculated that Cuba might be hit with oil and food shortages. A Western diplomat informed JMWAVE that he had learned from a minor government functionary that Che Guevara was alleged to be under house arrest for plotting to overthrow Castro. The wife of a Western diplomat told JMWAVE about a lunch conversation her husband had with Castro, who waxed eloquent on Cuban sugar production. One agent radioed JMWAVE that he had spotted Chinese troops. A skeptical station responded with a coded message to this agent: "We must have exact data on why you believe troops that landed at Mariel . . . are Chinese. There are several slant-eyed type people in Russia. Can you describe uniforms?"

In the wake of the assassination, Shackley continued to seek fanciful means to undermine Castro. One program he supervised aimed to flood Cuba with 14,000 letters advising the recipients on how to sabotage the sugarcane and cotton harvests. To provide cover for this onslaught, JMWAVE front groups in Miami mailed to Cuba 10,000 Christmas cards —presumably in envelopes similar to the ones containing the sabotage instructions.

The postassassination stand-down order from Langley regarding sabotage did not last long. In early December, Shackley began planning how to transport weapons to Cuba for the AMTRUNK and AMLASH operations. The shopping list he compiled in conjunction with headquarters was lethal: two sawed-off shotguns, two Wellrod pistols with silencers, two .357 magnums, ten fragmentation grenades, ten phosphorous grenades, two rifles with silencers, ten pounds of plastic explosives with firing devices. For another operation, Shackley requested headquarters approval to purchase four Italian Baretta 12-gauge pump shotguns.

A weekly situation report Shackley sent Langley on December 7 reflected how busy his station was—and how the burgeoning CIA bureaucracy demanded quantifiable dispatches. The sitrep cited five "intelligence highlights." Three were secret-writing letters from agents who reported, respectively, that a Cubana aircraft *might* have been sabotaged, that Castro *might* be making a trip to Moscow, and that a flight out of Cuba *might* have involved a Venezuelan military crew. Two other agent reports noted that forty light tanks and ten large crates had arrived in Havana and that two Soviet and fifteen Cuban military officials had apparently left Cuba in a hurry. These were hardly significant intelligence achievements.

Under the heading "operational developments," Shackley informed his superiors that a station operative was heading to Mexico to debrief and assess a source and that a diplomatic pouch delivery had been received in Havana. He also reported that a sabotage team, code-named AMADDER, had left to blow up a railroad bridge in Las Villas province —an operation that apparently never came off.

Looking to the week ahead, Shackley noted that seven paramilitary agents were to be exfiltrated out of Cuba, trained and reinfiltrated, that two JMWAVE assets were to sneak into Cuba to set up a "rat line" (an escape route), and that a four-man AMTRUNK team would land on Cuba and start recruiting others. He noted that the technical services branch of the station had in the previous week processed thirty-nine secret-writing messages, trained three agents in secret writing and four agents in operational photography, made 1,015 enlargements, and issued sixteen sets of Cuban documents and three Cuban militia berets.

As he oversaw covert war schemes, Shackley was forced to tend to bureaucratic matters large and small. He was ordered to cut his staff by twelve positions, bringing JMWAVE's personnel allotment to 197 people. He petitioned headquarters and won approval to lease an additional twenty-seven cars. His station tracked bank wires for hundreds of thousands of dollars and handled medical insurance claims for operatives— including payments as little as two dollars.

In mid-December, Shackley's own sabotage squad mounted another successful combat operation. Operation Duck was based on a legendary trick of British commandos. Grayston Lynch's crew of exiles infiltrated Cuban waters near a naval base. The agents planted powerful, time-delayed explosive charges underneath two Cuban PT boats; on one of the vessels they set an additional small charge. They also dropped mines into the surrounding waters. The CIA team then detonated the smaller charge. That prompted Cuban patrols to chase after the intruders. One Cuban boat struck a CIA mine. The JMWAVE team raced back to Florida.

The saboteurs did not hang around to see the next phase. The explosives placed underneath the Cuban vessels were timed to go off shortly after daybreak. The idea was that come the morning a host of Cuban vessels would turn out to inspect the scene of the crime. All these vessels —and their occupants—would be caught in tremendous explosions. The scheme seemed to work, for the Cuban government announced that a Navy patrol boat was blown up at its berth and that several Cubans were killed or wounded. But for Lynch and others in Shackley's PM wing, it was a last hurrah. Though they did not realize it at the time, this was the final JMWAVE sabotage raid against Cuba.

In the past year, Shackley's station had planned eighty-eight missions to Cuba, of which fifteen were canceled. Of the rest, only four directly involved sabotage, and ten others led to encounters with Cuban forces. At the Miami station, there were discussions about new commando raids, but with President Lyndon Johnson not yet decided on how to handle Cuba, there was no action. Weeks went by and no sign of Johnson's intention came—a sign in itself.

Shackley's station received permission only for intelligence-gathering operations. The cowboys were impatient. Some drank, a few PM instructors got into a barroom brawl. A despondency started spreading through the Agency's outfit in Miami. JMWAVE officers could see that the Cuban show was not going to remain an A-1 priority. Shackley, though, maintained his around-the-clock pace. His devotion was constant.

Shackley's station became a frustrating post for anyone who desired to be deep in the action. Some officers looked toward Vietnam. There lay the next romantic adventure for the cowboys: helicopters, jungle warfare, a fight against communist guerrillas. But the foreign intelligence crowd had to push on, though their job had become even more challenging. Each year, Castro's Soviet-assisted security forces improved. Losses at this stage were "tremendous," according to a headquarters official who supervised collection. "This guy of yours would disappear, then that guy would disappear," a JMWAVE espionage officer recalled. "A radio wouldn't come on again. That would be it." In one disastrous episode, the Cubans rolled up a network of 150 agents and informants run by a former Cuban politician recruited by the Agency. "The high living and immoral behavior of one of the principals," a CIA report later noted, "attracted the attention of the Cuban security service." After his arrest, every single member of the net was apprehended and convicted of espionage.

Early in April of 1964, President Johnson officially decided to discontinue CIA sabotage raids against Castro. At an April 7 meeting of the

Special Group, Rusk noted that the sabotage raids had been unproductive. McCone defended the work of Shackley and others, claiming their sabotage schemes were well planned. Bundy, in a bout of self-criticism, observed that since the previous June "policymakers . . . had turned sabotage operations on and off to such an extent that [sabotage] simply does not, in the nature of things, appear feasible."

The next day, McCone fired off a memo decrying the cutoff of sabotage. To do so, he complained, would "abandon the basic objective of bringing about the liquidation of the Castro Communist entourage and the elimination of the Communist presence in Cuba." Johnson, McCone thought, was throwing in the towel.

But not all action was turned off. In March and June of 1964, Shackley delivered arms to Cubela, the unstable CIA agent known as AMLASH. According to CIA cables to and from Shackley's office, Langley asked the JMWAVE chief to supply Cubela with rifles and telescopic sights— equipment suitable for assassination. Questioned about these shipments years later by congressional investigators, Shackley insisted that he did not recall being ordered to send such supplies to Cuba. Queried about the cables (which the investigators possessed and which plainly detailed JMWAVE's involvement), Shackley answered that he did not remember ever having seen them.

On April 2, 1964, Shackley sent a report to Des FitzGerald to boast of an accomplishment: he had bagged Al Burt, the influential Latin America editor of *The Miami Herald.* In a long dispatch, Shackley described how he had succeeded. In the fall of 1962, his station began contacting representatives of the local news media in an attempt to ensure reporters did not disclose the activities of KUBARK—the Agency's code name for itself. And Shackley noted, "when a relationship was established with [a *Herald* employee], it was carefully cultivated in order that JMWAVE might be able to use this contact at the [*Herald*] as a means [to] give JMWAVE an outlet into the press which could be used for surfacing certain select propaganda items."

A *Herald* representative, according to Shackley, offered to notify Shackley's station if his reporters uncovered any negative information about the Agency's anti-Cuba program. In return, the *Herald* expected to receive tips to hot stories.

Eventually, the point man for Shackley at the *Herald* became Burt, code-named AMCARBON, who, Shackley reported, cooperated with the station in several ways. Burt, according to the dispatch, withheld news coverage of exiles disliked by the CIA. He located an expatriate for Shackley. He informed Shackley when his paper chased stories of interest to the CIA. He wrote, at Shackley's urging, a series on an Agency-favored Cuban defector. He assigned articles on the basis of suggestions from Shackley. Burt, Shackley noted, even shared with the CIA chief his conversations with exile leaders, politicians, and other journalists and identified his sources.

This operation violated the proscription against CIA domestic activity. Agency propaganda efforts were supposed to be aimed at foreign targets, not American newspapers. But since Shackley's massive JMWAVE program entailed wide-ranging domestic actions, it was not odd he showed no qualms about mucking about with American-based journalists. To FitzGerald, Shackley enthusiastically recommended AMCARBON "be developed and harnessed for exploitation, bearing in mind that he does have long-term potential" as "one of the leading Latin American specialists in U.S. journalistic circles."

Shackley's account of the AMCARBON operation smacked of hyperbole—and might have bordered on fabrication. Years later, Burt offered an utterly different recollection of the matter, one suggestive of Graham Greene's classic spy novel *Our Man in Havana,* in which a British intelligence officer fills his agent list with the names of prominent locals with whom he has no contact.

The *Herald*'s relationship with Shackley, according to Burt, began one day in late 1962 when George Beebe, the paper's managing editor, was lunching with William Pawley. Across the room in the restaurant was Shackley. See that man over there? Pawley asked. You should know him; he's the CIA chief in Miami and the fellow who fed information on the missiles to Hal Hendrix. Before the Cuban missile crisis, Hendrix, a reporter for *The Miami News,* had written a number of articles on the presence of Soviet missiles in Cuba—scoops that would win him the Pulitzer Prize. Beebe was eager to meet Hendrix's source, and Pawley introduced the newsman to the chief of station. Shortly after that, Beebe passed Shackley to Burt.

Burt thought his relationship with Shackley was nothing unusual. They met for lunch. He occasionally called the CIA man for information. "You never felt like you knew him very much," he recalled. "This was a normal news contact." If Shackley ever asked him a question, Burt claimed he answered it courteously, without compromising himself or a source. In no way did Burt consider himself a Shackley asset. And he wrote a number of articles for the *Herald* that detailed Artime's paramilitary operation and the Agency connection to the project—subjects Shackley wanted under wraps. "Calling me a propaganda outlet was bureaucratic boasting on his part," asserted Burt, who left the Latin American beat in 1965 and never lived up to the potential touted in Shackley's memo.

No one in Langley was in a position to challenge Shackley's description of Burt as a hard-won and influential propaganda asset. His superiors had no way to tell if Shackley was misportraying his contact with the reporter. Only Shackley and Burt knew the truth about their relationship. If Shackley wanted to exploit an ordinary contact to score points with the brass, not much could stop him. In his line of work, there often were opportunities to claim successes that did not exist.

Shackley's own boom-and-bang program was over. But Johnson's cease-and-desist order—whether he knew it or not—did not stop the exile groups supported by the Miami station. In the spring of 1964, the JMWAVE-backed JURE tried to infiltrate Manuel Ray and a band of commandos into Cuba. The mission was a nightmare. Ray and his JURE comrades spent days at sea ducking bad weather and Castro's patrols. The exiles landed at Anguilla Cays, forty miles away from Cuba. They were arrested by the British for illegal entry into the Bahamas, fined fourteen dollars each, and told never to trespass again. Within the exile community, Ray now was a joke. Another attempt ended when Ray's boat developed motor trouble seven miles off the coast of Cuba. After this, the Agency decided he was worthless and cut him off after delivering a $75,000 severance payment.

The Agency's surrogate-of-choice, Manuel Artime, was no more effective. Artime's operation mounted a number of raids, but his men never did much but irritate Castro's security forces a few times. One commando team blew up part of a sugar refinery. (A State Department spokesman said the U.S. government had no connection to the raiders.) An MRR attempt to assassinate Castro failed. "I never saw such disorganization," recalled a Costa Rican who tried to assist Artime's army.

In September of 1964 the Artime gang outdid itself in incompetence —and proved that Shackley had been right to fear freebooters operating outside of his control. An MRR team seeking to attack the *Sierra Maestra,* the flagship freighter of the Cuban merchant marine, mistakenly assaulted a Spanish vessel, killing the captain, injuring much of the crew, and disabling the ship.

In Shackley's station, the top officials no longer took the Artime endeavor seriously. Months after the *Sierra Maestra* screw-up, the Agency yanked the subsidy for Artime's paramilitary operations. But the station continued to dispense Artime $15,000 each month to support his political endeavors. "They never managed to get much done," Tom Clines observed of the MRR, "but then neither did the CIA."

Though the Agency quashed Artime's PM program, it still had a use for his band. Some of its boats and men were transported to Africa for use in the Congo, where a CIA paramilitary program supported a Western-leaning regime against a coalition of disparate rebel forces.* As for Artime, the Agency had the perfect assignment for him. It covertly arranged for him to become a partner in conspiracy with its agent Cubela. AMLASH had become more insistent that assassination of the Cuban leadership was the essential first step of a coup. The CIA told him that it could not be part of this first step, but in early 1965 it placed him in touch with Artime. The two brainstormed ways to kill Castro and to launch an insurrection—neither of which were to come. In June of 1965, the Agency cut off all contact with AMLASH, after discovering that an associate of his was in clandestine contact with Cuban intelligence. Agency officers wondered whether Cubela had been a double agent all along.†

To some in the Agency, by late 1964 it was time to call it quits and shut down Shackley's empire. "I made myself damn unpopular by suggesting it was too big and had gone on for too long," said a headquarters official. "We had reached a point of diminished returns. Taxpayer money was being wasted. I was never aware of any singular PM accomplishment. An awful lot of money had been spent on running in and running out. The operation was just festering. We didn't need to be subsidizing the city of Miami." Throughout 1964 and 1965, an increasing number of JMWAVE officers were reassigned to Southeast Asia. There was a series of farewell cocktail parties.

Shackley's days were consumed with the task of decommissioning various elements of the Agency's largest station in the world. That had to be done carefully. Safe houses and boats needed to be sold. Warehouses had to be shut down. Arms and ammunition amassed by the station had to be disposed of, perhaps forwarded to new covert battlegrounds. Personnel had to be transferred. Operatives recruited by JMWAVE needed to be terminated. No one in the Agency wanted embittered ex-assets running about town and telling all.

Shackley departed Miami in June of 1965. The Cuban show was done, and there was nothing to show for it. When John Dimmer replaced Shackley as chief of JMWAVE, he and his staff found that they had inher-

---

* At the end of this civil war, in which the Agency-backed side was victorious, the leader of the government would be the dictator Joseph Mobutu.

† Cubela was arrested toward the end of 1965. At his trial, during which he stood accused alongside AMTRUNK recruits, Cubela called for his own death; but after Castro intervened, the former Cuban hero was sentenced to twenty-five years.

ited few intelligence assets to build on. Months later, John Hart, the deputy chief of the Western Hemisphere Division for Cuban Affairs, toured Agency stations in Latin America and complained to case officers that the CIA practically had no agent sources reporting from inside Cuba. It was relying on electronic coverage and aerial surveillance. Shackley and his officers had left little behind.

But the legacy of Shackley's station lasted long. Conspiracy theorists —some wide-eyed, others more discerning—would for decades ask if Shackley's program in Miami had anything to do with the assassination of the President. On a more tangible matter, the Cuban operation yielded a disposal problem. The JMWAVE station churned out hundreds of persons well trained in the arts of smuggling, sabotage, and gunrunning. These individuals were now free to apply their talents wherever they chose. Some joined Agency battles elsewhere. Others turned to more entrepreneurial endeavors, most notably mercenary work and drug-trafficking.

As far as the public record shows, no one in Miami or Langley gave much thought to demobilizing the secret army of exiles—certainly not the CIA men whose work had produced covert warriors and smugglers. "That was not our problem," Grayston Lynch said. "It was a national leadership problem. It was their duty to consider it." But it soon became a problem for Lynch. In 1971, he became a federal drug agent and encountered narcotics traffickers once on the Agency payroll. "A lot of drug smugglers," he observed, "learned their skills" via Shackley's station. "This is the bitter fruit."

Many bad apples fell from JMWAVE. In July of 1968, Cuban exile terrorists in Los Angeles bombed the offices of the Mexico Tourist Department and companies that did business with Cuba. Their explosives came from the CIA in Miami. Michael Townley, the assassin who in 1976 blew up former Chilean diplomat Orlando Letelier and assistant Ronni Moffit on Embassy Row in Washington, noted how easy it was to find the tools of his trade in Miami, long after Shackley was gone: "In the early seventies, late sixties . . . due to all the stuff that they had obtained from the CIA . . . you could buy plastic explosives on any street just like you'd buy candy—weapons, explosives, detonators, anything you wanted— and it was exceedingly cheap." Humberto Lopez, who served with Artime's CIA-subsidized force, was arrested in 1973 when federal agents raided his home and discovered a cache of weapons. Many of the weapons seized in his home, he said, were "leftover gifts from the CIA."

The links in the chain that started in Miami extended far. Rolando Martinez, a boat pilot for Shackley's station, was collecting a monthly retainer of $100 in 1972 when he was arrested as one of the five Watergate burglars caught breaking into the offices of the Democratic National Committee. Three other members of this crew had cut their teeth with the Agency.

Ramon Milian Rodriguez, a convicted drug money launderer, testified in 1988 before a Senate subcommittee that he was trained in his craft in the mid-1970s by associates of Manuel Artime. Rodriguez said that after Artime died in 1976 he started washing drug dollars for several of Artime's longtime followers who had become narcotics smugglers. He rapidly scaled the career ladder as a launderer until he was processing up to $100 million a month for a Colombian cocaine cartel.

For Shackley, the losing battle against Castro produced rewards. He received a Distinguished Intelligence Medal for his Miami tour. Within the Agency, there now was a small coterie of officers devoted to him: Tom Clines (who eventually had warmed to Shackley), Warren Frank, Dave Morales, Mickey Kappes, and others. Through his tour at JMWAVE, he impressed the senior men of the CIA. Des FitzGerald was telling Agency people that Shackley was heading toward the Director's chair.

Ultimately, the Agency—Shackley included—failed in a prime task. Castro remained in power. His position in Cuba might have even been strengthened by the CIA campaign against him and his success in fending it off. As for the intelligence mission, years after he left Miami, Shackley, choosing his words carefully, judged his station's espionage endeavors as "quite good" regarding exiles but "limited" concerning targets in Cuba—hardly a ringing endorsement. The chatty exiles were easy pickings. Penetrating Castro's regime was the real challenge. Through the years, JMWAVE officers claimed credit for helping to discover the Soviet missiles. But the most compelling piece of human intelligence was discovered by a routine interrogation at the Opa-Locka refugee center. More importantly, the policymakers of Washington never seemed to receive the message that Castro was well established in power.

But within the Agency, an important measure was how one did the job, almost regardless of results. Shackley faithfully executed the President's bidding. He ran a shop that oversaw extensive covert action. He demonstrated that he could supervise whatever clandestine or underhanded activity his superiors wanted performed. With Shackley as chief of the sprawling station, there were few embarrassing flaps. He had managed well. He had been a good bureaucrat. In the hallways of Langley, he was widely recognized as a comer.

John Kennedy and his CIA—no matter that they had at their disposal the creative eccentric Ed Lansdale, the hard-nosed Bill Harvey, the driven sophisticate Des FitzGerald, the serious FI chief Warren Frank, experienced case officers like Tom Clines, the do-or-die paramilitary cowboys, the hundreds of other committed professionals, the thousands of eager Cuban exiles, and the coldly efficient and dependable Ted Shackley—could not dislodge Castro and communism from Cuba. The United States, which chose not to resort to open military intervention in Cuba, was now turning to another Third World stage, its policymakers hoping that they could achieve ten thousand miles away what they could not do ninety miles from their own shores. And Shackley would be called upon to manage the newest doomed enterprises.

CHAPTER FIVE

LAOS: A SECRET WAR

I

IT was late in the spring of 1966 in Washington, when a young Agency case officer received a call. Ted Shackley wanted to meet him right away. The case officer was recently back from Laos, where the CIA was waging a truly secret war. This operation was not a collection of minor hit-and-run raids, fanciful assassination schemes, and wishful invasion plans. In Laos, the Agency furtively was nurturing and guiding a guerrilla force of over 20,000 tribesmen. The enemy was the Pathet Lao, a small nationalist and communist force supported by the fierce North Vietnamese Army. This was a war, not on the scale of the conflict next door in Vietnam, but a war nonetheless.

For the past four years, this young officer had lived with an army of Hmong tribesmen and operated out of its secret headquarters in the spectacular jagged mountains and lush, triple-canopy jungle of the north. He provided supplies, weapons, and advice on how to wage guerrilla attacks on the communists. He used the tribesmen, in small bands, to collect intelligence on the enemy for the policymakers of Washington. He celebrated their victories—a successful reconnaissance mission, a blown-up bridge, an ambush of the Pathet Lao. He mourned the losses of the tribal warriors, his comrades-in-arms.

When his second tour ended in 1966, he wanted more. He arrived in Langley, expecting to return soon to Laos. But William Colby, the OSS veteran who now headed the Far East Division, had other plans. Colby explained: if you go back to the excitement of Laos, you will end up dead or go native; no more jungle daring for you.

Shackley, though, was soon to depart for Laos to be chief of station. When Colby had needed a new man in Vientiane, he asked Des FitzGerald, now deputy director for plans, for a recommendation. FitzGerald touted Shackley as one of the Agency's best officers. Colby reviewed Shackley's credentials—he was among the few Agency men with experience in managing secret warfare—and judged him right for this most important of postings.

Shortly before he was to leave for Southeast Asia, Shackley dropped by the young officer's home for dinner to receive a firsthand account of the Laos operation. He struck the younger man as intelligent but cold and businesslike. Shackley listened carefully, without reaction, as the officer related his experiences. Shackley praised the program to date but showed no enthusiasm and disclosed no opinions about the hidden war—the course of which he would affect profoundly. The young officer did not mention to him Colby's fear for the fate of those seduced by Laos. For Shackley, it did not seem relevant.

Shackley was in Washington fresh from a truncated tour in Europe. About a year earlier, Langley had assigned Shackley to an old haunt: the Berlin base. Shackley reached Berlin in July of 1965, with his wife, Hazel, and two-year-old daughter, Suzanne. The Berlin Wall had changed all. It impeded the flow of people between East and West that Shackley had tapped in the 1950s. Yet spying continued as a leading trade of the city. The proprietor of West Berlin's most elegant brothel had been arrested recently on espionage charges for telling East German intelligence who visited his parlor. Every few months another Berliner was found guilty of spying on behalf of either East or West.

But Berlin was no longer the spy's paradise Shackley had once known. The Berlin base, crammed with 200 employees in the 1950s, now employed about 60, its output down precipitously. Shackley was determined to overcome the obstacle of the Wall. At his first staff meeting, he pointed and declared, I'm here to tear down that Wall. Damn, thought one officer present, we're finally going to be able to get something done.

Shackley's base managed to maintain about a dozen reporting assets inside East Germany. None were high-level; a couple were employed in midlevel government positions. Many were suspect. "Guys we hadn't seen in five years would all of a sudden show up with production figures," recalled one of Shackley's officers. "The East Germans were playing them back at us." After the end of the Cold War and the collapse of East Germany, files of the Stasi, the East German security service, indicated that most every U.S. agent in East Berlin after 1948 was doubled.

Neither did sex work. Shackley oversaw a sophisticated honey-trap operation. One of his officers placed an advertisement in a local newspaper: Wanted, a young, educated woman for a public relations position. But the women who reported to a small downtown office were not greeted by a PR executive. Instead they were screened by a base officer, who passed the right candidates to another case officer. The second officer would explain to each woman that the Poles, Czechoslovaks, and Soviets were running around West Berlin trying to make trouble. Americans and West Germans had to band together to thwart them. Would she help recruit spies? By the way, the CIA officer always added, she would make good money if she said yes.

While case officers vetted and recruited women, other Shackley men looked for targets, usually Polish or Czechoslovak military officials. Through surveillance, telephone taps, and electronic eavesdropping, they searched for an East bloc official experiencing problems with his wife or someone eager for fun. When a target was selected and his daily schedule ascertained, one of the recruited women was directed to ride on the streetcar the mark used each morning and sit near him but not pay him any attention. After weeks of this, one day when it was raining, she would ask him to walk her underneath his umbrella to her office. If all went well, a liaison started. The Agency had set her up in an apartment, so the two could meet privately. "How far did these things go?" one base officer remarked years later. "It depended on the girl. It was up to her. Usually she got so caught up in the spirit she wanted to go faster than the case officer liked."

Shackley's base nabbed no Czechoslovaks, Poles, or Soviets with this system. There were near-misses. But the targets were merely interested in a one-night stand or too scared to accept the women's request that they do a favor for a friend. "In the intelligence business," lamented the Shackley aide who directed this operation, "nothing works very well."

The free-and-easy days of the 1950s were long gone. "Probably the most discouraged people in West Berlin today," one journalist wrote in 1966, "are the numerous intelligence experts whose job it is to collect and evaluate information about conditions on the other side of the Wall." One intelligence analyst complained: "We work like chess players —*blindfolded* chess players. We have to rely on speculation, instinct, judgment. We know more about what is going on in Prague, Warsaw, and Budapest than we do about what is going on five miles from here over the Wall. . . . I've read *The Spy Who Came in from the Cold,* and I only wish we had an agent like that."

Shackley possessed one agent worthy of le Carré: the Czechoslovak intelligence chief in East Berlin. Shackley inherited him when he took over the base. Years ago in another European country, the Czech had volunteered his services to the Americans for cash. He was, in appearance, a perfect spy: bland, mousy. He looked like a timid bank teller. But at meetings in the CIA safe house, the Czech proposed daring schemes. When another Czechoslovak intelligence officer was about to meet an agent in West Berlin, he suggested the CIA intercept the Czech officer and pitch him. An Agency man had to remind the Czech intelligence chief that since he (the Czech) was one of three people aware of this meeting, it was not a good idea for the Americans to let the Czechoslovak service see they were wise to it.

The Czech spy was a true catch. After he had first walked in on the CIA, he was called to Prague to assume a high-ranking post in headquarters. From there, he sent the CIA volumes of microfilmed material. In East Berlin as the Czech resident, he was less valuable. He turned over the names of Czechoslovak agents, but his best material was the gossip he picked up in the hallways back in Prague. He remained active into the 1970s, until forced to retire due to age. His betrayal, as far as the CIA knew, never was discovered by his own service.

Many of Shackley's targets were people and groups on his side of the Wall. The Berlin base gathered information on political developments within West Berlin. The base had agents in the two major parties—primarily reporting assets, not covert operatives—and zeroed in on the left wing of the Social Democratic party, which was promoting closer ties to the East. "We didn't like that," said one senior Berlin base officer. "We did intelligence collection against them. We had penetrations of Mayor Willy Brandt's government."

There was a long list of Berliners for Shackley's base to watch. One Shackley deputy maintained contact with aides to Axel Springer, the influential right-wing publishing magnate who allegedly received millions of dollars from the Agency in the 1950s to help build his media empire. Some base officers massaged press contacts, hoping to squeeze out stories favorable to Washington's efforts in Vietnam. Shackley subsidized a small news service run by an alcoholic. Shackley's staff pored over intercepted letters, seeking potential recruits and tracking individuals of interest. His base bugged the West Berlin office of Wolfgang Vogel, the East German lawyer whose unconventional practice included brokering spy swaps between East and West. As student unrest flared at the Free University in West Berlin, Shackley and his men sought recruits in student groups. The Berlin base hoped to uncover proof of a link between protesting students and Moscow, but the search was in vain.

As he had done so far in his career, Shackley impressed and intimidated. "One had a great feeling of confidence in watching him at staff meetings," recalled Arthur Day, the deputy chief of the U.S. mission in Berlin. "In a personal sense, he was genial enough, but he never gave anything away. He was very self-contained. He was not an easygoing guy, but one doesn't expect that from the CIA." John Mapother, a reports officer in the base, viewed the same qualities from a different perspective: "Shackley had a great ability to organize information. He loved charts. He was a great map reader. He could take people in. He would never screw up a briefing by admitting there was something he didn't know."

Mapother had worried when Shackley arrived in Berlin. Mapother was a classic espionage man and shared the purist's bias against large covert operations. Information, not sabotage plans, was the currency of an intelligence service. Mapother questioned whether Shackley, now known for his management of JMWAVE, could understand the finer points of intelligence. He soon saw that Shackley, who had spent most of his career in the espionage line, knew and respected that end of the business.

But Mapother's initial fear was replaced by another. His new chief appreciated intelligence, but intelligence that could be packaged in tangible signs of accomplishment. Shackley stated his desire to see the number of reports go up. Mapother had no objection; he would be thrilled to pouch to Langley a bundle of intelligence reports, if the base could gather good enough material. Shackley pressed Mapother for more and more reports, and the two sparred repeatedly. Mapother dreaded what was coming: quotas that could only be met with substandard reports. Shackley was an aggressive manager of intelligence operations. But he had the touch of a bean-counter. He wanted it all reduced to numbers—figures that would earn Shackley and his base credit with the number-watchers in headquarters.* The CIA, Mapother believed, was in danger of becoming a bureaucracy where administrators and the untalented spend their days trying to preserve their jobs, looking good in the year-end evaluations. Mapother did not want his shop turned into a reports mill.

It did not come to that. After less than a year in the divided city, Shackley was called to Washington to prepare for the Laos assignment. Before leaving Berlin, Shackley engaged in a heated discussion with Arthur Day and a few other State Department officers. "We went on

---

* Shackley's tendency toward quotas was confirmed by Richard Dane, who was in charge of FI in the Berlin base immediately following Shackley's departure. Dane's officers told him that Shackley had demanded one report a week out of each of them.

endlessly," Day recalled, "about who represented what we called the real business end of American relations with the Soviet Union. Shackley made it clear that the CIA and intelligence operations were the real business end. The diplomatic end was just tea parties, people who traveled, shook hands, and didn't do anything." Now Shackley was off to where diplomatic endeavors were little more than charades and where the Agency was doing battle at the request of its commander in chief. Berlin was the past. Southeast Asia was the major front in the war against communism. And Laos was the secret battlefield.

II

Laos was an odd place to be fighting for the future of the United States and the world. But for centuries this land-locked, key-shaped country of some 3,000,000 people, squeezed in between Thailand, China, Cambodia, Burma, and Vietnam, had obsessed geostrategists. Greater powers which envied Laos' strategic location—such as the ancient Siamese and Vietnamese kingdoms—had long fought over the small nation. In the modern era, Western anticommunists worried that this sliver of a country offered Red China a land route through which it could project southward and dominate Southeast Asia. The remoteness of Laos would be an advantage for foreign powers which waged war within its borders. "This is the end of nowhere," an American official remarked in 1960. "We can do anything we want here."

Laos is a country blessed with dramatic and beautiful—nearly magical—terrain. It is a land of wild elephants, tigers, and buffalo; tropical rain forests; soaring mountains; fertile lowlands in the southern half where the Mekong River runs along the border; and tremendous plateaus topped by rolling grasslands, with the Plain of Jars in the northern central area the most striking of these. In the nineteenth century, Laos was a collection of small principalities. Beginning in 1887, France organized the kingdoms and turned the state of Laos into a colony. After the Second World War, Lao politics were dominated by two half-brothers, both princes in the royal house of Luang Prabang, who embarked on divergent paths. Prince Souvanna Phouma reached an accommodation with the French and in 1951 became premier of a French-dominated government. Prince Souphanouvong sided with the nationalists and communists of the Viet Minh of neighboring Vietnam. His followers formed the Pathet Lao movement.

France could not hold its position in Indochina. After the Viet Minh delivered it a humiliating military defeat at Dien Bien Phu in 1954, Paris began handing over the whole Indochina mess to Washington. Following the Geneva agreements of that year, the central political conflict in Laos was over whether or not to live with the communists.

Souvanna Phouma, a plump, pipe-smoking, sharp-dressing bridge player, believed that communists and noncommunists, if left alone by outside forces, could work everything out and create a truly neutral Laos. A rightist faction, strong in the military, was less forgiving regarding the Pathet Lao, which controlled northeastern provinces. Led by General Phoumi Nosavan, a CIA favorite, the anticommunist military insisted on the defeat of the Pathet Lao and the outright destruction of its political party.

Eisenhower's cold warriors did all they could to prevent a resolution between the factions headed by the two princes—and planted seeds of war. Washington desired an uncompromising anticommunist and pro-West enclave between Red China and reddening Vietnam. But Laos was not a coherent nation with a political and social infrastructure that the United States could effectively aid. The country was sharply divided along regional, religious, and ethnic lines. The economy barely functioned on a national level. The rugged terrain and absence of modern roads isolated sections of the country from each other.

"In this environment," Douglas Blaufarb, a CIA chief of station in Laos in the mid-1960s, later wrote, "the United States found that all its efforts to build a solid Lao government trickled off into the sand." But Washington carried on. It provided the sole financial support for the rightist-led Lao army of 25,000 that was incompetent, but effective enough to develop a reputation for repression in the countryside. An immense U.S. economic program was wracked by profound corruption.

A coalition government knit together by Souvanna Phouma in the late 1950s was opposed by the Eisenhower administration. CIA officers supported a group trying to whip up anti-Red sentiment, which failed to establish itself as a ruling power. When Washington held up its monthly subsidy to the government of the open-minded Souvanna, his coalition toppled. General Phoumi led a coup, then backed down and ran for office in 1960. Western journalists reported that Agency men were spotted passing out money to buy votes. Phoumi's forces won in a contest grossly rigged, and that fraud triggered a coup led by Kong Le, a paratrooper captain and a staunch neutralist who wanted to end all foreign meddling in Laos. He named Souvanna Phouma to head the government.

As General Phoumi regrouped his troops, the CIA in November of 1960 dispatched Bill Lair, a laid-back Texan, to the general's side. Lair brought with him five teams of Thai advisers to help Phoumi's army. The next month, Phoumi marched on the capital city of Vientiane and pushed out the army of Kong Le. Souvanna Phouma fled to Cambodia and denounced Eisenhower's anticommunists for failing to understand his country. Kong Le took the logical option—a move to which he in part had been driven by U.S. policy—and formed an alliance with the Pathet Lao. With the help of the Soviets and the Pathet Lao, his army drove Phoumi's troops from the Plain of Jars. As the bright-eyed, hopeful men of the Kennedy administration were moving into their offices at the start of 1961, a crisis was brewing that pitted a U.S.-backed army against Soviet-supported troops.

Another military player existed within Laos: a secret army of several thousand tribesmen, mostly Hmong, organized into irregular units. And the Agency was its midwife. The Hmong were hill people who had moved into northern Laos from southern China.* They found homes in the mountains, practiced slash-and-burn agriculture, and relied on opium as their best cash crop. The Hmong viewed with animosity all lowlanders, Vietnamese and Lao alike, and sought the precious right of being left alone.

The tribe first earned CIA notice as part of the indigenous army the French stitched together in the early 1950s to resist the Viet Minh throughout the region. To pay the bills for this tribal army, Colonel Roger Trinquier had turned to an innovative source of funding: drugs. As he later acknowledged, in a project sinisterly named Operation X, Trinquier bought the Hmong's entire crop of opium, shipped it to Saigon, and sold it to the Emperor Bao Dai at a high markup. The profit subsidized the war.

The ingenuity of the French counterinsurgency campaign, not necessarily its financing, intrigued Agency officials. The CIA provided weapons and assigned a case officer to Trinquier. After the Geneva agreement of 1954, Trinquier hoped to keep his tribal soldiers armed, and appealed to the CIA for assistance. The Agency declined. But the CIA kept an eye on the *armée clandestine* and its leader, a short captain named Vang Pao.

In December of 1960, Bill Lair, the Agency man assigned to General Phoumi's forces, went looking for Vang Pao. He found the Hmong leader and about twenty-five guerrillas hiding near the Plain of Jars. If you give us guns, the Hmong leader told Lair, we will keep with the fight. Without outside support, he could not go on. With help, he asserted, he could raise an army of 10,000. Lair believed the Agency bureaucrats would not accept Vang Pao's unusual offer. But the higher-ups embraced the notion of arming a faraway rebel force to fight communists.

The Agency began sending Vang Pao weapons, and he kept his word.

---

* The tribespeople called themselves Hmong, which means "mankind" in their language, but foreigners and other Laotians referred to them as the Meo, a contraction of a Chinese word for "barbarians." CIA people generally used the term "Meo" but were ignorant of the slur it conveyed.

Come July of 1961, about 9,000 Hmong tribesmen were equipped for guerrilla operations by a small contingent of Agency and Special Forces officers. Among CIA officers, the Hmong troops developed a reputation for ferocity. With their resentment of the Vietnamese and their hardy physical capabilities, they were made to order for U.S. policymakers in search of surrogates. Washington's goal was not militarily ambitious: create a small irregular force, loosely allied with General Phoumi, that could harass the Pathet Lao and collect intelligence. But the neat plans of the geostrategists would not work out that way.

Neither Washington nor Moscow desired another hot spot. The two had arranged a cease-fire in May of 1961, and an international conference convened in Geneva to neutralize Laos. The Geneva Accords, signed in July of 1962, called for all foreign parties to remove their military forces from Laos and for establishing a coalition government including right-wingers, communists, and neutralists, led by the ever-hopeful Souvanna Phouma. Technically the unity government ruled the nation; in actuality the Pathet Lao governed the territory it controlled in the north, and a de facto partition cut Laos along the lines of the cease-fire. The United States and the Soviet Union mostly complied with the withdrawal provisions. North Vietnam did not. Several thousand North Vietnamese Army (NVA) personnel remained in Pathet Lao country.

The Kennedy administration still was anxious to preserve Laos as a buffer zone between strife-ridden Vietnam and the rest of Indochina. But what could it do about the NVA? Hanoi was set on maintaining its presence in the sparsely populated, eastern portion of Laos so it could control supply routes into South Vietnam. North Vietnam displayed no intention of marching on Vientiane, yet Hanoi was not going to yield territory crucial for its war against South Vietnam. The Kennedy men needed a quiet way to stay involved in Laos, where they had on their hands their own tribal force. The CIA was the answer. It was a civilian agency; the presence of its employees would not technically violate the Accords. Its officers could secretly tend to the tribal army.

Months after the Accords were signed, the CIA resumed supplying the Hmong with modest amounts of ammunition. The United States also began providing Hmong refugees in the mountains with 300 tons of rice a month, 2,000 blankets, 4,000 kettles, tons of cement, and other supplies at a cost of several million dollars. The Hmong irregulars, guided by the CIA, blew up bridges and staged raids against Pathet Lao positions. For their American patrons, the tribesmen obtained intelligence on the North Vietnamese in Laos. In July of 1963, Kennedy approved enlarging the CIA's irregular army.

The Accords held; the peace did not. The various Laotian factions clashed. The communists left the coalition government, and in 1964 fighting resumed on the Plain of Jars, where the Pathet Lao forces nearly pushed Kong Le's army off the Plain.

The enemy, as far as Washington saw it, was the North Vietnamese, with the Pathet Lao no more than a front for Hanoi. But CIA intelligence showed that it was Pathet Lao troops that battled the neutralists, even if the Pathet Lao villages and supply lines were full of North Vietnamese. U.S. air strikes—another departure from the Accords—signaled that any further Pathet Lao move westward might spark more direct U.S. intervention. The Accords were no longer a true constraint, though all parties continued to pay official homage to them.

As fighting continued in Laos, the conflict came to be a mirror-image of the developing war in Vietnam. In that divided nation, the United States was aiding the regular and not very proficient Army of the Republic of Vietnam (ARVN) against the insurgent, unconventional forces of the North Vietnamese–backed Viet Cong. In Laos, the communists had the regular army, while the Agency directed unconventional tribal forces.

A pattern of warfare emerged. The better-equipped Pathet Lao and NVA units, dependent on roads, took the offensive in the dry season, which occurred between November and May, and gained territory. When the rains came, the tribal guerrillas attacked the immobilized communists, often causing them to abandon newly won positions. Underlying this annual exchange seemed to be a tacit policy. Both sides avoided targeting objectives of critical importance to the other or striking too far into enemy territory. The North Vietnamese appeared to care most about creating their own buffer zone, so they could dominate the corridor—known as the Ho Chi Minh Trail—that ran to South Vietnam. The U.S. mission even discouraged the royal forces from assaulting Pathet Lao positions if such an attack might provoke a strong response.

For Washington decision-makers, Laos evolved into a sideshow. U.S. policy regarding this land came to be dictated by the demands of the growing war in Vietnam. But such a geostrategic nicety was not shared with the Hmong and other indigenous tribes recruited by the Agency. The Hmong had their own reasons for fighting. A CIA report assessed the tribe's motivation: "Primarily it is economic and rests on the determination of the Meo to protect their homeland and their opium-rich poppy fields from outside incursions. Secondarily, it is political in the sense that the Meo are determinedly anti-Communist as they recognize that Communist domination would inevitably upset their entire tribal system. Finally, it is characteristic, because of the rugged individualistic and tribalistic outlook of these mountain people." With encouragement from the Americans, the Hmong were willing to battle their local enemies. But they made the commitment anticipating that Washington would arm and supply them, improve their lives, and bolster their standing in Laos. In this marriage of geopolitical convenience, each partner had its own reasons for warring. Only one would have to live with the consequences.

Gradually the Agency built the irregulars into a force of over 20,000. Chief of station Doug Blaufarb dryly observed years later that the "foresight which might have suggested that, regardless of the extent of U.S. aid, Meo forces could not be equalized with those of North Vietnam, did not exist."

In the spring of 1966, William Sullivan, the U.S. ambassador to Laos, arrived in Washington for consultations. An Ivy League–educated, former Navy man in his early forties, Sullivan, at the time of his appointment to the Vientiane post, was the youngest ambassador in the U.S. diplomatic fleet. But his shock of white hair and commanding manner afforded him an air of authority. On this visit to Washington, a prime concern for Sullivan was the replacement for Blaufarb, who was due to end his tour. Sullivan drove to Langley to talk to Richard Helms, the new Director of Central Intelligence. The Director told the Ambassador that Ted Shackley was the best man in the Agency for the job. Helms disclosed he was grooming Shackley to head the Directorate of Plans. There was one hitch. Shackley was not regarded as a team player, and Vientiane was a place where teamwork was essential. Placing Shackley there, Helms mused, might be good for him. The Director informed Sullivan that if the Ambassador ever gave the word, Helms would yank Shackley out of Vientiane. With such an escape clause, Sullivan accepted Shackley.

Shackley landed in Vientiane with his family in July of 1966. Sullivan was surprised. After Helms's description, he had expected a wild man. Shackley was almost owlish, with thick glasses, a square face and a serious, intense demeanor. Sullivan told the new man of his agreement with Helms. Shackley acknowledged that he understood. He then went right to work.

Vientiane in the mid-1960s was a quaint town. News correspondents who passed through reached for the same words to describe the administrative capital of Laos on the edge of the Mekong River: dusty and sleepy. It did not look like a city at war. Only a few signs were discernible. Tanned and boisterous Americans in short-sleeve shirts sat in the bars of Vientiane sucking down beers. If a stranger dared ask what they did, they went silent. A grimy block called the Strip was home to a line of taverns, whorehouses, and the few remaining opium dens. (Opium smoking was legal in Laos, but the authorities had shut most of the parlors in Vientiane.) French old-timers composed an expatriate community full of shady characters with their mitts in opium trafficking, gold smuggling, or some other under-the-table enterprise. All the warring factions in Indochina had missions in Vientiane: the United States, the Soviet Union, China, Taiwan, both Vietnams, and even the Pathet Lao.

The Lao people struck most Americans as a generally pleasant, easygoing lot, perhaps too easy. "We described it as the 'power of yes,'" recalled Mark Pratt, a senior embassy officer. "The Lao would say, 'yes, yes, yes, yes' to everything and then not do it." The Lao did not approach government seriously. More tribal than ideological, they were not tough practitioners of geopolitics, disappointing anticommunists. Their relaxed approach to life might have arisen from their respect for the *phi*— animistic spirits found everywhere, in the earth, in water, in households. Almost anything that happened in Laos was ascribed to the *phi*. The result was a pervasive sense of fatalism.

In a run-down business district, a short walk from the Mekong, the U.S. embassy and the CIA were housed in a modest French colonial house on a secluded side street, part of a compound that included a swimming pool, restaurant, bar, and an air-conditioned movie theater. The Agency got the top floor. A few miles outside of town, mission officers lived in a near-perfect replica of an American suburb—streets with look-alike ranch houses separated by fences, American cars in the driveways, bicycles strewn on front lawns.

Shackley once again had another secret fiefdom to run. There were CIA bases throughout the country, but they were dwarfed in size and importance by a place some called Spook Heaven. In the mountains south of the Plain of Jars, the secret CIA-financed city of Long Tieng had grown. It had no paved streets, almost no cars, yet a 3,000-foot runway divided the city and ended at the base of a mountain. Its tribal population—mainly Hmong and Lao Theung—topped 45,000. Thatched-roof huts dotted the foothills. Americans toiled in buildings covered by corrugated metal roofs. Trees jutted out of the sheer sides of the steep surrounding mountains. The ground was thick with red mud in the wet months. After the rains passed, wildflowers bloomed throughout the valley.

Those who visited Long Tieng described it as a Shangri-La. In the shadows of mist-draped mountains, naked children played in dirt roads, blocks away from buildings that sprouted the antennae of sophisticated telecommunications equipment. Hmong women in traditional black costumes adorned with colored sashes and bright jewelry shopped at the market, while troops milled about, airplanes zoomed in and out,

American pilots on secret assignment (dressed like surf bums or jungle adventurers) waited for orders, and Shackley's officers wearing polyester slacks and polo shirts hustled between offices and barracks planning a covert war.

The man who ruled in Long Tieng was Vang Pao—V.P. to the Americans. Now a general, Vang Pao was a true warlord, his power reinforced by the Americans. He arranged for food drops to villages and held up deliveries to areas that did not produce enough fighting bodies. To his people, the mighty Vang Pao made rice fall from the sky. He brought flying machines into the lives of those who had never seen a car. He produced strangers who made the doomed rise from their sickbeds by sticking a needle into them. He held the hopes and the future of over 100,000 tribespeople.

To the Americans fed up with the incompetents of the royal military, V.P., a charismatic and bold military leader, was a godsend. A man of slight build, with an oval-shaped face, he was a fierce, demanding (sometimes ruthless) and dedicated commander, never bashful about ordering the death of prisoners. Without him, the CIA program could not exist. "As long as Vang Pao said to his people cooperate," one CIA man noted, "they cooperated."

Tribal officers, CIA men, and undercover U.S. Air Force pilots gathered at Vang Pao's house in the evenings to dine, sitting cross-legged on the floor, and plan their next moves. At wild parties in V.P.'s home, there were drinking contests, as the locals and their American friends danced in circles to Hmong music. Afterward, the Americans could drop in at a local bar. Next to the tavern, a cage built into a hill was home to a honeybear named Floyd, who fancied beer and scotch. CIA men at the base wrestled with Floyd until he grew to be too much for them. When a U.S. military attaché passing through Long Tieng asked one American how one kept his sanity in northern Laos, the American replied, "You stay drunk."

The other side of a mountain ridge, in the village of Sam Thong, the U.S. Agency for International Development (AID) officials ran a major operations center, hand-in-glove with the Agency. Planes and helicopters came and went with rice and other supplies on their way to the Hmong and other tribes. The master of Sam Thong was Edgar "Pop" Buell, a retired crusty Indiana farmer who came to Laos in 1960 as an agricultural volunteer and then signed on with AID. As the war had expanded, he became a one-man supply corps for the CIA's secret army, arranging airlifts to tribal units and their families. On occasion he directed Hmong guerrillas to dynamite bridges and mountain passes.

The logistical center for Shackley's program was based at the Udorn Air Base in Thailand and fell under his authority. To preserve the fiction that Washington was adhering to the Geneva Accords, the United States could not maintain a support base for the Hmong in Laos itself. Since 1962, Agency officers had supplied the irregulars from Udorn. By the mid-1960s, Udorn was a full-fledged air facility, home to fighter squadrons, recon squadrons, a flight training school. A collection of whorehouses surrounded it. The number of Agency people there remained small. But that would change with Shackley.

Shackley's tribal troops and most U.S. programs in Laos depended on two highly unorthodox civilian air transport firms, Air America and Continental Air Services. Officially, Air America was a private company, but it was an open secret that Air America was a CIA front, owned entirely by the Agency. As its number one "customer" in Laos, Shackley de facto supervised much of its operations. Its pilots flew in and out of combat zones, hauling tribal and Lao troops, the wounded, unidentified CIA officers, VIPs, weapons, ammunition, and livestock. Continental Air was not owned by the Agency, but the firm argued it was improper for Air America to win all the available contracts. The threat was implicit: either the Agency hire Continental, or Air America's cover would be blown.

Ed Dearborn, the director of operations of Continental and a former Agency hand, disliked dealing with Shackley. Dearborn, who had been in charge of the Agency's secret air war in the Congo, was accustomed to camaraderie existing between the CIA officers on the ground and the covert airmen. But Shackley was all business. Dearborn's meetings with Shackley in the chief's nondescript embassy office were like corporate sessions, the only concern being the bottom line. "Shackley would ask us to go where people shouldn't go," Dearborn recalled. "He asked us to do things that we were not able to do with the type of equipment we had. We were just pilots, not fighter pilots. But he had his requirements and didn't care how it was done. Shackley's attitude was, 'Do this, and I don't care if you get back.' "

In Laos, Shackley was to command present and future Agency legends. The most notorious was Tony Poe. A large, rough-looking fellow with a booming voice, Poe had helped create Vang Pao's army. As more Americans settled into Long Tieng in the 1960s, he pushed further into the remote reaches of Laos to run operations out of the northwest corner. There "Mr. Tony" directed tribal units and became the subject of many bizarre and mostly true tales. He had aided Burmese insurgents, when Washington officially was favoring the government of Burma. He kept heads of slain enemy soldiers in jars of formaldehyde. And Tony Poe, according to a case officer who served with him, used to collect ears.

Poe had offered his tribal irregulars a bounty for enemy ears—a dollar a pair. When mission officials once questioned Poe about his claims of a large enemy body count, he stapled a batch of fresh and bloody ears to a report and sent it to the station. Eventually, he discontinued this program when he discovered it provided too much encouragement. At one airstrip, he had found a small boy with no ears. "My father took them to get money from the Americans," the boy said.

Poe, who married a Yau princess and spoke several local dialects, embodied the term "gone native." Within the DDP, he was well known and admired, even if grudgingly. But one case officer who worked with Poe in Laos considered him a tragic figure, a sad symbol of U.S. policy: "an interesting man who was very confused, very sick, and very good, extremely good, working with local people, enormously brave. He loved what he did. He simply lost touch with reality."

Shackley would develop his own particular rep as a pro. "Oh man, was Shackley weird," a CIA officer who was in Laos recalled, providing a slightly exaggerated description of his chief. "Tall, thin, real tall. And cold, man, real cold. Calm, quiet, he just kind of looked at you in this weird way. And real white skin, real white. He never went out in the sun, man, he never went out in the sun."

Word of Shackley had preceded his arrival in Vientiane. One senior embassy officer heard from those who had worked recently with Shackley in Berlin that he was too ready to sacrifice means for ends, the means sometimes being people. To his colleagues in Vientiane, it was apparent from the moment Shackley entered the embassy that he would be a different sort of CIA chief than his predecessor Doug Blaufarb. A graduate of Harvard and Columbia Journalism School, Blaufarb possessed an academic bent. A soft-spoken intellectual, he mulled over the nuances of policy, more the analyst than the operator. He had been content to let the boys at Udorn handle the nitty-gritty.

Shackley had been dispatched to Vientiane to run the war. He was there not to contemplate the murky grays of Laos, but to get things done. And he was not shy about letting everyone know that. He came into meetings, embassy officer Mark Pratt recalled, "and spoke as if he were the Lord Almighty with nothing but the highest truth, and everyone else was badly informed until he spoke." It was all can-do. "I wondered if he ever reflected at any time on why he was doing all this," said Emory "Coby" Swank, the deputy chief of mission. Sullivan saw no reason to wonder. It was clear to him that Shackley had no time for qualms about his job and purpose. Shackley was not a person to share his deeper thoughts. "One can only see him," Pratt observed, "from the outside."

Compared with Vietnam, the war in Laos was a small production. When Shackley arrived, Agency personnel numbered a few dozen. The annual cost of U.S. military operations in Laos was running in the $500 million range, maybe even less. Most of the tab was covered by the

Pentagon, with the CIA picking up the cost for about 10 percent. Sullivan was doing all he could to keep the war small. But he was fighting a losing battle—especially since the U.S. military in Vietnam constantly pressed him to take actions to assist its endeavors there. Shackley's presence in Laos, as some of his Agency colleagues would realize later, marked the end of that battle.

Sullivan and Shackley were largely free to handle the war as they deemed fit. "The situation in Laos was so confused and confusing, so unattractive that the Joint Chiefs really didn't want to take it on," Sullivan recalled. "We got practically no instructions whatsoever from Washington." And the assignment to Laos could be intoxicating. "It was great fun," one of Shackley's superiors said. "You sit in the Ambassador's office, deal with leaders of the Lao government, arrange for Thai artillery strikes, map out strategy, decide what moves Vang Pao's army should make, send orders to field commanders. It had everything."

III

When Shackley had arrived in Laos in the summer of 1966, the non-communist forces were in chaos. A quarrel between Prince Souvanna Phouma and the National Assembly over his budget proposals led to the Premier dissolving the legislature and calling for new elections. Then the commander of the neutralist army, General Kong Le, flew off to Thailand after being challenged by three of his officers. In October, rebellious units of the Laotian air force bombed the army's headquarters. A massive flood reduced rice crops by about 35 percent in government-controlled territory.

Souvanna Phouma, who had hurried back from a European excursion at the news of the air force revolt, held a press conference at the end of October. He voiced support for Kong Le and apologized for his delay in speaking out. He would have done so sooner, he explained, but it had taken him a week to determine what was happening in Laos.

Souvanna Phouma had more to deal with than who was overthrowing whom. The economy was running a $20 million deficit, despite $50 million in U.S. aid and another $10 million in other foreign assistance. Nearly 200,000 refugees had fled toward the south. At least the war resembled shadowboxing more than all-out combat. "Often enough," one U.S. official told a reporter, "one side shoots just to warn the other side that it is coming so the enemy can get out of the way." Some military men in Vientiane dubbed the overall situation a "successful mess."

Shackley's presence in Vientiane coincided with a change in the program, which soon would mean trouble and tragedy for Laotians, especially the tribal allies of Langley. CIA operations in Laos, to date, had not been designed to win a war. The original goal was to aid a guerrilla force that harassed the enemy, gathered intelligence, and occupied NVA troops that might otherwise inflict casualties on South Vietnamese and Americans. The point had been to wage a holding action for a few years. After that, matters in Vietnam presumably would be settled.

Shackley ushered in a new war. "Most of us in Laos were supportive of the pre-Shackley handling of the war," recalled Mark Pratt, reflecting a prominent view among embassy officers. The number of Americans in the country was kept low; conventional engagements were largely avoided. Blaufarb had been respected by embassy colleagues for ensuring that the Agency program assisted the irregulars and did not dominate them. With Shackley came an expansion in ambitions. "Shackley wanted more people, more assets, more everything," noted Dean Almy, the head of the Thai-Burma-Laos desk in Langley, "and he got it."

The U.S. military also was pushing for more in Laos, as a way to improve its prospects in Vietnam. Shackley was in sync. Acting on the wishes of the policymakers of the Johnson administration, he, too, wanted an ever-growing program. To embassy officers, such a change was conveniently consistent with Shackley's personal desires. "He was well prepared to see an expansion," Pratt asserted, "because it was an expansion of what he was doing. There was an ego operating."

Vang Pao also was eager to widen his activities. The general had begun to think he was more powerful than he was. "All the attention he got from the Americans and the American air support—it was quite insidious," one Agency man said. After capturing a few artillery pieces, Vang Pao's army wanted more. His successful small-squad forays against the enemy led to more ambitious battalion-size assaults. This escalation was to earn a commensurate response from the enemy, which increased its forces and armaments to maintain its position in Laos. With Agency sanction and support, Vang Pao was ratcheting up—in the direction of a conflict that he would not be able to sustain.

"There was a very conscious decision," said a CIA officer in Laos, "to turn this very effective and competent guerrilla organization into something far more conventional that served the purposes more of Vietnam than Laos, the purpose of tying down more and more NVA soldiers in Laos. That was the price that Ted Shackley and William Sullivan paid. In order to keep the program from going over to the military, they juiced up the Hmong to fight in the more conventional manner, and it would be a total fucking disaster for the Hmong."

Shackley poured people into the Udorn base, which in 1965 had been home to only a dozen or so Agency officers. This concerned Bill Lair, the veteran base chief at Udorn, who was married to a Thai and devoted to the people and cultures of Southeast Asia. "Up to then, the whole Laos program was working extremely well with a small amount of people and an unbelievably modest Agency budget," Lair recalled. But Washington was getting desperate about Vietnam. Someone there apparently had hit on the idea that if the secret war worked so well, then add more money and people and it will do that much better. Shackley ordered the construction in Udorn of a million-dollar, two-story concrete headquarters with state-of-the-art communications. "Then we had to fill it full of people," Lair said. Shackley was turning Lair's country store into a supermarket.

Lair hoped the secret war could stay modest, that the irregulars could remain an invisible hit-and-run force, a hard target for the mightier NVA. But since Washington wanted to increase the pressure on the North Vietnamese and was not willing to dump American soldiers into Laos, the CIA had to recruit others to supply the bodies.

After a few months in Laos, Shackley returned to Washington. He looked up Tom Clines, his former JMWAVE comrade. The convivial Clines had departed Miami in the summer of 1964 and joined the Special Operations Division as the deputy chief of its maritime branch, supporting Agency operations in the Congo and in the Dominican Republic. In a Langley office, Shackley explained the Laotian program to his friend. His primary task was doing whatever possible to interdict the flow of North Vietnamese troops and supplies that traveled through Laos on their way to South Vietnam. The second main responsibility was managing the war in northern Laos. The two jobs, he told Clines, were largely separate.

With the U.S. military pressing the CIA to stop traffic on the Ho Chi Minh Trail, Shackley's station was running road watch teams—tribal spotters who sneaked close to the Trail and observed what was coming down the path. The information they gathered was forwarded to U.S. military officials who planned bombing raids. The military was not pleased with the operation: the watch teams hit the Trail at long intervals of forty to fifty miles, and the information came back slowly. Even worse, the road watch teams got in the way. The U.S. Air Force could not napalm a section where an Agency squad was operating.

Shackley informed Clines his goal was to blanket the Trail with teams, ideally one every five miles or so. The team members would use a special type of radio to send their intelligence out immediately. These radios had buttons corresponding to the objects one might see coming down the trail—a truck, a tank, a brigade of troops. The illiterate tribesmen would push the right button every time one of these passed.

To Clines, Shackley boasted of another Vietnam-related program in the north. Atop Phou Pha Thi, a steep mountain in northeastern Laos, the Air Force had installed a navigational aid that guided U.S. bombers in and out of North Vietnam. The CIA-supported units of Vang Pao guarded the site. The war in the north, an optimistic Shackley asserted to Clines, was progressing well. But what was most important were the programs that used tribal assets to aid the U.S. effort in Vietnam.

Shackley confided that he was disturbed about the gang at Udorn. Under Blaufarb, Bill Lair had been the principal CIA contact with Vang Pao. Lair was in Long Tieng almost every day, seeing to the details of the secret war. Shackley wanted to be in charge, to have his own men in key posts. He asked Clines to be the deputy base chief at Udorn. To make room for Clines, he intended to boot Pat Landry, Lair's deputy. Shackley was irked by Lair's informality and fondness for parading about Udorn in pajamas and flip-flops. Clines did not want to replace Landry, an old friend. He convinced Shackley to retain Landry, and Clines accepted the post of chief of operations at Udorn. Shackley would later install as chief of the Pakse base Dave Morales, his PM chief in JMWAVE. For his deputy in Vientiane, Shackley had James Lilley, a Yale graduate considered a Shackley yes-man by the officers in the field.

Lair and Landry had not been heartened by Shackley's initial trip to Udorn. The new chief talked at the pair for what seemed two hours. He asked no questions. When he left, Lair looked at Landry and said, that young fellow is going to learn a lot more in the next two years than we will. From the start, Shackley was not a popular chief in Laos. His charge-through-the-brambles approach upset other officers. "Shackley didn't care whose face he slapped," complained William Young, a case officer with years of experience in Laos. "People became thumbtacks and numbers to him." Agency men peeved by him shocked embassy officials by knocking on their doors in search of commiseration.

Shackley adopted the same know-it-all tack with the Hmong. He would fly to Long Tieng with a plan in mind and in thirty minutes lay it out for tribal officers, who stared blankly at him. He did not realize they were not absorbing it. Vang Pao at first could not bear him. Shackley spoke to V.P. in a high-handed manner. Often after a visit from the station chief, Vang Pao threw a tantrum, shouting, I do not want this man up here any more. But Shackley won over V.P. by showing him his power. Vang Pao received plenty of air support, if Shackley liked his operation. Shackley boosted the Agency's pay of the tribal irregulars and gave them corrugated sheets of metals with which they could build homes. Vang Pao came to realize that Shackley got things done, and slowly Shackley learned how to deal with tribesmen, who did not possess his passion for organization.

Shackley was not in Laos for long, when he was handed an important political task. Senator Stuart Symington, a member of the influential Armed Services Committee, was coming to town. Shackley was to show

him what a good job the Agency was doing. The senator was wavering
on the war. Prior to leaving for Asia, the Missouri Democrat had called
Walt Rostow, the national security adviser to Johnson, and said, "You
and I have been hawks on Vietnam since 1961. I am thinking of getting
off the train soon." Rostow replied that he hoped Symington would
spend enough time in Indochina to understand why the mood of Americans serving there was up-beat. Shackley was to share his optimism with
Symington.

After Symington arrived, Sullivan took the senator to see Souvanna
Phouma, who explained why he did not want any open acknowledgment
of the war in Laos. That would complicate relations with the Soviets and
the Chinese and undermine the potential for a future political solution.
Then it was Shackley's turn.

The chief of station had continued to develop his reputation as a
skilled briefer—even if his facts and figures occasionally seemed selective. He could go on in a briefing about a great military success of the
Hmong without mentioning the casualties the battle had produced. "At
embassy staff meetings," Mark Pratt recalled, "we'd say to him, 'Sure the
Hmong have the force strength to do this or that, but that's only because
you included twelve-year-olds in your force estimates.'" After Shackley
had been in Vientiane only weeks, Ambassador Chester Bowles visited
Laos, and Shackley briefed him. The CIA man astounded Bowles with
his apparent grasp of the country. At the end of his stay in Laos, Bowles
pronounced this newcomer to Vientiane the most impressive man in
the whole embassy.

Now Shackley wowed Symington. The chief of station escorted the
senator to Spook Heaven. He introduced Symington to Vang Pao. The
senator chatted with pilots back from a combat strike. In Langley, John
Mapother, who recently was in Berlin under Shackley, read the reports
of Shackley's briefing of Symington. The senator had bought Shackley's
hard sell. "I was a little astonished by that," Mapother recalled. Symington invited Shackley to Washington to perform in front of the Senate
Armed Services Committee—an offer Shackley accepted months later.
After that private session with Shackley, Symington and other senators
praised the Laotian program. It was a sensible way to fight a war, Symington declared, and the Agency was spending in a year what the U.S. Army
in Vietnam consumed in a day.

Vientiane was a dream city for a spy. Everyone was there: the Chinese,
the Soviets, the North Vietnamese. South Vietnamese intelligence spied
on the North Vietnamese—and vice versa. They all were targets for
Shackley's station. If an Agency man strolled into a bar, on the next stool

he might find a Soviet intelligence officer. Across the room there could be a Chinese spy. Shackley's station ran agents, bought up secret diplomatic papers, conspired with the Lao intelligence service. His officers bugged restaurants frequented by the diplomats and intelligence officers of other nations. One favorite trick of Shackley's station was to arrange an automobile accident involving a Soviet embassy car. In the ensuing confusion, an operative attempted to snatch whatever materials the Soviet passenger was carrying. Agency assets broke into embassies in the hope that they might find code pads. His officers watched for Soviets who were drinking more than their fair share on the Strip or cavorting with local bar girls. For an intelligence officer, it was a wide-open town. Tom Clines loved to visit Vientiane and soak up the intrigue. Often he accompanied V.P. to the capital; when he did, Clines carried an attaché case containing a submachine gun and ammunition.

At the many fancy diplomatic affairs and receptions, Shackley's officers easily picked up champagne-induced information. Non-Agency Americans watched on amused as Shackley (whose cover was as an embassy officer), Jim Lilley, or other Company officers charged after sitting ducks. It was well known through Laotian and diplomatic circles that Shackley was America's chief spy in Laos.

The station tracked the internecine maneuvers within the government. There was an attempted coup nearly every year. Senior embassy officers thought Shackley could do a better job at sniffing out possible moves against Souvanna, and they did not see evidence of any major espionage coups during Shackley's tour. But if Shackley ever did reel in a Soviet diplomat or Chinese spy, he would not have shared his catch with the pin-striped crowd.

His station subsidized the civilian Laotian intelligence service. It supported a shortwave broadcasting station in Long Tieng. The power was weak, but the radio station's programs—news, native music, and hortatory material broadcast in Lao, Hmong, and other tribal languages—reached most tribal areas in northern Laos, where the Agency had distributed transistor radios. The Agency air-dropped into Pathet Lao territory counterfeit money and leaflets advertising for defectors. The material enticed few turncoats.

As for the political scene in Laos, Shackley did not need a secret agent to penetrate the inner reaches of the government. The Lao generally talked to anyone. "The whole thing was a little operetta, a charade in many ways," recalled Oliver Silsby, an Agency case officer who handled contacts with leading Lao. "There weren't many secrets to find." Most information could be gathered overtly. Mark Pratt, a vivacious fellow who spoke several languages, ran his own one-man intelligence outfit for the embassy. He maintained friendships with colonels, clan leaders, government officials. By trolling the gossip mill, he closely followed the political intrigues that wracked the government and the Lao elite. Pratt proved that a smart diplomat who knew his turf well could outcollect the spies.

No intelligence target in Laos was more important than the Ho Chi Minh Trail. U.S. officials obsessed over it. In Laos, Shackley ordered intelligence operations against the Trail and the NVA and sent out the tribal road watch teams that spotted trucks and troops flowing down the Trail. CIA-supported action units occasionally ambushed and destroyed enemy trucks, ammunition, and petroleum and seeded the Trail with antitank mines. Harry Aderholt, a U.S. Air Force officer supporting Agency operations in Southeast Asia, used the road-watch intelligence to plan raids by his Thailand-based bomber wings. But, he discovered, there was no way to verify that the information he received was accurate, that the station's tribesmen were pushing the right buttons on their special radios. Aderholt estimated that only 60 percent of Shackley's take was sound.

Every few weeks, General William Westmoreland, the commander of U.S. forces in Vietnam, and a bevy of aides flew to Udorn to meet with Sullivan and Shackley and others to ponder attacks on the Trail and related matters. Present at the sessions was Colonel John Singlaub, head of the top-secret Studies and Observation Group. Singlaub's outfit, which comprised about 8,000 Indochinese and 2,000 Americans, waged covert sabotage raids against Laotian portions of the Trail, where Americans were not supposed to be fighting. Singlaub kept Shackley posted on the SOG's actions in Laos. He appreciated that Shackley raised no protest about SOG's incursion into his turf. The problem was that damned ambassador, who was trying to keep the war in Laos under control and maintain the facade of the Geneva Accords. Sullivan had to okay all the proposed actions of Singlaub's teams. "And every time one of my teams took out a lucrative target on the Trail a few kilometers from their approved area of operations," Singlaub recalled, "we'd get a rocket of a telegram from the embassy in Vientiane." Sullivan did not understand that war did not always fit neatly within the borders of a map. When Singlaub dealt with Shackley, he was talking with someone on the team. It was too bad, Singlaub thought, that Shackley had to answer to his ambassador.

The high-level meetings at Udorn were tense occasions. Westmoreland and a slew of colonels usually demanded that the station do this or that—send a road-watch team to a particular point or deploy a tribal paramilitary force against an NVA unit—in support of the war in Vietnam. "Westmoreland and the other military men did not give a damn about what was happening in Laos for Laos' sake," recalled Tom Clines, who attended these discussions. The Agency managers of the secret war in Laos pushed for more air support for their own operations. There was constant friction, arguments about priorities and targets for the bombing campaign. At one gathering, an angry Westmoreland and Shackley quarreled over whether or not the Laos station had sent a vital piece of intelligence to Westmoreland. Shackley recited the number of the transmittal manifest—a long series of digits—from memory. Then one of Westmoreland's colonels located the report in a briefcase. "For a moment," Clines said, "it showed everyone that the bureaucracy was smothering itself in Vietnam."

Vietnam was America's first high-tech war, and Shackley tried to employ as much state-of-the-art gadgetry as he could. The station devised a program in which Vang Pao's operatives contacted Hmong tribespeople forced to work for the Pathet Lao and secretly supplied them a piece of equipment—perhaps a walking stick—that contained a miniature beacon. Agency technicians then monitored the whereabouts of the unit and targeted it for bombing. To make sure the Hmong with the beacon knew when the attack was coming (so he could escape), Shackley's officers broadcast a code phrase on the radio station it ran in Long Tieng —and assumed their man on the ground received the message.

One day Carlton Swift, Jr., one of the technical eggheads of the Agency's supersecret Staff D, showed up at Shackley's station. Heir to the Swift meat-packing fortune and an amiable gadget man, he dropped by to scope out the war and see if he could be of any help. After a brief review, Swift had one idea. What you should do, he told Shackley, is set up listening posts to track the enemy's radio transmissions.

The need for this type of intelligence had increased over the years, since the station's agents in and near North Vietnam had dried up. Under Swift's plan, the station would eavesdrop on the battlefield signals of the enemy. If it picked up an uncoded signal or one that could be deciphered, it would have instant intelligence. But merely by analyzing the pattern of the traffic—coded or uncoded—Swift's officers could tell Shackley where certain troops were and how active they might be. Headquarters was chary about stationing Agency communication experts too far into the field. But Shackley was all for it, and the program began.*

---

* In 1970, tycoon H. Ross Perot, a champion of U.S. prisoners of war, visited the Vientiane embassy and met with CIA officers who told him that they had broken the Pathet Lao radio system and discovered information relating to the whereabouts of captured Americans.

As a preliminary move, Swift flew in an Air America helicopter to northwestern Laos near the China border where a listening post might be established. A squall blew in, and the pilot brought the copter down in a Hmong village. The local chief arranged a minor feast. The girls of the village performed a dance for the VIPs. Right after Swift and his pilot lifted off, a squad of enemy soldiers raided the village looking for the Americans. Swift did not tell Shackley or anyone else about the close call. He possessed too much classified information to have been there in the first place. Swift continued his tour through the countryside and discovered that the secret war was graced with its own unique touches of absurdity. At one site he inspected, a Chinese general was inexplicably present. "No one knew where he had come from, or where he was going," Swift recalled. "It was odd."

In the northwestern corner of Laos, Shackley's station managed an elaborate and highly secret espionage program that had little to do with Laos. Since the 1950s, the CIA had employed locals for intelligence-gathering forays into southern China. For years, this effort was overseen by William Young, a case officer born in the nearby Burmese Shan states. Young and the CIA had friends in the area. In the early 1950s, the Agency had served as wet-nurse to an irregular army composed of Chinese Nationalists opposed to Mao's revolution and based in the southern Shan states. The Agency, using Civil Air Transport, an airline it secretly owned, had shipped arms to the ragtag force of the Kuomintang (KMT). Two KMT attempts to invade China failed miserably. Afterward, several thousand KMT remained in the Shan states territory and went into the local business: the opium trade. In the early 1960s, the CIA recruited KMT troops to patrol the China-Burma border area. Then William Young began sending small bands of CIA-trained Yao and Lao Theung tribesmen into China's Yunnan province to collect intelligence.

Young's cross-border project operated out of Nam Yu, an isolated base in a small mountain valley. From that site, his teams of two to fifteen tribesmen were flown fifty-five miles due north. In rubber rafts, they paddled across the Mekong River and hiked miles through the Burmese jungle to a base. A few days' trek brought the tribal operatives to a forward base miles from China. Team members tapped Chinese telegraph lines, watched roads, and sought information to forward to Shackley.

The CIA teams depended on security provided by Shan forces and shared jungle bases with the KMT, roguish armies both active in the opium trade. Agency operatives used immense opium caravans as cover for their trips to and from China. None of this perturbed Young. The mission came first; fretting about the locals' opium-running was counter-productive.

The high-risk cross-border program—which resulted in dead agents
—produced "very marginal stuff," according to Peter Dyke, an officer at
the Vientiane station. Even Young conceded it did not yield any earth-
shattering findings. But "it sure was sexy in Washington to say that you
got something from inside China," Pratt recalled. Sadly for the cold
warriors, the project failed to establish one fact they hoped to prove:
that China was exporting heroin for foreign exchange. In northeastern
Laos it was the CIA that profited from the narcotics business by recruiting people in the trade for operations against the communists.

From Vientiane, Shackley supervised such daring and imaginative
projects. But he remained more a bureaucrat than a swashbuckler. When
it came to intelligence production, his administrator's urges reigned.
He wanted easy-to-see results, and the best indicators were numbers.
Shackley delivered a message to his chief reports office. He wished to
boost the number of reports sent to Langley each month. He even
dictated the precise number of reports he expected his station to produce. To reach that amount, the reports officers resorted to an old trick:
break up one report into two or three pieces and put each out as a
separate report. The chief reports officer devilishly decided to follow
Shackley to the letter. If Shackley wanted one hundred reports a month,
the chief reports officer would send exactly one hundred. After a few
months of this, the clerks who tally the statistics in Langley would realize
what was happening. But Shackley caught on to the scheme and changed
the routine to prevent such a telltale sign. It was hard to outfox the
chief.

IV

"During my service in Laos," Shackley wrote after the war, "we developed fishponds, established pig breeding centers, and managed voca-
tional schools which taught carpentry, brickmaking and auto
mechanics." The U.S. program in Laos built hospitals and schools, dug
wells, introduced new types of livestock. Such civic action, Shackley
noted, produced results: "It won and kept the hearts and minds of the
majority of the hill tribes on the side of the royal Lao government." But
do-goodism clashed with the demands of war. Shackley demonstrated
this to AID officials when he stomped on one of their most ambitious
programs in Laos.

In 1964, AID initiated in the Sedone Valley in southern Laos a "village
cluster" project. Locals were brought into "clusters" for rural development programs. Some participating villagers were armed and trained.
The program flourished for two and a half years, according to Douglas
Blaufarb, who as Shackley's predecessor heartily backed it. Vegetable

gardens were planted, roads constructed, militias created. The Agency contributed funds and officers to the military side of the endeavor. A 1966 AID report claimed that the "village cluster" program was so successful that requests for the organization of additional clusters exceeded the resources of the U.S. mission.

Shackley inherited the project from Blaufarb, and did not think it worthy of his time and American money. In 1967, with the approval of headquarters and Sullivan, he withdrew Agency support. Shackley decided it was more important to use the resources for programs targeting the nearby Ho Chi Minh corridor. That would deliver a bigger bang for the buck—and contribute more directly to U.S. aims in Vietnam. AID personnel working on the program were upset. In their view, Shackley had engineered a unilateral withdrawal from a long-term commitment.

Shackley ordered that the recruits for the Sedone Valley program be turned into Trail watchers. "He would have defended his move by saying it provided useful intelligence," Blaufarb observed. "Others said that the men stayed in safe places, made up reports and sent them back in by radio." Shortly after the plug was pulled, several battalions of Pathet Lao and NVA troops overran the region. "Villages in the area which had cooperated with the government," Blaufarb noted, "suffered at the hands" of the Pathet Lao and NVA.

The war in Laos had continued its weather-dictated cycle. But each year brought an increase in the firepower and troops fielded by the Pathet Lao and an increase of U.S. support for the Hmong. The great equalizer on the Hmong side came from the air: American warplanes carrying tens of thousands of tons of bombs. In a U.S.-operated and -funded program initiated in 1964, Thai pilots, taking off from Udorn and Vientiane, flew World War II–vintage T-28s with Royal Lao Air Force markings in secret raids to support Vang Pao's army. The following year, the U.S. Air Force began bombing Pathet Lao and North Vietnamese positions in Laos. The U.S. bombing program in Laos, conducted in official secrecy, was essentially two campaigns. One in the panhandle, controlled by U.S. officers in Saigon, targeted the Ho Chi Minh Trail; the other, in the north, supported the Laotian army and the CIA's tribal forces.

Shackley and his subordinates "developed" targets—bases, depots, troop locations—for the bombing that assisted the tribal irregulars. From the perspective of the U.S. managers of the war, the bombing program went splendidly. Without a costly investment—especially in terms of American lives—the United States bolstered the Hmong's efforts. But the addition of airpower encouraged the ongoing change in the Hmong's role. No longer were they guerrilla irregulars harassing a better endowed enemy. Increasingly they were performing like conventional infantry and attacking fortified positions, with aid from the air. The loss of life for the tribespeople was heavy. But their initial success at this type of warfare led to an exaggerated sense—in Long Tieng, Vientiane, and Washington—of what they could do, and it hid a nasty truth: the irregulars, in the long run, could not succeed against a competent and larger conventional force.

As the sorties ordered by Shackley and other U.S. officials increased each year, the bombing of civilians took place—"an unfortunate excess in an originally sound and closely-controlled program," Blaufarb commented in a 1972 report.* The U.S. mission in Vientiane hoped that air raids on enemy installations close to civilian centers would block NVA and Pathet Lao advances. "That assumption is difficult to confirm," Blaufarb wrote, "but one certain result was the obliteration" of many towns on and near the Plain of Jars.

Jerome Brown, an Air Force captain and chief targeting official in Laos in 1967, was disenchanted with the bombing program. Every Tuesday he traveled to Udorn to discuss the week's bombing raids with Air Force officials and Shackley's men. Brown was angered by the Air Force's lax attitude toward the bombing that supported the CIA's tribal army. The bombing was often inaccurate: "You had bombs dropping all over the countryside, had bombs going anywhere from one-fourth of a mile to five miles off target. And five miles off target could conceivably be a village." At one point in 1967, Brown alleged, Shackley's station ordered the bombing of a village in northeast Laos that was supposedly a transshipment point for the NVA, even though Ambassador Sullivan had withheld permission for the attack.

Throughout 1967, the bombing campaign grew more intense. That year, American bombs dropped on Laos topped 128,000 tons. (The next year, the total figure would reach nearly 240,000 tons.) Sullivan assigned a junior embassy officer the task of ensuring civilian targets were not hit. But a United Nations adviser noted that by 1968, "the intensity of the bombings [on the Plain of Jars region] was such that no organized life was possible in the villages."

Refugees reported that civilians bore the brunt of many air attacks. A thirty-nine-year-old refugee, once a farmer, recalled for an interviewer how an American aerial assault in 1967—perhaps one of the many authorized by Shackley and Sullivan—changed the life of his village:

---

* Decades later, Blaufarb was more critical: "What they thought were roads and military concentrations—all they were were thatched huts. It was hard to tell what they were. . . . It was really a dubious proposition to use modern jet aircraft in that type of situation, when you are bombing jungle."

War planes of the type T-28s and AD-6s, along with F-105s and four-engine planes and many kinds that I didn't recognize, flew through the sky over my village. They made a spectacle the likes of which my village had never seen. . . .

At first, these planes shot at the different mountains. We thought that our people had nothing to do with these matters, we thought we could watch to our heart's content and continue living as we always had.

But just then they started to shoot along the road to the village, which dismayed us because they were shooting without aim and everyone became frightened and ran out to hide in the fields. At night we returned to the village and things continued as usual until March 14, 1967. . . . Four planes of the jet type dropped their bombs together to destroy my village and returned to shoot twice in the same day. They dropped eight napalm bombs, the fire from which burned all my things, sixteen buildings along with all our possessions inside, as well as maiming our animals. Some people who didn't reach the jungle in time were struck and fell, dying most pitifully. By the time the fire died down it was dark. Everyone came out of hiding to look at the ashes of their houses. Even the rice was all burnt. Everyone cried at once —loudly and agitatedly. . . . The other villagers and I got together to consider this thing. We hadn't done anything, nor harmed anyone. We had raised our crops, celebrated the festivals and maintained our homes for years. Why did the planes drop bombs on us, impoverishing us in this way?

One evening, Frank McCulloch, the Time-Life bureau chief in Saigon, was in a bamboo bordello-bar on the raunchy Strip of Vientiane. He got to talking with a group of rowdy, drunk Americans. Two boasted they were Air America pilots and were flying opium out of Laos—and Ted Shackley had approved their enterprise. McCulloch was stunned they would so brazenly discuss this with a stranger, even if opium smuggling in Laos was an open secret. But he did not pursue the lead. The part about Shackley seemed merely talk; maybe the drug pilots were looking for cover. Besides, McCulloch was already busy investigating the involvement of South Vietnamese officials in the Laotian opium business. But he was one of the first to encounter the ugly rumor that would haunt Shackley and the Company for years to come: that in Laos the CIA actively participated in narcotics trafficking.

Laos was a country that produced few goods in demand beyond its borders other than opium. Northern Laos was part of the Golden Triangle, which included Thailand and Burma and accounted in 1967 for 50 to 75 percent of the globe's illicit opium crop. That year, 100 to 150 tons, about 10 percent of the Golden Triangle production, were harvested by the tribes of Laos, some of whom had been recruited by the CIA for the war on communism. Opium brought the country $2 million a year, as the top export earner. Of the Laotian opium destined for export, a portion ended up as heroin in the veins of American GIs stuck in Vietnam.

Everyone in Laos knew the Hmong traded opium. Where the tribe went, so went opium. And opium collection, transportation, and protection was always a priority for the Laotian military. Within Laos, the opium business was legal. There was an internal demand for the product. But the real money was made by selling to buyers engaged in the international heroin trade, many operating in South Vietnam. Air America planes, Doug Blaufarb conceded, "without doubt" transported opium in the packages brought aboard by passengers and this "probably happened frequently. Seldom, however, was it done knowingly or did the [American] pilot benefit."

Rumors of Air America personnel trafficking in drugs became so persistent that in September of 1972, the Inspector General of the CIA would launch an investigation. The subsequent report became a holy writ for Shackley, the Agency, and its champions. The I.G. declared there was "no evidence that the Agency, or any senior officer of the Agency, has ever sanctioned or supported drug trafficking as a matter of policy." Neither was even "the slightest suspicion" found that any Agency officer, staff, or contract personnel in Laos was involved in the narcotics trade. As for the CIA-owned Air America, the I.G.'s pronouncement was carefully phrased: "We found that it has always forbidden, as a matter of policy, the transportation of contraband goods aboard its aircraft."

Policy is not always reality. Air America hauled what its customers put on its aircraft, and it did not possess the capacity to check each parcel. "We knew that we hauled a lot of dope," recalled Jim Parrish, an Air America pilot, "although we didn't do it intentionally. . . . Some damned Lao general would be the customer who had called up a plane and you had to carry what he wanted."

But the Air America connection was not the only Agency contact—wittingly or not—with narcotics smugglers. The CIA did work with agents and Lao officials involved in the drug trade, according to the I.G. report, among them General Phoumi Nosavan, the right-wing leader and onetime CIA favorite, and General Ouane Rattikone. Shackley's officers and U.S. military men routinely confronted evidence that their allies in the Laotian military were moonlighting as opium traders. One time, Eli Popovich, the CIA base chief in Luang Prabang, suspected an American airplane was ferrying a drug shipment to the landing strip he oversaw. He sent a local asset to spy on the unloading, and this man reported to him that the freight suspiciously was taken straight to the basement of a house belonging to General Ouane. Popovich could not stop such activity. On a visit to Laos, Dean Almy, a CIA desk officer, went up-country to a landing strip. As he watched an Air America plane on a mission for a top Lao general, the local CIA adviser said to him, that plane is loaded with opium but we can't do anything about it.

During the so-called Opium War that occurred in the summer of 1967, the U.S.-backed Laotian Air Force pounded Chinese Nationalist and Burmese Shan units fighting each other within Laotian territory over a large shipment of opium. The Chinese Nationalists and the Shans retreated, and General Ouane collected the opium—up to 12 tons, according to reports received by the U.S. embassy. The Chinese Nationalists were the same KMT forces helping Shackley's station acquire intelligence in China. "This was where the CIA was clearly involved with opium," said embassy officer Mark Pratt, referring to station programs that relied on KMT and Shan assistance.

The I.G. report acknowledged that Shackley's station was fully aware that many Laotian military officers were drug-traffickers. "Yet their goodwill," the report added, "if not actual cooperation, considerably facilitates the military activities of the Agency-supported irregulars." In one case, the station maintained an agent believed to be in the narcotics business because he was an influential government official.

CIA veterans, eager to protect their wartime tribal comrades, have asserted that Lao government and military figures were the true culprits who earned fortunes, while the Hmong received the small sums typically paid growers. "We found no evidence of organized trafficking by the Hmong who were involved in our paramilitary program," Shackley maintained. "The paramilitary forces controlled certain areas. Was there opium use in those areas by the civilian population? The answer is yes, there was. . . . Was opium processed and shipped by the Hmong clans into the international markets? Again, the short answer is yes. But these Hmong were not tied into our operations and were not supported by us."

But some of Shackley's tribal officers cashed in. In 1968, John Everingham, a war photographer, visited the village of Long Pot, thirty miles northwest of Long Tieng. One night he shared a house with an officer of Vang Pao's army. Early in the morning he was awakened by a commotion. Villagers were bringing in bamboo tubes full of black, sticky opium. The officer was paying the locals for it. This went on for a few mornings. The locals told Everingham the opium was transported to Long Tieng on Air America helicopters. In 1971 Long Pot villagers informed a visiting reporter that they regularly sold the opium to officers of Vang Pao's army. The rice drops they received courtesy of the United States, they explained, allowed them to forsake rice farming and devote their energies to the more lucrative opium production.

During and after the war, Shackley's best asset in Laos, Vang Pao, drew accusations that he had dabbled in the drug trade. In one 1988 television documentary, Tony Poe, the irrepressible, ear-collecting CIA officer, charged Vang Pao with "making millions" through heroin. But the evidence against V.P. has not been strong, and most Agency men who worked closely with him—even those who did not like him—swear they never had reason to suspect V.P. himself was in the business. Yet Vang Pao and his American friends knew that his tribe's economic health depended on opium. "He had to let opium get through for some of his people," said Pratt, the embassy man. No American held that against him. With the flow of U.S. aid into the country, there was much opportunity for money-making on the side, besides opium. Agency officers realized V.P. and his officers could be raking off profits from the Xieng Khouang Trading Corporation that the CIA established for the Hmong or pocketing the extra pay Shackley's station provided for the tribal soldiers.

In the mid-1960s, Shackley and the Agency did not see drug-trafficking as a threat to national security. The opium business in Laos, recalled Thomas McCoy, a senior CIA officer in the Far East Division, "was never a topic of serious discussion within the Agency." As the I.G. report later observed, "The war has clearly been our overriding priority in Southeast Asia and all other issues have taken second place in the scheme of things."

There were token Agency efforts to impose a measure of distance between their irregulars and the drug business. CIA men occasionally warned V.P. to make sure his officers were not smuggling opium. The Company-run radio station in Long Tieng aired antidrug messages— until somebody blew it up. But nothing was done by Shackley's station or any other U.S. agency to interfere with the movement of opium from the hills to the market. One of Shackley's case officers in Laos put it simply: he was "under orders not to get too deeply involved in opium matters since his primary mission was to get on with the war and not risk souring relations with his indigenous military counterparts by investigation of opium matters." As Douglas Blaufarb noted, "The policy of the American agencies working with the Meos was to turn a blind eye to the Meo involvement with opium."

There has been no evidence that any Agency officer in Laos turned dealer or that the CIA developed its own version of France's Operation X of the early 1950s. But Shackley and his Agency knowingly supported and associated with persons involved in the opium and heroin trades. This undeniable fact left a nearly indelible stain on the CIA. It became Company lore, an arrow in the quiver of Agency critics, the stuff of movies and novels. "It's one of the things that I think probably irritates me more than any of the allegations against the Agency, and that is that we were involved in the drug traffic at any time," Richard Helms protested after he left the CIA. "We never were! After all, the people who ran the Agency, the people who worked in various places on the operational side all over the world, were perfectly decent Americans."

Vang Pao's forces reached their apogee in 1967 and occupied terrain near Pathet Lao headquarters in Sam Neua. At this point he commanded 22,000 irregulars and 7,000 regular Lao forces. His army, throughout the first months of 1967, had blunted the annual dry season offensive of the Pathet Lao and the NVA. But V.P.'s successes did not breed optimism for all. In the spring of 1967, Emory Swank, the deputy chief of mission, bailed out of Vientiane, opting for a post in Moscow. "I just didn't see any particular solution to the Vietnam-Laos problem," he recalled. His years in Laos had been frustrating. What are we doing here? he wondered. Are we really helping these people? The AID program, a magnet for unceasing corruption, was wasting time on projects that seemed silly in the midst of a war: instructing locals in nutrition, teaching sound hygiene habits. He was not sympathetic to the clandestine war. He recognized the rationale: the North Vietnamese were running their secret war in Laos, so the United States had to have its own. But it was clear to Swank and other embassy colleagues that, no matter what the theory was, Washington was not going to triumph. They were drawing the small nation of Laos further into the hopelessness of Vietnam.

Not a doubter, Shackley was trying to turn the tribal guerrillas into a force with more muscle. In May, CIA-backed irregulars in the south were assigned—apparently with Shackley's permission—the dubious mission of interdicting the Ho Chi Minh Trail. "I and the Americans wanted to test the irregular forces in a company-sized, airmobile operation," Brigadier General Soutchay Vongsavanh of the Royal Lao Army later noted. "Up to this time, [the irregulars] had operated only as squads and platoons." One hundred of Shackley's tribesmen were loaded into Air America helicopters. In the early morning hours, they attacked an NVA position on the Trail. The NVA reacted swiftly and overran the hapless guerrillas before the Americans could arrange for air support. Within twelve hours of the landing, the company was wiped out. Only fifteen of the CIA's surrogates managed to escape and return to headquarters in this "test."

In Luang Prabang, the royal capital and a city of temples where water buffalo slept in the streets, CIA base chief Eli Popovich was dubious about Shackley's war. An old OSS hand who had fought in Yugoslavia and Burma, Popovich directed his own band of tribal irregulars. This army of several hundred waged guerrilla operations in the northeast, staging many out of the garrison in the valley town of Nam Bac. Popovich was fond of his unit, but he realized that it could achieve little. His warriors were hindered by their supposed allies in the Lao military, who seized CIA-supplied weapons from the guerrillas. Consequently, Popovich had a tough time convincing the tribal troops to do anything to support the overwhelmed Lao military.

Popovich was frustrated. In his two years in Luang Prabang, as Shackley prodded him on to action, he was not able to pull off a single outstanding paramilitary operation. Since he was not allowed to accompany his troops on their forays, he had no way of determining if they were accomplishing the small raids he assigned them. He provided one team with a simple point-and-shoot camera and directed them to take photographs of their mission, which was to hit enemy supply lines on the Nam Bac River. The troops assaulted a set of supply boats, and a tribesman photographed it all. But there were women and children on the boats. The photographs that landed on Popovich's desk showed his CIA-backed irregulars gunning down women and children in the river. These were not the types of photos he wanted. He took the camera away.

As a battalion, Popovich's recruits "didn't do a goddamned thing," he recalled. Guerrillas, he knew, cannot function in a large unit. He divided his army into smaller squads: long-range reconnaissance teams, support teams, fifteen-man action teams. Shackley objected; he was not interested in small units. He desired sizable components that demonstrated the CIA was backing large-scale combat operations. "Shackley wanted to show that we had some major assets up country working against the enemy and that they were accomplishing something," Popovich explained. "The battalions looked good on paper."

Within headquarters, there was little second-guessing of Shackley. The Agency program in Laos was widely regarded as quite the success, especially when compared with the morass in Vietnam. The talk often was of "Shackley's operation in Laos." NVA units were being occupied, but the U.S. presence was minimal. American soldiers were not dying. For the time being, the heroic and ferocious tribesmen were preserving the status quo in Laos. Vietnam was a black hole, sucking up U.S. resources, respectability, and lives. The challenge in Laos was infinitely easier: keep at bay the communists, who showed no sign of moving against Vientiane and the heart of Laos. Nevertheless, several dozen

Agency officers supporting a secret army of 30,000—that was a program of which to be proud. And it was Shackley's.

Yet Shackley and Sullivan were creating and accepting policies that could only provoke serious enemy retaliation. The people who would pay for this would not be Americans but the tribespeople cheered on by the CIA.

At Shackley's insistence, the war changed. After a successful guerrilla operation close to the North Vietnamese border, someone in the mission hatched a bright idea: to beef up the government's military presence in the north. If the embassy could establish several combat battalions in the north, Washington would be ecstatic. A detailed plan emerged, and Shackley became a driving force behind it. The Nam Bac garrison, sixty miles north of Luang Prabang, would be built up as a forward bulwark. Nam Bac sat forty-five miles southwest of the North Vietnamese border and near the southeast tip of China's Yunnan province. Government forces had occupied the town since October of 1966. Under the plan, a large number of government troops and some irregulars would be deployed to Nam Bac.

Nam Bac marked a new tactic. The point was to take the war to the NVA, "to really bloody the nose of the North Vietnamese," as one embassy officer recounted. Shackley and the embassy's main U.S. military attachés talked of establishing an "iron arc" of bases in northern central Laos. But outside the country team meetings, enthusiasm about Nam Bac was not widespread. As the buildup proceeded, the common chat in official Lao circles was that a debacle was in the making. Nam Bac is surrounded by mountain peaks full of caves that could well protect enemy artillery. The location bore an eerie similarity to Dien Bien Phu.

Sullivan held ultimate responsibility for Nam Bac, but embassy people regarded it as Shackley's folly. Senior mission officers speculated that Shackley embraced it as an opportunity to expand his own influence. "I never thought that Shackley was satisfied with the important but limited role he had," recalled one senior embassy official, "to use the Meo in the north for the war and the tribesmen in the south to monitor the Ho Chi Minh Trail. His judgment was clouded because of his ambition."

Shackley explained the scheme to Bill Lair, the chief of Udorn. What do you think? he asked. Lair told him it was a mistake. The U.S.-backed forces would be a tempting target for the NVA, and there was no commander in Laos capable of running an operation with its demanding logistics. The theory was not bad, Lair thought. The problem was that Shackley wanted to place the Lao military and the irregulars into a situation far beyond their capability. This would obviously lead to a siege of Nam Bac, and the larger, better-trained, better-supplied NVA would be able to put in whatever it needed for victory. Give the NVA a target and it will take it. Lair was not the only Agency doubter. "All the guys in Udorn said don't do that," Clines recalled. Shackley pressed ahead.

One embassy officer who had listened to Lao colonels predict failure at Nam Bac demanded a reevaluation of the plan; Shackley objected. The officer won a pro forma review, but it failed to derail the scheme. Shackley, as Sullivan put it, had a "pretty much single-minded" goal: "to get the North Vietnamese off Lao territory as quickly as possible, and those who didn't get off, get them killed." And on the matter of Nam Bac, Shackley had Sullivan's support.

Over a course of months, several thousand Lao and a small number of irregular forces arrived in the isolated valley of Nam Bac. Enemy forces in the area increased. By mid-October, the situation was critical; an NVA–Pathet Lao assault seemed imminent. On December 22, 1967, the U.S. embassy cabled Washington that a withdrawal from Nam Bac would hurt military and civilian morale and signify "abandonment of the important goal." The Laotian army and Shackley's irregulars had to stand firm.

A few days later, as government commanders at Nam Bac enjoyed a Christmas celebration, NVA artillery shells slammed into their quarters. The battle, or the nonbattle, of Nam Bac had begun. The first reports to Vientiane were misleadingly optimistic. At a meeting of senior embassy personnel, a U.S. military attaché pronounced everything was proceeding as smoothly as a military exercise. The 4,500-man government force used U.S.-supplied 105-mm howitzers to strike the Pathet Lao and the NVA. Laotian T-28 bombers soared over the valley, unleashing napalm on enemy mortarmen pounding the airstrip. American C-123 transport aircraft from the Udorn base dropped ammunition and rice. Air America helicopters dodged enemy fire to fly in supplies. Wounded were airlifted by the helicopters. U.S. Air Force jets bombed and strafed enemy supply lines. But Colonel Bounchanh Savophaipha, the commander of the Nam Bac garrison, declined to mount a major counterattack against the NVA and Pathet Lao.

Shackley looked for assistance. He asked Lair to arrange for Vang Pao to dispatch troops to Nam Bac, but the Hmong army was too far away. Shackley radioed Eli Popovich in Luang Prabang and ordered him to send his irregulars toward Nam Bac. But there was no way for Popovich to get the troops there; the airstrip at Nam Bac was surrounded by the enemy. Shackley issued a similar directive to Tony Poe in Nam Yu. Poe knew better than to send men into this crucible. He liberally interpreted

Shackley's message for help and called in Laotian T-28 air raids on targets in China, perhaps hoping that would provide a distraction or hit supply lines. The Chinese issued a statement charging that "pirate planes of United States imperialism and its lackeys" had struck Yunnan, killing and injuring several Chinese. The Pentagon refused to confirm that the air raids had occurred.

Less than a month after the shelling began, on January 13, some of the ill-trained and poorly equipped government forces began withdrawing and soon others had the same idea. (Many of the Laotian soldiers had never fired their rifles before finding themselves facing the battle-toughened Hanoi regulars; many of the Lao had been stationed in Nam Bac for months without relief.) The remaining government troops were not ready for a fight when the NVA launched its final assault. Early one morning, with thick mist obscuring most of the landscape, the NVA hit Colonel Bounchanh's command post. He lost contact with his troops. Left on their own, most of the Nam Bac soldiers fled. About 200 were killed.

The retreat turned into a rout. Two thousand of the Nam Bac troops scattered into the surrounding hills, as the NVA chased after them. Following the collapse, Laotian T-28s returned to bomb the howitzers and ammunition left behind by the fleeing Lao. A haggard and drawn Bounchanh escaped to Luang Prabang, where the hospitals overflowed with injured. He was inconsolable. Of the 3,278 men at the garrison when the last battle began—the men whose deployment was encouraged by Sullivan and Shackley—only one third were accounted for.

Shackley and Sullivan had miscalculated. They had given the North Vietnamese a target not to be ignored. The country was at war, but the reality of Laos was that the political restraints against the North Vietnamese were more potent than the military ones. To fight its war against the superpower United States, North Vietnam had run roughshod over Laotian neutrality. But Hanoi had refrained from striking into the Mekong Valley, which contained much of the population of Laos. Most senior embassy officials believed the NVA did not storm through Laos because such a move would be too blatant a violation of the Geneva Accords and perhaps provoke Washington to deploy troops in Laos. The diplomats at the mission saw no alternative but to maximize the political protections; the military prospects appeared so dim. The NVA could lose ten men for every Lao soldier or irregular and still triumph. But Shackley and the U.S. military attachés were scornful of a solution that did not rest on power. "Shackley wanted to be a successful military commander," embassy officer Mark Pratt observed. "How can you do that if you don't have a few big battles, your Gettysburg?"

Nam Bac decimated the Lao military, destroyed its morale. It never

recovered. A small army already, it literally lost two thousand men in
Nam Bac. Lao commanders, who believed they had been talked into
making this stand by the Americans, griped that they had not received
enough help from the United States. Many leading Lao considered Nam
Bac proof of a troubling suspicion: their American friends were using
Laos for their own purposes. "It was a terrible waste of people," remarked a senior embassy official, "and basically because of Ted's ambitions." The collapse of the royal Lao forces at Nam Bac had deadly
implications for the tribal irregulars. From this point on, the Hmong
and other tribesmen would assume more of the burden of fighting the
Pathet Lao and the North Vietnamese.

One morning after the disaster at Nam Bac, a senior embassy man
came to work and found a memo drafted by Shackley that was to be
sent to Richard Helms in Langley. The memo explained what had happened at Nam Bac, and Sullivan had approved its transmission to headquarters. The officer began to read it and filled with rage as he saw
what was heading toward Washington. Shackley attributed the defeat to
technical failures, the fault for which rested with Lao military officials. If
they had done their job right, the memo suggested, the embassy plan
would have succeeded. "It was," this career diplomat said later, "the
most dishonest piece of political-military reporting I had ever seen in
my life."

Shackley's report claimed that "the defeat at Nam Bac could have
been prevented had [the Lao military] taken a more aggressive stand
against the enemy initially and supplied its men with stronger leadership." He claimed that the "lack of leadership [in the royal Lao military]
essentially negated all of the plans that had been designed to save the
Nam Bac situation." Nothing had been wrong with the decisions Shackley had made. "The real tragedy of Nam Bac," Shackley wrote Washington, "is that it should not have been lost. With any real effort on its part
[the royal Lao military] should have been able to hold Nam Bac."

The offended embassy officer took the matter up with the ambassador. He was shocked that Sullivan, whose judgment he admired (with
the notable exception of Nam Bac), had okayed the report. When the
officer insisted that he write his own report on Nam Bac, Sullivan put
up no fight. But the two never got along after that. In Washington, a staff
member of the National Security Council received Shackley's report and
sent it to national security adviser Walt Rostow with a laudatory note: "I
commend to you the attached. It is the best thing I have ever seen of its
kind. I agree with its substance—and am dazzled by its crisp literary
style and total lack of waffles." Shackley's self-serving explanation for
the debacle was accepted. Washington would not hold him or Sullivan
responsible.

After Nam Bac, Bill Lair wrote a report of his own. The episode had depressed him. Nam Bac was a disaster that could have been avoided. The plan had been too ambitious. The Laotians could not have pulled it off, and Shackley had been warned. Lair committed his feelings to paper. But he did not send the report to anyone. What good would it do now? he thought. The die was cast. The program in Laos was changing, and the forces at work were too large to confront. He placed the report in his safe at Udorn.

There was one piece of Nam Bac business left to resolve. Washington requested that the station find out what had prompted the bombing raid that struck China before the final collapse. For weeks, Shackley periodically ordered his men in the field to investigate and report back to him. The gang at Udorn—Lair, Clines, and Landry—knew that the anything-goes Tony Poe had ordered the bombing. Poe's defense was simple: Shackley wanted him to do something, so he did. None of the field officers were anxious to squeal on their legendary colleague. They kept neglecting Shackley's request for information, offering various excuses and hoping another crisis would soon displace the chief's attention. Eventually, Shackley dropped the matter.* "We all referred to Nam Bac as Shackley's operation," one Agency man said, "and we used to laugh about it." This is what happens, Shackley's officers joked, when a logistician tries to be a field marshal—a superpower is bombed.

V

The buildup at Nam Bac showed that the Americans like Shackley were not merely munificent guardians nobly assisting the Lao and the tribespeople in their fight against the encroaching communists of the Pathet Lao and North Vietnam. It was not the only action supported by Shackley that changed the tenor of the war.

In 1966, the mission in Vientiane had reluctantly agreed with a U.S. Air Force proposal to install a navigational beacon on Phou Pha Thi, a 5,000-foot-high mountain with sheer sides fifty miles from the border with North Vietnam and long a Hmong stronghold. The directional aid guided U.S. bombers to their targets in North Vietnam. To the Hmong, the mountain was a landmark of profound spiritual power, which they were willing to defend to the death. Surrounded by scarlet poppies, it also was prime territory for opium cultivation.

Like Nam Bac, the navigational base at Phou Pha Thi—Site 85—was a

---

* When Poe returned to the United States in the 1970s for an Agency retirement ceremony, the message from the bureaucrats was clear: thanks for a job well done, now go back to Thailand and leave us alone. Poe returned to his Yau wife and the life of a farmer.

target the North Vietnamese could not afford to leave alone. For years, the inaccessible mountain had not been worth the bother for the NVA —until the addition of the Air Force base rendered it one of the most important strategic sites in all of Indochina. Here was a direct contribution to the American war effort in Vietnam that Shackley could trumpet. The site, guarded by his Hmong, bolstered the bombing campaign in North Vietnam. It was, as Blaufarb later noted, "more of a provocative act than we realized at the time." And Phou Pha Thi was not a secure site. After Tom Clines inspected the facility, he concluded that a group of determined Girl Scouts could take the hill.

Throughout the first months of 1968, undercover U.S. Air Force pilots flying recon missions and CIA ground watch teams reported that the Pathet Lao and North Vietnamese were building a road toward Phou Pha Thi. Villages nearby were falling to the enemy. It was obvious what was under way. Shackley reported this to Washington and ordered Major Richard Secord, an Air Force officer assigned to the CIA and stationed at Udorn, to "stop the road."* Secord fought with the Air Force bureaucracy to schedule bombing raids against the road, but the daytime assaults did not halt the construction. Each night hundreds of roadworkers crawled out of shelters and mended the craters.

There was time to abandon the base and pull out the U.S. Air Force technicians there, as well as prevent V.P.'s men from taking a big hit. In late February, Shackley produced an unofficial estimate that noted that it was not possible to predict the state of security at Phou Pha Thi beyond March 10. He asked headquarters for guidance. The message came back: "You will hold the TSQ Site at whatever cost. It is of vital importance." Washington's decision-makers were willing to take the risk. Secord begged for Special Forces to be sent to Phou Pha Thi; his request was denied. The Air Force even dispatched five more technicians to the site, bringing the total number of Americans there to seventeen.

Shackley's prediction was on target. At three in the morning on March 11, 1968, the Pathet Lao and NVA struck. The Agency-supported Hmong and Thai troops protecting the facility were guerrillas, not soldiers capable of holding a position. They were overrun. Three Americans, including the senior officer, were killed immediately. The other Americans

* Secord was well versed in secret warfare. In the early 1960s, he flew covert air strikes against the Viet Cong; in 1963 he helped the Iranian military to suppress a Kurdish insurrection. He then was sent to Southeast Asia and eventually placed in charge of all tactical air operations in support of the CIA war in Laos. One time, the Agency ordered Secord to drop dishwashing detergent on the Ho Chi Minh Trail to make it too slippery for the North Vietnamese to use. But when the rains came, the soap washed away. The NVA was not inconvenienced at all.

scrambled for safety and failed to trigger the detonation devices set up to destroy the sophisticated equipment to prevent its capture.

In Udorn, Secord, using an unsecured phone line, screamed at Air Force officers in Saigon who would not send a helicopter gunship to the site. U.S. jets and Laotian T-28s were eventually called in. Air America helicopters rescued some base personnel and carried out the defeated irregulars. The U.S. Air Force, which had pushed for the base, would not commit its own rescue helicopters, for fear of having one shot down in a country where the U.S. military supposedly was not operating. Eleven of the seventeen Americans were killed. For a week afterward, the U.S. Air Force returned to bomb what once was its own site, hoping to deny the enemy the sophisticated, high-tech equipment left behind.

Not only was the loss of the sacred mountain a blow to all Hmong forces, the attack marked the initiation of a major offensive that would drive Vang Pao's irregulars out of Sam Neua province and inflict many losses on his warriors. The day Phou Pha Thi fell, Sullivan cabled Foggy Bottom, "It appears we may have pushed our luck one day too long in attempting to keep this facility in operation."

Life in Vientiane—despite the defeats at Nam Bac, Phou Pha Thi, and the ongoing enemy offensive—continued its gaiety. One evening, the Rotary Club of Vientiane held a soiree, under the patronage of Souvanna Phouma. At the ball, Boris Kirnassovsky, the Soviet ambassador, provided his own rendition of a sinuous Laotian dance. A few blocks away, another party was under way at the Pathet Lao headquarters. Restaurants and nightclubs thrived in the capital city. Scores of American bohemians gathered nightly at the Psychedelic House or The Third Eye to smoke grass and drink beer. "The survival of Laos," a visiting reporter wrote, "all knowledgeable observers agree, depends on a proper disrespect for reality." Annual casualty figures had reached 15,000 on each side of the war, but Americans and Lao still hoped the war in Laos would not follow the path of the conflict in Vietnam.

Shackley did not take advantage of the free-and-loose atmosphere of Vientiane. A workaholic, he devoted most of his time to his job. Festivals, marked by tremendous drinking sprees, were common at Long Tieng. But Shackley, unlike many of his compatriots, was not a boozer. If he had to join in with a *baci* in Spook Heaven, he first trundled off to the mess hall and ate a chunk of butter, believing that this home remedy softened the impact of the local brew.

Shackley's top field men were hard-drinking, self-styled tough guys, and after their monthly meetings with the chief at his Vientiane home they invaded the local taverns. One night after the band finished their presentations for the boss and were heading out the door, Shackley pulled Tom Clines aside and asked why they never asked him along. Clines offered an invitation—that annoyed the rest—and six secret warriors, including Tony Poe, piled into a Chevy for a night out. They raised hell at several bars. In one, as a nude woman danced in front of Shackley, he tried to brief his men on this and that. At five-thirty in the morning, the night was winding down, Shackley was exhausted, and his officers were heading to the airport. On the way to the airfield, the spy-filled Chevy passed the White Rose annex, a spin-off of Vientiane's most notorious bar. Let's have one more, someone in the car shouted. It's closed, Shackley remarked. The Savannakhet base chief volunteered to get out and check. He walked up to the door and kicked it open. Bargirls asleep on the floor awoke. Someone turned on the jukebox, and the CIA men and their chief trooped in for a very late nightcap. After that, Shackley never asked to go out with the gang again.

Come April of 1968, it was clear the Pathet Lao and the North Vietnamese were not sticking to the old give-and-take game plan. Throughout the first half of the year the combined strength of the NVA and the Pathet Lao doubled to over 110,000 troops. "We are concerned," said one American official, "that there has been some change of strategy on their part. They are now attacking towns and taking terrain, they are willing to accept and inflict a hell of a lot of casualties and they have brought in a whole new range of weapons, 140-mm rockets, 120-mm mortars, anti-tank weapons, B-40 rockets, the works." The annual seesaw ride was over. The unofficial dead count on the government side for the offensive —and it was not clear if this figure included the Hmong—was a record 3,000. North Vietnamese and Pathet Lao units slashed across northern Laos and captured twenty-seven outposts and airstrips run by the Hmong. Nearly 10,000 refugees fled south. Americans worried for their tribal allies. "We're bugging out on our damn commitment to the little guys," a U.S. official griped to reporters. V.P. was losing up to twenty men a day. "We did not expect," the U.S. official noted, "a conventional offensive of this kind."

The army of V.P. staved off the Pathet Lao and NVA offensive at a few positions, including Site 36. Set in a valley, northeast of Long Tieng, Na Khang was one of the CIA-backed army's most important bases and another one of those positions difficult to defend. V.P. did not believe it could be held. Nevertheless, Shackley approved a plan to bolster it. About 1,500 Hmong soldiers were assigned to the site, which, after the fall of Nam Bac and Phou Pha Thi, was now the most northerly base for tribal activity.

Shackley put Clines in charge of the Na Khang operation. Clines installed wire fencing around the perimeter. The tribal irregulars did not appreciate being left with no escape route and cut holes in the barricade. On surrounding hills, Clines directed Agency technicians to install beacons that could facilitate bombing raids. The tribesmen knocked down the beacons so they could place artillery pieces on the same spots.

After Phou Pha Thi, the Agency had been insistent that the U.S. Air Force do its share to protect this base. But there was an obstacle. On March 31, President Johnson announced that he would not run for reelection and that he had ordered a bombing halt on targets north of the 20th parallel. Site 36 was north of the 20th. When the battle began there, Shackley and Secord requested B-52 strikes. Helms replied from Langley: the bombing halt covered assaults on Site 36. An outraged Secord and Clines flew from Udorn to Vientiane to complain to Shackley. The chief showed them a cable to Helms that he had drafted to protest the decision. But Shackley had accepted the decision as "inevitable." Do you like the cable? he asked. "Frankly, I don't," Secord snapped. Shackley threw a pad at him and told him to compose a better one.

Secord wrote a blistering message to Helms arguing that respecting the bombing halt in Laos was absurd, since the United States did not even acknowledge it was fighting in Laos. Shackley signed his name to it and forwarded the cable to Langley. The Pentagon responded quickly. B-52 strikes were still out, but Shackley's station could have up to 300 tactical air strikes per day. "We felt," Secord recalled, "like starving men suddenly shoved into a banquet."

U.S. jetfighters pummeled the territory surrounding the site. The bombing drove the Pathet Lao and NVA back. The fighting at Na Khang was a small morale boost for the Hmong in a miserable and deadly season.*

The irregulars were renowned as guerrillas, but they were lousy when it came to fighting from a defensive position. "They were told to stand and fight, and a guerrilla by definition doesn't do that," Clines noted. At other spots, Shackley's Agency had to wire them into a position. The tribal warriors cut the wire as fast as it went up. "We got them into engagements where they were nose-to-nose with North Vietnamese infantry units," Lair said. "They couldn't afford the casualties. They did not have that many people." Lair and other Agency men began to notice smaller boys in the ranks of the irregulars. And Vang Pao was getting a swelled head. "We made him believe that he was a more formidable force than he was," Lair said. "They got away from doing what they did best."

But what was the point in complaining? Lair wondered. Shackley was

---

* Na Khang would fall the following year after a bloody battle.

following the direction from Washington. It had become clear that the United States was in real trouble in Vietnam, and the chief was under pressure to do something. Until 1968, the irregulars had done well against the NVA. "When we started concentrating more irregulars together, that played into the hands of the NVA," Lair noted. "It got the irregulars to stand still." To be targets.

Dr. Charles Weldon, a doctor working for AID at Sam Thong, felt anger throughout the spring of 1968 as he treated young tribesmen with bullet wounds and shattered limbs. "The whole northern region is falling to the Communists," he said at the time. "They're fighting harder this year than they've ever fought before, and they're using their first team. The situation is hopelessly mixed up with the Vietnam War, and these poor people are taking a beating. Once we Americans had assumed an obligation to help them, we shouldn't have allowed them to suffer because of the situation in Vietnam. We should have defended them and helped them for their own sake."

Pop Buell, the chief AID officer at Sam Thong, was peeved as well. Buell unleashed his wrath in front of an American journalist: "People in Washington may call what's going on here in Laos 'the forgotten war,' but some of us will never forget it. General Vang Pao told me six years ago, 'O.K., we're willing to do our part because we feel it's for the free world and it's our duty, and all we ask of you is that you support us.' But that's the last damn thing we've done! The only real weapons the troops have are what they've captured from the enemy. Otherwise, they've just got old Second World War stuff—carbines and some mortars—which may have been all right four years ago but can't do anything against the new AK-47 automatic rifles the North Vietnamese have now. V.P. has lost at least a thousand men since January 1st—a thousand killed, that is. I don't know how many more wounded. Was it their war at Pha Thi? We asked them to go in and defend our lousy communications installation because of the Vietnam war. Why didn't we defend it? We destroyed part of their homeland to keep that installation secure, and now it's lost anyway."

Buell had been out in the field with V.P.'s officers, who were rounding up fresh recruits. Thirty percent of the new blood was fourteen years old or less. Another thirty percent was fifteen or sixteen, and the rest were thirty-five or older. "Where are the ones in between?" an agitated Buell asked. "I'll tell you—they're all dead. Here were these little kids, in their camouflage uniforms that were much too big for them. . . . They're too young and they aren't trained, and in a few weeks ninety percent of them will be killed. For what?"

When in June the sky burst open and gray sheets of water fell on Laos —the start of the rainy season—the Pathet Lao and the North Vietnamese offered no signs they intended to abide by the old routine and halt their advance. They now controlled 75 percent of the land of Laos, territories that included about one quarter of the nation's population. One of ten Laotians were refugees.

At Shackley's insistence, a stressed and demoralized Secord took some R&R. Secord, Lair, Pat Landry, and a few other CIA men went to Bangkok and got drunk, hoping to forget much of the previous months. Shortly after their return, Secord, Lair, Tony Poe, and Shackley were invited to Bangkok for a secret ceremony at Thai army headquarters. There the Prime Minister presented the Americans with the Most Exalted Order of the White Elephant, the highest honor awarded to foreigners, for their "heroic defense" of Phou Pha Thi and other actions. After the medal was pinned to his civilian jacket, Secord whispered to Shackley, "Sonofabitch, Ted—this is the first time I ever got a medal for failing."

Throughout the summer of 1968, the Lao military was useless. In the north, as a result of the Nam Bac defeat, the CIA's paramilitary units, according to a U.S. embassy report, could "do little more than pass in an occasional intelligence report while they regroup from enemy sweep actions." Pathet Lao and NVA forces were stronger and better equipped than in previous years. "It would appear imprudent," the U.S. embassy reported, "for friendly forces, both regular and irregular, to attempt anything more than carefully planned, relatively small-scale operations."

Vang Pao was worried. The general confided to Clines that he saw himself annihilating his own race. "It was all slipping through his fingers," recalled CIA officer Jack Shirley, who worked with V.P. "He needed help. His people were getting killed. He said to me that he missed the old days, when it was just a few of us." Still, V.P. carried on. And by the end of the summer, with the help of 700 U.S. Air Force sorties, Vang Pao recaptured some territory lost during the enemy's 1968 offensive. But the future did not look bright.

In July of 1968, Bill Lair left Laos terribly disappointed. Shackley's arrival had marked the start of a bad stretch. "We spent a lot of money and got a lot of people killed," Lair remembered, "and we didn't get much for it." His like-minded deputy, Pat Landry, drew up a chart that plotted year-by-year the amount of funds and number of Americans devoted to the Laotian program against what was accomplished. Starting in 1966—the year Shackley took over—the numbers on the resources side soared, but there was no parallel rise in successes.

Lair hated to cut out on his tribal comrades. "I'm a do-gooder," he explained later. "All my years out there I thought everything I did was helping the downtrodden. The Laotians had been run over by the French and everyone else. I was helping not just the United States but the people of Laos." But his friend Shackley was not a do-gooder. He wanted to rise to the top, he wanted a big show, he was there for America not Laos. "What I wanted to do," Lair said, "is to do things as quietly as possible and afterward say it all happened without the United States being involved." Lair desired a true covert action—one small enough to stay secret. He thought that was what the Agency had in Laos until Shackley landed. Once that course was no longer possible, Lair found no reason to remain.

Clines saw that Lair could not stomach what was occurring in Laos: "He was so closely intertwined with the people of Southeast Asia, the Thai and the Lao. It was hard for him to take. He heard young case officers saying, we're out here to save as many American lives as we can and to hell with all else. That hurt Bill." Shackley viewed a different world. "Ted focused on how many Americans were being killed in Vietnam," Clines explained. "He looked at the big picture. There were American casualties. To him the question was, how quickly can we turn that off? In terms of our national interest, he was right. Bill and Pat Landry—their concept of national interest was too Lao-oriented."*

Lair kept the cause for his departure from Shackley. Telling the chief, he believed, would do no good. Before he left Udorn, Lair reached into the safe in his office, pulled out the report he had written on the debacle at Nam Bac—an event that symbolized what had gone wrong in Laos— and burned it.

Shackley's tour in Vientiane impressed those who counted most, his superiors in Langley. They had a new assignment for him: Saigon. William Colby, who had left his post as chief of the Far East Division to oversee pacification programs in Vietnam, was officially on leave from the CIA in 1968. But he still wielded clout and arranged for Shackley's assignment to Vietnam. Colby had been favorably struck by Shackley's performance in Laos. Here was more proof Shackley was the guy to handle the big, important operations of the CIA. Des FitzGerald, a great promoter of Shackley, was dead; he had collapsed the previous year on a Washington tennis court during a match with the British ambassador. But when he had recommended Shackley to Colby for the Vientiane post, FitzGerald anticipated Shackley would graduate to Saigon and,

---

* Lair and Landry were not the only Agency men to feel this way. Nearly twenty-five years later, Jack Shirley recalled, "In the early years when Bill Lair ran the project, the toll on the Meo was negligible. When things expanded the toll became greater. It was unacceptable in the last few years.... It was not fair to the people doing the fighting. Ted, rightfully or wrongfully, went along. They expanded the war, and it was not necessary."

after that, move on to be the Deputy Director for Plans and then, perhaps, the Director of Central Intelligence. So far, it was going as planned.

Shackley asked Clines to share in his good fortune. Come with me to Vietnam, he said, and I'll put you in a job that will bring promotions. Clines demurred. Vietnam was a deepening pit. Several hundred thousand American troops had been sent there, and the war was not being won. An inept, sprawling U.S. military was in control. Clines did not want to spend his days squabbling with a bunch of Pentagon generals and battling a runaway bureaucracy. He also hoped to avoid becoming one of those Agency officers pegged as so-and-so's guy, in this case Shackley's. What he really wanted was to run the Long Tieng base, so Shackley arranged for him to be the Agency's top man there.

Before leaving Vientiane in October of 1968, Shackley went up to Long Tieng to say good-bye to General Vang Pao. According to the story that later made the rounds in the American community of Vientiane, Shackley flew to the CIA's Shangri-La the day before his flight out of Laos. The farewell festivities became a wild, rough party, with the tribal moonshine flowing all night. Shackley left magical Long Tieng the next morning horizontal—or close to it. In Vientiane, instead of checking on to a flight, he hit a hospital. The episode amused those Americans in Vientiane who knew Shackley. He finally had let his hair down—and did so with his Hmong.

VI

Shackley was fortunate. During his days as the chief spook of Laos, the secret war in Laos mostly remained a secret in the United States. The snoops of the U.S. press corps were largely absent from Laos. Hundreds of reporters covered the war next door, but few knew much about what was happening in the Other Theater. Not until 1970 would any American journalists witness Spook Heaven at Long Tieng. The Pathet Lao, the North Vietnamese, the Chinese, and the Soviets were aware that Washington was underwriting and guiding the war. The American people were in the dark.

A year after Shackley departed Vientiane, on October 20, 1969, in a room in the U.S. Capitol, Senator Stuart Symington called a secret hearing to order.* The subject was Laos. Symington was outraged that the United States was conducting a war in secrecy there. He accused "high government officials" of withholding from Congress information about its secret operations in Laos. The proceedings of this executive session

---

*A month earlier, *The New York Times* began publishing a series of articles detailing U.S. involvement in the war in Laos. Previously, there had been some coverage of the war in the media, but nothing extensive.

would be declassified and made available to the public months later. The cloak was off.

The legal experts of Langley scrambled to justify the Agency's actions. In a memo to Helms, Lawrence Houston, the general counsel, asserted, "I know of no definition [of war] . . . which would consider our activities in Laos 'waging war. . . .' We have no combatants as such, although the Air Force pilots doing the bombing come close." Damn close, the resident of a bombed Laotian village might think. True, the United States had not fielded uniformed American ground troops in Laos, but Shackley and others, on behalf of presidents, had armed troops, ordered bombing raids, and directed troop movements—all activities that fall under a reasonable definition of waging war.

Symington's outrage galled officers in Langley. They remembered he was briefed both in Laos and in Washington by Shackley and other CIA officers. "I couldn't figure out what all the fuss was about," Shackley recalled. In 1967, Symington had praised the Company's unpublicized, unacknowledged endeavors. Then in 1969, riding the crest of popular opposition to the Vietnam War, he was suddenly shocked that the United States was engaging in covert warfare. Symington insisted that significant details of the CIA's program in Laos had been kept from him. After Symington went public, the Agency reported that it had briefed as many as 67 senators on the secret war since 1963. "I knew we were doing a little of this and a little of that in Laos," said Senator J. William Fulbright. "I had no idea it was a major operation of this kind."

The Executive Branch had engaged in dissembling. In late 1968, for instance, during a secret session of the Senate Foreign Relations Committee, Ambassador Sullivan testified that the United States does "not have a military training and advisory organization in Laos." It did—the CIA. And the Air Force maintained a secret staff of over 100 advisers in Laos. Sullivan also said the only bombing in the north was being done by the Laotian air force. But as part of the Agency-run war, the U.S. Air Force was blasting targets in Laos.

The legislators were culprits as well, for most had turned a blind eye to the war in Laos. Those who were aware of some of the facts, like Symington, had raised no public objection nor had they pressed the matter. "The Congress," Symington's subcommittee confessed in 1970, "did not inquire into, nor was it kept informed of, United States military activities in and over Laos." Shackley and his colleagues, taking advantage of Congress's lack of diligence, managed an operation—an undeclared war—that arguably was unconstitutional.

It would be several years after Shackley's departure before the army of Vang Pao faced ultimate defeat and the government of Laos fell. In the meantime, V.P. would achieve some battlefield successes. But he and the Agency were stuck in a losing cause. A month or so after Shackley's departure, Pop Buell estimated that of all the Hmong who had taken up arms, one quarter of them were killed in action. Civilian casualties at that point totaled 40,000 men, women, and children—almost one out of every ten Hmong.

The Hmong were on the path toward decimation. The Agency's image was to be tarnished by its conduct of a secret war and its association with opium-dealing Laotians. The bombing in Laos was wreaking a horrible toll. The Laos program had become wed to the deepening problem of Vietnam. But the Agency's actions in Laos were touted as successful by those who ran the war and other Agency loyalists. In 1972, Douglas Blaufarb, the former chief of station, reflected on what he, Shackley, and others had accomplished in Laos: "If one grants that the U.S. purpose in Laos has been to fight a low-cost, low-profile delaying action to preserve the Lao buffer zone against North Vietnamese pressures, then the United States during 1962–1970 largely achieved its aim."

But Blaufarb was honest enough to qualify his assessment: "Of course, this was partly due to Hanoi's apparent disinclination . . . to mount an all-out takeover effort." The secret war was, Blaufarb maintained, the most efficient of all U.S. ventures in Southeast Asia: "In terms of cost effectiveness, the casualties and other losses inflicted upon the North Vietnamese would show a favorable balance for the U.S. effort in Laos as compared with Vietnam. But the costs to the Lao have been far greater, both in human suffering and in the destruction of towns and villages caused by bombing."

Policymakers kept their eyes on the bottom line when they evaluated Shackley's program. The U.S. operation in Laos, U. Alexis Johnson, the former undersecretary of state, told a Senate committee in July of 1971, is "something of which we can be proud as Americans. It has involved virtually no American casualties. What we are getting for our money there . . . is, I think, to use the old phrase, very cost-effective." Colby, in his memoirs, proudly noted that only five Agency employees lost their lives in Laos.

The cost-benefit calculations of Langley did not include the tens of thousands of Hmong casualties. "These grim statistics raise the question of whether the tribesmen would have chosen the same course had they foreseen the consequences to themselves and their communities," Blaufarb observed. But he defended the Agency's role in Laos. After all, who could have known at the start how sad and deadly the results would be? The Laos sideshow, he argued, was a miscalculation that was part of a larger miscalculation—Vietnam.

But one did not have to be a grand visionary to have predicted problems. "Arming the tribesmen," Roger Hilsman, a former senior State

Department official, wrote presciently in his 1964 book *To Move a Nation*, "engendered an obligation not only to feed them when they were driven from their traditional homelands but also to protect them from vengeance. This was an obligation that in some circumstances could never really be discharged. . . . Arming tribesmen sounds like a tough and realistic policy, even a generous one of helping brave fighters defend themselves. But it might in fact be not only unwise but unfair to the tribesmen themselves, those to whom it was seemingly designed to help."

CIA officers in Laos grew attached to their tribal allies. When Jim Lilley's wife once casually uttered a critical remark about the Hmong at a party, Shackley's deputy shot back at her: You don't know the sacrifices these people are making. Shackley's two years in Laos left a deep imprint on him. No matter what others might have thought, he developed a strong bond with the tribespeople. He did not believe he had exploited them unfairly for the greater good of the United States and anticommunism.

Decades after the war, Shackley asserted that the relationship between Washington and the tribes was forged in honor—but the United States then deserted its partners. The United States, he noted, had a "commitment to those who had struggled in partnership with us to maintain the independence of the Lao nation [against] an expansionist-oriented Hanoi. . . . When [policymakers] make this kind of commitment, to engage people in these kinds of activities, they have to have a contingency plan for what do they do for these people if it is not a success."

But it had not occurred to Shackley when he was in Vientiane to guarantee contingency plans existed to ensure the welfare of his tribal warriors and their families. "We had contingency plans," Shackley explained, "but our contingency plans never envisioned defeat. You couldn't ask government officials to plan for defeat. We were confident we were going to win or that we would get a solution which would permit the tribal people to live in harmony with others in the political process."

Even if Shackley and the rest of the secret warriors—Sullivan, Lilley, Lair, Landry, Young, Clines, Secord, and the others—actually believed that honor underwrote the alliance between Washington and the tribespeople, they could not have delivered on that honor. They were part of a system operating to achieve the national security objectives of the United States. In Shackley's case, no one ever accused him of allowing those objectives to fall from his sight. Compassion was not the reason the CIA was in Laos. Secret wars are not charitable enterprises. "The Hmong got shafted," complained William Nelson, who in 1968 replaced Colby as head of the CIA's Far East Division. "We can be cruel as a country in deciding what our national interest is. There is not much room for sentiment."

In the early days of the secret war, Ray Cline, a senior Agency official, argued with other government officials about the rapid growth of the CIA program. Too many tribesmen were being recruited and drawn away from the work needed to keep their villages intact. Cline's superiors did not want to hear this. The tribesmen were eager to kill North Vietnamese, and the cost of supporting them was much less than the price of intervening with the U.S. military. The message was, the tribespeople came cheap, so let's get as many as we can. "That was disgraceful, and we destroyed them," Cline, an Agency champion, remarked decades afterward. "It's one of the black marks of our history." He then paused, perhaps realizing that a few moments earlier he had praised Shackley's performance in Laos. "But you can't blame Ted Shackley for that," Cline added. "He did what he was ordered to do."

For Shackley, there were no regrets about his actions. Years after his time in Laos, he dedicated a slim book on counterinsurgency to the "heroic Meo hill tribes . . . who fought the full military power of North Vietnam to a standstill." He continued with his hyperbolic paean: "The fruits of their battlefield victories were ultimately lost to Hanoi's puppets, the Pathet Lao, in the political arena. . . . The Meo could not withstand Hanoi's assault when their primary ally, the United States, had lost the political will to sustain them in their battle for survival." Shackley found nothing intrinsically wrong with the policy he had carried out in Laos. The flaw was a lack of spine on the part of the politicians in Washington. He and his CIA colleagues could not be blamed.

"I had a lot of respect for him," Ambassador Sullivan said of Shackley. "You may not like his business. But we needed his business." Not everyone in the embassy was so gracious. "He was an apparatchik," recalled Peter Lydon, an officer in the embassy's political division. "He was pure personification of his mission, and it wasn't good. He was not a figure we should have more of in the United States." Another embassy man, embittered by the Nam Bac episode, was more biting: "Ted Shackley's tenure was marked by excessive bloodletting that could have been avoided. He was chasing delusions of a victory that was not possible." But he had to admit Shackley did a wonderful job of organizing. In Langley, a sharp-tongued wag dubbed Ted Shackley "the butcher of Laos."

Shackley's promotion to Saigon was a sign that headquarters believed he had served ably in Laos. He remained a comer. After hearing Shackley was off to Saigon, one Vientiane embassy officer, who believed South

Vietnam was destined to fall, dropped by Shackley's office to offer friendly advice. You might consider, he said to Shackley, developing intelligence assets that could stay behind when the war goes bust. Shackley refused to consider the notion. He was off to a country where the world's most important battle against communism was occurring, where his say would affect the disposition of billions of dollars, hundreds of thousands of troops, and millions of lives. Shackley would not head into such a job thinking he was going to lose.

CHAPTER SIX

SAIGON:
INTELLIGENCE AT WAR

I

ONCE a month the ROICs gathered in Saigon. Each man—a regional officer in charge—was chief of CIA operations in one of the five sectors into which South Vietnam was divided. In a conference room at the U.S. embassy, where the top floors were reserved for the Agency station, the field officers, long-timers with the Company, waited for the appearance of what they called the "zero chart."

During their monthly visits to Saigon, the ROICs conferred with assorted division heads and unit chiefs of a station that was a sprawling bureaucracy packed with managers, analysts, clerks, secretaries, and advisers. The most serious and to-the-point discussions occurred with Ted Shackley, a busy man, at the helm of the Agency's largest station.

Dressed in a dark suit, Shackley strode into the room with charts and graphs. He loved devices that reduced the imperfect and subtle craft of intelligence to numbers. In the sessions with his senior field officers, Shackley inevitably turned to a chart that listed every province and district in the country. Sent to Vietnam in December of 1968, Shackley was assigned, not to fight a war, but to help preserve the Saigon regime and to discover what he could about the enemy and its plans. It may have been a little late in the game for the United States to mount, for the first time in Vietnam, an intelligence offensive against a foe it had battled for years. But that was what Shackley was tasked to do. So he pressed his subordinates to recruit assets, run operations, and churn out reports, lots of reports. He wanted more intelligence dispatches from the provinces. Headquarters kept count of the reports that stations produced. Shackley yearned for big numbers for his Saigon outfit. He demanded high-level penetrations, spies in the upper regions of the Viet Cong, the underground communist apparatus.

But the chart did not lie. Shackley read down the list of the provinces and districts and noted the number of penetrations of the VC: zero, zero, zero, zero. Once in a while he might reach a "one" for a district, meaning the CIA had found a district-level agent. But then Shackley returned to the stream of zeros. The ROICs did their best not to be bothered by Shackley's recitation. They were the men on the ground, the ones who knew how daunting it was to practice espionage within a war—especially against an enemy that was disciplined, motivated, organized, highly compartmentalized, and that possessed decades of experience in maintaining an underground organization. After these meetings, they joked among themselves about Shackley's zero chart and then returned to the reality of Vietnam.

For over two decades, the CIA and its predecessor had been on the prowl in Vietnam. In the latter years of World War II, OSS operatives forged an alliance with Vietnamese nationalists—particularly the League for the Independence of Vietnam, or Viet Minh—in the war against Japan, and cooperated closely with Ho Chi Minh, the Viet Minh leader and a founder of the Indochinese Communist Party. But after the war, Washington's cold warriors supported France's bid to regain its colony —an effort that led to war between the Viet Minh and the French.

After the French defeat at Dien Bien Phu in 1954, an international conference produced an artificial settlement. The country was divided into two military zones, with the Viet Minh in control of the northern one. General elections for the whole nation were to be held in two years. The United States moved fast to find a suitable leader for the southern zone. It chose Ngo Dinh Diem, an ascetic Catholic bachelor living in Europe, who had served under the French. With the imprimatur of the Americans, he returned to Saigon in June of 1954 to become the prime minister of South Vietnam.

Washington was not counting on Diem alone. There was also the CIA. In 1954, Edward Lansdale arrived in Vietnam on assignment for the Agency. His orders were straightforward: stop the communists. Lansdale pulled together a unit that waged paramilitary operations and political-psychological warfare against the Viet Minh. A Lansdale team based in the north, and run by Lou Conein, Shackley's former office mate in Nuremberg, sabotaged Hanoi's buses and railway equipment. In South

Vietnam, Lansdale bribed religious and political sect leaders to support the aloof Diem.

There was little doubt Ho Chi Minh would triumph in national elections. In October of 1955, as a preemptive move, Diem held a referendum to ratify his own presidency and proclaim South Vietnam a republic all its own. With help from Lansdale, Diem won 98.2 percent of the vote. The new president declared he was not bound by the Geneva Accords plank that mandated elections to reunify Vietnam. Months later, he initiated a campaign against former Viet Minh activists, in which tens of thousands were arrested. Lansdale pressed his friend Diem to allow the political opposition to operate freely. Diem ignored the advice. By early 1956, a discouraged Lansdale wanted out of Vietnam. He worried that Washington was promoting "a fascistic state."

In subsequent years, Diem tightened his government's control of South Vietnam. The Agency helped by awarding a secret $25 million contract to the Michigan State University School of Police Administration to train different South Vietnamese security forces, which developed reputations for repression. Diem's heavy-handed methods did not win his government support among countryside residents, who had many reasons to dislike the regime: the return of land to old landlords, government corruption, conscription, the resumption of high taxes, official extortion, and arrests. One village chief estimated that the ills of Diem prompted 80 percent of the people in his area to support the resistance, the Viet Cong.

In Saigon, CIA station chief William Colby notified Washington of the growing concern within Saigon's political community over the Diem regime's authoritarian actions. But Colby's station strove to prop up Diem. It helped create the Central Intelligence Organization for the Saigon government. Colby steered the Saigon station toward political and paramilitary programs. He considered "pacification"—the term that applied to the hodgepodge of psychological and paramilitary programs aimed at countering the Viet Cong underground—a vital component of the war. The Agency armed and organized tribespeople, mostly the Montagnards. Some tribesmen were sent on long-range patrols through the mountains to locate enemy supply routes. The CIA trained and paid local "strike forces." The growing station guided Vietnamese Special Forces operations that included commando raids into Laos and North Vietnam.

Classic intelligence—espionage—took a backseat to pacification and secret warfare. Rather than serve as the eyes and ears of Washington and do all it could to penetrate the enemy and understand the complexities of Vietnam, the station was fighting its own version of the war.

In September of 1960, the ruling communist Lao Dong (or Workers

Party) of North Vietnam called for a coalition organization to "liberate the south," and three months later, the National Front for the Liberation of South Vietnam was formed. The NLF was dominated by communists and its operations were largely directed by Hanoi, but some Front participants were independent nationalists continuing the long-running fight for a united and independent Vietnam. Yet Washington portrayed the conflict as a case of an external communist force attempting to subvert the government of a noncommunist (and pro-American) state. The armed forces of the resistance—guided by a headquarters called the Central Office for South Vietnam (COSVN, to Americans)—grew and continued to clash with Diem's military, often getting the better of the Army of the Republic of Vietnam (ARVN).

After John Kennedy took office in 1961, he approved increasing the size of ARVN, boosting the U.S. annual budget for Vietnam to over $250 million, deploying more U.S. military advisers, and running covert missions against North Vietnam. The resistance continued to swell, and as a 1961 intelligence estimate put it, 80 to 90 percent of the 16,000 guerrillas were of southern origin, not troops from the north.

Colby and many of his CIA comrades believed the war could be won if Washington deployed imagination and did not rely on a conventional military response. With paramilitary and civic action programs designed to counter communists in the countryside, the Saigon station hoped to change those aspects of Vietnamese society that aided the VC. This supposedly sophisticated approach clashed with a let's-clobber-them, military plan of action. But it was predicated on two dubious premises: the dire threat was subversion emanating from outside the south, and Diem's government was not rotten beyond reform.

In 1962, Saigon initiated its strategic hamlet program, which forcibly relocated villagers into settlements surrounded by barbed wire and guarded by government troops. The program had emerged from conversations Colby held with government officials. The theory was that this would deny the Viet Cong the support of the local population that guerrillas need. (It would create much resentment among those relocated.) ARVN mounted division-sized search-and-destroy operations against the guerrillas, but failed to accomplish true victories. Diem continued his repressive ways, jailing Buddhist opponents. In August of 1963, Agency-trained and -funded Vietnamese Special Forces raided pagodas.

Diem, several Kennedy advisers concluded, was now more a problem than a solution. Officials in Washington argued over whether the United States should okay a military coup. Top CIA officials asserted Kennedy should stick with Diem. But the President decided it was time for Diem to go. Toward the end of October of 1963, the ubiquitous Lou Conein was given funds to disperse to insurgent generals. The coup proceeded, and on November 2, 1963, Diem and his brother were killed.

As the United States increased its commitment in Vietnam under President Johnson, the Saigon station collected information useful in determining how U.S. troops could best be deployed and which targets should be struck by American bombs. But addressing military priorities overshadowed efforts to collect intelligence on the political plans and activities of the Viet Cong and the North Vietnamese. With few officers skilled in Vietnamese or knowledgeable about Vietnamese culture, the station rarely penetrated the enemy. At a July 21, 1965, White House meeting, Admiral William Raborn, who had replaced John McCone as Director of Central Intelligence, was forced to concede to the President that the CIA had few agents in North Vietnam. When Johnson asked why the United States could not do better, Raborn lamely replied that he was working on it.

In 1965 the CIA station helped create South Vietnamese Census Grievance units that visited villages to elicit the residents' complaints and improve relations between villagers and Saigon. Another new CIA program was less warm in intentions: the counter-terror (CT) teams. The CT squads were born out of frustration. The regular army could not do much against VC guerrillas who harassed, attacked, and killed Vietnamese civilians allied with Saigon. The CT units—funded, trained, and guided by CIA officers—were small paramilitary groups outside the normal military chain of command. Their goal, chief of station Peer DeSilva wrote in his memoirs, was "to bring danger and death to the Vietcong functionaries."

The Agency had adopted the tactics of the enemy. Eventually Langley rechristened the teams Provincial Reconnaissance Units, a less suggestive name. PRU members, all Vietnamese, developed a reputation for ferocity—and for conducting atrocities. The Agency also built Provincial Interrogation Centers for the Special Branch of the National Police in each province capital. With the PICs, the station intended to promote professional interrogation of higher-level VC prisoners, but PICs became places of torture—with the South Vietnamese employing the torture—and produced little worthwhile intelligence on the VC.

In the name of efficiency, the Agency in 1967 established an outfit to coordinate all intelligence on the VC and gave birth to what would become the most notorious CIA venture of the war: the Phoenix program. Under Phoenix, field representatives of different U.S. and South Vietnamese agencies swapped intelligence and decided how best to "exploit" the material. Exploitation meant capturing or killing suspected VC leaders, ambushing Viet Cong couriers and suppliers, raiding VC strongholds. The intent of Phoenix was to develop lists of VC cadres and a solid picture of the VC network, so the CIA-backed PRUs and other forces knew where and whom to hit. The program, most CIA veterans have claimed, was not set up as an assassination unit. But deaths mounted, as suspected VC were killed by the PRUs and other units.

The CIA did all it could to control the circus of politics that took place in Saigon. From 1966 to 1968, John Sherwood headed the political action division. "We were giving money to every group," he recalled, "labor, youth, veteran, women, Seeing Eye dog groups, you name it." His unit dispensed funds to sway elections. "We pretended," he noted, "there was a real government we could influence."

In Vietnam, the CIA, while seeking hearts, minds, and enemy bodies, was supposed to be an objective observer of a world foreign to most Americans. Once again, the Agency was assigned a dual mission: to record events and intentions, and to create change. In wartime, the two goals clashed even more than usual. The press of combat frequently pushed aside the patient and dispassionate collection of unbiased information.

Generally, the Agency's U.S.-based Vietnam-watchers were not as hopeful as the Agency field officers. In 1964, a CIA special mission to South Vietnam noted that the VC were gaining. Agency analysts generated a series of gloomy estimates, predicting continued decline in the Saigon government. A 1965 estimate concluded that the insurgency in the south "has substantial capabilities independent of Hanoi" and that the Viet Cong, though heavily dependent on Ho Chi Minh's government, could carry on by itself. McCone irritated Johnson with his dire warnings that U.S. ground troops would have limited effectiveness against guerrillas and that Washington was heading toward a military defeat—unless Johnson committed to heavier bombing. A March 1966 CIA report wrote off the results of the Rolling Thunder bombing campaign as insignificant, but boldly recommended a bombing crusade of greater intensity.

In 1967, a holy war broke out when the CIA and military analysts could not agree on the enemy order of battle—that is, how many persons they were fighting in Vietnam. Sam Adams, a rumpled analyst in headquarters who had studied captured VC documents, ended up with a figure in the neighborhood of 600,000—more than twice the 270,000 the U.S. military was claiming. The Pentagon challenged Adams's accounting. Heated discussions ensued in Washington and Saigon.

The matter was crucial. If the military accepted Adams's figures, extrapolated from a small but not insignificant sample, then the light at the end of the tunnel was an illusion. Adams considered lower estimates by General Westmoreland and his staff a deliberate disinformation campaign designed to prove they could win the war. The dispute illustrated a fundamental dilemma: the U.S. government did not know who the enemy was. CIA Director Helms ordered his men to accede to the military's calculations.*

Four months later, in February of 1968, Adams won grim vindication. The VC launched its Tet offensive, the intensity of which surprised U.S. intelligence and demonstrated to a shocked American audience that the war was bigger than its government had acknowledged.† In early 1968, the analysts of Langley could offer only a bleak assessment of the war. They were not predicting defeat. The Viet Cong and the North Vietnamese, they believed, could not drive the U.S. military out of Vietnam in the near future. But as one report noted, "It is equally out of the question for U.S./[South Vietnam] forces to clear South Vietnam of Communist forces."

By the time Shackley took over the station in Saigon in December of 1968, the Vietnam War had undone Johnson's presidency, derailed the Great Society, soiled America's image for many people throughout the world, divided bitterly the United States, and claimed the lives of tens of thousands of Americans and countless residents of Indochina. Shackley had not asked for the assignment. He had been content with his position in Laos and expected to stay there for another two-year tour. He did not know how or why he had been chosen for the post. Nor did he realize that this was the path the late Des FitzGerald had laid out for him several years earlier. But Shackley was not at all apprehensive about the assignment. "There was," he later said, "no reason not to go."

II

Saigon was an occupied city, overwhelmed by war, heavily populated with the American military. Military trucks (loaded with unkempt GIs), jeeps, motorcycles, ratty-looking cabs, and small Japanese cars crammed the streets. Billboards hawked Seagram's, Sony, and Philco. The Presi-

---

* Adams went public with his tale in a 1975 article in *Harper's,* which led to a 1982 CBS documentary that charged Westmoreland and others with conspiring to suppress critical intelligence. The general sued for libel, but agreed to a very weak settlement before the trial was complete.

† In the years following the war, many CIA officers who served in Vietnam offered anecdotes that suggested the Agency had picked up whiffs of the Tet offensive in the making. But a senior CIA official at the time noted, "We didn't forecast Tet with any degree of definiteness."

dential Palace of Nguyen Van Thieu was guarded by Vietnamese soldiers armed with submachine guns. A twin-spired Catholic Church looked over a square—named for John F. Kennedy—that opened up to raunchy Tu Do Street, a procession of open-front bars, strip joints, brothels, and trinket shops. Rock and roll poured out into the street.

Blocks from the Catholic cathedral and Tu Do Street was the U.S. embassy compound. Marines patrolled the grounds, which were surrounded by a wall. The main building's facade was covered by a concrete artillery shield. People on the inside could peer out of portholes but not see much of the country they were hoping to save. The top three of the embassy's six floors belonged to the CIA station. The walls were pale green, the floor linoleum, a typical government workplace. The chief's office was on the top floor, near the situation room. On his floor, CIA people could hear the rattle of incoming helicopters and feel the vibrations emitted by the rooftop incinerators that incessantly burned mounds of classified garbage.

The CIA maintained offices and annexes throughout the city. A few blocks from the embassy, the Duc Hotel passed as home to many CIA men. A poker game was frequently in progress there. Raucous parties raged. Agency veterans sat at the hotel bar and waxed nostalgic about the good old days in Saigon, before the military stole the show from the spooks.* Randy Agency fellows often were in the company of a friendly local. Senior officers, like Shackley, lived in the villas left behind by the French. His was guarded by a fence and watched over by MPs.

At night, spies, diplomats, military officers, and war correspondents —the new breed of skeptical reporters and old Asian hands—gathered at hotel rooftop bars and watched parachute flares descend over the rice fields beyond the city and listened to the distant thunder of B-52 air strikes. The most common pieces of everyday America were readily available in what had once been the Paris of Southeast Asia: Budweiser, smog, Dairy Queen, *I Dream of Jeannie.* "There was such a dense concentration of American energy there, American and essentially adolescent," correspondent Michael Herr wrote, that "if that energy could have been channeled into anything more than noise, waste and pain it would have lighted up Indochina for a thousand years."

The incongruities of Vietnam burdened some CIA officers, but Shack-

---

* Lou Conein, having been tossed out of the Agency in 1967 for hosting a party at the Duc that got out of hand, lounged around Saigon and was involved in some unexplained business enterprise. He usually could be found in a Corsican bar, feeding peanuts to a vicious dog and mumbling lines like, "It will be the person you trust the most who will blow you away."

ley was impervious to the surrealism of Saigon. Too busy for ironies, he did not ponder the metaphysics of Vietnam. In the station, his all-business attitude set the tone, and officers, following their chief's lead, toiled long hours. As far as anyone could tell, Shackley was not tempted by the free flow of wine and native women. Frank Snepp, a station analyst, once asked Shackley what he did for relaxation. The boss replied, "I do my work."

Befitting his position as the top U.S. spook in the hottest spot on the globe, Shackley struck an imperial manner. He drove through the crowded streets of Saigon in a large chauffeur-driven armor-plated American car. The floor was steel-reinforced to protect against detonated mines. A security guard sat in the front seat with a shotgun. Bodyguards were always close by. One never saw Shackley strolling the streets. He carried a .45 in his briefcase. There was talk among the junior officers that his briefcase contained steel plates. In the event of any trouble, he could flip it open and duck his head in.*

His secretary, Dana Meiggs, zealously guarded access to Shackley's barren office. To her favorite officers, she slipped useful bits of intelligence, such as which parties Shackley planned to attend. She had a code name for the boss. "Daddy wants to see you," she would tell a subordinate, or "Daddy is mad at you." In his office, Shackley kept a stack of yellow legal pads on his large desk. They were for his officers. When he called someone in and issued an order, he wanted the subordinate to write it down.

Shackley desired complete control of the 600-person station. He insisted that base chiefs send reports to Washington through his office. He closely watched the finances. There was a constant stream of personnel problems: an alcoholic officer who wrapped a car around a tree, a pregnant secretary. On some days, Shackley had to race off to a meeting at the Presidential Palace. Once the Nixon administration settled in, Henry Kissinger was always on Shackley's back.† Shackley briefed VIPs, including members of Congress, Vice President Spiro Agnew, and foreign dignitaries. "On these occasions, he had to have his charts," recalled Joe Lazarsky, Shackley's cigar-chomping deputy. "He used to bug me about the charts and maps."

---

* For the first part of Shackley's Saigon tour, his wife Hazel and daughter Suzanne lived in Hong Kong. When the security situation in Saigon later improved, Hazel and Suzanne moved there.

† During a Kissinger visit to the station, a senior officer asked if he were satisfied with the intelligence he received. As long as it supports my policy, Kissinger said, I am satisfied.

Shackley carefully cultivated his relationship with U.S. Ambassador Ellsworth Bunker, a taciturn, formal septuagenarian and career diplomat. Shackley was always deferential and precise in the senior man's presence. At the daily morning country team meetings, Shackley took his place at the table with Bunker, top military officers, and the heads of other civilian agencies, such as William Colby, who was director of Civil Operations and Revolutionary Development Support (CORDS), the U.S. entity that managed pacification endeavors. Shackley was dealing with the elite of America. One time in Vietnam, he was in a meeting with several of the most senior men of the U.S. government. The conversation turned to alma maters. As each person in the room noted where he had attended college, the names of the finest schools, Ivy League institutions, flew across the room. When it was Shackley's turn, he reported he was a graduate of the University of Maryland. As his family later came to hear the tale from Shackley, an uncomfortable silence descended upon the room.

Shortly after Shackley took over the station, James Graham and Paul Walsh, two senior analysts in headquarters, came to Saigon to brief Bunker on a contested intelligence question: how much enemy materiel was transiting the Cambodian port of Sihanoukville. CIA analysts led by Walsh believed the flow of supplies was modest; the military's estimate was double that of Walsh. The issue was important, for the new Nixon administration was weighing how to deal with the enemy's use of Cambodia territory.

While escorting Graham and Walsh to Bunker's office, Shackley asked what they planned to tell the ambassador. Graham replied that they intended to report the truth: there was no clear answer yet. Shackley became indignant. You can't do that, he declared. You have to have an answer. Graham was not surprised. He had seen Shackley brief officials at headquarters on the program in Laos. Everything was crisp. There was no element of doubt. That was what Shackley wanted now. Graham told Shackley that he did not work that way. "Shackley said that this was not good enough," Graham recalled. "You can't go into the ambassador and say you don't know."*

Shackley nurtured good relations with General Creighton Abrams, the head of American armed forces in Vietnam, and Thieu's top aides—especially General Nguyen Khac Binh, who rose with CIA backing to become head of the National Police, and General Dang Vang Quang, Thieu's security adviser and reputedly the most corrupt general in the

---

* This issue was resolved when the CIA recruited an agent with access to shipping data. The agent's reports indicated the amount of goods moving through Sihanoukville was close to the military's estimate.

country.* Quang and Binh were touted by Shackley's station as valuable assets. They may, however, have played the station better than they were played. Quang continued his apparently corrupt ways. And both men, according to Snepp, told Shackley and their other CIA contacts what the Americans wanted to hear. "Our reliance on these two men had terrible consequences," Snepp complained. "Not only was our intelligence adversely affected, but so too was our moral and political position among the Vietnamese. By virtue of the wealth and prominence we bestowed upon them, both Quang and Binh became symbols of American-inflicted corruption and decadence that ultimately provided the Communists with their best propaganda weapons."

Shackley struck up friendships with a small number of journalists, the older Asian hands who were mostly sympathetic with Washington's aims in Indochina. The core group of those the chief favored included Robert Shaplen of *The New Yorker,* Keyes Beech of *The Chicago Daily News* and later *The Los Angeles Times,* George McArthur of the Associated Press and then *The Los Angeles Times,* and Bud Merick of *U.S. News and World Report.* Shackley had little time for the young turks of the press corps who reported the war with a mistrust previously unknown to mainstream American media.

The chief became a guardian source for the believers—but totally off the record. If one of the gang needed to file a story on the latest strategy indications out of Hanoi, Shackley graciously arranged for a briefing with a station officer. Shackley was more generous with his preferred reporters than with fellow U.S. government employees. Douglas Pike, an embassy expert on the Viet Cong, scheduled lunches with Shaplen and Beech to find out what Shackley and other station officers had told them but not disclosed to him. He complained to his embassy supervisors that journalists were being handed sensitive information. The CIA, he was told, had the authority to provide classified information to reporters—particularly, Pike thought, if it made Shackley and the CIA look good.

At the end of each week, Ted Shackley sent a situation report— someone tagged it a "Shackleygram"—to headquarters, hailing the station's accomplishments of the week. Snepp, a young, cocky analyst, often collected material for the reports. "They were really self-congratulatory,

---

* In 1971 Quang was accused by NBC News of being "the biggest pusher" of heroin to GIs in Vietnam. Similar charges had long been hurled at Vice President Nguyen Cao Ky. The U.S. embassy repeatedly denied such allegations. But an embassy official told one journalist no evidence was found because Bunker's embassy and Shackley's station avoided looking for any. He maintained that it was an unwritten rule that during mission discussions on the heroin trade, nobody could mention high-ranking Vietnamese officials.

so puffed up," he noted. (Snepp was a native North Carolinian who majored in Elizabethan literature at Columbia University before joining the CIA to escape the draft. But some Agency friends, as a prank, submitted an application in his name for a job in Vietnam, and he was called to take it.) Snepp also wrote briefings for Shackley. His sessions with the chief were highly ritualized. Snepp arrived at Shackley's house late in the day and asked, Mr. Shackley, what do you want me to say? Shackley guided Snepp to a chair with a bright light by it, as if Snepp were to be interrogated. He never offered a beer or a drink. Standing off in the shadows, Shackley told Snepp what he desired written.

It was in Saigon that one of Shackley's underlings created a romantic nickname for the intimidating spy-bureaucrat: the Blond Ghost. Supposedly a woman analyst in the station with a mild crush on the chief coined the phrase. She was part of a bevy of women in the station who admired Shackley and fancied him a handsome and dashing figure. At CIA parties, they huddled to discuss how their chief looked that evening. They all began referring to him as the Blond Ghost.

The name was physically accurate, but a moniker better suited to a stealthy field man, whose world is a collection of covert nooks and crannies from where he plots in secrecy. Shackley was a specter in complexion only. Throughout Saigon he was well known as the chief of station. The mystery-soaked Blond Ghost tag did not circulate far; it was a private joke shared by a few CIA people. Only in later years, after Shackley became immersed in public scandal, would this melodramatic nickname become widely known and enhance a notorious reputation.

Shackley landed in Saigon with a specific set of orders from Director Helms. He was to extricate the Agency from most of the paramilitary and pacification programs—Phoenix, Census Grievance, and the like—that had distracted the station from its intelligence mission. Helms hoped to pass much of this activity to the Pentagon and William Colby's CORDS. His main objections were bureaucratic: These programs demanded too many resources. He expressed no concerns about their probity, but he realized the more brutal operations would tarnish his Agency's reputation. To some subordinates in the field, there was another reason for dumping these programs: most were not working.

Orrin DeForest, a wiry, mustachioed former Army investigator hired by the Agency, arrived in Saigon about the same time as Shackley. He was astonished by a conversation with the station officer in charge of the Census Grievance program. The units ostensibly had been formed to collect complaints from peasants so the Saigon government could address their concerns. But the program became a way of encouraging peasants to supply information on the Viet Cong, a kind of mass, low-level intelligence program. Since the Agency had no Viet Cong agents, the station officer told DeForest, the Census Grievance program was one of the Agency's main sources of information. "I found it difficult to believe my ears," DeForest later noted. "Could the Census Grievance director actually be saying that we had no agents of our own in Vietnam? No spies? . . . How the hell, I thought, could we possibly win a war with no spies? And was he telling us that the Census Grievance program simply accepted (and paid for) information from peasants it had signed up? It seemed the perfect target for any double agent: any of these peasants could be Viet Cong; no doubt many of them were. Many more were undoubtedly Viet Cong sympathizers. And the Agency was paying them for their services and accepting what they said as intelligence?"

Shackley had become the CIA's best manager of elaborate covert operations, but he would follow Helms's lead and stick to the new emphasis on espionage. Shackley could go either way: run a secret war or manage intelligence collection—or do both at once. That was what made him so valuable to his superiors. He was not seen as a champion of any particular program. He implemented what his bosses wanted. It was the way to be a good Company man, the way to move closer to the Director's chair.

Once in Saigon, Shackley reviewed all the CIA programs. "It became clear to me then," he said afterward, "that the pacification programs had come of age . . . that the Agency contribution was no longer required. So my original proposal was to see about getting others to manage these . . . programs, to free up CIA resources to improve the quality of the intelligence product, to penetrate the Viet Cong, and the NVA supporting them, and to concentrate more against the North and the VC and the NVA in Cambodia." Foremost on the list of things to go was Phoenix. Shackley began transferring management responsibility for Phoenix to the military and CORDS. Within six months, the transition officially was complete. But in Vietnam the official did not always match the actual. When the Phoenix program later became a subject of great controversy, the Agency would not be in the clear.

Before Shackley hit Saigon, paramilitary and political programs claimed roughly 75 percent of the station's resources; intelligence collection received the rest. And the station's prime target for intelligence was its ally, the Thieu regime. The Saigon station had to guarantee that U.S. officials were aware of all the intrigue and internal crises that whirled about the Presidential Palace. The enemy in the field came second. "It was a fact of life," Shackley deputy Joe Lazarsky noted, "that we did not have good enough intelligence on the VC—who they were and what they were up to." Shackley passed the word to his ROICs, who spread it to their province officers: the Agency was phasing out participation in the psychological and paramilitary activities. It was now time to start focusing on the VC. Go figure out who is VC and what they are doing.

Recent history provided Shackley and his hundreds of subordinates little guidance. The Agency had been involved intimately in Vietnam for two decades, yet it had never approached Vietnam in true intelligence fashion. "Quite frankly," Colby recalled, "over the years we had not done all we should have with clandestine intelligence operations. We were preoccupied with PM problems and national political problems." Penetrating the VC structure, learning about the enemy, and discovering its plans had not been the top priorities for the station.

No one knew that better than George Allen, for years a Directorate of Intelligence specialist on Vietnam. On a trip to Saigon in 1960, Allen had been startled to discover that not one officer in the station was more than marginally interested in intelligence on the burgeoning insurgency. Everyone was occupied with the survival of Diem's regime. Four years later, Clark Clifford, a Johnson adviser, visited Saigon and urged the station to increase its efforts to penetrate the enemy. For the next year or two, there was the occasional meeting at Langley or in Saigon, a cable here and there, each urging more attention be devoted to the insurgents. The Agency-constructed Provincial Interrogation Centers, with their torturers and poor results, were part of this moderate push and supposed to generate intelligence through the questioning of captured VC. But not much actually happened. "There were no real intelligence operations going on at this time," recalled Jack Horgan, the ROIC for Region V in the delta in 1966 and 1967.

Espionage against the VC was too hard. Few CIA officers spoke the language, and they were too conspicuous. A civilian American walking down the streets of a district capital stood out. The notion of conducting surreptitious meetings in this setting was laughable. "It was very frustrating," said Lewis Lapham, Shackley's predecessor as station chief. "It was very difficult to have agents who were well placed in the Viet Cong, given the fact that you had to recruit them through cutouts* and this required working with the South Vietnamese. We had an extremely tough time figuring out who was and wasn't reliable."

Better intelligence would not come simply because Ted Shackley

---

*A cutout is another agent or operative who acts as a conduit between the U.S. intelligence officer and the actual VC agent, e.g., a South Vietnamese citizen or officer in contact with a Viet Cong spy. The Agency officer usually received reports from the cutout, not the agent.

desired it. Shackley could designate intelligence the new priority; he could not vanquish the obstacles. His field men still lacked the requisite knowledge and language skills necessary for sophisticated espionage operations in wartime. They had to collaborate with the locals, mainly the Special Branch, full of bumblers, corrupt officers, and VC agents.

In early 1969, Orrin DeForest, now chief of interrogation for Region III, learned this firsthand when he toured the CIA-built Provincial Interrogation Centers. Before DeForest departed Saigon, Shackley's man in charge of the PICs briefed DeForest and repeatedly used the phrase "We must make the PICs work." He was obviously nervous about the prospects. "The chief's watching this one closely," the PIC officer explained. Shackley was determined to turn the PICs into a foundation of the revived drive to infiltrate the enemy.

DeForest's colleague had cause for concern. The two flew up to Qui Nhon to inspect the most active PIC in Region II. The interrogations they witnessed were dismaying. The Special Branch officer who questioned the prisoner was incompetent. There was no rhyme or reason to his queries. In the Nha Trang PIC, prisoners were held in squalid conditions. The place stank of urine and feces. Not one of the captives admitted to being VC. "All [the PIC officers] had the ability to do was beat the shit out of these people," DeForest observed, "and then what would they know?"

Visits to other PICs convinced DeForest that the program was not yielding any useful intelligence. After his tour, DeForest had to provide a written report to Shackley. The PICs were a waste of time and money, but Shackley considered the PICs a vital starting point for his campaign to produce more intelligence. DeForest did not want to contradict the strong-willed chief. In his report, DeForest merely observed that there was room for improvement. At that point, he later wrote, "I had seen absolutely nothing there to suggest that the Agency brass [in Saigon] had any real sense for what went on in the field."

After settling in Bien Hoa, DeForest realized that his boss, Daren Flitcroft, the ROIC for Region III, was a bit lost. "I'll tell you," Flitcroft said, "half the time we don't have any idea what's going on." The intelligence reports that came out of the PICs or the Special Branch were penny ante. While visiting the Bien Hoa PIC one day, DeForest saw four Special Branch police officers questioning a young girl, as one shoved a broomstick into her vagina.

For Shackley, the PICs remained underused Agency assets. The Company had paid for their construction, and the chief believed it should derive something from them. He urged the field men to use them to process the VC and NVA defectors who responded to the Saigon government's Chieu Hoi program.* "The problem was," Flitcroft explained, "that the way you make the Chieu Hoi program work is the enticement. The PICs had a terrible reputation." Using them as a processing center did not encourage defections or reassure defectors.

Flitcroft was aware the CIA-advised Special Branch practiced torture in Agency-supported PICs—the program Shackley kept pushing. "What can you do?" he asked years later. "It's their institution. We saw it as counterproductive to everything we were trying to do. You can't torture people and get information. It was not part of our way of thinking. That's not true with the Vietnamese. Their job was to stamp things out. Their job was not to penetrate [the high levels of the Viet Cong] but to kill the guy at the hamlet level. You could see the marks [on the prisoners] and the instruments. . . . You agonized over it. You didn't want to be associated with it. . . . The publicity was so damaging. You talk to the [Special Branch officers] running these institutions and they would decry the practice. What do you do? Hit them over the head? What are you going to do? Withdraw support? That's what we were stuck with?"†

DeForest decided that if he wanted to produce intelligence he had one choice: forget working with the South Vietnamese and Shackley's PICs. With Flitcroft's permission, he established his own covert, unilateral interrogation operation, based at the regional center for the Chieu Hoi program. There were 1,300 defectors with whom DeForest could start. Solid interrogations with them would produce material on the local Viet Cong organization and indicate which VC officials should be targeted for recruitment. When another officer asked Flitcroft what he intended to tell Shackley and the station, the ROIC replied, "Fuck 'em. I'm not even going to mention it to them." The Region's budget was juggled to provide the funds.

Shortly after the system was going, Shackley visited the Bien Hoa base, only fifteen miles north of Saigon. He was not bashful about showing his displeasure with Region III. In a talk to Flitcroft and his senior subordinates, he complained that their area had only one VC agent in development. Regions I and II in the north had none, but Region IV, the delta, was working on fifty potential agents. "What exactly is wrong with Three Corps, Mr. Flitcroft?" the chief asked. "You people seem to be batting zero out here."

Shackley demanded a briefing on the PICs. During the presentation,

---

*Between 1963 and 1973, "Open Arms" (Chieu Hoi) brought in about 160,000 deserters, about 30,000 of them VC.

† Dean Almy, ROIC for Region II, acknowledged that the PICs were places of brutality. Roger McCarthy, ROIC for Region I, called them "a waste of time." He added, "We never got anything worthy out of that effort."

DeForest steered clear of disclosing to Shackley anything about his unilateral interrogation operation. He tactfully reported that the Special Branch and the PICs were generally ineffective. Shackley's face registered disdain. Another officer jumped in to note that the Special Branch intelligence reports were not reliable and that because they refused to make their agents or agent-handlers available, the Agency officers could not verify the reports. Shackley did not want to hear this. The Special Branch was the core CIA intelligence program. Look at Region IV, Shackley responded sharply. They were doing just splendidly down there. Perhaps the problem here was not the Special Branch but the CIA people running Region III. The meeting ended, Shackley left, and DeForest never saw him again.

But DeForest's operation prospered. Its files grew to contain thousands of cards, each covering a suspected VC. Its interrogations produced reports on VC activity in the region. Some material was encouraging. VC capabilities seemed to be down. Some units were short on food, ammunition, and recruits. Intelligence was passed to the Air Force for targeting B-52 raids. Yet, at the same time, information from the defectors showed that the Viet Cong had penetrated deeply into the South Vietnamese army.

DeForest's ultimate goal was to develop spies. He had none yet. But he was pleased with the early returns. A lot could be done if he did not have to adhere to Shackley's set-in-stone preference for the PICs. Then in the summer of 1969, Nixon announced his policy of Vietnamization. The role of U.S. ground troops would be limited. It now was up to the South Vietnamese to win what was supposed to be their war—albeit with plenty of U.S. support and air power. DeForest was moving in the opposite direction. His project worked. But what was the point in an all-American effort? It was an admission that a fundamental premise of the war—the Saigon government was functional—was incorrect.

Shackley was inflexible. But perhaps he grasped an essential truth: if the South Vietnamese could not run their own government and security apparatus, the United States surely would suffer its first military defeat.

Across South Vietnam, Shackley's officers shifted their attention toward espionage. The hope was to score strategic intelligence—the overall plans of the Viet Cong and the NVA. The prime target was any VC official with access to COSVN, the floating enemy headquarters. But Shackley's officers had to settle for less.

Flitcroft's Region III managed to recruit a VC prisoner who returned to Hau Nghia province and collected not-very-sensitive information about COSVN directives. In the delta, Dan Mudrinich, Shackley's ROIC for Region IV, was dissatisfied, even though he was in charge of the area that Shackley held up as an example to others. In each of his sixteen provinces, his men were working around the clock, yet little intelligence was coming back. In some provinces, literally nothing was happening. The liaison relationship with the Special Branch was worthless.

Gradually, Mudrinich's officers developed unilateral recruitments—assets obtained separately from the joint programs with the South Vietnamese. During his tour, his men ran about twenty agents of varying value. By paying merchants who routinely crossed the border (in one case, a drug smuggler), Mudrinich's officers eked out reports on the condition of enemy troops in Cambodia. But his field men had no luck searching for what Shackley most desired: high-level reporting sources who could say what the enemy would do next.

For all the frustrations, one of Mudrinich's operations succeeded brilliantly. Among the many elusive targets for Shackley's station, the Viet Cong in the U Minh forest ranked high. Located in Kien Giang, a southern province, the dense, triple-canopy jungle provided cover for VC storage sites, underground bunkers, and operations centers. The Viet Cong ruled the forest. The Agency was clueless as to what went on underneath the foliage. Then one day a CIA officer met a woman who lived in the province. Her daughter was sick, and a grandchild was going blind due to an ailment. She also had a son who was a senior VC official in the U Minh, and she visited him every few months.

Over the course of almost a year, Mudrinich's officer befriended the woman and procured for her grandchild the medical treatment needed to save the child's sight. He offered the woman gifts and money. Then, after one of her trips to U Minh, the officer asked her a seemingly innocuous question. How many people did you see at the VC headquarters? She answered. Following subsequent visits, he posed additional questions, until she felt comfortable being debriefed. After one trip, she noted that her son had asked her to find him a used typewriter. Don't worry about it, her CIA friend said, I'll get one for you.

Soon afterward, the woman again rode a sampan down the river into the U Minh forest, and she carried with her a typewriter. In the sky above, American aircraft followed. Shackley's station had planted a homing device in the typewriter. Eavesdropping helicopters and planes tracked the typewriter as it moved through the forest. When the signal showed that the typewriter had been still for several days, the Air Force unleashed a massive bombing raid on that spot. Navy SEALs dropped into the bombed-out site for a quick look and were amazed to discover enormous underground chambers that served as a local headquarters for VC. There was much damage. Mudrinich and Shackley had an operation about which they could boast, one that had contributed directly to the war effort.

Shackley's station did not call on the woman again and never learned if her son had survived the assault. "We didn't tell her," Mudrinich said, "that we were going to hurt him."

Other Shackley ROICs were not as fortunate as Mudrinich. Dean Almy, who trained with Shackley in 1951, was the senior man in Region II, which included most of the northern half of the country and covered tough mountainous terrain. It was strategically important territory, but there was little population for the CIA men to mine in this largely rural area. "We didn't have any good agents in II Corps," Almy said. The most productive assets were Vietnamese woodcutters who returned from forays into the jungle and reported on NVA movements.

In Region I, the northernmost part of the country, Shackley's officers targeted the VC and sources on the other side of the demilitarized zone. But during Roger McCarthy's tenure as ROIC, Region I developed no spies in the north. Nor did it find any high-level penetrations that would earn a mark on Shackley's zero chart. At best, McCarthy's outfit squeezed out the same sort of low-level intelligence collected elsewhere. One of the better agents was a young woman who agreed to play the role of VC supporter. Like many southerners, she despised the northerners, all ideology aside. The woman visited communist-controlled portions of the region and returned to report to her handlers on basic VC activities: what they were doing in the villages, what was their propaganda line of the moment; what troop movements were occurring. Her information was always a week or two old, useful but not crucial. Still, any agent was better than none, and the Agency continued to encourage her ventures into enemy turf. On one of those trips she was shot to death in a free-fire zone.

Charles Yothers, the operations chief for Region I, was ever desperate to gain access to a potential source and please the hard-driving Shackley. He wooed a twelve-year-old girl, whose father was a district-level VC officer living in a communist area. The girl often visited her father. Through her, Yothers delivered the father a message: the Americans would help his daughter if he supplied information. There was no threat involved, but it was understandable if the father imagined something bad might befall his child should he tell the Americans no. He agreed to answer questions brought to him by his daughter.

Yothers could not rely on the girl to remember all the queries he wished to pose to his new agent, and it was dangerous for her to carry openly a list of questions. To reach her father, she had to pass through VC and U.S. Marine checkpoints, where civilians were searched. The technical officers of Shackley's station had the solution: a special pair of panties. In the crotch, an Agency seamstress had sewn a hidden pouch. Yothers, using an interpreter, composed a list and put it in the pouch. The girl slipped on the underwear and headed to enemy country.

"We got some information," Yothers recalled. "Nothing I would consider valuable." The operation continued for four or five months. Then one day the girl never came back.*

The one singular success McCarthy and Yothers achieved only provided cause for pessimism. A joint program with a Marine counterintelligence team unearthed VC intelligence archives. The records were discouraging, indicating that the enemy had numerous penetrations of South Vietnamese labor unions, political parties, the National Police, and Special Branch. And a general survey of Region I produced more dark news. Conventional wisdom on the U.S. side held that as a result of the Tet offensive of 1968, the Viet Cong was spent. McCarthy did not see it that way. Pacification was not progressing, and the real situation did not match the optimistic reports that the local CORDS officers sent to Saigon. In McCarthy's region, the VC and NVA regularly bombed, raided, burned, and pillaged refugee centers. The VC was reestablishing itself. "That became more and more evident," McCarthy recalled. "But nobody wanted to put it out, recognize or believe it. That was flying in the face of what Washington wanted to hear."

McCarthy, though, had no compunctions about forwarding reports containing such information to Saigon. "Shackley and I had a few heated exchanges about this," McCarthy noted. His dispatches suggested the U.S. policy of limited warfare in Vietnam was not working. McCarthy never knew what happened to the reports he sent to Saigon, but he suspected that they never were relayed to Washington.

Vietnam was a war of numbers: body counts, bomb tonnage, neutralizations, pacified hamlets. The American inclination to quantify ran wild. Shackley's approach to intelligence fit perfectly. He demanded production and to see it in numbers. He notified CIA people he expected a certain amount of reports each month. To many of the field officers, Shackley's guideline was a rigid quota, proof that he had the soul of a

---

* Twenty-two years later, Yothers, sitting in the basement office of the Washington apartment building he managed, paused at this point in the story. His voice cracked. "I assumed," he continued, "that she got hit by a mortar, zapped by a plane or an artillery shell, or hit by the VC"—while traveling through no-man's-land for a CIA officer anxious to bolster his reporting output and gain Shackley's favor. Yothers no longer remembered her name.

bureaucrat. There was an argument in favor of establishing concrete expectations. Shackley was in charge of overseeing hundreds of officers spread out across forty-four provinces. Being in command, however, was not the same as being in control. How could he really know what was going on outside Saigon? Quotas guaranteed work would be done. But Shackley wielded this bureaucratic tool with the same heavy hand that characterized his entire management style.

As they did with the zero chart, the ROICs tried not to pay too much notice to the chief's demand for numbers. "Shackley liked to keep score," Mudrinich said. "He liked statistics. It cranked people up. . . . There were bad operations to fill out the numbers. That will happen. There is no question about it. But we didn't have the luxury of taking three or four years to recruit someone. . . . It irked a lot of people: numbers, numbers, numbers."

It was not only the numbers that upset some of Shackley's people. Certain reports counted less than others. Charles Yothers discovered that when a reliable contact in the South Vietnamese military told him that Vietnamization was not proceeding smoothly, his record of the conversation did not qualify in the eyes of Shackley's station as a report. If five proven sources told him the same, then maybe Yothers could turn the material into a report deemed suitable for dissemination in Washington. But he could not report on this discouraging subject too often. "There were certain things that D.C. and Saigon didn't want to hear," he explained. "You develop a sixth sense about that, and that included anything negative about Vietnamization. You might send it in once and then get a memo back: we've already heard about this. In effect, you don't report on this any more. The name of the game in reporting is to get a report to the White House, to have somebody respond, 'This is interesting material, can you get something more?' If someone in Saigon says don't give us any more on this, you just know you will have trouble getting it out of the country. And then you won't meet the reporting requirement for the month. My goal was to meet the goal levied on me. I wanted Region I recognized as a better region for reporting. I was competing."

III

By the time Shackley became chief spook there, Vietnam meant many different things: a tragedy, a disaster, geopolitics gone mad, a noble stand against the communists, the ugly-but-unavoidable imperative of the domino theory. Though most Agency people accepted the mission without question, there were nonbelievers. Earlier one officer quit the service rather than take the job of chief of station. Now Vietnam was a posting accepted with little enthusiasm. The Far East Division literally drafted bodies to send to Vietnam. It was not uncommon for an officer accustomed to meeting contacts in the Place de la Concorde to be dumped into a rural province and told to produce spies. The results were predictable.

Charles Yothers, who worked on the Guatemala coup in 1954 and tracked Soviet intelligence officers in Vienna, hated Vietnam every day he was there. "I didn't speak the language," he explained. "There were such cultural differences. Corruption and bribery were increasing. You end up cursing the fools you're trying to help. And you pull back into a position: I'm going to sustain my career and move forward." Everywhere he turned, he encountered one more reason to wonder what the hell he was doing in Vietnam. Unshaven GIs were running around in head-bands. Soldiers were dealing heroin. News from home—the protests, the division, the anger—was depressing.

Some Agency people shared the more laid-back view expressed by another officer: "I didn't mind. I was in Saigon, not with the troops in the jungle. I was well-housed, had a nice office. It was a very pleasant experience." But profoundly negative reactions were not uncommon. Ralph McGehee, a station officer who conducted liaison with the Special Branch, fell into a deep, dark funk. "Every waking moment I fought an internal battle of doubts and contradictions," he said. "I couldn't sleep, my head ached all the time, the tension was terrible. . . . I had no one to talk to about my distress. . . . All I wanted was to be home with my family and away from this awful place."

An officer who worked in Saigon with Shackley had his pessimism reinforced during an interrogation session. A captured VC cadre told him that one night, a U.S. helicopter was shot down near his village. The local Viet Cong leaders assumed the chopper contained a homing de-vice, which would allow U.S. forces to track it. Fearing an attack, the villagers spent the whole night burying the helicopter. "They actually buried a helicopter in one night," this officer recalled. "For some rea-son, that really hit me. It showed that these people would do anything."

Shackley's war was in Saigon. For many Agency people, it was possible to spend two years in Vietnam and never see more than the raunchy, crowded capital. Shackley rarely left the city, which set some senior field officers to grumbling. The ROICs also complained about Shackley's proposal to maintain a six-man team in each province—even where the targets were few. But Shackley had it all worked out: more officers in the field meant more intelligence. "Let me tell you the latest from Sai-gon," Flitcroft griped to an associate. "Ted Shackley . . . is now personally making all assignments, at all levels. I no longer have any control. You want to know what else? He's got a new concept. He just declared that from here on out each province is going to have a six-man team. . . . I

Ted Shackley was an intense and confident young man. This year-book photo was taken in 1950, the year before he joined the Central Intelligence Agency. (Courtesy of *The Terrapin*, University of Maryland)

Ted Shackley (third from the right in the rear) stands with the History Honors Society at the University of Maryland. (Courtesy of *The Terrapin*, University of Maryland)

ABOVE: Lucien Conein (standing on left) was one of Shackley's first CIA colleagues, when the two worked together in the Nuremberg base in the early 1950s. (Courtesy of Lucien Conein)

William Harvey, the legendary CIA spymaster, selected Shackley for a tour of duty at the prestigious Berlin base in the 1950s and then assigned him to the secret JMWAVE base in Miami in 1962.

In the 1950s, the CIA's Berlin base was home for the elite of the CIA. There Shackley and scores of ambitious case officers waged mostly futile espionage programs against the Soviet bloc. (Jan Rohl)

From the JMWAVE base, Miami station chief Shackley in the early 1960s supervised dozens of case officers and hundreds of agents plotting sabotage and espionage operations against Cuba. Though the station achieved little success, Shackley impressed the CIA's top brass and came to be considered a potential leader of the Agency. (*Harper's*)

Richard Helms, CIA Director from 1966 to 1973, chose Shackley as station chief for Laos. Helms worried that Shackley was not a team player, but he believed the posting to Vientiane would teach him how to work with others. (AP/Wide World Photos)

BELOW: Shackley stands on the runway at the Long Tieng base in Laos. Here he ran a secret war that left tens of thousands of tribespeople dead or displaced.

Known as Spook Heaven, the Long Tieng base in Laos was the secret headquarters of the Hmong tribal army that Shackley directed. (Gary and Brenda Peters)

General Vang Pao (center), the paramount leader of the CIA-backed tribal army, reads about the Vietnam War in *Newsweek* in 1968. At first, Vang Pao could not stand the demanding Shackley, but the two ambitious men soon formed an effective partnership in covert warfare. (Gary and Brenda Peters)

From the CIA's station within the U.S. embassy in Saigon, Shackley directed a sprawling intelligence operation that failed to penetrate the enemy and that overlooked the weaknesses of the Saigon regime. (AP/Wide World Photos)

In 1972, CIA headquarters ordered Shackley from Saigon to Washington to become chief of the Western Hemisphere Division. His prime task was to rid the division of all traces of Philip Agee, a former case officer who was writing a tell-all account of his CIA days. Shackley relentlessly prosecuted a purge and oversaw a spying operation against Agee.
(Courtesy of Philip Agee)

William Colby, CIA Director from 1973 to 1976, talks with Senator Frank Church (left). In 1973, Church ran an investigation into CIA activity in Chile—an inquiry that Shackley conspired to mislead.
(AP/Wide World Photos)

Shackley (seated in the rear on the far left) joins several U.S. officials, all grasping for reasons for hope, in a meeting with President Thieu (far right) in the last days of South Vietnam. At the table are U.S. Ambassador Graham Martin and General Frederick Weyand (second and third from the right, respectively). (David Hume Kennerly)

As an officer in the Saigon station, Frank Snepp wrote reports and briefings for Shackley. After the fall of Saigon, Snepp concluded that Shackley and the rest of the CIA were whitewashing the Agency's poor performance in Vietnam. Snepp resigned to write a book and became the target of a spying campaign directed by Shackley and other senior officers. (Courtesy of Frank Snepp)

ABOVE RIGHT: Thomas Polgar succeeded Shackley as Saigon station chief and with Shackley shared responsibility for the faulty intelligence that came out of Saigon in 1975, the final year of the war. (AP/Wide World Photos)

RIGHT: Rogue ex-CIA officer Edwin Wilson exits a federal courthouse in 1982 after being found guilty of arms-smuggling. Shackley's curious relationship with Wilson led to the end of Shackley's CIA career. (UPI/Bettmann Newsphotos)

For over twenty-five years, Shackley rose quickly through the CIA—until President Jimmy Carter appointed Admiral Stansfield Turner to be CIA Director. Turner had an uneasy relationship with Langley's old guard, including Shackley, whom he pushed out of the operations directorate. (AP/Wide World Photos)

LEFT: After being driven out of the CIA, Shackley wrote a slim book, *The Third Option,* advocating the greater use of covert warfare. For many years, this 1981 book jacket portrait was the only publicly available photo of the Blond Ghost.

LEFT: Years after he worked with Shackley in Laos, retired Air Force General Richard Secord became a central figure in the Iran-Contra scandal and was called to testify before Congress. (AP/Wide World Photos)

Shackley tried to recruit Iranian businessman Albert Hakim as a CIA asset in 1976. After he left the Agency in 1979, Shackley entered into a business arrangement with Hakim—an endeavor that drew Shackley into the Iran-Contra affair. (AP/Wide World Photos)

Tom Clines, a lifelong friend of Shackley's, worked with him in Miami, Laos, and Washington. After both were tarred by the Edwin Wilson affair, they went into business together. Clines then joined Secord and Hakim in running the secret Contra operation and aiding the Reagan administration's covert arms sales to Iran. He was the only Iran-Contra player to serve a jail sentence. (Courtesy of Tom Clines)

Shackley eluded the Iran-Contra congressional committees and an independent counsel, but he became the chief target of a highly publicized lawsuit filed by the Christic Institute. A company that produced Iran-Contra trading cards devoted one card to Shackley. (© Salim Yaqub, from *Iran-Contra Scandal Trading Cards,* Eclipse Enterprises, 1988)

Following years of exposure and controversy, Shackley faded from public sight. But he attended reunions of old spooks and spoke at the occasional conference. In 1991, he gave a talk on Capitol Hill sponsored by a conservative foreign policy group, where this photograph was taken. (Brad Markel)

was just about to close up half our province offices, but instead we are not only going to keep them open, we're going to beef them up. The first batch is coming in [to] Song Be [in Phuoc Long province]. Six guys living in [a] little shack up there waiting for mortars every night and the good chance of getting overrun every day. If anyone can explain that, please do. Personally it seems pretty obvious Saigon doesn't know what the fuck's going on."

In the spring of 1969, as part of his six-man policy, Shackley sent George French, a case officer, to Tay Ninh province, a hot area that bordered Cambodia and was a center of VC activity. French moved into the old villa that served as the local Agency post. He and his colleagues tried to make it out to the villages to check on VC and NVA action, but they could not travel the roads due to enemy action. (One time a mortar round hit the CIA villa and knocked out its radio.) Night after night, B-52 raids shook the countryside. "The bombs would level the whole country," French recalled, "and then the NVA would come out from under the ground." What he saw in Tay Ninh disenchanted French. This war was not going to be won.

Nevertheless, French attempted to use Agency-controlled Provincial Reconnaissance Units to attack the local VC infrastructure. The Americans at the base tried to cultivate their own intelligence networks. But French and his comrades achieved little. They devoted most of their time to staying alive. After he had been in Tay Ninh for several weeks, French saw Shackley in Saigon. "You're not getting much," the chief said sharply. French had no reply for him. He was glad his tour in Vietnam was near its end.

Despite all the paper-shuffling regarding Shackley's withdrawal of the CIA from Phoenix, the chief maintained a watch over the program. The men who headed Phoenix—in succession, Evan Parker, Jr., John Mason, and John Tilton—all came from the Agency, and Shackley was in close contact with each. In the provinces, Shackley's officers still participated in Phoenix. "Shackley was happy to have CORDS be identified as the mother hen [of Phoenix]," Roger McCarthy, the ROIC in Region I, recalled. "But the Agency was very much involved in the Phoenix program." Some CIA province officers directed the local Phoenix activity. In his area, McCarthy attempted to raise the standards, so that only suspects authenticated as VC or communist collaborators were grabbed by the PRUs and other security units. As expected, the number of people apprehended fell. "I didn't play the numbers game," McCarthy noted, "and that did not endear me to Brother Ted."

Phoenix remained a program rife with problems and ripe for popular misunderstanding. In late 1969 and early 1970, a string of media reports brought Phoenix to the American public's attention, with accounts describing it as an assassination campaign connected to the CIA. About this time, a DDI analyst assigned to Shackley's station surveyed the Phoenix program and did not like what he encountered. "I got disgusted when I tried to find out how they authenticated their information," he recalled. "They captured people. And how did they determine what kind of enemy they were? The provincial police would say so-and-so is a secret VC and we have to neutralize. Well, how did they know? We couldn't get authentication. It was a rampant problem throughout the war. By mid-1969, a lot of innocent people were being captured by South Vietnamese security and disposed of."

Shackley had transferred responsibility for Phoenix to the U.S. military and CORDS, but his officers were mired in its muck. And Shackley retained control of the program that to many observers represented Phoenix and that often was the source of the deaths and excesses attributed to Phoenix: the Provincial Reconnaissance Units.

Ever since the Phoenix program became a subject of controversy, its apologists have argued the point, with some justification, that Phoenix was merely a clearinghouse for intelligence. The action arms of the counterinsurgency effort—which used Phoenix information for their operations—were the National Police, the Special Branch, local military units, and the paramilitary PRUs. Most were controlled by the South Vietnamese and guided by American military officers. But the PRUs, reputed as the best VC hunters of the bunch, belonged to Shackley's station. Their members were Vietnamese, some NVA defectors, some former VC, some ex-convicts; their advisers were often Agency officers. These small bands were supposed to answer to the local South Vietnamese civilian province chief. The Agency, though, controlled them in the way that counted most: money. The Saigon station's bill for the PRUs averaged $7 million a year. They were a private army, directed by Shackley and his lieutenants.* In Saigon, Tucker Gouglemann, a big and noisy former Marine, supervised the PRU program. His deputy, William Buckley, oversaw the day-to-day operations of the PRUs.†

As the war was different in each province, so were the PRUs. In some places they were corrupt bumblers. Certain PRUs, according to their CIA advisers, were stand-up outfits that went by the book. Others were filled

---

* The PRUs were a Nixon favorite. At a Washington meeting in 1969, a White House aide suggested funds for the PRUs be cut. "No," Nixon said. "We've got to have more of this. Assassinations. Killings. That's what they're [the enemy] doing."

† Years later, Buckley would be kidnapped, tortured, and killed in Beirut, Lebanon, and become one of the most famous CIA officers in history.

with brutal warriors deserving of their harsh reputation. Stories spread of PRUs that sliced off the ears or cut out internal organs of the suspected VC they killed. The PRUs, Shackley's ROICs asserted, generally were not out to murder people but to collect VC suspects and intelligence. "But," Flitcroft admitted, "they did kill people." Mudrinich, the ROIC in Region IV, made the same point: "They killed a lot of people, but their primary purpose was to pick up VC in their home or village, bring them out and debrief them for intelligence." And Dean Almy, the ROIC in Region II, noted, "The idea was not to go out and kill people but to capture people. But, of course, there was a war going on. With the PRUs people got killed, and I'm sure there were innocent people getting killed."

Were these deaths CIA assassinations? They certainly were rung up by the local Phoenix office and Shackley's station as "neutralizations." In December of 1969 in Quang Tri, the northernmost province, a PRU mounted a raid that killed seven VC suspects and captured eight. Several of the captives were district-level cadres. But the PRU did not bother to exploit the prisoners for intelligence purposes. Instead, it shot five of the suspects in the head. This was, literally, an execution funded by Shackley's station.

Years after the war, Shackley provided his own version of the PRU program. The PRUs, he wrote, were well-disciplined, smooth-running units that used "solid intelligence" to conduct "surgical" operations "to capture or eliminate a particular Viet Cong cell." In one six-month period, Shackley boasted, his PRUs captured 3,000 VC and killed about 700, while suffering only 60 or so deaths. They attacked, he poetically observed, "with the suddenness of a thunderclap." His account did not refer to the conflict in the program's goals—intelligence gathering versus neutralization—or the messiness that ensued in Quang Tri and many other locales. Shackley proudly considered his PRUs a textbook case of how to fight communists.

On the evening of June 20, 1969, Thai Khac Chuyen sat alone in an interrogation room in a military compound in Nha Trang. Two men entered. One held him down, the other administered two shots of morphine. The pair bound him, carried him to a truck, and drove to a nearby military boat launch. With the help of two others, they placed Chuyen in an assault boat. Three of the men jumped aboard. Under cover of a moonless night, the boat chugged down the dark river and out to the South China Sea. Chuyen started to stir. One of the three struck him with a .45.

Close to midnight the boat stopped. As the vessel bobbed, two of the men attached a chain and four tire rims to Chuyen. One placed a silencer-equipped .22-caliber pistol against Chuyen's head and pulled the trigger. Chuyen's skull exploded. Two of the men heaved the body overboard. It sank into the sea.

One more death in a war that had claimed scores of thousands—but one with a difference. The men who murdered Chuyen were Green Berets, and they were acting, they believed, with the tacit approval of Ted Shackley. With the execution of Chuyen, they precipitated the worst scandal to strike the Saigon station during Shackley's tenure.

The episode began weeks earlier, when a darkroom technician at the Nha Trang headquarters of Detachment B-57 of the 5th Special Forces —the elite Green Berets—printed a shot from a roll of film captured after a battle. The photo showed a group of North Vietnamese soldiers. One man with wide ears in the front row looked like Chuyen. Detachment B-57 was an intelligence unit that, in coordination with Shackley's station, conducted highly sensitive operations to support Nixon's secret war in Cambodia. Chuyen, a South Vietnamese citizen, was an interpreter and operative for a B-57 sergeant named Alvin Smith.

Smith took the photo to his superiors, Captain Budge Williams and Captain Bob Marasco. There was a resemblance, but it was by no means definitive. As the Green Berets studied the earlobes of the man in the photo, they pondered a ghastly question: Was Chuyen an enemy penetration? Captain Lee Brumley, head of counterintelligence for the Green Berets, and Major David Crew, the new chief of B-57, were informed of the potential problem.

On June 10, 1969, Crew and Williams had a routine meeting in the Saigon station with two of Shackley's officers: Bruce Scrymgeour and Clement Enking. Crew and Williams reported they might have a double agent in their midst. Turning him over to the South Vietnamese, Crew and Williams explained, would be a disaster. He might blab about B-57's unilateral operations. Could Shackley's station put Chuyen on ice somewhere, until the Green Berets figured out his story? No, the CIA men replied, as they puffed on their cigarettes.

Shackley's officers recognized the dilemma. If Chuyen was bad, he could compromise the most secret side of the war. What should they do? the Green Berets asked. Enking exhaled smoke and, according to the Green Berets, said: "Well, you know, the most effective course of action may well be to get rid of him." He then quickly added, "Officially, we can't approve anything like that." Crew and Williams departed, believing they had as clear a sign as one could expect in the murky intelligence business.

Chuyen was polygraphed, shot with truth serum, deprived of sleep, interrogated. His answers were inconsistent, suggesting that perhaps he had been in touch with the North Vietnamese. But there was nothing conclusive, no confession. The Green Berets contacted the local CIA.

Dean Almy, the ROIC for Region II, and his deputy were out of town. That left Harold Chipman, the operations chief, in charge. Having served with Shackley in Berlin and Miami, he was considered a protégé of the chief.* On June 17, Chipman showed Crew and Brumley into his office. The two asked once more if the Agency would take Chuyen off their hands. Chipman said no. Crew noted that Enking had suggested that eliminating Chuyen might be the only course. What would Shackley think of that? Crew asked. According to the Green Berets, Chipman replied, "He won't have any objections to this, considering all the people that disappeared when he was in Laos."

Crew and Brumley then reported to Colonel Robert Rheault, commander of all the Green Berets. The two explained their problem with Chuyen and recounted the informal advice they had received at Shackley's station. Pressed by Rheault, Crew recommended executing Chuyen. Make up a plan, Rheault ordered, and obtain a clear line of guidance from Shackley's station.

The next day, Crew and Brumley twice visited Chipman, in search of an unambiguous signal from Shackley. Chipman had none for them. The following morning, he sent a priority cable to Saigon asking for a response to an inquiry he had forwarded previously. Perhaps, the Green Berets thought, this was the Agency's way of delivering a message. They had queried Shackley's men repeatedly for permission to execute Chuyen. No one in the Company had said no.

In Saigon for a meeting, Dean Almy on June 19 received a cable from Chipman. His operations officer, whom Shackley had touted as a star, was screwing up. Why didn't he just tell the Green Berets to find their own way out of the jam? The Green Berets, Almy thought, should turn Chuyen over to some locals who would know what to do with him. Well, Almy concluded, Chipman was Shackley's guy, so let Shackley handle this. An annoyed Almy took Chipman's cable to Shackley, but Dana Meiggs, Shackley's protective secretary, would not let him into the chief's office. Shackley was in a vital meeting. This was important, Almy protested. Meiggs took the envelope with the cable in it, plopped it in her desk, and said she would make sure that Shackley received it.

That day the Green Berets again pressed Chipman, who could only report there was no response from Shackley. This was damn ridiculous,

---

* Almy did not think much of Chipman. "Shackley surrounded himself with yes-men," he recalled. "It was his biggest weakness. They always got him into trouble. Chipman had poor judgment."

the Green Berets thought. No response had to mean something; it had to mean "go." The next morning, June 20, Crew paid another visit to Chipman. The operations man had nothing to say. Later in the day, Crew returned to the CIA's Nha Trang compound with Brumley. Almy was back. Had Shackley gotten their message? the Green Berets asked. He got it, Almy said, though he knew there was a chance the cable was sitting in Meiggs's desk. "There's nothing we can do for you," he remarked. "I'm sorry."

The two Green Berets left, realizing that the Agency still had not told them *not* to kill Chuyen. Later that night Chuyen was murdered. Brumley, Williams, and Marasco were on the boat; Marasco pulled the trigger. Crew supervised the operation, and Warrant Officer Edward Boyle helped.

The next day, Chipman gave Crew a telex from Shackley. Advise the Special Forces, Shackley had written, that the Agency had no interest in the Chuyen case, that eliminating him "is no solution to the problem, that it is immoral and has the highest flap potential." Shackley noted that if his officers in Nha Trang could not obtain the assurance that Chuyen was safe, then he had no alternative but to bring this affair to the attention of General Abrams and Ambassador Bunker. Crew informed Almy and Chipman that Chuyen had been sent on a secret mission and could not be reached.

When Shackley read the response from Nha Trang—Chuyen was somewhere in Cambodia and could not be recalled—he smelled a cover story. The man must be dead, he thought. Now Shackley had to make sure his backside was protected. He brought his suspicions first to Bunker and then to Abrams. In Abrams's bungalow, Shackley explained to the general that this was an Army problem. I'll get back to you, Abrams said. Don't bother, Shackley replied. He did not want anything else to do with this.

Shackley was prescient. One of the biggest scandals of the war was about to kick off. When Abrams queried Rheault on the matter, the colonel lied and stuck to the cover story. For a week, the story held. Then Sergeant Smith, Chuyen's handler, cracked. He had opposed Chuyen's murder and now feared his colleagues planned to do to him what they did to Chuyen. His nerves frayed, he headed to the CIA office in Nha Trang, requested asylum, and revealed that Chuyen had been killed. Smith's account triggered a full-fledged investigation. Two Army investigators soon pieced together what had occurred.

On July 13, the two Army detectives, Frank Bourland and Bob Bidwell, sat in a U.S. Army briefing room with three generals, Shackley, and Clement Enking. The detectives noted that their interviews with the

Green Berets indicated that perhaps the B-57 officers were encouraged, if not directed, by the CIA to kill Chuyen. "I advised Major Crew that eliminating Chuyen could not be approved," Enking explained to Bourland and Bidwell. "However, I did say it was the most efficient course of action." Bidwell asked Shackley if he could question him and Enking. "I'm not being interviewed by a military policeman," Shackley declared. And what about Enking? Bidwell asked. "We'll see," Shackley said and left with Enking. The next day when Bidwell stopped by Shackley's station and asked for Enking, a receptionist told him that Enking was no longer in Vietnam.

On July 14, Crew was apprehended and taken to the military stockade in Long Binh. He was soon joined there by Brumley, Marasco, and Williams, as well as Major Tom Middleton, who had participated in the planning of the murder. On July 21, Colonel Rheault, the man in charge of the Army's most prestigious branch, was arrested for murder.

The subsequent legal proceedings posed serious problems for Shackley. On July 31, in the Long Binh chapel, the Army opened a preliminary hearing. During the secret session, lawyers for the defendants presented a list of persons they wanted to call to the stand: Clement Enking, Bruce Scrymgeour, Harold Chipman, Dean Almy, and Ted Shackley. With rain pounding on the chapel's tin roof, the attorneys requested a large amount of CIA information, including "a list of all terminations with extreme prejudice since 1961 [and] a list of all terminations with extreme prejudice in the Provincial Recon Unit." Captain John Stevens Berry, a defense attorney, explained that termination with extreme prejudice is what happened to agents who outlived their usefulness. The lawyers for the Green Berets wanted to pin the rap on Shackley's CIA. If that did not work, they planned to make this trial as uncomfortable for the Agency as possible.

During the proceeding, Kenneth Facey, Rheault's deputy, testified that if Shackley's station knew a man was about to be eliminated and did nothing, that was, for all practical matters, a go-ahead from the CIA. After all, the money that paid for the Green Berets' agents, like Chuyen, came from the Agency. Army detective Bidwell detailed how Shackley had blocked his efforts to investigate the CIA role in the case.

Up to now, the Green Beret affair was a secret. But it turned into front-page news after George Gregory, an attorney for one of the accused, spilled the basics of the case to reporters—but with a twist or two. In Gregory's account, the CIA had confirmed Chuyen's status as a double agent and suggested that he be either isolated or "terminated with extreme prejudice." This term, *The New York Times* reported, "is said to be an intelligence euphemism for execution."

It was not. But the phrase was to be enshrined in popular spook lexicon.* The press jumped on the story. It had all the elements: murder, intrigue, spies, dashing soldiers, interservice rivalry. Throughout August, stories appeared in papers and newsmagazines. One running theme in the press accounts was, what was going on behind the scenes? What was the CIA's part in this mysterious affair? Did Shackley's station routinely terminate with extreme prejudice? Why all the bother over this one suspected spy? There had to be more involved, journalists speculated, than a foul-up.

But that was most of the story. The Green Berets had botched a counterintelligence case, and Shackley's subordinates fouled up by not turning off the murder plan. Then Shackley handed the Green Berets legal ammunition by not cooperating with the investigation.

In Washington, members of Congress from the districts of the accused Green Berets decried their treatment at the hands of the Army. Heavy-weight civilian lawyers joined the defense team. The case was getting big, and the CIA was caught in the wringer.

On the night of August 19, Stanley Resor, the Secretary of the Army, was in a field headquarters in Bien Hoa, when an aide told him that Shackley was outside and wished to have a word with him. Resor joined Shackley, and the two walked into the shadows. The CIA had not ordered the murder, Shackley explained. So would the Army be good enough to issue a statement clarifying matters? Resor rejected the request. The facts would have to come out at the trial. Resor could not clear the Agency. Shackley's face twitched, and he moved off into darkness.

The next morning, Harold Chipman took the stand at the continuing pretrial hearing in Long Binh. Chipman testified that the CIA never assassinates. Defense attorney George Gregory asked Chipman what he knew of "a Phoenix operation." "It is a program," Chipman answered and dodged further questions about it. When Gregory ended his questioning, an exasperated Chipman declared, "You just don't shoot an agent."

Chipman was right. The CIA was not in the habit of disposing of agents in that fashion. But the defense attorneys were eager to muddy waters. Phoenix did involve murders—even if (as CIA people asserted) only as unintended consequences of planned snatch operations. But the targets were Viet Cong suspects, not double agents. Toward the end of Chipman's testimony, Henry Rothblatt, another defense lawyer, asked if

---

* In the 1980 film *Apocalypse Now,* the protagonist is ordered to "terminate with extreme prejudice" an American warlord in the jungles of Indochina.

he had told Major Crew that Shackley had been responsible for 250 political killings in Laos. "I can't answer that," Chipman replied.

Langley dispatched John Greaney, one of its lawyers, to Saigon. Get this case off my back, Shackley demanded of him. The affair was consuming his days, and a terrible possibility loomed: Shackley in the witness chair in a public trial. Not only would he be asked about all those secret programs his station was running in Vietnam, the defense lawyers surely would question him about operations in Berlin, Cuba, and Laos.

Shackley's position, on points, was strong. When he had learned of the problem with Chuyen, he ordered the Special Forces to return their agent to duty. When they replied that Chuyen was on a secret mission, Shackley reported his suspicions through channels. But Greaney was telling him that, in order for the defendants to receive a fair trial, he might have to submit himself to a slew of queries. "Jesus Christ, you Benedict Arnold," Shackley said. "What are you trying to do to me?"

On September 18, the Army declared the court-martials would begin in October. The announcement followed an assurance from Langley that the defense could call Agency officials as witnesses. But Nixon was discomfited by the prospect of a trial that might reveal aspects of his secret war in Cambodia. He sent a note to Kissinger: "I think Helms should be made to take part of this rap."

Responding to Nixon's wishes, the Agency reversed itself; it would not permit its men to testify. On September 29, Army Secretary Resor, noting that the defendants could not receive a fair trial without being able to call CIA witnesses, ordered that all the charges be dropped. The case was over. Ted Shackley would not have to testify. But his station was taking the fall. The public could only guess what odious CIA connection to the case had prevented the court-martial of the Green Berets. The Agency's move appeared to back defense contentions that Shackley's station had something to hide. The antiwar movement obtained more fodder. Working relations between the CIA and both the Green Berets and the U.S. Army were now strained. The CIA was further soiled. But Shackley was safe.

Despite the distraction of the Green Beret case, station operations continued, and by late 1969 Shackley finally had what he most desired —a penetration of COSVN, the enemy command. This spy, the only true prize that Shackley's station would produce, had been in development for several years by officers in Tay Ninh province, where Agency operations were mostly a bust. Charles Stainbach, a career officer previously stationed in Afghanistan and Pakistan, arrived in Tay Ninh in the summer of 1969 as the province officer in charge and found a disaster. The finances were in disarray, the reporting atrocious.

Stainbach was not high on the war. "By this point, we had no business being there," he reminisced. "We were supporting a Saigon government that did not represent the people of South Vietnam." But his job was to produce reports on the VC, not worry about the grand picture. In the administrative clutter of the base, he discovered that it had for years participated in a Special Branch operation that ran an agent, a South Vietnamese man in his thirties who lived in Tay Ninh and had VC relatives. But he had been handled sloppily, and his reporting was a jumble of opinions and observations. What the base had in this second-rate source was the best agent Shackley's station would ever know.

Code-named HACKLE, the agent was the brother of a district-level Viet Cong official and had close access to the VC province chief. Since Tay Ninh was so near COSVN headquarters, which moved about in the area over the border in Cambodia, the VC officers there were the first to receive directions from COSVN. HACKLE could tap into the pipeline early. The original contact with HACKLE had occurred through a family connection. HACKLE's primary motivation was political. He held no affection for the corrupt government of Saigon, but he disliked the interlopers from the north who dominated the VC.

Stainbach moved to transform HACKLE into a professional spy. The agent passed a polygraph. He was taught to be a dispassionate observer. He was instructed on the basics, such as emergency contact procedures. HACKLE met with his South Vietnamese Special Branch control officer a few times a month, never with Stainbach. If Stainbach should fall into enemy hands, he did not want to be able to identify Shackley's best spy. To protect the agent, Shackley's station shared little of the take from HACKLE with the various South Vietnam intelligence outfits. The Agency even persuaded HACKLE's South Vietnamese handlers not to report on HACKLE through their own official channels.

The material from HACKLE was the best intelligence of the war. He returned with verbal reports and documents on VC plans and policy guidance. "This was as close as we got to having somebody working in the equivalent of Hitler's bunker," analyst Frank Snepp said. HACKLE's penetration of COSVN was limited, since enemy operations were still highly segmented. He did not learn much about communist activities in the northern part of the country. But a few times HACKLE produced advance word of a pending attack.

One of HACKLE's most important contributions was verifying captured VC documents. His confirmation of COSVN Resolution No. 9 was an important success for Shackley. The document was found by a U.S. military patrol in the second half of 1969. The long paper contained the communists' pessimistic assessment of the Tet offensive of 1968 and following events. It indicated that the Viet Cong were planning to rebuild for several years. "We have not yet produced any leaping development of decisive significance in our struggle against the enemy," the document read. It listed the problems: slow development of guerrilla forces, combat inefficiency of its conventional troops, and a disappointing level of recruitment for its political organizations. If true, this was encouraging news for Washington, an indication that the enemy intended to build up its forces and shy away from direct military confrontation. It signaled it was safe to continue with Vietnamization.

Shackley ordered an all-out effort to confirm the authenticity of the paper. As part of that, HACKLE was asked to find out if Resolution 9 was real. He reported to the CIA that it was genuine. HACKLE also told his patrons that the North Vietnamese had no plans to step up the infiltration of guerrillas into the south and would reduce their battalion-size units in the delta. Shackley was able to forward to headquarters the most welcome of intelligence, that which supported Washington's policy. HACKLE was a bold mark for the chief's zero chart. Shackley informed his officers the White House was impressed with this operation.

Intelligence material does not always lend itself to one interpretation. HACKLE's reports contained promising information for the short term. But they also reinforced Stainbach's pessimistic impression. The VC were still rebuilding after Tet. There was no decrease in will. Much of the reporting out of Shackley's station proclaimed improvements in the security of the countryside. In Tay Ninh, Stainbach saw, the VC remained active, but for the time being were ducking confrontations. The enemy was neither gone nor defeated.

Shackley strived to send Washington reports that bolstered confidence. He was part of the team that was supposed to win the war. One paper produced by his station in December of 1969 declared that the "initial stages of Vietnamization have been achieved successfully." But the study could not avoid all reality. "Much of the population and many in the armed forces," it noted, "have not yet developed a strong commitment to the governmental structure of South Vietnam. These well-known handicaps do not yield easily to the assistance and pressure of U.S. influence." This report, read carefully, suggested that after years of fighting and political maneuvering, Washington was battling for a government that lacked the support of its own people. "But," the paper concluded, "Vietnam is stronger militarily and politically today than ever before."

Near this time, a case officer in the delta, a Shackley favorite, had formed an association with a Vietnamese citizen who was close to a regional Viet Cong functionary. The potential existed for another espionage coup. The subject eventually agreed to spy for the Americans. From his desk in Saigon, Shackley issued specific orders on how the agent should be handled. The agent twice failed polygraph examinations. Yet Shackley insisted the operation proceed.* By the summer of 1970, this new agent was producing intelligence on COSVN and enemy supply routes. Not too long afterward, he was exposed as a fabricator. In the field, Agency officers viewed the affair as a profound embarrassment for their chief. "Shackley had distinguished himself as a manager," said one of his province officers, "not as a recruiter or a runner of operations. The sense among people was that he was taken in by all this because it was not part of what he was good at. He could run an organization of hundreds, but he got really suckered on this."

IV

In the middle of 1969, Shackley traveled to Langley to brief his comrades. Sam Adams, the obsessive doom-saying analyst who had ruffled feathers during the VC order of battle controversy, was not allowed to attend the session. But he prompted a friend to ask Shackley how many Viet Cong agents had penetrated the South Vietnamese army. "Well," Shackley replied, "the South Vietnamese Military Security Service has about 300 suspects under consideration. I think that about covers it." Shackley's answer was way off, according to Adams. He and another analyst had been studying captured documents regarding a Viet Cong unit that recruited agents in the South Vietnamese army and National Police. The two had discovered references to 1,000 VC agents. When Adams had mentioned this to Langley's Vietnam branch chief, the officer replied, "For God's sake, don't open that Pandora's box. We have enough troubles as it is."

Adams did not heed the warning. Extrapolating from the documents, he and his partner, Robert Klein, estimated that the VC had 20,000 agents in the army alone, not the 300 to which Shackley referred.

Counterintelligence was the weakest part of the Saigon station's performance in Vietnam. Enemy spies were everywhere. The CIA could protect its own ranks from penetrations. But how could it do the same for the various South Vietnamese security services and the entire Saigon

---

* The use of polygraphs in Vietnam was the subject of a long-running argument within the station. Many officers believed they were ineffective with Asians, due to cultural differences. The lie-detector debate climaxed in 1971, when a number of agents recruited under Shackley failed the flutter. Shackley, usually a stickler for by-the-book security regulations, ordered that the agents' development be continued.

government? CI is troublesome business, particularly when it involves a wartime ally.

Ralph McGehee learned that in 1969, when he was working with the Special Branch in Gia Dinh, the province that with Saigon composed Region V. For more than a year, McGehee's office had supervised a Special Branch project—called the Projectile operation—that targeted a suspected spy ring in the highest reaches of the Thieu government. The information was flimsy and the key source dubious, but the implications were explosive. Two members of the ring, the main source said, were Huynh Van Trong, Thieu's special assistant for political affairs, and Vu Ngoc Nha, Thieu's close friend and unofficial adviser. After new evidence came in, McGehee told the Special Branch he thought it was time to roll up the net. But the Special Branch was not eager to end its best case. Neither was Shackley's station. The ROIC for Region V, who had served under Shackley in Berlin in the 1950s and 1960s, argued that this could be a communist operation aimed at provoking unwarranted arrests of top government officials.* The ROIC told McGehee to review the case.

At this time, the ROIC, whose son had been killed in Vietnam, was directing an extensive campaign against the North Vietnamese intelligence service, the Cuc Nghien Cuu, and VC operatives in Saigon—and enthralled with it. "Most people in Saigon couldn't wait to serve two years and go home," he recalled. "This was the easiest place to operate in I've ever been. It was where I had the most degree of success in my entire career." For years, the Cuc Nghien Cuu had waged elaborate operations in Saigon, with at least five staff officers present in the capital city. (That was a feat the Agency could not match in Hanoi.) The North Vietnamese penetrated every relevant agency of the Saigon government and set up *cums,* or cells, of up to thirty people. The ROIC and his officers, working closely with Colonel Nguyen Mau of the Special Branch, went after the *cums.* In one case, a Cuc Nghien Cuu courier was on the police's payroll. Special Branch teams followed him and trailed his contacts. Joint Agency–Special Branch teams then arrested various members of the spy ring.

Over the course of ten months in 1969, this counterespionage op-

---

* The ROIC for Region V, a Shackley friend, was interviewed for this book, but he agreed to talk only if his name did not appear any place in the book. (Other confidential sources were only promised they would not be identified as the source of particular quotes or information.) At the time of the interviews, the ROIC was a businessman living in a country where U.S. business people were subject to kidnappings. He worried that if his past Agency connection became public, he and his family would be at risk.

eration, overseen by Shackley, broke up several *cums* and captured three or four clandestine radio sets, as well as code pads. With the code pads, National Security Agency analysts deciphered previously intercepted radio messages and tried to identify Hanoi's sources in the south.

Shackley's station conducted a similar crusade against the Viet Cong in Saigon. At the start of 1969, each month Saigon experienced several dozen bombings, shootings, and assassinations. The Viet Cong engineered many of these attacks from bunkers in Tay Ninh province, about fifty miles outside of Saigon. This area was off-limits to the South Vietnamese military. But when the Special Branch picked up a VC, Shackley's station secretly placed a tiny beacon in his sandals and arranged for an escape. U.S. aircraft tracked the signal. Once this VC reached a spot likely to be an enemy base, an air strike was called in to knock out what the CIA officers could only presume was a VC bunker. Eventually, the VC ordered people entering their turf to strip.

To counter the VC sappers in Saigon, the Agency-assisted Special Branch went to extremes, and Shackley's favorite ROIC deliberately looked away. Arrested VC suspects were submitted to brutal questioning sessions at an interrogation center. "The Vietnamese were a very ruthless people," the ROIC said by way of explanation. "The people were so consumed with hate, south and north, and took pleasure in inflicting pain on each other. It was a sick place." The ROIC practiced a selective morality. The professional North Vietnamese intelligence officers he tried to spare. "They were people like me," he remarked. "As for the professional [VC] murderers, what did I do? I looked the other way. I had no mercy with them."

No Americans, the ROIC maintained, were involved directly in the "rough stuff." But Shackley and his officers knew that many VC suspects brought to the interrogation center did not survive questioning. But such harshness led to the results Shackley and the ROIC sought. By year's end, VC sapper incidents had fallen to only several a month.

The ROIC, a tall, slim man with a shock of white hair, found his daily Vietnam experience unreal. He lived in a nice apartment near the cathedral downtown. He had a driver, maid, and cook. He awoke at six in the morning, put on a suit, and ate breakfast with his section chiefs. Some had been out all night with Special Branch arrest teams. Next the ROIC attended Shackley's morning meeting and shared with the chief what his unit had accomplished the previous evening. After that, the ROIC usually played tennis until lunchtime. Following lunch, he and his section chiefs planned that night's operations. After dinner, he returned to his office to finalize the arrest lists. Then he went to a rooftop bar, had a drink or two, and watched the fighting in the distance. Snipers fired on aircraft coming into Saigon. Helicopter gunships in search of the snipers set off flares. Machine-gun fire rattled the night.*

In search of the hard evidence needed to convince the ROIC and Shackley to roll up the *cum* penetrating Thieu's palace, Ralph McGehee turned toward a filing cabinet full of old reports in his office. Among all the paper, he found a discolored, ratty-looking document, an abominable translation of a police report from 1962. McGehee discovered that it referred to a similar spy net that years earlier targeted the Diem government. Several of the Projectile suspects had been part of that group.

Shackley and the ROIC now agreed it was time to apprehend the suspected spies. But Thieu had to be convinced. Shackley dispatched a subordinate to inform the President about the network and the pending arrest plans. Thieu became upset. Let's just dismiss the spies quietly, he suggested. The President worried the publicity would undermine his government. The CIA officer shook his fist at Thieu and asked, How in the hell can the United States justify the expenditure of American lives and money, if communists are everywhere and you take no action against them? An unhappy Thieu yielded.

In July of 1969, Colonel Mau organized a successful raid. Fifty persons were arrested, including Nha (who later confessed), Trong, other government and military officials, and businessmen. House searches unearthed microfilm of secret documents, code pads, invisible ink, and miniature cameras. News of the arrests hit the front page in the United States.

Projectile was a winner, but double-edged for Shackley's station. "While our Projectile operation had been successful beyond any of my dreams," McGehee explained, "this was obviously not the kind of success that the CIA's top officials wanted to see. For the report of the Projectile operation showed that our ally in this longest of wars had a government so riddled by enemy spies that they were able to operate under the nose of the President. It provided further evidence that the CIA had not only stubbornly refused to see the strength of the enemy but also had never acknowledged the weakness of our 'friends.' "

---

* More than two decades later, the ROIC expressed no regrets about his time in Vietnam: "I studied in seminary before I became a soldier and a CIA officer, and what we did does not bother my conscience at all. We were not murdering Vietnamese but saving American and Vietnamese lives. I don't understand all this flagellation about the Phoenix program. We in the CIA did not dump napalm on villages. We did not round up people as was done at the My Lai massacre. We did not conduct random violence. No one suffered from us who wasn't guilty. We just caught the guilty people and punished them severely. Terrorists are not deterred by the thought of sitting in jail for years. What deters terrorists is the idea of swift and summary punishment."

Months after the roundup of this net, Shackley promoted the ROIC to head the Liaison Operation Division, which was in charge of all CIA–Special Branch programs. Shackley hoped his friend would duplicate his Saigon success nationally. But the Special Branch was staffed by incompetents and corrupt officials. Others were tired and burned-out. Shackley's grand expectations went unfulfilled.

In headquarters, analyst Sam Adams had not let go of the bone. He was promoting his conclusion that the Saigon government and military were infested with enemy spies. He was not alone in this concern. On May 11, 1970, NSC aide Laurence Lynn, Jr., sent Kissinger a top-secret memo referring to VC penetrations. He reported that the enemy had possessed advance knowledge of the recent U.S. invasion of Cambodia.* "Although agents have been uncovered," Lynn wrote, "the CIA estimates that no more than 50% of the enemy's agents in the Saigon area have been neutralized. It is possible that the VC still have agents in the highest levels in the [Saigon government]." Lynn prepared a memo for the President from Kissinger. It offered a distressing picture of an ally riddled with thousands of agents and incapable of dealing with the problem. Even the assistant chief of ARVN's counterintelligence bureau, the memo noted, had been a VC agent. The White House fired an order to Richard Helms instructing him to investigate the situation.

Adams continued to press within the bureaucracy his belief that about 30,000 VC agents had burrowed into Saigon's armed forces and government. In September of 1970, the Directorate of Intelligence issued a classified report that embodied Adams's argument: 30,000 enemy agents in the South Vietnam military. "These agents range from highly trained and dedicated agents," the report noted, "to unproductive fencesitters."

If Adams was correct—if Thieu's army was so infiltrated—all of Shackley's endeavors were essentially pointless. The analyst sent a draft copy of his report to Shackley's station for comment. Shackley directed his reports and analysis office of the station to repudiate Adams. But Shackley was not able to control the damage. In October of 1970, an earlier version of the paper leaked to the press. "CIA Says Enemy Spies

---

* In April of 1970, Nixon sent troops into Cambodia. In the United States the move, seen by many as contradictory to the winding-down of the war that Vietnamization purportedly marked, provoked more antiwar protest. Nine months later, Nixon mounted something of a repeat. South Vietnamese troops invaded the Laotian panhandle. Hanoi, according to documents later captured, had been aware of the minute details of the invasion. The offensive turned into a rout, as the NVA ambushed Saigon's troops and forced a chaotic retreat. More than 9,000 South Vietnamese were killed, wounded, or missing; the casualties included 317 Americans.

Hold Vital Posts in Saigon," exclaimed a front-page headline in *The New York Times*. The *Times* article noted that the penetrations undermined the essence of Nixon's Vietnamization program. The study made the whole Vietnam situation look foolish. How could Washington support an ally so infiltrated? The *Times* also noted that the United States and South Vietnam had nothing comparable.*

Whether Adams was right or wrong in the particulars and the degree, the counterintelligence dilemma was real—and largely ignored by Shackley's station and the rest of the Agency. "We never developed a proper counterintelligence operation in Vietnam," said James Graham, a senior Agency analyst in Langley. "By 1970 it was recognized as a problem, but there didn't seem to be the will or resources to do anything about it." In headquarters, James Angleton, the powerful head of counterintelligence, crusaded for more CI in Vietnam. But some officers feared a stronger CI effort was one with the paranoiac Angleton leading the charge. "It was a blindspot," acknowledged Sam Halpern, then an assistant to DDP Tom Karamessines. "I'm sorry we didn't force more CI on the station. It was not just Ted's fault. We didn't do it."

Shackley was in a sort of competition with communist spies, for he, too, was conducting operations against the Saigon government. Shackley had to track what President Thieu was thinking and doing, and he needed to follow all the ambitious South Vietnamese officials who thought they could do a better job than Thieu. The last thing Ambassador Bunker wanted was a coup. Toward this end, Shackley's officers recruited agents in the Special Branch, the Military Security Services, the Central Intelligence Organization, and other agencies of the Saigon government. "We had quite a few high-level paid agents," Lewis Lapham said. "We were not just relying on two or three people, and these agents tended to have a shelf life of years."

The CIA had the government wired. Before Shackley was appointed chief, the Agency had bugged the Presidential Palace by presenting Thieu with television sets and furniture containing hidden microphones. Only the most important American officials in Saigon and Washington saw the "eyes only" transcripts and reports produced by this program.

---

* Adams scored his third assault on the CIA establishment in 1971 when he turned toward studying the number of Khmer Rouge guerrillas in Cambodia. Once again, his figures were dramatically higher than those of others. He concluded the size of the Cambodian communist army was not 5,000 to 10,000 but more in the range of 100,000 to 150,000. "Ted Shackley and everyone else in the Far East division hit the fucking roof on that one," Frank Snepp recalled. Adams left the Agency in 1973. He hoped to write a book on the CIA and Vietnam—to be titled *Who the Hell Are We Fighting Out There?*—but died before completing it. His half-finished memoir was published in 1994, under the title *War of Numbers*.

Shackley supervised all details of the enterprise. He knew that if it were ever uncovered by the Vietnamese, a firestorm would ensue. Not only was it unseemly to bug an ally, disclosure of the eavesdropping would suggest that American soldiers were fighting and dying for a government it did not trust.

Shackley carefully watched the political machinations of Saigon and the noncommunist opposition to Thieu. At parties and receptions, he regularly chatted with Tran Van Don, a senator and a prime opponent of Thieu. Several Shackley subordinates scorned their chief as "Tran Van Shackley" for his seeming reliance on Don for political intelligence. Tran Van Don happily spoke with Shackley, hoping he could demonstrate to the chief that the United States was wrong to throw so much muscle behind Thieu. Not unexpectedly, Don was disappointed. "I had some problems with Shackley," he recalled. "He didn't want to know exactly what was our war. He didn't listen to all the right people, especially the [South] Vietnamese fighting for the people and peace. He was too much in support of the government. Instead of trying to know all the opinions of people in South Vietnam." Don kept Shackley apprised of his plans, calculating it was better for the CIA chief to receive the information firsthand than to obtain it through paid informants. He wanted Shackley to be assured that he was not a communist, a label too often attached to Thieu's opponents. He received little sympathy from Shackley. "At one social engagement," Don said, "he told me, 'We are in South Vietnam to support Thieu's government, not to support the opposition.' I was not glad to hear that."

On the political front, Shackley deployed officers that flitted about Saigon's political circuit. They placed on Shackley's payroll agents of influence—journalists, politicians, and others, including a senator who was paid to support legislation that CORDS wanted. Shackley's political officers funneled funds to the National Social Democratic Front, a pro-regime coalition, but most of the cash ended in the pockets of Thieu's cronies. Station personnel helped Tran Quoc Buu, who led South Vietnam's labor federation, write American labor leaders in search of support for Saigon. "No one in the station's front office," Snepp observed, "seemed bothered by the fact that this was a violation of the CIA charter, which prohibits the Agency from dabbling in U.S. domestic politics." One of Shackley's men, William Kohlmann, persuaded Buddhist leaders to refrain from conducting demonstrations that could embarrass Thieu. Did they accept Kohlmann's advice because he slipped them Shackley-authorized funds? "I'd rather not answer that," Kohlmann said afterward. The Buddhists were relatively quiet during Shackley's tenure, accounting for one of the main successes of his political unit.

Shackley had handed most hearts-and-minds programs to the military and CORDS, but his station ran its own covert actions: propaganda schemes, phony broadcasts, and the like. In the delta, the South Vietnamese picked up infiltrators who kept diaries covering their trip down the Trail. Shackley's men found the best sections—a fellow describing the hardships of life on the Trail—and broadcast them at the enemy courtesy of an Agency-supported radio station called Mother Vietnam. Station officers aired black radio programs—broadcasts that appeared to be originating from Radio Hanoi or a VC station—that contained doctored news stories devised to discourage enemy troops listening. The Agency men hired an astrologer to read on-air fake horoscopes for North Vietnamese leaders. Shackley dropped by the Saigon office of Operation 38, the propaganda outfit, once or twice a week, often with an item for the radio broadcasts. Since some North Vietnamese defectors cited discouraging radio broadcasts as one reason for jumping sides, Shackley and his Op 38 gang believed they were making a difference.

During the 1970 Tet season, Tran Ngoc Chau was on the run. The forty-six-year-old Chau had been the Kien Hoa province chief, the mayor of Da Nang, the head of a CIA-backed pacification training program, and then the secretary-general of the National Assembly. Now he was unfairly denounced by the government as a spy. He expected his old friends in the CIA to help. But Shackley refused.

For years, Chau, a Viet Minh commander who became an anticommunist, had tried to convince American and South Vietnamese officials of what he believed was the essential, but largely ungrasped truth of Vietnam: the conflict was about politics, not military strength. The key, he had been saying for years, was not to kill the VC guerrillas but to win over the Vietnamese people by addressing legitimate complaints. As province chief, Chau pioneered the Census Grievance unit and Counter-Terror team, both of which evolved into CIA programs. It was one of many Vietnam ironies that Chau's projects grew into the Phoenix program, which came to symbolize the murderous side of pacification.

Chau had found a small following among those American advisers who shared his view on this "other war": Edward Lansdale, Daniel Ellsberg, John Paul Vann. But Chau was never a favorite of the U.S. establishment in Vietnam. Nor were his opposition efforts appreciated by Thieu. In the National Assembly, Chau railed against the corruption of Thieu's regime and advocated negotiations with the communists in order to turn the war into a political struggle.

As Chau's countrymen observed Tet, he was dodging Thieu's security officers, for Thieu had discovered a means to bring Chau down. The opportunity came after the Special Branch in April of 1969 arrested an enemy intelligence officer. Under interrogation, Tran Ngoc Hien admitted that he was Chau's brother and that he had been in contact with Chau between 1965 and 1968. Thieu's cronies accused Chau of being a spy and began a campaign to strip him of his parliamentary immunity so he could be imprisoned by a military court. General Quang, Thieu's corrupt aide and one of Shackley's most valued contacts, plotted the moves against Chau. Few Americans in Vietnam could thwart Thieu. But one who could was Ambassador Bunker; another was Ted Shackley. Neither did anything to save Chau.

In 1965 and afterward, Chau had seen his brother, who asked him to help establish a direct channel of communication between Washington and Hanoi. Chau told his close friend John Paul Vann of Hien's request. He also informed a CIA officer of his contact with his brother, but he withheld from the Agency man the information that Hien was a relative. Both the embassy and the CIA station were not interested in this overture.

After Thieu initiated his anti-Chau campaign in mid-1969, Chau's American friends unofficially rallied support for him. John Paul Vann drummed up press reports about Thieu's vindictive crusade against Chau. But no signs of official assistance came from Bunker's embassy or Shackley's station.

When Richard Moose and James Lowenstein, senior aides for the Senate Foreign Relations Committee, visited Saigon at the end of the year, they stopped by Shackley's office to discuss the Chau affair. "We raised hell with him," Moose recalled. Shackley was unmoved. He told Moose and Lowenstein that Chau was working with the communists. "He said that our notion of a Vietnamese nationalist was close to what a loyal American would call a VC," Moose noted. Shackley was not going to intervene. At a dinner Moose attended, he heard Shackley issue a flat statement: Chau is a communist.

The remark was near to a death sentence. If the highest U.S. officials in Vietnam were saying that Chau was a Red, then Thieu could do what he wanted with him. During his stay in Saigon, Moose argued with Shackley. Go back and talk to your own people who had worked with Chau, he urged. Shackley brushed off the suggestion. Moose was outraged: "I didn't see how they could just throw people overboard." Chau's problem was that he fit in nowhere. He opposed communism and supported nationalism. But he wanted to be neither an American puppet nor part of a corrupt regime detached from the populace. The CIA and the embassy had little use for him.

In Washington, officials realized the Chau case was another public relations disaster in the making. In late December of 1969, Elliot Richardson, the undersecretary of state, sent Bunker a cable telling him to stop Thieu's persecution of Chau. Bunker sidestepped the order. Chau could count only on friends. Keyes Beech, the conservative *Los Angeles Times* correspondent, hid Chau from the Special Branch in his own home and wrote several articles based on conversations with Chau, including one that charged that Shackley had tried to buy off Chau. (Start a political party and we will bankroll you, two CIA officers had told Chau. There was only one condition: the party must support Thieu. Chau declined.) In one dispatch, Beech quoted Chau as saying, "If this is a sample of the way the Americans treat their Vietnamese friends, I wonder about the future of thousands of other Vietnamese who have cooperated with the Americans."

Beech pleaded Chau's case with both Bunker and his friend Shackley. If everybody in South Vietnam who has a communist relative were locked up, Beech argued, then most of the country would be behind bars. Neither man was swayed. Shackley, though, was annoyed by the stories Beech was writing. The episode threatened to rupture their close relationship. One day, Shackley came to Beech's home for lunch. While the two Americans ate, Chau, one of the most sought-after persons in Saigon, quietly sat in the next room—his presence a secret to the chief of station.

In February of 1970, John Paul Vann and Evert Bumgardner, a pacification officer, spirited Chau out of Saigon and devised an escape for him into Cambodia. But Chau returned to Saigon, still convinced that neither the embassy nor the CIA would permit Thieu to imprison him. Shackley's station, though, was working against him. After Jean Sauvageot, another friend and pacification officer, tried to convince Colby, the director of CORDS, that Chau should be helped, a Shackley subordinate called Sauvageot to the station and told him to stay out of the Chau business.

Shackley was not necessarily in a position to wave a wand and save Chau. But his pronouncements on Chau made a difference. John Paul Vann told Daniel Ellsberg that Shackley had described Chau to Bunker as a communist sympathizer, and Bunker accepted his station chief's judgment.* At one point during the Chau controversy, Richard Helms came to the office of Senator William Fulbright, the chairman of the Senate

---

* According to Ellsberg, then an analyst at the Rand Corporation, the Chau case was part of what motivated him to leak the Pentagon Papers—the largest intelligence leak in U.S. history. In the summer of 1969, Vann invited Ellsberg to Vietnam to help Chau. To come right away, Ellsberg needed an official invitation. Colby and another embassy official nixed that, apparently because of Ellsberg's developing opposition to Washington's Vietnam policies. Ellsberg stayed put in America and soon began copying the Pentagon Papers. "Had I gone over then," Ellsberg recalled, "I probably would not have done anything so drastic."

Foreign Relations Committee, to talk about Chau. Many of his facts were wrong, according to committee aide Lowenstein. To Lowenstein, it was clear that Helms had been misinformed by Shackley.

In mid-February, Colby and Vann testified before the Senate Foreign Relations Committee about the pacification effort. When the subject of Chau arose, Colby artfully deflected the questions. Vann stated that his friend was "a dedicated nationalist anticommunist," but he could say little more. Ambassador Bunker had ordered him to refrain from speaking out on Chau's behalf. In one exchange, Senator Symington revealed that Shackley—"who happens to be a friend of mine, and one of the best men I know in the business"—had told him that Chau was *not* a communist. Indeed, months earlier, Shackley had informed Symington that he did not believe Chau was a Red. Then Shackley dramatically changed his mind. "Something happened in the intervening time," committee aide Moose later said. "Ted Shackley would have you believe that he found something out. But I believe it simply became expedient for the Agency to turn its back on Chau. This enraged me about Shackley."

On February 23, 1970, Chau came out of hiding. Two days later, a military court tried Chau in absentia and judged him guilty of associating with a North Vietnamese spy. On the afternoon of February 26, police hauled him off to prison. Chau was sentenced to ten years at hard labor. On March 6, a top Saigon official said Chau's prosecution might have been averted had the embassy confirmed publicly that Chau had worked with the CIA.

Bunker's nonchalant attitude toward the event was summed up in a cable he sent to Foggy Bottom: "At the core of the Chau case probably lies President Thieu's belief that he must gear up his people and army for a long war, and that to do this it is necessary to take a strong and unequivocal anticommunist stance." A few weeks later, Senator Fulbright excoriated the embassy on the Senate floor. "The Embassy seems to have been obsessed with appearances and the maintenance—at any price—of good relations with the Thieu regime," he declared. Bunker and Shackley had acceded to Thieu's use of political terror.

Decades afterward, Chau was remarkably gracious in his judgment of Shackley: "Ambassador Bunker wanted to protect Thieu. That was the main point of interest for the United States. Mr. Shackley was part of the machine. He had to do what the machine wanted."

In early May of 1970, Shackley sent a cable to headquarters reporting on the Saigon political scene. He observed that opposition to Thieu was increasing. Student protests were the big problem. But the chief reassured Langley that tougher measures employed by Saigon's security forces against demonstrators should deter future actions. Then Shackley had the nerve to note that the Tran Ngoc Chau case was one of several developments that "contributed to a rising tide of criticism and dissatisfaction." The threat, however, was not imminent. "The opposition," Shackley observed, "is still fragmented and continued U.S. support should deter anyone of a mind to move against the Thieu government." Thieu, the station chief predicted, would survive his present difficulties. Beyond that, Shackley could not say: "The longer term outlook is not so clear."

V

In March of 1970, Felix Rodriguez arrived in Vietnam, once again to serve Ted Shackley. After JMWAVE's covert war against Cuba cooled, Rodriguez fought on against communism for the Company. In 1967, he advised the Bolivian military during its successful jungle hunt for Che Guevara, who had left Cuba to bring revolution to South America. Rodriguez failed to fulfill his orders from Langley: bring back Che alive. The Bolivian military unit he assisted killed Che. The CIA next dispatched Rodriguez to train military units in Ecuador and Peru. Then he volunteered for Vietnam, where he was assigned to be deputy field adviser to Shackley's PRUs in Region III.

Before starting his job at Bien Hoa, Rodriguez met Shackley, whom he never encountered in Miami. To Rodriguez, Shackley resembled a professor more than a covert warrior. Rodriguez soon picked up all sorts of stories about Shackley. He possessed a near-photographic memory; he was obsessed with quantifiable results. Shackley supposedly had convinced an astrologer, whom Thieu consulted, to encourage the President to authorize an army operation near Cambodia.

In Bien Hoa, Rodriguez developed a specialty—using helicopters in tandem with PRUs. Viet Cong targets were developed from intelligence sources. Then Rodriguez in a chopper searched out the enemy positions, often by drawing fire. He marked the spot with smoke grenades. Next gunships and PRUs converged on the target. In one case, Rodriguez led a PRU team against the base of an NVA colonel in charge of rocketing Saigon. "We would have preferred to capture [the colonel] alive," Rodriguez claimed, "but that didn't happen."

Despite Shackley's emphasis on espionage over paramilitary activities, his PRUs in Region III were more a classic counterinsurgency operation than an intelligence program. His officers in the region attempted to penetrate the VC command. But the results were disheartening. Once they apprehended the secretary to a local Viet Cong military commander. She provided the names and addresses of scores of VC officials and supporters. Through her, the CIA tried to recruit one of the commander's comrades. The plot failed when the target refused the pitch. Immediately afterward, the VC questioned him; there had been a leak.

Rudy Enders, a former JMWAVE officer and now Rodriguez's supervisor, investigated and discovered that the local PRU commander was a VC agent. The episode convinced Donald Gregg, the current ROIC, to all but give up on penetrations. "I decided," he recalled, "I couldn't penetrate."

Gregg knew that Shackley was pressing for intelligence penetrations, but he focused instead on going after—and neutralizing—the known VC. One PRU raid conducted by Enders and Rodriguez during Tet of 1971 nabbed twenty-three VC suspects. Interrogations with these prisoners led to the identification of nearly a hundred members of the local VC network. One was valet to the South Vietnamese civilian province chief, another worked for the police. A Viet Cong village secretary defected and disclosed the names and whereabouts of the entire VC structure of his village. Rodriguez and his PRUs mounted a helicopter operation that rounded up twenty-eight of his former colleagues.

But the village secretary was a painful reminder of what the entire U.S. establishment in Vietnam was facing. Using information from the secretary and other sources, Orrin DeForest (who was still running in Bien Hoa his unilateral operation in defiance of Shackley's wish that officers rely on the PICs) calculated that in one district up to 10,000 people were active participants in the VC. Extrapolating from these figures yielded frightening statistics: 100,000 VC in Region III; almost a half a million nationwide. Shackley's station was not reporting such intelligence to Washington.

Within Shackley's station, some officers came to question the intelligence they processed. By mid-1970, Phil Jones had been in Shackley's station for about a year. "I visited DDP officers in the provinces and for the life of me couldn't see what they all did," Jones said. "I had seen similar things in the CIA's work on China. They have to present a credible front that they are engaging in major support of the war. They had to be able to tell Congress and the top military command that they were doing something." Jones saw that a lot of the case officers were scurrying to meet Shackley's quotas and "running largely spurious agents and operations."

Jones, an analyst, was a skeptical consumer of the intelligence Shackley's station collected. "I would ask [a case officer] how did you authenticate the agents, do they exist," he explained. "Often they didn't deal with the agent directly but with a local police chief who said he had an agent. When I finally realized how insecure the authentication of their sources was . . . well, there was nothing they could do about it. It was the system."

Jones was not alone in his skepticism. "We never came up with any intelligence that affected the national security," recalled Richard Dane, a senior officer in Region V. "Maybe they would find some arms in a hay cart. It was a lot of bullshit." Still Shackley demanded reports from Dane that pumped up the Agency and could be used in the weekly Shackleygram that trumpeted his station's most recent successes.* "Shackley didn't have to do that," Dane recalled. "He was the most competent senior officer I ever worked for. But he always had some puffery about him."

Shackley dealt not with piddling, low-level agents or corrupt and inept Special Branch officers. His concerns were larger—a top item always being the preservation of Thieu's presidency. As part of this brief, Shackley assigned a veteran officer to watch over Madame Ngo Ba Thanh, a prominent opposition leader. A member of a notable family, she had studied law at Columbia University and now headed a feminist organization and cochaired the antigovernment People's Front Struggling for Peace. Shackley's man visited Thanh in her home, dodging Thieu's security officers who surveiled her. Shackley did not want Thieu to know the Agency was in contact with Thanh.

The officer and Thanh discussed her plans. She told him when demonstrations were scheduled. He received her complaints about government corruption. Thanh, like many opposition figures, wanted to share her criticisms with Agency people, believing her comments would reach U.S. policymakers and affect their thinking. (Such beliefs were overly wishful.) The case officer, in return, supplied Thanh political advice, sympathy, medicine, and cigarettes.

In the embassy, Agency and State Department officers debated Thanh's sincerity. Some considered her another commie agitator or sympathizer, which was what Special Branch officers were telling the station. The Agency man who met with her defended her as a bona fide dissident.

In the summer of 1971, Thanh was arrested and charged with engaging in "activities harmful to the national security," creating an illegal organization, and distributing materials that "undermine the anti-Communist potential of the people." Thanh's CIA contact worried about her. Forty years old, she suffered serious asthmatic attacks while imprisoned. In an episode reminiscent of the Tran Ngoc Chau case, he asked Shackley if the Agency could do something for her, perhaps advise Thieu

---

*As a deputy ROIC and then the ROIC, Dane worked closely with the Special Branch and did not enjoy the company of its officers. "All that stuff, the torture, was true," he recalled. "Those cockroaches were stuffing Coke bottles in women's vaginas."

to lay off. She was not a communist, he asserted, and she had cooperated with the Agency. Couldn't Shackley help her?

It couldn't be done, Shackley explained. Any move made in that regard might indicate to Thieu that his station was interested in Thanh and perhaps even regarded her favorably. Intervening could complicate the always delicate relations between the Americans and the Saigon government. It might even cause an insecure Thieu to treat Thanh more harshly. Our hands, Shackley said, are tied.

The CIA man could not argue with Shackley's logic. He watched as Thanh, whom he considered a friend, languished in a Saigon prison. Even worse, he had to wonder if his conversations with her had been discovered by Thieu and had prompted Thanh's arrest.*

The arrest came during a political season. A presidential election was scheduled for October 3, 1971, and the station and the embassy had been busy for months guaranteeing that Thieu would win reelection. At the start of the campaign, the conventional line in Saigon was that Thieu faced an easy race if Vice President Nguyen Cao Ky, his rival, declined to run. The other likely candidate, General Duong Van ("Big") Minh, a coup-plotter in 1963 and now the leader of a potential "third force," did not appear a strong contender. (In a December 22, 1970, dispatch, Shackley had predicted that Ky would withdraw from the race on his own accord and that Big Minh would pose "the greatest threat.") Thieu's political strategy was simple: keep Ky out. In early 1971, he rammed through the legislature a bill rendering it difficult for Ky to gain a spot on the ballot. Then, in concert with Shackley's station, Thieu pressured legislators who might support Ky.

Throughout the spring and summer, U.S. officials, including Nixon and Secretary of State William Rogers, claimed they were doing all possible to ensure an honest and impartial election. Few in Saigon believed that. Shackley, according to Frank Snepp, forwarded cables to Washington boasting that the CIA had helped round up enough votes in the legislature to keep Ky off the ballot. George McArthur, then a correspondent for *The Los Angeles Times,* went to his good friend Shackley and asked how much money the station was spreading about. "You're a damn fool to ask me that question," Shackley replied.

As Shackley's station endeavored to influence the election, he realized the danger such activity carried. In a June 12 cable—in which he now predicted that Ky and Minh would stay in the race—Shackley observed

_____

* Thanh was released in September of 1973 and returned to waging opposition politics. After the war, she was locked up by the communists, but then she obtained a position in the Vietnam government and maintained a correspondence with the CIA man who had been her contact.

that if Ky and Minh withdrew, the international standing of the Thieu government would be severely damaged and the election considered a joke. A Shackleygram the next month reported that Thieu's political lieutenants were employing "all means, fair and foul," to achieve victory. There now seemed "little doubt," the chief added, that Thieu would win.

On August 6 the supreme court of South Vietnam ruled that Ky was disqualified from the campaign. Shortly afterward, General Minh obtained a document, marked "Top Secret," that outlined a proposed systematic election-fraud scheme to be waged on Thieu's behalf. Big Minh bowed out of the contest. (A report filed by Shackley on September 13 noted that Minh had collected much evidence of "irregular" campaign practices waged by Thieu's organization.) Thieu would win—but not in any fashion that would allow him or Washington to claim he was the people's choice.

Bunker and Shackley needed to dress up the elections. The ambassador visited Big Minh and offered him a large bribe—CIA money—to stay on the ballot. Minh declined to be a shill.* On October 3, Thieu triumphed in the one-man election. Bunker and Shackley had failed in an impossible task—to stage-manage a contest that appeared democratic but ensured the success of Washington's preferred candidate. The whole exercise was more proof that neither Saigon nor Washington was genuinely committed to democracy in South Vietnam. Shackley's early cables were right: there was no reason for anyone to take the election results seriously.

In September of 1971, Bill White, the new man in the small analytical branch of the Saigon station, was saddled with writing the weekly Shackleygrams. For his first report, White collected material from the various divisions and composed a dispassionate summation of the week's activities. Before the report went out, Shackley whistled White into his office. This is totally unacceptable, Shackley yelled at him. Go back and ask your supervisor how to do it right. "I discovered that it had to be written in a way to make it look as if Ted Shackley was winning the war in Vietnam," White recalled. "You could not say such-and-such happened,

---

* Snepp claimed the amount offered Minh was $3 million. Confirmation of the attempted bribe occurred in 1978 during a deposition of a CIA official, in which a document was produced that indicated Shackley had bugged Minh. "[Deleted] listened to the tapes . . . in which Ambassador Bunker offered to finance [deleted] race for the presidency," the Agency document said, "[Deleted] noted that the amount of $3 million was not mentioned in that conversation, although the basic report by Snepp is true."

and that the enemy did this or that. Instead of an objective account, he wanted a report that said [the enemy] did something, but we caught them at it and we took decisive action." It was de rigueur to boast of the number of intelligence reports the station filed that week and the percentage increase that marked. White thought this was inane. But he went along.

White frequently clashed with Shackley. "He was always bitching about my work," White said. "He didn't like the way I put things. He wanted color, embellishments." White included in the weekly reports information on corruption in the South Vietnamese ranks, but Shackley demanded that inefficiencies and corruption be played down. He was not eager to show the shortcomings of Washington's allies. Shackley was promoting the view that there was light at the end of the tunnel; White considered Vietnam a bottomless pit. Shackley insisted that the reporting put a positive spin on ARVN's general performance, the bombing campaign, and efforts to slow down the supply lines of the Trail. "This all probably tended," White asserted, "to skew to some extent the picture for the people back home."

Presenting an accurate picture of what was going on in Vietnam was what Shackley was supposed to do. His crusade to recruit and report led to a rise in the number of agents and an increase in production. By force of will, Shackley was able to impose some direction on the unwieldy station. For that, he earned from station officers both appreciation and derision. The number of reports generated by the station jumped from about 100 each month to roughly 500. But some wondered about the quality of the reports. "Most of it was trash," claimed McGehee, the disenchanted case officer, who in 1971 was serving in Thailand and stewing about Agency activity that supported the military dictatorship there. "Every single day you could pick up reports of planned [local] VC action. Normally this low-grade stuff would be ignored. Now it was disseminated as a report." McGehee realized that in Vietnam and elsewhere "policy-supportive intelligence" received a free ride: "Intelligence that questioned policy was subject to scrutiny. So you have a case officer who knows that to get a promotion he has to crank out intelligence. He has no real intelligence, so he puts out a report, based on an arrestee or some so-called penetration, saying that VC morale was low. That type of stuff would go out immediately. And he would get a mark on his scorecard. Others would rewrite Special Branch reports. It was a big paper mill."

Complaints about Shackley circulated within the Company. The chief of station in Thailand, who had previously served in Vietnam, routinely encountered officers who bitched about Shackley. The gripes had a consistent theme: Shackley had established reporting requirements to make the station look good and there was little substance to many reports. Joe Lazarsky, the deputy chief of station, left Vietnam believing that Shackley's station fared poorly on the espionage front. "We were not able to come up with sufficient intelligence to pinpoint enemy actions," Lazarsky remarked. The information the Agency did gather was not encouraging. "The enemy was not pacified," he said. "Their morale was still high. There was determination down to the rank and file from Hanoi. They all believed, regardless of cease-fire negotiations, 'We will rule.'"

Vietnam was bureaucracy run amuck. Shackley rode at the top of an entity that fielded hundreds of officers who funneled information into the national security behemoth in order to facilitate informed and wise decision-making. But was anybody listening? The history of Vietnam was one of policymakers, including presidents, ignoring the findings of their spies and analysts. Ambassador Bunker certainly appreciated the inside dope captured by the bugs in Thieu's office, but generally he did not display enthusiasm for intelligence Shackley's station brought him. "As for learning what was going on inside the enemy headquarters and what their plans were, I don't think we had much of a handle on that," recalled Charles Hill, a special assistant to Bunker. "Overall, U.S. intelligence was not very successful. They never were any good at finding out what was going on in the minds of anyone else." And Bunker did not really care. "His view," Hill explained, "was if you start spending your time trying to figure out the motives of the enemy, you will waste your time. If you know what you want to do, you do it. Don't concoct theories about what's going on in the headquarters of the other side." Bunker realized hundreds of Americans were running around trying to discern such matters. Intelligence officers have to collect; analysts have to tell you what the situation is. "He considered CIA intelligence," Hill noted, "largely tangential."

In the lower ranks and in the field, other non-Agency officials expected little of the Agency. "The CIA put a lot of officers into the Vietnam program who knew nothing about Southeast Asia," noted Fred Z. Brown, who in the early 1970s was consul general in Da Nang. "Some of the guys they had didn't have a clue. I was cynical about the value of what was being reported. I felt all along that America's ability to get at the truth of what was happening was limited. I could fly out in a helicopter and see the NVA building a four-lane highway and a sixteen-inch pipeline. Our position in the north was militarily indefensible. In this context, running agents to find out the Viet Cong infrastructure of a district becomes a ridiculous exercise."

In Washington, Lou Sarris was not impressed with the intelligence from Vietnam he reviewed. For a dozen years he had dwelled on the Vietnam dilemma as a State Department intelligence analyst. Sarris believed that the intelligence community never obtained a firm grasp of Vietnam. He saw that Shackley was making a difference as the chief of station. The Agency was focusing on the VC, the politics and psychology of the enemy. More material from a wider range of sources was pouring in. But "more" did not mean "better." The tone of the reporting he read—and individual reports ran the good news–bad news gamut—promoted the line that the Viet Cong were on the decline and the staying power of the North Vietnamese was slipping. Sarris thought that this was a case of wishful thinking. He questioned the intelligence from Shackley's station that highlighted heavy VC losses and projected further enemy setbacks. His analysts agreed that the VC were not really gone. They were lying low and watching for Washington's response.

Few government bureaucracies produce objective information. An intelligence service is supposed to; that is its purported reason for existence. But like other government agencies, the CIA had in its ranks opinionated Cold War missionaries, don't-rock-the-boat careerists, and bureaucrats who believed that the key to advancement is telling superiors what they want to hear. When these sorts are at the controls, the system is likely to yield skewed intelligence. Within the intelligence community, accusations of rigging intelligence are easy to come by and difficult to prove—especially on a controversial matter like Vietnam. With the intelligence flow so massive, there was plenty of material on which to build a case that Shackley was misleading Washington about the reality of Vietnam. But whether Shackley actually conspired to impose a too-rosy spin on reports to Washington, his officers certainly learned what *not* to report to Saigon.

The way Shackley managed the station bred self-censorship, and that tilted the intelligence Washington received. Officers who served in different capacities under Shackley realized this. Bob Wall, who in 1970 handled liaison with the Special Branch, collected discouraging information from its commander, Colonel Mau, on Vietnamization. "You knew it wouldn't get out of Vietnam that way, because it was bad news," Wall maintained. "You knew Shackley wouldn't approve it. To avoid his wrath, you would write what he wanted."

By the time his tour came to an end in 1971, Charles Yothers, the operations chief in Region 1, was a full cynic and upset by what he perceived as a good-news bias in Shackley's station: "As Vietnamization went on, it was clear the VC would take the region back, and Washington is blaring to the world that Vietnamization is working. I didn't see it working. The local military commanders and province chiefs did not believe it would. And I couldn't report that. Washington didn't want to hear it."

Yothers left Da Nang concluding he had achieved little. The intelligence had improved marginally. But he did not view this progress as relevant to the outcome of the war. Everything he learned through his intelligence indicated to him that the South Vietnamese would not be able to withstand the North Vietnamese. "You just couldn't see Vietnamese commanders manning front-line firebases," he said, "or leading troops on an airdrop into the jungle canopy." That overarching notion was not being conveyed to the policymakers of Washington, who were unreceptive to receiving such information. When Yothers returned to Langley, a personnel officer decided he had done such a fine job he ought to return to Vietnam. There was only one way to duck the assignment. Yothers resigned from the Company.

Bill Kohlmann, a case officer in the political branch, shared the belief there was a fundamental problem in reporting: "A strong-willed guy like Shackley would report progress because it was his job to bring about progress." Shackley was determined to notify Langley that his station was doing a bang-up job. If Kohlmann tried to report a remark made by a Vietnamese senator that was critical of the regime, his superiors said who cares what this senator has to say. But if the senator uttered something positive, the response was, let's get this out in a report to Washington. "Shackley was a strong character, and he persuaded himself of the rightness of what he was trying to do," Kohlmann recalled. "Most chiefs of station do the same thing. He was just a stronger and more intense person than most."

Toward the end of 1971, Langley informed Shackley that his stay in Vietnam was soon to end. In his three years in Saigon, Shackley had imposed some order on the chaos. Intelligence reports were flowing. PRUs were racking up neutralizations. There had been some unfortunate public relations disasters on his watch. The Green Beret case was an ugly mark for the Agency. The Chau affair was another one, but it had faded from public sight. Phoenix was forever in disarray, but Shackley had moved to put some official distance between the Agency and that tar baby. Most important, at the end of 1971, anyone in Washington who wished to see hope could find reasons to believe. The security situation in certain parts of South Vietnam appeared improved. The VC were lying low. Negotiations with North Vietnam had started. Maybe, just maybe, the cold warriors of the United States were going to escape Vietnam with some face. Early 1972 was a good time to leave Vietnam.

In headquarters, Shackley's tour was widely judged another of his successes, according to William Johnson, a Vietnam desk officer.* "His tenure was seen as one of accomplishment," Tom Polgar, his replacement, explained. "He had come to Vietnam after the Tet offensive. Now everything seemed in better shape both in the country and with the overall intelligence picture. He came out of Vietnam with the aura of having done things well." Shackley thought he had done an excellent job. "He anticipated going all the way to the top," his friend, reporter George McArthur, recalled.

Shackley had succeeded in the primary mission: to manage. "I presume that during his tour in Laos, he came to consider himself a serious candidate to be DCI," his CIA colleague Jamie Jameson said. Now he had effectively done the bidding of the President and Kissinger and sat at the table with the leading men of the military and the diplomatic corps. The rumor spread within the Agency that Shackley was returning to Washington to head the Soviet Russia Division, a most prestigious assignment and a true sign of upward mobility.

Shackley was honored with the usual round of farewell visits and parties. During one celebration, his Agency comrades staged a skit that poked fun at Shackley clichés: Always be forward-leaning. Always be ahead of the curve. At a big bash at Shackley's home, McArthur was surprised to find a host of South Vietnamese officials—military men and police officers—whom he never realized were Agency-connected. "It was a pretty gamey crowd," he recalled. "It was spooky."

The atmosphere of the station changed the moment Tom Polgar assumed command in early 1972. Polgar was more relaxed, less pretentious. He dispensed with the bodyguards that had protected Shackley from unseen enemies. Polgar allowed base chiefs to file reports to Washington without first sending them to the station—a move unthinkable for Shackley. He got rid of quotas for reports. He dumped the weekly Shackleygram.

Shackley left Polgar with a well-organized station—and a lot of lousy agents. "There were burn notices being circulated," Frank Snepp recalled, "saying everything this agent has produced should be put into the shredder. Polgar felt the station recruitment list had been pumped

---

* "Shackley may not be the most honest man in the world, but he's a pro," Johnson said years later in a puzzling remark. "He always had the reputation for being just a little unscrupulous. Not with money, but with operations. It was totally an in-house feeling. It doesn't relate to his competence." Johnson, who claimed to be an admirer of Shackley, refused to elaborate.

up and that sources were not reliable." Polgar's after-the-fact estimation was more diplomatic: "When I came in . . . there was a great deal of hypocrisy and self-delusion [regarding operations]. People are very eager to produce, and in many cases the wish becomes the father of the thought. . . . Most agents were low-level. Very few were high-level, whose contributions made a real difference."

Ultimately, Vietnam—from the start, through Shackley's tenure, and onward—was an intelligence failure. U.S. officers there and in Washington did not comprehend the country. No amount of managerial skill could change that. "We didn't understand the people," said Hill, the Bunker aide. "We didn't understand Vietnamese nationalism. We didn't understand our Vietnamese allies." After the war, Richard Helms, the man responsible for U.S. intelligence, offered a stunning indictment: "We were dealing with a complicated cultural and ethnic problem which we never came to understand. In other words, it was our ignorance or innocence, if you will, which led us to misassess, not comprehend, and make a lot of wrong decisions, which one way or another helped to affect the outcome." Ideally, Shackley's CIA was the government entity that should have done the most to ensure that the men running the war in Washington really understood Vietnam. It did not come close.

Shortly after Shackley returned to Washington, he lunched at one of those ersatz country-inn restaurants in suburban Virginia with Frank Snepp and another officer who had been in Vietnam. Shackley was in a poor mood. He voiced worries about Vietnamization. Saigon's army was having trouble. The South Vietnamese intelligence apparatus was foundering. He wondered about Polgar's ability to run the station. He was concerned that the station had not done enough recruiting. "This was a very strange Ted Shackley," Snepp recalled. "A Shackley shorn of his PR pretensions, less characteristically optimistic, one of the few times I ever heard him reflect any pessimism."

Shackley also was fretting about his career. He had not been called home to become chief of the Soviet Russia Division. His new job was to clean up the rubble of an intelligence disaster. Only recently the Agency had discovered that a former case officer in the Western Hemisphere Division was considering revealing all the secrets he possessed. Shackley's new assignment was to shut down all operations and dump all officers and assets known to the ex-Company man. It was a terrible task.

At lunch, Shackley agitatedly discussed this turncoat. In all his positions, Shackley was extremely mindful of security. Now he was being handed someone else's screw-up. Such a situation would never have developed on his watch, he asserted. He would have found out about the renegade and somehow preempted him. He was irate that he had left the prestigious post of Saigon station chief to be tossed into a cesspool. Shackley did not know then that this nasty business would mark the beginning of a bad stretch for him and the Agency. At this moment, wracked with pessimism about Vietnam and anger over the Agency defector, Shackley did not seem invincible.

CHAPTER SEVEN

WASHINGTON:
THE ENEMY WITHIN

I

THE problem apparently began when Philip Agee fell in love with a woman who idolized Che Guevara.

Agee, a square-jawed, dark-haired fellow with dashing looks, had joined the Agency in 1957. A child of privilege, he had grown up in Tampa, Florida, and attended Jesuit secondary school and then Notre Dame. In 1960, the CIA sent Agee to South America. For six years—first in Ecuador and then in Uruguay—he ran all the classic operations: recruiting Communist Party members; tapping telephones; collaborating with state police forces; penetrating Soviet and Cuban missions. Years of such toil took their toll. His marriage to his college sweetheart fell apart. In 1967, the Agency assigned him to the Mexico station as a special assistant to the ambassador for the 1968 Olympics game.

In Mexico, Agee met an older American woman who worked for the Olympic organizing committee. She was a free spirit and an admirer of Che Guevara. The two fell in love. When the Cuban revolutionary was murdered by Bolivian forces in October of 1967, she complained to Agee. The CIA man squirmed; he had not revealed to her his true identity. Soon afterward, Agee wanted out of the CIA. He had enough of the double life. His political doubts were growing. He desired a new start with his new love. In the spring of 1968, he informed Winston

Scott, the lordly chief of station in Mexico City, that he intended to resign after the Olympics.*

Agee left the Agency amidst a nasty battle with his wife over the custody of their two sons. He remained in Mexico City. His romance failed. He drifted toward a circle of left-leaning artists and writers. He began to consider writing about his time in the Agency. In early 1971, François Maspero, a Frenchman who had published Che Guevara's Bolivian diary, offered to help Agee and arranged for him to use research facilities in Cuba. In the spring of 1971 Agee arrived in Cuba.

Agee refused to think of himself as a defector, and in later years he ardently claimed he had not supplied any secrets to Cuban intelligence —an assertion no one in the Company took seriously. He stayed on the island for several months, writing his book. He also drafted a letter to *Marcha,* a political weekly in Uruguay. Agee identified himself as a former CIA officer once stationed there, warned how the Agency might intervene in upcoming elections, and disclosed that he had begun a book on his CIA days. Before leaving Cuba for Paris, Agee handed the letter to Cubans helping him. Do with it what you want, he said.

Agee settled into a cheap hotel in Paris. One evening around Christmas of 1971, Keith Gardiner, a CIA officer, showed up at the door. Gardiner and Agee had gone through training together. Agee's letter to *Marcha,* published in November, had shocked Langley. "There was bewilderment," Gardiner recalled. "It was mind-boggling. What on earth is going on? we asked. Why is Phil saying these things? Who would have thought that an intelligence officer would go public and try to hurt your organization?" No one in the Agency had any plan for this sort of thing.

At a dark bar near Agee's hotel, Gardiner asked for an explanation. "Look, Keith," Agee said, "I'm not the same person you knew in the Agency. I've changed. I think the Agency's operations in Latin America are wrong—wrong from every point of view except that of the rich minorities they help." Gardiner stared across the table at Agee. "I didn't understand," Gardiner later said. "He had done quite well within the Agency. He came from a conservative background. There were no signs of disaffection. I couldn't see what had made him change. I looked for a cause, an external cause, and I couldn't find one."

Agee told Gardiner that he had delivered a 700-page manuscript to Maspero. (This was not true; Agee wanted Langley to believe it could

---

* Years later, CIA people would claim that Agee's reasons for quitting had more to do with his divorce, alcohol consumption, and dalliances than any political beliefs. They maintained his new girlfriend was a suspected Cuban intelligence operative— even though an investigation uncovered no conclusive evidence she was a Cuban asset.

not stop him.) The book, he said, showed that the CIA was supporting repressive governments against people struggling for change. He revealed he had been to Cuba and admired Castro's revolution. "When [headquarters officials] find out you spent six months in Cuba they're going to flip out," Gardiner exclaimed. Don't worry, Agee said, I'm going to submit the manuscript to the Agency for clearance. But as he said that, Agee knew he was lying.

Gardiner's cable to headquarters set off alarm bells. The assumption within Langley was that everything Agee knew about the CIA was now in enemy hands. The Agency would have to decimate its Latin America programs, and it needed to initiate an all-out spying operation against Agee, in the faint hope that it could prevent publication of his work. The man in charge of all this would be Ted Shackley.

Shackley returned to Washington from Saigon in February of 1972. He had not been stationed in headquarters since 1961. In the intervening years, secrets had been revealed, and the Agency's image had begun to tarnish. In 1964, Random House published the first significant exposé of the Agency, *The Invisible Government.* Written by Washington journalists Thomas B. Ross and David Wise, the book spilled details of the botched Bay of Pigs invasion. It offered the first authoritative accounts of the CIA-backed coups in Iran and Guatemala. Ross and Wise suggested that the national security state had gone too far and that policymakers had become too reliant on the quick fixes of covert action.

Three years later, a series of articles in *Ramparts* magazine revealed the CIA's secret support of the National Student Association, proving that Shackley's colleagues were meddling in domestic affairs. Similar revelations followed in other media outlets, including *The New York Times,* which disclosed CIA connections with corporations, trusts, research centers, universities, and individuals. Some members of Congress grumbled that the CIA needed to be reined in. And Vietnam stained the Agency. The Green Beret case caused some Americans to wonder what the Agency was doing in their name. When William Colby returned to Washington and the CIA in 1971 after overseeing the Phoenix program, he encountered posters that cried, "Colby—Wanted for Murder." As Shackley and his family settled into Bethesda, Maryland, an affluent suburb of Washington, the Agency was entering what for CIA people would be a very dark period.

Shackley had little cause to be happy with his assignment to the Western Hemisphere Division. CIA people did not hold the division in high repute. It was considered a sleepy part of the DDP. There were few active Soviet operations. Many of the division's original officers were former FBI agents, who as a group were looked down upon by the more sophisticated, better educated CIA men. The real action of the Cold War was in Europe. There had been the campaign in Guatemala, and Castro's revolution had changed the equation. But the second-class status of the division lingered. Too many of its officers thought intelligence gathering entailed taking an influential Latino to lunch at a university club and then reporting the comments to Langley.

To the officers of the Western Hemisphere Division, Shackley was an interloper. He had headed the Miami station in its heyday, but he had not risen through the division ranks. And his reputation was that of a heavy-handed manager. Now that hand was to be applied to the sensitive Agee matter.

Shackley inherited as his deputy James Flannery, a longtime division officer. Flannery, a wry Texan, considered it his chore to let Shackley know how things were done in the division. It was, he found, not an easy job. William Broe, Shackley's predecessor, had been a quiet, personable chief, popular with his staff. Shackley did not remind many of Broe. His detractors in the division assigned him the inelegant nickname "Ted Shitley." As his deputy chief explained, "Shackley wanted to yell 'shit' and watch everyone squat."

Shackley moved to make the division his own. He placed his favorites in key positions. Shackley named his ROIC for Region V in Vietnam to the chief of operations post for the division and assigned him to oversee the anti-Agee program. He wanted somebody in that job who absolutely had no ties to Agee. Shackley put Tom Clines in charge of the Chile desk. Around this time, Dave Morales, a fervent Shackley loyalist, was shifted to Latin American operations.*

The new division chief was in a tough spot. The top brass expected the forty-five-year-old Shackley to clean up a division compromised by the CIA's first turncoat. There was no question that Agee knew a lot. When Agee was based in Mexico City, chief of station Winston Scott

---

* Morales had a story he told of his Latin American days. He was assigned to develop a relationship with a rising Panamanian military officer: Manuel Noriega. Morales offered to refinish the desk in Noriega's office. Noriega accepted the gesture. The desk was renovated, and CIA technicians added something extra: one of their most advanced bugging devices. The desk was returned, but Agency monitors failed to pick up Noriega's chatter. Morales investigated and discovered another desk in Noriega's office. Noriega explained he did not like the way the old one looked. Now the Agency had to find the desk and the bug. The CIA station traced it to a used-furniture store, where it sat at the rear of a room full of desks. CIA men tried to purchase it, but the proprietor said they had to choose a desk from the front. To buy their desk, the Agency officers had to pay for all the desks between them and the one they sought.

maintained in a large fireproof vault a legendary but relatively unsecure filing system. His records contained secrets about CIA activity throughout Latin America. And Agee had access to all this material. "If I had the slightest interest I could have learned everything," Agee recalled. "But by then I was so tired of it all." Yet Shackley had to assume that Agee had spent hours taking notes in the vault.

Shackley approached the clean-up job with the relentlessness he applied to all assignments. He could not know which officers, agents, and operations Agee had already blown or might do so in the future. He had to assume the worst. If he left anyone in place who subsequently proved to be compromised, it would be his fault. He would have to swing his axe far and wide. There was a ruthless logic in such a strategy, and in temperament Shackley was no pruner.

In headquarters, Shackley's chief of operations set up the division's anti-Agee project. With a staff of three analysts, he scrutinized Agee and his career. They examined his preemployment interviews. They pored over the assessments from his training classes and every fitness report on Agee. They reviewed all intelligence reports Agee had submitted. Two key questions demanded answers. Was Agee a spy inside the CIA before he resigned? Had he left behind a compatriot, a mole?

The operations chief and his staff vetted every officer who had come into contact with Agee. The list of persons with substantial links to Agee numbered about 100. Officers who knew Agee were called to headquarters and pumped for any insights. Shackley's staff tracked down women whom Agee had dated. All were asked to reveal every detail about their relationship to the former spy. The operations chief composed his own portrait of the target: an operator, a social animal, a popular fellow, ambitious and bright but not hardworking. He had been disappointed that he had failed to turn his high-flying social contacts in Mexico City into a lucrative job.

Agee's former colleagues tried to imagine what had prompted Agee to betray the CIA. His own explanation—he came to see the Agency as an instrument of oppression—was not acceptable to those who served proudly. "Not a single person ever thought Agee did what he did because of philosophical differences with the Agency and its mission," the operations chief said. "Only after Agee's world fell apart did he develop ideological misgivings." An Agency shrink drew up an assessment of the defector. "The ideological conversion of which Subject speaks," the psychological profile concluded, "would seem to rest on a rather shallow base. It is probably his rationalization for this self-aggrandizing act." The Langley psychiatrist, like other Agency people, could not believe that Agee was sincere in his disgust with the CIA and U.S. foreign policy.

Shackley's operations chief and his aides discovered no evidence that

Agee spied for the Cubans or Soviets before he left the Agency. "When he was in Mexico City," the operations chief said, "Agee was supposed to work on Soviet operations. His branch chief told us Agee was one of the laziest guys he had ever seen. The station had some good technical operations—taking pictures of people going in and out of the Soviet embassy. If Agee were a spy, he would have been most interested in it. But he never showed any interest."

The operations chief's conclusion—that Agee had not been an enemy spy—earned him a fight with James Angleton. The hypersuspicious counterintelligence chief was convinced Agee was a mole and had left behind a cabal within the Agency. Angleton constantly called the operations chief—often late in the afternoon after Angleton had consumed a few drinks at lunch—and berated Shackley's deputy. His speech slurred, Angleton accused Shackley and the operations chief of being too thick to see the deception being waged by the Soviets. "I kept telling Angleton there was no evidence," the chief of operations noted. "Agee never went into the vault in Mexico City. 'Oh,' Angleton said, 'that's small stuff, they already knew all that.'" While Shackley and his ops chief believed Agee was now in league with Cuban and Soviet intelligence, they would not sanction an internal witchhunt on the possibility that Agee had gone bad before he left the CIA.

But Shackley and the operations chief were about to turn the division inside out. The operations chief's analysis showed that dozens of assets, operations, agents, and officials could be blown by Agee. CIA operatives might be approached by Soviet or Cuban intelligence and threatened or recruited. Some might be killed. Shackley saw no choice but to order massive terminations and reorganization. The Ecuador and Uruguay stations were out of business. Much of the Mexico station's operations were suspect.

The officers of the Western Hemisphere Division watched in horror as Shackley decommissioned operations, dismissed agents, and reassigned Agency personnel. Officers grumbled that the new chief was going to extremes. They argued that Agee might be disaffected but that he would not blow operations and endanger assets and his former colleagues. People were reluctant to give up the few successful operations they had. The operations chief fired off unsentimental cables ordering officers to stop this operation, pay off that agent. A few men in the field fought back. Shackley told the Brazil station to end its best operation: a high-level penetration of the Brazilian Communist Party. There was no evidence Agee knew directly of the infiltration. But it was such a winner that many in the division had chatted about the operation for years. The chief of station violently objected. Thanks to this agent, the CIA knew how Moscow was secretly passing the party money. Shackley would not yield. Terminate the agent, he declared. With the operation over, the Agency informed the Brazilian intelligence service of the route of Moscow's courier. Next time the bagman crossed the border, he was arrested and tens of thousands of dollars were confiscated. The Agency relocated its Brazilian communist agent to Portugal.

Joseph Burkholder Smith, an officer in the Mexico City station with two decades of experience, received a stream of get-rid-of messages signed by Shackley. It was dismal work. "I was disturbed," he recalled, "to have to dismiss so many loyal men and upset to have the defenses I kept putting up to try to salvage something of their old lives summarily dismissed by the Star Chamber conducting the purge in Washington." Smith was already unhappy with the Agency, and this bitter episode provided another reason why he should quit the service: "I could not treat people as unimportant spare parts to be used up and thrown away as administrators like Shackley could." According to hallway gossip Smith had picked up, at a dinner party in Mexico City Shackley pointed to an officer, another Agee casualty, and abruptly said, you're no longer of any use to me. Smith requested early retirement and began to reevaluate his days as a cold warrior.

Tom Gilligan, another officer in Mexico City, was angered by Shackley's attack on the division. He had arrived in Mexico in July of 1969 and inherited several agents and three NOCs—CIA officers who worked outside the station under nonofficial cover. Two of the NOCs handled "technical operations"—wiretaps, bugging, surveillance. One had pulled off a daring task. When several communist diplomats were staying in a Mexican hotel, the NOC sneaked into a malodorous ventilation shaft, and while balancing on a ladder and holding a flashlight between his teeth, he managed to tap their phone lines. Gilligan urged John Horton, now the chief of station in Mexico, to buck Shackley.* Agee, Gilligan asserted, did not really know much of the station's activities; the defector had focused on the Olympics when he was in Mexico. But Horton would not fight the division chief.

Gilligan was forced to fire his NOCs and agents. The agents, he later wrote, "had come to work for CIA in their late twenties and were now in their forties, with no transferable commercial skills and no way to get

---

* Gilligan later wrote that Shackley was "a man with a reputation for being absolutely decisive. He had made a name for himself out in Southeast Asia, in good part because he could play the body count and numbers game to the satisfaction of the American military. Most who had worked with him said he was mean and emotionless, a man who drove himself and others unceasingly."

a letter of reference from their long-time employer, CIA. Some found that when they could not provide such a reference, prospective employers were convinced that they had been in prison. . . . We were firing individuals Agee could not have identified. . . . Mr. Decisive [Gilligan's name for Shackley] had gone overboard."

In Paris, Agee continued writing. At a café, he befriended Sal Ferrera, an American journalist in his twenties who wrote for underground publications in the United States. Agee took a brief trip to Cuba—only to do research, he claimed—and then decided he needed to use the newspaper library of the British Museum in London. But money was running low. Ferrera had an idea. He would interview Agee and sell the story to *Playboy.* The two would split the large fee. Agee agreed and unknowingly entered into a project being run by Shackley's division.

As a correspondent for the antiwar College Press Service, Ferrera had filed stories from Paris on the Vietnam peace talks and hobnobbed with leftist leaders, antiwar activists, and other radicals. Along the way, Ferrera had become an asset of the counterintelligence staff of the CIA— and now Shackley was putting him to good use.*

Agee was scared. Surveillance teams followed him. (The watchers were French security officers helping out the Paris station.) He imagined meeting the most dreadful of ends. Within Langley, officers screamed for the head of this traitor. "Of course, there was talk about how to stop him," Shackley's operations chief recalled. "Some people said, why don't we blow him away? I would have no more moral concern [regarding killing Agee] than I would for swatting a fly, but there are laws and no one in the Agency would ever give authority for us to do that." There were already rumblings about murderous Agency activities in Vietnam. And though the Agency years earlier conspired to kill heads of state, knocking off an American was deemed a different and riskier endeavor. There would be no way to keep it quiet, and if anything happened to Agee, the whole world would believe the Agency was behind it. "Ted and I never would have been dumb enough to get involved in something like that," the operations chief said. "Ted had his eye on a higher

---

* In 1977, a *New York Times* article would identify Ferrera as a CIA operative. That year, John Foster Berlet, a College Press Service colleague of Ferrera, received, in response to an FOIA request, information the Agency had on Berlet and CPS. Berlet's careful reading of the material suggested that the Agency's source had been Ferrera. The CIA withheld from Berlet three documents, asserting that their disclosure would compromise an Agency employee. The officer who rendered the final determination on withholding the information was Theodore Shackley.

goal"—moving up within the Agency—"and he was not about to let this foolishness with the Agee case screw it up."*

The interviews with Ferrera dragged on. Agee was anxious to get his money. He could not even afford a typewriter, he complained. Ferrera loaned Agee a small amount of money and provided him a typewriter.

In mid-June, Agee was reading a copy of *The International Herald-Tribune*. Several burglars had been arrested in the Watergate office of the Democratic National Committee. The story revealed that the address book of one of the men contained the name and telephone number of E. Howard Hunt, a consultant at the White House and a former Agency officer, who worked at the Robert R. Mullen public relations firm. Agee bolted to Ferrera's apartment. Agee had information that might be explosive. He knew that the Mullen PR firm had long provided cover to CIA officers in the field. Maybe the Hunt-Mullen connection meant that the Agency was involved in the break-in. Let's get this interview out immediately, Agee said. Ferrera, oddly, was not enthusiastic. As Agee left, his friend invited him to dinner at an Italian restaurant a few nights hence.

It was poetic that on June 17—the day of the Watergate break-in—Ted Shackley was in charge of the Western Hemisphere Division. Three of the five men who broke into the Democrats' office were Cuban exiles, past foot-soldiers in the covert war against Castro; another was an American veteran of the anti-Cuba campaign. They had been enlisted for the Watergate job by Hunt, who helped organize the Bay of Pigs invasion and now was part of the Nixon White House's undercover, dirty-tricks Plumbers unit. One of the five, Eugenio Rolando Martinez, was still on Shackley's payroll—another headache for Shackley and the Agency.

The day after the break-in, Shackley received a cable on Martinez from Jacob Esterline, his chief of station in Miami. The previous November, Martinez had mentioned his association with Hunt to the Miami station. But Martinez did not disclose the full extent of his contact—most notably, that he had participated with Hunt and the Plumbers in the break-in at the office of Daniel Ellsberg's psychiatrist. And in March of 1972, Martinez had told Esterline that Hunt was skulking about Florida for

---

* "I prayed Agee wouldn't get hit by a truck," Jim Flannery, Shackley's deputy, maintained. "I half-seriously suggested we send a couple of guys to Paris to protect him." Years afterward, Agee claimed a former CIA officer told him that in early 1972 people in Langley were pondering specific ways to make Agee literally disappear.

the White House and asked if the chief was aware of all the Agency activities in the Miami area. Clearly, Martinez thought Hunt was still with the Company—and that Esterline might be out of the loop. A worried Esterline wrote headquarters requesting information on Hunt's ties to the White House. The March 27, 1972, reply from Cord Meyer, the assistant deputy director for plans, was brusque: don't worry about Hunt in Miami; the ex-spy is on White House business. "Cool it," Meyer ordered.

In his dispatch to Shackley after the Watergate break-in, Esterline sought to preserve a cover story. The chief of station noted, accurately, that Martinez currently had two responsibilities for Shackley's division: reporting on maritime operations against Cuba and gathering intelligence on possible demonstrations at the Republican and Democratic conventions, both scheduled to be held in Miami. But Esterline deliberately kept out of his report information about Martinez's prior—and worrisome—references to Hunt's suspicious activities. Esterline did not reveal that the CIA had caught a whiff of the scandal to come and did nothing.

Had either headquarters or the station pursued Martinez's curious activities and his relationship with Hunt, the Agency might have stumbled upon the Watergate break-in plans. For his part, Esterline wondered why no one in headquarters—Meyer, Shackley, or anybody else—had ever instructed him to terminate the CIA's relationship with Martinez after Esterline had reported that Martinez was in league with Hunt.

On June 20, Shackley wrote Esterline, chiding him to maintain better track of his operatives. That same week, Shackley ordered Martinez's Miami case officer reassigned to headquarters for several months. There was good reason for Shackley to keep this man close to home. The officer possessed evidence that Shackley's division could have had foreknowledge of Watergate.

Shackley was slow, perhaps purposely, to deal with another Martinez problem. On June 19, a Miami station operative reported that Martinez's car was parked at the Miami airport and contained compromising documents. The CIA waited two days before sharing this information with the FBI, which was investigating the Watergate caper. Congressional investigators later termed this delay highly suspicious. A report produced by the minority staff of the Senate Select Committee on Presidential Campaign Activities—the Watergate Committee—noted, "Our staff has yet to receive a satisfactory explanation regarding the aforementioned time lag and an accounting of Agency actions during the interim." Langley refused to make one Miami officer who worked with Martinez available to the committee staff. Nor was the staff given access to the contact reports regarding Martinez filed by several Miami officers. The committee requested documents on the debriefing of the officer whom Shackley had called to Washington, but the CIA refused to supply the material. The minority staff report recommended that the Martinez matter be further examined and that Shackley be interviewed as part of that inquiry. But no follow-up probe was ever initiated. Shackley would not face questioning. If there were any shenanigans—any CIA cover-up involving Martinez and Miami—Shackley and his colleagues got away with them.

Days following the Watergate break-in, after a fine meal at an Italian restaurant in Paris, Sal Ferrera steered Phil Agee into a British-style pub. An attractive woman in her twenties took the stool next to Agee. She said she was an American named Leslie Donegan and was spending the summer in Paris. She mentioned that she had been raised in Venezuela, that her parents were dead but had left her some money, and that she thought U.S. foreign policy in Latin America was a disgrace. She gave Agee her phone number. She, too, was a spy for Shackley.

Prior to joining the Western Hemisphere Division, Shackley's operations chief had put in a brief stint at the Swiss-Austria branch. There he supervised a program that recruited young Americans to penetrate leftist and student groups in Europe. For the project, the operations chief interviewed a number of young Americans who had applied to the CIA, but he found no one who truly had the right stuff—except one. "Once in your lifetime you run across a beautiful lady in the spy business," he reminisced. "This person was the only one I met in twenty-eight years. Most of the people we deal with in the Agency are creeps, opportunists."

Her name was Janet Strickland. She was blond, pretty, and twenty-three years old. She indeed had grown up in Venezuela, where her father was an oil executive. When the ops chief moved to the Western Hemisphere Division, he realized he had the perfect asset to target against Agee. Langley ordered the young, beautiful Janet Strickland to head to Paris. Her cover name was Leslie Donegan.

Agee and Donegan had dinner, and days later he told her of his book project. She offered him 1,000 francs and asked to see what he had written. Agee, desperate for cash, gave her a copy for a few days. She returned it and informed him she would finance his project.

As soon as she had the manuscript, Donegan passed her copy to her case officer in the CIA's Paris station. Chief of station David Murphy immediately sent a copy to Shackley and the operations chief. Shackley was pleased to see the draft. It confirmed his worst fears—Agee did intend to disclose precious secrets—but justified Shackley's actions in clearing out much of the division. In the Western Hemisphere Division, people heard that Shackley had acquired Agee's work-in-progress. His accomplishment won him respect, but not any affection. Many officers still carried a fierce hatred of Shackley due to his relentless purge.

Leslie Donegan left Paris, and Agee used her studio apartment as a workspace. He enlisted a friend, Therese Roberge, to type his manuscript. The two met each day at Donegan's apartment, and Agee lived in secrecy at another apartment. Donegan sent money and several times invited Agee to join her in Majorca. He declined and plowed ahead with his book. By October of 1972, Agee had 500 pages finished.

Shackley and his operations chief were trying to get Agee a book contract. The operations chief traveled to New York City to meet with publishers. He was hoping to convince one of them to buy Agee's book. The intent was to string Agee along. After the publisher acquired the book, it would help the Agency by repeatedly requesting rewrites from Agee until it finally dumped the project. The operations chief found one publishing house that agreed to assist the CIA in the scam. But before the operation was launched, Cord Meyer heard about the plan and halted it. "Cover publishing" was one of Meyer's areas of expertise. He did not appreciate the turf invasion, and he also thought the potential for a public controversy was too high.

Agee was dependent on Donegan for financial support. But the former CIA man had suspicions about his patron. She had told him she thought it was wrong for him to expose names of CIA officers. She suggested he go to the United States to see publishers. (Agee was staying clear of the legal reach of the Agency.) She repeatedly asked where he lived.

Sal Ferrera was another concern for Agee. He refused to give Agee copies of photographs he had snapped of the surveillance teams. He would not tell Agee where he had obtained the typewriter Agee was using. And Ferrera was taking his time with the *Playboy* interview. But Agee could not cut the pair off. He needed Donegan's money. He put his fears aside and arranged for the three of them to go to England, where they would finish the book together.

At a café on a cold, rainy afternoon, Donegan, relaying a message from Ferrera, told Agee the unidentified owner of the typewriter wanted it back. But she had with her a replacement. Agee brought Donegan's typewriter to his apartment. Days later, he stumbled across a man and woman in trench coats standing outside the apartment's door. The man had what looked to be a hearing aid in his ear; something bulky was under their coats. Agee heard a beeping sound. As he entered his apartment, the pair departed. Agee wondered about the beeping. Then it struck him—the typewriter. He took it apart; beneath the cloth lining of the lid was a collection of transistors, batteries, and an antenna.

Shackley and the CIA had found him. Donegan had planted a bugged typewriter on Agee. Shackley hoped that by bugging Agee he could answer the question obsessing the Agency: was Agee plotting with Soviet or Cuban intelligence? With the typewriter, Shackley discovered Agee's hiding place and eavesdropped on his most private conversations—but only for a few days. Shackley and his operations chief picked up little valuable information through the bug. And they never would obtain any evidence that Agee was in contact with the other side. (Yet the operations chief later declared, "There was not a chance that he wasn't in touch with the bad guys.") Shackley could report to his superiors that he had penetrated Agee's circles. But due to the operation, he lost his best assets in the anti-Agee program.

Agee assumed both Donegan and Ferrera were CIA operatives. Donegan's apartment must be bugged as well, he figured, so the Agency had all his conversations with his typist Therese Roberge. It knew he planned to name names. But, at least, Agency money had supported him for the past few months. Donegan already had given him funds for his upcoming trip to London. "The irony was that CIA money got me through the worst time in my life," Agee recalled. "If I hadn't gotten the CIA money I couldn't have continued." Maybe—just maybe—without the money from Shackley, Agee's book project might have faltered and died.

Agee did not confront Ferrera and Donegan and headed to London. Over the course of the next few weeks, Ferrera and Donegan repeatedly asked Agee to travel to Spain. What did they want? he wondered. Was his former employer trying to lure him somewhere? Perhaps the Agency was planning to plant drugs on him. Perhaps, he imagined, something more sinister was brewing.

Years later, Agee collected one piece of evidence to support his fears of those days. In records he obtained from the Justice Department, he read that the Department between 1975 and 1979 pondered whether to bring criminal charges against him. One document observed that "prosecution is impossible without disclosing the illegal acts." The "illegal acts" reference went unexplained, but suggested that the Agency—possibly Shackley himself—had been too enthusiastic in its pursuit of Agee and had crossed some line.

Agee remained in London. The British secret service, responding to a request from Langley, followed Agee wherever he went. Penguin Books furnished him a contract and a £2,000 advance. He cut his ties with Ferrera and Donegan and continued to write his book—which Agee envisioned a contribution to socialism and international revolution. He wanted to stop the CIA.*

II

Philip Agee was not the only Agency enemy Shackley needed to neutralize. Another was the U.S. Congress.

On March 21, 1972, shortly before Shackley took over the Western Hemisphere Division, syndicated columnist Jack Anderson disclosed that the CIA and the International Telephone and Telegraph Corporation had been involved in "a bizarre plot" to block the 1970 election of leftist Chilean President Salvador Allende. According to documents leaked to Anderson, William Broe, who in 1970 headed the Western Hemisphere Division, schemed with ITT officials to cause economic chaos in Chile, hoping this would spur the Chilean military to pull a coup and prevent the democratically elected Allende from coming to power. The ITT papers indicated that John McCone, the former CIA chief and now a director of ITT, was a key participant in the conspiracy. Anderson further reported that ITT, panicked by the prospect of Allende seizing its holdings in Chile, had offered the White House $1 million to use in any anti-Allende campaign.

Here was a looming PR disaster for the Agency. The CIA had engaged in underhanded business since its inception. But intervening in the democratic process overseas—that seemingly was not the American way. This sort of activity had been going on for years, but the American public had not been supplied evidence of such intrigue.

As Shackley moved into the office of chief of the Western Hemisphere Division to deal with the Agee troubles, U.S. senators were considering whether or not to investigate the Anderson revelations. Up to now, the Agency had generally been treated gingerly by its overseers on Capitol Hill. The committees with jurisdiction over the CIA—the armed services committees and the military appropriations subcommittees—were protective of the Agency. (There were yet no full committees devoted to

---

* In 1976, Agee learned Leslie Donegan was working in Geneva at the International Labor Organization of the United Nations and that her real name was Janet Strickland. He and two photographers from Le Nouvel Observateur, a French newsweekly, sandbagged Strickland in her office. When the flashbulbs started popping, she fled her office. Le Nouvel Observateur declined to publish Agee's article on Strickland. But The Sun, a British tabloid, picked up the story and tracked Strickland to her parents' mansion in Palm Beach, Florida. She denied ever having worked for the Agency. After the Agee operation, Shackley's operations chief visited his agent and her parents at their Park Avenue home in New York. He took Strickland to lunch. "If every agent I ever handled was as good as Janet," the operations chief noted, "my life would have been much easier."

intelligence.) Their chairmen, mainly conservative southerners, did not pry too far. But with the ITT scandal, the committee seeking to do the prying was the Senate Foreign Relations Committee, which was not in the pocket of Langley, and the member pushing the probe was Frank Church, a liberal Democrat from Idaho who chaired the Subcommittee on Multinational Corporations.

Acquiescing to the Nixon White House, Church agreed not to hold hearings on the ITT affair until after the 1972 presidential election, and in September the investigators of his subcommittee started interviewing dozens of ITT employees, CIA officers, and U.S. officials. Shackley and others in Langley worried about what the investigators might find. The Company men realized that the ITT thread threatened to unravel much more, for Anderson had uncovered but an exceedingly small slice of the CIA's Chilean operation.

The Agency worked its friends on Capitol Hill. Helms, whom Nixon had canned as CIA head but nominated as ambassador to Iran, testified before the Senate Foreign Relations Committee on February 5, 1973, as part of his confirmation hearings.* Two days later he appeared at an executive session of the committee. In both encounters, he downplayed the whole ITT-CIA business. There had been no exchange of funds, he explained, and at no time had the Agency and ITT plotted to affect political events in Chile. Asked by Senator Symington, a friend of Helms, if the CIA had tried to overthrow Allende, Helms answered, "No, sir."

About this time, John Maury, the Agency's legislative counsel, told one member of Congress that Langley was not worried about Watergate. ITT was another matter. This affair, he said, could be "misunderstood," especially if that liberal Church tried to use it for his own purposes. In the White House, Nixon and his aides looked on anxiously. On February 9, 1973, John Dean, the counsel to the President, called James Schlesinger, the new head of the CIA, and discussed Church's snooping into the ITT episode. This could be "rather explosive," Dean told Schlesinger.

---

* Helms was fired by Nixon in November of 1972. CIA partisans reasonably assumed he was dismissed because he had not cooperated fully with Nixon's attempt to stonewall the Watergate investigation. Days after the break-in, Helms's deputy, Vernon Walters, at the instruction of the White House, had told L. Patrick Gray III, the acting FBI chief, that the Bureau's Watergate inquiry might trip over Agency projects. Walters noted that it might be best for Gray to "taper off the matter." A week later, Gray told Walters the FBI had to investigate further, unless the CIA officially declared the FBI probe endangered national security. The CIA would not do that. Helms and Walters had taken a stab at stopping the FBI, but their refusal to go all the way led the vindictive Nixon and like-minded aides to consider Helms disloyal.

Helms's testimony in early February did not satisfy Church's investigators. Church requested Helms's presence at a hearing of his Subcommittee on Multinational Operations. For Shackley and the CIA brass, that was going too far. They had stood by and watched as the staff of this new subcommittee had poked into Agency business by privately questioning Agency and ITT officials. Now Church, by pursuing Helms and the ITT controversy, was threatening to embarrass the Agency. Shackley decided it was time to shut Church down.

On February 23, Shackley conferred with Senator Henry "Scoop" Jackson, a hawkish Democrat the Agency counted as an ally. Shackley tried to persuade Jackson to block Church from conducting further investigations and—scariest of all prospects—public hearings. When he returned to his office, Shackley wrote a memo recounting the conversation. A few years later, portions of the memo—without Shackley's name—were included in a congressional report as evidence of how the Agency maneuvered to withhold information from Congress.

"Senator Jackson's advice to us," Shackley wrote, "was as follows":

1. Senator Jackson felt strongly that the first order of business for CIA in terms of handling the basic issues that were involved in the Senate Foreign Relations Subcommittee on Multinational Corporations asking the Agency about its activities in Chile in 1970, was to discuss the problem with the White House. [Jackson] was quite explicit that this conversation should be carried out by Schlesinger and that he should talk with no one other than President Nixon and [White House chief of staff] Mr. [H. R.] Halderman [sic]. The Senator stressed repeatedly that the Church Subcommittee on Multinational Corporations had focused on ITT only in the sense that this was the top of the iceberg. . . .

2. Senator Jackson felt that the ultimate solution to the problem facing the Agency . . . could be found in getting Senator [John] McClellan [chairman of the Intelligence Operations Subcommittee of the Appropriations Committee], acting on behalf of Senator [John] Stennis [chairman of the CIA Subcommittee of the Armed Services Committee], to . . . [privately] look into the nature and scope of the CIA's activities in Chile in 1970. Once that was accomplished, the [McClellan subcommittees] would handle the Foreign Relations Committee. Senator Jackson repeatedly made the comment that in his view the [McClellan subcommittees] had the responsibility of protecting the Agency in the type of situation that was inherent in the Church subcommittee. As a result of this conviction, Senator Jackson would work with the Agency to see that we got this protection. . . .

4. Once the [McClellan subcommittees] had heard the details provided on the CIA's involvement, the Agency could send a brief statement to the Church subcommittee staff members in response to the questions which they had previously posed to CIA. Senator Jackson

agreed that the following statement would be perfectly adequate for the purpose.

"The testimony of Mr. Helms on 5 and 7 February before the Senate Foreign Relations Committee clearly established that CIA neither gave to nor received from ITT funds for use in Chile in 1970 for support of political parties. In addition, Mr. Helms' testimony brought out the fact that there were no joint action programs established in the context of the 1970 political developments in Chile. CIA regards Mr. Helms' testimony on this topic to be accurate thus, no further elaboration is planned." . . .

9. *Comment*. Senator Jackson was extremely helpful throughout 23 February on the issue of the Agency's problem with the Church subcommittee. Senator Jackson is convinced that it is essential that the procedure not be established whereby CIA can be called upon to testify before a wide range of Congressional committees.

The chief of the Western Hemisphere Division was trying to stone-wall, with a senator as an accomplice. For years, the CIA only had to answer to friendly subcommittees. Church was undermining this comfortable status quo.

Adopting Shackley's advice, Schlesinger sent a frosty letter to Church that included almost word-for-word the paragraph Shackley suggested in his memo. Those nosy members of the Senate Foreign Relations Committee had gotten their crack at Helms. That was enough.

Shackley was trying to exploit the jurisdictional fights that routinely occur between congressional committees. At first, Shackley's plan appeared to be working. "We heard that Jackson was moving to limit our investigation," said Jack Blum, a Church subcommittee investigator. Then McClellan called a showdown meeting with Church and other members. Now, you know, Frank, the old Arkansan Democrat said, you're intruding into the areas covered by other senators. Why are you pushing so hard here? Church realized he could not simply claim he wanted to know what the Agency had been up to. But he had a powerful argument ready. ITT had applied to recover almost $100 million from the U.S. Overseas Private Investment Corporation, which guaranteed a portion of the firm's Chilean investments expropriated by the Allende government. If he could demonstrate that the company had connived with the Agency to interfere in Chilean politics, Church explained, then perhaps OPIC and U.S. taxpayers would not have to honor the claim.

McClellan leaned back in his chair and put his feet up on his desk. He placed his hands behind his head and slowly said: "No one ever told me about a potential $100 million claim. Frank, you go ahead and do whatever you think is necessary."

Church went ahead. His subcommittee called in Helms for a private session. Helms was crafty. He reformulated questions he was asked and then answered his version of the questions. Still, Church and Clifford Case, the ranking Republican on the subcommittee, caught Helms in a few contradictions. The session was not going well for the former spy chief. "Helms was becoming more desperate by the minute," recalled chief counsel Jerome Levinson. Then Symington intervened. Not long ago Symington had engineered a big stink about the CIA's secret war in Laos. But he had always liked Helms. A Director of Central Intelligence, Symington remarked, cannot be expected to remember everything. Let's bring in whoever was head of the Western Hemisphere Division when all this happened. Symington was doing Helms a favor, but he had discomfited the Agency. The subcommittee staff had not expected to obtain anything more than the testimony of the former CIA director. This was a whole new ball game—the testimony of an Agency line officer—and one more dilemma for Shackley.

On a winter's day, Shackley drove to Capitol Hill for unpleasant business. In Church's office, Levinson and Blum were amused to meet this man. Levinson had heard from his CIA contacts that some spooks referred to the blond fellow sitting across from him as the "Butcher of Laos." He looked more like an uptight businessman—tough, but no secret agent. He was stiff, no-nonsense all the way. He made no small talk. He was there to discuss the ground rules for what would be a historic occasion: the public testimony of a CIA officer.

Shackley was not taking this well. "He was very nasty," Levinson recalled. "He thought this was all a great mistake. We had to keep reminding him that we had an agreement." Helms for William Broe—that was the deal. Shackley kept attempting to set limits on what the subcommittee could ask Broe. The committee lawyers did not accept his conditions. When they said, here are the questions Broe must answer, Shackley could not say no.

But there was something that Shackley could do: rig the information provided to the subcommittee.

His all-important task was to preserve the cover story that while senior officers of ITT and the CIA in the United States had brainstormed on how to get rid of Allende—the ITT documents were irrefutable—CIA and ITT men in the field had not schemed together. Shackley could only do that with the cooperation of Hal Hendrix and Robert Berrellez, ex-newspapermen on the ITT payroll, who had been in contact with the CIA in Chile in 1970. Fortunately, he had a close tie with one. Hendrix was the former *Miami News* correspondent who supposedly had used information from Shackley to write his Pulitzer Prize-winning articles on the missiles in Cuba.

The subcommittee was interested in what Hendrix and Berrellez had to say about CIA-ITT collusion. As Jack Anderson had reported, the two in September of 1970 had sent a report to ITT executives noting that U.S. Ambassador to Chile Edward Korry had received a "green light" from Nixon to block Allende's election. Levinson and Blum were curious how the ITT men had learned this. The investigators suspected that the source for the cable included local CIA officers, and they believed the cable was proof the CIA and ITT in Chile had cooperated in anti-Allende activities.

For Shackley, it was crucial to keep Church's investigators far from any trail that led them toward the highly secret doings of the very active station in Santiago, Chile. Hendrix's talks with station chief Henry Hecksher were not more scandalous than those in the United States between Broe and ITT corporate executives. But if the subcommittee started to delve into Agency actions in Chile, the CIA would be in deep trouble. At almost any cost, that had to be prevented.

Shackley assigned the case to Jonathan Hanke, chief of covert action for the division. He told Hanke to advise Hendrix what to say when called to testify. Jim Flannery, the deputy chief of the division, opposed sending Hanke to contact Hendrix. Let's stay away from Hendrix, he argued, so there is not even the appearance of collusion. Shackley ignored Flannery's recommendation. Shackley "insisted," Flannery recalled, "we were not telling [Hendrix] what to do. 'They're just steering tips,' he said. That was b.s. It was part of his ability, if he deemed something to be useful, to resort to moral or legalistic sleight of hand." Shackley was conspiring to mislead Congress.

Hendrix told Shackley's emissary not to worry. He would deny to the subcommittee that he had learned of the "green light" from Hecksher.* Hanke also contacted Berrellez, who also promised to falsely tell the subcommittee he had not known any CIA officers in Latin America. In early February of 1973, Hendrix and Berrellez met with Levinson and Blum of the Church subcommittee. As Shackley hoped, the pair said they had no contact with the CIA in Chile.

To protect his small but vital secret, Hendrix had needed the help of

---

* Hanke held a meeting with Hendrix on May 11, 1972. Over breakfast at the Marriott Hotel in Rosslyn, Virginia, they discussed how they could find Anderson's source for the ITT papers. Hendrix reported on ITT's internal reaction to the Church subcommittee's request for documents. He noted that several ITT lawyers had become familiar with the key papers and would not support destroying the incriminating records. The pair, according to a subsequent CIA memo, talked about ITT's continuing covert funding of the Chilean opposition and referred to two payments of $100,000 each. Hendrix remarked that his daughter's fiancé had encountered a problem while applying for an Agency job and asked Hanke to check on the situation.

Hanke and Shackley. Hendrix's plan was to inform the subcommittee he had learned of the "green light" from another source—not Hecksher. He had the perfect candidate for the fake source: a dead Chilean. But before proceeding, Hendrix needed to be sure this fellow was deceased and to know whether this man had been in Santiago at the time crucial to the cover story. Shackley's division ran a check on this individual. It passed the results to Hendrix: the man had been in Santiago and, yes, he was dead. It supplied Hendrix with a physical description of the person and a list of his habits, in case Hendrix had to prove his connection to the deceased. With this information in hand, Hendrix told the subcommittee that he had obtained the "green light" information from a Chilean acquaintance in a hotel coffee shop.

On March 20, 1973, in the Dirksen Senate Office Building, Senator Church convened the first of seven days of public hearings. ITT officials testified about their anti-Allende scheming in 1970 and the related conversations between Broe and top ITT officers. When Hendrix appeared before the subcommittee, he stuck to the story he had developed with Shackley's division. Asked about the source of the information he placed in his September 1970 "green light" report, Hendrix claimed his source was a Chilean highly placed in the Christian Democratic Party. After Berrellez testified, Hanke wrote a memo—presumably for Shackley—that reported that Berrellez also had successfully evaded the truth.

On March 27, Shackley and other top officials at Langley could only watch as a piece of unpleasant history occurred: for the first time, a CIA officer would testify under oath before a congressional committee and that testimony would become public. Broe, now the Inspector General of the CIA, took his place at the witness table in a small room in the Dirksen Building. Present were Church, five other senators, and Levinson and Blum. The public was not allowed in, but a transcript of the session was to be released the next day.

Broe discussed his contacts with ITT officers in 1970. Contradicting the earlier testimony of McCone and Berrellez, he noted that the company had offered the Agency money to be passed to an Allende opponent. Broe said he had approved a list of anti-Allende actions proposed by Berrellez and Hendrix. (ITT officials testified they never put the plan into operation.) Church asked the CIA officer if there were anything else the senators ought to know. Broe replied no.

"Someone is lying," Church declared after Broe's testimony. The senator had in mind the allegation that ITT had offered the CIA funds for anti-Allende activity. Moreover, Charles Meyer, a former assistant secretary of state, had testified that the Nixon policy was not to intervene in Chilean politics. His testimony suggested—wrongly—that the CIA had run off on its own, half-cocked. "We must assume," Church said, "that what was being done by the CIA was being done on its own. CIA was being lobbied by ITT and they had a little thing going."

A *little thing going*—Shackley, Hanke, Broe, and their comrades had, in the immediate sense, not done such a bad job. As shocking as the hearings might have been, the sessions showed only that stateside CIA officers participated in talk, not action. The Agency's only contacts with ITT, according to the evidence presented, were discussions about hypotheticals. The direct contacts between ITT and CIA officers in Chile were, thanks to Shackley and Hanke, successfully cloaked. Most important of all, there was no evidence that the CIA actually took steps to destabilize the elected government of Chile.

The spies had trumped the interlopers from Capitol Hill. But it was a Pyrrhic victory. The secrets—the real secrets about the Agency's activities in Chile—were, for a time, safe. But Shackley and his colleagues had planted one big landmine, soon to explode and change the Agency they aimed to protect.

The ITT case was but a footnote to what the Agency had done—and was still doing—in Chile. At the precise moment Shackley sat down with Church's investigators and argued over what they could ask Broe on the narrow subject of CIA and ITT joint actions during a three-month period in 1970, Shackley was overseeing an extensive covert action program in Chile. The effort, one of the largest in the Agency's history, was part of a decade-long offensive waged by the Agency to mold Chilean politics to Washington's fancy. Church barely had hold of the tail. There was so much more to the story.

Ten years earlier, John Kennedy had launched a massive covert program in Chile. The CIA was then dispensing $230,000 in secret funds to Chile's centrist Christian Democratic Party to oppose the leftist coalition behind the presidential candidacy of Salvador Allende. It funneled cash to the right-wing Radical Party and spent over $2.6 million to help the 1964 presidential campaign of Eduardo Frei, the Christian Democrat candidate.

To stop Allende that year, the Santiago station mounted an extensive clandestine propaganda campaign. Agency dollars produced a flood of newspaper stories, television programs, radio broadcasts, and thousands of posters hostile to Allende. One of Shackley's most prominent JMWAVE assets, Juana Castro, toured South America and spoke out against Allende. "If the Reds win in Chile," she warned, "no type of religious activity will be possible." This was one of the most effective propaganda campaigns the Agency had ever run. Frei won a clear majority and became President.

In the five years following Frei's elections, the CIA spent $2 million on covert actions in Chile. It continued to fund the archconservative Radical Party. Case officers used $350,000 to influence the 1969 congressional elections. The station had a number of journalists on the take. Between 1964 and 1968, CIA officers infiltrated the Chilean Socialist Party and the cabinet of the Chilean government. They paid assets to challenge leftists within student groups and labor unions. They supported a host of civic, cultural, and intellectual organizations deemed friendly to U.S. interests.

Come 1970, Allende was again running for President, and his platform called for nationalizing copper mines, socializing major sectors of the economy, accelerating agrarian reform, increasing wages, and improving relations with socialist countries. The CIA expended about $1 million on a new anti-Allende propaganda campaign, reminiscent of its 1964 masterpiece. The message was similar: an Allende victory would bring violence and repression. Langley's prognosticators were right. Violence and repression would follow Allende's victory. But they would come from the forces who had been supported and egged on by the CIA.

On September 4, 1970, Allende squeaked to victory with 36.3 percent of the vote. "The CIA had had its nose rubbed in the dirt in Chile," recalled a CIA officer who monitored the results. "We had staked our reputation on keeping Allende out. [The] loss hurt the CIA's standing [in the White House] and its pride." In the White House, Nixon and Kissinger were beside themselves.

Their reaction was not commensurate with on-the-ground reality. Days after the election, an interagency group that included representatives of the CIA, the Pentagon, State, and the White House issued a memo on the meaning of the election. Yes, it was, the group noted, a psychological setback for Washington and a win for the Reds. But the paper concluded that the United States had no vital interests within Chile and that the Allende victory did not alter significantly the global balance of power, nor did it pose a threat to peace in the region. But this analysis did not convince those with power. Nixon and the CIA had seven weeks until the Chilean congressional ratification of the election to take another stab at stopping Allende.

On September 15, the President called Helms to his office. Do whatever it takes to prevent Allende from assuming office, Nixon ordered. "Make the economy scream," he declared. Organize a military coup. Ten million dollars is available, more if necessary. And, Helms was told, do not inform the Department of State or the Pentagon about this secret "Track II" program.*

At first the Agency hoped to bribe Chilean congressmen to vote against Allende's ratification, but its convoluted scheme collapsed. Agency-funded journalists produced stories that predicted economic collapse should Allende assume office. As part of Track II, Langley did all it could to promote an easy way out—a military coup. Between October 5 and 20, Agency officers made at least twenty-one contacts with key military and police officials inclined to stage a coup. These Chileans were assured that Washington looked forward to their success. Helms sent two longtime CIA operatives to Chile to help instigate a coup. Agency officers provided cash and weapons to two different bands of military plotters who planned to kidnap General René Schneider, the army chief of staff and a strict constitutionalist, as a prelude to a coup. One group tried to snatch him and failed; the other moved against Schneider and mortally wounded him. But the coup did not come off. The Chilean Congress, many of its members outraged by the attack on Schneider, confirmed Allende as President. Helms and the CIA had let Nixon down.

After Allende became President, the Agency poured money into various covert actions in Chile. It underwrote the Christian Democrats. CIA officers slipped funds to opposition candidates. In 1971, the White House okayed a $700,000 covert donation to *El Mercurio,* the leading opposition paper. The Santiago station passed the Chilean military fabricated material suggesting Chilean police were conspiring with Cubans to dig up dirt on the Chilean army high command. Agency loyalists argued for years afterward that CIA projects in Chile following Allende's inauguration sought merely to preserve the political opposition. But the desired result of the disinformation plot was obvious: convince the military it should get rid of Allende.

III

By the time Shackley moved into the Western Hemisphere Division in April of 1972, the secret Chile program had become routine. From behind his always-clean desk in Langley, Shackley was now one of the officers who reviewed projects and decided where the Agency should place U.S. taxpayer dollars to undermine the government of Chile.

As had been true in other instances, the analysts of the Directorate of

---

* Track II was also hidden from Congress. Of the thirty-three covert action programs undertaken in Chile between 1963 and 1974 with the approval of the White House, only eight were disclosed to Congress in some fashion.

Intelligence did not perceive a great threat from the target of the covert action crowd. In June of 1972, the Directorate of Intelligence issued a National Intelligence Estimate that found the prospects for democracy in Chile were better than at any time since Allende's inauguration. Legislative, union, and student elections were transpiring in normal fashion. When progovernment forces lost, they accepted the results. Congress, controlled by the Christian Democrats and the National Party, curtailed Allende's power. The news media included vocal critics of Allende. The DDI reported that Allende did not share Castro's revolutionary goals. The NIE noted that Allende had sought to avoid irreparable damage to his relations with Washington. Democracy was not threatened in Chile, but for the Nixon administration democracy was not the issue. The CIA was intervening in Chile for the sake of U.S. financial and geopolitical interests, real or imagined. Shackley and his fellow officers were not missionaries for democracy.

Once Shackley was running the division, Nixon's national security team authorized another $965,000 for *El Mercurio,* the opposition newspaper. But the intelligence that crossed Shackley's desk showed Allende had no evil designs on *El Mercurio.* One agent's report maintained that Allende considered *El Mercurio* generally objective in its news and that the President often defended the newspaper from other leftist leaders who wanted to move against it. This source reported that Allende was telling associates he fully intended to have free and democratic elections in 1976 and turn the presidency over to whoever won.

Such intelligence did little to change Shackley's task. He approved continuing propaganda projects. The Santiago station produced magazines, books, and studies. His division developed articles and stories to be placed in *El Mercurio* and on radio stations and television shows. Agency-promoted stories routinely alleged the Reds were plotting to disband or destroy the armed services and that the Soviets were eager to develop a submarine base in Chile. Overall, the CIA dumped $8 million into Chile between 1970 and 1973, with $3 million expended in 1972 alone.* In this period, the White House authorized Shackley's division to dish out nearly $4 million to opposition parties.

A summary of CIA intelligence on Chile prepared in July of 1972 for a congressional briefing portrayed a situation not to Washington's liking, but hardly a bleak one demanding an extreme response. The opposition to Allende remained viable. The economy was expanding at about 7 percent, twice the rate under the previous administration. Unemployment had been drastically reduced. Anti-Americanism within Chile was

---

* These figures are at official exchange rates. Through the black market, the Agency could buy Chilean *escudos* at one-fifth the official level.

"only a passing point." The military was even growing accustomed to Allende, who was supplying the armed services decent pay for the first time in many years. Talk of a coup was at a low ebb.

Nevertheless, Shackley had his CIA officers in Chile prepare for a coup. They compiled lists of persons who would have to be arrested and a roster of civilian and government installations that would need protection in the event the military moved against Allende. Through agents within the government, Shackley's division obtained Allende's plans for dealing with a military uprising. The CIA later maintained it never shared this booty with the Chilean military. But Shackley's men in the field were in close contact with the Chilean military, ostensibly for the purpose of collecting intelligence. The station penetrated a group of military men considering a coup. One case officer communicated with the leader of a cabal. There is no evidence of direct station involvement in coup planning, but as a congressional report later noted, "the U.S. government's desire to be in clandestine contact with military plotters, for whatever purpose, might well imply to [the plotters] U.S. support for their future plans."

By September of 1972, the domestic scene in Chile had undergone a severe turn. Strikes had besieged Chile. Food shortages prompted various antigovernment popular outbursts. In October—as Allende declared a state of emergency to deal with a national trucking strike and widespread protests against the government—Shackley's officers were given $100,000 to distribute to anti-Allende business organizations. The money was supposed to be limited to activities related to upcoming congressional elections. (One of these private sector groups passed the modest amount of $2,800 in Agency money to striking truckers, in violation of Agency rules. Shackley's division chastised the group, but continued to fund it.) Nixon also authorized Shackley's officers to provide more than $1.4 million to opposition political parties and private groups to influence the congressional elections scheduled for March 1973. Once more, the CIA had another chance to do in Allende.

As part of his usual practice of placing his most trusted allies into critical posts, Shackley put the affable Tom Clines in charge of the Chile desk. After Shackley had left Laos in 1968, Clines had stayed for nearly two years as the senior CIA man in Long Tieng. He returned to Washington burned out. He wanted out of the Agency life of long hours and short pay. His superiors convinced him to cool off and spend a year at the Naval War College in Newport, Rhode Island. Refreshed after that, Clines arrived in Langley ready for action.

Clines harbored strong notions of how he wanted to handle things in Chile. Shortly after he took over the Chile desk, he told the chief of station in Santiago he intended to send some of his paramilitary guys to

Chile. He had in mind several trustworthy Cubans from the days of JMWAVE. We can get the situation settled quickly, Clines said to the chief. The station chief declined the offer and explained to Clines the plan was to work covertly through the political system. They would buy votes, stir up the political pot. "They did not want to run this thing into a war," Clines recalled. "That turned me off. I wanted to settle it my way."

For a while Clines did it the other way. The chief of station sent him messages: I need so much money for this or that asset. Requests came in from the station to set up bank accounts in Switzerland and Israel through which cash was funneled into Chile. When large amounts were concerned, Clines went to Shackley for an approval.

Toward the end of 1972, political turmoil was increasing in Chile. Allende called out tanks, his cabinet resigned, and the government instituted food rationing, claiming opponents engineered food shortages. The more unrest the better for Shackley and the Agency. They hoped to pack the Chilean Senate with a two-thirds majority of anti-Allende members, who could impeach the President. In the months before the March 1973 elections, Shackley and his officers schemed to dispense $1.5 million to Allende's opposition.* In February, the White House gave the CIA another $200,000 to pass to the opposition. That month, Shackley's officers asked for additional funds. Ambassador Nathaniel Davis, who supported the thrust of the U.S. program, opposed the request. The influence-peddling, he believed, was going beyond reasonable limits.

In the March congressional elections, the opposition retained its majority in both houses but fell short of the number of seats needed to oust Allende. Shackley and his colleagues had failed. In Washington, Nixon and his men, even if distracted by the demands of Watergate, Vietnam, and the ITT scandal, continued to search for a way to knock off the socialist Allende.

The Agee nightmare, the ITT scandal, Watergate, destabilizing Chile —it was a busy time for Shackley. When not tending to these matters, he handled the more mundane tasks of intelligence. He was determined not to let crises dominate his first tenure as a division chief. As chief, he pushed his subordinates to recruit Soviet agents. But the number of potential targets was small. "Ted Shackley and other people who had

* Around this time, the CIA asked the FBI to "reinstitute coverage" of the Chilean embassy in Washington—that is, to bug it. The public record does not reveal who in the CIA in late 1972 asked for the "coverage" to resume.

served in Europe were used to having the Soviets around," recalled Jim Flannery, his deputy. "But there were not a lot of Soviets in Latin America. There were some in Mexico, Cuba, and maybe Chile." So Shackley's division focused on others: left-of-center groups, political organizations, guerrillas, and governments. It was, Flannery noted, "second-tier work."*

As he had done elsewhere, Shackley demanded more and better reports. In Berlin, Laos, and Vietnam, he prompted grumbling with his incessant call for larger numbers. More is not always better, officers griped. Maybe Shackley took those complaints to heart, for in the division he instituted a grading system for reports. From now on, reports in the division were evaluated not only on quality but on the difficulty the officer had faced in obtaining the information. If a case officer in Montevideo merely took his local police contact to lunch and then wrote up what the cop told him about an internal split within the local Communist Party, that report was graded differently than one produced as the result of a long-term, tough operation.

Despite the emphasis on quality, Shackley wanted to see big numbers. "This was typical of Ted," said Clines. "We used to say, with Ted Shackley, you take an intelligence report and you make five out of it. He wanted numbers. We gave him numbers." Shackley was calling for more intelligence while he was, thanks to Agee, eviscerating the division.

Jim Adkins was one case officer glad to see Shackley in control. He had served under Shackley in Laos and considered Shackley an impressive leader. He now was stationed in the Dominican Republic. Soon after Shackley came along, Adkins began receiving the guidance cables the chief wired all his stations: Do more. Be more aggressive. That was what Adkins was waiting to hear. He had arrived in Santo Domingo a year before Shackley became division chief, looking to recruit members of the Dominican government, particularly officers of its security ser-

---

* Shackley's insistence on more Soviet operations had a large payoff. Shortly after he left the division, the Agency recruited a Russian in the Soviet embassy in Colombia. The Agency opened a Swiss bank account for the Russian, who was called back to Moscow and assigned to the secretariat of the Foreign Ministry. There he photographed hundreds (perhaps thousands) of cables and documents for the Agency. One cable he passed to the Americans covered a discussion between Kissinger and a Soviet official before President Jimmy Carter took office in 1977. Kissinger bitterly complained that a naïve Carter would be unable to manage international relations. By the time this report was received in Washington, Carter was President. Eventually, the Russian was caught. When KGB officers came to his office to apprehend him, the Russian spy grabbed a pen Langley had provided him and stabbed himself with the lethal potion it held. He died immediately.

vices. But for unexplained reasons headquarters refused to grant him permission. Perhaps it was skittishness due to the Agee predicament. Shackley said, go to it, and Adkins assembled a roster of agents.

With Shackley prodding from a distance, Adkins did more than recruit. He helped the repressive government of Joaquin Balaguer as it tracked down and killed an enemy of the state.

On February 4, 1973, the Dominican armed forces announced that a small band of eight rebels in a sailboat named *Black Jack* had landed on the island. Press reports immediately speculated that the troops were commanded by Colonel Francisco Caamano Deno. The constitutionalist Caamano had been a popular leader of the 1965 effort to restore President Juan Bosch to power, after he was ousted by a right-wing military cabal. A civil war had ensued, and Lyndon Johnson had dispatched Marines, who helped the anti-Bosch military put down the rebellion. When the fighting ended, Caamano was shunted off to a post in London. He disappeared in 1967 while on a trip to the Netherlands. Some rumors claimed he was in Cuba.

Reports of Caamano's mini-invasion in 1973 prompted a crisis in the Dominican Republic. Balaguer's regime announced it found on the sailboat documents that linked Caamano to Bosch and other opposition leaders. Bosch's home and that of others were raided, and the former president, who denied any tie to the tiny insurrection, rushed into hiding. Military personnel were sent to newspaper offices and radio stations. Tanks surrounded the autonomous university of Santo Domingo. Troops chased after Caamano.

No one in Langley thought Caamano had much of a chance. But one could never be too careful, especially when dealing with what might be a Cuban-backed operation. When the Dominican government turned toward the Company for help, the CIA was happy to oblige.

Every day, Adkins, with the approval of Shackley, met with a Dominican opposite and supplied him with advice on how to deal with Caamano's rebellion. Adkins had years of experience in the jungles of Laos, directing a tribal guerrilla force. Adkins, in return, learned from the liaison officer and other sources precisely what progress was being made by the troops. His reports back to the division earned him praise.

Over the course of two weeks, Balaguer's troops and Caamano's small band clashed several times in the southern mountains, as Adkins continued to assist from Santo Domingo. The government's goal was no secret. "If they captured him, they would make sure he was dead," recalled Flannery, who had served on the island in 1965. "They wouldn't take him alive."

On February 17, the Dominican military announced Caamano and several of his comrades had been gunned down on a highway by government troops. Bosch's party later raised a series of questions about the government's account of Caamano's final battle, implying Caamano was killed after capture. Whatever the truth, Caamano was dead. Shackley and others in Washington were pleased with Adkins's contribution.

Shackley's division provided assistance to other pro-America regimes in Latin America.* In the fall of 1972, Shackley sent Felix Rodriguez, the battle-scarred Cuban exile, to Buenos Aires. Rodriguez was a gift to an Argentine the Agency would have been happy to have as an asset: General Tomás Sánchez de Bustamante, a senior military commander who controlled the First Army Corps and the Federal Police and who was a leading figure in the unpopular military junta ruling Argentina. By 1972, Sánchez de Bustamante was perhaps second in power only to General Alejandro Lanusse, the head of the military regime, and he was not looking forward to the transition to civilian rule scheduled for 1973.

Sánchez de Bustamante had met Rodriguez during a tour of South Vietnam. He requested the CIA man be assigned to him as an adviser on counterterrorism and low-intensity warfare after Rodriguez finished his Vietnam stint. Now the general had another reason for reuniting with Rodriguez. He feared he was targeted for assassination and confided his concern to the chief of station. Shackley sent Rodriguez to develop a security system for the general.

Argentina was gripped by political chaos. The military government faced a small but increasingly popular leftist insurgency, and the right sponsored its own violence.† In the summer of 1972, large antigovernment protests throughout the country were met by troops commanded by Sánchez de Bustamante. The press and the parlors of Argentine society buzzed with rumors about generals who were not pleased with Lanusse's decision to hand the government to civilians. The wild card was Juan Perón, the deposed president who was preparing to return to his homeland after seventeen years of exile in Spain.

In Argentina, Rodriguez proffered advice to Sánchez de Bustamante and sat in on many of the general's meetings. Shackley's man lectured the general's officers on the dangers of communism. As the March 1973 election approached, Sánchez de Bustamante remained a pivotal figure in Argentine politics. This CIA-aided general was urging his fellow offi-

---

* Occasionally the Agency wanted to do more than a foreign government. Shackley proposed the CIA provide bounties for the capture of Tupamaros guerrillas in Uruguay. The branch chief told him that the Uruguayan government would reject such an offer.

† A 1973 cable from the U.S. embassy in Buenos Aires to State Department headquarters reported that "the guilt [for violence against civilian politicians] rests more accurately on the shoulders of hard-liners within the military government who were seeking the same end as the terrorists."

cers to retain control of the government should the Peronists win at the
polls. (A politician named Hector Cámpora was running as a stand-in for
Perón.) Shortly before the election, Sánchez de Bustamante convened a
meeting of military men at an armored unit base in Buenos Aires. There
he proclaimed that his respect for democracy was limited: "Peronism
says, 'Cámpora to government, Perón to power.' I say, 'Cámpora to
government, the Army to power.' "

Cámpora won the election. A month later, the military government,
citing left-wing violence, declared a state of emergency. But Cámpora
was inaugurated in May. He resigned in July, paving the way for Perón's
return to the presidency. The Peronists forced out Langley's ally, General
Sánchez de Bustamante. The new government moved to improve relations with Cuba.

Shackley's CIA courted friends throughout the security services of
Latin America. One bright prospect was Manuel Noriega, a rising Panamanian officer whose contact with U.S. agencies stretched back to his
days as a cadet at the Peruvian Military Academy in 1958. In the early
1960s, as a second lieutenant in the National Guard, Noriega had become a protégé of then-Major Omar Torrijos. With the help of U.S. Army
intelligence, Noriega established an intelligence-gathering operation to
monitor communist influence among banana plantation workers. In
1967, he attended U.S.-run intelligence courses in Panama and the
United States. Noriega caught the attention of the CIA. During one of
Noriega's trips to Washington, Jake Esterline, the deputy chief of the
Western Hemisphere Division in the late 1960s, had Noriega to his
house for dinner to demonstrate the Agency was interested in him.

After Torrijos overthrew the government in 1968, he rewarded Noriega with a series of posts that culminated in Noriega's appointment, in
1970, as head of the country's military intelligence. Noriega was now
more important than ever to the CIA. Washington fretted about the
future of the Panama Canal. Torrijos had dared to suggest that the canal,
long in the hands of the Americans, should revert to Panama, and in
June of 1971 the two nations began a series of talks on the 1903 canal
treaty. Equally annoying to the Nixon administration was that the general
had renewed relations with Cuba. Noriega was Torrijos's loyal servant,
but he was an ambitious man of his own. One day he might be in charge.
He seemed a good investment for Langley. On Shackley's watch, Noriega
continued his rise as an Agency asset.

The CIA supplied the future strongman with funds. A string of division
chiefs, like Shackley, signed off on using Noriega. The money was officially justified as "support for 'institutional cooperation,' " Noriega declared years later in a legal filing, "but in fact it was a slush fund." He
was expected to use the money to bolster intelligence programs and to

pay agents who produced intelligence for the CIA. But there were no invoices or budgets. Noriega took a liberal view of what he could do with Langley's money.*

The CIA's best contact in Panama was considered a threat to America by another part of the U.S. government. U.S. drug enforcement officials had identified Noriega as a narcotics trafficker. According to evidence collected by federal agents in the early 1970s, Noriega accepted payoffs from traffickers in return for allowing them to smuggle their wares through Panama. While Noriega was providing information to Shackley's division, some federal drug agents proposed killing Noriega as a means toward countering the narcotics trade—a suggestion that was dismissed. Noriega continued on, playing all sides, making alliances with drug dealers and providing information to Cuba, U.S. military intelligence, narcotics agents, and the CIA.

To Shackley's division, Noriega was worth the money. When Torrijos visited Cuba in early 1973, Noriega accompanied the general. Upon his return to Cuba, Noriega provided his CIA contact a detailed briefing on the trip. He reported that Torrijos believed there were clear differences between his brand of nationalism and Cuba's socialism. He passed along a comment Torrijos uttered while in Cuba: "Every country has its own brand of aspirin. Panama's brand is [the American-made] Bayer." In Langley, that was a piece of intelligence Shackley could assume would sit well with the White House. As much as Torrijos might raise a fuss about the canal, he was not ready to turn his back on the power to the north.

The Agency would support the thuggish Noriega for years. His extra-curricular activities could be tolerated. The CIA had dealt with former Nazis in Europe and drug smugglers in Southeast Asia. If the drug-fighting agencies of the United States passed their intelligence on No-riega to Shackley, the division chief could brush aside the reports with the time-tested rationale that spying is a business in which one cannot be squeamish about using certain tools.

IV

In the early 1970s, there was a new enemy for the CIA. President Nixon had declared a war on drugs, and he ordered Langley to the front lines. Shackley was instructed to deploy his officers against drug dealers. They were to collect intelligence on dealers in Latin America and pass it to the officers of the Bureau of Narcotics and Dangerous Drugs (BNDD),

---

* After the U.S. invaded Panama in 1989 and killed hundreds of civilians on its way toward capturing Noriega, the general maintained that he had received a total of $11 million from the CIA over the years.

the precursor of the Drug Enforcement Administration. Neither U.S. narcotics officers nor CIA people were enthusiastic about the Agency's entry into this business. It was a clash of cultures. The narcs' job was to arrest the dealers; the spies were to develop secret intelligence on the smugglers. The two tasks might at first seem to jibe. But spying depends on stealth, on not shaking things up. Drug-fighting requires busts, which are hardly secret and blow sources of information.

As the sophisticates of Langley saw it, the drug officials were heavy-handed, not versed in clandestine operations, and a pain to deal with. The CIA would track a drug suspect and share its intelligence with drug agents who then told too many others about the Agency information. "Surveillance should not be made known," Jim Flannery remarked. "Our people could get caught." There was a distaste in Shackley's division for anything that smacked of law enforcement. Intelligence officers thought of themselves as an elite force challenging the ultimate enemy: the evil communists bent on world conquest. Drug dealers were secondary, and they were scum. The CIA was descending into the international gutter. "We didn't like the damn thing," Flannery said. "You think you deal with sleazy types as spies. But when you get into the drug milieu, you're really dealing with sleaze."*

The feeling was mutual. BNDD officers were not happy to be collaborating with the close-mouthed, turf-jealous spies of the CIA—particularly Ted Shackley. Gerry Strickler, head of the Latin American desk for the BNDD, conferred regularly with Shackley. The Western Hemisphere Division chief demanded that the drug fighters hand over to the CIA their case files, lists of informants, and cable traffic. Using the BNDD leads, Shackley's division then recruited BNDD targets as CIA assets—and did so without telling the BNDD.

Coordination was supposed to be the watchword for the assorted bureaucracies involved in the war on drugs. But often turf came first. Shortly after Shackley entered the division, he called a summit meeting with his people, Customs, and BNDD. At a reception afterward, Strickler told Shackley that he thought the session had been beneficial. Shackley replied, I couldn't care less. His people had been handed the drug-

---

* In October of 1972, the Miami station chief asked Shackley for permission to recruit a Bay of Pigs veteran who was in the gambling business and close to mobsters Santos Trafficante and Meyer Lansky. Recently, one of the subject's partners in a gambling venture in Colombia had been arrested for drug-trafficking, and another of his associates was deported from Panama to the United States for being part of a cocaine-smuggling ring. "Although [his] contacts make him a possibly interesting target," the station chief reported to Shackley, "he will be a difficult and wary one. However, we are encouraged that we are right on target in trying to get closer to him."

fighting brief and he just wanted to make sure they produced. Strickler concluded that Shackley did not care about the overall effort. Shackley was out to ensure that his division looked good to those watching from above.

Strickler put up with a constant stream of irritations caused by Shackley's division. When would-be informants visited U.S. embassies and asked to talk to someone about narcotics, the visitors were directed to the CIA. The BNDD sometimes was not informed about these sources. CIA officers posed as narcotics agents for cover. "High-ranking foreign policy officers called our offices in the middle of the night, demanding an explanation for some operation that did not work out," Strickler recalled. "It would not be ours but the CIA's." But the narcs' main grievance was that their CIA colleagues recruited the same people the drug agents were attempting to arrest.

It was only natural for the spooks to do so. They had been trained to penetrate enemy organizations by recruiting participants—an officer of a foreign intelligence unit, a Communist Party functionary, an official of an armed service. You want intelligence on drugs, you recruit a drug-runner. "We were making cases on some of the [CIA recruits]," Strickler noted. "We'd arrest some in joint operations with foreign police and the suspect would say, 'I'm working for the U.S. government.' We wouldn't know if they were trying to dupe us. We would then have to conduct an investigation to see who was controlling them. A couple of times we thought about indicting a CIA officer. It was infuriating." The basic problem, from Strickler's perspective, was that Shackley's intelligence collectors were too concerned with demonstrating they could obtain information. They sacrificed busts to do so. Their main interest was a steady intelligence flow, not removing the targets from action.

The drug busters found themselves competing with Shackley's officers for sources. In one annoying case, U.S. drug agents managed to convince a Latin American dealer to supply information crucial for a big operation. But suddenly the dealer disappeared. The CIA offered to help find him. At first, Strickler was told by Langley that the Western Hemisphere Division possessed strong leads on the whereabouts of the vanished informant. Then, all of a sudden, the Agency lost him. Later Strickler discovered that the CIA had located the man and recruited him for its own purposes.

Shackley's division did share its narcotics intelligence with the BNDD, copies of which went to the White House. "The White House was very impressed with the intelligence," Strickler noted, "and wanted to know why we weren't doing more with it." The BNDD officers, as might be expected of a rival bureaucracy, found a host of flaws in the CIA intelligence. They concluded the Agency was being snookered by many of its sources, whose revelations were fabrications. "Initially we tried to act on a lot of their information," Strickler recalled. "But as time went on we found out it did not pay to spend time and effort on it. One time we were able to talk to a CIA source, and during that encounter he admitted that he had been lying to them. It got to the point where we would have little to do with the CIA. They would get our documents, steal our informants, and send over faulty intelligence reports. They were not just spinning wheels. They were causing damage."

The ultimate aggravation for the BNDD officials was that CIA participation in a drug case might hinder its prosecution. Agency involvement in a narcotics case could not be disclosed in any legal proceedings, so cases had to be dismissed to protect the Agency. "Consequently, it became more important for us," Strickler recalled, "that the CIA not be involved."

In May of 1973, John Murray, the chief of the Mexico branch, forwarded a collection of explosive documents to Shackley. At William Colby's urging, Director James Schlesinger had sent a memo to all CIA employees requesting they report any past or present activities "which might be construed to be outside the legislative charter of this Agency." (The order was prompted by news accounts that former CIA officer Howard Hunt, using Agency equipment, had broken into the office of Ellsberg's psychiatrist.) If the seventh floor wanted the dirty secrets, Murray had a few.

Murray became a Company man in 1948 and served in several African stations. In 1961, while deputy chief of station in Sudan, he mounted what would become a legendary operation. The CIA had discovered that the Soviet-backed government of Antoine Gizenga in the Congo was due to receive from Moscow a large sum of money to pay its troops. It also learned that the Soviet courier and his armed escort were transiting Khartoum. The night before their arrival, Murray memorized the plan of the airport. The next day he sat in a terminal lounge and waited. In came the bag man guarded by several armed men. When the courier put down the satchel of money, the guards were supposed to watch it. But Murray saw they were distracted. He walked over to the bag, picked it up, and left the airport. No one tried to stop him. The loss of the payroll contributed to the subsequent collapse of the Gizenga government. In the mid-1960s, Murray shifted to the Western Hemisphere Division. For several years, he worked in headquarters, preparing for a major overseas assignment. Then Shackley disappointed him.

In December of 1972, Shackley informed Murray he would be the next chief of station in Haiti. The posting was not a prestigious one. Murray already had served abroad in four hardship posts. He worried about medical facilities for his family. He wanted something better and told Shackley he would not accept the job. Shackley accused Murray of placing family ahead of the service. In early January of 1973, Shackley said Murray would be expelled from his position as chief of the division's Mexican desk. Murray heard gossip that Shackley intended to award that spot to a friend. "The whole experience leaves me wondering if I am a senior officer of the CIA or a Viet Cong suspect!" Murray wrote in a memo. "I feel like a Kafka character."

When Murray received the Schlesinger memo in May of 1973, he was in limbo and mad at Shackley. He was also suspicious of Shackley's travel to Mexico City and Miami shortly after the Watergate break-in. (Although he was chief of the Mexico branch, Murray was not informed of the details and purpose of the trips.) And he knew he had something of interest to the Director.

Two years earlier, in February of 1971, Bruce MacMaster, a CIA officer in Mexico, had come to see Murray in headquarters. MacMaster eagerly told stories about Tony Sforza, a veteran CIA operative. MacMaster and Sforza had gotten into a bloody brawl at Sforza's home in Mexico City on New Year's Eve.* Before Murray, MacMaster went on about Sforza: he had used station officers to collect duty-free liquor; he had exploited Agency pouches to ship contraband; he had sent a large package of hard-core pornography to the Mexico City station; he had gotten drunk and shoved the chief of station in Mexico. A disgruntled MacMaster had more than petty complaints. He told Murray about a sensitive operation that had occurred in 1970—in Chile. Both MacMaster and Sforza had met with members of the Chilean military group led by retired right-wing General Roberto Viaux, which was plotting Allende's overthrow. MacMaster's highly sensitive mission, Murray wrote in a memo, "was to help create a situation which would encourage the Chilean military to activate a military takeover of the Chilean government." He and Sforza apparently had encouraged the Viaux band to move against General Schneider, the constitutionalist assassinated following Allende's electoral victory. MacMaster informed Murray that Chilean military

---

* Following the fistfight, in a breach of security and professional conduct, MacMaster, according to a CIA memo, contacted a Mexican official, told him that Sforza had insulted the Mexican president, and revealed that Sforza handled Cuban matters for the Agency. He asked that the Mexicans toss Sforza out of the country. The Mexican —cited in CIA documents as LITEMPO-12—informed another station officer of his talk with MacMaster and complained of what he termed MacMaster's womanizing.

officials who knew of the CIA role in their murderous plotting had asked him for $250,000 in hush money. After this 1971 meeting with MacMaster, Murray reported MacMaster's remarks to his superiors. These revelations, he wrote in a memo, "could conceivably have serious implications for the Agency." But Murray never heard back from the higher-ups.

In May of 1973, Murray, still chief of the Mexico branch, received another chance to report this potentially scandalous information—CIA involvement in an assassination—which was then a highly guarded secret. Responding to Schlesinger's invitation for embarrassing material, he pulled out the memos he had written on MacMaster and Sforza in 1971 and sent them to Shackley.

The chief of the division could not have been pleased to receive Murray's material. He had dedicated much of the past year to preventing secrets of the Chilean operation from being revealed during the Church subcommittee inquiry. Now one of his own men was launching into the paper trail sensitive documents on this very matter. Moreover, Sforza was a friend. He had worked for Shackley in Miami and became one of the small group of officers fiercely loyal to the JMWAVE chief. (In the late 1950s, according to Agency lore, Sforza had operated in Havana under the cover of a professional gambler and cultivated contacts with the Mafia in Cuba. After the revolution, he was based in Miami and reported to Warren Frank, Shackley's chief of foreign intelligence.) Due to Murray, Shackley had a dilemma. Should he pass on the information to higher levels in Langley?

Murray never learned what happened to the memos. But no one ever asked him about them. He assumed Shackley sat on the material. Right after he forwarded the bothersome documents to Shackley, his chief ordered him out of the country. Murray was to serve as acting chief of station in Jamaica.* It seemed to Murray that Shackley wanted him away from headquarters.

In the next few years, Murray found it hard to obtain promotions. He came to believe that Shackley, who placed in Murray's personnel folder a poor performance evaluation, had sabotaged his career. He thought Shackley worried that Murray knew too many of Shackley's secrets. A

---

* In Jamaica, Murray replaced Tom Clines as acting station chief. ("I talked to [Michael] Manley every Friday," Clines recalled, referring to the leftist prime minister. "I hated that meeting.") When Murray arrived in Kingston, he could not locate Clines. Shackley's friend was finally found by the pool in a resort sitting with several Jamaican women. During his four months in Jamaica, Murray oversaw an electronic bugging of the Chinese mission.

determined Murray would wage a campaign to rehabilitate his file and to convince his superiors that Shackley could not be trusted.*

Much to Murray's dismay, on May 20, 1973, Shackley, after a year of cleaning up the division and blocking a congressional inquiry, received his second Distinguished Intelligence Medal. Following the presentation ceremony, Shackley and Hazel drank sherry with Bill Colby. Both men, due to Nixon's growing entanglement in Watergate, were about to receive career boosts.

A week earlier, the President had announced that Jim Schlesinger, who had been DCI only since February, would leave Langley to become Secretary of Defense. His departure was part of a Nixon reorganization plan designed to win the beleaguered President political breathing space. To demonstrate that the Oval Office was not inhabited by an underhanded paranoiac, Nixon named William Colby, the mild-mannered, career Cold War missionary, to be the new director. That triggered a chain of moves. Colby picked William Nelson, the longtime chief of the Far East Division, to be deputy director for operations. (Schlesinger had renamed the Directorate of Plans.) Shackley was promoted to be chief of what was now called the East Asia Division. Of all the division chief posts, only head of the Soviet Russia Division bore more prestige. And the East Asia position seemed to be the true stepping-stone. Shackley was following closely behind Colby and Nelson. He was heading toward the Director's chair.

Shackley's promotion was not prompted by a stellar record on intelligence production. His division had achieved no great successes during his year-long tour as chief. On the all-important target of Cuba, Shackley's section gathered little intelligence of value. "I think he was tired of dealing with Cuba," Flannery said. "And it was not going so well." Shackley's plate had been full with the Agee operation and clean-up, the covert program in Chile, and the ITT cover-up. It was a year of crisis management, not intelligence accomplishment.

---

* In 1974, Inspector General Donald Chamberlain issued a memo requesting all Agency offices to review their files for materials relating to Watergate. On Murray's copy of the document, he scribbled three items he apparently intended to report and provided no further explanation:
  —Political Conventions in 1968
   Bugging ops against candidates—N. Rockefeller
  —Chile Operation—1970
  —White House (implementation of listening devices—joint Secret Service–CIA operation)

As Shackley prepared to shift offices, Agee was settled in England, book contract in hand, busily writing. Shackley could not stop the book. Agee's *Inside the Company: CIA Diary* would be published in England in late 1974; an American edition followed months later. A paperback version became a best-seller. Most of the book was devoted to dispassionate descriptions of operations, replete with names of scores of agents and CIA officers. It provided what to date was the most detailed account of the inner workings of the CIA and the life of a U.S. intelligence officer. Only toward the end of the book did Agee let loose with his prorevolution fervor. "The CIA is," he wrote, "one of the great forces promoting political repression in countries with minority regimes that serve a privileged and powerful elite." One method to undermine the Agency, he suggested, was to expose its officers. He pledged to continue doing so.*

The covert program against Allende continued until Washington got what it wanted: the end of his leftist regime. On September 11, 1973, a military coup overthrew Allende.

Shackley had left the Western Hemisphere Division by then, but his colleagues had carried on. Throughout the summer of 1973, the CIA received intelligence on the plans of the military group that was to carry out the coup. CIA officers maintained contacts with Chilean military men supposedly to gather intelligence, but according to a somewhat mysterious reference in a congressional report, the Agency officers "went beyond the mere collection of information." The report wondered "whether those [CIA] contacts [with the Chilean military] strayed into encouraging the Chilean military to move against Allende."

The 1973 coup prompted the inevitable question: was the CIA involved? There was circumstantial evidence of direct U.S. participation in

---

* When Agee exposed officers after the publication of his book—by examining public State Department records, he and other anti-Agency activists could identify CIA employees stationed overseas—the Agency asked the Justice Department to consider legal action against Agee. The U.S. government never brought charges against Agee, possibly because a trial would expose information about the "illegal acts" conducted in connection with the Agee case. But in 1979 the State Department revoked Agee's passport. In 1991, responding to Agee's attempt to regain his passport, CIA Director William Webster and another Agency official declared that the Agency possessed evidence that Agee had received money from Cuba in return for his anti-CIA endeavors—evidence never obtained during Shackley's investigation. In 1992, a Cuban intelligence officer who had defected to the United States five years earlier, claimed he once heard another top Cuban intelligence officer discuss making payments to Agee. Agee denied the charge and suggested he was the victim of a disinformation plot.

the coup and critical events that preceded it. A group of striking truck drivers told a *Time* magazine reporter that money for their lavish meals came from the CIA.* The U.S. military was reportedly active the day of the coup; U.S. ships off the coast participated in maneuvers with the Chilean Navy. A young American named Charles Horman talked to several Americans—both civilian and military—near the port of Valparaiso that day and later told friends that his countrymen claimed they were in Chile to get a job done, presumably the coup. A few days after the coup, Horman was arrested. He was shot to death in the National Stadium.

Congressional investigators years later unearthed no evidence of CIA participation in the final coup. But life is not a courtroom. In his memoirs, Colby explained it simply: "Certainly having launched such an attempt [in 1970], CIA was responsible to some degree for the final outcome, no matter that it tried to 'distance' itself and turn away well before 1973."

Salvador Allende died during the coup. When the smoke cleared, General Augusto Pinochet, the head of a military junta, was in dictatorial control. Political parties, including Langley's favored Christian Democrats, were banned. Congress was closed. Elections were suspended. The press was censored. Allende supporters and opponents of the junta were jailed. Torture centers were established. Executions replaced soccer matches in Santiago's stadiums. Bodies floated down the Mapocho River. Due in part to the hard work of Shackley and dozens of other Agency bureaucrats and operatives, Chile was free of the socialists.

Following the coup, Senate Majority Leader Mike Mansfield urged an investigation. He wanted to know what the CIA had been doing in Chile. Press reports maintained that the Agency had aided the strikers and helped set the mood for a coup. But at the time of the military rebellion, the CIA's Chile campaign was still a secret. Then William Colby spilled the details and undid the handiwork of Shackley and the others who had manipulated the Church subcommittee.

On April 22, 1974, Director Colby trundled into a committee room to secretly brief a House intelligence subcommittee on his agency's activity in Chile. In a clinical tone, he described the details of the Chilean operations and their extent. Afterward Representative Michael Harrington, a liberal critic of U.S. foreign policy and a member of the House Foreign Affairs Committee, demanded to see the transcript of the Colby session. The congressman was allowed to read the transcript but not

* One congressional report noted, "It remains unclear whether or to what extent CIA funds passed to opposition parties may have been siphoned off to support strikes. It is clear that antigovernment strikers were actively supported by several of the private sector groups which received CIA funds."

permitted to jot notes. He was astonished by what he saw. No hint of such a massive years-long campaign had emerged during the previous year's ITT hearings. Harrington tried to convince colleagues to further investigate Langley's intervention in Chile. A letter from Harrington to another legislator describing Colby's private testimony was leaked to both *The New York Times* and *The Washington Post*. (Harrington later admitted to being the source of the *Post* leak.) On September 8, 1974, both papers ran front-page stories describing the multimillion-dollar CIA crusade against Allende. In the letter, Harrington expressed dismay that Nixon and the CIA had not been at all deterred by the ITT hearings. Whether he knew it or not, Harrington was referring to Shackley.

The revelations caused a furor on Capitol Hill. We've been lied to, legislators exclaimed. A State Department spokesman repeated the assertion—made previously in the congressional testimony of its officials —that the United States had stuck to a policy of nonintervention during the Allende years. Senators Symington and Stennis, two of the old boys who oversaw the CIA, claimed surprise at the Colby disclosures. Senator Edward Kennedy accused both the Nixon and Ford administrations of deceiving Congress and the American public. Lawmakers called for a new investigation.

Senator Frank Church was outraged. During the ITT investigation of 1972 and 1973, the Church subcommittee aides had heard gossip about CIA activity in Chile. But they had not been able to pursue the rumors. That was outside their jurisdiction. Church now realized that when he and his staff were pressing the CIA—Shackley included—to level with them about the ITT episode of 1970, Shackley and the rest were up to their necks in covert action in Chile. The senator and his aides saw they had been navigating in the dark past one big iceberg.

Shackley, Broe, and Helms in 1973 had no obligation to disclose the Chilean operations to Church and his investigators. The Chile program was secret information, only to be shared (which much of it was not) with the few senators and congressmen charged with what passed for oversight of the Agency. Nevertheless, Church felt suckered. The ITT business was minor stuff when compared with what the Agency had been doing in Chile for over a decade. It's time, Church told his aides, to take a thorough look at the Company. Let's see what Langley really has been up to.

After *New York Times* reporter Seymour Hersh in December of 1974 exposed CIA spying operations that targeted Americans and other domestic programs that arguably violated the Agency's charter, Church had more cause for a full-scale probe of the CIA. On January 27, 1975, the Senate passed a resolution that established a committee to examine intelligence activities and to determine if the nation's spies had been involved in "illegal, improper, or unethical activities." The House of Representatives followed suit.

When he left the division, Shackley seemingly had deserved praise from his superiors for not letting the ITT investigation get out of hand. But the ultimate result would not be a happy one for Langley. "All that really did was get Frank Church pissed at us," observed Tom Clines, "and gave him more reason to go ahead with his investigations. He got stonewalled so much. It really hurt us in the long run." In the Senate, the Democratic leadership named Church to head the committee, an appointment which was to become a nightmare for many an intelligence officer, including Ted Shackley.

The ITT cover-up yielded other fallout. After Colby's secret testimony on Chile became public, Church asked for a perjury investigation to be initiated against Richard Helms, Henry Kissinger, William Broe, and ITT officials with whom Shackley had colluded. Helms, for one, had told a secret session of the Senate Foreign Relations Committee that the CIA had not passed money to Allende's opposition.* Kissinger had downplayed the role of the CIA in Chile during a secret hearing a week after the 1973 coup. The others, Church believed, had lied to his subcommittee. (Shackley had not testified and was safe from a perjury charge, though he conceivably was vulnerable to a conspiracy charge for misleading Congress.) If these cases went forward, Shackley might find himself a witness in a public trial being asked about his efforts to torpedo congressional oversight of the CIA.

Few officers in the Western Hemisphere Division were sad to see Shackley vacate the chief's chair. His relentlessness in cleansing the division had not been appreciated. His ambition remained obvious. There were few doubts among fellow officers that Shackley desired to be DCI. A small number hoped that would come to pass, for he had continued to foster a following among a small circle of subordinates. "Wherever Ted Shackley went, he left a trail of great loyalty and great animus," recalled Jim Flannery, his deputy. "It was hard to be neutral with Ted. He didn't want people to be neutral." At the end of Shackley's watch, morale within the division was low. David Phillips, Shackley's successor as chief, attributed the atmosphere to lingering doubts among

---

* Helms was already in trouble. In response to an internal complaint—perhaps one made by John Murray—a three-man Inspector General team had investigated Helms's testimony. The trio concluded Helms perjured himself. In December of 1974, the Agency had sent the team's report to the Justice Department, which began investigating the former CIA chief.

officers about the Agency's role in scandals and Shackley's authoritarian management style.

When Shackley left the division, an obligatory farewell party was held. The doors between a few adjoining offices were opened, and division employees gathered. At one point, Shackley stood virtually alone at one end of the suite, while partygoers congregated at the other. For that moment, no one seemed to want to talk to the fellow who had taken care of the Agee problem, the officer who had handled the Church subcommittee, the bureaucrat who had signed off on various interventions in Chile, the man still on his way up—who now was to oversee the finale of the worst miscalculation ever made by the cold warriors.

CHAPTER EIGHT

THE WAR AT HOME

I

ON April 30, 1975, a muggy Washington day, at the end of a chaotic and emotional shift, Ted Shackley attended a cocktail party with his wife, Hazel. The mood was downbeat. Driving home to his red brick house on a pleasant street in Bethesda, Shackley pondered events occurring in a different world, thousands of miles away. This was one of the worst days in his life.

For the past two years, Shackley, as chief of the East Asia Division, had overseen Agency activity in Vietnam. After U.S. ground troops had withdrawn, the CIA remained, doing all it could to aid the hapless South Vietnamese security services, to bolster (and spy on) the corrupt Thieu regime, and to discern the intentions of Hanoi. From his Langley office, Shackley managed all this and other operations throughout the Pacific region. Now Washington's Vietnam enterprise finally had collapsed. The enemy had taken Saigon. The Agency's performance during the last days of South Vietnam soon would become a subject of controversy. A handful of Agency officers and outside observers would wonder, had the CIA lost Saigon?

That question did not yet trouble Shackley, as he arrived home. He found his eleven-year-old daughter, Suzanne, in front of the television watching film clips of U.S. helicopters evacuating Americans and South Vietnamese from the roof of the U.S. embassy. This was where Shackley had imperially run the CIA station and earned his Blond Ghost nickname. The United States in retreat—it was an ignoble and disgusting sight. With this defeat in mind, Shackley later wrote that the end of a counterinsurgency program brings "agony . . . not unlike that of watching a child die."

In his living room, with his only child by his side, Shackley, three years shy of fifty, watched the humiliating images. He did not say anything. Suzanne turned from the television and gazed at her father. He was crying.

When Shackley took over the East Asia Division in May of 1973, the war was technically finished. In the summer of 1972, Henry Kissinger and Hanoi's chief negotiator, Le Duc Tho, had hammered out a draft peace agreement. The provisions included a cease-fire in place, withdrawal of all foreign troops, a restriction on outside military aid, and an exchange of prisoners of war. In the south, the Provisional Revolutionary Government would be recognized, along with Thieu's government, as one of two "administrative entities." But Kissinger had obtained for the United States no more than a negotiated retreat from Vietnam, a deal that could have been reached four years—and tens of thousands of deaths—earlier.

After President Nixon in December ordered one last spasm of bombing, the agreement was signed. The last U.S. combat troops were out by the end of March of 1973. Thieu's army kept fighting, its soldiers exhausted and short of supplies. The armies of Hanoi avoided direct engagements and constructed highways toward Saigon. The air war over Cambodia continued. Urban unemployment in South Vietnam hit 40 percent; southerners faced food shortages. Officially, the war was over. Not settled was who would control South Vietnam.

Shackley's officers in the field knew the clock was running. "A grim, sad mood took hold in Bien Hoa," recalled Orrin DeForest, the maverick contract officer who, against Shackley's wishes, had set up his own unilateral intelligence processing system. "It affected everybody, Americans and Vietnamese alike, though for us as Americans the sadness was mixed with shame. . . . For all the rotten corruption in the Saigon government, we were still talking about leaving an entire people to its fate."

DeForest and other case officers continued to seek intelligence to relay to Shackley in headquarters. DeForest's outfit ran five agents and pumped out sixty or so reports a month. Reports from defectors indicated the NVA was stockpiling its units in the South and that the flow of materiel on the Ho Chi Minh Trail was on the rise. DeForest, like many other case officers, forwarded to Saigon a steady stream of reports on military corruption and received little feedback: "The abuses were so widespread that they were putting the region at risk. But it was like shouting into the void."

When Don Gregg, then chief of station in South Korea, passed through the Bien Hoa base in mid-1973, a local colonel told him that if nothing was done to curb corruption and deal with the economic crisis, the south was doomed. Gregg replied that he had already reported this to Shackley. The colonel was not reassured.

In Tay Ninh, the agent code-named HACKLE still churned out the best intelligence reports on the enemy. In the summer of 1973, his Agency handler in the province shot himself dead. A thirty-six-year-old CIA officer named John Stockwell, a veteran of three tours in Africa, was rushed to the province to replace the suicide. Stockwell, proud to be part of this important assignment, was disturbed by one aspect of the job: the local police chief was a sadistic torturer. A longtime recipient of CIA money, the policeman mutilated prisoners in an Agency safe house. (This also had gone on during Shackley's years in Saigon.) Stockwell sent Saigon a memo, expecting that chief of station Tom Polgar would take discreet steps to transfer the police chief. Stockwell received no answer from Saigon. He encountered Polgar at a cocktail party. The police chief's transfer could not be arranged, Polgar explained, because of a little torturing.

Stockwell was aware he was working for Shackley. He had never met the man, but he had been hearing stories about Shackley for years. He had encountered dozens of complaints about the report quotas Shackley imposed when he was Saigon station chief. So Stockwell was surprised when the division chief visited Bien Hoa to meet officers from the region. In the base headquarters, a villa overlooking a river, Shackley asked probing questions about the HACKLE operation, as Vietnamese servants brought in lunch. He impressed Stockwell. He was alert, confident, in-charge. He was not the bully Stockwell envisioned, nor the bureaucrat he expected. Perhaps this was because Shackley was dealing with the men who ran the most important espionage operation in Vietnam—the HACKLE program. Shackley eagerly listened to a report predicting the recruitment of more communist agents. But he brushed aside the comments on government corruption and incompetent allies. Just keep up the good work, he said. We may well come out on top when this whole business is over.

Push on. More reports. More agents. Stay ahead of the curve. It can be done. That was Shackley. The system works.

. . .

One of the best intelligence sources Shackley had on North Vietnam was over 6,000 miles from Hanoi: the CIA-bugged embassy of North Vietnam in Paris. Before Shackley became East Asia Division chief, the Agency had wired the embassy and begun collecting taped conversations of North Vietnamese diplomats. Shackley inherited the operation, managed by a small unit his division maintained within the Paris station.* The bugging operation, a pet project for Kissinger, produced information useful for the ongoing talks between Washington and Hanoi. The project was a bright feather in the Agency's cap. But its glory was short-lived, due to a low-level screw-up.

As was customary, the Agency had set up a listening post in an apartment near the embassy. The station recruited a German fellow once convicted of fraud to service the apartment: to maintain its appearance, to check the recording equipment, to gather the tapes. Good "trade-craft"—as spies call it—demanded that Americans stay away from the listening post, so as to not tip off the other side or the French intelligence service.

It was the operative's proclivity for fraud that caused the operation's undoing. One of Shackley's case officers who handled the German discovered errors in the financial accounts. Apparently, the German was pocketing a modest amount of the money earmarked for expenses. The case officer threatened to fire him. The German, now insulted, collected the recording equipment and tapes and stormed off to the Vietnamese to show them they had been bugged. But he was so agitated when he arrived at the embassy that no one would see him. He piled everything into his car and headed out of the country, as the CIA looked for him. At the border, French customs officials searched his car and found the suspicious equipment and tapes.

French intelligence soon had the whole story, and the chief of the French service sent a message to the CIA: that was marvelous stuff we received from you, *merci*. The French forced the German to identify CIA officers with whom he had worked, and the French asked them to leave. In Langley, Shackley was outraged. Because of a few hundred dollars, one of the Company's best operations had cracked.

To know what was happening in Vietnam, Shackley depended on Thomas Polgar. A short and squat Hungarian-American, Polgar was an Agency veteran who had served in Germany in the 1950s, where he encountered the young Shackley. In Saigon, Polgar won a reputation as a smart and diligent man. But Shackley worried about Polgar's ability to do a good job, and Polgar had mixed feelings about his boss. Polgar

---

* Asked about the bugging project twenty years later, Eleazar "Lee" Williams, who directed the Paris unit, exclaimed, "I can't comment on that operation!"

complained about the quality of reporting Shackley bequeathed him, and upon his arrival in Saigon he had feared Shackley would constantly second-guess him. But Shackley was fully supportive of his station chief —perhaps too much so, for Polgar and his decision-making were to become controversial.*

Polgar maintained less control than Shackley had over the intelligence flow from Vietnam to Washington. But he too fell victim to that occupational risk of the intelligence trade, the temptation to report good news over bad. "He saw his job in terms of a balancing act," recalled a friend. "He felt he was straddling a fence between forces on the one side that demanded a scientific description of the world around him and those on the other that required that he put it into language that would have a desired effect." Polgar was not blind to the problems in South Vietnam. But he was a half-full man, when it was not clear to all in the station that even that much water was in the glass. "Polgar would say the Thieu government is functioning all right," recalled Bill White, an analyst in the station, "that it was delivering the mail, collecting taxes. You could say to him, 'But, sir, you can't go out at night.' 'Well,' he would respond, 'they're used to it.'"

When Shackley came through Saigon on an inspection tour in mid-1973, Polgar aimed to impress him. He knew what Shackley liked: computerlike rhetoric, numbers, hard facts. Because Frank Snepp previously had compiled figures and facts for Shackley, Polgar assigned the confident and fast-talking analyst the task of briefing the division chief. (Polgar, with his slow and thickly accented monotone voice, was not an ideal briefer.) As had Shackley, Polgar embraced Snepp as a bright light of the station.

Snepp believed he had Shackley pegged. When it came time for the presentation to Shackley, he brandished charts, whipped out a pointer, and laid on statistics-studded statements proving the successes of the station. As he briefed, Snepp realized he was mimicking his old boss. Shackley praised the briefing. Polgar was so delighted he decided to use Snepp as his principal briefing officer. From then on, Snepp wrote many of Polgar's field appraisals and personal communications to Shackley. In a later series of cables, Polgar heaped praise on the analyst, recommending a pay raise and a promotion.

---

* Some CIA people saw Shackley and Polgar as competitors. Polgar, years afterward, dismissed that notion. But when he talked about Shackley, his comments had an edge: "Helms was a great fan of Shackley, but he had a realistic appreciation of the problems one might have with Ted Shackley. [Shackley] returned from Saigon in more fortunate circumstances than I would, and that gave him a step-up. But I would outlast him."

Shackley the organization man had come to Saigon bearing a new bureaucratic philosophy: management by objective, or MBO. It was an idea William Colby was pushing. In the embassy "bubble"—a highly secured, bug-proofed room-within-a-room composed of transparent walls—Shackley crisply explained to station personnel that under this scheme, the Agency would set key objectives—say, finding out what enemy X intended to do about situation Y—and then key intelligence assets on this target. Resources were limited. The Agency simply could not do everything. He ticked off subjects that were to receive less priority in Vietnam: drug-trafficking, prisoners of war.* Political covert action was no longer a top item.†

Field officers in South Vietnam and elsewhere bemoaned the lack of flexibility MBO demanded. But it suited cost-conscious bean-counters who wanted quantifiable results. Snepp thought it was madness. The right objectives were not being identified—particularly the political and military weaknesses of the Thieu regime.

As East Asia Division chief, Shackley spent most of his time in Langley, where he had more to worry about than Vietnam. In early August of 1973, Shackley received from Don Gregg, chief of station in Seoul, a cable containing some of the hottest intelligence in the world. It showed that a foreign intelligence agency close to the CIA was about to murder one of South Korea's most famous citizens.

On the afternoon of August 8, Kim Dae Jung had disappeared from his hotel suite in Tokyo. Kim was the leading political opponent of the dictatorial regime of General Park Chung Hee, another repressive anticommunist ally of Washington. For years, the Korean Central Intelligence Agency, which had been established with technical and financial

---

* Narcotics was a responsibility that had not been embraced throughout the CIA. "The priority it received was minus-zero," recalled one East Asia Division officer who specialized in the field. "Sociologically, the Agency as a whole had its priorities geared too much against the communist threat. It didn't give a rat's ass about opium." This headquarters officer tracked drug money; he followed it through financiers in Vietnam to banks in Bangkok to banks in Switzerland. But no one in Shackley's division was excited by his discoveries.

† Shackley did not eschew all political operations. His division secretly slipped $350,000 to a Vietnamese think tank to support its publications. The South Vietnamese embassy in Washington distributed the think tank's magazine to Americans, including members of Congress, some of whom cited its articles in floor debates. Shackley was funding a propaganda effort aimed at the American public—an ostensible violation of the CIA's charter. A congressional report later cited this covert action as an example of how the Agency tried to "manipulate public and congressional opinion in the United States to support the Vietnam War."

assistance from the Company, relentlessly had harassed Kim Dae Jung and other dissidents in South Korea, the United States, and across the globe.

In August of 1973, Kim Dae Jung was in Japan politicking among Koreans there. During the trip, he vanished. His friends and supporters reasonably feared he had been snatched by the KCIA. When the CIA station in Seoul learned of Kim's disappearance, a young case officer named C. Philip Liechty thought he could discover what had happened. Until recently, Liechty had been disillusioned with his tour in South Korea. His first chief of station in Seoul had been a lush who accepted gifts of women and liquor from his KCIA friends. The Koreans had the chief completely under their control. Any reporting that cast Park's government in a negative light was not allowed out of the station. Liechty's reports on political repression were buried. In recent weeks, the station's atmosphere had changed. Shackley had sent Gregg to be the chief in Seoul, and Gregg had unlocked the gate. Liechty and others were free to send their reports to Langley.

Encouraged by the new boss, Liechty sought out intelligence on Kim's disappearance. He contacted a South Korean government source he had been cultivating. The Korean, who possessed access to intelligence records, confirmed that the KCIA had Kim Dae Jung and provided the names of the KCIA officers who had grabbed him, their aliases, their passport numbers, and the details of their travel. He told Liechty that the KCIA goons had smuggled the dissident onto a boat and planned to kill him soon at sea.

Liechty wondered if he might have trouble sending this news back to Shackley. It was dangerous intelligence. If the CIA (and the Nixon administration) knew that the KCIA intended to assassinate the dissident, then uncomfortable questions could not be avoided: What do we do about it? Do we try to stop it? It was not inconceivable to Liechty that Gregg—or maybe Shackley—would ask him to verify the information, to double-check these inconvenient facts, and to do so slowly. But, to his delight, Gregg immediately forwarded a priority cable to Shackley and headquarters, and his report was accepted. "A lot of people there were unhappy about this," Liechty recalled. "Most people in headquarters, Shackley included, were sympathetic to the Park government and the KCIA."

U.S. Ambassador Philip Habib called on the Korean government. In straight language, he told the Koreans that Washington would not countenance the killing of Kim Dae Jung.

A day or two after he was seized, Kim Dae Jung, who had been drugged, lay on the deck of a high-speed boat in the middle of the Sea of Japan. He was tied to weights. He heard his KCIA captors discussing their intention to toss him overboard. He began to say his final prayers. Then an aircraft approached. Kim heard someone shouting. Afterward, he was untied and fed. Another day or two later, he was dumped on a street near his home in Seoul. Shackley's officers had saved the life of the major opponent to an important Washington ally.

After the Kim Dae Jung episode, Liechty resumed his usual espionage duties, free to report on the dark side of the Seoul regime. One matter, though, was not pursued: KCIA activities in the United States. The Seoul station of the CIA was aware that its fellow service was courting members of Congress in Washington, intimidating Koreans abroad, and trying to acquire political influence in the United States. But it did little to collect intelligence on these fronts. "It was clear," Liechty noted, "that people running things in headquarters—and I presumed that meant Shackley—did not want it."

Shackley's position took him back into the thicket of Laos, as a distant manager of the last days of the now not-so-secret war there. That side-show had proceeded after Shackley's departure from Vientiane in 1968. In the years that followed, the Pathet Lao and NVA forces gained ground with only an occasional setback—until they threatened the CIA's secret base at Long Tieng.

The war had continued to wreak suffering on Laotians. The bombing that Shackley once helped coordinate had increased in ferocity. Vang Pao, with the help of his CIA friends, had fought on valiantly. But increasingly his cause seemed to be a losing one. A cease-fire implemented in February 1973 put an end to two years of especially fierce warfare. These battles had achieved little for the Hmong of Vang Pao and the CIA. "The principal effect" of those engagements, former station chief Douglas Blaufarb noted, was "to force most of the population that supported the resistance back into refugee status at a painful price in suffering and death." As Pop Buell lamented in the summer of 1973, "Runnin' and dyin', runnin' and dyin', that's all the Hmong have known. And now there's no place to run." Thirty thousand Hmong were dead from the CIA-encouraged war. More than 120,000 were refugees. (Another 250,000 Laotians were homeless.) "When there was trouble in the old days," Buell recalled, "the Hmong used to say, 'There's always another mountain.' But not anymore."

The Laotian truce was followed by the establishment of a coalition government favoring the communists. Aided by Shackley's officers, Vang Pao still directed attacks against what he considered to be encroachments on Hmong-controlled territory. Unhappy with the cease-fire, he wanted to maintain the fight. Shackley continued to send to Laos case officers to guide the doomed tribal efforts.

In the northwest of Laos, CIA contract officer Gary Parrott directed nine battalions of warriors from nineteen different tribes—1,500 men in all. "I was a warlord," recalled Parrott, a former Navy SEAL and Agency PRU adviser in Vietnam. His orders from Shackley: stop the tidal wave. Despite the truce, the Pathet Lao and the NVA were pushing the tribesmen from one position to the next. The irregulars were taking a pounding from North Vietnamese artillery.

Parrott and Shackley's other officers in country could do little for the longtime allies of Washington. Slowly, the fighting in the countryside came to a halt. Like other CIA officers who had followed Shackley's orders in Laos, Parrott was disillusioned. When he finished his tour in 1974, he complained to his superiors in Shackley's division that the whole Laos program had been a con. Many of the tribespeople had risked their lives believing they were fighting for an autonomous state —not U.S. geopolitical interests. They had been misled by the CIA.

With most of the fighting finished, the station in Vientiane turned toward the more classic task of intelligence collection, with the prime target Pathet Lao plans and intentions. "We were not really able to get anything," lamented Roger McCarthy, the deputy chief of station. "We had some moderate successes. But it was not what we hoped."

Shackley's scope was wide. He was responsible for directing spying efforts throughout the Pacific, in more than a dozen countries, and his most formidable target was the behemoth Red China. It was Shackley's job to squeeze whatever intelligence he could out of that closed communist society of one billion people.

Richard Helms, when he was Director, had declared Chinese intelligence a top priority. But that designation had not increased the Agency's production of valuable material on China. The country long had posed a quandary for the spies of the CIA. In the late 1960s, Ralph McGehee, while on the China desk of the Directorate of Plans, observed that all the motion produced little output. "Ghosts of case officers past roamed the halls," he later wrote, "carrying pieces of papers that gave purpose to their eerie missions. . . . Every day did bring a few cables and dispatches from China units scattered around the world. Most such documents noted the efforts of case officers to spot and assess people with access to Chinese officials serving overseas. [The China branch] had begun to realize the near impossibility of recruiting a Chinese official to be our spy."

After Nixon's opening to China in 1972 led to the establishment of the U.S. Liaison Office in Beijing, staffed by thirty people, the CIA finally could assign its own officers inside China. A few slots in the Liaison Office were Shackley's to fill. Jim Lilley, Shackley's second in Vientiane, received the honor of being the first chief of station in Beijing. Lilley landed in China in July of 1973.* But having his own men in China did not help Shackley a lot. As one senior CIA officer put it, "what the hell can you do as a small isolated contingent with the enemy all around you?" The Liaison Office and the Americans were under constant surveillance. If a CIA officer could evade the total surveillance, he did not have many leads to follow. "We had," one of Shackley's superiors recalled, "very few decent penetrations of the Chinese government."

The best way to get at the Chinese was to do so outside of China. Spy satellites and high-tech communication intercepts yielded most of the Agency's intelligence on China. As for human intelligence, the CIA station in Hong Kong took the lead. A steady stream of unsavory characters approached station officers to peddle information on China. In one instance, the Hong Kong station recruited an agent who appeared to be a treasure trove of useful information on events in China, but then the Agency discovered he was merely providing reports based on Chinese newspapers.

Shackley's division concentrated on Chinese missions around the world. It planted bugs in Chinese embassies and consulates. "But these did not provide much," a senior officer said. "There was little information of intelligence use and lots of squeaky bed springs. We had hours of reels of tapes with nothing on them."

Shackley turned to his six or so officers in Paris to find sources on China. In the fall of 1973, the station in Paris thought it had a potential agent. Kenize Mourad was a twenty-nine-year-old French citizen born in India. A journalist for *Le Nouvel Observateur,* she was raised by an order of nuns and at some point had been befriended by a Swiss diplomat who was ambassador to Beijing. Her nephew was a third secretary in the Pakistan embassy in Paris. Mourad knew diplomats from India, Pakistan, Bangladesh, and China. Shackley authorized an approach to Mourad. She accepted the Agency's pitch, according to a CIA cable. The CIA dubbed her UNPOLO/1 and placed her on the payroll. After a few months in the job, Shackley could claim an agent with access to Chinese diplomats.

But Shackley's luck did not hold. One month later—before Mourad could be productive—she quit the Agency. Mourad sent a note to her case officer in Paris: "The idea seemed exciting, but I finally realized it

---

* Over a year later, George Bush, the scion of an establishment family who had served in Congress, as U.N. ambassador, and as head of the Republican Party, was named U.S. envoy to China, a position in which he worked closely with Lilley and the CIA.

was going deeply against my feelings. . . . It would be a constant struggle in my mind." It was a typical scenario: agent found and recruited, operation launched, operation crashed.*

China was tough, and no one in the senior ranks of Langley expected much out of Shackley. He and the Agency eventually received solace from an unlikely source, a Soviet agent. This agent, the Foreign Ministry employee whom the CIA had recruited in Colombia, was supplying his Agency handlers with material on Soviet intelligence efforts against China. His reports allowed CIA people to reach a somewhat comforting conclusion: the Russians don't know anything more about the Chinese than we do.

As he had as chief of the Western Hemisphere Division, Shackley demanded Soviet penetrations. He tried to set quotas. Stations had to report so many Soviet recruitments a year. Some officers shrugged; others complained to one another. Many were posted to stations that had not seen a single Soviet-related success in years. But this was the Shackley they all had heard about.†

Afterward there would be conflicting accounts of who authorized one of the dumbest dirty tricks ever waged by the Agency. News reports, perhaps encouraged by Agency-friendly sources, suggested a rogue officer in Thailand had run the operation on his own. Yet the officer said he had clearance from Washington. And a senior CIA man claimed the division had signed off on the operation—that is, Shackley had okayed it. In any event, Shackley, as chief of the division, bore responsibility for a ploy that sparked anti-U.S. protests in Thailand, threatened a rupture in relations between Washington and Bangkok, and made the operators of Langley look like rank amateurs.

Toward the end of 1973, someone in the CIA decided to pull a fast one on the leftist insurgency based in northeastern Thailand. The communist rebellion had been sputtering along for years, and the CIA had long

---

* In September of 1979, the Agency renewed contact with Mourad, but the case officer did not identify himself as a CIA employee. Passing himself off as an embassy officer, he hoped Mourad would introduce him to leftist journalists and provide material about Iran, to which she traveled on business. At that time, probably without realizing to whom she was speaking, Mourad supplied the Agency information on Iran.

† "As always, Shackley ran the division by the numbers," said Bill Kohlmann, an officer on the Singapore-Malaysia desk. "When you are not trying to win a war and just trying to get intelligence, this approach did less harm. He did get people to work hard."

supported Bangkok's counterinsurgency program. But the CIA now wanted to take a shot at the communist insurgency on its own.

In December of 1973, the government of Premier Sanya Dharmasakti received from an insurgency leader, who went by the nom de guerre of Chamras, a letter proposing a cease-fire. Come negotiate, Chamras wrote. But he demanded the Thai government permit the guerrillas to set up a government in the territory they controlled. Immediately the government plunged into a debate about what the offer meant. Maybe it signified a rift in the rebellion's leadership. Perhaps the insurgents planned to shift their tactics from armed resistance to political struggle. Whatever it signified, the letter was not welcomed. Since the government obviously would reject the offer, Thai officials feared the communists would gain a propaganda win.

Creating confusion in Bangkok was not the intent of the letter writer, for the proposal had been forged by one of Shackley's men in northeastern Thailand, the CIA base chief in Sakhon Nakhon. The letter was also mailed to several Bangkok newspapers. The base chief's hope was to foment dissension within communist ranks by producing "evidence" that Chamras was attempting to cut his own deal with the government.

The base chief in Sakhon Nakhon miscalculated. The letter probably caused more discomfort within the government than among the insurgents. But the problem was not merely that a bad idea backfired. Shackley's base chief had committed a terrible mistake in tradecraft. He had handed the forged letter to a Thai employee to mail. At the post office, the Thai was asked if he wanted to register the letter. He provided the post office with the address of the CIA base.

Industrious Thai reporters traced the letter back to Sakhon Nakhon. The reporters discovered it was mailed by a Mr. Pisit, the CIA employee. He admitted posting copies of the letter but knew nothing of the contents. Ask my boss, the American, he said. The journalists confronted the American base chief. He refused to offer a full explanation but he asserted that whatever was done was carried out according to orders from Washington.

The resulting stories landed on the front pages in Thailand. The Thai government protested CIA "interference in the internal affairs of Thailand." Members of the Thai government and military called for eliminating CIA activity in their country. Editorials and columnists demanded the CIA be booted out of Thailand. Communists and student dissidents cited the incident as more proof that the Thai government was in the pocket of the United States.

The blowup came at a sensitive time. Thailand was a crucial ally in Washington's Indochina program. It had provided "volunteers" for the war in Laos and allowed the United States to station forces and aircraft in its country. But in October of 1973, months before the forged letter scandal erupted, the pro-Washington military regime had collapsed, after a series of student protests. A civilian government had taken over. The following month, Nixon appointed William Kintner to be the U.S. ambassador to Thailand. Student groups were outraged by the move. Kintner, once a colonel in the U.S. Army, had been assigned to the CIA in the early 1950s. "Because he previously worked for the CIA, Mr. Kintner will tend to interfere in the internal affairs of Thailand," one student leaflet declared.

The forged letter was perfect ammunition for the opposition. After the Thai press revealed that the CIA was behind the letter, 4,000 Thai demonstrated at the U.S. embassy. They demanded Kintner's departure and an investigation of Agency activities in Thailand. The U.S. embassy took the unusual step of publicly admitting that the Agency was responsible for the letter. Ambassador Kintner tendered his apologies to the government and told his staff he wanted to end the "gung-ho attitude" of the CIA. He promised the Thai nothing of this sort would happen again.

In Washington, a disgusted and furious Shackley yanked the base chief from his post* and closed the Sakhon Nakhon base. Because of the botched operation, Shackley's officers would have less latitude in this strategically important land.

Months after the episode, John le Carré, the spy novelist, visited Sakhon Nakhon to mine raw material for his books. He prowled about the deserted house that once housed Shackley's team. With a *Washington Post* reporter in tow, le Carré spoke to locals about the two Americans who had worked there. "They never said what they actually did," one resident said. "When you asked them they would say, 'Oh, a little of this and little of that.'" Le Carré discovered that when Shackley's men departed suddenly on New Year's Day of 1974, they left behind equipment that the locals assumed were radios and encryption devices. The machinery sat for weeks until unidentified Americans retrieved it. As le Carré toured the site, the *Post* reporter peppered him with questions. Was it really possible, the journalist asked, for a first-rate intelligence service like the CIA to commit such a stupid blunder as to allow a local employee to register a supposedly covert piece of mail? "Oh yes, quite possible," the novelist replied with delight. "It happens all the time. When in doubt about something like this assume a screw-up."

* Years later, the career of the base chief, an Irish-American, would be resuscitated when the so-called Irish mafia ran the Agency during William Casey's tenure.

II

In January of 1975, Shackley received a report from Tom Polgar. The cable asserted that Thieu was so firmly in control of South Vietnam that he would probably face reelection in October without significant challenge. Polgar proposed the CIA begin cultivating a token opponent. Officers in headquarters laughed at Polgar's report. Looking that far ahead, they believed, was absurd. A return message arrived in the station —presumably Shackley signed off on its content—politely informing Polgar his estimate had been trashed. Let's not worry yet about Thieu's political future, it advised.

Polgar and his station consistently had relayed reports to Shackley that bolstered the case for maintaining U.S. aid to Thieu's regime. (U.S. Ambassador Graham Martin was pressing Polgar for evidence that additional U.S. assistance would yield a payback.) Polgar's optimism shocked some of his subordinates. When Polgar visited the Bien Hoa base and told officers he foresaw no major problems in 1975, Orrin DeForest and his colleagues were astounded. "We were," DeForest recalled, "on the edge of disaster."*

Throughout 1974, the general thrust of Polgar's reporting to Shackley had been that all was not lost, that Saigon and Washington were still in the game. Polgar, a man of some professional integrity, was not so brazen as to report outright falsehoods to Shackley. Instead, he engaged in what one CIA colleague dubbed "creative intelligence gathering." He applied tight quality-control standards to reports of corruption and security problems, so that few were cleared for release. He did allow his regional officers to send cables directly to Washington and avoid the tilt of Saigon. But, according to analyst Frank Snepp, Polgar made certain to forward to headquarters rebuttals that discredited reports that highlighted corruption and inefficiency in the South Vietnamese government and army. Undoubtedly the reporting system was freer than in Shackley's day. Yet Polgar's opinions remained the most important. "The result," Snepp claimed, "was that we seldom troubled Washington with any news of the very foibles and weaknesses that were setting our allies up for the kill."

In headquarters, Ralph McGehee was one of those officers who won-

---

* Reports from the agent code-named HACKLE were a strong basis for pessimism. His information was used in a national intelligence estimate, issued in late December of 1974, that reported that Hanoi's military was more powerful than ever before and that an increase in NVA action was likely in 1975. But this and subsequent estimates failed to note the soon-to-be-apparent deep weaknesses of the South Vietnam military.

dered if Shackley's division was sleepwalking off a cliff. A year or so earlier, he had written a memo criticizing Shackley's management of the Saigon station and was chastised for doing so by Inspector General Gordon Stewart, the Agency veteran who sent Shackley to Nuremberg in the early 1950s. McGehee was then assigned to a do-nothing job in Langley. In November of 1974 he came across two cables from officers in Region IV. One reported a high rate of defection to the Viet Cong of South Vietnamese military and government personnel. The other noted that the communists controlled much of an entire southern province. Polgar, as could be expected, dispatched his own cables challenging this intelligence. But drawing on these reports, his own experiences in Vietnam, and his increasing pessimism, McGehee compiled a year-end report warning that South Vietnam was in danger of imminent collapse. He sent it to Shackley and William Nelson, the deputy director for operations. McGehee heard nothing in response.

"I always hoped that something I said would make a difference," McGehee recalled. "But policy was always in control." A washed-out troublemaker, though, was the last person to be heeded by Shackley and other senior officers. More important, given the choice between nay-saying intelligence and can-do reports that supported the aims of Nixon and Kissinger—and in the complex muck of Vietnam one could find either—it was only natural for Shackley to embrace the material that showed Washington was not on the road to defeat. No one expected him to buck the bureaucracy and the senior men of the administration. Officers who confronted the system never got too far. If the leaders of the United States and the top policymakers were imprisoned by their assumptions and desires, Shackley was not the man to bust them loose.

As Snepp viewed it, Polgar was maintaining a double policy. He grasped for good news suggesting the war would end through negotiations not tanks, but at the same time, Polgar—hoping for additional congressional aid—maintained a drumfire about the military threat. When the Defense Attaché Office of the embassy began updating the embassy's 400-page evacuation plan, the station chief declined to participate. He did not believe South Vietnam would have to be abandoned. But DeForest's intelligence operation in Bien Hoa had growing evidence that major enemy military action loomed ahead.

In early March of 1975, the NVA attacked the key highland city of Ban Me Thuout, which quickly fell. The North Vietnamese could barely keep up with ARVN's collapse. "By the third week of March," Snepp recalled, "I was churning out an appraisal per day to help keep Washington abreast of [the] nightmares-in-progress." His reports to Shackley, signed by Polgar, raised the prospect of a decisive defeat for Saigon. Polgar had told Snepp he wanted to be on the record with a bleak view, in case the worst did happen. But the chief still emphasized that more money and equipment might save the day. That was a terrible mistake. "Instead of convincing colleagues in Washington of the gravity of the military situation," Snepp asserted, "we succeeded only in persuading them there was still an out. For the optimists back in the State Department and the CIA could always assure themselves after reading our analyses, 'Well, yes things are going badly out there, but Polgar and his boys say aid is still the answer.' It was the beginning of a last fatal illusion."*

The high command of the CIA—Shackley and others—were slow to accept the grim assessments that came out of Saigon. A national intelligence estimate produced at the end of March declared the South Vietnamese army was strong enough to hold the new defensive line north of Saigon through the beginning of the rainy season in May. On March 25, as Da Nang fell, Snepp penned a memo summing up the deteriorating military situation. The NVA leaders had not envisioned such a weak reply to their 1975 offensive and were exploiting it as best they could. "The entire complexion of the Vietnam war has altered in a matter of weeks," Snepp wrote in a report bound for Shackley's desk, "and the government is in imminent danger of decisive military defeat."

Shackley went to witness the nightmare-in-progress. Senior decision-makers in Washington were questioning the credibility of the doomsday intelligence. President Gerald Ford and Kissinger, ever distrustful of the CIA, ordered General Frederick Weyand, the army chief of staff, to Saigon to render an independent evaluation. Erich von Marbod, a senior Pentagon official, saw the risk inherent in such a trip. If Saigon fell after Weyand's trip, the general could be blamed for whatever mistakes he did not foresee. The solution was simple: create a team. If blame ever had to be cast, there would be several pairs of shoulders to carry it.

Shackley, Weyand, Ambassador Martin, George Carver, a veteran Agency Saigon-watcher, and other U.S. officials lifted off from Andrews Air Force Base in a C-141. During the long flight, Shackley and team members huddled around a conference table discussing whom to see and what to ask once they hit South Vietnam. They seemed to believe that with the right decisions made, the proper actions taken, the situation could be rectified.

When Shackley and the Weyand team touched down in Saigon on

---

* In defense of his actions years afterward, Polgar noted, "I advised Washington as early as the 14th of March . . . that the ultimate outcome of the Communist offensive is not in doubt, 'because South Vietnam cannot survive without U.S. military aid as long as North Vietnam's war-making capability is unimpaired and supported by the Soviet Union and China.' " Polgar reported all was lost—if more U.S. aid did not materialize. Snepp's position was unqualified: all was lost, period.

March 28, Da Nang and much of Region I were in the process of being lost. Less than half of the Agency's 500 Vietnamese employees in the area managed to escape. And Cambodia, where the United States had backed the government of Lon Nol, was coming apart. The arrival of the Weyand mission was greeted with sarcasm by Agency officers who recognized that the end was approaching. "It was sadly ironic," Snepp noted, "that they should have arrived in Saigon in the very midst of the final dissolution of the army in [Regions I and II], for having so much to comprehend, and so little time to do it, they would never fully appreciate how close we were to the final reckoning."

Shackley, once the prime briefer on Vietnam, was now on the receiving end. He and team members gathered in the embassy to get the truth from representatives of the CIA, the State Department, and the U.S. military. The military and Agency men were in agreement: nothing much could stop the North Vietnamese. Polgar and Snepp now concurred that only new U.S. intervention or a negotiated surrender could prevent total communist victory in the next few weeks. Deputy chief of mission Wolfgang Lehmann, echoing Ambassador Martin, stuck to the rosy claim that with more ammunition and support Saigon could pull through.

Snepp found that the Washington team had trouble accepting the notion that it might be over. That was not unexpected. They all had possessed a role in the making of the mess at hand. Shackley had spent five and a half years of his life in Laos and Vietnam, and another two years in Washington directing the efforts of Polgar, Snepp, and scores of others. "To have convinced such committed 'experts' that Saigon was finished," Snepp later wrote, "would have taken months, perhaps even years, of persuasion."

Within the Saigon station, several officers hoped negotiations might avert a total military defeat and prevent Hanoi from overrunning the south. But on April 1, in a safe house near the embassy, an agent fresh from the field told Snepp that Hanoi was on a "blood scent" and saw no reason to stop shy of total victory. Its leaders might even reject a negotiated surrender. At lunch, Snepp shared the agent's observations with Polgar and Shackley. Polgar did not buy it. The communists would not choose battle over a negotiated surrender. Shackley, too, was skeptical.

Yet Polgar was realistic enough to request authority from Shackley to start shipping out family and household effects of CIA officers and to grant early departure to Agency people close to finishing their tours. The station began compiling lists of Americans and third-country nationals whom it would assist in an evacuation.

Shackley snatched hours from the schedule of the Weyand team to help Polgar deal with the disintegrating situation. "This was a pressure-packed period in my life," he later said. He flew to various spots around the country to be briefed by his own officers and Vietnamese officials. He was a different man than the one who had commanded the Saigon station. He was nervous and seemed off-balance.

At one CIA base outside Saigon, a somber Shackley met with field officers. He was not eager to hear them talk about the weaknesses of Thieu's rule. The officers saw that Shackley was in tune with Polgar's policies and believed, like the station chief, that should this be the end there would at least be a decent interval that would permit the United States an orderly withdrawal. These officers did not buy that line, but no one was willing to contradict Polgar. "There's nothing in it," one recalled, "for us to say to Shackley that our boss [Polgar] has been lying to you."

On April 3—a day on which Ambassador Martin announced to news reporters, "There's no danger to Saigon"—Shackley and the Weyand team trooped to the Presidential Palace to confer with Thieu and his aides. The Americans and Vietnamese traded handshakes and forced smiles, as cameramen and photographers recorded the scene, and then they sat down at a mahogany table in the situation room. Once the journalists were ushered out, Martin asked his colleagues to brief Thieu on their findings. He turned to Shackley to start. Shackley noted that he saw a possibility for a turnaround. Saigon, he said, needed to focus on how the rest of the world viewed Vietnam. "There is a need for your government to address itself to the refugee problem and make it apparent to the people of Vietnam and the world that the government cares for them and that the problem is being well handled," he commented. "The refugee problem can be used to generate sympathy for Vietnam." The situation in Vietnam only had to be framed properly: "There is a need to present to the American public that this is a clear-cut North Vietnamese invasion and there are not simply more Viet Cong coming out of the woods." Too many Americans considered the current military activity the culmination of a civil war.

Shackley droned on. The Vietnamese shifted in their seats and looked disappointed. They knew the problems. From the Americans they wanted just two things: aid and a resumption of bombing. But after Shackley finished, George Carver pressed the same theme, noting that the true story of the NVA invasion had not been told. He talked about inviting opponents of the war to see for themselves what was happening in Vietnam. This is unbelievable, thought Nguyen Tien Hung, a top Thieu aide. The enemy was at the gate, and the men of the CIA were talking public relations.

When it was Weyand's time to speak, the general criticized Saigon's military command. But he vaguely promised, "We will get you the assistance you need and will explain your needs to Congress." That did not buoy Thieu and the Vietnamese, whose appeals for B-52 bombing went unanswered. The Americans filed out. Thieu remained behind, looking deflated and sad.

On April 5, the U.S. military aircraft carrying the Weyand team back to Washington landed in Palm Springs, California, where President Ford was vacationing. In the hours before touching down, Weyand, Shackley, and the team drafted a report for Ford. As soon as they were off the plane, Weyand, Shackley, and the others briefed Ford and Kissinger. Their report could not avoid reality. "The probability of the survival of South Vietnam as a truncated nation in the southern provinces is marginal at best," it noted. "The [government of Vietnam] is on the brink of a total military defeat." But Weyand and the rest stopped short of saying the war was about to end. No one wanted to pronounce the final judgment. "The social and political structure of the country," the report said, had been dealt a setback, but it added, "it is hard to tell" to what extent. As for the enemy, the best the team could do was to observe the obvious. North Vietnam had two options: a complete military takeover or a lopsided negotiated settlement. Which course Hanoi would choose they dared not predict. On the question of what to do next, the report proposed morale-boosting actions such as positive statements from Ford and more trips like the Weyand mission. (Its members were under the mistaken impression that their presence had reassured the South Vietnamese.) On more concrete matters, the report proposed $722 million in emergency aid and recommended B-52 bombing runs. No one was willing to pull the plug.

Kissinger had been advocating one final spasm of U.S. aid. His argument was simple: if Saigon went under after the aid, then no one could say that Washington had been stingy. The Weyand report, not surprisingly, agreed with the Secretary of State's reasoning. "The governments of the world . . . ," it stated, "will see any present inability to support the Vietnamese . . . as a failure of U.S. will and resolve. If we make no effort, our future credibility as perceived by ally and potential adversary alike will be lost for years to come." Here at the end of a tragic experiment in geopolitics—in which war had been waged in large part to demonstrate Washington's willingness to wage war—image was all that was left.

The Weyand report was classified, but media stories noted it was gloomy. In Palm Springs, official White House photographer David Kennerly, who had accompanied the Weyand mission, summed up the inspection tour for reporters: "the worst thing that ever happened to me in my life. . . . It is really shitty and you can quote me."

Shackley always wanted more intelligence reports. Now the Saigon station was flooded. Hundreds of reports were pouring in from the field officers. Snepp was churning out a situation report every day, which was immediately cabled to Shackley. In Washington, the top honchos of the Ford administration argued over how much aid they should request from an unenthusiastic Congress. In South Vietnam, Company officers were waiting for the finale. Bill and Pat Johnson, a husband-wife team in the station, made a pact. If they were not able to escape the final North Vietnamese push, he would shoot her with his .38 and then turn the gun on himself. CIA people who already drank hard, began to drink earlier each day. Polgar ordered the destruction of classified files. Secretaries fortified themselves with Bloody Marys as they fed the shredding machines. Station employees collected arms, helmets, and flak jackets. Polgar walked about with a gun tucked underneath his jacket.

The station continued to put out material that downplayed the threat of an NVA invasion of Saigon and that exaggerated the strengths of the South Vietnamese regime. Polgar possessed some basis for his hopes. For months, he had socialized with Hungarian delegates of the International Control and Supervision Commission, which monitored the peace agreement of 1973. When Shackley earlier questioned this close relationship, Polgar had claimed his Hungarian friends promised to provide him with advance warning of major NVA offensives. By the first week of April, the Hungarians were telling Polgar the war did not have to end with a military takeover of Saigon. Polgar set as his grail a negotiated settlement, a new truce that would permit the United States a tidy departure. He cabled Shackley that the station had, as he later put it, "little time or flexibility to execute evacuation schemes which combine safety, dignity and satisfaction of our moral commitments to hundreds of thousands of Vietnamese." He urged the commencement of new negotiations while South Vietnam maintained some leverage.

Snepp's reading of agent reports was that the NVA had no intention of stopping short of Saigon. One of the station's better agents reported that a new COSVN resolution called for the "liberation" of all territory north of Saigon in April and a move against the capital city after that. The agent also asserted that all talk of a truce or negotiated settlement was a ruse. Snepp held up this report as the truth that ought to guide all actions—and prompt a thorough evacuation of Americans, their Vietnamese employees and agents, as well as the complete obliteration of all South Vietnamese and American intelligence files. Polgar and Martin judged his view as alarmist. The report Snepp was allowed to dispatch to Shackley and CIA headquarters was toned down.

DeForest's agents were saying the same thing: the final push was on. DeForest wanted to evacuate his Vietnamese employees and their families. Polgar would not yet authorize such action. Instead the order from Saigon station called on field officers to assemble a prioritized list of "key indigenous persons," who should be moved out in case of an emergency. DeForest was enraged: this was a list of the "Station's contacts and friends . . . generals and police officials and politicians"—not the persons who had done the work for the CIA bases.

In Tay Ninh, John Stockwell, the last officer in charge there, started to pull together his own evacuation plan. The reports he received from HACKLE convinced him there was little time left. The Americans had to get their employees and agents out. But Polgar and Martin did not want any evacuations. The overly persistent Stockwell was ordered out of the country by Polgar.

On April 17, Snepp met in a Saigon safe house with HACKLE. Sipping a Budweiser, the Agency's best agent in Vietnam reported that Hanoi was determined to take Saigon by May 19, the birthday of Ho Chi Minh. There would be no negotiations, no coalition government. Snepp returned to the embassy and briefed Polgar. There's no need to report this, Polgar responded. We've heard it all before. Snepp was stunned. He pleaded with the chief to be allowed to send his notes on the conversation to Washington through "operational channels"—which meant the report would be regarded as low-level material and not disseminated widely. Snepp's cable went out this way. But CIA officers in Washington bumped it out of the "ops channel," and the report was circulated throughout the national security bureaucracy.*

Polgar, who still prayed for a negotiated settlement, was not the only one to downplay this important piece of information. The intelligence evaluators of Shackley's division rated Snepp's prescient cable as being of only modest value.† Shackley, who was far from the on-the-ground reality, was in no position to enter the fray and make the bureaucracy see the light as Snepp, DeForest, Stockwell, and others saw it. Polgar was in charge, and Shackley was standing by his station chief's judgment.

On April 19, Polgar heard from a Hungarian contact that a deal might be possible. If Thieu resigned and the U.S. ceased its military support,

---

* Polgar took issue with Snepp's overall account of Polgar's performance during the last weeks of Saigon. In a 1977 letter he noted that Snepp's charge that Polgar suppressed information is "just about the worst accusation one can level against a professional intelligence officer." Snepp's allegation, he continued, "is devoid of truth." He dismissed Snepp (whom he once commended) as a "medium-grade analyst who, a few times, was permitted to talk with sources."

† After the war, Ambassador Martin testified to Congress that Polgar had not paid much mind to this report, which was soon to be proven accurate. Martin, though, at the time was no more receptive to this piece of bad news than was Polgar, according to Snepp. A postwar CIA memo, looking for bright spots, took credit for Snepp's work, boasting that its April 17 Daily Intelligence Publication reported that "our most reliable source of communist intentions"—meaning HACKLE—disclosed Hanoi's call for the "final" assaults.

then the final battle would be forestalled and Washington would not be pushed into a humiliating retreat. Polgar quickly cabled his report to Shackley. Senior officials of State and the CIA grasped at Polgar's straws. Shackley protested another gloomy intelligence estimate that asserted Saigon was doomed and, relying on Polgar's reporting, he told Director Colby an opportunity for a political settlement existed.

Shackley was stuck behind a desk in suburban Virginia, trying to evaluate the intelligence from Saigon. Only he knew if all the years he had put into Vietnam affected his judgment. Intelligence officers are supposed to keep emotions far from evaluations. But doing so requires great discipline, especially in those cases where officers are supposed to both observe and shape situations. It was not only Shackley's and Polgar's job to observe what occurred in Vietnam; they had to promote and preserve America's standing there. Their reporting embodied more than dispassionate comments on events in Vietnam; it reflected their efforts to safeguard U.S. interests. The pressure was enormous to transmit information that showed the CIA was performing well. In Vietnam, from start to finish, the collection of good intelligence was compromised by the dual nature of the CIA.

The last-ditch U.S. aid never came. Neither did the negotiated settlement. Shackley had to deal with the disposition of two decades of U.S. involvement in Indochina, as an evacuation began in haphazard fashion. After the Pentagon withdrew permission for the CIA to use several of its air transports, the deputy chief of the station asked Shackley to authorize a shift of all Air America transports to Taiwan, Thailand, and Singapore. It was a sly move. If Shackley said yes, each outgoing flight could be turned into a passenger lift for Vietnamese whose contacts with the Agency were now deemed life-threatening. Shackley denied permission. Neither Thailand nor Singapore, he asserted, would allow such a massive influx of CIA-linked Vietnamese. Agency officers in the field were aghast, believing the station was cutting it too close. If they did not get out all their Vietnamese employees and agents, these people would be lost to the communists.

As an ad hoc evacuation continued, Polgar and Martin remained hopeful that a total retreat would not become necessary. On April 27—after the NVA attack on Saigon had begun—Shackley sent a series of cables to Polgar urging him to quicken the withdrawal of nonessential CIA personnel and key Vietnamese. Station staff were besieged with calls from Vietnamese who wanted out. CIA officers were forced to decide whom to help and whom to leave behind. Of those not lucky enough to be invited to the evacuation were 800 or so Vietnamese employed by the CIA-supported Central Intelligence Organization and the Special Branch. No one at the station assumed the task of determining whether South Vietnam intelligence had cleaned out sensitive files. In Bien Hoa, the National Police fled their headquarters and left behind files identifying agents developed by Orrin DeForest and his team.

HACKLE, the CIA's only high-level agent, was offered the chance to leave. He chose to stay in Vietnam. CIA people later heard that HACKLE was executed after a South Vietnamese security officer betrayed him. In the last days of Saigon, Tucker Gouglemann, who had served in Saigon under Shackley and then retired, returned to search for Vietnamese friends.*

One of the thousands of Vietnamese looking to flee was Tran Ngoc Chau, the former opposition legislator and CIA ally whom Thieu had railroaded in 1970 while Shackley stood by. Thieu had released Chau in 1974. With Saigon's collapse pending, Chau sought help from his friend Keyes Beech, the journalist. Beech called the CIA station to see if it could tend to Chau and his family. "Why not ask us to evacuate Ho Chi Minh?" an officer snorted. Another station officer agreed to help Chau. But, come April 29, Chau had heard nothing further from this officer; he was stuck. Weeks later, troops surrounded his home. He was taken to a reeducation camp and treated as if he were a CIA agent. Chau spent two years in the camp. In February of 1979, he and his family escaped Ho Chi Minh City (what was once Saigon) by pretending to be Chinese refugees. With the help of newsman George McArthur, they settled in America.

Years after the Vietnam War ended, Keyes Beech heard a disturbing piece of news from Frank Snepp: Shackley in headquarters had vetoed Chau's evacuation. Shackley was a neighbor of Beech and occasionally dropped by. On one visit, Beech asked his friend if he had blocked Chau's departure. Shackley answered obliquely: I'll have to check the back channel cables on that, but I can assure you he was not one of my priorities. Beech interpreted that to be a yes. "I didn't think anyone would do a thing like that, I really didn't," Beech later remarked.

Chau never figured out what precisely had gone wrong. But as he frantically searched for a way out of Saigon during the closing days of April of 1975, he realized the CIA had screwed him, again. "They tried to destroy me," he said two decades afterward. "That is history. I am not

---

* Gouglemann would miss the final airlift and be captured by the North Vietnamese. After Saigon's fall, William Buckley, who had managed the PRU program with Gouglemann, frantically made the rounds in Washington to find someone who would order a rescue of Gouglemann. But Shackley and others turned Buckley down. Gouglemann was tortured, interrogated, and killed by the North Vietnamese.

angry with them. They were people who were so ignorant, ignorant people who did a lot of bad things to both my country and the United States."

The fall of Saigon arrived April 30. Polgar, Snepp, and other station officers were consumed with the task of evacuating the CIA's favorite Vietnamese. The chaotic streets were full of Vietnamese desperate to leave. They gathered wherever helicopters landed to pick up designated evacuees. There was plenty of heroic action. But hundreds of Vietnamese who had toiled for the Agency—who had been spies, who had run the Duc Hotel, who had staffed CIA offices, who had translated for the Americans—were left behind. Voices kept coming over the radio in headquarters: "Save me, save me, save me." Finally CIA communications officers took axes to the high-tech radio gear. Hours after darkness descended, the last dozen or so Agency people in Vietnam headed to the roof to be airlifted to the U.S.S. *Denver.* Polgar and his deputy remained behind to help supervise the final details of the retreat.

In Langley, Shackley and the others could only wait for the next cable updating the evacuation. The final message Shackley received from Vietnam came shortly before Polgar became the last CIA officer to leave the Saigon station. Prior to hustling onto a helicopter, Polgar paused to deliver a philosophical exegesis:

> It has been a long fight and we have lost. This experience unique in the history of the United States does not signal necessarily the demise of the United States as a world power. The severity of the defeat and the circumstances of it, however, would seem to call for a reassessment of the policies of niggardly half measures which have characterized much of our participation here despite the commitment of manpower and resources which were certainly generous. Those who fail to learn from history are forced to repeat it. Let us hope that we will not have another Vietnam experience and that we have learned our lesson.
>
> Saigon signing off.

It was the type of cable Shackley might have fired off. Those damn politicians had not let the military and the intelligence services do the job right. The cause had been unquestionably just. The waste of Vietnam —the lives lost, the years sacrificed—was not the fault of men like Polgar and Shackley. They were victims, too.

In Washington, Colby immediately signaled that such victims as Polgar and Shackley would not suffer careerwise. His final message to Polgar was full of hubris: "I would like to record Agency's pride and satisfaction with the job that its representatives did there, and at no time during its twenty-odd-year history is this more true than in these past few weeks. The courage, integrity, dedication and high competence the Agency displayed in a variety of situations over these years has been fully matched and even surpassed by your performance during this difficult final phase."* Colby, a politic and polite man, did not choose this occasion to reflect on the numerous intelligence failures that were an integral piece of the whole Vietnam debacle.

III

Wars may end in clear victory or defeat, but murky battles over blame often remain. Shackley was about to be pulled into a nasty one, courtesy of his onetime aide, Frank Snepp.

After escaping Saigon, Snepp relocated to Thailand, where for a short spell he debriefed journalists and refugees from Vietnam. He also wrote articles on Vietnam that the Bangkok station sought to place in the local press. He then returned to Washington. The analyst who had impressed both Shackley and Polgar soon was distressed. He discovered that of the station's 1,900 Vietnamese employees, only 537 had been evacuated. Worse, he figured, about 30,000 Vietnamese who worked with the Agency—Vietnamese intelligence officers, PRU members, agents, translators, defectors—had been left to the enemy. Intelligence files of the Saigon government, which identified CIA operatives, had not been destroyed. The evacuation, Snepp concluded, was "an institutional disgrace."

Snepp was a loyal Company man; he believed the system would address the fiasco in appropriate fashion. He arranged to see Shackley in the chief's office. As Shackley sat placidly, Snepp asked if the division was going to conduct an after-action report to identify the Vietnamese the CIA had abandoned. Snepp was sure Langley was planning some sort of rescue operation. When Snepp finished, Shackley uttered some noncommittal remarks. The meeting was over.

Shortly after that unsatisfying audience, Snepp was told to fill out a questionnaire Shackley's division was distributing to all Saigon veterans. Its introduction was all too telling. "We recognize," it read, "that not all the individuals who were on the [evacuation] list were evacuated due to a variety of reasons. It was unfortunate that the phased flow was interrupted by heavy local enemy action and we recognize that there was of necessity a change in emphasis at that point, with a greater effort being made to evacuate American personnel. It is not our design to seek

---

* Afterward, Colby conceded that many Vietnamese were abandoned and that documents were left behind—not Agency records but those of the CIA's friends in the South Vietnamese police and the Phoenix committees.

scapegoats or to assign blame or discredit to any individual." Snepp read the message loud and clear. Shackley was rigging a whitewash. Sure, the questionnaire asked respondents to note who was left behind, and it requested that officers identify cases with "flap potential." But Shackley was not going to rake anyone over the coals for the last screw-ups in Vietnam. Snepp refused to fill out the form.

Snepp wanted a real "damage assessment" conducted. But no one in Shackley's division, including the chief, was interested. Shackley did have loose ends to tie up. Responding to inquiries from the State Department and Congress, he ordered officers to study several specific questions: Were CIA documents destroyed? What happened to Saigon government records? Was money in the Agency's possession returned? Who exactly was brought out of Vietnam? But there was no overall study to evaluate the evacuation.

Shackley's chief of Vietnam operations (VNO)—the fellow who was ROIC V for Shackley in Saigon and then his chief of operations in the Western Hemisphere Division—had to sweep up the remains of Vietnam. (In Langley, CIA people gossiped about an artifact this Shackleyite had brought back from Vietnam and hung in his living room: a blood-stained VC flag.) "People were coming back the debris of a defeated Agency," the VNO chief recalled. "All came out very bitter. Many were bitter at Polgar. They had lost furniture and possessions. And they complained about the strict orders [from Polgar] to hold agents in place in the provinces, at the insistence of Kissinger and the White House. In the last analysis, people were left behind and ended up in camps or were murdered." This troubled the consciences of many case officers. "The Agency is not the Boy Scouts," the VNO chief said. "But if you recruit somebody, you feel an enormous sense of responsibility for them. If they stayed in place at your instruction and then couldn't make it to the airport and get out, it's on you. Instead, the airplanes came back full of black marketeers and whores. It was a bad scene."

One day Snepp came knocking. He had been wandering the halls of Langley searching for someone willing to take a hard look at what went wrong in Vietnam. He pressed Shackley's VNO chief to review the reporting out of the station and Polgar's handling of the evacuation. The VNO chief recognized there was a lot of truth in what Snepp said. He too believed Polgar had been suckered by his Hungarian contacts into believing Hanoi would allow Washington a graceful exit. But the VNO chief had no desire to assume this gargantuan headache. Don't tell me, he said to Snepp. Take it to the inspector general. A frustrated Snepp left. As he watched the young officer leave, the VNO chief thought, there are too many sour people around here.

The VNO chief was not looking behind. Under Shackley's supervision, he was busy resettling officers throughout the Agency. And Agency assets in refugee camps demanded attention. Lieutenant General Dang Van Quang, for one, was sitting in a camp in Arkansas. In Vietnam, the notorious Quang was known as the most corrupt official in Thieu's circle and a dabbler in the narcotics trade. He also was a key contact for Shackley and Polgar.

Quang's presence at the camp was not appreciated by fellow refugees outraged by the stories of his war booty. His life was threatened. A frightened Quang appealed to Shackley to get him out of the camp. His plight was discussed at the interagency task force on refugee policy, where Shackley's VNO represented Agency interests. Publicly, a task force spokesperson said Quang merited no special attention. Shackley and the VNO chief, though, wanted to assist Quang (while the Drug Enforcement Administration desired to speak to him). But without Shackley's help—according to the VNO chief—Quang arranged his own speedy departure and headed to Montreal, before DEA officers could chat with him.

Once Quang settled in Canada, he complained to his old CIA friends of financial difficulties. "Shackley and I talked this over," said the VNO chief. "We were very careful about sending money to him. We didn't want to display any undue CIA favoritism. We gave him $5,000 once or twice." Agency officers, with Shackley's approval, slipped nontraceable cashier's checks to a man suspected of drug dealing.

Shackley directed the VNO chief to initiate operations to obtain intelligence on the new Vietnam. The VNO chief tried to establish an intelligence effort on Vietnam out of Thailand, but the project fizzled. He conducted a review to determine if any American prisoners of war were in Indochina and concluded that no POWs remained.* Agency people like the VNO chief could shake off the dust of Vietnam and proceed with their careers. Frank Snepp could not.

Despite their difference of views in Saigon, Polgar had invited Snepp to join him in Mexico, where he was to be posted as chief of station. Snepp put aside his feelings about Polgar's mistakes in Vietnam and accepted the offer. But the two were not to be reunited.

In mid-August, Snepp delivered a lecture to cleared State Department officials on the evacuation of Saigon. He told them it had been a disaster. Shackley was angered by Snepp's presentation. But Snepp would not shut up. His embittered complaints circulated through Langley's hallways. He was not the only dissenter. In October, Colby told the inspector general that "there is a feeling among a certain number of our people

---

* After serving as Shackley's VNO chief for a year, this officer was sent by Shackley to Manila to be chief of station for the Philippines.

who served in Saigon that the reporting from there was in some fashion edited or selected to present a favorable picture, and to suppress an unfavorable one, of the likely strength of the South Vietnamese." The Director asked the I.G. to "do some interviewing...to determine whether there is any general impression in this regard, and, if so, the degree to which it represented a conscious policy rather than an unconscious development."

Colby was tiptoeing around an explosive subject. The accusation was that Polgar had rigged the intelligence. If so, Shackley had failed as division chief to ensure that the intelligence he distributed to policymakers was honest. These were allegations that ruined careers.

Colby's request to the I.G. came two days after the completion of an internal CIA study on the "Effectiveness of U.S. Intelligence Analysis on Vietnam, December 1974–April 1975." The paper evaluated reporting from Saigon that had been overseen by Shackley and praised the intelligence community for its "continuous, voluminous, and high quality input to U.S. policy makers." The report's authors boasted that a December 1974 intelligence estimate accurately assessed North Vietnamese plans for 1975, particularly an increase in military action. But the complimentary memo acknowledged "minor" deficiencies. It observed that the CIA in 1974 and 1975 overestimated the resiliency of the South Vietnamese military and underestimated Hanoi's ability to exploit the situation. The paper could not ignore an obvious shortcoming: "It should be noted that like the North Vietnamese, the U.S. Government also did not anticipate the rapidity of South Vietnam's collapse against a less than all-out offensive."

The comparison with North Vietnam was absurd. Unlike Hanoi, Washington had tremendous access to the Saigon regime. If Shackley's division had been able to assess anything correctly, it should have been the strengths and weaknesses of the army and government of South Vietnam. Being correct about Hanoi's plans mattered less, since the Agency missed the mark on Thieu's military and government, the easier targets. Shackley and senior officers had been too close to their subjects.

Responding to Colby's request, Donald Chamberlain, the inspector general, called in Snepp and eight other officers from Vietnam. To Norman Jones, an I.G. official, Snepp railed about Polgar for nearly two hours. Polgar, Snepp asserted, had trouble accepting Thieu's weaknesses and the low morale in ARVN. Snepp complained that whenever the station was asked to evaluate ARVN, a CIA officer would leave his villa, play tennis with a South Vietnamese general, and report back that things were fine. As for corruption, Polgar believed that this was a way of life in Asia, nothing about which to bother Washington.

Snepp asked to write a report on the Saigon station's performance.

Jones waved off the idea, noting, Snepp later claimed, that the I.G. was collecting information to help Colby fend off critics on Capitol Hill.* Snepp now decided he had to take action on his own. Shackley and the I.G. had failed in a basic bureaucratic task: allow a would-be whistle-blower to let off steam.

The I.G.'s office produced a five-page memo—Shackley was not inter-viewed—that cleared Polgar of any wrongdoing. But the report con-tained one passage that came close to supporting one of Snepp's key charges: "It is possible that to win Mr. Polgar's approval, some categories of information, such as reports of poor morale in the South Vietnamese military, may have required more elaborate source validation than sub-jects of lesser importance." In support of Polgar's management of the station's intelligence reporting and the final evacuation, the memo noted, "All of these decisions were of necessity based on very incom-plete information" as to both "enemy intentions and the possible reac-tions of our South Vietnamese allies." In a strange way, Chamberlain defended Polgar by referring to an intelligence failure. The I.G. report was nothing of which Polgar and Shackley needed to worry.

Chamberlain's inquiry was not the thorough investigation Snepp de-sired. After attending a December awards ceremony for Vietnam veter-ans in the bubble-shaped auditorium at headquarters—in which Colby defended U.S. policy in Vietnam and handed out medals—Snepp de-cided to write a book.

As went South Vietnam, so went Laos. In the spring of 1975, enemy troops encircled Long Tieng—Spook Heaven. Vang Pao's forces had suffered disastrous defeats. Shackley's officers in Laos argued that he would be more effective as a leader in exile than a martyr on the battlefield. The Hmong general consented to a CIA plan to extract him. On May 18, 1975, Vang Pao left Laos. Cargo planes ferried hundreds of his closest supporters to Udorn, Thailand. "The Meo were a strong people who never cried before," the general said. "Now when the peo-ple see me, they cry over our losses." His departure from Long Tieng was followed by an orgy of looting.

After years of fighting under the guidance of Shackley and other

---

* Norman Jones in 1978 told his superiors that Snepp did not ask to file such a report. He also denied that he told Snepp the I.G. was procuring material to defend itself against congressional inquiries. But Colby was desperately concerned with the Agency's image. In November of 1975, he met with Marvin and Bernard Kalb, two journalists working on a book about the fall of Vietnam. Colby then authorized Shackley to continue to brief the Kalb brothers. Shackley spoke with them a few times, but he later claimed he did not discuss Vietnam with the pair.

Americans, Vang Pao's people were decimated. Tens of thousands had perished due to the war. Many more were refugees. Thousands poured over the border into Thailand to reside in squalid refugee camps. Vang Pao's tribe was no more. Most of the Hmong close to Vang Pao fled the country before the end. But many tribespeople who had worked with the Agency were left behind. By the end of the year, the Pathet Lao were fully in control of the government.

Roger McCarthy, deputy chief of station in Vientiane at the end, was depressed as one of the Agency's most prominent covert actions drew to a close: "We bore a great deal of responsibility. This was not our finest hour or our finest effort. Ultimately, the Hmong was unable to do much as a military force. They needed incredible support. We destroyed their tradition of being nomadic. They had to hunker down to meet the big iron birds that came in and dropped off rice and tin roofing. It was the usual case of mistaking fantasies and dreams for what could be done. It should never have been done."

"Those of us who had worked with the Meo were very unhappy," recalled a senior DDO official. "They had put out a lot for us. We distributed some funds in the millions-of-dollars range as a form of severance, tipped our hat and said good-bye. I don't think we ever had thought ahead as to wonder what would happen to the Hmong tribe."

Nineteen seventy-five was not a good year for anybody who had devoted his or her life to the Central Intelligence Agency. Shocking revelations in the media of CIA domestic spying had prompted President Gerald Ford in early January to establish a commission, headed by Vice President Nelson Rockefeller, to investigate the Agency. Weeks later, the Senate unveiled a committee to investigate the intelligence community. The House of Representatives created its own panel. At the helm of the Senate inquiry was Senator Frank Church, who months earlier had been enraged to learn that Shackley and others had misled his subcommittee during the 1973 ITT probe. Several other liberal critics of the CIA were assigned to the Senate committee. The Church Committee's broad mandate included discerning whether the Agency ever had engaged in illegal or improper activities and determining whether the American intelligence system served the national interests. That the legislators even had to ask such questions was an insult to Shackley and his colleagues. CIA people grumbled about the snoops who soon would come calling.

While the Rockefeller Commission and the congressional committees delved into the crevices of the CIA, leaked news of Agency deeds and misdeeds spilled out. The Justice Department was reported to be examining Richard Helms's 1973 testimony on Chile for perjury. Newspapers across the country carried the account of a 1968 CIA attempt to raise a Soviet nuclear submarine that had sunk in the Pacific Ocean. (The multimillion-dollar operation raised part of the sub, which then split up and carried its intelligence treasures—warheads, guidance systems, codes—back to the ocean floor, but the project retrieved valuable material about Soviet technology.) There were disclosures that the CIA had spied on members of Congress, that the Agency and Gulf Oil had contributed funds to Bolivian politicians in the 1960s, and that—most scandalous of all—the Agency had plotted assassination.

In June, the Rockefeller Commission released its report. It was full of soiled linen. The President's panel revealed that the CIA had tested LSD on unsuspecting subjects, spied on American dissidents, physically abused a defector, burgled and bugged without court orders, intercepted mail illegally, and engaged in "plainly unlawful" conduct.

On Capitol Hill, the Church Committee was conducting private audiences with Richard Helms, John McCone, Richard Bissell, William Harvey, and lesser-known Agency colleagues. (The House committee inquiry stalled, amid bickering over its leadership.) Colby was cooperating with the congressional inquiries and handing over the Agency's darkest secrets. Shackley, who two years ago had blocked the inquiries of the Church subcommittee, was one of many Agency people who watched with disbelief as Colby graciously passed secrets—some related to Shackley's own activities—to the prying headline-hogs of Congress. "But once the decisions were made," Shackley claimed, "the organization supported him."

That is the myth—the dedicated professionals saluting and doing the Director's bidding, even when it pained them. Sam Halpern, a former senior DDO officer called out of retirement to deal with the investigators, found that some offices in Langley, conveniently, could not locate relevant materials. It was obvious to him that documents were being lost as they were being requested.*

In July of 1975, Shackley had to withstand another Agency scandal—one that rattled his own division. An agent he had inherited was exposed as a suspected drug smuggler. As with many episodes, Shackley's name

---

* When Congress demanded information on an Asian topic, Richard Fuller, a DDO officer who gathered information for Congress, contacted Shackley's deputy, who then assembled the relevant papers. But Fuller had no way of guaranteeing that Shackley's division was providing all available information. On one occasion, when Fuller asked another division for material on an assassination program, the division claimed the operation ended at a certain date and supplied no information beyond that. But one of Fuller's colleagues happened to know the program had continued, so Fuller was able to go back and demand the rest of the file.

never became publicly attached to this affair. But this was his turf, his problem. The result was another CIA cover-up in which Shackley was implicated.

That month the CIA admitted in a letter to Senator Charles Percy that Puttaporn Khramkhruan, a thirty-year-old Burmese employed by Shackley's division in Thailand to obtain intelligence on the narcotics trade, was an alleged member of a multimillion-dollar opium ring. It had been his contact with the CIA—he had been paid $144.58 a month —that saved Khramkhruan from a lengthy stay in prison.

Khramkhruan was a reporting source for the East Asia Division, when Shackley became division chief in 1973. (Years previously, Khramkhruan had been a captain in the Kuomintang army of nationless Chinese anti-communists and led opium caravans in the Golden Triangle.) When U.S. Customs officers in early 1973 discovered a parcel of 59 pounds of opium mailed to the United States from Thailand, they found among the packing materials an envelope with Khramkhruan's name and address in Chiang Mai, Thailand. Several months later—near the time Shackley took over the division—a Customs agent visited the CIA base in Chiang Mai and asked about Khramkhruan. The CIA agent was gone. He had flown to the United States to attend a business seminar as part of an AID program. Shackley's division had loaned him the $1,600 for the airfare.

Khramkhruan was arrested in July of 1973. He eventually announced he would wage a stiff defense and claim his smuggling was known to and supervised by his CIA boss. For his defense he would need CIA documents. With a trial approaching, the top brass at Langley—Shackley included—huddled to decide how to react.

In April of 1974, the CIA told the Justice Department that under no circumstances would it cooperate with the prosecution of the case. It would not turn over documents to the prosecution or the defense. This decision achieved what Langley wanted: the case was dismissed. Khramkhruan went free and so did the main player in the drug ring.

The affair had not become a public matter. But a year later Senator Percy wrote the CIA about the case. (He probably had been tipped off by a source close to the U.S. attorney's office.) The response from the Agency conceding that one of its spies in Thailand had been arrested on drug charges yielded headlines and led to yet another set of congressional hearings.

On July 22, 1975, a House Government Operations subcommittee opened five days of hearings. Shackley was not questioned by the investigators or asked to appear. But he could not have been pleased with the spectacle: more liberal legislators decrying the Agency—and his portion of it. The hearings disclosed that at the time of Khramkhruan's arrest, the agent was due to receive additional training from Shackley's division. But no witness disclosed what further use the division had expected to put Khramkhruan to.

For Shackley and the CIA, the Khramkhruan case was one drop in a bucket overflowing. Church was casting secrets everywhere. At a public hearing in September, the committee publicized the discovery of a secret Agency cache of deadly poisons. Another hearing disclosed that the CIA illegally opened the mail of American politicians. At this session, senators excoriated James Angleton (who had been canned by Colby in late 1974), for having told the committee privately that he found it "inconceivable that a secret intelligence arm of the government has to comply with all the overt orders of the government." The slim white-haired cold warrior hunched over the microphone was not a good advertisement for the Agency.

In Langley, morale among the spies plummeted. The refrain, "What am I supposed to tell my children?" echoed within headquarters. CIA people eyed comrades warily, wondering who was giving up what secret to the committees, who was leaking to the media. The more paranoid officers speculated that the puppetmasters of Moscow were behind all this. Throughout the fall, the Church Committee hearings and those of the Pike Committee on the House side continued. Every few days brought another exposé in the media.

For months, the investigators had come. Longtime spooks bristled as young congressional aides pressed them to reveal details of past operations. The inquisitors were probing the most sensitive areas: assassinations, drug tests, Cuba, Laos, the murder of John Kennedy. The snoops had questions for Shackley.

Several times in 1975, committee staff interviewed Shackley on Capitol Hill. He was not a major target, but the investigators realized Shackley was a serious figure in the DDO. Before a meeting with Shackley, Frederick Baron, counsel to the Church Committee, expected to see a grizzly character fresh out of a spy movie. William Harvey, for one, had lived up to expectations. When Baron and others visited Harvey in his Indiana home, they encountered a caricature of the hard-boiled covert operator; the retired Agency officer had guns on his coffee table. Baron had heard much about Shackley, and his staff had learned that some Agency employees called Shackley "the Butcher of Laos." The investigators expected to meet a younger Bill Harvey. But when Shackley arrived for his first meeting with Baron—the subject at hand was Operation Mongoose —Baron was surprised by the CIA man's boyish, clean-cut, all-American looks. This is not a spy, thought Baron. This man is an accountant who played high-school football.

Shackley, Baron found, was a tough witness. The East Asia Division chief hated appearing before the committees. He was determined not to disclose one piece of information more than he had to. "He felt he was a particular victim," said his Agency friend Jamie Jameson. "He was concerned about his own personal survival." With Baron, Shackley let nothing slip. Any material he revealed was premeditated. "He was," Baron recalled, "a very impressive operator." After the interview ended, Baron concluded that he did not know much more about JMWAVE operations than he did at the start of the session.

One time Shackley briefed Church aides on the activities of his East Asia Division. Shackley tried to impress by recounting the number of assets and reports his division had produced. "My business is producing spies," he announced. "If I wanted to produce widgets, I'd be in private enterprise."

As inquiries proceeded, John Murray, the Western Hemisphere Division officer who had confronted Shackley, and his wife, Dolores, a former Agency operations officer, looked on and hoped the past was about to crash on top of Shackley. To push this process along, Dolores was sending letters full of disclosures—many relating to Chile—to a leading newspaper reporter. The notes overflowed with vitriol aimed at Shackley, whom she feared Colby would appoint head of the clandestine service. In one 1975 letter, she revealed that Shackley and others were scared that the current investigations might unravel their cover-up of the 1973 ITT controversy and that the congressional committees would learn of Tony Sforza's and Bruce MacMaster's close contacts with the military cabal that killed General Schneider in Chile in 1970. Especially frightening to Langley was the prospect that Sforza might be called before the Church Committee.

"Shackley is frantically trying to bring Sforza back from overseas so they can give him . . . retirement for the 'good of the service,'" Dolores Murray wrote. ". . . They are really worried about Sforza but Shackley thinks he is too personally loyal to Shackley to do anything like testify. Everyone who testified before Congress [in 1973] about CIA involvement in Chile is guilty of perjury and they are really uptight."*

John Murray also plotted against Shackley. He covertly contacted William Miller, the staff director of the Church Committee. The two met. Murray unloaded a host of secrets. Shackley and Helms, he told Miller, had arranged in 1970 to keep the CIA from being implicated in the official inquiry into the 1968 My Lai massacre in Vietnam. (Some evidence suggested the slaying of several hundred Vietnamese civilians by a U.S. Army unit was related to Agency activity with the Phoenix program.) And, he added, Shackley had rigged the testimony of witnesses before the Church subcommittee. Both Murrays believed that if they got

---

* The committees never learned Sforza's secrets.

out the truth of how Shackley had handled the ITT inquiry, his spectacular rise through Agency ranks would halt. They were to be disappointed.

IV

As democracy intruded upon the CIA at home, an intelligence disaster
loomed for Shackley in Australia.

On November 2, 1975, Australian Prime Minister Edward Gough Whitlam, a tall, silver-haired figure, took the stage at a political rally. The
liberal Whitlam accused opposition leader Doug Anthony and his right-
wing National Country Party of having received CIA money. The next
day, the Australian papers burst with controversy. Some press reports
noted that Whitlam's charge came from information his government
recently discovered showing that the conservatives had accepted Agency
funds in the late 1960s. Anthony denied the allegation, but a story in the
Financial Review reported that Anthony years earlier had befriended
and rented a house to Richard Lee Stallings, a CIA officer in Australia. In
Langley, Shackley read the cables from Australia with great unease.

For years, Shackley and his colleagues had fretted about Whitlam. In
December of 1972, Whitlam's Australian Labor Party, campaigning on a
platform that decried foreign interests, won power for the first time in
twenty-three years. At the time, Colby considered Whitlam's rise a crisis
for the Agency. Whitlam's party was not sympathetic to Australian intelligence, one of the Agency's best partners. (The intelligence services of
the United States, England, and Australia cooperated closely under an
arrangement called the UKUSA Treaty.) A 1971 ALP national conference
nearly voted to abolish the Australian Security Intelligence Organization
(ASIO), a counterespionage service. When Whitlam assumed office and
learned that two Australian intelligence officers were assisting the
Agency's anti-Allende operation in Chile, he ordered their removal.*
Such actions and Whitlam's criticism of U.S. policy in Vietnam irritated
Washington and Langley.

What concerned U.S. intelligence most was the future of the American
electronic spy base at Pine Gap, near Alice Springs. In the desolate
center of the continent, American personnel collected data from satellites orbiting over the Soviet Union, China, and Europe. From Pine Gap,
the Americans monitored Soviet missile launches and intercepted radio,
radar, and microwave communications. The base, one of the most important U.S. foreign outposts, conveyed communications from the Pentagon to nuclear submarines. The CIA, the Navy, and the National Security

---

* The Agency, according to Colby, occasionally called on its Aussie friends for
help, especially in Chile, Cuba, and elsewhere in the Caribbean. "Sometimes they
could be where we couldn't have a person," he said.

Agency had outposts there. "We had a lot riding on this thing," Colby
noted. Early in his administration, Whitlam informed U.S. ambassador
Walter Rice that he would allow the base to continue its operations.
But, he added, "if there was any attempt . . . to 'screw us or bounce us,'
inevitably these arrangements would become a matter of contention."

Langley was not reassured. In March of 1973, Whitlam's attorney general raided the offices of ASIO in search of intelligence he believed the
counterespionage service was withholding from the government. The
raid, recalled Jim Angleton, "threw confusion into the ranks of all Western counterintelligence services." Within his own party, Whitlam defended the presence of U.S. bases in Australia. The Australian
intelligence service continued to collect intelligence and cooperate with
officers of Shackley's division on such topics as political intrigue in
Saigon, the Thai military leadership, Chinese government directives,
and the Khmer Rouge insurgents in Cambodia. But Shackley and his
colleagues remained wary. They were waiting for trouble.

It arrived with Whitlam's 1975 accusation that the CIA had supported
his political opponents. The charge came in a season of political turmoil.
The two major parties were deadlocked on budgetary legislation. Whitlam's opposition was exploiting the "loans affair"—an attempt by the
Whitlam government to borrow $4 billion in Arab cash that prompted
true and untrue press stories implicating cabinet members in wrongdoing.* The *Financial Review* reported that its own investigation of the
CIA in Australia uncovered no evidence of Agency funding of the National Country Party. But it maintained that CIA money "flowed into
Australia aimed at influencing Australia's domestic political situation
with a view toward protecting America's interest." Most of this money,
the paper noted, went to projects designed to secure the continued
existence of U.S. bases in Australia and to preserve an amenable environment for U.S. business.

During a November 6, 1975, television interview, Whitlam claimed
CIA money had influenced Australian domestic politics. The next day,
Whitlam sacked Bill Robertson, the head of the Australian intelligence
service. Whitlam's actions and accusations sent shudders through Langley. An ally was charging a friendly intelligence service with mucking
about in his country. Press accounts in Australia were identifying Agency
officers—Shackley's own men. In his office in suburban Virginia, Shackley concluded that Whitlam's antics were threatening the future of Pine
Gap and other bases. Shackley did not want to see the CIA lose Australia
on his watch. Whitlam had to be stopped.

---

* The Australian press reported that leaked documents discrediting the Whitlam
administration were forged and planted by the CIA.

On November 8, Shackley sent a biting message to ASIO's man in Washington. It was practically a declaration of war:

On 6 November the Prime Minister publicly repeated the allegation that he knew of two instances in which CIA money had been used to influence domestic Australian politics.

Simultaneously press coverage in Australia was such that a number of CIA members serving in Australia have been identified—Walker under State Department cover and Fitzwater and Bonin under Defense cover. . . .

On 7 November, fifteen newspaper or wire service reps called the Pentagon seeking information on the allegations made in Australia. CIA is perplexed at this point as to what all this means.

Does this signify some change in our bilateral intelligence security related fields?

CIA cannot see how this dialogue with continued reference to CIA can do other than blow the lid off those installations where the persons concerned have been working and which are vital to both our services and countries, particularly the [Pine Gap] installation at Alice Springs. . . .

CIA feels it is necessary to speak also directly to ASIO because of the complexity of the problem. . . .

CIA can understand a statement made in political debate. But constant further unraveling worries them. Is there a change in the Prime Minister's attitude in Australian policy in this field?

This message should be regarded as an official demarche on a service to service link. It is a frank explanation of a problem seeking counsel on that problem. CIA feels that everything possible has been done on a diplomatic basis and now on an intelligence liaison link. They feel that if this problem cannot be solved they do not see how our mutually beneficial relationships are going to continue.

The CIA feels grave concern as to where this type of public discussion may lead. The [Director General of ASIO] should be assured that CIA does not lightly adopt this attitude.

In none too subtle language, Shackley was asking, what is going on? He was also threatening to toss the Aussie spooks out of the club—the UKUSA pact—if they did not pull their act together. In between the lines was the strong suggestion that someone should rein in the liberal Prime Minister who had the audacity to question Agency intervention in his own land.

The Agency had taken the unusual step of publicly denying the charge it meddled in Australian politics. But a young man working below ground in a vault in California knew that the disavowal was a farce. A year before Whitlam had raised hell, Christopher Boyce, a twenty-one-year-old college dropout, began working at the aerospace firm TRW in Redondo Beach, California. His true employer was the CIA, his job monitoring equipment in a code room linking CIA headquarters and the Pine Gap base.

Over the course of 1975, Boyce read cables that indicated the Agency was trying to manipulate politics in Australia. He saw cable traffic covering CIA attempts to infiltrate Australian railroad and airline unions, hoping to prevent strikes that might disrupt the movement of equipment and personnel to Pine Gap. The United States preached democracy over communism, but, he concluded, it was as underhanded as the enemy. His newfound contempt, Boyce later claimed, helped push him to the brink. In the spring of 1975, with his childhood pal Andrew Daulton Lee, a small-time drug dealer, Boyce began selling satellite secrets to the Russians. Boyce's reaction to CIA operations in Australia apparently contributed to one of the biggest espionage coups ever achieved by Moscow.*

In the second week of November of 1975, Whitlam did not lay off the Agency. He proposed to confirm in Parliament that Richard Lee Stallings, the American associate of opposition leader Doug Anthony, was a CIA officer. More alarming to Shackley, the Prime Minister now threatened not to extend the Pine Gap lease, due to expire on December 9.

But Shackley and the CIA had a friend in Australia's Governor-General, John Kerr. The Queen's representative, Kerr, appointed by Whitlam to the largely ceremonial post, looked upon the parliamentary impasse that prevented the passage of a budget with much disapproval. He also was troubled by Whitlam's stance on security and intelligence. (During World War II, Kerr, an intelligence officer, was assigned to the OSS. In the 1960s he ran a foundation secretly funded by the CIA.) On November 11, Kerr delivered, intentionally or not, a gift to the CIA. He sacked Whitlam. The move—dubbed a "constitutional coup"—stunned most political observers in Australia. Kerr justified the step by citing Whitlam's inability to win approval of the budget bill, and he placed opposition member Malcolm Fraser in charge of a caretaker government.

Australian and British press accounts maintained that throughout 1974 and 1975 officers of the CIA and the British MI-6 had discussed how to resolve the Whitlam problem. According to some reports, the CIA's concern expressed in Shackley's cable was passed directly to Kerr. Ray Cline, a former top Agency officer, told one Australian journalist that officers of Shackley's division had supplied opposition politicians with

---

* Boyce and Lee would not be caught until January of 1977. Their exploits were then chronicled in the book and movie *The Falcon and the Snowman*.

negative information on Whitlam and had induced Australian civil servants to pressure Kerr. He later asserted to an American reporter that there was no CIA campaign to damage Whitlam "within his own country." Years following the affair, Admiral Bobby Inman, a former director of the National Security Agency and deputy director of the CIA, acknowledged that "dirty tricks" had been played against Whitlam.

After the Christopher Boyce trial in 1977 splashed allegations of CIA activity in Australia across front pages in the United States and Australia, President Jimmy Carter sent Deputy Secretary of State Warren Christopher to see Whitlam. Christopher made clear, according to Whitlam's memoirs, that Washington would "never again interfere in the domestic political processes of Australia." Christopher (and Inman and Cline) was seemingly—and obliquely—referring to the handiwork of Shackley and his associates in 1975.

Because of Kerr's extraordinary action, the intelligence establishments of Canberra, Washington, and London were rid of a pest. In a bad year, Shackley had something to celebrate and, possibly, for which to claim credit.

On February 6, 1976, Shackley, recently back from a two-week trip to Asia, received a cable with upsetting news from Thomas Polgar, now chief of station in Mexico. Frank Snepp had submitted his resignation and told Polgar he intended to write a book on Vietnam. Snepp, Polgar observed, had become "increasingly irrational . . . and may be under pressure to make money quickly. For this and other reasons which [are] probably best analyzed in psychiatric terms, [I] believe that we may have a real problem on our hand, even though Snepp repeatedly has stated that he is not going to be another Agee."

Another Agee—Shackley did not want to go through that again. Worse, Snepp, unlike Agee, had stories to tell about Shackley. Once more Shackley had to contemplate a damage control operation. He asked the Agency's security office to "discreetly monitor" Snepp's activities.

There was reason for Shackley to fear. Ten days earlier, Graham Martin, the last U.S. ambassador to South Vietnam, had testified before a House subcommittee. It was his first public statement since the collapse of Saigon, and late in the day, Representative Lee Hamilton, the subcommittee chairman, asked Martin about a media report that the CIA had received information from a source—meaning the agent HACKLE—that indicated that Hanoi by the end of March 1975 had decided to push for a total military victory instead of a political settlement.

"It is true that information did come which indicated that . . . the

North Vietnamese were now determined to press a strict military solution," Martin answered. "Now, I hesitate to say this, but it is true that [at] that time that report was not given much credibility by the CIA station chief. It was not sent back by the CIA station chief in the normal reporting channels. It was not until he was pressed by the officer who was in direct contact with this particular penetration to do so, that this man was allowed to send it back through operational channels."

Martin was referring to Snepp, and he was presenting an unflattering view of Polgar and the CIA—and Shackley by extension. An immediate question for Shackley was, how to respond to Martin's testimony? Shackley and others also wondered what it meant that Snepp was in the audience during Martin's testimony.

Shackley's division quickly reviewed the reporting that had come out of Vietnam in April of 1975. Shackley's officers found that two HACKLE reports from the Bien Hoa base had indicated clearly that the North Vietnamese were committed to a military triumph. Both had received high evaluations in headquarters. Two additional reports based on Snepp's interview with HACKLE were indeed forwarded to headquarters in the less-important operations channel. Shackley's officers, though, disagreed with Martin's charge (and Snepp's belief) that the handling of the reports showed the CIA did not take the information seriously. Once again, the bureaucrats found nothing to criticize.

Shackley decided not to respond to Martin's testimony. It had received only slight attention in the media, and his comments regarding CIA reporting were absent from the major news accounts. An attempt to challenge Martin, according to a cable Shackley approved, would "magnify [the] importance [of] Martin's comments and add fuel to what is otherwise [a] one-day happening." Polgar, who was stewing over Martin's remarks, wanted to contact Hamilton and testify. Shackley ordered Polgar to do nothing. Polgar's pride would have to be sacrificed for the good of the institution.

There was still the question of Snepp. Shackley was hearing from Agency people that Snepp was trying to interview former colleagues for his book. Shackley put out the word to officers who served in Vietnam: Snepp was persona non grata. Both the Agency's security office and Shackley's division tracked Snepp's actions. They quickly saw that he was not going to fade away.

As Shackley pondered Snepp's intentions, the results of the congressional investigations became public. The Pike Committee report was completed in mid-January of 1976, but the committee voted to suppress it. A copy leaked to the press. The first line was alarming: "If this Committee's recent experience is any test, intelligence agencies that are to be controlled by Congressional lawmaking are, today, beyond the lawmaker's scrutiny." The committee reported it had confronted delays in receiving information from the intelligence community. Relevant material was deleted from documents. Witnesses were silenced. Briefings on important matters had been "selective." "Perhaps the most difficult problem in developing information about intelligence activities," it observed wisely, "is knowing the right question to ask."

The committee then presented a host of findings, large and small. The budget for foreign intelligence was three or four times more costly than Congress had been told. A CIA station in a small country had devoted $41,000 one year to liquor. The Agency had used taxpayer dollars to arrange female companionship for heads of state. Ten billion dollars was being spent by a handful of people, the report noted, with little independent supervision and inadequate controls. The report outlined a number of embarrassing intelligence failures, including the CIA's misses in calling the Tet offensive, the Soviet invasion of Czechoslovakia in 1968, Egypt and Syria's attack on Israel in 1973, the left-led coup in Portugal in 1974, India's 1974 explosion of a nuclear device, and the Greek overthrow of Cyprus' democratic government in 1974. "The American taxpayer," the committee judged, "clearly does not receive full value for his intelligence dollar."

Regarding covert actions, the Pike Committee report found they had been "irregularly approved, sloppily implemented and at times have been forced on a reluctant CIA by the President and his National Security Adviser." It threw one important bone in the direction of Langley: "All evidence in hand suggests that the CIA, far from being out of control, has been utterly responsive to the instructions of the President and the Assistant to the President for National Security Affairs." Shackley and other CIA lifers could consider this conclusion an answer to Frank Church's famous pronouncement that their Agency was a "rogue elephant." No, their misdeeds and mistakes often occurred as the result of an executive request.

In April of 1976, the Church Committee released its final report—the product of an investigation that occurred partly in response to the cover-up on Chile directed by Shackley. The introduction quoted Justice Louis Brandeis, in a dig at all the Ted Shackleys of the covert world: "The greatest dangers to liberty lurk in insidious encroachment by men of zeal, well-meaning but without understanding." The report was harsh: "It is clear that the growth of intelligence abuses reflects a more general failure of our basic institutions." The committee noted that Congress had failed to assert its oversight responsibility. It presented a history of intelligence gone amuck, propelled by a blinding anticommunism. It accused the intelligence community of too often focusing on secondary issues and targets. It exposed details of and criticized several operations for which Shackley shared responsibility: the anti-Castro program, the secret war in Laos, the Allende operation. It probed allegations of the CIA's association with drug-traffickers in Laos.

Many of the secrets had already made news. But the report again referred to CIA assassination plots. It disclosed that the Agency was using journalists accredited with American news organizations as agents, and was secretly funding scholars (who sometimes were unaware they received CIA money). According to the committee report, Agency officers in the 1950s and 1960s picked up Americans in bars and slipped LSD into their food and drink as part of mind-control experiments. The report expressed a skepticism toward all covert actions, charging that administrations relied on them for quick fixes and that many were self-defeating. It revealed that committee members had considered proposing a total ban on all covert actions but flinched, deciding that the United States needed to preserve its options. The committee backed the call for vigilant congressional oversight committees.

The report identified few officers. Anyone who read the multivolume set did not stumble across Shackley's name. It did not appear in the scores of newspaper accounts based on material released or leaked by the committee. The report did not reveal how Shackley and the Agency had manipulated testimony to the Church subcommittee in 1973. It did not threaten Shackley's standing in Langley.

In a statement attached to the report, Church declared that in this "dangerous world" the United States needed a strong and effective intelligence organization. Information was necessary for the development of sound foreign and defense policies. But, he added, covert actions had gone too far—a result of a troubling development: the growth of a fright-driven Cold War mentality that depicted the world in blacks and whites and placed ends over means. "It was only after our faith gave way to fear," Church explained, "that we began to act as a self-appointed sentinel of the status quo. Then it was that all the dark arts of secret intervention—bribery, blackmail, abduction, assassination—were put to the service of reactionary and repressive regimes that can never, for long, escape or withstand the volcanic forces of change. And the United States, as a result, became even more identified with the claims of the old order, instead of the aspirations of the new."

If Shackley ever bothered to read this statement, he would have been insulted, probably enraged. According to Church, Shackley and thousands of others had been working the wrong side of history for years. These patriots had not only been counterproductive; they had brought shame on their nation.

Amidst all the fuss, another intelligence flap went overlooked in the United States. But within Langley, officers heard that one of Shackley's favorites had botched a recruitment and landed on the front page of the newspaper of Guam.

During the JMWAVE days, Robert Wiecha handled propaganda and publishing operations for Shackley's Miami station. Some Agency colleagues did not respect Wiecha's clandestine skills. Nevertheless, Shackley had sent him to Guam, a U.S. territory in the Pacific, to find spies. In the fall of 1975, Wiecha, undercover as a navy officer, visited Ruth Gilliam, a resident of nearby Palau and a part-time correspondent for *The Daily News* of Guam. He asked her to report on events in Palau, an American trust territory. She said yes, and he later dropped by with her employment forms. He also gave her two bottles of vodka, told her she would be paid $500 each month, and invited her to attend a training session in Japan. He noted that he most wanted information on a specific Palauan legislator and two newspaper owners, all nationalists critical of the pro-Washington government of the trust territory. Soon, he added, you will hear from one of my subordinates.

Shortly after the recruitment, people started telling Gilliam they knew she was working for the CIA. Somehow Wiecha had mishandled the enlistment. Her recruitment fast becoming a public fact, Gilliam decided not to be a spy. Not surprisingly, she took her story to her newspaper. Months later, *The Sunday News* of Guam disclosed Wiecha's effort to spy on Palauans. Wiecha's operation—undoubtedly authorized by Shackley—apparently violated the rules that prevent the Agency from spying on Americans. The residents of Palau, a trusteeship of the United States, supposedly enjoy the same rights as Americans.

The newspaper article also revealed that Wiecha had offered a payoff to the high chief of Palau, who refused the money, and that Wiecha was attempting to penetrate a Japanese intelligence ring based in a Guam hotel. When a reporter for the paper had called Wiecha and inquired about the recruitment of Gilliam, Wiecha slammed the receiver down. Shackley's man had screwed up in a big way. Thankfully for the Agency, the U.S. media, feeding on information from the congressional hearings, never caught on to the story. The Agency looked foolish only in Guam, in the trust territory, in Japanese intelligence cables, and in Langley where CIA people traded gossip about a silly operation gone bad.

Shackley was a manager who demanded fast results, but he recognized the necessity of long-term planning. One personnel decision Shackley rendered brought the CIA one of its truer accomplishments of the 1970s.

Shackley approved extensive training for one of his officers in Chinese, spycraft, and nuclear engineering, in preparation for the assignment Shackley had authorized: a stint in Taiwan collecting intelligence on nuclear proliferation. The man Shackley already had spying on the nuclear ambitions of the Taiwanese was not one of the Agency's best. Averse to embassy life, this officer hated the diplomatic social circuit, where potential agents were to be found.

The Taipei station had picked up hints that Taiwan was diverting to a bomb-building program nuclear materials and technology it received from the West for a civilian energy program. But Shackley's antisocial case officer failed to find any conclusive intelligence. He was reassigned and replaced by the other officer. Shackley would soon be gone from the division—but the work of this case officer would be a positive legacy.

Once in Taipei, the new man established his cover as the U.S. embassy officer on technology and prowled for intelligence on Taiwan's secret bomb program. He soon found a credible source who disclosed that a heavy-water reactor, acquired from Canada and used for civilian re-search, was producing plutonium for a weapons program. Twice a team of American civilian nuclear experts visited the research facility and gave the Taiwanese a clean bill of health. But the CIA officer's agent revealed that the Taiwanese were removing the uranium inner cores of the reac-tor, which contained plutonium, and separating the plutonium in a dan-gerous procedure.* For several years, the CIA man would file reliable reports detailing the ongoing Taiwanese efforts to obtain the bomb.

By the spring of 1976, Bill Nelson, the deputy director for operations, had had enough. A scholar-turned-spook—he had studied at Harvard with the famous sinologist John Fairbank—Nelson had entered the CIA in 1949. He had devoted his life to the Agency, with a career exclusively in East Asian matters until his promotion to DDO in 1973. Now seemed an appropriate time for him to bow out. The previous year had been physically and emotionally exhausting. The work of his lifetime was subjected to criticism and, often, ridicule by members of Congress, journalists, and Agency critics. Nelson had been a gentleman-spy, the old breed. He was well regarded within the bureaucracy. He was no ideologue. He had believed in the mission and regretted the excesses. But the world was a nasty place, and even spy services make mistakes. He was confident that his had been an honorable stint in an honorable

* The intelligence reports on Taiwan's nuclear weapons activity were leaked to *The Washington Post,* which noted that Washington did not confront Taiwan for fear of revealing the source of the intelligence. But the Taipei station managed to steal government files and plans and covertly block Taiwan's purchase of sensitive parts.

profession. But try explaining that to friends, family, neighbors, and the American public. The same day the Church Committee released its final report, Nelson announced at a staff meeting that he had submitted his resignation to the new CIA chief, George Bush. His quitting set in motion a chain of promotions that would lift Shackley a step closer to the Director's office.

The previous November, Colby had been called to the Oval Office early on a Sunday morning—he had to put off going to Mass. President Ford fired Colby and explained that his dismissal was part of a wider reorganization. Colby reasonably viewed it as punishment for his release of too many secrets to the antagonists of Capitol Hill.

Colby had been one in a series of senior officers who had guided Shackley's career: Bill Harvey, Des FitzGerald, Dick Helms, Bill Colby, and Bill Nelson. Now all were gone, but Shackley was still ascending. George Bush, Colby's replacement and a newcomer to intelligence, promoted William Wells, Nelson's assistant, to be the deputy director for operations, the chief of the clandestine service. To fill the slot of associate deputy director for operations, Bush tapped Ted Shackley. At the age of forty-eight, Shackley, the master intellcrat, was second-in-command of all CIA covert activity. His rise through the ranks, a product of untiring dedication, undeniable intelligence, and relentless self-promotion, seemed inexorable. It was a time of trouble for Shackley's Agency. But he had ridden out the rough waters. He even had prospered. The CIA would survive, and the day could well arrive—perhaps soon—when Ted Shackley controlled a revived Central Intelligence Agency of the United States of America.

CHAPTER NINE

THE END OF THE CLIMB

I

ON the morning of April 12, 1977, Admiral Stansfield Turner sat at the breakfast table and stared at the banner headline on the front of *The Washington Post*. Turner, who had taken over as Director of Central Intelligence only five weeks earlier, barely could believe what he read. A story by Bob Woodward reported that a past CIA officer, Edwin Wilson, had procured the timing devices for the car-bomb murder of Orlando Letelier, a former Chilean ambassador to the United States. In September of 1976, the expatriate Letelier and an assistant had been killed while driving along Massachusetts Avenue in Washington. The ex-CIA man, according to Woodward, also had plotted with Agency-trained Cuban exiles—graduates of the Miami station—to assassinate an opponent of Libyan President Moammar Qaddafi. The DCI's exasperation heightened when he reached the following sentence: "There is some evidence that Wilson may have had contact with one or more current CIA employees."

What had he walked into? Turner, a straitlaced Navy man with little experience in the intelligence business, had been chosen by President Jimmy Carter to manage a CIA held in suspicion by portions of the American public and the new Democratic administration. Years of media and congressional investigation had left the Agency with a lingering PR problem. Turner, a prim outsider, wondered if the shady reputation was deserved. "Do we have disloyal or dishonest people inside the CIA?" he asked himself when he put down the paper.

Getting to the bottom of the Wilson business became priority number one. As soon as Turner entered his office on the seventh floor of CIA headquarters, he ordered his top aides to find out what this Wilson business was all about.* The information Turner received left him aghast. Two midlevel CIA men had worked with Wilson on deals that might be illegal. Worse, two senior officers had been associating with Wilson. The admiral sat at his desk stunned. How could anyone in the Agency hobnob with an assassin-for-hire? The senior officers were either crooked or dumb. They were the type who had brought disgrace onto the CIA, the ones who supplied ammunition to Agency critics. Had they learned nothing from the spasm of wrenching scrutiny the Company recently experienced? As long as Turner was at the helm, neither of the pair stood a fool's chance of promotion. One was Tom Clines, a senior officer in the training division; the other, Ted Shackley, the associate deputy director for operations.

When Shackley became ADDO a year earlier in May of 1976—continuing his arc toward the Director's office—George Bush had been running the CIA for four months. Part cheerleader and part caretaker, Bush was no details man and assumed as his chief priority the soothing of the bruised egos of America's spies. Much of Bush's time was consumed by treks to Capitol Hill where he defended his new family. Bush won significant increases in the budget for spy satellites and signal intercepts. He tried to turn off the spigot of disclosures. When the Defense Intelligence Agency discovered that Manuel Noriega had purchased intelligence information from three U.S. Army noncoms in Panama, Bush elected not to prosecute the Americans. Doing so would expose sources and the embarrassing fact that a CIA asset was spying on his patrons. CIA people generally were glad to see Bush in charge. As Tom Clines put it, "Bush didn't say no to anything."

Shackley's immediate boss, Deputy Director for Operations William Wells was a longtime Asian hand. He had headed the European division before becoming number two to DDO William Nelson. A low-key and

---

*Woodward actually had picked up on crossed wires. At the time, the FBI was investigating Wilson for possible involvement in an assassination overseas and other matters. Some FBI agents had speculated that Wilson might be involved in the Letelier job, but Justice Department lawyers handling the Letelier case did not see any Wilson connection. Of all Wilson's sins, killing Letelier was not one of them.

competent manager, Wells was popular in the clandestine service. An OSS veteran more attuned to espionage than covert action, "Wild Willie," as Agency people called him, generated a flood of ideas on how to gather intelligence. "He always had three or four suggestions on how to do any given thing," a former DDO said of Wells. "One out of four would be good; the rest would be terrible."

Shackley was ambitious. He yearned to lead the clandestine service, while Wells seemed a reluctant Deputy Director. Wells enjoyed the work, did a fine job, but was not driven—a good station chief who, by luck of the draw, ended up directing the outfit. The unflappable and intense Shackley made a good sidekick to Wells.

The ADDO is akin to the Vice President. His office is next to the DDO's office, down the hall from the Director's. He does not have direct line authority; the division chiefs answer to the DDO, not him. But he manages key responsibilities for the DDO, and in the DDO's absence, he assumes the position. While Wells juggled big-picture management issues—crunching numbers for the Agency budget, guiding the Director through sessions with Congress, meeting with leading officers of foreign services—Shackley often handled the day-to-day running of the directorate and its espionage, counterintelligence, and covert action programs. As second to the clandestine service's top spymaster, he had his hand in everything, the directorate's accomplishments and its failures.

Shackley was viewed by some officers—especially the small band of diehard Shackley loyalists—as a more experienced operator than Wells. "You couldn't see Wells ever saying okay to some Russian or Chinese operation somewhere without Ted Shackley saying it was a great idea first," Clines noted. "Wells generally left things up to Shackley, including any sophisticated type of operations approval. Shackley really ran the operations directorate when he was ADDO." Whenever Clines had an operation, he brought it to Shackley, not Wells.

Shackley's style had not changed. He remained demanding, ever vigilant in compartmentation. He once called in a division chief, an old, trusted friend from Miami days, and held out a note from the White House. Paragraph number three concerns you, Shackley told his colleague. But before he allowed the division chief to read it, he covered the other paragraphs with pieces of paper. He refused to talk with Agency people about what they did not need to know. There were officers who took aside a colleague and said, did you hear about this operation we pulled off in such-and-such a country? Shackley did not share such shop chat.

Hundreds of pages crossed his desk each day—a flood of cables, dispatches, and memos on operations, administrative concerns, and personnel matters. Traditionally, the associate deputy director for operations screens traffic for the DDO. But an ADDO possesses some discretion as to how much of the paper stream to sort through himself. An ADDO can fob off reams on subordinates. But Shackley was renowned as one of the most prolific cable-readers in top management. He read as much as he could. The more he read, the more he knew, the more influence he possesssed.

One matter, a personnel dispute, threatened Shackley's all-important relationship with Director Bush: the John Murray case. Murray still was convinced that Shackley covertly had been ruining his career because Murray knew too much about Agency operations in Chile and the subsequent cover-up directed by Shackley. Harold Fiedler, a personnel officer, examined Murray's file and found that somehow it had been mishandled and that Murray had not been promoted as he deserved. But Fiedler did not know what to make of Murray's claim that Shackley was the cause of the trouble. Better not to pursue that piece of the mystery, he decided. But he was championing Murray within Langley's byzantine promotion bureaucracy. Murray, though, searched for more clout than Fiedler could supply, and he went outside Company circles to find it.

Murray and his wife, Dolores, contacted Senator Thomas McIntyre, a New Hampshire Democrat on the Armed Services Committee. In a letter to the senator, Dolores Murray claimed Shackley bore a vendetta against her husband, recently diagnosed as having terminal cancer. She portrayed the ADDO in dark terms:

> Mr. Shackley's wide knowledge of past activities of many CIA senior officers puts him in a position of "great influence." Indeed, on the day after President Ford announced the firing of William Colby as Chief, CIA, Mr. Colby promoted Mr. Shackley to an executive schedule position—a promotion never before made for a Chief of an area division in the Directorate of Operations. It also made Mr. Shackley of equal grade to his supervisor, the Director of the Operations Directorate. Obviously, nobody in the Operations Directorate dares to "take Mr. Shackley on."

She accused Shackley of fiddling with Murray's personnel file and ordering his subordinates and cronies to deny Murray promotions. Shackley, she claimed, "is, in effect, running the Directorate of Operations no matter whose name is officially on the door. . . . We are determined that Mr. Shackley and his friends be curbed."

McIntyre was concerned enough by Murray's tale to ask Bush about it. After a month of review, Bush wrote McIntyre to inform him that Murray would immediately be assigned a good position. But Bush defended Shackley as a brilliant and honest officer who in no way had impeded Murray's promotion. It all had been a minor management foul-up, Bush explained.

At a May 18, 1976, meeting in his Senate office, McIntyre shared with Murray his skepticism about Bush's comments regarding Shackley. The senator speculated that Shackley did know too much to be disciplined or dismissed. His interaction with Bush, McIntyre told Murray, had per-suaded him that the new Senate intelligence committee should closely monitor Shackley and the crew across the river. How old is Shackley? he inquired. Forty-nine, Murray replied. The senator assured Murray he would keep an eye on Shackley. He promised to ask other senators, including Daniel Inouye, the chair of the intelligence committee, that they do the same.

Murray shook the Senator's hand and left. In the evening darkness, Murray, weak from his cancer, struggled with the walk down Capitol Hill to where his car was parked. He thought about the meeting. After years of fighting, he had rehabilitated his file, but Shackley had gotten off. At least he had warned the right people.*

Bush did not heed the warning. Had he, the Agency might have been spared another embarrassment, for as Bush was defending Shackley to Senator McIntyre, his new ADDO was associating with Edwin Wilson.

Wilson embodied everything Agency critics believed was wrong with the CIA. Born poor in Nampa, Idaho, in 1928, he joined the Marines in the early 1950s and shipped off to Korea. In 1955, he returned to the States and joined the Agency. Wilson, a big, garrulous man, was first assigned to the Office of Security and guarded the planes and pilots of the U-2 program. He conducted security investigations and assisted eavesdropping operations against Americans. But he was ambitious. Guarding people, running background checks—that's not what real spies do. In 1960 he talked his way into the International Organizations Division, which penetrated student and labor groups, created political fronts, and supported pro-Western media. He became a deep-cover con-tract agent and joined the staff of the Seafarers' International Union of North America, which sent Wilson to Belgium. The Seafarers' officers were not informed that Wilson's true master was the CIA.

Wilson spied on labor unions. He monitored cargo shipments leaving

---

*Murray soon was promoted to chief of the directorate's career management group, where he served for several months and received laudatory performance evaluations. He then was assigned to the NSC but could not take the job due to his cancer.

Antwerp for Cuba. He paid off Corsican mobsters to lean on communist dockworkers. He returned to the United States, and the Seafarers appointed him a lobbyist in Washington. Then he moved to the International Department of the AFL-CIO in 1963.

The next year, Wilson jumped to the Special Operations Division, which was in charge of covert actions. First, he served as an advance man for Hubert Humphrey's vice-presidential campaign, allowing the Agency to keep tabs on Johnson's running mate. After the election, Wilson opened a front business: Maritime Consulting Associates, an ocean freight forwarder that handled sea logistics for CIA programs. The Agency man in charge of Maritime was Tom Clines, deputy chief of the division's maritime branch.

Wilson ran Maritime Consulting as if it were a regular company. He recruited a figurehead president and worked hard: weapons to Angola, communications equipment to Morocco, materiel to Laos. He also found non-Agency business to conduct—activity that put cash in his pockets. For Langley's fronts, profits meant better cover. Wilson had a golden gig. There was little auditing of his books. No one noticed when he padded his costs. He could be both a secret agent and a wealthy man.

Wilson and Clines were an appropriate match. Both hailed from modest origins. Neither had entered the Agency through the blue-blooded Ivy League route. They did time as grunts; Wilson, a guard, Clines, who was two years younger, a courier. Both were large men, schmoozers and schemers, each a bit reckless, who enjoyed a good time. They each had big ideas about their futures.

Clines relied on Wilson to transport arms and equipment—including surplus from Shackley's JMWAVE station—to the Congo and the Dominican Republic. Clines and Wilson traveled together to Libya, where they tried to recruit a Russian shipping agent by providing him a lucrative contract. Over drinks, the two regularly swapped spy stories. Clines, usually strapped for cash, hit up Wilson for small loans. Wilson, with his expense account, always had money.

It was natural that Clines would introduce Wilson to his friend Shackley. Clines saw both as strong, driven men. Perhaps they all would be running the CIA someday. Years later, Shackley could only remember encountering Wilson once or twice in Washington during this period. To Shackley, Wilson might have seemed another one of the hundreds of officers he routinely ordered about.

In 1966, Clines was recruited by Shackley for the secret war in Laos. Wilson acquired a new case officer and continued on the same path. He collected a set of high-powered Washington contacts, including Robert Gray, one of the town's most influential PR men, and Senators Strom Thurmond, John McClellan, and James Eastland. He developed sources who supplied him with inside information on Pentagon contracts. With CIA encouragement, he transformed Maritime Consulting into Consultants International and engaged in business beyond shipping.

But in 1970, the Agency was ordered by the Office of Management and Budget to rein in its free-wheeling proprietaries. Wilson, whose net worth now topped $200,000, was not eager to rejoin the Agency fold at a government pay scale. Wilson made the Agency an offer: give me a year's pay as severance and let me retain Consultants International as my own firm. Langley agreed. Wilson left the Agency in February of 1971.*

Two months later, Wilson was back in the intelligence game, thanks to Clines. His friend had told Wilson about Task Force 157, a small secret unit of naval intelligence. This outfit ran agents—dockworkers, seamen, shipping agents, and port prostitutes—to monitor traffic on the seas, particularly that of Soviet ships. Task Force 157, which conducted many operations through proprietaries, was a perfect home for Wilson. He signed up with the group, and in June, he purchased an estate, the Mount Airy Farm, in northern Virginia hunt country.

Wilson opened up more fronts. His navy intelligence case officer often had no clue what Wilson was doing. He bought a trawler to cruise the Persian Gulf and scout for nuclear weapons the Russians might be shipping to Iraq. He purchased a freighter and used it to measure magnetic fields, collecting data necessary for aiming nuclear missiles on U.S. submarines. As cover, the ship searched for oil deposits, and Wilson sold the geologic information at high prices to oil companies. The money flowed.

A string of congressmen, Capitol Hill aides, generals and admirals came to Wilson's estate and savored his boundless hospitality. So came the spooks and the secret warriors. The affable Clines was a regular, enjoying the free flow of food and spirits. Richard Secord, introduced to Wilson by Clines, visited, as did Erich von Marbod, a top Pentagon aide in charge of logistics.† Among Wilson's guests was Shackley, a rising CIA star.

Shackley had not seen Wilson in years. The two became reacquainted at a party of Agency people in 1972 or 1973. Shackley was intrigued by

---

* One account of Wilson's departure from the Agency noted that his exit was hastened when the inspector general discovered Wilson had listed one of his CIA fronts on a net-worth statement submitted as part of a personal mortgage application.

† In an FBI interview in 1981, Secord said he could not remember ever having been to Wilson's farm. Three months later, he told the FBI he had visited Wilson's estate several times.

this shady covert operator. "He was on the fringes of what I call the twilight zone," Shackley recalled. He enjoyed talking with Wilson, who knew the international arms market. Wilson traveled much and often returned with fascinating tidbits of information. And the Wilson and Shackley families got on well. Wilson's wife, Barbara, and Hazel Shackley became close. Suzanne Shackley befriended one of Wilson's sons. The families shared Thanksgiving. The Shackleys frequently drove to Wilson's farm for a cookout. Wilson and Shackley, both gun enthusiasts, shot together, firing at targets made of bulletproof material. Shackley would adopt a classic pose—one hand on his hip, his other arm extended—and shoot away.

Suzanne loved to ride, and Wilson generously sold Shackley a horse for $100 and boarded it for free. There was much to bond the families: genuine friendship between the wives and children, mutual need between the men. Shackley, the ambitious intelligence officer, found in Wilson a high-flyer moving in circles of interest to Langley. For Wilson, who collected influential people like keepsakes, Shackley was a catch, one of the most senior officers in the operations directorate, a man who might one day be Director.

Over the next few years, Shackley, now chief of the East Asia Division, and Wilson discussed spook stuff. Wilson conveyed global gossip about captured American equipment in Vietnam: who was selling it and where. One time Wilson told Shackley that he might be able to obtain a Soviet missile. Shackley told Wilson to go ahead and try. "Ted was interested in what Wilson could do," said Mickey Kappes, a CIA officer close to both. Wilson informed Shackley of his plans to sell security systems to various governments. There was talk of a minefield cleaning operation in Libya. Shackley later declared he never considered Wilson an "intelligence source." He was merely a window on a netherworld in which Shackley held a deep professional interest.

Wilson was all over the map. In 1975 he was spending time in Iran peddling high-tech spy equipment. He cooperated with two Indonesia-based CIA men—presumably officers of Shackley's East Asia Division—in a weapons deal that directed thousands of weapons and millions of rounds of ammunition to Africa, possibly to the CIA-backed forces in Angola. A mysterious, Agency-linked bank in Australia, the Nugan Hand Bank, participated in this transaction.* During this period, Douglas Schlachter, the overseer of Wilson's farm and a guy-Friday, often chauffeured Wilson to Agency headquarters for meetings. In another scheme,

---

* A 1981 report in the *Wilmington News Journal* maintained that Wilson used Task Force 157 to provide funds for anti-Whitlam operations in Australia.

Wilson recruited CIA contract operative Felix Rodriguez, who had come recommended by Clines, to create teams to penetrate Palestinian camps in Lebanon.*

Eventually Donald Nielsen, a new Task Force 157 commander, developed suspicions about Wilson's far-flung enterprises. He checked twice with the CIA. Each time the Agency vouched for its former employee. A Navy review of Wilson's operations uncovered nothing derogatory. Nevertheless, Nielsen sensed something amiss. He turned Wilson's permanent contract into a temporary one set to expire April 30, 1976. Wilson carried the issue to Admiral Bobby Ray Inman, head of Naval Intelligence. At a February lunch, Wilson pitched Inman. Let me set up my own operation, he requested. He boasted of having covert sources around the globe. He dropped a long list of names, including his "good friend Ted Shackley out at CIA." I know Naval Intelligence is having budgetary problems, Wilson told the admiral. If you back me, you'll get all the money you need out of Congress. Inman was shocked. One of his subordinates was trying to bribe him. Inman decided to shut down Task Force 157.

Then Inman heard from Shackley. Wilson could not be dismissed, Shackley asserted. The reason: national security. Inman did not buy this. If Wilson was so important, the CIA could pick up his tab.

Before the task force was disbanded, the Navy asked the CIA if it were interested in jointly assuming Task Force 157 operations with Naval Intelligence. DDO Bill Wells passed. Wilson, despite Shackley's effort, was a free agent, a spook without a service.

II

On August 4, 1976, Shackley lunched with Albert Hakim, an Iranian businessman, at the Jockey Club in Washington. The encounter had been arranged by Ed Wilson. Shackley found Hakim an interesting character. Iran was in a state of flux, and Hakim was familiar with the territory and boasted plenty of contacts there. The next day, Shackley sent Wells a memo on Hakim. The ADDO thought he would make a good source for the Agency. With this memo, Shackley also was helping Wilson.

Oil-rich Iran was an important target for the CIA. The United States ran in Iran secret eavesdropping installations trained on the Soviet Union. The Shah, who had been returned to the throne in 1953 courtesy

---

* Shortly after the Lebanon mission, Rodriguez left the Agency. With the help of Shackley, he was able to retire openly—that is, acknowledging his past relationship with the Company. Shackley had steered Rodriguez's request for open retirement through the bureaucratic maze. On his last day at Langley in early 1976, Rodriguez had what for him was an emotional farewell meeting with Shackley.

of the Agency, was considered Washington's best ally in the Muslim world. The United States supplied him with the latest in American weaponry; it advised the Shah's 350,000-man army. The CIA cooperated with SAVAK, the brutal secret police. The Shah needed help. Students, leftists, and Islamic fundamentalists were protesting his harsh, undemocratic rule. Demonstrations were mounting. The Shah's grip—though neither the Agency nor the State Department realized the danger—was weakening.

The CIA was failing in Iran. For the past year, the Tehran station had not filed a single report based on sources within the religious opposition. Shackley's officers in Iran were concentrating on other targets, mainly the Soviets. This was because U.S. policy explicitly discouraged direct contacts with opposition elements. The Agency shied away from such reporting, a 1979 congressional report noted, because it feared "that the Shah, suspecting a CIA conspiracy against him, might deny U.S. access to its technical collection sites or restrict other forms of intelligence cooperation."

Here was another instance in which the CIA's mission of collecting intelligence clashed with its desire to preserve a friendly government—in this case, a government that allowed it to spy on the Soviet Union. As the congressional report observed, "The danger that CIA's action responsibilities might color its intelligence performance in Iran is implicit in the dual task assigned to CIA. On the one hand, CIA had historically considered itself the Shah's booster. On the other hand, it was supposed to provide sound intelligence analysis of the Iranian political situation."

The Agency had no clue it was lost. A 1976 review of reporting from Iran (an exercise in which Shackley's office played a part) pronounced the output as "very satisfactory." But it noted a "continuing need for more first-hand information about opposition elements." The CIA, the report suggested, might be too dependent on intelligence from SAVAK. But the shortcomings were not rectified. In 1977, Agency analysts, relying in part on DDO reports, would proclaim that the "Shah will be an active participant in Iranian life well into the 1980s."

With the CIA in need of better information on Iran, it was prudent for Shackley to cultivate a source like Hakim. He saw a chance to break free of SAVAK, to develop his own agent in Iran. But Hakim was a scoundrel looking to cash in.

In his August 5 memo on Hakim to Wells, Shackley noted that Hakim, who specialized in military and intelligence electronics, was trying to score big with sales to Iran's army and SAVAK. In particular, he was pushing a communications surveillance system. To improve his prospects, Hakim was casting about for persons in the U.S. government with whom, Shackley wrote, "he can find a mutuality of interest." Shackley smelled an opportunity. If the CIA helped Hakim, Hakim could assist the CIA.

At the same time, Hakim was developing a partnership with Ed Wilson the spy-turned-entrepreneur. The previous December at a Christmas party for past and present spooks, Wilson had met Frank Terpil, another former CIA man trying to strike it rich in the international security field. (While in the Agency, Terpil was suspected of smuggling gems and was caught in a money-changing scam.) Terpil and Wilson talked about making millions by joining forces. Terpil bragged he had a good line into Libya through a cousin of Qaddafi. He explained he was using his old Agency contacts to peddle surveillance equipment around the world through a subsidiary of Albert Hakim's Stanford Technology Corporation.

Wilson had tried to sell SAVAK a surveillance system, exploiting his friendship with Richard Secord, now a major general in Tehran overseeing U.S. military assistance to the Shah. The deal had failed. But maybe something could be worked out through Hakim. By the summer of 1976, Wilson and Hakim were discussing business, and Wilson shared his new associate with his good friend, the ADDO of the CIA.

Shackley, as ADDO, usually did not get caught up in details regarding reporting sources. But the Hakim case motivated him. In an August 16 memo, he outlined a scheme for Wells and others. Hakim was on his way to Tehran, hoping for a sale. Shackley proposed that his old friend Tom Clincs, who also had met Hakim through Wilson, introduce the Iranian businessman to two other Shackley compatriots in Tehran: Richard Secord and Erich von Marbod, the senior defense representative of the U.S. mission in Iran.*

Shackley, Clines, Secord, and von Marbod—this was a fraternity of the secret war in Laos. Clines and Secord were at the Udorn base when Shackley was chief of station in Vientiane; von Marbod at the Pentagon handled logistical arrangements for the Laotian operation. All four had

---

* Von Marbod was not in a position to do Hakim much good. Months earlier, the Shah, upset with the management of the vast U.S.-Iranian arms program, had asked that von Marbod be fired. General Hassan Toufanian, the Shah's chief aide for weapons procurement, complained that von Marbod was acting as if he were an agent of U.S. arms firms. In fact, in 1975 von Marbod had been reprimanded by James Schlesinger, then Secretary of Defense, for accepting hospitality at a Northrop hunting lodge in Maryland. In mid-August of 1976, Richard Helms, now the U.S. ambassador in Tehran, told a U.S. businessman that, in regard to the program von Marbod oversaw, he had never seen "so many people out of control in the Pentagon."

enjoyed Wilson's munificence at his Virginia estate. Now Shackley was pushing to make Hakim part of this circle.

Shackley proposed that Secord and von Marbod brief Hakim on the specifications for a perimeter security system the Iranians planned to install at their military bases. "Mr. Clines' introduction of Mr. Hakim to Mr. von Marbod and General Secord would give Mr. Hakim no commercial advantage *per se,*" Shackley wrote. "Given the Middle East style of business, however, the fact that Mr. Clines had made an introduction . . . should result in Mr. Hakim being willing to respond to a request for assistance from Mr. Clines." That request would be for Hakim to become a source for the CIA. Shackley's plan was good for Wilson. Whether Shackley knew it or not, Wilson and Hakim had agreed that if any money came Hakim's way through this arrangement, Wilson would receive a cut.

By this time, Wilson and Terpil had consummated an unholy alliance. The pair had signed a deal to provide the Libyan dictatorship with plastic explosives and 500,000 sophisticated timing devices. As he put the deal together, Wilson was aided by his CIA buddies. Clines recommended I. W. (John) Harper, an explosives man and JMWAVE veteran. William Weisenburger, an Agency officer in charge of exotic equipment, helped Wilson obtain demonstration models of the timers. When Wilson decided to expand his business, he again drew on his Agency contacts for the right talent; he needed an assassin.

The Libyans wanted a dissident residing in Egypt killed. The man Wilson had in mind for the job was Rafael Quintero, one of the Company's best Cubans. As an operative of Shackley's JMWAVE station, Quintero had worked closely with Clines. Wilson called Quintero to Washington. In a parking lot in suburban Virginia, Wilson and Terpil explained the million-dollar job to Quintero. The Cuban figured this was an authorized hit—one okayed by Langley—and said he would find the men to do it.*

As Wilson was spinning out of control, Langley sent a cable to the station in Tehran, asking for its thoughts on Shackley's proposal to help Hakim. In a brief reply, the station chief notified headquarters that Hakim's Stanford Technology had previously signed a contract to supply the Iranian air force with a communications surveillance system. But the Iranians discovered Hakim had cheated the air force by unloading a

---

* Clines sometimes took Quintero to CIA headquarters to see Shackley, according to Shirley Brill, Clines's girlfriend then and a CIA employee herself. In 1987, Shackley told congressional investigators that, to the best of his recollection, he did not meet Quintero until after he (Shackley) had left the Agency.

large quantity of unneeded, oversophisticated equipment at exorbitant prices. The Iranian officer in charge of the suspicious contract had okayed the deal without the clearance of his superior, and the Iranian military command terminated the shady arrangement.

"In view [of the] unsavory reputation of STC here," the station chief wrote, he preferred not to go ahead with the Shackley plan. The station, he noted dryly, "appreciate[s] headquarters having identified this opportunity." Shackley had failed to set up Hakim as an asset. Wilson had failed to broker a deal.* But the episode was not a total bust. Connections had been made, connections that would lead Shackley, Secord, Clines, and Hakim to profits and, then, scandal.

Kevin Mulcahy spent most of September 7, 1976, drinking in his home in Vienna, Virginia. Late at night, he picked up the phone and called Langley. He demanded to talk to Shackley.

Mulcahy had grown up in an Agency family. He had put in five years as a CIA computer and communications officer in the 1960s. But drinking drove him out of the service. In April of 1976, Wilson had hired the thirty-three-year-old Mulcahy as his administrative aide. Soon Mulcahy was worrying about the probity of Wilson and Terpil's efforts to peddle machine guns overseas. Mulcahy informed agents of the Bureau of Alcohol, Tobacco and Firearms about the scheme. But the deal fell through. Then Wilson told him about the pending Libyan plan: explosives, sophisticated timing devices, military training, all for what Wilson claimed was a Libyan antiterrorism program. Everybody was going to make a mint, and the enterprise would produce intelligence for their friends in Langley.

It wasn't so farfetched to Mulcahy. He knew how the CIA worked. It could piggyback on an Edwin Wilson. And Wilson, who was always quick to hint he was deep-cover Agency, regularly spoke with CIA officers. On Friday nights, he often hit the bars in suburban Virginia that served as hangouts for Agency men, sometimes in the company of Tom Clines, well known in Agency circles for his friendship with Shackley. Mulcahy even had accompanied Wilson on a visit to Shackley's home in Bethesda in late May of 1976. Tagging along was Harry Rastatter, a business associ-

---

* Eleven years after these events, Shackley provided a false account to congressional investigators. Asked if he had recommended any action after meeting Hakim, Shackley replied, "No." He claimed that he had sent the Near East Division a memo only describing Hakim and that the division then notified Shackley it was not interested in Hakim. At a second interview, Shackley was presented with documents outlining his proposal. He then acknowledged suggesting Hakim be assisted.

ate of Terpil's recently back from Iran. For Mulcahy, the visit to Shackley's house sealed the matter. Here they were in the living room of the number-two man in the CIA's clandestine service. Shackley accepted information Rastatter had obtained from SAVAK. Wilson mentioned he was off to Libya. If Shackley knew, it had to be all right.

But after Mulcahy lost a $4,000 cash payoff he was supposed to deliver to a Wilson contact in a defense firm, and Wilson threatened to have his head, Mulcahy rifled through papers. He discovered the secret proposal for the Libyan project. Wilson was supplying Qaddafi the training and equipment for use in covert sabotage operations, not antiterrorism, as Wilson had maintained.

Mulcahy had to tell someone. Fortified by booze, he phoned the duty officer at Langley and asked for Shackley. An hour later, Shackley returned the call. Mulcahy told Shackley he had to see him right away. The two met, and Mulcahy showed him a copy of the secret Libyan project proposal. Was this a CIA operation? he asked. After the conversation, Shackley wrote a memorandum reporting in a low-key tone what Mulcahy had said. He noted that Mulcahy had been drinking. He sent the memo through channels.

Whatever Shackley told Mulcahy, it did not provide comfort. The next day Mulcahy went straight to the FBI and told them all. He did the same when Thomas Cox from the CIA inspector general's office called on him, as a result of Shackley's memo.*

Meanwhile, Quintero and two Cubans he had recruited for Wilson's murder job—Raoul and Rafael Villaverde—were moving ahead. They saw Wilson and Terpil in Geneva on September 15 and began preparing for a trip to Libya, but not without hesitation. Wilson was talking about a million dollars for the assassination. The Villaverdes, like Quintero, were Agency veterans, and the Company rarely threw around money of that quantity. Maybe this job wasn't okay with Langley. These diehard anticommunists also were put off by Wilson and Terpil's offer to train Libyans in demolition skills side by side with Soviet and Chinese advisers. Quintero, to be on the safe side, reported his conversations with Wilson to Clines, his old case officer.

Clines had no choice but to write it up. The Cubans might be telling other people that Wilson was pulling together assassin and sabotage packages for Libya. Clines had to cover himself. But in the memo Clines drew as much a distinction as he could between Wilson and Terpil. It was Terpil, Clines claimed, who had requested the assassination of the

---

* A month earlier, John Harper, an ex-Agency demolition expert who worked for Wilson, had contacted the CIA about Wilson's activities. The Agency sent him to the FBI and Bureau of Alcohol, Tobacco and Firearms.

Libyan dissident and proposed the Cubans train the Libyans in explosives work. In a separate report to the I.G.'s office, Clines wrote, "Quintero thought that he was involved in an Agency operation from his first contact with Mr. Ed Wilson even though Mr. Wilson stated it was not. . . . He was sure that Mr. Wilson would do nothing against the interest of the United States Government. . . . Frank [Terpil] was playing the pivotal role in this entire matter." Clines was helping two of his best friends. Wilson called off the assassination; Quintero continued to do other business with Wilson.

By the fall of 1976, the CIA knew something of Wilson's unorthodox activities. The FBI had a piece: Its officers spoke with Quintero and the Villaverdes and questioned Shackley and Clines.* The BATF had been alerted. The office of John Waller, the inspector general at Langley, was poking about. But no real investigation materialized. When questioned by the I.G. investigators, Shackley downplayed Mulcahy's allegations. The man, after all, was a drunk. Waller did not consider Wilson's business a top priority for his staff. This was more a matter for the FBI. "We didn't want to muddy the waters with a dual investigation," Waller claimed. Besides, Wilson was no longer within the CIA. Waller was not especially curious about Wilson's current connections to the Agency. "We did whatever the FBI asked us to do," Waller noted. "Whatever we did, we took our cue from the Bureau."

Waller did not do much. According to Admiral Bobby Inman, who became deputy DCI in 1981 and then reviewed the Wilson case file, Waller's officers had relied almost wholly on personal interviews. They did not bother to assemble documents. "It's hard to dignify what happened with the word 'investigation,' " Inman concluded. "The people running it seemed more interested in drawing the wagons in a tight circle around Ted Shackley and Tom Clines than in getting at the truth."

As ADDO, Shackley had to contend with much more than Hakim, Wilson, and Iran. In addition to his routine duties—overseeing efforts to recruit Soviet agents, to penetrate the Chinese government, to spy on allies around the world, to mount covert actions—Shackley's workdays were marked by crises and controversy. The Agency was struggling with how to respond to claims by indicted drug-dealers that they were with

---

* After Clines first heard from the FBI, he contacted Shackley. His friend quickly issued Clines advice: call the inspector general and get a piece of paper saying you are not involved in Wilson's misdeeds but are willing to tell the Bureau what you know about him. That's what I'm going to do, Shackley said.

the CIA. The Justice Department wanted Agency personnel to testify in such cases when the claim was false; Shackley was pushing for a policy that would exempt CIA officers from testifying. (CIA general counsel Anthony Lapham urged a less absolute position.) Shackley was overseeing Agency endeavors in Europe tracking black-market sales of weapon-grade uranium. Justice Department lawyers were on the trail of the ITT cover-up. Snepp was stirring up old dust.

In October and November of 1976, a series of press leaks, apparently engineered by Agency employees, noted that the CIA and the FBI had concluded the Chilean junta was not behind the recent car-bomb assassination in Washington of former Chilean ambassador Orlando Letelier and his assistant, an American named Ronni Moffit. In what smacked of a disinformation campaign, unidentified intelligence officials told a *New York Times* journalist that the investigation was pursuing the possibility that left-wing Chileans bombed Letelier to disrupt U.S. relations with Pinochet. A *Washington Post* article, citing "informed sources," claimed Bush had told Kissinger that Pinochet's military government had nothing to do with the executions. (At the same time, the CIA station in Santiago made no attempt to determine if the Chilean government was behind the killing.) While the misleading leaks poured out of the CIA, inside headquarters officers in the operation directorate worried that the murders had been executed by right-wing Cuban exiles who might boast past ties to the Agency.

The truth was that the Chilean security service, DINA, had used Cuban rightist terrorists for this hit. A subsequent investigation uncovered evidence that the Agency, prior to the assassination, had received information about the killers' intentions to travel to the United States on a mission—its purpose was not clear—and did little in response.*

The CIA "has weathered the storm," Director Bush declared before a gathering of former intelligence officers. The congressional muckraking was done, but the flow of unpleasant disclosures had not ceased. Jack Anderson revealed that the CIA condoned illegal activity conducted in the United States by the intelligence services of Chile, South Korea, and Iran. One news account declared that the Agency in 1971 had supplied anti-Castro operatives with the swine fever virus, which was released on Cuba and created a nationwide animal epidemic. The socialist Ethiopian

---

* In 1989, Robert Scherrer, an FBI agent who worked on the Letelier investigation, disclosed that a senior CIA officer had admitted to him that the Agency mishandled a cable from the embassy in Paraguay. The cable contained information about Chilean agents on their way to the United States. If the CIA had dealt with it correctly, Scherrer said, Letelier and Moffit might still be alive.

military government charged the CIA was supporting opposition elements—but offered no proof. In Jamaica, Prime Minister Michael Manley accused the Agency of encouraging political violence.*

Jimmy Carter's election as President in November of 1976 drew no cheers from Shackley and Langley. Prior to the election, Shackley had confided to his childhood friend Norman Hamer that he thought he might be in line for the DCI job, should Ford win reelection. On the hustings, Carter, a Georgia Democrat, had campaigned as a Washington outsider promising to bring trust back to the American government, and he had cited three national disgraces: Watergate, Vietnam, and the CIA. Shackley was directly connected to two of the three.

III

As Agency people wondered what Carter had in store for them, Shackley had to be pondering his own future. Ghosts were afoot. He was not facing trouble for having run secret wars and covert actions. He was at risk for pulling a fast one on Congress during the 1973 ITT investigation, when he and others conspired to mislead Senator Frank Church's subcommittee about Agency intervention in Chile. In the fall of 1976, Justice Department attorneys were combing through the testimony that CIA and ITT officials had given the Church subcommittee, looking for perjurers and Agency officers who had encouraged them.

A year ago, in December of 1975, the Justice Department had requested from the Church subcommittee its entire file on the CIA-ITT inquiry. This move suggested that all Agency people connected to the Church subcommittee inquiry were potential targets. A federal grand jury began hearing evidence in the summer of 1976. William Wells feared the worst. In July, he ordered a subordinate to perform a "damage assessment" and review the potential consequence of indictments against "one or more CIA officers." The subordinate was instructed to compile a file on all officers involved. Shackley must have been on the list.

Bush was trying to protect Shackley and others. He objected to Justice Department plans to call CIA and ITT officials as witnesses before the grand jury or in any trial that might ensue; he protested the use of CIA

---

* Manley won reelection in the December national elections. In 1977, *Penthouse* magazine published an article that quoted anonymous intelligence sources disclosing the details of a massive CIA plot to undermine Manley in 1976. Years later, Tom Clines, who was once acting station chief in Kingston, observed, "Everybody in the CIA liked [Edward] Seaga [the right-wing Jamaica Labour Party leader and Manley's opponent]. I'm sure they helped him during the elections."

documents as evidence. If Bush's position stood, a White House memo noted, the investigation would have to be aborted. Bush privately complained that public exposure of his officials—people like Shackley—would compromise operations and cause morale at Langley to tumble. But President Ford in October of 1976 directed the CIA to cooperate with the Justice Department.

Bush instructed his officers to assist government lawyers.* Subpoenas arrived at Langley—forty-five of them. Justice Department attorneys wanted to talk to William Broe, the former Western Hemisphere Division chief who had appeared before the Church subcommittee. They were interested in his secretary. They demanded to interview Jonathan Hanke, the officer Shackley had used to arrange misleading testimony. The lawyers asked to see Jim Flannery, Shackley's deputy in the division. They also wanted to question Shackley. He was called before the grand jury in late November of 1976.

By now, many in the operations directorate knew CIA officials had rigged testimony during the Church subcommittee inquiry. Agency people talked about potential perjury charges. Hanke was nervous. He borrowed money for a lawyer. He had done Shackley's bidding, now his career was threatened.

A bad sign arrived when the Justice Department in November charged Hal Hendrix, the former ITT official, with withholding information from the Church subcommittee. Hendrix pled guilty to a misdemeanor as part of a plea bargain. His testimony had been coached by Hanke on Shackley's instructions. Now he was telling all. If the Justice Department learned that Hendrix had deceived Congress at the Agency's request, Hanke and Shackley might face conspiracy charges. For the investigators, Helms and top ITT officials remained the primary targets, but Shackley and other senior CIA officials were in the crosshairs.

As Justice attorneys dissected the CIA-ITT cover-up, another Shackley operation was exposed. In December, *The Washington Post* revealed that the Agency for several years had bugged leaders of Micronesia, a group of Pacific islands the United States administered as a colony. Micronesia fell under Shackley's purview when he headed the East Asia Division. His luck in the region had been mixed. A case officer he had

---

* Bush managed to defend Shackley on another front. After the remains of John Rosselli, the mob-linked hood and CIA asset, were found in an oil drum floating near Miami in August of 1976, Florida police posed a series of questions to the Agency. Rosselli's participation in the CIA's anti-Castro plotting was now public information, and the police asked if they could talk to whoever was Miami station chief in the early 1960s. Bush refused to provide them Shackley's name or allow them access to him.

dispatched, Robert Wiecha, was caught trying to recruit an American.* But the bugging operation in Micronesia—initiated in October of 1973 at the request of Henry Kissinger—produced reports on the islanders' strategies in the ongoing negotiations with Washington over the colony's future status. Shackley even had obtained an agent within the negotiating committee. The problem was, the Agency was not supposed to spy on Americans. Micronesians are not U.S. citizens, but under the U.N. trusteeship arrangement they were to be afforded the same rights as Americans.

The CIA had more image trouble: the mighty United States spying on tiny Micronesia in order to better the colony at the bargaining table. Shackley was one of those responsible, though, as always, he escaped public notice.

But John and Dolores Murray had not forgotten about Shackley. John Murray was forced by his cancer to retire in November of 1976. But he still brooded over Shackley's influence within the clandestine service. Months earlier when Murray and Senator Thomas McIntyre had discussed Shackley, the two agreed that the only hope for reforming the CIA lay in a change in the White House. That had happened, and Dolores Murray was working on Jimmy Carter's transition team in the office of Hamilton Jordan, soon to be White House chief of staff. On December 17, she sent Jordan a long memo on the CIA, much of it devoted to Shackley.

Dolores Murray reported that Shackley had managed the ITT cover-up and that he controlled a network of loyal officers placed throughout the directorate. "Mr. Shackley," she wrote, "recently drew a line through the names of officers carefully and competitively selected through panels for promotion to supergrade level. He then calmly wrote in the names of several men of his own choosing whom nobody had considered for promotion. No one could do anything about it. The Director doesn't know it goes on and anyone reporting such violation of regulations will not only finish his career but will be harassed." The promotion system—the heart of the bureaucracy—was crooked, Dolores Murray claimed. If Agency people had to kowtow to powerful officers like Shackley, the integrity of the system was compromised.

She had another piece of disturbing information for Jordan. After Carter won the election, she reported, Wells had called in his senior officers to discuss what they could expect. The Agency would have to

---

* After Wiecha botched the Palau job, he was awarded, with Shackley's assistance, a plum post: Israel branch chief. CIA people marveled at the promotion, proof that Shackley tended to those loyal to him. The appointment provided Shackley influence over Langley's Israeli account.

put up with sanctimonious bullshit for six months or so, Wells said, but by then the Agency should be able to impress Carter with all its bells and whistles. After that, the CIA will have the same relationship with Carter as it had with other presidents. Dolores Murray was issuing an alert: watch out for Langley, especially Wells and Shackley. She hoped her memo would be passed to Carter's yet-to-be-named Director of Central Intelligence.

Meanwhile, Frank Snepp had not gone away. Shackley's promotion from East Asia Division chief to ADDO did not rid him of anxieties about his past subordinate. On May 31, 1976, shortly after Shackley had moved into his ADDO office, *The Washington Post* reported that the North Vietnamese Army, during the 1975 fall of Saigon, captured South Vietnamese military, police, and intelligence files full of classified data. The sources for the story were the memoirs of NVA General Van Tien Dung and the confirming on-the-record recollections of Frank Snepp. In the article, Snepp attributed the failure to destroy vital documents to the wishful thinking of station chief Thomas Polgar and Ambassador Graham Martin, who believed a negotiated settlement to the war was possible. He accused them of ignoring intelligence that contradicted their own wishes. Snepp disclosed he was writing his own book on the collapse of Saigon.

In headquarters, senior officers contemplated what to do about Snepp. Shackley was to be a point man. Polgar flew from Mexico to Washington. He discussed the Snepp crisis with both Shackley and Wells. And he had lunch with Snepp. At a Washington-area restaurant, Polgar defended his performance in Saigon and questioned Snepp's patriotism. It was a melancholy moment, the last meeting of two former colleagues. Afterward, Polgar returned to Mexico and cabled a report to Wells and Shackley. Polgar observed that Snepp had been in a "highly emotional state." Snepp, he wrote, "is developing considerable feelings against the Agency. [He] is not acting from disloyal motives but is disappointed, frustrated and perhaps even desperate about being thwarted in his attempts to prove that he was right and if only we had listened to him, hundreds perhaps thousands more South Vietnamese" could have been evacuated. At lunch, Snepp had told his old boss he had wished only to write a history of CIA involvement in Vietnam. When Shackley and others had said no, he decided his only choice was to quit and do it on his own. But, Snepp added, he had no desire to hurt the Agency and harbored hopes the Agency might supply him material he needed for his book.

Polgar was inclined to assist the young man. "I think Snepp is basically honest, very capable but emotionally somewhat unstable and under great strain," he wrote. "He is not doing well financially, and he feels driven into a corner. When the pressures on him become great enough he will lash out against whatever he can. At this point he has not been, and does not intend to become, disloyal but he can cause great damage even without such intentions." Polgar's recommendation was simple: bring Snepp back by providing him the intelligence produced by the Saigon station: "He should be given [an] opportunity to blow off steam." Such advice did not rest well with Shackley.

On June 30, Shackley met with deputy DCI E. Henry Knoche, Inspector General John Waller, and other senior officials to discuss Snepp. The group decided to review Snepp's FOIA requests—Shackley called for a *careful* review—and to establish a control officer for Snepp. From now on, Bob Layton, an assistant national intelligence officer covering Southeast Asia, would be Snepp's CIA contact; he also would spy on him.

Throughout the summer, Layton monitored Snepp and sent memos to higher-ups on Snepp's progress. He reported on Snepp's trip to Paris, his visit to the Vietnamese embassy, his efforts to interview General Dung. Layton met with Snepp, who griped about the Agency's rejection of his request for cables. Snepp complained that Marvin and Bernard Kalb were granted access to sensitive information for a book on Vietnam. In a memo, Layton noted that Knoche, Shackley, and others needed to keep in mind that Snepp knew a lot, had many contacts within the Agency, and was a talented intelligence officer. Layton doubted Snepp could be defused completely. But he suggested that the Agency throw Snepp some scraps: show him the information the Kalbs got, supply him sanitized versions of the cables.* Confronting Snepp would only set off a bigger explosion.

But at a September 28 meeting with Knoche and others, Shackley declared that Snepp's request for the cables had been denied. There would be no sanitized versions released to placate the troublemaker.

More meetings occurred, as Shackley, Knoche, Layton, general counsel Anthony Lapham, and security director Robert Gambino considered how to stop Snepp. Shackley was intent on preventing Snepp from telling classified tales—especially now that Joseph B. Smith, another disgruntled CIA man, had circumvented the Agency review process to publish memoirs of his twenty-two years in the clandestine service. Smith's book, *Portrait of a Cold Warrior,* opened with a reference to Shackley's purge of the Western Hemisphere Division and depicted Shackley as a ruthless bureaucrat who installed his own henchmen in positions of authority. Shackley, whose name had not surfaced publicly

---

* In one memo, Layton wrote, "Mr. Snepp is essentially right on this matter [regarding Bernard Kalb]; Mr. Kalb was shown, but was not allowed to retain, a copy of [a classified document on Vietnam]."

during years of scandal and investigation, was now exposed. He was enraged. And Snepp was more familiar with Shackley than Smith.

In late December, Layton called Snepp and asked if he intended to submit his manuscript for review. Snepp said he did not. Layton sent a memo to Shackley, noting that a "crunch point . . . was fast approaching."

Enough already, Shackley decided. At a January 3, 1977, meeting in the Director's conference room on the seventh floor, Shackley announced it was time to set the law on Snepp. The former officer had signed the standard secrecy oath, pledging never to disclose Company secrets without first submitting to an Agency review. Now he intended to break that sacred oath—a vow that preserved the most necessary characteristic of any intelligence service: secrecy. If the oath did not stand, if anyone could reveal what he or she had done for the Agency, the CIA could not continue. Shackley advised that immediate legal action be taken to force Snepp to provide the Agency a copy of the manuscript for review. The others agreed with Shackley.

After months of watching institutional hand-wringing, Shackley had become the first top officer to formally recommend that the Agency sic the Justice Department on Snepp. Shackley's advice would not be taken for some time—and too late to protect his reputation.

In March of 1977, Shackley saw Snepp at a cocktail party at the house of journalist Bud Merick, whom both men had known in Saigon. In a subsequent memo, Shackley noted that he had run into Snepp at the soiree. But the Snepp-Shackley encounter was prearranged. Merick and *Los Angeles Times* reporter George McArthur had schemed so that Shackley and Snepp could meet. No one in the Agency other than Snepp's designated contact was supposed to talk to the former analyst. But Shackley wanted to make Snepp one final pitch: just let the CIA conduct a pro forma review of the book so that the Agency's authority would be preserved.

As Shackley recorded the event for the bureaucracy, Snepp sought him out at Merick's home and started talking about his book on his own initiative. Shackley asked which firm was publishing the book. Snepp, worried the Agency might hurt him or interfere, refused to say. "Mr. Snepp," Shackley wrote, "was quite vague on . . . how the Agency might 'hurt' him." Shackley confronted Snepp: Do you plan to submit the book to the CIA for a security review? Snepp dodged the question. (Shackley did not mention in the memo any attempt to entice Snepp with an offer of a pro forma review.) In the memo, Shackley again asked, "Where do we stand on the issue of getting Snepp to honor his secrecy agreement?" He was pushing for action.

· · ·

On March 9, 1977, Admiral Stansfield Turner was sworn in as the twelfth Director of Central Intelligence, and for Langley's old guard—of which the forty-nine-year-old Shackley was now one—another bad spell was at hand. Turner had been a classmate of Jimmy Carter's at Annapolis and was serving in Italy as commander of NATO's southern flank, when the new President called him to Washington. The silver-haired admiral hoped that his old friend was ready to promote him to a senior military post. Instead Carter offered him Langley.

In the years after his rocky tenure, Turner claimed that he arrived at Langley with few preconceived notions about the Agency. As a military officer, he had always sought out CIA intelligence. Stationed overseas during the Church Committee period, Turner had not followed closely the recent Agency controversies. But he realized he was taking over an organization with serious problems. Turner was determined not to let the CIA get into the same jam again. His job was to protect the CIA from itself.

Turner expected the Agency to salute sharply and follow his lead. "I came in naive," he recalled. "In the Navy, we were used to shifting commands and, when that happened, you change your loyalty. That was not the case in the CIA." It would not be the case in most bureaucracies. Turner's intentions toward the CIA—reform the organization and re-store public trust in the institution—were admirable. But he lacked the political clout and bureaucratic skills needed to achieve the arduous task he had in mind: to foment change from within the closed community of the CIA, a world in which Turner was out of place.

Turner was at odds with the institution immediately. He let it show that he had little faith in the Agency's elite—a move that no matter how justifiable undermined his authority from the start. From Turner's perspective, his distrust was fully warranted. Shortly after settling into his Langley office, Turner concluded that senior officers in the operations directorate—the old boys—were not playing straight with him. When he posed questions to Bill Wells, the usual reply was, I'll look into it. "It was very unsettling," Turner noted. "These were things he should have had answers to." In the Navy, Turner asked subordinates for information on operations and received immediate responses. The delays he encountered at Langley fueled his suspicions.

His apprehensions were further buttressed by a report on how the Agency had handled one of its most sensitive cases. Early in Turner's tenure as DCI, Robert "Rusty" Williams, a special assistant the admiral had brought with him from the Navy, came to the Director's office carrying a file inches thick. He shoved it at his boss and said, you have to read this.

It was the file on Yuri Nosenko, a KGB officer who had defected to the CIA in 1964. He came bearing the news that the KGB had had no substantial contact with Lee Harvey Oswald, the assassin of John Kennedy. (Oswald lived in the Soviet Union from 1959 to 1962.) Nosenko's defection seemed too coincidental to the hypersuspicious minds of James Angleton's counterintelligence shop. Within the Agency, debating Nosenko's bona fides became something of a parlor game. For over three years, the Russian was held in solitary confinement in a small, windowless prison built for him, while he was interrogated as if he were a KGB plant. He was allowed no contact with the outside world. His diet was meager; he was drugged. Nosenko never changed his story.

Turner found this incredible. There had been no legal basis for holding Nosenko. His review of the Nosenko file dramatically affected his view of the Agency. "The message of the case," he recalled, "was that lots of people knew this was going on but no one was willing to stand up and say this is wrong." Turner concluded that if that had happened in the Yosenko affair, it probably had happened in others—cases that Turner would never learn about. More frightening, it could happen again.

CIA people immediately resented Turner. He seemed insecure, afraid of being outfoxed by Agency veterans. He surrounded himself with naval cronies who knew little of the Agency. The old boys swapped stories about the new guard's inexperience: did you hear that Williams asked somebody to explain how a safe house works? Turner ordered about officers as if he were morally superior to these disgraced government officials. His distrust showed. Some Agency people considered him smug and self-righteous. They saw the same high-handed moralistic attitude in Rusty Williams, who was ever on the prowl for Agency misdeeds. One time he visited a station overseas and questioned Agency employees about the social behavior of their coworkers. Williams complained to George Kalaris, the counterintelligence chief, that there was too much divorce in the Agency. He wanted a worldwide decree that all case officers spend at least three nights a week home with their families. Turner and Williams were certainly a pair, Agency people thought. They even prayed together.

Senior Agency people soon had themselves to blame for Turner's intractable attitude, for Turner's suspicious bias regarding the clandestine service was fixed into place by the Wilson affair—particularly by Shackley's role in it. When in mid-April the admiral read in the Post of Ed Wilson's connections to Agency employees, he called inspector general John Waller and demanded an immediate investigation. Turner wanted results within a week. Waller reported to Turner that afternoon. The Agency knew all about Wilson's contacts. Patry Loomis, a deep-cover case officer in Asia, moonlighted for Wilson. William Weisenburger, the Agency logistics officer specializing in high-tech equipment, helped Wilson obtain sensitive technology. Turner was surprised. The Agency was aware of these connections, yet none of the senior career officers were upset. No one had bothered to inform him of the problem when he came aboard.

The next day, Turner questioned Loomis and Weisenburger. They made excuses; he did not buy any. A few days later, the Director convened a meeting of his top people: Knoche, Wells, Shackley, Waller, Williams, and others. Gentlemen, he said, the question is what to do with Loomis and Weisenburger. The choices were exoneration, punishment, or dismissal. He went around the table. Shackley and the other career men suggested dishing out moderate punishments. Dismissing the pair, they argued, would demoralize the Agency. Only Rusty Williams said the pair ought to be canned. Turner looked at his top officers—he could not believe their attitude—and said sarcastically, "Majority wins. They're fired."

Most startling to Turner was the report from the I.G.'s office that Shackley and Clines had associated with the rogue Wilson. Clines, now an officer in the training division, was preparing to go to Jamaica as station chief. Clines, according to the I.G. report, had been spotted in a restaurant with Wilson and Loomis. Bring me Clines, Turner ordered. Clines hurried to Shackley and Wells. They advised him to sign a letter of resignation before he met with the admiral. Then, they explained, he cannot fire you. But Clines believed he could bluff his way through this rough patch.

In the Director's office, the quick-talking Clines told Turner there was nothing to fret about. He had no business relationship with Wilson. In fact, he had been assigned the task during the Bush years of penetrating the Wilson gang. Turner did not believe him. He thought Clines was in neck-deep with Wilson, but he had no hard evidence. Clines was safe from the axe. But the admiral shuddered at what Clines could get away with in his own station. He killed the Kingston assignment.

Shackley's contacts with Wilson were even more disturbing. "It was beyond my imagination," Turner exclaimed later, "that the number-two man in the DDO would be spending his weekends with an accused gunrunner." Turner called Shackley into the Director's office. Shackley was ready with a defense. His contact with Wilson was purely social. Their wives were friends. We never talk about business. Turner could not believe that an ex-CIA man sits down with a senior CIA officer and they never discuss their overlapping worlds. Turner did not have any proof to the contrary. But he worried about the example Shackley set. "What did it say to an organization just accused of doing all sorts of bad things by the Church Committee?" Turner remarked. "It was unconscionable. Yet Bill Wells would keep Shackley on as his number two. There was a total indifference to the world around them."

Turner was unsure what to do about Shackley. He already felt he was in the midst of a DDO mutiny. He feared that firing the ADDO—Turner's natural inclination—would be viewed as a major strike against the directorate and exacerbate his predicament. Nor could he punish Shackley and leave him in place. How can you have someone occupying a high position who engaged in action that warranted disciplining? Turner thought about shoving Shackley into a prestigious post abroad, perhaps chief of station in Paris. But he did not want to hand someone he did not trust an important overseas assignment. Shackley would have to stay put. But Turner would keep looking for a dumping ground.

IV

Frank Snepp was now Turner's problem. The CIA learned from former officers whom Snepp had contacted that he intended to use real names of CIA officers in his book. And on April 10, 1977, *The Washington Post* published an open letter to Stansfield Turner from John Stockwell, who had recently resigned. After serving in Vietnam, Stockwell in 1975 had been appointed chief of the Angola task force, as it was preparing to arm anticommunist rebels. His tour on the task force had completed a long process of disillusionment. In his letter, Stockwell let loose with a string of disturbing revelations about Vietnam and Africa. (Agency operations in Vietnam, he wrote, were often fabrications, "but were papered over and promoted by aware case officers because of the 'numbers game' requirements from Headquarters for voluminous reporting.") What made it worse for top CIA people was that Stockwell and Snepp were in cahoots.

Days after Stockwell's letter appeared, Snepp told Agency officers he had placed Stockwell in touch with the newspaper. But, Snepp said, he was doing all he could to make sure that Stockwell did not go too far. Don't push Stockwell, he advised, unless you want another Agee.*

But even as Snepp claimed to be doing a favor for the Agency, he raised the ante—and did so at Shackley's expense. Snepp complained to a senior Agency officer, William Parmenter, that in the early 1970s—while Shackley was in Saigon—the base chief in Nha Trang created a phony network of informants and embezzled the money he supposedly used for the network. The man was never prosecuted for this age-old intelligence scam. Snepp demanded to know why Shackley and others had let him off the hook. Snepp told Parmenter he was not threatening

---

* Stockwell soon learned from an Agency contact that Snepp was passing information on him to the Agency. Mad about that, he accused Snepp of a breach of faith.

anyone, but Parmenter certainly had cause to assume otherwise. Shackley, who received a stream of memos on Snepp's contacts with the Agency, must have wondered too. What skeletons might Snepp reveal?

Snepp shared his upset with the Director. In a memo to Turner, he outlined a number of concerns. Was the CIA considering taking legal action against him? he asked. Why had the Nha Trang base chief been allowed to resign and escape prosecution? ("It is not too much to say," Snepp wrote, "that [the base chief's] misuse of funds contributed to a monumental intelligence failure, one that affected the very heart of American policy in Vietnam.") He reported that before he had helped Stockwell publish his letter of resignation he called Shackley to see if Stockwell's complaints could be registered through official channels. When Shackley failed to return the call, Snepp went ahead in assisting Stockwell. (In a subsequent memo, Shackley claimed Snepp had not contacted him.) Snepp reiterated his complaint that Shackley, as chief of the East Asia Division, had turned a blind eye to the problems of the evacuation of South Vietnam and that the "Agency attempted to discourage any soul-searching on the Vietnam fiasco." He accused Shackley of offering help to a favored journalist working on a Vietnam book. Snepp asserted to Turner that he had decided to go public only after the Agency refused him a say internally.

The top brass hustled to respond to the charges. Knoche reported to Turner that the Nha Trang base chief was forced to retire and repay the funds but that, as Snepp alleged, the CIA had not referred the case to the Justice Department. He advised Turner not to get mixed up in the Snepp affair.

But Turner wanted to hear out the young man. The two met on May 17, 1977. Much of the hour-long discussion centered on Snepp's belief that the Agency assisted preferred journalists with classified leaks. He knew of one journalist willing to swear that Shackley had offered this reporter sensitive information. Only weeks earlier, Turner had decided —due to Shackley's relationship with Wilson—that the ADDO was a man of poor judgment. He was not going to take Snepp at his word. But here was more reason for the admiral to be wary of his ADDO.

After the meeting, John Morrison, Jr., the deputy general counsel, observed that Snepp's "aggrieved feelings" might be mitigated if Snepp were allowed to express them. But it was too late for that. Shackley had such an opportunity two years earlier, and he had passed.

Turner, after months in the job, still believed Wells, Shackley, and others were resisting him. Getting answers out of the old boys seemed harder than recruiting Soviets. Turner wanted an abridged version of the Nosenko report to be assigned reading in seminars for senior officers. Well, the top career men replied, we can't get it into the next round of classes, but maybe we can distribute it in subsequent sessions. Turner kept over a dozen people on Wells's staff busy with a constant stream of inquiries about operations. It was a maddening process. After Turner received a memo on a given subject, he sent it back to Wells covered with questions written in red ink. Who is this? What is this a reference to? What is this agent going to do? Wells's staff compiled the answers. Another memo would come zooming back with more questions about the responses. Such a hands-on Director drove Agency people nuts. But Turner felt he had to cover every minor point because he could not trust Wells and Shackley.

Turner found that few operations were going on, because the Agency was in a state of shock in the wake of all the investigations. "The covert action cupboard was bare," he recalled. A take-no-chances mentality reigned. Shackley and Wells occasionally came to Turner with a proposed operation, but most were of questionable merit. Further discussion usually led to scratching them. "They never left my office denied to do something they still wanted to do," Turner claimed.

The admiral was skeptical of many covert actions. Distributing propaganda behind the Iron Curtain, planting a pro–United States news article, funding a civic group—none of this engaged him. But he did back a program to create a radio station to broadcast into a country deemed anti-American. As for political actions intended to undermine an unfriendly government, Turner did not believe his officers were capable of mounting such a campaign. "They would sometimes talk about it," he recalled, "but nothing would come of it."

Shackley, though, viewed Turner as a bumbling amateur. Turner ordered Agency officers to prepare scenarios for paramilitary actions. One asked whether paramilitary skills and supplies could help Yugoslavia repel a Soviet invasion. This seemed foolish to Shackley. Anyone could see that Yugoslav guerrillas could not win a war of attrition against a conventional Soviet army, reasoned Shackley. (This was the same man who years earlier was criticized by Agency colleagues for placing Hmong irregulars in the path of the North Vietnamese Army.) Another Turner assignment called for studying whether CIA personnel could be brought out of Langley to direct a commando raid against a military target. Shackley scoffed at this, too. CIA officers did not run such operations. Turner had seen too many movies. Agency PM specialists worked with local insurgents; they were not combat leaders.

A conspiratorial Shackley suspected Turner of being ridiculous on purpose. "The end result," Shackley asserted, "was that Turner's scenarios were so far removed from world realities that subordinates con cluded he either was obtuse or wanted to convince them to junk the CIA paramilitary capability as unworkable."

Shackley thought Turner might be purposely undermining the covert action wing. The admiral thought Shackley and Wells were cowed and inept. The two camps could not communicate with each other. Turner also saw a cautiousness in the operation directorate's reading of new regulations regarding whom it could spy on. (Americans could only be targeted when they were involved in activities related to foreign intelligence.) Turner thought the rules were too tight and prevented necessary espionage. He wondered if he should relax them. But when he contemplated a change, his thoughts shifted to Shackley: How would these guys, who are so injudicious as to consort with suspected criminals, respond if I ease the restrictions? With Shackley in mind, Turner allowed the tight interpretation to stand.

The Director was further rapped by his subordinates—Shackley among them—for not being an aggressive advocate of human intelligence. He was too hung up on technical intelligence, satellites, communications intercepts, and other nuts-and-bolts. The DCI, Shackley later griped, had "little feel for . . . the human source aspect of intelligence gathering." Turner did believe that technical intelligence produced more consistent results and that back-alley espionage was largely an affair of luck. A talented officer could skillfully execute an operation, but whether the agent was hooked, or whether the agent gained access to desired information, was a matter of fortune. Turner thought the old-fashioned espionage crowd at Langley was stuck in the past. Sure, you can't get rid of the spies, they serve a purpose—when you're lucky enough to have one in the right place. But satellites are more reliable. This attitude made Agency people livid.

The atmosphere at Langley deteriorated so much that deputy DCI Hank Knoche decided to do something about it. While Turner was out of town, he called several hundred top Agency people to the auditorium and spoke to them about Turner. When Turner returned, Knoche insisted he read the transcript. That's okay, Turner said, I trust you. Knoche pressed the Director to review it. As Turner sat in his house and flipped the pages, his anger increased. The general drift of Knoche's remarks was that Stan Turner was not such a bad guy; it's only that he did not understand the way we do things here at the CIA. In time, he'll come around. Knoche thought he was sticking up for his boss. Instead, his speech prompted Turner to ask for his resignation. Knoche complied with the request. Turner wanted to send a signal: he was not going to respond to the wishes of the organization; the organization would respond to him.

Months later, Turner replaced Knoche with Frank Carlucci, a Foreign

Service officer serving as U.S. ambassador to Portugal. Just what Langley needed, Shackley thought, a second-in-command who, like his boss, possessed no in-depth experience in intelligence.

Pushing satellites over people, micromanaging operations, disciplining wayward officers, doubting the honor of senior officers—all of that was nothing compared with what Turner had in store for the DDO bureaucracy: staff reductions. When Turner declared his intention to trim the bloated clandestine service, Agency people considered it an announcement of war. The old guard, Shackley included, saw Turner bent on self-emasculation. The enemy was no longer at the front gate. He was inside, and he was swinging a cleaver.

Since moving into Langley, Turner had met periodically with employees from the guts of the CIA: low-level analysts, communications officers, secretaries, and junior officers of the clandestine service. He heard from the latter that they were fed up with all the old people supervising them. The DDO, with its 8,000 employees, was overmanaged and overstaffed at the top. There were not enough slots into which the younger officers could be promoted. These complaints bolstered Turner's own impressions. Too many old-timers were hanging on. He learned that a recent Directorate of Operations management study had suggested cutting 1,350 positions over five years. Turner decided it was time to execute the suggestion. But 1,350 jobs were too many. He settled on 820 as a target number, to be cut over two years.

On August 7, 1977, Turner assembled his top people in the auditorium to reveal his plan. Since the end of the Vietnam War, he said, the Agency had not reduced proportionately. The point was to make the clandestine service leaner, more effective, and to provide more opportunity for those in its ranks. All effort will be made to reduce the numbers through attrition and early retirement. Only those employees ranked poor in performance will be affected. The cuts will target more senior than junior officers.

The news rumbled through Langley. Some officers perceived Turner as more a threat than the CIA's enemies on Capitol Hill and in Moscow. Enraged officials referred to him as *Stanislav* Turner. Shackley thought Turner was destroying his directorate, but he did not speak against the plan. No one in the DDO directly challenged Turner. "Had they put up a real battle," Turner recalled, "I would not have been able to go ahead."

But CIA employees did not go along smoothly. Many veterans who served with Shackley in Berlin, Miami, Laos, or Vietnam, approached the ADDO and asked him to stop all this. Some viewed the strong-willed Shackley as more a natural champion of the directorate than Wells. "This made his burden especially acute," said his friend Jamie Jameson. "It was a crisis in his life." But Shackley did not envision a way to mount a successful end run. There was nothing for him to do shy of resigning in protest—and that he did not do.

It was up to Wells to decide who should go. For three months, he, Shackley, and others worked on the plan. The pink slips went out on October 31, 1977. "Beat Navy" signs appeared on Agency bulletin boards before the Army-Navy football game. Keepers of the secrets broke their vow of silence and turned to the media. Newspaper articles reported on the "Halloween Massacre" at Langley. Reflecting the arguments of horrified DDO employees, media accounts claimed that Turner was striking at the heart of the service, that he was jeopardizing its covert action capability, that he was cruelly dumping patriotic Americans.

Letting go of 820 spies was a major move. Station chiefs in London, Bonn, Vienna, Ottawa, and several Latin American capitals were being "separated." But, as Turner later claimed, only seventeen people were fired. One hundred and forty-seven were forced into early retirement (which to many felt like dismissal). A few dozen were transferred to other parts of the Agency. The rest of the cutbacks occurred through attrition. But rumor and gossip spread quickly: the CIA was in a shambles, its espionage operations devastated. "Why did this legend build up?" Turner reflected. "Because this change was seen by the DDO as my taking control of the DDO. These people really sincerely believed that no outsider could understand and manage something as sensitive and unique as the DDO. There is no question in my mind that if you can't, then the whole government is in trouble."

Shackley, who had drawn accusations of ruthlessness for years, later wrote that Turner's greatest sin was his absence of compassion—a fair charge. There was, Shackley recognized, a case for personnel reduction. "What troubled the CIA's senior managers and employees most, however, was Turner's failure to grasp the significance of the human factor that is such an integral part of a well-balanced intelligence organization," he observed. Shackley asserted that Turner rejected the "compassionate solution" of a gradual reduction and forfeited the confidence and respect of his officers.

The tangible consequence of Turner's cuts was not so dire. The staff reductions did not diminish the CIA's espionage ability, according to John McMahon, a senior Agency man who later took over the clandestine service. Turner's move did hit hard on the paramilitary side of the CIA —but the PM crowd did not have much work these days. The cutback was no "real disaster," McMahon said. The impact was in spirit, not effect.

Days after the Halloween Massacre, another blow came. Richard Helms, the former Director who had sent Shackley to Laos, Vietnam, and the Western Hemisphere Division, appeared in a federal courtroom in Washington and pleaded no contest to the charge that his 1973 testimony to Congress on Chile and the CIA was inaccurate. "You now stand before this court in disgrace and shame," district judge Barrington Parker told Helms. It was as if the entire CIA was in front of the judge, as he lectured the patrician Helms: "There are those employed in the intelligence security community of this country...who feel that they have a license to operate freely outside the dictates of the law and otherwise to orchestrate as they see fit. Public officials at every level, whatever their position, like any other person, must respect and honor the Constitution and the laws of the United States." Parker fined Helms $2,000 and handed him a suspended sentence of two years. Minutes after the hearing ended, Helms proclaimed his conviction "a badge of honor."

The former DCI had arranged a plea bargain: two misdemeanor counts, no admission of guilt, and no trial. The no-trial stipulation was beneficial for both sides. Helms was spared the embarrassment. The U.S. government was spared the necessity of making CIA witnesses and documents available to the Helms defense team. Agency people, perhaps Shackley, no longer had to worry that they would be forced to testify against their former colleague.

The disposition of the Helms case suggested that the Justice Department had no stomach for pursuing other CIA officers. But Shackley was not in the clear yet.

It was a lousy autumn for an Agency loyalist—firings in the DDO, Turner at the wheel, Helms scolded. Then came Snepp's book. In mid-November, copies of *Decent Interval* were released. Snepp had not submitted it to the Agency for review; he and his publisher, Random House, had handled publication in strict secrecy. The book's allegations that the CIA had committed major intelligence blunders in Vietnam made the front pages. The main villains were chief of station Tom Polgar and U.S. Ambassador Graham Martin. But numerous pages of Snepp's long, detailed account were devoted to Shackley, his heavy-handed reign in Saigon, his spooky and demanding demeanor, his interaction with Polgar, and his role in the Agency's final failures in Vietnam. It was the most complete portrait of the ADDO then available to the public. It was not flattering.

Finally, the Agency took Shackley's persistent advice and initiated legal proceedings against Snepp. Shackley had recommended such a move a year earlier, when perhaps it might have prevented publication. But the lawyers of Langley had decided against bringing a suit, which would have challenged a strong prevailing presumption in American law against prior restraint. Now Justice Department lawyers, representing the CIA, charged Snepp with breach of contract for violating his secrecy oath. For that, the government lawyers wanted all the money Snepp earned from the book. They would not accuse Snepp of disclosing classified information, merely that he had broken the sacred oath. Snepp could not be stopped. But maybe future Snepps could be. For Shackley that was the only consolation.*

V

After the Halloween Massacre, Turner went after the top. The Director thought it was time for Wells to go. The impersonal way in which Wells had handled the cutbacks—people were informed of their termination in two-sentence notices—had made him unpopular in the directorate and undermined his position as its head. Of more concern to Turner, newspaper reports—leaks from CIA officers—were undercutting the Director. Posters poking fun at Turner appeared on bulletin boards in Langley. "Wells was not willing to stand up to them and say, 'This guy is our boss and you do what he says or get off the boat,' " the admiral recalled. Turner offered to find Wells another post. Wells declined and agreed to leave.

Wells's departure led to a showdown between Turner and Shackley. The ADDO once was on the fast track to be Deputy Director for Operations. But now it was a different world. The CIA was in the hands of an outsider who did not abide by the old rules and who did not trust Shackley. The Wilson affair was an indelible stain. Turner found it easy to justify his feelings about Shackley. When he asked a group of senior officers who should succeed Wells, "ninety percent of those people said anybody but Shackley," Turner later noted. "Ten percent said Ted Shackley—and they shouted it." Shackley evoked tremendous loyalty in a small number of officers, but after decades of working with him many CIA people resented Shackley's imperial manner, his rampant ambition, his success, his manipulation of facts. After almost thirty years in the Company, Shackley drew little support from the ranks. And he had run out of superiors to impress.

Not for a moment did Turner consider Shackley for the DDO post. Instead, Turner chose John McMahon, a long-time Agency careerist. McMahon, who had little experience in the operations directorate, took

---

* On February 19, 1980, the Supreme Court ruled six-to-three that the secrecy oath was an enforceable contract and that Snepp had violated his obligation by not submitting his manuscript for review. The court ordered Snepp to turn over all earnings from the book. The majority rejected Snepp's defense, presented by the American Civil Liberties Union, that the secrecy agreement was a restraint on the constitutionally protected right of free speech.

the job—but with reluctance. "Ted Shackley should've had that job," McMahon said years afterward.*

Turner had to do something about Shackley. After being passed over, Shackley could not be expected to stay in the associate slot, and the Director wanted an all-new management team for the directorate. For months, he had been thinking about where he could shuffle Shackley. Then the perfect opening appeared: a position at the National Intelligence Tasking Center (NITC), which coordinated the collection activities of various intelligence services. For a senior operations officer who retained high hopes, the assignment was akin to a bureaucratic Siberia.

Shortly after Christmas, Turner called his top officers to his conference room. Shackley and Wells were not there. I've asked Mr. Wells and Mr. Shackley to step aside, the Director announced. He praised the contributions each had made to the organization. They have done a marvelous job, Turner said. He offered no more explanation other than it was time for new blood. He introduced McMahon and the new ADDO, John Stein.

After the session, one of the attendees dropped by to see Wells. The outgoing DDO was packing up his office. What do you think happened? the senior officer asked. It's those damn young turks, Wells replied. They got to the admiral. They think they ought to replace the old codgers. They want to make room at the top. The senior officer shared his own theory with Wells: Turner was an admiral who had not witnessed combat. He was full of complexes. He could not work with men like Wells, old OSS veterans who once parachuted behind enemy lines. Wells and Shackley knew more about the intelligence business than Turner, and the admiral could not stand that. Neither mentioned Turner's major complaint: he had absolutely no faith in Wells and Shackley.

Turner's decision to replace Wells and Shackley immediately leaked to *The Washington Post*. Unidentified CIA people complained about both Turner and Wells. It seemed as if the Agency was in chaos. The account noted that Shackley and Turner had tussled over management policy. At one point, after one nasty confrontation, Shackley had stormed out of the Director's office. Right after that, Dana Meiggs, Shackley's longtime secretary, had called the logistics office to prepare for the removal of the secured communications equipment installed at Shackley's home.

In February of 1978, Shackley departed a demoralized clandestine

---

* McMahon felt a little uncomfortable as DDO. At his first staff meeting with senior directorate officers, he said, "One of you guys should be sitting in my seat."

service and became associate deputy to the DCI for collection tasking. His office was no longer down the hall from the Director's. Now each day, Shackley reported to the National Intelligence Tasking Center in downtown Washington. There officials representing the CIA, the National Security Agency, the Defense Intelligence Agency, and other intelligence services coordinated intelligence collection among the various players of the national security bureaucracy. The assignment, recalled a Shackley colleague, was "death for Ted."

The NITC was a Turner innovation. Its goal was to produce less overlap and more efficient collection. Once again, Turner ran into resistance, this time mostly from the military, which was reluctant to share its own collection assets. Turner also knew that the CIA disliked disclosing its capabilities to other intelligence services—to say, for instance, we have an agent in Poland who can try to find out what is coming out of that factory spotted on satellite photographs.

Shackley's new home was "a doomed endeavor," remarked Fred Feer, a CIA analyst assigned to the NITC. Turner used his own people to run the center, and he had placed retired Lieutenant General Frank Camm, another outsider, in charge. "The more they pushed, the stronger the intelligence community veterans resisted," Feer said.*

Shackley was in exile. But he joked to friends that he had the best office in town. The NITC, based in the former Selective Service headquarters, across the street from the Old Executive Office Building, had been renovated as a downtown base for Turner. The furniture was plush leather. On the wall of Shackley's office hung a photograph of an airstrip in the Laotian jungle. He pointed it out with pride to visitors. Shackley told people Turner had hinted that after a stint at the NITC he might be brought back to the clandestine service. The choices were limited for someone as senior as Shackley, with the main options the four elite chief of station postings: London, Paris, Bonn, and Tokyo. The most successful senior officials often capped off their careers in these spots. If Shackley won one of the coveted jobs, he would be back on the team, rehabilitated, and perhaps in the running for a higher post in another administration.

His friend Tom Clines, though, had tired of waiting for the clouds to lift. Turner had derailed his career by nixing his assignment to Kingston.

---

* By the time he reached the NITC Feer was skeptical about the whole intelligence game. "The typical defense of intelligence officers is that you only know about our screw-ups," he said. "You don't know our successes. But the successes are not all that many, and most of those are not all that dramatic. The question is how such good people—bright, motivated and sometimes caring—get it wrong so often."

Clines enjoyed his current job as DDO liaison with the Pentagon, in which he regularly met with military intelligence chiefs to discuss their proposed clandestine operations, which had to be approved by the Agency. A CIA man distrusted by his own director, he was transmitting Agency gospel to the U.S. military. But Clines realized he was not going anywhere in the CIA as long as Turner remained in charge.

In early 1978, he resolved it was time to punch out. He thought Shackley also had overstayed his welcome. Clines sat down with his friend and put it to him bluntly: "Both of us—so long as Stansfield Turner and Jimmy Carter are alive—are dead meat. Let's get the hell out of here." Shackley did not want to leave. He told Clines he still hoped he could get his CIA career on track. With twenty-seven years invested, Shackley was not ready to jump.

Clines did not leave just yet. While still a Company man, he hatched a plan with Edwin Wilson to make a bundle by helping Nicaraguan strong-man Anastasio Somoza stay in power. (A Turner ban on all Agency contacts with Wilson did not stop Clines.) The idea was to sell Somoza a massive, ready-to-roll countersubversion program. Clines brought into the deal his old comrade Rafael Quintero; neither was dissuaded by Wilson's work for Qaddafi or Wilson's attempt to contract an assassination.*

Clines, Quintero, and Tina Simons, a former Capitol Hill secretary working for Wilson (her task was to flirt with Somoza), jetted to Managua to present Somoza the details. But Clines did not want the Agency, especially Turner, to know what he was doing. He had told the CIA security office he was off to the Caribbean for the weekend. The next morning, the trio met with Somoza and handed him a six-page proposal.

"Our company was formed to negate subversion," the proposal stated. "We have developed the basic techniques needed to apply flexible, graduated and covert responses that will avoid a potentially embar-

---

* Since Wilson's brush with the law in September of 1976, the former CIA man had supplied Qaddafi over 42,000 pounds of C-4 plastic explosive and had enlisted U.S. Green Berets to train a Libyan commando team. Wilson, who had broken with Frank Terpil, provided Libya with U.S. intelligence he obtained from a DIA official. In December of 1977, the Department of Justice decided not to prosecute Wilson for those activities it knew about: an earlier shipment of explosive materials and the conspiracy to murder the Libyan dissident. But E. Lawrence Barcella, Jr., a top lawyer in the U.S. attorney's office for Washington, decided to pursue his own case against Wilson. In January of 1978, he brought before a grand jury Kevin Mulcahy, the former Wilson employee. Quintero also testified before the grand jury. Barcella's hunt for Wilson was on, when Clines and Quintero entered this business deal with Wilson.

rassing overt commitment on the part of the Nicaraguan government."
In other words, we will do the dirty work for you. They offered to set
up "secure intelligence nets" and "an excellent counterintelligence
force" and to conduct psychological warfare. The project would penetrate subversive groups and identify their leaders "so that government
forces can neutralize them." The proposal promised to provide Somoza
"with an excellent intelligence organization enabling your personnel to
carry out 'search and destroy' missions against your enemies in the most
effective way."

Somoza read the paper carefully. He liked its ideas, but he said he
had a problem with page six—where the cost estimates were listed.
Clines, Wilson, and Quintero were asking for $650,000. That's too much,
Somoza said. I'll put together an operation like this on my own. Thank
you. To Simons, he added, I'll call you later.*

The wheels kept turning. After the Nicaraguan plan collapsed, Clines
started to set up his own business. With Quintero and Ricardo Chavez,
another former CIA contract officer, Clines established API Distributors.
The plan was to sell drilling equipment to PEMEX, the Mexican state oil
company. Chavez had connections in Mexico that the three hoped to
parlay into contracts. Wilson provided API space in his Houston office.
Company literature eventually would list Ted Shackley as a consultant.

Clines filed his retirement papers. While they were being processed,
Jimmy Carter on August 16, 1978, flew by helicopter to Langley to deliver
a pep talk to CIA employees. In recent months, there had been more
disclosures: the Agency had infiltrated African-American groups in the
1960s, misled Congress about its covert war in Angola in the mid-1970s,
and used Nazi war criminals as agents after World War II. To hundreds
of Company people assembled outdoors, Carter said that CIA officers
must be "more pure and more clean and more decent and more honest" than other government workers. He praised his audience: "There
is a growing appreciation for what this agency does. . . . There is now a
stability in the CIA."

Three months later, Carter would criticize the leadership of the
Agency—Shackley included, though not by name—for failing to warn
of the anti-Shah revolution in Iran and order his national security aides
to improve the quality of intelligence reaching his desk.

---

* Clines later said that Shackley was unaware of his trip to Nicaragua. But while
Clines was conniving on the Agency's dime—and consorting with Wilson—he and
Shackley entered into apparently their first joint business venture. The two purchased as an investment a $70,000 bungalow in McLean, Virginia—about a mile
from CIA headquarters.

• • •

Shackley was not out of trouble for the ITT cover-up. In March of 1978, the Justice Department had filed six-count felony charges against two ITT officials, accusing them of lying to the Church subcommittee in 1973. Both Edward Gerrity, Jr., a senior vice president, and Robert Berrellez, ITT's PR man in Latin America in 1970, allegedly had conspired with Hal Hendrix to block the Senate inquiry into the anti-Allende alliance forged between the Agency and ITT. Berrellez's indictment noted that he had met a CIA official in 1972 and pledged that he and Hendrix would deny ever having contact with the Agency in Latin America. This lie had been essential to Shackley's effort to prevent the subcommittee from digging too deeply into CIA activity in Chile. Jonathan Hanke, the man Shackley had put on the case, was named repeatedly through the indictment. Hanke, Shackley, and other CIA people escaped indictment themselves—Hanke was granted immunity for his testimony—but the Justice Department's case promised to drag them into the public light of a courtroom and reveal them as conspirators in a cover-up.

In the summer of 1978, the Justice Department served Shackley notice that he could expect to be a witness in the Berrellez trial. The Agency was being squeezed from both sides. Justice considered putting in the witness seat not just Shackley but a long line of his colleagues: William Broe, Henry Hecksher, Jonathan Hanke, Thomas Polgar, and Jacob Esterline. If it did not, then Patrick Wall, Berrellez's attorney, might call them to the stand. Wall also was demanding access to classified CIA records in order to mount his defense.

The morning of October 23, the first day of the Berrellez trial, *The Washington Post* reported that prosecutors intended to call both Richard Helms and Frank Church to the stand. But, the paper noted, the real attention-grabbers in court would be a group of less-well-known Agency men, including an officer named Ted Shackley.

Shackley and the rest were saved by Wall's wile. The trial began with a secret proceeding before Federal District Judge Aubrey E. Robinson, Jr. Justice Department lawyers were asking for a court order instructing Wall not to reveal during the trial certain CIA information without prior approval. Prosecutor John Kotelly noted that they feared that Wall, while defending Berrellez, would divulge the names of CIA agents and officers beyond those that the government was prepared to see exposed. Wall opposed the motion, and Judge Robinson declined to issue the order.

In the same hearing, the government lawyers then objected to Wall's subpoena of certain Agency documents. Wall explained he needed the documents to present one of the defenses—"that through at least one, if not more of its [officers], the Central Intelligence Agency in effect assisted and requested that Hendrix and Berrellez give the testimony they gave." He was directly referring to Hanke and suggesting Shackley and others were plotters as well. Wall signaled his intent to reveal in open court that Hernan Cubillos, the current Chilean foreign minister, was a CIA asset who had conspired with Berrellez and Hendrix. (Wall said he had seen Agency documents confirming Cubillos's relationship with Langley.) If he could show Cubillos was an agent, Wall asserted, he could enhance his argument that the CIA had encouraged Berrellez to lie to Congress. The judge quashed Wall's subpoena.

The government lawyers petitioned Robinson for a closed session in which they could ask Wall what sensitive information he intended to use in his defense. The attorneys bickered over this. With the matter unresolved, the court adjourned.

The next day, the CIA and Shackley got lucky. At a bench conference, the lawyers again argued over the protective order the Justice Department wanted and Wall's request for classified information. Nothing was worked out. Judge Robinson dismissed the jury. This trial was over. Robinson gave the government six days to decide what it desired most: another trial or the protection of Agency secrets.

The Justice Department urged the U.S. Circuit Court of Appeals to direct Robinson to adopt the protective order and retry the case. *The Washington Post* editorialized about the problem of "graymail"—the ability of persons charged with national security-related wrongdoing to dodge prosecution by threatening the release of secrets. But the appeals court turned down the Justice Department's petition. In February of 1979, the Justice Department, citing fears that secrets would be exposed, dropped the cases against Berrellez and Gerrity. Shackley would not have to testify.

Senator Frank Church—the man who had been lied to by CIA and ITT officials—denounced the Justice Department's decision as "outrageous." Secrets were not as important as justice, he declared. But to the CIA they were the most important things. Shackley's role in the cover-up would remain one of those secrets.

Several times Shackley approached Turner and asked if there might be a more suitable job for him in the intelligence community than his post at the tasking center. Turner always waved him off. In mid-1979, Frank Camm announced he was resigning as the head of the NITC. Shackley believed he was in line for that post. It was not a prestigious job, and the center was stumbling along. But if he became its director, Shackley would have a fiefdom of his own. Maybe he could transform the NITC into an effective organization and turn the chief's position into one of influence.

The promotion did not come. It was painfully obvious: Turner was not about to hand him Paris, London, Bonn, or Tokyo. Shackley had hung on for over a year since vacating the ADDO's office. His patience was exhausted. He was going nowhere in Turner's service, and he was anxious about the direction in which Turner was leading the Agency. After twenty-eight years, Shackley decided it was time to exit the Central Intelligence Agency.

There was a farewell ceremony at headquarters for Shackley. The man who once hoped to command the entire U.S. intelligence community was awarded his third Distinguished Intelligence Medal.

During his final days as a CIA officer, Shackley stopped by Turner's office to say good-bye. I don't understand, he told the Director, why you and I never got along. Shackley said he was sorry for that. Turner had the good grace not to respond directly. The reason for Turner's attitude toward Shackley was clear: Ed Wilson. The Director never could believe that Shackley had allowed himself to get close to such a thug. How could it have happened? Was Shackley duped by Wilson, or was Shackley hiding something? In either event, he had little sympathy for Shackley. Turner in his memoirs later mused on the impact of the clandestine life on CIA people: "Hiding your accomplishments, leading a double life, regularly facing difficult moral issues, and being subjected to criticism for doing what was acceptable at the time one did it can all take their toll. In many ways, a clandestine career can be said to deform the person involved." But the contact between Shackley and Wilson was wholly unacceptable. That was it for Turner; no sympathy, case closed.

With Shackley in front of him for the last time, Turner kept these thoughts private. He muttered some meaningless remarks. Shackley turned to leave. Turner chuckled to himself. This man who had spent his entire adult life within the CIA really did not seem to understand the problem. That said a lot about the Agency.

CHAPTER TEN

IN THE COLD

I

IN a suburban Virginia office, a proud Thomas Clines had something to show Ted Shackley. Look at this, Clines said, as he handed Shackley a piece of paper. Shackley studied it and became upset. Clines had placed a picture of a rifle on the checks for one of the companies Clines had created, a firm for which Shackley was a consultant. That was a damn stupid thing to do, Shackley told his friend. What's the big deal? Clines responded. This is going to be a weapons-trading company. But Shackley knew it is not always advantageous to identify an arms firm as such. The name of the corporation, Systems Services International, was innocuous. People who needed to know it was a munitions company would not require a rifle-bearing check. This was poor tradecraft.

In his new line of work, Shackley intended to be as discreet and cautious as he had been as an intelligence officer. Such care would serve him well in the years ahead, when Shackley would become the elusive target for federal investigators, journalists, and private sleuths.

Shackley was in the cold, no longer a high priest in a closed community. But where do old intelligence officers go? Many of their acquired skills—running agents, arranging secret payoffs, suborning journalists and political officials, bargaining with indigenous tribal warriors—do not translate easily into mainstream business. Those who toiled in the clandestine service cannot tell prospective employers of their previous accomplishments. The Agency routinely holds retirement seminars for departing officers. Counselors warn retirees-to-be that the adjustment might not be smooth, and they advise how to go about finding new jobs.

Shackley did not need this. He was about to join a tightly knit subculture: former Company men who put their intelligence skills to use for private business and foreign governments. And he had a friend who had been waiting for him on the outside, Tom Clines.

After leaving the Agency in 1978, Clines, the back-slapping, fast-and-loose schemer, incorporated a variety of companies. He had a host of strike-it-rich ideas: oil equipment in Mexico, foodstuffs in Latin America, arms all over the world. But he needed the help of Edwin Wilson. In 1978, Clines started his API Distributors with Wilson's assistance. Then in 1979, Clines required half a million dollars to get his business empire going. Wilson came through with the funds.

The loan was set up by Edward Coughlin, a Geneva-based attorney for Wilson. In a memo, Coughlin wrote of the loan: "It is proposed that an offshore corporation be organized with, eventually, five equal shareholders. Four of these 20% shareholders are individual U.S. citizens, and the fifth would be a foreign corporation, not controlled by U.S. persons." The shareholders were not named. Their identities one day would be a mystery for government investigators and others to consider.

The funds secured, Clines opened the blandly named International Research and Trade, Limited, a Bermuda corporation, which became an umbrella for API and Systems Services International. In the spring of 1979, he met Hussein Salem, a former Egyptian official with a line on a large contract for shipping U.S. military hardware to Egypt. (In the wake of the Camp David peace accords, billions of dollars in American arms were flowing to Egypt.) In a month or so, Clines had a deal. He would be a 49 percent partner in the Egyptian American Transportation and Services Corporation; Salem would own 51 percent of EATSCO. Soon afterward, EATSCO won an exclusive contract from Cairo to ship U.S. military equipment to Egypt. Clines's business would submit its bills to the Defense Security Assistance Agency, where Erich von Marbod, an associate of Shackley, Clines, and Secord, was acting director. Clines had scored. He soon would be loaded like Wilson—raking it in, jetting around the world, doing well with the ladies.

Clines invited Shackley to share the ride. In September of 1979, a month after he had left the Agency, Shackley became a consultant to API Distributors. Clines was concentrating on EATSCO and asked Shackley to manage API, which was still not yet off the ground in the oil equipment business. Clines also signed up Shackley as a consultant to the Wilson-funded IRT, and he gave Shackley $2,000 a month to write reports for EATSCO on the political situation in Egypt and other countries.

All told, according to Clines, he paid his former boss about $50,000 a year. "I was trying to give him a jump start," Clines said, "like what I got from Ed Wilson."

Shackley was aware that Clines had borrowed money from Ed Wilson. Oddly, he was not concerned. Shackley's relationship with Wilson had virtually ended his decades-long rise in the Agency. He had been warned that Wilson was aiding and abetting Qaddafi. He knew of Wilson's attempt to solicit Quintero to commit a murder. But the Wilson loan to Clines did not trigger any alarms for Shackley. Though he harbored hopes of returning to the intelligence field, Shackley joined a set of endeavors supported by a person soon to be the most notorious Company man in the world.

Shackley the businessman was moving in circles full of shady ex-spooks. He chatted several times with Bernie Houghton, a mysterious Texan connected to the Nugan Hand Bank, a shadowy Australian financial concern doing business with former intelligence operatives and drug dealers. (Houghton frequently huddled with Wilson in Geneva.) When Michael Hand, a founder of the bank and a former CIA operative in Indochina, passed through Washington, he and Shackley talked business, but, by Shackley's account, nothing evolved. The Nugan Hand Bank collapsed in 1980, after cofounder Frank Nugan was found shot to death in his Mercedes outside Sydney. His death was ruled a suicide. In the ensuing scandal, Hand disappeared.

There was no clear link between Shackley and the bank's activities, but his friends and associates were implicated directly in the affair. Near the time of Nugan's death, Clines and Quintero visited Wilson's office in Geneva. According to a subsequent Australian government investigation, the pair rifled through a bag of material left by Houghton. They found one document and removed it. "We've got to keep Dick's name out of this," Clines reportedly said at the time, possibly a reference to Secord. The Australian investigators never explained the significance of the episode.* After Nugan's death, the enigmatic Houghton—a restaurateur before signing up with the bank—tried to arrange the purchase of another bank, which would allow the Nugan Hand operation to continue. The buyer-to-be was Ricardo Chavez, the former CIA operative who worked with Shackley at API Distributors. Australian investigators later suspected that Chavez was fronting for Clines, but the Corporate Affairs Commission of New South Wales, which probed the bank, expressed frustration at being unable to decipher fully the Nugan Hand

---

* A year later, Secord became a deputy assistant secretary of defense. In this post, he oversaw U.S. weapons deals in the Middle East and South Asia.

affair. Crucial to solving the mystery, it noted, was discerning more about Chavez, Houghton, Hand, and Wilson. Each of these men was connected to Shackley. The Australian investigators, though, failed to find answers to many riddles of the Nugan Hand scandal.

Officially Shackley did not remain part of the Clines consortium for long. API Distributors was not much of a going concern, and Shackley was irritated by the attitude of his longtime subordinate. Throughout their years in the Company, Shackley had called the shots for Clines. Now Clines was in control. Shackley complained to Agency friends that Clines had misled him. What Shackley had believed to be a partnership was a Clines-dominated venture.

Shackley left Clines in mid-1980 and formed his own firms. With his wife, Hazel, and Jamie Jameson, a former CIA Soviet specialist, Shackley created Research Associates International, what he called a risk analysis company.* Around the time Shackley and Jameson were launching RAI, the pair met with Peter Karlow, who had run CIA technical services in Germany in the 1950s when Shackley was stationed there. At a restaurant in downtown Washington, the two asked Karlow if he wanted to join their private sector intelligence service. "Ted was ticked off at Stan Turner," Karlow recalled. "He was going to set up a competitive business. He was all steamed up." Some intelligence watchers came to wonder if RAI was an Agency front. But Shackley and his associates worried that the Agency was spying on them, that the NSA was monitoring their telexes.

Shackley also established TGS International. He termed it a "logistics problem-solving company." The firm's endeavors were hardly the work of former spies: remodeling homes, selling modular storage equipment, brokering international food deals. One time it tried to find 747s for an Italian company doing business in China. It sold groceries and canned meats to a supermarket chain in the Bahamas. Shackley worked with an Italian trying to sell helicopters in Latin America.

Shackley and his companies eventually settled into the top-floor suite of an office building in Rosslyn, Virginia, across the Potomac from Georgetown. To reach Shackley, visitors had to ride the public elevator to the thirteenth floor and transfer to a small private elevator that carried them to the fourteenth floor. Then they approached a large, heavy door

---

* "Political risk assessment is to business what intelligence is to government," Shackley wrote in a 1983 article. Most information needed for risk assessment, he noted, comes from open sources, such as newspapers, government reports, trade association papers. But what "separates the men from the boys in the risk analysis business" is access to nonpublished data.

with several locks. To gain entrance, visitors identified themselves through a sophisticated intercom system. There even seemed to be a small television camera that spied on visitors.

Though he threw himself into private enterprise, Shackley believed he could reenter U.S. intelligence. He even contemplated returning as DCI, and he had cause for encouragement. In the early phases of the 1980 presidential campaign, George Bush, the former CIA Director, was a contender for the Republican presidential nomination. Candidate Bush was surrounded by campaign aides who were former Agency officers. Hazel Shackley worked for his primary campaign.

Bush lost the nomination to Ronald Reagan. But in August, Reagan selected Bush as his running mate. Past and present spooks could again hope that their former colleague soon would be in the White House.

Shortly after Bush was named to the Republican ticket, Shackley and Hazel visited Jameson at his family's country house in Maine, near the Bush clan's summer estate. Bush was in Maine then, and Shackley asked Jameson, whose family was friendly with the Bushes, if Jameson could arrange for him to see Bush. "Ted was not sure how to plug in," Jameson recalled. But he was looking for a way back.

On a Sunday afternoon, Shackley and Jameson spent a few hours with Bush at his home. They sat in a living room, with a large window that looked out on a cove. As Barbara Bush served hors d'oeuvres and drinks, they chatted about Stan Turner and Shackley's departure from the Agency. Shackley made it clear he preferred the days of Bush's tenure. Returning to the CIA was on Shackley's mind, but he did not raise the subject explicitly. "There was no real discussion of that," Jameson noted. "Ted had hopes that might occur. Part of [the reason for seeing Bush] I presume was to remind Bush that he was still out there."

Shackley later claimed he was not lobbying Bush for any job. As far as Jameson said he knew, this was the only discussion Shackley held with candidate Bush. But within the spook world the belief spread that Shackley was close to Bush. Rafael Quintero was saying that Shackley met with Bush every week. He told one associate that should Reagan and Bush triumph, Shackley was considered a potential DCI.

Shackley was not just waiting to see what happened in the election. He resolutely sought business opportunities and found a receptive audience for his unique talents in Italy. He did so by hooking up with Michael Ledeen, a scholar-journalist-spook. Ledeen, a bearded forty-year-old world-class bridge player, had crafted an unusual career. In the early 1970s, he was denied tenure at Washington University in part due to questions about the integrity of his scholarship. He moved to Rome and became a correspondent for *The New Republic,* filing stories on the perils of Eurocommunism. In 1977 he settled in Washington and joined the hawkish Center for Strategic and International Studies and started penning articles on intelligence and terrorism for *New York* magazine. In one alarmist piece, he declared that a Soviet mole might have penetrated the highest levels of the U.S. government.

Along the way, Ledeen cultivated Shackley as a source—and treated him kindly in print. In a March 3, 1980, *New York* piece, Ledeen slammed Stansfield Turner for mismanaging the CIA. In the article, Ledeen touted Shackley as "one of the most talented members of the DDO." Turner's failure to promote Shackley, Ledeen wrote, proved he was an unfit Director. Months after the story appeared, Ledeen and Shackley were business partners; their client was Italian intelligence.

General Giuseppe Santovito, head of SISMI, the military intelligence service of Italy, feared his spies were not sufficiently skilled in obtaining information quickly overseas. Santovito turned to Ledeen, for whom he had been a confidential source. Ledeen recruited Shackley for the project. The two devised a sort of war game and flew to Rome to "play" with SISMI officers. In the scenario, a prominent Italian abroad fell into a jam, and the Italian spies had to discover what had happened as fast as possible. With Shackley as the lead expert, he and Ledeen guided the Italians through the process: this is what you can ask the host intelligence service to do for you, this is how you can use diplomatic channels. It was basic stuff. Shackley pocketed about $20,000 and placed it in a bank in Bermuda. There was, Ledeen insisted later, nothing sinister in any of this.

But near the time of this exercise, Shackley's partner was involved in true intrigue. Ledeen was chasing a story that would reveal that Billy Carter, the President's brother, had visited Libya in 1979 and accepted from the Qaddafi government a $50,000 payment and a $220,000 loan related to an oil deal. According to a later indictment in an Italian court, Ledeen obtained information for this story from his and Shackley's client, SISMI. Shortly before the 1980 U.S. presidential election, Ledeen had, courtesy of Italian intelligence, a major scoop that might help the prospects of conservative champion Ronald Reagan.*

The story, which Ledeen cowrote with conservative journalist Arnaud de Borchgrave, appeared in *The New Republic* and prompted a row in the U.S. media over "Billygate." Ledeen failed to mention in his author's identification that, thanks to the help of Shackley, he was a paid consultant to Italian intelligence. Such a disclosure would have prompted the query: had Italian intelligence sought to affect an American election?

Spies turned entrepreneurs do what all business people do: exploit

---

* General Santovito, Ledeen's friend and the head of SISMI, was a prominent member of the international right-wing, secret Masonic lodge called P-2.

contacts. After twenty-eight years in the CIA, Shackley's range of contacts centered on spooks. Using Felix Rodriguez as a broker, he attempted to sell modular storage equipment in Venezuela. He and Rodriguez tried to peddle drone missiles—which could be used for military or civilian missions—to a firm in Caracas. Shackley renewed his acquaintance with a man he had failed to enlist as a spy: Albert Hakim.

The Iranian-American contacted Shackley in the fall of 1980. Hakim was figuring a way to make a buck off the vicious Iran-Iraq war. He knew that the Abadan oil refinery in Iran had been damaged. Anyone with a proposal for repairing the refinery once the war was done would be well positioned to draw large profits. Hakim had heard that Shackley was now in the oil equipment business. The two got together, bruited business ideas. Soon Shackley joined Hakim's payroll as a risk analyst. His monthly retainer topped $5,000. Shackley was not deterred by the fact that Hakim—as reported in 1976 CIA cable traffic—had earned an unsavory reputation in Iran.

On December 5 and 6, 1980, a few dozen former spooks, journalists, Capitol Hill staffers, and foreign intelligence officers gathered in a Washington conference room. They had all been invited by the National Strategy Information Center, a conservative think tank, to participate in one of several conferences designed to shape the intelligence agenda of the 1980s. The mood at the gathering was hopeful. Jimmy Carter had been trounced by Ronald Reagan, who favored unleashing the U.S. intelligence community. George Bush, the former CIA Director, was about to become Vice President. The dark days of Turner were ending.

The subject at hand was covert action: what type of dirty tricks would be needed in the 1980s? There were a series of presentations. Vernon Walters, a former deputy DCI, covered the use of political and propaganda covert actions in the decade ahead. Jamie Jameson predicted the Soviets would mount covert actions on a grand scale. Among this set, there was little disagreement on the need, effectiveness, or legitimacy of such clandestine activity. With Reagan in the White House, the participants believed, covert action would be a growth industry in the spy business.

Before his fellow ex-spies, Shackley read a paper on paramilitary covert actions in the 1980s. "As the decade of the 1980s opens," Shackley began, "Cuban mercenary armies sustain dictatorial governments in two large African nations, Angola and Ethiopia. In the Western Hemisphere, Cuban and Soviet-trained revolutionaries rule in Nicaragua. Their comrades threaten to seize neighboring El Salvador. Guatemala is in turmoil for it knows it is next in line to receive priority attention from Havana's and Moscow's guerrilla movements." The list went on: Soviet forces in the south of the Arabian peninsula, threatening the West's supply of oil; a Soviet army in Afghanistan; the Moscow-backed forces of Vietnam fighting small armies in Cambodia and Thailand; Soviet-supported rebels in Honduras and Namibia. The real threat from the Soviets, Shackley declared, was not a nuclear one; it was conventional warfare and insurgency.

Here was a cold warrior's view of the world. All trouble emanated from Moscow. The Kremlin was on the march—and achieving its dastardly ends through propaganda, deception, agents of influence, bribery, and guerrilla warfare. The United States had to respond in kind, otherwise the unthinkable would be at hand. "Failure to confront and repel the challenge posed by these techniques of international political warfare," a melodramatic Shackley pronounced, "is dangerous, recklessly so. Indeed, such failures might well lead ultimately to a nuclear confrontation between the Soviet Union, controlling much of the world, and an isolated, embattled United States turning to its nuclear arsenal in convulsive desperation." If the United States did not heed his warning, it might find itself with no choice but to wage nuclear war.

There was a way out: to fight the bastards with their own means. The conventional view toward international crises was either send in the Marines or do nothing. But there is, he said, another choice, "the third option, the use of insurgency and counterinsurgency techniques and covert action to achieve policy goals." The United States must embrace paramilitary action. It could not afford the luxurious belief that it had no right to meddle secretly in the affairs of another country. The degree to which Washington policymakers employed PM actions would indicate if they had the will to protect U.S. interests.

His geopolitical sermon finished, Shackley offered a basic briefing on how guerrilla insurgencies operate and how the United States could exploit them. But most of his presentation concerned how to counter those insurgencies directed from Moscow. His recommendations were straight out of Vietnam. Washington should help threatened governments create elite counterinsurgency units, set up Phoenix-like programs, establish population control, organize local self-defense forces, and develop civic action programs. But thanks to Turner, the Agency, Shackley griped, was no longer equipped to do so. He expected that to change. "The will to take these decisions has been rekindled in the land," Shackley proclaimed. ". . . In the 1980s we will see paramilitary operations become once again an integral part of our defense arsenal."

After Shackley finished, the audience joined the discussion. One former intelligence officer raised a delicate point: what happens to indigenous groups aided by the CIA and then later left on their own?

Obviously, the officer had the Hmong in mind. Shackley had not mentioned the tribe and its demise during his talk.

Shackley's presentation to the former spies was not an exclusive. Since leaving the CIA, Shackley had been writing—not as a past insider telling tales, but as a strategic prophet and proselytizer of paramilitary action. He found a publisher for his doom-and-gloom view, the *Reader's Digest* imprint of McGraw-Hill. The result was a slim volume titled *The Third Option: An American View of Counterinsurgency Operations,* released in March of 1981.

"I am not alone," Shackley declared bitterly at the start of the book. "Since 1976—and the election of President Jimmy Carter—approximately 2,800 American career intelligence officers like myself have retired, many of them prematurely. They were a natural treasure. . . . These men and women were professionals. Their expertise and dedication were unquestioned. They have not boasted of their accomplishments; they are true to their oaths of silence. They deserve more than a warm handshake when they walk through the doors of the Central Intelligence Agency . . . into retirement and the outside world." Shackley was licking his wounds. He believed he deserved more than that handshake when he was edged out of the CIA. He had been discarded.

Now he was joining the public battle. He decried the investigations of the Agency that cast it as "a shadow government run amok; a nest of fascists." All this scrutiny undermined the effectiveness of the Agency and caused foreign intelligence services to avoid working with the leaky Americans. "It was not unlike watching," Shackley commented, "someone busily sawing at his own wrists with a dull razor blade." He assailed the "lackluster performance" of a CIA he had run. It had not caught wind of the revolution in Iran or the Soviet invasion of Afghanistan. The geopolitical landscape looked bleak. Nicaragua had been taken over by "pro-Cuban revolutionaries," the Angola anticommunist rebels (led by strongman Jonas Savimbi, a onetime Maoist) were no longer supported by Washington, and leftist guerrillas grew in strength in El Salvador.

"Make no mistake," wrote Shackley. "We—all of us—*are* locked in a struggle for survival."

Shackley asserted the third option was the only path open to Washington as it faced a powerful Soviet Union bent on global conquest. He defended the prolific use of covert action. He again argued that a failure to employ such methods against Moscow might lead to a situation in which U.S. leaders had no choice but to go nuclear. Americans could not afford to be queasy at the thought of secret warfare or the necessary restraint of civil liberties, such as freedom of the press. The Soviets did not care about such niceties.

Shackley, who had cleared his book with the Agency, described the intricate details of insurgency.* He hailed operations he had once over-seen: the Provincial Reconnaissance Units in Vietnam; the secret war in Laos; penetrations of the Viet Cong. He dedicated the book to the Hmong. He expressed no second thoughts, no misgivings.

Shackley pitched a number of recommendations: restrict the use of the Freedom of Information Act; limit congressional oversight; and do away with the CIA. In its place, he envisioned a Foreign Intelligence Service that would perform most tasks assigned to the CIA. History, he noted, had not been kind to the name "CIA." A cosmetic change was in order—so that the spies of America could continue to do what they always had done, but under an untarnished banner.

Adopting a hard line against the Soviets was fashionable in Washing-ton. In *The Washington Post,* reviewer Peter Osnos, a former correspon-dent in Vietnam, called the book "pretty light weight" but added, "Given the current political climate, it is a fair bet that somewhere—and soon —[Shackley's] theories will be tested." He noted that spook scuttlebutt held that Shackley was in line for a top post in Reagan's CIA.

Some of Shackley's former Agency colleagues were surprised by his book. It was strident, archly ideological, the product of a die-hard cold warrior. No one ever had mistaken Shackley for one of those woolly-headed liberals who joined the Agency to be a do-gooder. But few considered him an extreme ideologue. He was regarded as more the executive than the geopolitician. Shackley's explanation for what to oth-ers seemed a change was benign. "I found," he wrote, "that retirement offered me the luxury to think about America's choice of policy options ... in a way that I could not while I was on active federal service." Agency people saw more to it than that and considered the book a signal that Shackley was angling to be a player again.

II

That was not to be. Ed Wilson was back. For years, federal officers quietly had been investigating Wilson. On April 23, 1980, the U.S. attor-ney's office in Washington had filed a sealed indictment against Wilson and Terpil for shipping explosives, soliciting a murder, and failing to register as foreign agents. In the following months, Wilson operated out of Europe and holed up in Tripoli, as assistant U.S. attorney Larry Bar-cella plotted his capture.

---

* In one case study, he praised the CIA-supported operation in the Bolivian jungle to nab Che Guevara in 1967. But, he added, no American representative knew of the Bolivians' plan to execute the captured Che. Shackley was not telling the truth. His friend and Agency colleague Felix Rodriguez had passed the execution order from a Bolivian colonel to the Bolivian sergeant who shot and killed Che.

But everything had proceeded too slowly for Kevin Mulcahy, one of the ex-CIA men Wilson had roped in. He took his story to Seymour Hersh, a renowned journalist. Hersh produced a two-part series that ran in *The New York Times Magazine* in June of 1981. Of the Wilson-Terpil case, Hersh wrote, "It is a story of an old-boy network of former CIA operatives and military men, and a story of present and past CIA leaders who seem unable to face fully the implications of the case." He revealed Shackley's connection to Wilson—heretofore unknown to the general public. He disclosed that Shackley had downplayed the warning Mulcahy had provided him in 1976 about Wilson's activities. The only publicly available picture of the secretive ex-ADDO—the headshot on the jacket of *The Third Option*—appeared in the *Times* opposite a prison mug shot of Frank Terpil and a photo of Sayad Qaddafi, a Libyan intelligence officer Wilson had assisted. Shackley, Hersh wrote, had been questioned by federal prosecutors.

If anyone in the Reagan White House or William Casey's CIA was contemplating bringing Shackley in from the cold, the Hersh series provided reason to stop. He was damaged goods.

A few weeks after the Hersh articles, Barcella and other federal investigators conferred with Wilson and his lawyer in Rome. They were hoping to persuade the fugitive to return to the United States; Wilson wanted a deal. He told them much about his operations, and he made a big point of his contact with Shackley. Wilson asserted that between 1976 and 1979 he had regularly furnished Shackley with intelligence regarding Libya. He said that he had loaned Clines money to start a business. Wilson claimed he, Shackley, and Clines had discussed selling intelligence—all gleaned from public sources—to Libya. The meeting resolved nothing. But it provided more cause for investigators to be curious about Shackley.

The headlines did not cease. There were articles about a Wilson plot to kill a Libyan dissident in Colorado and Wilson's shipment of C-4 plastic explosive to Qaddafi. Shackley and Clines were thrown onto the front pages. A September 6, 1981, *New York Times* article exposed the corporate connections between Shackley, Clines, and Wilson. It all seemed a tangled web. Shackley, the *Times* asserted, had discouraged the Senate intelligence committee in 1976 from convening an investigation into Wilson and his ties to the Agency. Shackley told the *Times* he would not discuss his days at Langley.

Four days later, a front-page headline in *The Washington Post* made Shackley look like a fool: "Relationship With CIA Aide Gave Credibility to Arms Seller." Shackley's contacts with Wilson, the paper reported, had lent Wilson "an aura of respectability" that enabled Wilson "to convince his associates and clients that his arms exports and commando training were approved by high agency officials." Shackley stuck to his story: he had been manipulated by a friend, who never acknowledged the true nature of his activities. Federal investigators told the *Post* that Shackley was not a target of the ongoing probe, public absolution that did little good.

Wilson's exposure sent people running for cover. Clines showed up in the Geneva office of Wilson's lawyer Edward Coughlin. He had come to pay off the $500,000 loan from Wilson. One condition of the payment, Clines insisted, was that Wilson waive his right to acquire 20 percent of the company Clines had formed with Wilson's money. The company was worthless, Clines explained. Coughlin considered it strange that Clines cared about protecting a worthless firm but went along. Clines demanded that Coughlin let him keep the original copy of this release. He told Coughlin that he had to show it "to some other people right away." Hussein Salem, Clines's partner in EATSCO, moved to cut the ties between Egypt and Clines. Salem eventually provided Clines a generous buyout of over a million dollars.

The media continued to report on Wilson's various schemes. His contact with Shackley was mentioned repeatedly. "If there's an 'old-boy' network, it ought to be dissolved," declared House intelligence committee chairman Edward Boland. The Senate intelligence committee also investigated, but the only matter its staff probed was whether Wilson was officially connected to the Agency when he committed his sundry crimes. "It was not too thorough," recalled Robert Simmons, a former CIA officer on the committee staff. The documentary evidence available convinced the committee staff that Wilson was not on the Company payroll when he broke the law. Liberal Democratic senators on the committee wanted more: an inquiry into Wilson's association with Shackley and others. But Senator Barry Goldwater, the committee chair, nixed that. The Agency had suffered enough, he argued. Exploring Wilson's relations with Shackley and other spooks would only do more damage. Shackley was spared.

Larry Barcella wondered, too, about this old-boy network and Shackley's role in the whole jumble of deals and companies. He questioned the former ADDO several times. Wilson was only an information source, Shackley kept insisting. On one occasion, the usually cool Shackley accused Barcella of blackballing him and preventing his appointment to a top slot at the CIA. "You flatter me," Barcella said. He grilled Clines and Shackley about the money Clines received from Wilson. Shackley said he knew nothing about the funds. (Years later, he acknowledged he was aware that Clines had obtained money from Wilson.) BATF officer Richard Pedersen asked Shackley, how could you have anything to do with Wilson after you knew what Wilson was doing? Shackley did not reply.

In October of 1981, Barcella called Shackley and Clines before a grand jury. They were still not targets of his probe, but new information was coming in. Doug Schlachter, the former Wilson associate, told Barcella that Shackley, Clines, von Marbod, and Secord had conferred regularly with Wilson at Mount Airy. Barcella broadened his inquiry to include von Marbod and Secord—and to determine if Shackley and Clines were as innocent as they claimed.

On November 9, 1981, CBS News reported Secord had helped Wilson sell equipment to Iran. Secord was placed on administrative leave from his senior Pentagon job—a suspension that lasted ten weeks.* With Barcella interested in him, von Marbod, deputy director of the Defense Security Assistance Agency, abruptly resigned, citing narcolepsy.

Was all this just a bunch of spooks with overlapping career paths, or were these men part of a conspiracy with Wilson at its center? Doug Schlachter had told Barcella that Clines and Shackley had known all about Wilson's Libyan project. Then in December of 1981, Roberta Barnes, Wilson's girlfriend, was arrested in Dallas for smuggling silver into the United States. She soon described to Barcella a deal in which Wilson had supplied Clines with $500,000 to set up a company that would make a bundle shipping goods to Egypt. Shackley, von Marbod, and Secord—Wilson supposedly had told her—all possessed secret shares. But, Barnes warned Barcella, they were careful, there's no paper trail, you'll never prove it.

Were Wilson and his associates falsely implicating Shackley and company in some sort of graymail? Had he cooked up this tale of the secret sharers to beat the charges against him? There was, as Barnes said, little documentary evidence. There was a memo written by Wilson's lawyer (and not yet in Barcella's possession) noting that the Clines company funded by Wilson would be owned by four unidentified Americans and a foreign corporation. But the memo did not say who the owners were.

Barcella concentrated on capturing Wilson. Shackley, Clines, Secord, von Marbod—that was a sideshow. (Meanwhile, Clines's EATSCO had come to the attention of federal auditors who discovered extensive fraud in its past bills to the Pentagon.) With the assistance of a former intelligence operative, Barcella lured Wilson out of Tripoli to the Do-

---

* In his memoirs, Secord denied the account and downplayed his ties to Wilson. He claimed that since he had succeeded in ushering through Congress the controversial sale of AWACs surveillance aircraft to Saudi Arabia, the Israeli lobby had wreaked revenge by concocting the Wilson story.

minican Republic. Wilson, whose assets now topped $14 million, was immediately placed on a plane to New York City and arrested on June 15, 1982. In suburban Virginia, Clines and Quintero drove over to Secord's house to watch the news reports on Wilson.

The next year and a half for Wilson would be filled with trials. In the end, he would be found guilty of gunrunning, smuggling plastic explosive, and soliciting the murder of Barcella and others after his arrest. (Wilson also discussed with a prison informer killing Clines, but no case was brought against him for that, perhaps because the government did not want Wilson's relationship with the Agency probed during a trial.) The long sentences piled up. Wilson would never be a free man.

No charges were brought against Shackley. But the damage to his reputation was irreparable. In the years following the Wilson episode, Shackley crafted his defense. How could an experienced intelligence hand get caught up with such a scoundrel? That was what Stansfield Turner had wanted to know in 1977. Then federal investigators asked the same question. Then investigative journalists wondered—and so did members of the public who followed spook scandals.

"The Ed Wilson I knew in 1972 or 1973 was not the same man who was arrested in 1982," Shackley claimed. "It's a different guy. He changed. I knew Ed Wilson in the period of 1972 and 1973. My family and his had outings together. I came and had lunch with him. But certainly the Wilson of that time had no correlation with the [later] Wilson. . . . He distorted his contacts with me. It's clear that on some occasions when he would meet with me, he probably would say to somebody I'm going to meet with Shackley. . . . Yes, he could use that to infer or authenticate something to somebody else."

If no secret business cabal existed, there are two ways of viewing Shackley's relationship with Wilson. Either Shackley did not know what Wilson was doing and was duped by him—the experienced senior intelligence officer conned by a money-grubbing conniver—or Shackley was too smart for his own good. That is, he was aware of Wilson's criminal activities, attempted to play the sleazy Wilson as an asset, and was burned. Neither scenario is flattering for a senior intelligence man. In his own telling, Shackley played the victim. He was bamboozled. But, then, he had not fallen at his own hand.

Years afterward, Shackley was asked if he had made any mistakes in dealing with Wilson. In a sharp, defensive tone, his voice rising a bit, he said, "If I had been hanging out in bars and carousing around and drinking I probably would've picked up on some of those stories, and I could have put a stop to [my contacts with Wilson]. But that was not my lifestyle. . . . At the end of a long day at the office, I went home to spend the evening with my family. I'm sure if I heard some of these war stories that were discussed at some of these [bars], I could've put a stop [to the contacts]. So did I make an error in my lifestyle? I don't think so. Could I have done something to stop that? Yes, I could've been a boozer. But did I want to be one there and do I want to be one now? The answer is no."

Shackley's only problem, as far as he would admit, was that he had worked too hard and was not an alcoholic like his old man. Shackley's diligence had prevented him from learning the truth about Ed Wilson.

After Wilson was imprisoned, he continued to draw press attention. Two books would be written on him. And at the highest echelons of the government, the Wilson affair (including his relationship to Shackley) remained of sharp interest.

On March 21, 1983, shortly after the end of one of the Wilson trials, a meeting was held in the White House situation room. The topic was EATSCO—and Wilson and Shackley. The officials present are not publicly known. A memorandum detailing the meeting was released years later in response to a Freedom of Information Act request filed by Wilson, but significant portions were deleted. Gone was the name of the CIA officer who wrote it. Blacked out were the first two paragraphs and the final paragraph of the four-page memo. Nevertheless, the memo was a detailed account of shady dealings. The first nondeleted line read, "Appearance of EATSCO as the shipping agent was evidence of the conspiracy."

The Agency author noted that 600,000 documents related to EATSCO had been reviewed. Hussein Salem, Clines's partner, was described as a former Egyptian intelligence officer and the protégé of a former chief of Egyptian intelligence. The memo then stated:

> In the fall of 1978 Clines, Shackley, Secord and von Marbod were holding weekly meetings in northern Virginia to discuss ways to obtain contracts with U.S. Defense Department. In October 1978, Clines retired from the CIA. On 4 October 1978, the Defense Department received a letter from the Egyptians saying that Tersam of Panama [Salem's company] is the sole shipping agent for the [government of Egypt]. In January 1979 Wilson, Secord and von Marbod were in London together. Wilson gave von Marbod $10 thousand in cash according to an eye witness.
>
> In February 1979 Wilson loaned one-half million dollars to Clines (this is Wilson's part of the conspiracy). The money was to be used by Clines to form various business groups. All of the principals have 20 percent shares, and all but Clines' share are "SECRET."

The implication was obvious. With Wilson's money, Clines had formed a joint venture with a well-connected Egyptian, and Clines, Secord, von Marbod, Wilson, and Shackley were in it together: 20 percent for each—with those still in government secret partners. Then Egyptian officials handed EATSCO, which had no shipping experience, a tremendous contract and requested that the Pentagon provide a $15 million advance to EATSCO.

The CIA officer who wrote the memo appeared to believe that something untoward had transpired—kickbacks, contract-rigging, under-the-table deals, he did not say. The officer reported that in October of 1980 Clines had slipped a cash payment to von Marbod in Geneva and that Clines had delivered another suspicious cash payment in the $10,000 range to an unknown party. During the White House meeting, Wingate Lloyd, the director of Egyptian affairs at the State Department, noted that there was potential for great embarrassment for President Hosni Mubarak of Egypt.

The memo suggested Shackley was a party to a grand plot as one of the secret partners in a Clines hustle. But since the CIA deleted the opening paragraphs—where the participants would have been listed and the source of the memo's information noted—a definitive reading is impossible. Was someone passing along innuendo? Or was the Agency or Justice Department reporting verified facts? It is unlikely that an interagency gathering would convene in the White House to share gossip.

A month after the White House meeting, Stanley Sporkin, the general counsel for the CIA, sent a short note to DCI William Casey: "Here is another interesting memo on EATSCO. See page 2, paragraph B." The next two lines are deleted.

The "interesting memo" was composed by Wilson, sent to Libyan intelligence, and dated May 12, 1981—a year after his indictment. The portion Sporkin found intriguing concerned a Wilson deal with Egypt. Wilson had written:

> The undersigned is a 20% partner of the company Systems Services International, Inc. (SSI). This organisation was formed about three years ago, and the undersigned funded it with $500,000. Individuals setting up the company were Thomas Clines... General Richard Secord... Erich von Marbod.... Also in the Corporation is Theodore Shakley [sic], Former Deputy Director of the CIA [sic], and now Managing Director of SSI.

SSI, Wilson reported accurately, had given birth to EATSCO, which was shipping military equipment. In his memo, Wilson suggested that perhaps he could persuade this group—for a substantial fee—to assist Tripoli.

Here was another indication of a conspiracy. But could a document written by Wilson, a notorious liar, be accepted at face value? Wilson might have written the memo to impress the Libyans. He also could have fabricated the document. When he had met with Barcella in Rome in July of 1981, Wilson had spoken much about Shackley but did not mention a secret partnership. Maybe, if there were a covert business arrangement, Wilson at that point still hoped to profit by it; perhaps he was holding on to this secret as a card to play later. None of these actions and calculations were beyond him.

But even rogue CIA officers sometimes tell the truth. Roberta Barnes's statements, the White House meeting document, the loan memo from Wilson's attorney, Wilson's own memo—this was a lot of smoke, strong circumstantial evidence that Shackley, Clines, Secord, and von Marbod were in a clandestine and illegal business venture. Shackley and his friends were fortunate to be implicated by a man without credibility.

In the case of Tom Clines, the government did unearth concrete evidence of wrongdoing related to EATSCO, and on January 16, 1984, Clines pleaded guilty to having overbilled von Marbod's Defense Security Assistance Agency. The government charged that EATSCO padded its bills by $8 million between 1979 and 1981 and that Clines and SSI made off with $2.5 million of the phony charges. Clines had to pay $10,000 in a criminal fine and $100,000 in a civil settlement.

The Justice Department continued to conduct a bribery and conflict-of-interest investigation of Clines and Secord, stemming from their association with Wilson. The feds also probed Clines in another case, probably arising out of his aborted attempt in 1978 to peddle his and Wilson's services to Somoza. These investigations would be dropped by the Justice Department in early 1986. But soon after that, Clines, Secord, and Shackley would be targets of more investigations, and Wilson would return to haunt them all.

But in 1982 and 1983, with Wilson locked up, Shackley could go about his business. He advised Hakim on a plan to sell helicopters to South Korea; the pair knocked around other ideas—selling radar equipment to Trinidad and Tobago, peddling arms-related equipment to Egypt. He and Secord, now retired, discussed an oil concession in Sudan. None of this ever took off.

Connections—that was Shackley's business, finding people with inside information, intelligence, of any kind. It could be a tidbit about the political status of an oil minister in the Middle East, or a lead on a foreign purchasing agent and what sort of goods he was looking to acquire. Shackley called on anyone he could, including friends in Israeli intelligence. With the information he collected, Shackley could write his risk assessments or build business deals.

William Friedman, a Washington consultant to Wheelabrator-Frye, a manufacturing and engineering concern, was one of Shackley's early clients. Wheelabrator-Frye sought government contracts in Oman, and for that the firm needed contacts there. "We hired Shackley for a pretty good fee to develop personal contacts, using friends he had for years," Friedman recalled. There was some grumbling within the company. One corporate officer with intelligence connections complained about Shackley, citing Shackley's ties to Ed Wilson. Memos flew back and forth; finally, his worries were overruled.

With the help of James Critchfield, a former CIA Middle East specialist who had gone into the international consulting game, Shackley put Friedman's company in touch with two people influential in Oman: Tim Landon, a friend of the sultan of Oman; and a sheik with whom Wheelabrator-Frye eventually developed a joint venture.*

Impressed with Shackley, Friedman hired him to provide intelligence for Texas Pacific Oil. The firm was stuck in a dispute with the Thai government over the development of a natural gas field in the Gulf of Thailand, and it was looking to lobby the government. This time Shackley joined forces with Daniel Arnold, a former station chief in Thailand. They identified for the company which Thai officials were the most influential in this matter. But Texas Pacific got jittery after receiving a report from Arnold. Due to political considerations, he wrote, "export of Thai natural gas is out of the question for the foreseeable future." Yet Arnold had a solution befitting a former Agency man: "I therefore recommend that consideration be given to undertaking a series of overt and covert activities designed to accelerate the inevitable process for political change." Arnold's secret proposal confirms the suspicion of those spook-watchers who eye warily that small band of spies-turned-consultants. Such consultants, including Shackley, like to depict themselves as businesspeople, not private sector spies. Arnold's report shows how thin the line can be between consulting and CIA-like scheming. Texas Pacific reacted quickly to Arnold's suggestion. Joe Clark, the company's president, ordered Friedman "to disassociate" his firm from Arnold's proposal and to terminate Arnold's services. Friedman ended the company's relationship with Arnold, and he also stopped working with Shackley.

---

* Shackley hoped that TGS International would snag a contract to do work at an airbase the United States was building in Oman, but that did not happen.

· · ·

Much of Shackley's professional attention was devoted to a man of mystery. The chief client for Shackley's Research Associates International was one of the more controversial financial figures in the world, a secretive billionaire who profited from a close and clandestine relationship with the racist regime of South Africa.

Johannes Christiaan Martinus Augustinus Deuss is a freewheeler in the chaotic and cutthroat world of international oil. He has offices, banks, investment companies, trading offices, and villas around the world. A Dutch citizen who failed at a career as a car salesman, John Deuss became an oil trader in the 1970s and developed a megabusiness by assuming big risks and striking deals with unusual parties. He signed a $500 million contract with the Soviets, an arrangement that went awry, and the Soviets claimed Deuss committed hundreds of millions of dollars in fraud. Shackley's patron-to-be amassed much of his fortune from undercover transactions with South Africa. When Pretoria was the target of a global oil embargo, Deuss was one of its largest oil-runners.

The early 1980s were a tough time for Pretoria. With the fall of the Shah in 1979, South Africa lost its only steady supplier of oil. But Deuss privately negotiated a 60-million-barrel-a-year deal with South Africa and became its main supplier of oil. Between 1979 and 1983, his firm, Trans World Oil, brought at least 97 shipments of crude oil into South Africa, accounting for about a quarter of Pretoria's import demand. Much of the oil came from Saudi Arabia and Oman, both of which publicly adhered to the United Nations embargo against South Africa. Yet Deuss found Saudi and Omani officials happy to do business with Pretoria, as long as it occurred in secrecy.

For Deuss, a man who would trade with the communists of the Soviet Union or the racists of South Africa, Shackley followed world developments that might affect the oil business. He tracked tankers and production trends. Shackley and his staff studied open literature—foreign newspapers, specialty publications—but to prove his worth to Deuss, he needed to come up with information not freely available. He sought people around the world who could tell him what was happening in, say, Iran and how that might affect the nation's oil yield—a search that would draw him into yet another controversy.

Shackley advised Deuss's operations on security and helped Deuss in his dealmaking, which was not always in synch with U.S. interests. Once Shackley attempted to pull together a "countertrade" transaction in which Iran was to sell crude oil to a Portuguese company, which would supply weapons to Iran. Trans World Oil was to buy the refined oil from the Portuguese firm. Shackley met with the Iranian principals in Switzerland—at a time when Washington was decrying Iran as a terrorist state. The net result would have been arms for Iran, money for the Portuguese middlemen, and profits for Deuss. Shackley later claimed the scheme never went forward. But he discussed with Deuss the notion of using European cutout companies for Deuss's purchase of Iranian crude, and Trans World tried to develop more countertrade ventures involving arms. It advertised its oil-for-weapons expertise in military trade publications. Associates familiar with RAI operations estimated that Deuss paid Shackley at least $100,000 a year.

For his own company, TGS International, Shackley explored selling food to anti-America Iran. But Iran wanted no food made in the United States. Shackley considered shipping U.S. foodstuffs to the Bahamas, slapping a Bahamian label on the goods, then forwarding the food to Iran. But he did not go ahead with that plan.

TGS International did obtain at least one valuable overseas job. In 1982, at the request of the Kuwait government, the U.S. Navy awarded Shackley's firm a $1.2 million contract to rehabilitate a warehouse for the Kuwaiti Air Force. Shackley had little experience in this area, and he subcontracted part of the work to Robert Springer, Jr., who owned a small building firm in Georgia. In January of 1983, Springer flew to Kuwait to supervise employees he had dispatched. Over the course of the next two months, according to Springer, he and his men completed the job. But then, Springer said, TGS International refused to pay him.

Springer's side of the story suggests that Shackley had pull in Kuwait. On March 1, Vernon Gillespie, a former Green Beret and vice president of TGS International, ordered Springer to meet him at the American embassy.* The location puzzled Springer. Why there? Was Shackley the ex-Company man calling in some chits? At the embassy, Gillespie and a lawyer for TGS International ordered Springer to sign a declaration that he was withdrawing from the contract. If he did not, they would have him thrown in jail by Kuwaiti police. On what charges? Springer asked. Oh, something can always be trumped up, the two replied. In a Kuwaiti jail, they added, he could look forward to regular beatings. They would not let Springer leave the room to make a call. You have ten minutes to decide, the two said. Springer signed. He was frightened. "Shackley is in a position to pull people out of the past to scare your pants off,"

---

* Gillespie, a three-tour Vietnam veteran, previously had booked tours for the U.S. Marine Corps band and had been a partner in a firm that marketed Rhodesian sugar globally—but not in the United States, which was honoring the boycott against white-ruled Rhodesia.

Springer explained. Later that day, Springer, having been threatened again by the two Shackley associates, handed them all the cash he had, $7,000, and signed over a $20,000 bank account.

Back in the United States, Springer filed a lawsuit against Shackley and TGS International, alleging breach of contract, infliction of emotional duress, and false imprisonment. He demanded over $4 million in damages. In his reply, Shackley denied Springer was threatened. He maintained that Springer abandoned the job, submitted false invoices, and did not return money advanced to him.

The court papers do little to prove one side's case or the other. Before the suit could go to court, Springer suddenly dropped the action. Asked about this years later, he was scared to talk. "The CIA can be bad boys," he said by way of an explanation. "Why should I open myself, when I finally feel safe?" Only recently, he remarked, had he stopped sleeping with a gun beneath his pillow. Discussing the case, he said, would place him in jeopardy. You know Shackley's past? he asked. Enough said.

Shackley viewed Kuwait as a source of tremendous profits. By March of 1983, TGS had before the Kuwaiti Air Force several proposals that could bring it up to $200 million. What Shackley received was more modest, but nevertheless much money. Toward the end of 1983, TGS International signed a $6.3 million contract with the Navy to perform construction at the Ali Al-Salem Air Base, forty miles outside of Kuwait City. After beginning work on the site in early 1984, TGS soon began to fall behind schedule. "It appeared that TGS was not the kind of contractor that the Navy would have selected to do a job like this," recalled Charles Kubic, a Navy officer who oversaw the TGS contract. But Shackley's man in Kuwait, an ex-Marine named Johnny Carter, had sold TGS to the Kuwaitis. Even as TGS failed to meet the schedule, the Navy increased the contract to $15 million.

But in 1986 the Navy, citing delays and other performance issues, refused to pay $4.5 million TGS claimed it was due. Shackley appealed to the Armed Services Board of Contract. At a hearing on the case, Shackley presented his credentials by describing his tour in Laos: "I managed a 40,000 man guerrilla force structure. . . . I was responsible for building a lot of short take-off and landing airfields throughout Laos, building barracks, training camps and warehouses." His appeal was rejected.

III

Shackley's Virginia offices were full of dabblers. He tried putting together an oil deal that could have resulted in a $2.7 billion transaction —but did not get lucky. Jamie Jameson, his partner, and Felix Rodriguez sought an oil concession in Guatemala. Jameson pursued, but did not win, lobbying contracts with the governments of Guatemala and Peru. Jameson traveled to Central America several times with Newman Peyton, Jr., a right-wing conservative evangelist who visited heads of state. While on these trips, Jameson sat in on top-level meetings and gathered political intelligence of interest to Shackley's corporate clients. Through Peyton, Jameson met Daniel Ortega, the Sandinista leader of Nicaragua. It was a strange scene: Shackley's associate discussing world events with the man the Agency and Shackley's former colleagues were trying to overthrow.

The office suite that housed Research Associates International and TGS International was a magnet for weird characters. In 1983, Jameson and Gillespie met with Kevin Kattke, a maintenance engineer for a Macy's in Long Island who was a covert action hobbyist. Kattke and several colleagues had befriended a number of Caribbean exiles in the New York area and were promoting revolution in socialist Grenada. (Kattke and his associates had been referred to Shackley's office by an aide to Senator Jesse Helms.) By Kattke's account, Gillespie introduced Kattke to two private American security firms which Gillespie said could help trigger a coup in Grenada. Gillespie's contacts at each company were encouraging but ultimately declined to become involved with Kattke. Shortly afterward, Kattke and his Long Island chums were recruited by NSC aide Oliver North to help in the plans for the U.S. invasion of Grenada.*

Shackley attracted other covert players. In 1984, he was approached by Barbara Studley, a former Miami talk show host. With retired General John Singlaub (who had worked with Shackley in Laos), Studley had created GeoMiliTech, a weapons firm. Studley came to Shackley for advice on the arms market in Latin America. He was not an expert, but he shared information he did possess.

Such encounters were small stuff, part of the private-spook world in which Shackley and his office mates traveled. It was Shackley's more pedestrian work for oilman John Deuss that led him into the most serious government scandal of the post-Watergate era.

In mid-1984, Shackley flew to Los Angeles to see a potentially valuable source. Manucher Hashemi was a brigadier general in Iran in the days of the Shah and headed the counterespionage section of the brutal SAVAK. He fled Tehran shortly before the revolution and now lived in

---

* Kattke stayed in touch with Shackley's office for a couple of years. He maintained that he spoke with Novzar Razmara, an Iranian exile who worked for Shackley, about finding weapons and supplies for the anti-Khomeini opposition in Iran.

London. Novzar Razmara, a Shackley employee who had worked with Hashemi in Iran, thought Shackley and the old general should meet.*

According to Hashemi, Shackley poured it on thick when the two gathered in California. Shackley introduced himself as a former CIA official who was a businessman but also an intelligence adviser to Vice President George Bush. Shackley noted that his duties—perhaps those on behalf of Bush—included obtaining information about Iran, particularly what the Soviets were doing in that country. He shared his worry that lurking off-stage, ready to move should Khomeini die or lose power, were far-left clerics and radicals supported by Moscow.

As Hashemi recalled the meeting, Shackley was interested in more than the acquisition of information. *Our* aim, Shackley told Hashemi, is to establish better relations with Tehran. He hoped Hashemi could introduce him to Iranian officials. Hashemi, who had little contact with current Iranian leaders, agreed to do what he could.

Shackley later asserted he was only pursuing his private business interests, that he was no operative for Bush or the CIA. But Hashemi believed Shackley was representing more than his own firm. It may be that Shackley, adopting what spies call a "false-flag" ruse, pumped up his status to impress the general, calculating that Hashemi would cooperate more readily if he thought he was assisting Bush and not John Deuss. After the Los Angeles session, Hashemi called Razmara and said he had the right fellow to introduce to Shackley, a man well informed on the political scene in Tehran. They scheduled a rendezvous in Hamburg.

On the night of November 19, Shackley and Razmara arrived in the German city. They checked into the posh Four Seasons Hotel. Shackley called a government official he knew in Hamburg and asked if any prominent Iranians were in town. Shackley's friend checked and reported that no noteworthy Iranians were about.

The next morning, Hashemi introduced Shackley to Manucher Ghorbanifar, an overweight, boisterous, goateed Iranian expatriate. Ghorbanifar, echoing Hashemi's account, later said that Shackley introduced himself as a "very close" associate of Bush and hinted he might be the next CIA Director. That day, Shackley and Ghorbanifar met three times. During the second session, the pair were joined by two other Iranian officials, including Ali Shahabadi, the chief Iranian purchasing officer in Hamburg and purportedly a friend of Adnan Khashoggi, the billionaire entrepreneur and arms dealer.

Shackley afterward told congressional investigators he had gone to Hamburg simply to get together with Iranians who could supply him inside information on the Iran-Iraq war. But Hashemi's recollection

* Razmara had come to Shackley recommended by Hakim.

differed from Shackley's. He noted Shackley acted as if he still held an official brief and discussed with the Iranians renewing diplomatic relations between Washington and Tehran and ways to deliver to Iran weapons purchased by the Shah but withheld by the United States.*

If Shackley suggested he might be more than a private businessman, that was exactly what Ghorbanifar wanted to hear. The Iranian offered to provide the United States with Soviet military equipment Iran had captured. In return, Iran would want TOW antitank missiles. This unorthodox proposal did not faze Shackley. In Shackley's version, he told Ghorbanifar to forget the TOWs. Find something simpler. He asked Ghorbanifar if he had tried the CIA.

"We know the CIA in Frankfurt," Ghorbanifar replied with bitterness. "They want to treat us like Kleenex—use us for their purposes and then throw us out the window. We can't work with them as they are unreasonable and unprofessional. In fact, if you check on me with them, they will tell you I am unreasonable and undisciplined."

With a thick file on Ghorbanifar, the CIA had reason to be wary of him. Following the Islamic revolution in 1979, Ghorbanifar, the managing director of an Israeli-connected shipping firm, had fled Iran. Ever since then, he was dogged by rumors that he had been an informant for SAVAK and an asset for Israeli intelligence. Trying to sell himself in the West as a broker to Iran, he acquired a reputation as a dishonorable schemer. Yet in 1980, he became a CIA informant and was implicated in an abortive coup attempt in Iran.

His career as an Agency source was brief. In September of 1981, Langley concluded his information could not be trusted. In March of 1984, Ghorbanifar met with a CIA officer in Frankfurt and claimed he possessed information on the kidnapping of William Buckley. The CIA hooked Ghorbanifar to a lie-detector machine and determined he was lying. But Ghorbanifar was persistent. In June, he again contacted the Agency. This time he said he could deliver an Iranian official interested in talking to the United States. Ghorbanifar failed another polygraph exam. The CIA issued a "burn notice," warning that Ghorbanifar "should be regarded as an intelligence fabricator and a nuisance."

Ghorbanifar's next contact with anyone associated with U.S. intelligence came when he met Shackley. Sitting across from Shackley at the

---

* When all this became public, some former CIA people speculated that Shackley had been dispatched to Hamburg on an unofficial mission for the Agency to inquire about William Buckley (the Lebanon station chief then being held hostage by Iranian-backed militants) and the prospects of winning the CIA man's release. Buckley had worked on the Provincial Reconnaissance Unit program in Vietnam when Shackley was in Saigon. Shackley denied his Hamburg trip had such an agenda.

Four Seasons, he was at it again. Ghorbanifar did not stop with his offer to swap Soviet arms for TOW missiles. He raised the question of the three American hostages then held in Lebanon. Shackley later recalled he told the Iranian "it would be interesting" to determine the hostages' status. "I assume you're talking about tractors for prisoners exchange," Ghorbanifar said, referring to the successful U.S. attempt in 1962 to ransom the Cuban exiles captured at the Bay of Pigs. "I don't have anything specific in mind," Shackley replied.

A deal was in the air, at least for Ghorbanifar. In the evening, the two gathered for drinks. Ghorbanifar announced that he had made some calls and discovered an arrangement was possible: cash for the hostages. See how fast I can move, he told Shackley. The ball is in your court.

The next day, Shackley left Hamburg. As soon as he returned home, he wrote a memo on his discussions with Ghorbanifar. He noted that Ghorbanifar is a man of certain talents and skills but would be difficult to manage. Ghorbanifar, Shackley wrote, "could be kept on track if he were tasked via Hashemi." But Shackley had a concern: an official U.S. government follow-up to his dialogue with Ghorbanifar might imperil his business. He was happy to be of help, especially since Buckley was a friend. But business is business. He hoped government action "will not prejudice our relationship with General Hashemi and Mr. Ghorbanifar." Shackley noted that Ghorbanifar's proposal needed to be answered soon. He took the memo to the State Department, deliberately avoiding the CIA, and delivered it to Lieutenant General Vernon Walters, then ambassador-at-large and a former deputy director of the CIA.

At Foggy Bottom, Shackley's report moved through the bureaucracy. Officials there thought Ghorbanifar was trying to pull another scam. According to Shackley, on December 11, the State Department told him, thank you, but we will handle this problem via other channels.

Ghorbanifar did not give up. He made contact with two Israelis, Al Schwimmer, an adviser to Prime Minister Shimon Peres, and Yaacov Nimrodi, an Israeli businessman. He proposed that the Israelis secretly sell him TOW missiles for Iran. In return, he said, he would arrange the release of William Buckley. About then, Michael Ledeen, the onetime business associate of Shackley and now an NSC consultant, was trying to persuade Robert McFarlane, the national security adviser, to consider a joint U.S.-Israeli initiative regarding Iran. Ledeen's effort coincided with a reevaluation being conducted by the U.S. intelligence community of policy toward Iran. Government geostrategists were considering an opening to Iran, and a CIA memo suggested that arms sales through an ally could kick off a dialogue with Iran. Ledeen met with Prime Minister

Peres, who said that Israel wanted U.S. approval to sell armaments to Iran.

By now Shackley apparently was out of the loop. But in May of 1985, Shackley and Ledeen lunched together. You cover the Middle East, Ledeen remarked, do you have any bright ideas on how to get the hostages out? No, Shackley replied. But he had met an interesting Iranian last year and then notified the State Department, where no one was interested. Ledeen asked for a copy of Shackley's memo.*

Ledeen asked Shackley to check whether this Iranian channel was still open. Shackley had his friend General Hashemi contact Ghorbanifar. Could he or others still arrange the release of the Americans? On June 1, Ghorbanifar told Hashemi that Iranian authorities were no longer interested in a straight ransom deal; they wanted a dialogue with "a responsible American who can identify what he represents" and "a discussion of a quid pro quo that involves items other than money." Shackley wrote up a memo on this latest round and gave it to Ledeen, who then handed it to Lieutenant Colonel Oliver North, the NSC staffer responsible for counterterrorism.

Ghorbanifar must have been heartened by this back-channel communication from Shackley. He was working with the Israelis and, all of a sudden, Shackley, whom Ghorbanifar believed was close to Bush and the CIA, reappeared.

On a curious note, Ledeen later asserted to investigators that he did not read Shackley's memo before passing it to North and that in his chats with Shackley the two had not discussed Ghorbanifar by name. Ledeen's story was that he was ignorant of Ghorbanifar's role but continued working with the Israelis, who unbeknown to Ledeen were collaborating with Ghorbanifar. Weeks after his lunch with Shackley, Ledeen, on behalf of Washington, told Israel it could engage in a one-time arms sale to Iran. Ghorbanifar was to be the middleman.

Ledeen's claim that he did not read the Shackley memo served to distance his friend Shackley from a key moment in the initiative. It also allowed U.S. officials to maintain that they did not know that the dubious Ghorbanifar—a known fabricator—was a main mover at the origin of the Iran initiative. Only after the first sale of weapons to Iran was under way, Ledeen said, did the United States discover that Ghorbanifar was

---

* Two years later, congressional investigators asked Shackley why he had not mentioned his Hamburg trip to Ledeen earlier. "I keep my own counsel," Shackley snapped. "I don't run around and tell everybody that I meet for lunch everything I'm doing. Why? That's not my personality. . . . You seem to think I should be out there advertising this thing, I had a meeting; I reported it [to the State Department]. Bang! Finished!"

involved. Ledeen's hard-to-believe denial made Shackley's presence in this episode seem even more mysterious.* Was it merely one more odd, scandal-related coincidence for Shackley?

The Iran initiative quickly developed its own momentum. The arms sale to Iran, at first a one-shot deal, would snowball into an eighteen-month-long project.† It would become intertwined with the White House's covert and arguably illegal campaign to arm the Contra rebels fighting the leftist Sandinista government in Nicaragua. It would fail. When revealed, it would spark public outrage, congressional investigations, a grand jury probe, and several trials, and drag Shackley back to the public stage.

While Ledeen and others handled the Iranian operation—the others came to include Secord, Hakim, and Clines, who first had been recruited by North to aid the Contras—Shackley tended to business. There was intelligence to collect for Deuss, deals to consider.‡ As he went about transforming his unique government experience into private profit, Shackley in early 1986 did not know he was being pursued by a left-wing legal advocacy group called the Christic Institute—an opponent that would cause him more direct harm than any enemy he faced as a CIA man.

His main pursuer was Daniel Sheehan, a fiery-eyed, quick-talking, charismatic forty-year-old who fancied himself a foe of government wrongdoing. In Shackley, Sheehan believed he had a crusade.

Sheehan was a public-interest lawyer, a leftist legal Elmer Gantry, and a charlatan in his chase after Shackley. Decades earlier, he nearly had entered Shackley's world. As a young man, he had contemplated a life in the Special Forces. At Northeastern University in 1964, he enrolled in ROTC to prepare for the Green Berets. But the classes in how to kill the enemy disgusted him. He left Northeastern for Harvard College and went on to Harvard Law School. He practiced at prestigious law firms. He was a litigator for the American Civil Liberties Union. He attended classes at Harvard Divinity School and served as general counsel to the Jesuits' social ministry office in Washington. He worked on the Pentagon Papers case and was involved in the high-profile case of Karen Silkwood,

---

* When queried about this by congressional investigators in 1987, Ledeen had no good explanation for his purported failure to read Shackley's memo.

† Buckley died in captivity in late 1985.

‡ While Secord and Hakim were busy with their covert Contra business, Shackley was discussing with them a bid to sell aircraft shelters to the United Arab Emirates in return for oil. Nothing came of this.

the nuclear plant whistleblower who died in a suspicious car crash. (In describing his past, Sheehan often exaggerated his role in such cases.) In 1980, he became general counsel for the Christic Institute, a small public-interest group supported by religious organizations.

Shackley had become Sheehan's holy grail in roundabout fashion. Throughout 1985, Paul Hoven, a friend of Sheehan's and a Vietnam veteran, regularly attended parties of ex-Agency men and weekend warriors, some associated with *Soldier of Fortune* magazine. (Hoven worked at the Project on Military Procurement, an outfit funded by liberals and devoted to exposing Pentagon waste.) At a bash near Christmas, Carl Jenkins, a former CIA officer who had been assigned to Miami and Laos, introduced Hoven to Gene Wheaton, a balding middle-aged fellow.

Wheaton was an odd bird. As Wheaton has related his life story, he was a Marine in the 1950s and then joined the Tulsa police force. He was an army detective in Vietnam and in the mid-1970s a security officer at a top-secret CIA-Rockwell surveillance program in Iran called Project IBEX. In 1979 he returned to the United States, went through a string of security-related jobs, and became obsessed with the covert world and drug-trafficking. When he met Hoven, Wheaton, now representing a California aviation company, was scheming with Jenkins and Ed Dearborn, a former CIA pilot in Laos and the Congo, to win federal contracts to transport humanitarian supplies to anticommunist rebels, including the Mujahedeen of Afghanistan and the Contras. So far, the trio had failed to collect any. They had even complained to a State Department official that Richard Secord and Oliver North improperly controlled who got the Contra-related contracts. They badmouthed Secord, noting that he had been mixed up with Shackley, Wilson, and Clines.* One set of spooks was pissed at another.

At the *Soldier of Fortune* party, Hoven pegged Wheaton as someone who thought he was a player but who truly was not. Nevertheless, he agreed to assist Wheaton. Hoven set up a meeting with a congressional aide who followed the Afghan program. Hoven did not realize that Wheaton had more on his mind than contracts. Wheaton had spent much of the previous year hobnobbing with arms dealers, ex-CIA officers, and mercenaries, and he had collected information on past and present covert operations, including the secret Contra-arms project.†

---

* Jenkins had occupied space in Clines's suite of offices around 1980.

† Wheaton had a close connection to North and Secord's covert Contra program. Rafael Quintero, a key player in the operation, was a friend of Carl Jenkins, Wheaton's erstwhile partner. Either directly or indirectly, Quintero was a source for some of what Wheaton knew of this project.

Wheaton was obsessed with the 1976 assassination in Iran of three Americans who worked on Project IBEX. He believed the killings were linked to U.S. intelligence, that a ring of ex-spooks was running wild in Central America and elsewhere.

So when Wheaton met with the congressional staffer and Hoven, he skipped the presentation on supplying the Mujahedeen. Instead he launched into a speech about political assassinations related to U.S. intelligence. He rattled on about the mysterious IBEX murders. Hoven had a hard time following Wheaton. His claims were based on a mish-mash of speculative hearsay, fanciful information, and some actual facts. But Wheaton made his bottom-line point obvious: a rogue element in the U.S. government had engaged in a host of nefarious activities, including assassinations.

The congressional staffer wanted nothing to do with the rambling intrigue Wheaton was peddling. But Hoven was interested. He called Danny Sheehan, thinking he ought to hear Wheaton's tale.

Sheehan already had developed an interest in the murky community of mercenaries, Cuban exiles, and others secretly aiding the Contras. By early 1986, press accounts had revealed that a clandestine Contra-support network ran all the way into the White House and that Oliver North, a low-level aide, was involved—even though Congress had seemingly barred the administration from militarily aiding the rebels. (The White House claimed these stories were wrong.) Here was the perfect target for Sheehan: a furtive program supporting a covert war against a leftist government. He wondered if he could strike at it in the courts. He always was looking for cases that made good stories—ones in which he could be a hero. Then he met Gene Wheaton, who had a helluva tale for Sheehan.

IV

Sheehan and Wheaton sat down in the kitchen of Hoven's house in early February of 1986. It was magic. To a wide-eyed Sheehan, Wheaton, posing as an experienced operator, tossed out wild stories of clandestine operations and dozens of names: Wilson, Secord, Clines, Hakim, Singlaub, Bush. A whole crew was running amok, supporting Contras, conducting covert activity elsewhere. Drugs were involved. Some of this gang had engaged in corrupt government business in Iran and Southeast Asia. Now the same old boys were running weapons to Latin America. Central to the whole shebang was a former CIA officer named Ted Shackley. Sheehan was captivated. He had struck the mother lode.

Sheehan spoke a few times with Carl Jenkins. At one session, Sheehan listened as Jenkins and Wheaton discussed what Wheaton was calling the "off-the-reservation gang"—Secord, Clines, Hakim, and Shackley—

and the operations they ran in and out of government. According to Hoven, Wheaton and Jenkins wanted to see information about this crowd made public and saw Sheehan as the mechanism of disclosure.

Wheaton and Jenkins did not tell Sheehan that they hoped to settle a score with a band they believed had an unfair lock on the air-supply contracts they desired. But to Hoven it was clear that one faction of spooks was whacking another. Hoven was not sure who was on what side. He guessed that somebody somewhere—maybe even in the Agency itself—was upset with the freelancers and wanted to see them reined in. But if Jenkins or anyone else thought they could use Sheehan as a quiet transmitter of damaging information, they were as wrong as they could be.

Throughout the winter and spring, as Sheehan talked to Wheaton and Jenkins, he had something else on his mind: a two-year-old bombing in Nicaragua. On May 30, 1984, a bomb had exploded at a press conference in La Penca, Nicaragua, held by Eden Pastora, a maverick Contra leader who resisted cooperating with the CIA and the main Contra force. Several people were killed, but not Pastora. Afterward, Tony Avirgan, an American journalist who suffered shrapnel wounds at La Penca, and his wife, Martha Honey, set out to uncover who had plotted the attack. A year later, they produced a book that charged a small group of Americans and Cuban exiles—some with ties to the CIA and the Contras—with planning the murderous assault. One of the persons they fingered was John Hull, a Contra supporter with a spread in northern Costa Rica and a relationship with North and the CIA. Their report noted that some Contra supporters were moonlighting in the drug trade.*

Hull sued the couple for libel in Costa Rica. He demanded $1 million. Avirgan and Honey, who lived in San José, received death threats. They considered retaliating by filing a lawsuit in the States against individuals in the secret Contra-support network. But they could find no lawyer to take such a difficult case. Eventually Sheehan was recommended to them. They checked him out. The reports were mixed. But he had one undeniable positive attribute: he would accept the case. The couple retained him.†

Come late spring of 1986, Sheehan was mixing with spooks in the Washington area, and he was pondering how to craft a lawsuit for Avir-

---

* It was not until 1993 that a collection of journalists, including Avirgan and Honey, determined that the La Penca bomber was Vital Roberto Gaguine, a member of the People's Revolutionary Army (known as ERP), a collection of Argentine Marxists who freelanced for Nicaraguan intelligence. The simplest conclusion was that the Sandinistas had tried to knock off Pastora.

† With no help from Sheehan, Avirgan and Honey in May of 1986 won the libel trial in Costa Rica on technical grounds.

gan and Honey. He collected information on the Contra operation. He drew closer to Wheaton, who had a new tale every time they met. Then Sheehan made a pilgrimage to meet the dark angel of the covert crowd: Ed Wilson.

The imprisoned rogue officer made Sheehan's head swim. The essence of Wilson's story, Sheehan claimed, was that the Agency in 1976 had created a highly secretive counterterrorist unit modeled on the PRUs of Vietnam and had run this entity apart from the main bureaucracy. The mission: conduct "wet operations" (spy talk for assassinations). After the election of Jimmy Carter, this group was erased from the books and hidden in private companies, and Shackley was the man in charge of the unit both in and out of government. The program was divided into different components. CIA man William Buckley supposedly had directed one out of Mexico with Quintero and Ricardo Chavez. Another unit was headed by a former Mossad officer. Felix Rodriguez was involved in yet one more in the Mideast. Sheehan took Wilson at his word. "Wilson went into such detail," Sheehan later maintained. "It's not something that's being made up."

At one point after Sheehan met with Wilson, it dawned on him: everything was connected. The La Penca bombing, the North-Contra network, the Wilson gang, all those CIA-trained Cuban exiles, the whole history of Agency dirty tricks, the operations against Castro, the war in Laos, the nasty spook side of the Vietnam War, clandestine Agency action in Iran. It was an ongoing conspiracy. It did not matter if these guys were in or out of government. It was a villainous government within a government, a plot that had existed for decades, a permanent criminal enterprise. Sheehan had a unified field theory of covert U.S. history. And Shackley was the evil Professor Moriarty, the man who pulled all the strings. The avenging Sheehan now was determined to take Shackley down.

Sheehan melded the La Penca bombing case to his Wheaton-influenced investigation of the old-boy network. Avirgan and Honey shared with him all the information they carefully had developed on the Contra-support operation. Names and stories he threw at them—including Shackley's—were unfamiliar. They took it on faith that Sheehan knew what he was doing when he blended the results of their professional investigation with the grab-bag of information he had collected from Wheaton, Wilson, and others. "We saw John Hull as the center, and Sheehan saw it as Shackley," Honey recalled. "Shackley was the main ingredient. I don't know why Danny fixated on him. He told us he had lots of information on Shackley's involvement in La Penca. That was b.s. But what do we know, sitting in Costa Rica?" Sheehan was looking for a case he could play before a large audience. He repeatedly told Avirgan and Honey the public did not care about La Penca. But people would pay notice if the enemy was one grand conspiracy headed by a dastardly figure.

Sheehan applied the resources of his small Christic Institute to the case. Wheaton continued investigating the Wilson crowd and other covert sorts. He started telling Jenkins that he believed he was chasing a decades-old, top-secret assassination unit. Wheaton claimed it had begun with an assassination training program for Cuban exiles that Shackley had set up in the early 1960s. The target was Castro. The secret war against Cuba faded, but the "Shooter Team" continued. It expanded and was now called the Fish Farm, and Shackley remained its chief.*

Sheehan knitted together all this spook gossip and misinformation with a few hard facts, and on May 29, 1986, he dropped the load. In a Miami federal court, Sheehan filed a lawsuit against thirty individuals, invoking the RICO antiracketeering law and accusing all of being part of a criminal conspiracy that trained, financed, and armed Cuban-American mercenaries in Nicaragua, smuggled drugs, violated the Neutrality Act by supporting the Contras, traded various weapons, and bombed the press conference at La Penca. Sheehan's plaintiffs were journalists Tony Avirgan and Martha Honey. The conspirators were far-flung: John Hull in Costa Rica; Cuban exiles based in Miami (including Quintero); druglords Pablo Escobar and Jorge Ochoa in Colombia; arms dealers in Florida; Contra leader Adolfo Calero; an Alabama mercenary named Tom Posey; Robert Owen, a secret North aide; the unknown bomber at La Penca; and Singlaub, Hakim, Secord, Clines, and Shackley. Sheehan alleged that Shackley had peddled arms illegally, plotted to kill Pastora, and (with Secord, Clines, and Hakim) accepted money from drug sales for arms shipments. Sheehan demanded over $23 million in damages.

With this lawsuit, Sheehan believed, he could break up the Contra-support operation and cast into the light shadowy characters who had been up to mischief for years. Sheehan and Wheaton had stumbled across some real players and some real operations. But they both possessed hyperactive imaginations, and whatever truth they did uncover they had twisted into a false, cosmic conspiracy.

The filing—drafted sloppily by Sheehan—surprised Shackley and his fellow defendants. Hoven and Jenkins were stunned. Neither expected Sheehan to produce such a storm. Sheehan clearly was in this for politics and ego. He was not about to be a quiet disseminator of information. "I had been left with the assumption," Hoven noted, "that I was set up to pass information to Sheehan. But they"—whoever *they* were—"fucked it up because Sheehan was not playing it close to the script."

---

* Wheaton claimed that a senior CIA official had told him about the Fish Farm, but he has refused to name the source or put the source in touch with journalists.

Shackley learned about the lawsuit from one of his associates who read a news wire report about it. He understandably was upset. He called Secord to find out what was going on. Secord said he was checking into the situation. Days later, Shackley and his attorney met with Secord, Clines, and Tom Green, who was Secord's lawyer, at Green's office. While they discussed the case, Oliver North walked in. Shackley also chatted with Singlaub about the suit. I know why I'm in the suit, said Singlaub, who as a private citizen had been soliciting funds for the Contras. But I don't know why you are. Shackley wondered, too. There had to be some reason, he concluded. There had to be something behind all this.

In September, federal Judge James Lawrence King tossed out Sheehan's messy complaint against Shackley and the rest. But he gave the Christic Institute thirty days to try again. The Institute filed a revised complaint on October 4. The next day was a bad one for the covert crowd.

On October 5, 1986, a Sandinista patrol in Nicaragua shot down a C-123K cargo plane that was supplying the Contras. Eugene Hasenfus, the surviving crewman and an Air America veteran, told his Nicaraguan captors he thought the CIA was behind this operation, which was run out of an El Salvador air base by two Cuban-Americans. Reporters chased leads. One of the Cuban-Americans was Quintero, the other, ex-CIA man Felix Rodriguez, who, journalists discovered, was a close friend of Don Gregg, an old Agency hand now advising Vice President Bush. (Rodriguez had even met with Bush.) The White House declared that the U.S. government was not connected to this operation. Then in early November, a small Lebanese magazine disclosed the Iran initiative. For weeks, the White House put out conflicting accounts of the Iranian program. On November 25, Attorney General Edwin Meese III announced the startling news that profits from the Iran initiative had been diverted to the Contras. Reporters at the press conference were amazed.

Slowly facts emerged. North had directed his own unofficial covert unit, which had supplied weapons to the Contras, facilitated secret arms transfers to Iran, and planned for bigger and better things. It was an off-the-shelf mini-CIA, run by Secord, Clines, and Hakim—all friends of Shackley. Rodriguez and Quintero, both past associates of Shackley, were in charge in Central America. Shackley had had an early contact with the middleman of the Iran deal. Reporters checked clip files and noticed that the whole crew was once connected to Ed Wilson. A secret clique appeared to be running the nation's most covert programs.

On December 12, 1986, in the early heat of the Iran-Contra scandal, Sheehan submitted to the court an affidavit detailing the heart of his case against Shackley and the rest. Written in the first person, Sheehan's affidavit described how he had uncovered the grandest national security scandal of all time. The affidavit, a long, rambling document full of references to confidential sources, was a masterpiece of conspiracy theory. A few parts were true—even prescient; other portions were ridiculous and baseless. Much of it was demonstrably wrong and ahistorical.*

At the heart of Sheehan's opus lurked what he dubbed the "Secret Team," a collection of former CIA men, Pentagon officials, and arms merchants who supposedly specialized in covert political assassinations of communists and other enemies. Citing "Source 48," a former U.S. intelligence officer—in actuality, Gene Wheaton—Sheehan claimed Shackley and Clines were running a private assassination program that had evolved from projects they ran while Agency officials. He named Secord, Hakim, and Quintero as other Secret Team members. He maintained that Shackley and the rest were responsible for supplying the plastic explosives used at the La Penca bombing. He noted that "Source 49"—later identified as Carl Jenkins—had confirmed all this.

Sheehan wanted to do more than solve the La Penca case. He was out to rescue American foreign policy from the clutches of Shackley's foul squad. In Sheehan's secret history, Shackley and his comrades had conspired with the Mafia in Miami and then transferred to Laos where they allied themselves with a drug-dealing Vang Pao and used his dirty profits to fund a clandestine operation that assassinated over 100,000 civilians in Laos, Cambodia, and Thailand. Next Shackley and company directed the overthrow of Allende in Chile. Once that was accomplished, Shackley, as Saigon station chief, ran the Phoenix program and financed it with drug money from Vang Pao. Then in 1973, Shackley and Clines created their "own private anticommunist assassination and unconventional warfare program." They set up a base in Tehran and retained Wilson to head an assassination program. The Secret Team banked its drug money at Nugan Hand in Australia. It offered "assassination services" to Somoza in Nicaragua. The Shackley cabal formed EATSCO and supplied weapons to the Contras. When the Reagan administration decided to sell arms secretly to Iran, the White House turned to the professionals: Shackley's Secret Team.

---

* Rob Hager, a lawyer for the Christic Institute, had beseeched Sheehan to bring him affidavits from his spook sources, in which they would attest to the information Sheehan was presenting as fact. Instead, Sheehan wrote his own affidavit to detail how he had come to possess all this damning material. "He was intent," Hager recalled, "on filing an affidavit that had his name on it. . . . He was absolutely flipped out. There was potential for all that fame. It was like being in the middle of Watergate. He'd been around Washington all these years, waiting to be the center of attention. Plus, there would be money." Hager, disgusted with Sheehan, soon quit the case.

From start to finish, in Sheehan's warped view, it was Shackley, with Clines always by his side. The most notorious covert operations of the past twenty-five years were the doing of a handful of rotten spooks. From Castro to the Contras, Shackley had been the mastermind, trafficking in guns, drugs, and murders. Shackley was the evil genius of recent American history. "Shackley is like a black widow," Sheehan declared to a group of supporters. "[He] is the duomo of this whole operation. He has been running this thing, this specific type of operation basically since 1961, and he has gone everywhere."

But Sheehan's affidavit was riddled with errors. Names, dates, titles were off. He had Shackley and Clines—and others—at the wrong places, at the wrong times. He had no proof to buttress the sensational allegations. His account, predominantly based on the say-so of Wheaton and Wilson, conflicted with the historical record. The clandestine activity conducted by the CIA in Cuba, Laos, Vietnam, and Chile depended on the participation of hundreds—if not thousands—of Americans in the national security bureaucracy. These operations were all sanctioned by the President and his national security advisers; they were not the work of a covert coven.

On January 30, 1987, Judge King shocked Shackley and his fellow defendants. He ruled against their motion to dismiss the Christic complaint. They had argued that Sheehan had failed to meet the legal criteria required for a racketeering case to proceed. King did not agree. Sheehan would be awarded the power of discovery. He could take depositions and compel his foes to turn over records. The excitable Sheehan now had power akin to that of a government investigator.

Shackley's role in the Iran initiative—his meeting with Ghorbanifar, his discussion with Ledeen—made media reports. He claimed that after his initial talk with Ghorbanifar, he had no other participation in the Iranian initiative. His involvement was nothing more than happenstance. It was hard for some journalists to believe that the man who once was a potential DCI, who had associated with CIA rogue Ed Wilson, who ran what seemed a mysterious consulting business, happened to be the fellow who first made contact with Ghorbanifar. Perhaps there really was a Secret Team.

In *The New York Times Magazine,* investigative writer Peter Maas profiled the major figures in the scandal. With this article and a book he published a year earlier on the Wilson case, Maas introduced Shackley's Vietnam nickname—the Blond Ghost—to a wide audience. From this point on, within the community of journalists, government investigators, and spy hobbyists who follow intelligence issues, Shackley would be known by this label. It was the final revenge of Frank Snepp, who in his post-Agency days had spread word of Shackley's wartime moniker.

Both the House and the Senate set up select committees to investigate the Iran-Contra affair, and their staffs pursued Shackley. How could Shackley not be immersed in the Iran-Contra affair? He was a colleague and business partner of the main operators. He had been mixed up in the Wilson affair. Congressional investigators and journalists dusted off a 1983 Australian government report on the mysterious Nugan Hand Bank. The study, parts of which were still secret, noted that a whole cadre of covert operators had been associated with the bank, and the names were familiar: Secord, Clines, Quintero, and Shackley. Recent history suggested that Shackley must have had more than a cameo role in the latest chapter of this ongoing real-life spy story. But Shackley kept maintaining he had nothing to do with the scandal other than his meeting with Ghorbanifar in 1984.

The Iran-Contra scandal was a tangled affair, overflowing with plots and subplots. The controversy created a rift in the barrier that normally hides the world of covert operatives from prying outsiders. Reporters peering through the opening found a host of bizarre characters and leads. A *Miami Herald* investigation discovered that in 1985 Dr. Mario Castejon, the head of a conservative political party in Guatemala, who had a plan to create a Contra medical brigade, was referred by Vice President Bush to Oliver North. The story suggested Bush, despite his denials, had known of North's clandestine efforts.

In tracking the tale, the *Herald* reporters encountered Shackley. Two American associates of Castejon—one an arms dealer, the other a security consultant—told the *Herald* that a report based on Castejon's proposal was hand-delivered to Novzar Razmara in Shackley's office. The point was to use Shackley as a channel to the Agency, so CIA officers could review and informally approve the plan. The newspaper's sources also asserted that Bush was a regular visitor to Shackley's suites.

Shackley and Razmara completely denied the story. No report was delivered to them. They had nothing to do with Castejon. Bush "has never been in this complex," Shackley said. "... We have absolutely nothing to do with the CIA." In trying to sort out the claims and counterclaims, the *Herald* reporters discovered Edwin Hochstedt, a Baltimore businessman and longtime friend of Razmara. Hochstedt said he had seen Bush at Shackley's office meeting with Razmara. He noted his belief that Shackley's operation was connected to the Agency. But after speaking with Razmara, Hochstedt phoned the newspaper to say he was mistaken about the Bush-Razmara meeting.

It was a curious story, suggesting Shackley was more than a private business consultant. But it boiled down to Shackley's and Razmara's word against allegations from other spooks. A year after the story appeared, Jamie Jameson provided a different account of this affair: "Razmara had said [to me] he met somebody and he had some kind of proposal about medical assistance to the people in Central America and so we met and we talked and there was nothing we could do about it and that was it." This remark of Jameson's contradicted Razmara's and Shackley's earlier blanket denials about the Castejon plan. If they were not honest when they said they had absolutely nothing to do with Castejon, then perhaps their assertions about their ties to Bush were off.

Congressional investigators wanted answers about Shackley's role in the Iran-Contra scandal. They sent him a subpoena requesting all documents he had related to various companies and individuals. But neither the congressional investigation nor special counsel Lawrence Walsh would focus much on Shackley. The Iran-Contra committees did not even bother to take Shackley's deposition until after Congress had finished its extensive hearings on the affair. During that spectacle, Secord was defiant, and North became a folk-hero for conservative Americans. The committees did not consider calling Shackley to the witness table. He was deemed a peripheral character in this circus. But in September of 1987, as the investigation was winding down, he was brought into the chaotic Capitol Hill offices of the Iran-Contra committees for a two-day, tense deposition.

The deposition covered a wide patch of ground: Shackley's relationships to Clines and Hakim; his business activities; the Wilson scandal; various Iran-Contra odds-and-ends. Shackley said he had never heard of the Fish Farm—the assassination program Gene Wheaton claimed Shackley directed. On the key issues at hand, Shackley maintained he had not met North until after the Christic suit was filed in May of 1986, that he knew nothing of the Contra supply operation run by his friends, and that despite his contacts with Ghorbanifar and Ledeen he was unaware of the Iran initiative.

Cameron Holmes, the lead interrogator, did not believe him. How could Shackley be the one person in this mob unaware of what was going on? Why was he so insistent he had not picked up a single whiff of the Contra operation or the Iran initiative? There was no crime in knowing. Shackley proclaimed his ignorance too much. Holmes could only imagine why. But he possessed no evidence contradicting Shackley's claims.

Years later, some evidence did emerge. In a 1992 interview, Clines told a story that undermined Shackley's account. Clines recalled that in 1985, when he was based in Lisbon and purchasing arms for the Contras, he had received a call from his partner Secord. The retired general told Clines that Shackley claimed to know a better arms dealer in Lisbon than the one Clines was using. Shackley recommended that Clines switch his business to this fellow. (In his 1987 deposition, Shackley mentioned he had a Portuguese friend who represented a Portuguese arms firm.) Why change a system that's working? Clines argued. Nevertheless, he phoned the arms merchant Shackley was pushing. The man was out of the country, and Clines let the matter drop. "This indicates," Clines remarked in 1992, "that Shackley knew what I was doing and that Secord must have been talking to him."

Other evidence that Shackley may not have been straight with congressional investigators surfaced when Oliver North's notebooks were declassified and released to the public in 1990. North—whom Shackley claimed he never met until June of 1986—referred to Shackley several times in his diaries, and in ways that could suggest Shackley was connected to the scandal. On February 7, 1984, North had made a cryptic entry. (Many of his entries are cryptic.) He jotted a short list:

Sarkis—delivered weap[on]s *Gratis!*
Tom Cline [sic]/Shackley connection?
Felix Rodriguez—Miami
Quaddhaffi connection

At this point, funds for the Contras were dwindling, and North was scrambling for help. Sarkis Soghanalian was a Miami-based arms dealer who apparently gave someone a free supply of arms. The rest of the note is strange. Rodriguez claimed in his memoirs that he did not meet North until the end of 1984, and Clines and Secord did not become involved in the Contra operation until months after this entry. The list's meaning is not clear, but North was thinking about Shackley and Clines in the context of weapons.

North, on December 20, 1984, scribbled Shackley's name again. This time the reference was less oblique. North noted he had received a call from Duane "Dewey" Clarridge, chief of the CIA's Western Hemisphere Division. Shackley had known Clarridge in the Agency. But in a 1991 interview, Shackley declared, "I had absolutely nothing to do with Mr. Clarridge during the timeframe of Iran-Contra." North's note suggests otherwise.

After talking to Clarridge, North wrote, "Check as to whether Ted Shackley is helping in Portugal with arms—may be for South Africa." The rest of the entry was deleted by White House censors, with the explanation that it referred to a foreign intelligence service—probably South African intelligence. Portugal was where Secord and Clines were procuring arms for the Contras (and where Shackley had a friend in the arms business). And Clarridge, in April of 1984, had traveled to South

Africa and discussed with officials the prospect of Pretoria providing financial assistance to the rebels in Nicaragua. As with most of North's notes, this one only provides a hint of what was going on—but North seemed to believe, on the basis of his conversation with Clarridge, that Shackley was participating in a weapons-related deal.*

North mentioned Shackley a few more times. After talking to Ledeen on June 3, 1985, he wrote Shackley's home and office number in his diary. And on April 17, 1986—when North was concerned about the hunt being waged by Gene Wheaton and Daniel Sheehan—he talked to Secord and then scrawled, "Call Ted Shackley re Libya and Secord suit."

These notes do not indict Shackley, but taken with Clines's recollection they indicate that there is more to the story than Shackley admitted. Holmes's skepticism was warranted. But neither he, his fellow congressional probers, nor the independent counsel investigators, who shared the same suspicions about Shackley, would ever prove anything. The Blond Ghost eluded them all.

V

The Christics were still on the case, and they were demonizing Shackley. The Institute sold copies of Sheehan's affidavit, which portrayed Shackley as a drug-peddling leader of an international Murder, Inc. Its mass mailings and newsletters spread Sheehan's Secret Team theory across the nation. The Institute peddled a comic book version, in which Shackley was depicted as a black cat with bloody fangs. An enterprising entrepreneur produced Iran-Contra trading cards; on one Shackley looked like a vampire.

In churches, at schools, Sheehan spoke to audiences full of wide-eyed supporters. His denouncements of Shackley and the Secret Team brought standing ovations and offers of help. He appeared on one radio station after another. He dazzled thousands with his stirring oratory powers. Sheehan was a missionary with a message for those who worried about what their government did behind the veil. At one of Sheehan's speeches, a person stood up and said, "I'm so grateful. You know, I've known for twenty-five years that something wasn't right, and I couldn't figure out what was going on, and I thought I would die before

---

* Associates of Shackley claimed he stayed away from anything that went boom or bang. "Ted is hypersensitive about arms," maintained Jamie Jameson, his friend and partner. "He never came close to touching it. It was a matter of prudence not morality." But in 1983, Bill Kohlmann, an Agency analyst in Saigon under Shackley, had been traveling in Germany. At an old hotel on the Rhine, he ran into Shackley, who acknowledged he was part of a delegation of arms traders whom the Bonn government had invited to a weapons trade show.

I ever understood." In Washington, Sheehan talked of forcing the impeachment of President Ronald Reagan and, later on, President George Bush and Vice President Dan Quayle.

He mass-marketed his crusade. The Christic Institute solicited money in direct-mail from hundreds of thousands of liberal Americans. Tens of thousands contributed regularly. Hollywood celebrities and popular musicians, such as Bruce Springsteen, Jackson Browne, Don Henley, and Kris Kristofferson raised funds for the Christics. The Institute distributed a videotape of Sheehan presenting his Secret Team rap. Thousands of devotees held house parties and played the tape for friends and family. Sheehan attracted a cultlike following.

In the Institute's offices, two cluttered row houses in a run-down section of Washington, dozens of low-paid staffers and investigators toiled relentlessly and pursued countless leads. They fed information —some of it solid—to journalists. When friends, political supporters, dissident Agency veterans, congressional investigators, national security experts, and reporters criticized Sheehan's outlandish mangling of facts, he waved their concerns aside. He dismissed the pleadings of responsible Christic staffers who tried to correct mistakes in Christic material. Sheehan alone possessed the truth. He had a holy cause. He was brandishing the sword of righteousness, and his dragon was Ted Shackley. For scores of thousands of Americans, Shackley became a symbol of all that is dark, nefarious and wrong with the U.S. government.

Shortly before Christmas of 1987, Sheehan flew to the high-security federal prison at Marion, Illinois, to take the deposition of Edwin Wilson. But Wilson did not support Sheehan's claim that Shackley was running an assassination unit. Asked by Sheehan if Shackley had established a private, off-the-shelf covert operation, Wilson said yes. But Wilson depicted this entity as primarily a commercial enterprise to ship and trade arms—a firm in which Wilson, Shackley, Clines, Secord, and von Marbod were to be secret partners. Wilson said that the $500,000 he had loaned Clines was the start-up money for the endeavor, but Clines had cut him out by setting up EATSCO on his own. If there were a conspiracy between Wilson and the so-called Secret Team, it had been more about money than politics and assassinations.

That did not stop Sheehan. The Christic Institute churned out a steady stream of fund-raising appeals. "You and I," read one, "know that former CIA Associate Deputy Director *Theodore Shackley, and his assistant Tom Clines, set up the Secret Team* years before North ever set foot in the White House." The letter added, "Because of your support, our investigators now know that Ted Shackley has *five bases of operation around the world.*" The congressional Iran-Contra committees, the Christics

griped, had failed to uncover Shackley's covert empire. They had ignored the Contra-drug connection. (That much was true.) The Institute
pledged to expose and stop the Secret Team.

In the shadowy world of national security scandals, Shackley became
a favorite villain. The political cult of Lyndon LaRouche and the Liberty
Lobby, a right-wing populist organization, conducted "investigations"
that cited Shackley as the hidden hand in global oil intrigue and international drug-trafficking. (They failed to back up their assertions with per-
suasive evidence.) During the Iran-Contra investigation, two arms-
dealing brothers in Britain, Leslie and Michael Aspin, claimed that Leslie
had met with Shackley, North, and Ghorbanifar in Hamburg in 1984 to
plot secret missiles sales to Iran. But Michael Aspin had been charged
with conning several arms merchants regarding a fake $40 million TOW
missile deal involving Iran. The Aspin charges smacked of a concocted
tale meant to cover their actions.

Shackley was in an unusual position. He was one of a handful of CIA
officers to achieve public notoriety. Few Americans, few journalists,
could name more than a couple of Agency officials, and those known
mostly were directors. Any conspiracy peddler looking to tie the Agency
into a theory needed to link his allegations to a past or present Agency
officer. To an outsider, the choices were not many. But Shackley was
well known in the circle of CIA watchers, and what was most known
about him was his proximity to scandal.

In early March of 1988, Sheehan took Wheaton's deposition. For five
days in a federal courtroom in Washington, Wheaton rambled on, spout-
ing his jumble of facts and fantasies. He continued to claim Shackley was
overseeing an assassination outfit called the Fish Farm. During the cross-
examination, Wheaton refused to say which retired CIA official had told
him about Shackley and the Fish Farm. A defense attorney asked if
Wheaton possessed direct knowledge of Shackley drug-smuggling or
money-laundering, as Christic legal papers claimed Wheaton did.
Wheaton admitted he did not have "any direct knowledge." He knew
nothing about Shackley gunrunning to the Contras. He denied being
Sheehan's source for several key pieces of information, contradicting
Sheehan's affidavit.

Throughout his deposition, Wheaton came across as sincere and serious, but a man who could not differentiate between what he truly knew,
what he heard, and what he and others speculated. He certainly knew
something of the world of private spooks—but precisely what was impossible to determine. He was not a source to build a case upon.

After almost two years of this foolishness, Shackley was right to be
enraged. A bunch of leftists—the sort who always besmirched the
Agency—were turning him into a poster boy for government evil. He

had been fighting back by collecting depositions and statements from people who Sheehan claimed could attest to the Blond Ghost's worst deeds. One day Shackley and Vernon Gillespie showed up unannounced at the home of Paul Hoven, who had introduced Wheaton to Sheehan and now was listed as a source in Sheehan's suit. They wanted a statement from him. Hoven went with the pair back to Shackley's office. Shackley, according to Hoven, noted that his firm was working for a foreign manufacturer of armed personnel carriers and that there might be a related research job for Hoven. Hoven wondered if this was a bribe. But he did not need any such incentive. He knew nothing about Shackley's activities and signed an affidavit declaring that.

Shackley gathered affidavits from other figures in the case, some named in Christic legal papers as potential witnesses who could confirm Shackley's alleged illegal actions. Secord, Singlaub, Robert Owen, Adolfo Calero, and Douglas Schlachter all swore that they had seen no evidence that Shackley helped the Contras, smuggled drugs, or managed a political hit squad. Carl Jenkins, cited repeatedly by Sheehan as a source on Shackley's villainy, vowed he had no personal knowledge about such matters. "I am astounded that on the basis of his conversations with me," Jenkins stated, "Mr. Sheehan would swear under oath that I supplied him with any of this information."

These statements did not settle the matter. Some were from friends of Shackley, some from fellow defendants. But Sheehan had indicated in his court filings that these were the very people whose testimony could prove Shackley's malevolence. If they would not share such testimony, Sheehan's case would have to depend on the statements of Wheaton—which meant he had no case.

The Iran-Contra affair and Sheehan's exploits resurrected Edwin Wilson. Reporters called and visited the imprisoned ex-Company man. He had lawyers working on several fronts: challenging his convictions and suing the CIA and the Justice Department for the release of documents. He considered suing Shackley, Secord, Clines, von Marbod, and others for allegedly cheating him out of the money from their secret deal and then framing him. The lawsuit never took off. But Wilson's legal maneuverings produced statements that supported a few of his assertions about Shackley.

Wilson's lawyer acquired an affidavit from Lloyd Jones, a helicopter pilot who had worked for Wilson in Libya in late 1979.* Jones noted that he and other Wilson employees had collected information on Soviet

---

* Paul Blumenthal, an attorney for Wilson, maintained that he verified that Jones flew for Wilson in Libya. Several years after Jones provided his statement, he moved from his Oklahoma home and could not be located.

military activities in Libya and that Wilson passed this material to friends in U.S. intelligence. Jones swore he had smuggled this type of information out of Libya and once carried a package of papers to Shackley in the United States. Several times Wilson had asked Jones to call Shackley to see if he had gotten the information. "I was informed by [Shackley] that he had been receiving this information and that it was adequate," Jones stated.

All this activity supposedly had occurred after Shackley quit the Agency. Jones's affidavit, if true, led to serious questions. Was Shackley acting as a pipeline into the Agency for Wilson? Was he doing something else with the intelligence? Was he trying to fool Wilson into believing that he (Wilson) was still connected to the Company?

Even more fascinating—and damning—was a twenty-four-page 1988 affidavit signed by Shirley Brill, a former girlfriend of Tom Clines. A few years earlier, Brill had been spurned by Clines. Her recollections could be discounted as revenge, but much of her story jibed with the established record. In her telling, Shackley and Clines were lucky to be free men.

Brill, a CIA employee, met Clines in 1976, and the two lived together for a spell. She claimed that in 1977 Clines regularly had received overseas calls from Wilson. After Clines hung up, Brill recalled, he always phoned Shackley. She said that Clines and Shackley often discussed getting out of the Agency and making lots of money. Brill and Clines frequently traveled to Miami. There, she asserted, they stayed in a cabana owned by a Cuban exile, a friend of Quintero and someone whom Clines hinted was a drug dealer. After Clines left the Agency in 1978 and began to form his own businesses, Brill maintained, he told her that von Marbod was going to help "them" gain Pentagon contracts. To Brill, "them" meant Clines, Shackley, Secord, and Wilson.

Brill confirmed what Wilson had been saying for years: Clines, Shackley, Secord, von Marbod, and Wilson were all in it together. Brill claimed that she had heard Clines, Secord, Quintero, and Shackley plotting to frame Wilson.*

Brill's statement caused neither Shackley nor Clines any problems. There was no Wilson-related case pending against them. Her affidavit

---

* When called before the Iran-Contra committees in 1987, Felix Rodriguez had testified that Clines had told him that both Secord and Wilson were secret partners in his endeavors. (By this point, Clines and Rodriguez had experienced a bitter falling-out.) But Rodriguez also said under oath that he never had worked for or with Wilson. According to Rodriguez's own memoirs, Rodriguez collaborated with Wilson in 1975 to train the Lebanese military to penetrate Palestinian bases. Everybody connected to the Wilson affair suffered severe credibility problems—which has made it hard to sort out the conflicting assertions.

could have been payback for a soured affair. Her claims might have been overly influenced by the Wilson charges already in the public record. She was a dubious witness, and Wilson's appeal was going nowhere. What he and his witnesses had to say about Shackley did not matter. If Shackley and the others had gotten the best of him—and the evidence is far from conclusive—they did a good job.

On June 23, 1988, days before the Christic Institute suit was to go to trial, Judge King tossed it out of court, ruling that Sheehan had failed to demonstrate his case had any foundation. King declared Sheehan's allegations were "based on unsubstantiated rumor and speculation from unidentified sources with no firsthand knowledge." Sheehan and his followers had an automatic excuse ready: since King had not allowed the suit to proceed, Sheehan was not able to collect all the information he needed to prove his charges. The Christics hinted that King was part of a conspiracy so deep it even perverted the federal justice system. Shackley took his wife out to dinner to celebrate.

A dismissed case did not end the crusade. Sheehan filed an appeal. His fund-raising machinery continued to whir. He spoke at more campuses, on more radio shows, capturing new recruits. Shackley initiated legal action against the Christic Institute to recover his massive legal fees. (His friends estimated that the suit cost him up to $500,000.) He appealed to his fellow Agency veterans, via the newsletter of the Association of Former Intelligence Officers, and asked them to write anti-Christic letters-to-the-editor and to request that their representatives and senators press the IRS to examine the Institute's tax-exempt status.

To Shackley, the lawsuit was about something much larger than Shee-han's egotistical desire to be a giant-killer, Wheaton's urge to be a player, or Jenkins's resentment at being frozen out of transport contracts. "This attack," Shackley wrote, "is part of a long-range plan to weaken the entire U.S. intelligence community." The case was not merely Sheehan's doing. Dark forces had animated the assault. *The Journal of Defense and Diplomacy*—a publication for which Shackley wrote—published a scathing and anonymous attack on the Christics that suggested, with no real proof, that the Institute was influenced by Moscow and that Avirgan and Honey, as journalists, followed orders from the Soviets. In a media interview, Secord put it more plainly: the Christic suit is a case of "foreign intelligence services working through witting and unwitting parties, trying to use our own judicial system against us."*

---

* In his memoirs, Secord wrote, "The suit seemed to be the end product of a concerted effort to undermine . . . U.S. contra support, with roots in the Congressional opposition and possible assistance from foreign intelligence services—perhaps the KGB, but more likely . . . Cuban intelligence."

Shackley and Secord wanted to see the Evil Empire—even one in the process of reforming—as the true enemy and the unseen hand behind their troubles. Such an explanation enhanced their image as cold warriors, and elevated their own importance. But the made-in-Moscow theory was more farfetched than the mundane and simple explanation that the Christic case evolved from an intraspook squabble. Most likely, the obvious culprits—Danny Sheehan, Gene Wheaton, and Carl Jenkins—had acted alone.*

In February of 1989, Judge King ruled that Sheehan had brought a frivolous lawsuit and ordered the Institute to pay the defendants $955,000. This was one of the highest sanction orders in history and represented four times the total assets of the Christic Institute. From the Christic payment, Shackley recouped $148,296, but his out-of-pocket expenditures had totaled much more. The Christic Institute appealed the assessment of the fee. This motion and its appeal of King's dismissal were eventually rejected.†

The Iran-Contra investigations of Congress and Lawrence Walsh left Shackley relatively unscathed. His friends Secord, Hakim, and Clines fared less well. Richard Secord pleaded guilty to one count of lying to Congress and was sentenced to two years of probation. Hakim pleaded

---

* In 1989, Susan Huck, a conservative ex–Capitol Hill aide, produced, with Shackley's help, a book on the Christic case. Titled *Legal Terrorism,* it red-baited Avirgan and Honey and implied that the Christics were "good instruments" of Soviet disinformation, that their lawsuit advanced "Soviet interests," and that they have "devoted themselves to weakening the United States and supporting our enemies." Huck, reflecting Shackley's own thinking, wrote that Shackley possessed a "record of thwarting . . . Moscow and Havana for three decades, and it is not difficult to imagine that grudges are held. . . . There was no reason whatsoever for the inclusion of Shackley in the La Penca case. . . . Why did the Christics insist upon it? Was it merely Sheehan's fixation, or did he have a little help from his friends?" The book demonstrated that rightists could be as conspiratorial as leftists. Huck's work was published by a small business called New World Publishing, which later put out a book by Shackley on terrorism and shared an office with Intel Research, a military consulting firm.

† In early 1992, the Supreme Court refused to set aside the sanction, which bankrupted the Christic Institute. Sheehan moved the Institute to Los Angeles, where he had a funding base among gullible Hollywood liberals. He talked of selling a movie on Iran-Contra. Avirgan and Honey, who now considered Sheehan a fraud, filed a complaint with the bar association of Washington and hoped to see Sheehan disbarred. They also sued Sheehan to gain access to the legal papers he had spirited away to California. Gene Wheaton kept going as a freelance investigator, latching on to different cases across the country. Years later, he would still be pitching high-flying conspiracy theories involving Shackley. He even called Shackley about one, a case in which a Marine colonel supposedly involved in covert operations had died mysteriously. According to Wheaton, Shackley told him, "I don't think you and I have anything to talk about."

guilty to illegally supplementing North's salary, and a company Hakim controlled pleaded guilty to stealing government property by diverting Iran initiative proceeds to the Contras. Hakim received a $5,000 fine and two years of probation. (North was found guilty of destroying documents, obstructing Congress, and accepting an illegal gratuity; his convictions were thrown out by an appeals court, which concluded that North's immunized congressional testimony had tainted the trial.) Walsh charged Clines with underreporting his income from the Secord-Hakim enterprise by at least $260,000 and with failing to disclose on his tax returns that he had an overseas bank account.

During the two-week Clines trial in a Baltimore federal court in 1990, a matronly-looking woman from the CIA sat in the back row of the courtroom and took notes. Her job was to report to Langley what Clines was revealing. (The judge had prevented Clines from disclosing much of his Agency past.) The CIA observer talked little with the few reporters present. But toward the trial's end, she remarked, "I hate this man. He's a sleazebag. And he gives all of us a bad name." Clines was found guilty and sentenced to sixteen months and a $40,000 fine. Clines served several months in a minimum-security prison, the only Iran-Contra player to do time.

Shackley had triumphed. The Christic Institute was reduced to a shell. Sheehan never introduced in court any evidence to support his spurious charges against Shackley. But before tens—maybe hundreds—of thousands of Americans who had paid attention to the Christic Institute, Shackley was vilified.

Sheehan's prime mistake was to confuse a community with a conspiracy. There does exist a small brethren of covert operators. For decades, their paths have crossed in and out of government. They are the men who have been called on by the highest officials of the United States to conduct its most secret missions. Shackley was not only one of these men; he had been a leader in this fraternity. But he was no Professor Moriarty. He was a special breed of federal bureaucrat: one who directed paramilitary operations, recruited spies, conducted clandestine political activity, and oversaw cover-ups for his commander in chief.

Shackley did not head a decades-old Secret Team, yet he had managed the Cuba show, supervised a secret war in Laos, run the Agency in Vietnam, approved internal meddling in Chile, and associated with Wilson and other covert crooks. The Christics actually had chosen wisely in selecting Shackley as a symbol—but not because he represented a small, roguish unit. He stood for something bigger. After years of intelligence scandals and disclosure, the American public had a name to attach to the hidden people of the clandestine world. That name was Ted Shackley. He was a covert ghost flushed into the open.

With the Christic nonsense behind him, Shackley again tried to slip into the quiet life of a former intelligence officer and international businessman. He continued working for the notorious oil billionaire John Deuss and other clients. Shackley wrote another book, *You're the Target: Coping with Terror and Crime.* Coauthored with a former CIA officer and a retired Baltimore chief of detectives, the book was a how-to guide to protecting corporate executives—how to avoid being kidnapped, bombed, and so on. But Shackley could not resist preaching, and his geopolitics had not mellowed. In tracing the rise of terrorism, Shackley and his coauthors cited the activity of nonviolent political protest groups "from which terrorists and rural and urban guerrillas draw their support and replenish their ranks." Protest movements such as the international boycott against Nestlé (which marketed infant formula in Third World regions where its use was unsafe), the book claimed, create the right kind of "conditioning" for would-be terrorists.

In surveying potential terrorists, Shackley listed homeless advocates and "militant environmentalists" as threats to watch. In canvassing current political instability, he recalled the extremism of Chilean leftists in the early 1970s—"behavior so provocative, violent, and unconstitutional that it left the armed forces no alternative but to intervene." Nearly two decades after Shackley had headed the Agency division that targeted Allende, he was justifying the murderous military takeover, without mentioning the CIA's role. He viewed the tens of thousands of deaths in the El Salvador civil war as the sole responsibility of the leftist rebels, not the Washington-backed military and death squads which conducted massacres and killed far more civilians than the insurgency.

Shackley's outlook on the world was bleak. Urban guerrilla warfare loomed in western Europe. Covert Soviet expansionism—even in this time of perestroika and glasnost—fueled terrorism and political agitation worldwide. The powerful, anti-apartheid African National Congress in South Africa was in Moscow's orbit. (No doubt, his years of work for Deuss had influenced Shackley's opinion.) But most of the book covered tips on how the savvy corporate executive could evade trouble. Keep your profile low, Shackley advised. Try to be "the 'little gray man,' the one nobody notices."

After years of exposure and controversy, Shackley faded from public sight—becoming a "little gray man." But he did not go underground. He spoke at the occasional conference, including a gathering in Miami of Cuban-American alumni of JMWAVE and Operation Mongoose. He delivered a lecture at the Smithsonian Institution on the future of intelligence. (As his audience filed into the room, Shackley sat unnoticed at a small desk beneath an escalator and polished his notes.) He gave a talk on Capitol Hill that was sponsored by a conservative foreign policy group. He was active in the Association of Former Intelligence Officers and attended reunions of old spooks.

Shackley even participated in a job fair at American University in Washington, D.C., where his Research Associates International hoped to recruit students to be risk analysts. As young people strolled past the various booths, one student who followed intelligence controversies gazed at the name tag on the plain-looking fellow in a dark suit who was sitting behind a table on which were scattered RAI brochures. Surprised, the student blurted out, "Are you Shackley from the CIA?" "That's me," Shackley replied. The stunned student managed to say, "Oh, I've heard a lot about you." Shackley put his lips together and smiled tightly.

EPILOGUE

"I have great respect for Shackley. Like me, he was a loyal servant of the state."

—OLEG KALUGIN, A FORMER MAJOR-GENERAL OF THE KGB IN CHARGE OF FOREIGN COUNTERINTELLIGENCE

THEODORE G. SHACKLEY lived the Cold War. In the name of America, he sent foreign intelligence agents to their doom in Germany in the 1950s. He managed a small secret war against Cuba, then oversaw a larger one in Laos. He directed intelligence in Vietnam during a war of profound intelligence failures. In Washington, Shackley signed the orders for scores of espionage and covert action operations around the globe. He was responsible for ugly things: political payoffs, the suborning of journalists, the enlistment of spies, the misleading of Congress. His flight toward the Director's chair stalled. After he left the Agency he was ensnared in scandals that bared the seamier side of the clandestine struggle between the United States and the Soviet Union. Ed Wilson was a product of the intelligence system that was assembled to do battle with communists. The Iran-Contra affair was propelled by the calculations of geostrategists obsessed with achieving an edge over Moscow, even if that meant selling arms to a country they decried as a terrorist state or promoting a war in the jungles of Central America. But most of the actions for which Shackley bears responsibility—and they may be key pieces of Cold War history—will never be known publicly.

There is a cliché often spouted by Company veterans: the failures of an intelligence service are well known; its successes are not. It is a hard proposition with which to argue, since these mythical accomplishments are not open to outside evaluation. But much of what is known of Shackley's career are programs that did not work or went awry.

In the intelligence field, the law of unintended consequences reigns. The flurry of Agency activity against the Eastern bloc countries in the 1950s gave those regimes justification for adopting more totalitarian population control measures. Scores of American agents were captured and then doubled, imprisoned, or killed. Eastern European lives were sacrificed by Americans, in anticipation of a war that never came. There was much effort and sacrifice for little gain, little meaningful information. So much action was based on the assumption that Moscow was bent on overrunning western Europe—an assumption founded on fear more than fact.

In Cuba, Agency sabotage missions, which sometimes resembled Keystone Cop capers, played into the hands of Castro, whose intelligence service thoroughly penetrated the CIA campaign against him. For decades afterward, the Agency would have to cope with what is called in the spy business "the disposal problem": hundreds to thousands of exiles trained in clandestine warfare who were free to put their skills to use elsewhere.

The show in Laos ended in utter disaster for those people whom some CIA officers thought they were helping. The Hmong might have been better off had they never met anyone from Langley.

Agency efforts in Vietnam ultimately were pointless. During the conflict, the Agency developed a reputation for brutality that may have been exaggerated but was not wholly fictitious. The station's PRUs and its allies in various Vietnamese security forces did dirty work. Shackley's men, desperate to produce for their chief, recruited women and children as agents. The results were meager.

Chile ended a success, in that a socialist was replaced by a pro-America tyrant. But that operation—and the lies CIA officers told Congress about it—led to investigation and legal trouble, further stained the Agency's reputation, and inspired a new generation of anti-Americanism in Latin America and elsewhere. Iran was another mess. The Agency again was caught in the institutional schizophrenia between espionage and intervention. China was impenetrable—a constant source of frustration. As for the biggest, most important job—recruiting Soviet spies—the CIA built a spotty record. Many officers of the clandestine service devoted decades of their lives to this enterprise and, by the time of their retirement, could boast of no success against the Soviet target. If Shackley ever worked directly on an operation that bagged a significant Soviet spy, it has remained one of the better-kept secrets among CIA officers.

Ask CIA people about the value of their endeavors during the Cold War and you are likely to receive one of two types of answers. Some acknowledge that much of what they did was foolish. They had to look busy. They had to try. If you could not bring in a Soviet spy, then one could at least slip U.S. propaganda into a local paper or penetrate a communist party and have something to write home about. When you did not succeed in stationing spies in, say, Poland, at least you could count these operations a necessary, if somewhat cold-blooded, gain in experience. All told, the returns were minimal and, in some instances, counterproductive. But it had to be done; this was war.

Other CIA people hail Agency actions as pivotal and productive episodes. For instance, there was the discovery of the Cuban missiles. This operation supposedly helped save the world and, thus, was worth the entire CIA budget. The detection of the missiles, some argue (in the face of a contrary paper trail), was the by-product of a vital Agency espionage program overseen by Shackley.

Both answers, though, end up in the same place: all's well that ends well. The United States won the Cold War. The Soviet Union crumbled. The Agency must have done something right. The premise that Washington's actions, including the CIA's implementation of presidential decisions, might have prolonged the Cold War (while causing people around the world to suffer) can be brushed aside easily as speculation. We can never know what could have been. Shackley and his comrades in the clandestine community can pronounce themselves victors and justify the screw-ups and loss of life as noble sacrifices for a cause that triumphed. "It's hard for people to understand who have not been there," observed one of Shackley's loyal assistants, his ROIC in Region V and operations chief in the Western Hemisphere Division. "It's easy for people—especially people of another generation—to view what we did with their own perspective. I fought the communists for twenty-eight years. I did a lot of bad things for my country. But I loved my country and did what I thought best. Tell people that."

When I started to write this book, I hoped to find out what sort of person sent agents on missions that could end in death or sat behind a desk and plotted the details of a secret war. Some CIA people pointed to Shackley as an emblematic Agency man: a heartless, soulless bureaucrat who ignored the grays of the world and implemented the policies set by the cold warriors at the top. That was what he was there to do: put into action the orders of his President. It was not his job to second-guess the operating assumptions. Presidents and their advisers needed Shackleys and those like him in the trenches to make real what they willed. To his superiors—with the exception of Stansfield Turner—Shackley was the perfect Company man: a smart, competent, ambitious manager whom they could trust to get a project done. He was no ideologue, yet he embraced the guiding principles. Bureaucracies value such officers.

In my interviews with over 100 former CIA officials I came across few people who could tell me about Shackley's internal motives. Some suggested that his childhood as an orphan—an Agency myth—sparked his fierce identification with this organization and caused his relentless ambition, traits that would have been apparent in any field of work he chose. But was there anything more than the coincidences of life that propelled Shackley into a position where he coolly made life-and-death decisions behind a veil and justified all in the name of anticommunism?

I first contacted Shackley in June of 1989, at the start of my research. I informed him that I had a contract to write a book on his career and that I wanted to interview him eventually. The day my letter arrived, Shackley was being interviewed by a conservative author working on a book on the Christic Institute case. "Tell [Corn] thanks, but I already have several contracts on my life," Shackley said to the journalist. In his reply to me, Shackley was less sardonic. "I am a very private man," he wrote. "I have not sought publicity." He observed that it is "difficult . . . to see on what basis we could cooperate." But he was good enough to send a reading list and a copy of his book, *The Third Option*. For two years I tried to see Shackley, and he put me off. At one point—when I asked him to lunch at the Willard Hotel—he agreed to meet; then he refused to schedule a time. Finally, in June of 1991, Shackley consented to an interview—but on his terms. A letter from his lawyer listed the conditions: I had to submit all questions in advance; this would be a one-time interview and last no longer than three hours; it would be conducted in Shackley's office; only Shackley could tape-record the discussion.

The negotiations on the last point lasted several months, with Shackley stubbornly resisting other arrangements. We at last agreed that there would be two tapes of the interview. Shackley would get one; the other would be retained by a third party. I would have unlimited access to that tape but not be allowed to copy it. We then squabbled over who would be the bearer of the second tape but found an attorney known and trusted by both Shackley's lawyer and my literary agent.

The interview was anticlimactic. I arrived at his highly secured office in Rosslyn, Virginia. Dressed in a dark suit, Shackley looked like a corporate executive. Now sixty-four years old, his face drooped slightly. He wore bifocals. If there ever had been anything intimidating in his presence, it was no longer there. His manner was cordial but official. He introduced his wife, Hazel, who shook my hand and offered a forced smile. I was then shown to a windowless conference room. A large map displayed the world's key oil production facilities. Bookshelves held large black binders labeled with the names of various geographic regions. Shackley sat across from me at a long table. Next to him was Richard Finney, who had served under Shackley in the Agency and now was a Shackley employee. Finney, who was very deferential to his boss, was in charge of the two cassette recorders placed on the table.

In front of Shackley was a stack of papers. He picked up the first few sheets and began to read. He had several points to make. He reiterated that he had agreed to see me on a one-time basis for three hours. He noted the time to the minute. He declared his interest was to "insure" the accuracy of my work. "The matters that we discuss today will afford you access to the truth, while permitting me to continue to honor my obligations under the law," he said, referring to the secrecy oath he signed when he joined the CIA. He noted that he had presented to the CIA the 214 questions I had submitted to him so he could receive guidance on what he could discuss. He then asked me what was the thesis of my book.

I noted that I was not out to prove any "thesis." I believed that his life in the CIA, since it embodied many seminal episodes, provided something of a history of the Agency. My goal was to use his twenty-eight-year-long career in the CIA as a window into the world of intelligence. "Good biographies," I said, "tend to speak for themselves."

"That's an interesting thesis," he responded.*

By my estimate, over the next three hours, Shackley responded to fewer than one fifth of the questions I had sent him. His explanation was that he was only following CIA instructions. But he was silent on some subjects that had been declassified by the Agency, such as the Berlin Tunnel. When I pointed this out, he barely shrugged. How could I know, I asked, if he avoided a question because the CIA directed him not to talk about a subject or because his preference was not to discuss it? "You will have to be perceptive enough to come to conclusions on your own," he replied.

Shackley went on about the Christic Institute's unfair persecution of

---

* After the interview, a close associate of Shackley's informed me that Shackley could not figure me out. Shackley was convinced that there was a hidden agenda to my project, but he could not discern it. Decades in the intelligence field—and his experience with the Christics—had left him suspicious and, in this case, unable to recognize the obvious: I was writing a book about Shackley's Agency career.

him. "If you have a theory why they included me, I'd be interested in hearing it," he said. He defended his actions regarding Wilson, maintaining he had been duped by a man he considered a family friend. He defended the secret war in Laos, but refused to discuss details of his management of it. The Hmong people, he observed, had been abandoned by U.S. politicians.

Shackley was hard to penetrate. Wary of my intentions, he did not let any feelings show. When I pressed him for reaction to certain events, he never offered much. What were your impressions when you first visited Long Tieng? I inquired, referring to the secret Hmong base in the Laotian mountains. "Once you've seen one of these kinds of camps, they're all pretty much the same," he replied. He answered questions in a pedantic manner, and I recalled what one close associate of his had told me: "Shackley is not the type of man who is imaginative enough to run a global conspiracy. He is very intelligent, but to get from A to Z, he has to go through one letter at a time. If you're looking for a plotter, now Hazel, she would be the one." Shackley refused all opportunities to be reflective or introspective. As much as this might have been the result of his distrust of me, it was consistent with what many of his friends and colleagues had said of Shackley: he is not a contemplative man. He did not question his life in the Agency. And when he was running a secret war or a CIA division, he did not slow down to consider the larger issues. He was just right for the national security bureaucracy. Doubters are not appreciated. The existential questions are best left to those at the top. Let the President and his immediate circle wrestle with notions of right and wrong, the probity of intervention and subversion, the morality of intelligence work, the overall effectiveness of covert action and its influence on national decision-making. People like Shackley are there to make the system work. People who hold the secrets do not have to be deep or interesting.

I wanted to know what had pushed Shackley so hard all those years in such a rough profession as intelligence. Was it merely personal ambition? Was there some intellectual or philosophical principle involved? But he is not a man to be asked such questions directly. I took a stab at eliciting his thoughts in a roundabout fashion. I informed him that friends from adolescence and college recalled that Shackley in his younger days always appeared more patriotic than his peers, that he had a strong desire to serve his country in one form or another. "Do you know where that impulse came from?" I asked. What had made him so patriotic? Shackley stared at me for a moment. "I have no idea," he responded. "That was so long ago. I probably have become more jaded on that subject." He blinked. "I really don't know. I'd have to spend some time thinking about it. I don't really have an answer to that."

Shackley may have possessed an answer but wanted to keep it from this intruder. But suppose that he was speaking the truth, that he did not know what had made him the type of man who could unquestioningly devote his life to a government bureaucracy in which the end justifies the means, to a trade predicated on the premise that honorable goals require underhanded actions—and a trade that is not withering away with the end of the Cold War. Shackley's reluctance or inability to ponder such weighty matters might explain in part his rise in a field in which moral dilemmas are ever-present. There are no simple explanations to a man's entire life. But if Shackley is taken at his word, he unwittingly offers a clue to those who try to understand the past and future Shackleys of this world: Theodore Shackley did what he did because he was something of a mystery to himself.

ACKNOWLEDGMENTS

Penetrating the world of the Central Intelligence Agency is a task that cannot be accomplished on one's own. This book could only be written with the help of scores of others.

The most important contribution came from a string of research assistants who were interns at *The Nation* magazine's Washington bureau: Susan Saenger, Mark Judge, Danzy Senna, Amy Lowrey, Matthew Ruben, Jeffrey Young, Adam Freedman, Dawn Blalock, J. Alexander Knoll, Nancy Segal, Patrick Bryant, Nick Schou, and Michael Abowd. Seth Richardson also donated his research services. This lot examined obscure government records, pored over old newspaper articles, spent hours at heaving copy machines, tracked down legal material across the country, and searched for people around the globe. They were indispensable. Victor Navasky, the editor of *The Nation,* graciously allowed me to deploy the interns on my book project and to steal time from my *Nation* duties. I owe him much. He sent me to Washington and told me I was free to write what I wanted. He supported this project and provided valuable advice. He is an admirable conniver and a wonderful writer, and I have tried to learn much from him.

Any errors this book contains are mine; the responsibility for this volume's existence is shared. Special thanks go to Gail Ross, a literary agent, lawyer, counselor, and friend all rolled into one. She did not fade away once the contract was signed. She always quickly returned calls and listened to the woeful tale of the week. Bob Bender at Simon &

Schuster was a patient editor, who wanted the best, not the fastest, book. His reading of the manuscript pushed me to make it better when I wishfully and wrongfully thought that it was done. Bob's assistant, Johanna Li, was always helpful. Mark Perry, a Washington journalist and fellow spook-watcher, was the first to suggest I take on this project, and I chose to listen to him.

Kai Bird, Martin Andersen, and Peter Kornbluh read sections of the manuscript, when it was at a bloated stage, and supplied insightful comments. Peter and his colleagues at the National Security Archive provided me with armfuls of documents, suggestions, and fellowship. Without the Archive, a private nonprofit outfit that collects material on U.S. foreign policy, much of this book could not have been written. Let me thank the following persons at the Archive by name: Thomas Blanton, Sheryl Walter, Malcolm Byrne, Laurence Chang, David Wallace, Jeffrey Richelson, Jeff Nason, and Bill Burr. Scott Armstrong, the visionary founder of the Archive, was a constant source of encouragement.

The National Archives staff in charge of the John F. Kennedy assassination records collection was of great assistance. The CIA portion of these papers became available in August of 1993, and it included hundreds of documents—cables, memoranda, dispatches—written by Shackley or related to operations he oversaw. There is no other set of publicly available Agency records like this one. The historical records unit of the CIA is to be commended for its quick processing of these papers in response to the law passed by Congress mandating the release of the documents. Unfortunately, the Freedom of Information office of the CIA was not as responsive. I filed dozens of requests with this office and received little new material. (Some responses were ridiculous. When I asked for material on the Hmong tribe and its leaders, the FOIA office claimed no such documents existed.) Moreover, it took unreasonable lengths of time to pry from its grip copies of material previously released. A Cold War mentality still seems to dominate that office.

Frank Snepp kindly permitted access to the records of his legal case. William Dobrovir, a Washington attorney, shared with me papers he had obtained from the Justice Department relating to its investigation of the congressional testimony given by U.S. officials and ITT officers in 1970. Author John Prados traded with me documents he had on Laos for material I possessed. David MacMichael, a former CIA officer who worked for a time with the Christic Institute, supplied several documents related to the investigations he conducted for the Institute. Journalists David Martin, Christopher Robbins, Doug Valentine, and John Kelly supplied fruitful leads. Seymour Hersh, the best investigative reporter in the business, was helpful in a special way.

I am indebted to several authors whose books blazed trails I was to follow: Thomas Powers (*The Man Who Kept the Secrets: Richard Helms and the CIA*), Jeff Stein (*A Murder in Wartime: The Untold Spy Story That Changed the Course of the Vietnam War*), Peter Maas (*Manhunt: The Incredible Pursuit of a CIA Agent Turned Terrorist*), Joseph Goulden and Alexander W. Raffio (*The Death Merchant: The Rise and Fall of Edwin P. Wilson*), Zalin Grant (*Facing the Phoenix: The CIA and the Political Defeat of the United States in Vietnam*), and Jonathan Kwitny (*The Crimes of Patriots: A True Tale of Dope, Dirty Money, and the CIA*).

Terry Harpold was always there when I called with yet another computer nightmare. Daniel Brandt and his Public Information Research saved me countless hours with their incredible database: a compilation of thousands of names of national security–related individuals and companies referenced in government records and media publications. Daniel often fulfilled research requests at a moment's notice.

Most of all, I must thank the scores of people who granted me interviews, particularly those who served in the Agency. For many of them, the decision to talk to an outsider was not easy. As one told me, "I have been trained most of my life not to deal with people like you. It's a hard habit to break." This book exists because dozens of former intelligence officers believe that the demands of history outweigh the secrecy oaths they signed.

During the past five years, I was fortunate to receive from dozens of colleagues and friends generous amounts of support and encouragement, which were crucial to this book's completion. Past and present coworkers at *The Nation* top the list: George Black, Neil Black, Roane Carey, Elsa Dixler, Christopher Hitchens, Andrew Kopkind, Richard Lingeman, Judith Long, Peter Meyer, Jill Petty, Richard Pollak, Katha Pollitt, Dennis Selby, Bruce Shapiro, Micah Sifry, Katrina vanden Heuvel, Art Winslow, and JoAnn Wypijewski.

Others who deserve credit and who have my gratitude are Tony Alfieri, Kathi Austin, Brian Barger, Dan Becker, Eddie Becker, Mary Belcher, Susan Bellows, Seth Berg, Brenda Brock, Barbara Burr, Julie Burton, Joe Conason, Kathleen Conkey, Mark Feldstein, Elizabeth Fine, Robert Fink, Agnieszka Fryszman, Audrey Gerlach, Don Goldberg, Janlori Goldman, Bonnie Goldstein, James Grady, Ellen Grant, Judy Grayson, Christopher Harvie, Max Holland, Jim Hougan, Andrew Jennings, Jeremy Karpatkin, Jamie Kitman, William Klein, Paul Lashmar, Ed Long, Conrad Martin, Kate Martin, Michael Mawby, Elliot Negin, Craig Nelson, Michael Pollan, Steven Prince, Howard Rosenberg, Tina Rosenberg, Lauren Rothfarb, Knute Royce, Eric Scheye, Ricki Seidman, Jack Shafer, George Stephanopoulos, Gary Stern, Michael Waldman, Tim Weiner, David Weir, Jonathan Winer, and Steven Wolfson.

My family had to put up with this book. To them, I apologize for too often being distracted when the phone rang. I may not have acted as if I realized this, but knowing that they always are there and available made all the difference. Thank you, Barry, Steven, Samantha, Amy, Gordon, Diane, Ken, and Ruth, for your love and support.

NOTES

The government documents cited below came from a number of sources: Freedom of Information requests filed by the author and others with the CIA and the State Department, official and nonofficial archives, and confidential informants. Several collections were especially helpful.

Many of the memos and cables on the operations against Cuba (Chapter 4) were found in two collections: a group of documents obtained from the National Security Council under FOIA by the National Security Archive, a nonprofit research organization in Washington; and a set of records compiled in the late 1970s by the CIA to respond to a Congressional committee investigating the John F. Kennedy assassination. These CIA documents—called the "CIA Segregated Files"—now reside in the Kennedy assassination papers at the National Archives. Another copy is maintained by the nongovernmental Assassination Archives and Research Center in Washington.

Material related to the CIA coverup and the subsequent court case described in Chapters 7 and 9 came from a large group of documents Washington lawyer William Doborvir pried from the Justice Department using FOIA. But the transcript of the secret court session was received from a confidential source, as were the memos regarding John Murray.

Documents on the Frank Snepp affair (Chapter 8) were part of the discovery material produced during his court case. They are now held in storage by the Washington office of the American Civil Liberties Union.

CHAPTER 1. A SUBSTANTIAL MYSTERY

Page

15 *Sitting in a Capitol Hill:* U.S. Senate Select Committee on Secret Military Assistance to Iran and the Nicaraguan Opposition, U.S. House of Representatives Select Committee to Investigate Covert Arms Transactions with Iran, *Report of the Congressional Committees Investigating the Iran-Contra Affair,* Appendix B, Volume 25 (Washington: Government Printing Office, 1987), pp. 1–476. Hereinafter, Shackley deposition. Cameron Holmes, interview, November 30, 1990; Charles Kerr, interview, December 10, 1990; Joe Saba, interview, November 30, 1990; Timothy Woodcock, interview, November 30, 1990: Holmes, Kerr, Saba, and Woodcock were attorneys with the Iran-Contra committees and present for parts of the deposition. Confidential interview with an Iran-Contra committee staff member. Quotes from any of the above are from the interviews and the deposition.

16 *The scandal was composed:* See *Report of the Congressional Committees Investigating the Iran-Contra Affair.* Hereinafter, *Iran-Contra Affair.* This is the main portion of the committees' final document.

17 *The Iran-Contra scandal cast: Iran-Contra Affair,* pp. 163–168. President's Special Review Board, *Report of the President's Special Review Board,* February 26, 1987, pp. b-3, b-11–12. Hereinafter, *Tower Report.*

18 *He declared his belief:* Shackley deposition, pp. 7–8.

19 *Shackley avidly stuck:* Ibid., p. 204.

19 *At one point he grudgingly:* Ibid., pp. 376–386.

19 *He reminisced about his days:* Ibid., p. 256.

CHAPTER 2: ORIGINS

Page

21 *"This is a very tough":* Confidential interview with CIA officer who worked with Shackley.

22 *Armchair analysts:* Peter Maas, *Manhunt: The Incredible Pursuit of a CIA Agent Turned Terrorist* (New York: Jove Books, 1987), p. 30.

22 *"Some of our pop":* Bill White, interview, September 26, 1990.

22 *On September 4, 1925:* State of Connecticut, Bureau of Vital Statistics, marriage license. *The Palm Beach Post,* August 7, 1985, obituary of Eleanor Manning lists her age as 75, suggesting she was born in 1910, but census information from 1920 indicates that she was born in 1907. She probably shaved a few years off her age at some point.

22 *Sadova did not want anyone:* Confidential interview.

22 *Her husband, Theodore:* City of Springfield, Massachusetts, certificate of birth for Theodore George Shackley.

22 *His father, George:* City of Springfield, Massachusetts, marriage license for George William Shackley and Mabel S. Deane. City of Springfield, certificate of birth for Theodore George Shackley. 1920 Census information.

22 *Shortly after Lena Anna:* City of Springfield, birth certificate of Theodore George Shackley, Jr.

22 *Theodore was a drinker:* City of Springfield, death certificate of Theodore George Shackley, Sr., April 27, 1951. Confidential interview.

22 *Often Ellie, toting her son:* Confidential interview.

22 *One of her son's earliest:* Confidential interview.

22 *Two and a half years after:* Dorothy Manning, interview, July 25, 1990. Manning is the daughter-in-law of Eleanor Shackley's second husband. Hampden County Probate Court records, filed November 5, 1937, by Theodore George Shackley, Sr.

22 *Years afterward when she told:* Dorothy Manning, interview.

23 *Ellie Sadova Shackley, short:* Dorothy Manning, interview; Norman Hamer, interview, March 1, 1991.

23 *At some point, Ellie sent:* Confidential interview. U.S. Army personnel records of Theodore G. Shackley, Jr.

23 *As an adult, Ted Shackley:* Confidential interview.

23 *Whoever this woman was:* Confidential interview.

23 *As a youth, Shackley:* Confidential interview.

23 *One day on the job:* Dorothy Manning, interview.

23 *On November 5, 1937:* Hampden County Probate Court records.

23 *Justin Manning was lucky:* Dorothy Manning, interview.

23 *They finally wed:* Ibid.

23 *Asked if she practiced:* Ted Brown, Jr., interview, January 29, 1991.

23 *To other members:* Wayne Manning, interview, July 30, 1990. Wayne Manning is the younger of Justin Manning's two sons.

23 *The Manning household was:* Dorothy Manning, interview. Hamer, interview.

24 *"That caused a lot":* Loyal Gould, interview, September 22, 1993.

24 *With white wavy hair:* Ed Eissey, interview, January 24, 1991. Hamer, interview. Bill Zern, interview, January 24, 1991. Zern was a partner of Mizell.

24 *"He was the toughest":* Eissey, interview, January 16, 1991.

24 *Shackley's best friend:* Hamer, interviews, March 1 and March 13, 1991.

24 *"I had to remind him":* Hamer, interview, March 1, 1991.

25 *He dated a few:* Eissey, interview, January 16, 1991. Hamer, interviews. Brown, interview.

25 *"But it was always":* Eissey, interview, January 16, 1991.

25 *Hamer, too, was struck:* Hamer, interview, March 1, 1991.

25 *"He was always talking":* Eissey, interview, January 16, 1991.

25 *"Ted was," Brown observed:* Brown, interview, January 29, 1991.

25 *Shackley did not enlist:* U.S. Army personnel records of Theodore G. Shackley, Jr.

26 *On April 13, 1946:* Ibid.

26 *At the end of the Second World War:* Ian Sayer and Douglas Botting, *America's Secret Army: The Untold Story of the Counter Intelligence Corps* (New York: Franklin Watts, 1989), p. 268. V. R. Berghahn, *Modern Germany: Society,*

Economy and Politics in the Twentieth Century (Cambridge: Cambridge University Press, 1982), pp. 176–178.

26   *Anonymous propaganda:* CIC Region III, Weekly Report No. 53, for period ending November 16, 1946, p. 8.

27   *The primary CIC task:* Counter Intelligence Corps, *History of the Counter Intelligence Corps* (Fort Hollabird: U.S. Army Intelligence Center, 1959), Volume XXVI, p. 48.

27   *For example, on July 22, 1946:* Ibid., p. 75.

27   *"The CIC has more":* Sayer and Botting, p. xi.

27   *An official CIC history:* Counter Intelligence Corps, *History of the Counter Intelligence Corps,* Volume XXVII, p. 16.

27   *He was made a clerk-general:* U.S. Army personnel records of Theodore G. Shackley, Jr.

27   *There are no indications:* Interviews with more than a dozen men who served in the Corps at the same time as Shackley.

27   *But Shackley was selected:* U.S. Army personnel records of Theodore G. Shackley, Jr.

27   *Newcomers to intelligence:* Ted Kraszewski, interview, November 13, 1990. Kraszewski worked in the CIC training program.

27   *Shackley found himself:* Theodore G. Shackley, Jr., interview, October 30, 1991.

27   *After the courses:* Ibid. Confidential interview with CIA official who had access to Shackley's personnel record.

27   *Shackley did more than:* Shackley, interview.

28   *Under Operation Paperclip:* Counter Intelligence Corps, *History of the Counter Intelligence Corps,* Volume XXVII, pp. 95–96. See Christopher Simpson, *Blowback: America's Recruitment of Nazis and Its Effects on the Cold War* (New York: Collier Books, 1988).

28   *The most notorious instance:* Simpson, pp. xii, 49–51, 69–71, 170, 182–183, 185–198, 252.

28   *After spending ten months:* U.S. Army personnel records of Theodore G. Shackley, Jr.

28   *That short spell:* Brown, interview.

28   *As Klee remembered:* William Klee, interview, February 28, 1991. Klee was a fraternity brother of Shackley at college.

28   *An acquaintance from high-school:* Gould, interview.

29   *Secretary of War:* Daniel Yergin, *Shattered Peace: The Origins of the Cold War* (New York: Penguin Books, 1990), pp. 242–243.

29   *Clark Clifford:* Ibid., p. 244.

29   *Shackley left military:* U.S. Army personnel records of Theodore G. Shackley, Jr.

29   *Four days later, President Truman:* Arthur B. Darling, *The Central Intelligence Agency: An Instrument of Government, to 1950* (University Park: The Pennsylvania State University Press, 1990), introductions by Bruce D. Berkowitz and Allan E. Goodman, p. 176. This is an official history of the early years of the

CIA, written in 1953 by Darling, a CIA historian. The CIA declassified the study in 1989.

29   *Truman, though, abolished:* William M. Leary, ed., *The Central Intelligence Agency: History and Documents* (University, Alabama: The University of Alabama Press, 1984), pp. 19–20. This history was written for the Senate Select Committee to Study Governmental Operations with Respect to Intelligence Activities (also known as the Church Committee) and published as an appendix to its final report in 1976.

29   *The second director:* Darling, pp. 169–174, 177.

30   *The CIA was assigned:* Leary, p. 27.

30   *Before he and Norman Hamer:* Hamer, interview, March 1, 1991.

31   *The 1950 yearbook: Terrapin* (College Park, Maryland: University of Maryland, 1950), p. 299.

31   *Shackley entered:* Dorothy Ball, interview, April 24, 1990. Ball worked in the office of public inquiry at the University of Maryland.

31   *"This was a strong-willed":* Dean Steliotes, interview, July 23, 1990.

31   *"He was an operator":* William Bruce Catton, interview, May 14, 1990.

31   *He served in the ROTC:* Susan Huck, *Legal Terrorism: The Truth About the Christic Institute* (McLean, Virginia: New World Publishing, 1989), p. 61. Hamer, interview, March 1, 1991.

31   *In his junior year: The Diamondback,* April 14, 1950.

31   *Fred Stone: The Diamondback,* May 9, 1950.

31   *In a statement that ran: The Diamondback,* May 2, 1950.

32   *"I don't know how much":* Hamer, interview, March 13, 1991.

32   *Shackley's strategy failed: The Diamondback,* May 5, 1950.

32   *The summer before:* "Shackley-Brown," *The Palm Beach Post,* June 21, 1950.

32   *Shackley cut short:* Ball, interview.

32   *It isn't a pretty picture: The Diamondback,* January 19, 1951.

CHAPTER 3. GERMANY: SPYING

Page

33   *Usually it was at night:* Lucien Conein, interviews, April 21, 1990, September 25, 1990.

33   *During the war, he served:* William Colby and Peter Forbath, *Honorable Men: My Life in the CIA* (New York: Simon & Schuster, 1978), pp. 25–26, 35–37.

34   *Conein jumped into France:* George Crile III, "The Colonel's Secret Drug War," *The Washington Post,* June 13, 1976.

34   *After graduating early:* Shackley, interview.

34   *The notice arrived:* City of Springfield, death certificate for Theodore George Shackley.

34   *Shackley reported for duty:* U.S. Army personnel records of Theodore G. Shackley, Jr.

34 *Three months into his service:* Shackley, interview.

35 *Its personnel increased:* Leary, p. 52.

35 *"There was a sense":* Donald Jameson, interview, March 20, 1990.

35 *The fresh officers:* Dean Almy, interview, February 20, 1992.

35 *In his class:* Almy, interview.

36 *Considering the importance:* Colby and Forbath, pp. 86–87.

36 *Michael Burke:* Michael Burke, *Outrageous Good Fortune* (Boston: Little, Brown & Company, 1984), p. 157.

36 *"There was this feeling":* Confidential interview.

37 *"He wanted to go":* Hamer, interview, March 1, 1991.

37 *On September 18, 1947:* Darling, pp. 246–254.

37 *President Truman's advisers:* Ibid., pp. 257–258.

37 *The Agency's new covert:* Leary, p. 41.

38 *Clay reported:* Jean Edward Smith, *Lucius D. Clay: An American Life* (New York: Henry Holt & Company, 1990), pp. 466–467. Leary, p. 41.

38 *Eventually named the Office:* Leary, pp. 131–133.

38 *The OPC was let loose:* Colby and Forbath, p. 109. "The Pike Papers: House Select Committee on Intelligence, CIA Report," *The Village Voice,* a special supplement (n.d.), p. 28. This is a leaked version of the report of the House Select Committee on Intelligence, chaired by Representative Otis Pike.

38 *Under the leadership:* John Ranelagh, *The Agency: The Rise and Decline of the CIA* (New York: Touchstone, 1987), p. 218.

38 *The OPC in 1949:* See Nicholas Bethell, *Betrayal* (New York: Times Books, 1984). Harry Rositzke, *The CIA's Secret Operations: Espionage, Counterespionage, and Covert Action* (Boulder, Colorado: Westview Press, 1977), pp. 171–173.

38 *After the outbreak:* Leary, p. 43.

38 *In 1949, OPC's total:* Ibid., pp. 43–44.

39 *"A friend of mine said":* Jameson, interview, March 8, 1990.

39 *In August of 1952:* Leary, pp. 50, 53.

39 *A son of a Baptist minister:* Gordon Stewart, interview, October 2, 1990.

39 *His fellow CIA officers:* Confidential interview with CIA official.

40 *In 1948, after the communists:* Gordon Stewart, unpublished memoirs, p. 204. Hereinafter, Stewart memoirs.

40 *The CIA base in Munich:* Stewart memoirs, p. 206.

40 *"The collector risks":* Ibid., p. 222.

40 *Stewart saw it:* Stewart, interview, September 28, 1990.

40 *After the war, the CIA:* Stewart memoirs, p. 214. Stewart, interview, September 28, 1990.

40 *In 1952 Stewart sent Shackley:* Stewart, interview, September 28, 1990.

40 *"But money talks":* Ibid.

41 *When the CIA was founded:* David Martin, *Wilderness of Mirrors* (New York: Ballantine Books, 1980), p. 90.

41 *The Agency, pressed by:* Stewart memoirs, pp. 234–235. Stewart, interview, September 28, 1990.

41 *But Polish operations:* Stewart memoirs, p. 234.

41   *The stymied chief of Polish operations:* Stewart, interview, September 28, 1990.

41   *When Shackley arrived:* Conein, interview, April 21, 1990.

41   *Cross-border operations:* "Czechs Clearing Border," *The New York Times,* June 8, 1951. U.S. Embassy in Prague, cable, December 5, 1952. "Poles Being Registered," *The New York Times,* January 23, 1952.

42   *On November 27, 1951:* "Czechs Arrest Vice Premier, Former Party Boss, as Spy," *The New York Times,* November 28, 1951.

42   *But Slansky had been approached:* Confidential interview with CIA officer involved in the episode.

42   *Over 20,000 persons:* "Exiles Undergo a Rigid Scrutiny," *The New York Times,* April 29, 1955.

42   *A Czechoslovak media report:* Foreign Broadcast Information Service, Czechoslovakia, January 8, 1954, p. GG3.

42   *A camp director:* "Exiles Undergo a Rigid Scrutiny," *The New York Times.*

43   *"With a shrewd":* Stewart, interview, September 28, 1990.

43   *Every six or so weeks:* Conein, interview, April 21, 1990.

43   *"All intelligence operations":* Confidential interview with CIA officer in Germany.

43   *In one instance in 1952:* "Five More Spies Stand Trial in Warsaw," Foreign Broadcast Information Service, January 11, 1952, p. FF5.

43   *The Czechoslovaks released:* Press Section of the Ministry of Foreign Affairs, *Documents on the Terrorist Activities of American Agents in Czechoslovakia,* 1952, pp. 9–10.

43   *"In retrospect":* Confidential interview with CIA officer.

44   *Gordon Stewart's impression:* Stewart, interview, September 29, 1990.

44   *"No claim can be made":* Rositzke, p. 50.

44   *"This was one":* Jan Nowak, interview, April 9, 1990.

44   *In the fall of 1990:* Stewart, interview, September 28, 1990.

44   *On August 1, 1953:* U.S. Army personnel records of Theodore G. Shackley, Jr.

44   *Shackley decided to stay:* Shackley, interview.

45   *In 1953, the Agency helped:* Ranelagh, pp. 260–264.

45   *The following year:* See Stephen Schlesinger and Stephen Kinzer, *Bitter Fruit: The Untold Story of the American Coup in Guatemala* (Garden City, New York: Doubleday & Company, 1982).

45   *Its top man:* Leary, p. 57.

45   *Between 1953 and 1961:* Ibid., p. 58.

45   *One government task force:* Ibid., p. 65.

45   *"Most borders are":* Ibid., p. 144.

46   *Ted Shackley, twenty-seven years:* Thomas Polgar, interview, February 8, 1992.

46   *"Berlin had so many":* David Chavchavadze, *Crowns and Trenchcoats: A Russian Prince in the CIA* (New York: Atlantic International Publications, 1990), p. 185.

46   *To the imaginative copywriters:* "Berlin," *Time,* May 7, 1956.

47   *There was a tacit understanding:* Burke, p. 163.

47   *Between 1945 and 1961:* Peter Wyden, *The Wall: The Inside Story of Divided Berlin* (New York: Simon & Schuster, 1989), p. 94.

47   *When Shackley arrived in Berlin:* Joseph Wechsberg, "Letter from Berlin," *The New Yorker,* March 19, 1955.

47   "One Patriot": Dee Day, "Berlin: Safe or Sinister," *Travel,* May 1954.

47   *A pair of travel writers:* George Mikes and David Lagdon, *Uber Alles* (London: A. Wingate, 1953), p. 91.

48   *To the world at large:* U.S. State Department, *Biographic Registrar,* 1974, p. 310.

48   *Before Shackley's arrival:* Confidential interview with Berlin base officer.

48   *William Harvey, head of the Berlin:* John McMahon, interview, October 21, 1991. McMahon was at that time a midlevel officer in Frankfurt.

48   *Born in 1915:* Martin, pp. 28–68. The accounts of Harvey's personal history and the Philby case are drawn from this work.

49   *When a young officer visited:* Thomas Clines, interview, March 26, 1991.

49   *John Bross, chief:* John Bross, interview, December 14, 1989.

50   *Later that day:* Chavchavadze, p. 202.

50   *One officer upon arriving:* Confidential interview with Berlin base officer.

50   *"If you ever know":* Martin, pp. 68–69.

50   *"Shackley was very single-minded":* Polgar, interview, May 1, 1991.

50   *Shackley stayed off:* Clines, interview.

50   *Speaking years later:* Shackley deposition, p. 256.

51   *One favorite pool:* Confidential interview with CIA officer in Germany.

51   *"It took a lot of practice":* Confidential interview with Berlin base officer.

51   *"If you got a guy":* Polgar, interview, May 1, 1991.

51   *"We were very lucky":* Confidential interview with Berlin base officer.

51   *Shackley and a subordinate:* Confidential interview with Berlin base officer.

51   *In May of 1956:* "Czechs Hold 10 as Spies," *The New York Times,* May 12, 1956.

51   *In 1957, the Czechoslovak:* U.S. Embassy in Warsaw, cable, May 10, 1957.

52   *In a highly celebrated case:* U.S. Embassy in Prague, cables, April 2, 1957, August 9, 1957. A CIA officer who worked on Czechoslovak affairs confirmed that Vesely was an agent.

52   *In another episode:* Foreign Broadcast Information Service, Czechoslovakia, March 1, 1956, pp. HH4–5.

52   *In 1990, a retired:* Confidential interview with CIA officer.

52   *A case officer in another:* John Sherwood, interview, September 16, 1990.

52   *One ugly tale circulated:* Ibid.

52   *Two case officers, who were transferred:* Confidential interview with CIA base officer in Germany.

52   *"I stewed":* Ibid.

53   *For decades, Shackley:* Gus Hathaway declined to be interviewed for this book. Other officials who worked with him and Shackley confirmed that the two had clashed in Berlin.

53 *"Frankly, we didn't know"*: "Hope It Is True," *The Boston Post,* May 4, 1958.

53 *He handled liaison:* Peter Wyden, *Wall,* p. 100.

54 *The digging had begun:* Martin, pp. 78–79. U.S. Central Intelligence Agency, "The Berlin Tunnel," 1968.

54 *For a year:* Confidential interview with deputy chief of the CIA processing unit for the Tunnel.

54 *The price tag:* Martin, p. 90.

54 *One of the British intelligence officers:* "George Blake: Confessions of a Traitor," *The Sunday Times,* September 9, 1990. "Why I Betrayed Britain," *The Sunday Times,* September 16, 1990. See George Blake, *No Other Choice* (New York: Simon & Schuster, 1990).

55 *One case officer who toiled:* Confidential interview with Berlin base officer.

55 *Not only had Blake:* "The Confession," a BBC television production in association with Novosti Video, 1990. Tom Bower was the producer.

55 *Failures and roll-ups aside:* Stewart, interview, September 28, 1990.

55 *"He thought of himself"*: Confidential interview with Berlin base officer.

55 *"I had a sense"*: Polgar, interview, May 1, 1991.

55 *Alex Shatton:* Alex Shatton, interview, February 26, 1992.

55 *"None of us"*: Confidential interview with Berlin base officer.

55 *Once when Juliusz Katz-Suchy:* Shatton, interview.

56 *One time two Agency men:* Confidential interview with senior CIA officer.

56 *Shackley was in Washington:* Court papers, filed in *Elizabeth Ann Shackley vs. Theodore George Shackley, Jr.,* Fifteenth Circuit Court of Florida, Palm Beach County.

56 *A senior Polish military intelligence officer:* Ed Juchniewicz, interview, March 18, 1994. Confidential interview with CIA officer.

57 *"Ted was a superior manager"*: Jameson, interview, March 21, 1990.

58 *"Money was the great"*: Confidential interview with Czech desk officer.

58 *And of all the walk-ins:* Ibid.

58 *It proved an easy task:* Confidential interviews with Czech desk officer and another CIA officer. Ronald Payne, *Who's Who in Espionage* (New York: St. Martin's Press, 1984), p. 52.

59 *He admitted he had turned over:* Payne, p. 52.

59 *The Federal Supreme Court:* "Bonn Deputy Sentenced to 15 Years as Traitor," *The New York Times,* April 29, 1961.

59 *"If we could get"*: Confidential interview with Czech desk officer.

59 *"We had this guy"*: Ibid.

60 *While many in the Directorate:* Ibid.

60 *"Such operations were"*: Ibid.

60 *When Dean Almy:* Almy, interview.

61 *In 1953, the Agency began:* Ranelagh, pp. 202–210, 270–271.

61 *The Agency achieved a notable:* Ibid., pp. 285–288.

61 *And it was pioneering:* Leary, pp. 70–71.

61 *In 1957, the Agency assisted:* Joseph B. Smith, *Portrait of a Cold Warrior* (New York: G. P. Putnam's Sons, 1976), pp. 239–240, 248.

61 *At a secret site:* Ranelagh, p. 335.

61 *Throughout the 1950s:* Thomas Powers, *The Man Who Kept the Secrets: Richard Helms and the CIA* (New York: Pocket Books, 1979), p. 53. William Blum, *The CIA: A Forgotten History* (London: Zed Books, 1986), p. 20.

61 *In Costa Rica:* David Wise and Thomas B. Ross, *The Invisible Government* (New York: Random House, 1964), pp. 120–121.

61 *"I did not care":* Richard Kovich, interview, October 23, 1990.

61 *On April 28, 1960:* Court papers, filed in *Elizabeth Ann Shackley vs. Theodore George Shackley, Jr.* This account of the Shackley divorce is based on these records.

62 *Such a situation:* Burke, p. 167.

62 *"You certainly didn't bring":* Confidential interview with Berlin base officer.

62 *"He was very, very secret":* Ted Brown, Jr., interview, October 22, 1990.

62 *In Berlin, Shackley:* Confidential interview. Betts Shackley declined to be interviewed for this book.

62 *She was employed:* Confidential interview with an associate of Hazel Shackley.

62 *In the mid-1950s:* Confidential interview with Berlin base officer.

63 *Afterward, Shackley instructed:* Confidential interview.

63 *Whether or not Betts:* Confidential interviews with Berlin base officers.

63 *"When people become":* Confidential interview with Berlin base officer.

63 *Don't mess with her:* Richard Dane, interview, February 25, 1992.

63 *Within the Company:* Charles Yothers, interview, February 24, 1992. Yothers, an Agency officer who later served under Shackley, heard this story from several persons a number of times.

63 *Two months later, Hazel: James R. Burson vs. Hazel Tindol Burson,* Winston County Circuit Court, Alabama, Case No. 2371-D, July 19, 1960.

64 *This select assembly:* Papers of the "Conference on NATO Long Range Planning," September 8 to 11, 1961. All information about the strategy game, the scenario, and the participants not otherwise sourced is drawn from these papers.

64 *The Agency had failed to detect:* Wyden, *Wall,* p. 26.

64 *Schelling, the author:* Thomas Schelling, interview, March 11, 1991.

64 *In July of 1961:* Thomas C. Schelling, "Nuclear Strategy in the Berlin Crisis," July 5, 1961, p. 1.

64 *"We kept thinking":* Alan Ferguson, interview, March 21, 1991.

65 *He was on the control team:* Schelling, interview.

65 *"To those of us":* Ibid.

65 *Shackley, though, drew:* Shackley, interview.

65 *At a postgame meeting:* Schelling, interview. Ferguson, interview.

65 *A postgame memorandum:* "Memorandum for General Taylor; Subject: [Deleted] Exercise at Camp David, 8–11 September, 1961," September 23, 1961.

CHAPTER 4. MIAMI: COWBOYS, GUNS, AND SPIES

Page

67   *On April 21, 1962:* United States Senate, Select Committee to Study Governmental Operations with Respect to Intelligence Activities, *Alleged Assassination Plots Involving Foreign Leaders,* November 20, 1975, p. 83. This committee was better known as the Church Committee, named after its chairman, Senator Frank Church, a Democrat from Idaho. Hereinafter, *Alleged Assassination Plots.* J. S. Earman, "Report on Plots to Assassinate Fidel Castro," May 23, 1967. Earman was the inspector general of the CIA and drafted this report at the request of the director. In many sources, including CIA records, the name of the mobster is spelled "Roselli," but he spelled his name "Rosselli."

68   *After he and his comrades:* U.S. House of Representatives, Select Committee on Assassinations, *Report of the Select Committee on Assassinations,* 1979, p. 104. Hereinafter, *HSCA Final Report.*

68   *After a year of watching:* Ibid., pp. 104–105.

68   *The CIA began:* Warren Hinckle and William Turner, *The Fish Is Red: The Story of the Secret War Against Castro* (New York: Harper & Row, 1981), p. 48.

68   *The city turned:* "Miami Is Going Latin as Cubans Make Their Effect Felt in City," *The New York Times,* March 18, 1962.

68   *Starting in March of 1960: Alleged Assassination Plots,* pp. 72–73.

69   *The higher-ups:* Ibid., pp. 74–85.

69   *Deputy Director for Plans Richard Bissell:* Trumbull Higgins, *The Perfect Failure: Kennedy, Eisenhower and the CIA at the Bay of Pigs* (New York: W.W. Norton & Company, 1989), pp. 49–50.

69   *The misjudgments:* "The perfect failure" is the title to Higgins's book. For accounts of the invasion, see Higgins, and Peter Wyden, *Bay of Pigs: The Untold Story* (New York: Simon & Schuster, 1979).

69   *Privately the President:* Higgins, p. 155.

70   *Days after the debacle:* Jack B. Pfeiffer, "The Taylor Committee Investigation of the Bay of Pigs," November 9, 1984, p. 29. Pfeiffer produced this report as an official Agency historian.

70   *A Kennedy-commissioned: Alleged Assassination Plots,* p. 136. Pfeiffer, pp. 210, 219–220.

70   *The CIA and the State Department:* U.S. Department of State Bureau of Intelligence and Research and U.S. CIA Office of National Estimates, "Facts, Estimates, and Projections," May 2, 1961.

70   *"The Cuba matter":* Arthur M. Schlesinger, Jr., *Robert Kennedy and His Times* (Boston: Houghton Mifflin Company, 1978), p. 493.

70   *In July of 1961: Alleged Assassination Plots,* pp. 135–136.

70   *But in the months following:* Samuel Halpern, interview, June 21, 1990.

71   *A silver-tongued:* See Cecil B. Currey, *Edward Lansdale: The Unquiet American* (Boston: Houghton Mifflin Company, 1988). For the vampire story, see pp. 102–103.

71   *Collaborating with Bobby Kennedy: Alleged Assassination Plots,* p. 139.

71   *On November 28, 1961:* Director of Central Intelligence, "The Situation

and Prospects in Cuba," Special National Intelligence Estimate Number 85–61, November 28, 1961.

71   *Two days after its release: Alleged Assassination Plots,* pp. 139–140.

72   *In January of 1962:* E. G. Lansdale, "The Cuba Project," January 18, 1962.

72   *The next day:* Edward G. Lansdale, "Memorandum for Members, Caribbean Survey Group," January 20, 1962.

72   *In a postmeeting memorandum:* Ibid.

72   *Within a month:* Edward G. Lansdale, "Subject: The Cuba Project," February 20, 1962.

73   *It took Lansdale a day:* Edward G. Lansdale, "The Cuba Project," March 2, 1962.

73   *The Special Group (Augmented) permitted:* Director of Central Intelligence, "Memorandum for the Special Group (Augmented)," March 12, 1962, and "Guidelines for Operation Mongoose," March 14, 1962. Edward G. Lansdale, "Memorandum for the Special Group (Augmented)," March 13, 1962.

73   *In the basement:* Sherwood, interview, September 16, 1990. Sherwood worked on Task Force W. Confidential interview with Task Force W officer.

73   *At the start of 1962:* Confidential interview with senior JMWAVE officer.

74   *Bumping the JMWAVE chief:* Sherwood, interviews. Confidential interviews with senior JMWAVE officer.

74   *Shackley presided:* "How the CIA Operated in Dade," *The Miami Herald,* March 9, 1975. Henry King Stanford, interview, June 12, 1991. Stanford was the president of the university. Bradley Earl Ayers, *The War That Never Was* (Indianapolis: The Bobbs-Merrill Company, 1976), p. 26.

74   *Shackley's own office:* Sherwood, interview, September 16, 1990.

74   *Shackley's station was run:* Taylor Branch and George Crile III, "The Kennedy Vendetta," *Harper's,* August 1975. Hinckle and Turner, pp. 112–113. U.S. House of Representatives, Select Committee on Assassinations, *Investigation of the Assassination of President John Kennedy, Appendix to Hearings, Volume X, 1979,* pp. 6–7. Hereinafter, *HSCA Volume X.* Grayston Lynch, interview, March 5, 1991.

75   *Overseeing FI was:* Confidential interview with senior JMWAVE officer.

75   *The annual budget:* Schlesinger, p. 498.

75   *The paramilitary gang:* Mickey Kappes, interview, May 7, 1992.

75   *The most prominent:* Lynch, interview, March 5, 1991. Wyden, *Bay of Pigs: The Untold Story,* pp. 83–84, 229.

75   *Since the summer:* "The Kennedy Vendetta," *Harper's.* Thomas Clines, interview, August 8, 1991.

76   *Grayston Lynch:* Lynch, interview, March 5, 1991. Wyden, *Bay of Pigs: The Untold Story,* pp. 83–84, 229.

76   *One of the PM experts:* Bob Wall, interview, February 22, 1992.

76   *The pay for Cuban agents:* Felix Rodriguez and John Weisman, *Shadow Warrior* (New York: Pocket Books, 1989), p. 118.

76   *"To a Cuban a secret":* Justin Gleichauf, interview, August 8, 1991.

76   *"A Cuban":* Confidential interview with Task Force W officer.

76   *"Every Cuban, it seemed":* Gleichauf, interview.

76   *Felix Rodriguez, an agent:* Rodriguez and Weisman, p. 120.

76   *The Cuban show was a pet:* Hamer, interview, March 13, 1991.

77   *"He was an executive":* Jameson, interview, March 8, 1990.

77   *Clines had joined the Agency:* Clines, interviews, August 8, 1991, September 14, 1990, March 20, 1991. Thomas Clines testimony, *United States of America v. Thomas G. Clines,* United States District Court for the District of Maryland, 1990. Clines testified on September 14, 1990.

77   *When Shackley took over:* Clines, interview, March 26, 1991.

78   *In April of 1962:* Edward G. Lansdale, "Memorandum for the Special Group (Augmented)," April 26, 1962.

78   *Harvey personally watched:* Ibid.

78   *It was on this trip: Alleged Assassination Plots,* p. 4. Martin, pp. 121–122.

78   *Decades afterward, Shackley asserted:* Shackley, interview.

78   *After Harvey returned: Alleged Assassination Plots,* p. 154.

78   *Lansdale then reported:* Edward G. Lansdale, "Memorandum for the Special Group (Augmented)," May 3, 1962.

78   *In early May:* Edward G. Lansdale, "Memorandum for the Special Group (Augmented)," May 14, 1962.

78   *Havana announced:* Foreign Broadcast Information Service, USSR International Affairs, May 17, 1962, p. bb22.

79   *Shackley whipped off:* Edward G. Lansdale, "Memorandum for the Special Group (Augmented)," May 17, 1962.

79   *And days later:* Ibid.

79   *An enthusiastic Lansdale:* Edward G. Lansdale, "Operation Mongoose, Priority Operations Schedule, 21 May–30 June, 1962," May 17, 1962.

79   *During the first week of June:* Edward G. Lansdale, "Memorandum for the Special Group (Augmented)," June 27, 1962. "Cuba Tells of Battles Wiping Out Guerrillas," *The Miami Herald,* June 29, 1962.

79   *Lansdale inspected:* Edward G. Lansdale. "Memorandum for the Special Group (Augmented)," July 5, 1962.

80   *On July 11, 1962:* Theodore Shackley, "Operational [Deleted] Review and Analysis of [Deleted] Operation," July 11, 1962.

80   *"There was no shortage":* Confidential interview with senior JMWAVE officer.

80   *The station exploited:* Confidential interview with senior JMWAVE officer.

80   *All together:* Confidential interview with senior JMWAVE officer.

80   *His station was running:* Confidential interview with senior JMWAVE officer. "Castro's Sister Linked to CIA As an Informant for Four Years," *The New York Times,* July 3, 1964.

81   *In August of 1962, Shackley:* Sherwood, interview, July 19, 1991. Confidential interview with senior JMWAVE officer.

81   *In June of 1964:* "Castro's Sister Linked to CIA As an Informant for Four Years," *The New York Times,* July 3, 1964. Philip Agee, *Inside the Company: CIA Diary* (New York: Bantam Books, 1976), p. 396.

81   *For years afterward:* Author deleted, "[Deleted] Juana Castro," June 29, 1970. This memo was prepared for the CIA Office of General Counsel.

81   *Agency assets targeted: Alleged Assassination Plots,* p. 146.

81   *Harvey complained:* Schlesinger, p. 499.

82   *"It went down": Alleged Assassination Plots,* p. 144.

82   *Harvey and Lansdale:* Martin, p. 137.

82   *In one encounter:* Confidential interview with senior JMWAVE officer.

82   *Harvey routinely referred:* Martin, p. 136.

82   *He criticized:* Dino A. Brugioni, *Eyeball to Eyeball: The Inside Story of the Cuban Missile Crisis* (New York: Random House, 1991), p. 70.

82   *Halpern learned:* Halpern, interview, August 6, 1990.

82   *Bobby Kennedy, the overeager: Alleged Assassination Plots,* p. 150.

82   *Members of a JMWAVE:* Lynch, interview, March 6, 1991.

82   *In Shackley's station:* Clines, interview, March 26, 1991.

83   *In a memorandum to Lansdale:* Robert A. Hurwitch, untitled memorandum, July 19, 1962.

83   *But Brigadier General Benjamin T. Harris:* Benjamin T. Harris, "Memorandum for the Chief of Operations, Operation Mongoose," July 23, 1962.

83   *In Lansdale's own evaluation:* Edward G. Lansdale, "Memorandum for The Special Group (Augmented)," July 25, 1962.

84   *"The Cuban ground forces":* U.S. Central Intelligence Agency, "The Situation and Prospects in Cuba," National Intelligence Estimate 85-2-62, July 27, 1962.

84   *"It's a good thing":* Gleichauf, interview.

84   *Under Shackley's command:* Confidential interview with senior JMWAVE officer. Gleichauf, interview.

84   *Harvey visited:* Confidential interview with senior JMWAVE officer.

84   *He was "very demanding":* Jameson, interview, March 8, 1990.

84   *Lynch was astounded:* Lynch, interview, March 5, 1991.

84   *He insisted on approving:* Confidential interview with senior JMWAVE officer.

85   *"There was always":* Confidential interview with senior Task Force W officer.

85   *Rocky Farnsworth, chief of covert:* Wall, interview, February 22, 1992.

85   *He replaced Farnsworth:* Wall, interview, February 22, 1992. Kappes, interview. Clines, interview, January 14, 1992.

85   *"The exile community was penetrated":* Al Tarabochia, interview, July 26, 1991.

85   *Shackley was desperate:* Clines, interview, March 26, 1991.

85   *"Always be forward-leaning":* Confidential interview with senior JMWAVE officer.

86   *Dyke's task:* Peter Dyke, interview, September 25, 1991.

86   *In one instance, CIA excavators:* Confidential interview with senior JMWAVE officer.

86   *In 1963, the CIA used:* Walter Raymond, Jr., "House Select Committee on Assassinations (HSCA) Request for CIA Files on Teresa Proenza Proenza," July 20, 1978. Raymond was a senior officer in CIA headquarters. U.S. Central Intelli-

gence Agency, "Political Action Operations in Cuba—The Proenza Case," undated. U.S. Central Intelligence Agency, "Political Action Operations in Cuba—The Proenza Case," a draft memorandum, undated.

86 *Shackley's maritime unit:* Confidential interview with senior JMWAVE officer.

87 *JMWAVE-controlled front:* Donald M. Wilson, "Broadcasting to Cuba," September 11, 1962. Wilson was deputy director of the United States Intelligence Agency and wrote this memo for Lansdale.

87 *It even had an exile agent:* Theodore Shackley, "Operation [Deleted], Monthly Operational Report," July 13, 1962.

87 *At one point, the CIA:* Richard Helms, "Anti-Castro/Anti-Communist Organizations," November 6, 1962.

87 *Shackley assigned:* Clines, interview, March 26, 1991.

87 *At his desk at JMWAVE:* Shackley, interview.

87 *"Ted wanted to do things":* Kappes, interview.

87 *He urged approval:* Edward G. Lansdale, "Stepped Up Course B," August 8, 1962.

87 *On August 10: Alleged Assassination Plots,* p. 146.

87 *But at an August 21, 1962:* John McCone, "Memorandum for the File," August 21, 1962.

87 *Nevertheless, on August 23:* McGeorge Bundy, "National Security Action Memorandum No. 181," August 23, 1962.

87 *On August 30:* "The Kennedy Vendetta," *Harper's.*

88 *Shackley's station composed: Alleged Assassination Plots,* p. 337.

88 *Lansdale suggested it destroy:* Ibid.

88 *On September 19, 1962:* U.S. Central Intelligence Agency, "The Military Buildup in Cuba," Special National Intelligence Estimate 85-3-62.

88 *For months, Shackley's station:* Richard Helms, "An Address by Richard Helms, Director of Central Intelligence," *Problems of Journalism, Proceedings of the American Society of Newspaper Editors,* 1971.

88 *By the count:* "CIA Ignored Cuban Sightings of Missiles in 1962," *The Philadelphia Inquirer,* October 20, 1992. This article was based on a conference on the Cuban Missile Crisis held at CIA headquarters, at which Frank spoke.

88 *"We certainly had no":* Russell Jack Smith, *The Unknown CIA: My Three Decades with the Agency* (Washington, D.C.: Pergamon-Brassey's, 1989), p. 154.

88 *But come the summer:* Ranelagh, p. 395.

88 *One headquarters officer insisted:* Confidential interview with senior JMWAVE officer.

88 *That irritated Warren Frank:* Confidential interview with senior JMWAVE officer.

89 *Tom Clines ran:* Clines, interview, March 26, 1991.

89 *"It got to be a morale thing":* Confidential interview with senior JMWAVE officer.

89 *Shackley felt the reporting:* Confidential interview with senior JMWAVE officer.

89 *"I can't get my teeth"*: Clines, interview, March 26, 1991.

89 *Outside the administration:* "Congressmen Demand Strong Action on Fidel," *The Miami Herald,* September 7, 1962.

89 *With the missile controversy:* John McCone, "Memorandum of Mongoose Meeting Held Thursday, October 4, 1962," October 4, 1962. *Alleged Assassination Plots,* p. 147.

89 *As the policy shuffle:* Martin, pp. 143–144. "The Kennedy Vendetta," *Harper's.*

90 *Weeks later, Cuba disclosed:* "Cuba Reports Plotters' Arrest; Charges U.S. Trained Saboteurs," *The New York Times,* November 14, 1962. "Cuba Between the Superpowers, Transcript of the Meetings," Session 1, January 4, 1991, p. 11. The transcript is available at the National Security Archive, Washington, D.C. Wall, interview, February 22, 1992.

90 *After Orozco's capture:* Wall, interview, February 22, 1992.

90 *On October 18:* William K. Harvey, untitled memorandum, October 18, 1962.

91 *The Agency had received a secret-writing report:* U.S. Central Intelligence Agency, "Restricted Military Area in Pinar del Rio Province and Possible Missile Installation at La Guira," September 18, 1962.

91 *And six days earlier:* U.S. Central Intelligence Agency, "Comments of Cuban Pilot Concerning Presence of Guided Missiles in Cuba," September 20, 1962.

91 *At the Opa-Locka:* Justin Gleichauf, "Reds in Cuba: The Genesis of a Crisis," *Army,* November 1979. Richard Lehman, "CIA Handling of the Soviet Buildup in Cuba," November 14, 1962. This memorandum was written for McCone. In 1992, the CIA's History Staff released an excerpt of it.

91 *Between October 1 and 3:* Richard Lehman, "CIA Handling of the Soviet Buildup in Cuba."

91 *On October 3:* Walter Laqueur, *A World of Secrets: The Uses and Limits of Intelligence* (New York: Basic Books, 1985), pp. 164–165.

91 *Years after the crisis, several Agency veterans:* Brugioni, pp. 164–165. Confidential interview with senior JMWAVE official.

91 *But neither this report:* Richard Lehman, "CIA Handling of the Soviet Buildup in Cuba."

92 *A postcrisis analysis:* Laqueur, p. 161.

92 *In the midst of the crisis:* John A. McCone, "Memorandum of Meeting of Executive Committee of the NSC," October 23, 1962.

92 *After the crisis ended:* Roswell L. Gilpatric, recorded interview with Dennis J. O'Brien, May 5, 1970, John F. Kennedy Library Oral History Program.

92 *Without providing details:* Shackley, interview.

92 *Shackley ordered his case officers:* Rodriguez and Weisman, pp. 131–133. Clines, interview, March 26, 1991.

92 *Bob Wall, on Shackley's orders:* Wall, interview, February 22, 1992.

92 *Shackley dispatched officers:* Confidential interview with senior JMWAVE officer.

92 *Justin Gleichauf was ordered:* Gleichauf, interview.

93   *In the middle of the crisis:* Ranelagh, p. 388.

93   *But Shackley, acting:* Lynch, interview, March 5, 1991. Marshall Carter, "Mongoose Operations and General Lansdale's Problems," October 25, 1962. Carter was deputy director of the CIA.

93   *Yet when Bobby Kennedy learned:* Edwin O. Guthman and Jeffrey Shulman, *Robert Kennedy in His Own Words: The Unpublished Recollections of the Kennedy Years* (New York: Bantam Books, 1988), pp. 378–379.

93   *At a White House meeting:* Martin, p. 144.

93   *On October 24:* The National Security Archive, *The Cuban Missile Crisis* (Washington, D.C.: National Security Archive and Chadwyck-Healey, 1990), pp. 64–74.

94   *"In the spring of 1962":* Sergo Mikoyan, recorded interview, October 13, 1987, Conference on Cuban Missile Crisis, John F. Kennedy School of Government, Harvard University.

94   *Khrushchev later claimed:* Nikita S. Khrushchev, *Khrushchev Remembers* (Boston: Little, Brown, 1970), pp. 493–494.

94   *"The secret war":* Schlesinger, p. 526.

94   *A postcrisis Agency study:* U.S. Central Intelligence Agency, "Khrushchev's Cuban Venture in Retrospect," undated. It was transmitted to McGeorge Bundy, the national security adviser to President Kennedy, on December 7, 1962.

94   *Robert McNamara conceded:* Pierre Salinger, "Gaps in the Cuban Missile Crisis Story," *The New York Times,* February 5, 1989.

94   *On October 30, 1962: Alleged Assassination Plots,* pp. 147–148.

94   *Two days before that:* HSCA Volume X, p. 14. W. C. Sullivan, "Call from the Attorney General to Assistant Director Courtney Evans on October 28, 1962," October 29, 1962.

94   *Kennedy's no-invasion pledge:* Mario Lazo, *Dagger in the Heart* (New York: Funk and Wagnalls, 1968), p. 378.

94   *On October 31:* "Ten Cuban Exiles and Weapons Seized on Boat on Miami River," *The New York Times,* November 1, 1962.

95   *The feds then rounded up:* Hinckle and Turner, pp. 158–165. "U.S. Nabs Anti-Castro Fighters—Why?" *The Miami Herald,* December 5, 1962.

95   *"We were cut off":* Frank Sturgis, interview, August 13, 1991.

95   *Most anti-Castro crusaders:* "CIA's Cuban Network 'Leaks,'" *The Miami Herald,* November 20, 1962.

95   *A discredited Bill Harvey:* William Harvey, "Operational Plan for Continuing Operations Against Cuba," November 27, 1963.

95   *On December 29, 1962: HSCA Volume X,* pp. 66–67. "A Wave of Hope Sweeps Exiles in Orange Bowl," *The Miami Herald,* December 30, 1962.

95   *His administration had:* Peter Wyden, *Bay of Pigs: The Untold Story,* p. 303.

96   *To the man in charge:* Shackley, interview.

96   *"There is well nigh":* McGeorge Bundy, "Further Organization of the Government for Dealing with Cuba," January 4, 1963. This was a memorandum for the President.

96   *"We'd been working":* Guthman and Shulman, p. 378.

96 *"Mongoose was poorly conceived":* Schlesinger, p. 558.

96 *Lansdale, decades afterward:* Currey, p. 240.

96 *Operation Mongoose was terminated: Alleged Assassination Plots,* pp. 84–86, 170.

96 *Harvey was replaced:* Russell Jack Smith, p. 181. Schlesinger, p. 569. Guthman and Shulman, p. 379.

96 *Harvey was shipped off:* Martin, pp. 183–187, 216–220.

97 *Task Force W was transformed:* Ranelagh, p. 388.

97 *High-level oversight:* Thomas Parrott, interview, November 8, 1990. Parrott was a CIA officer assigned to the Special Group (Augmented) as a secretary.

97 *The stand-down issued:* Lynch, interview, March 5, 1991.

97 *But these raids:* Halpern, interview, August 6, 1990.

97 *The enthusiastic FitzGerald asked: Alleged Assassination Plots,* pp. 85–86.

97 *His operational hopes:* U.S. Department of State, "Assessment of New Reports of Revolution Against Castro," February 13, 1963.

97 *After the missile crisis, returns:* Confidential interview with CIA headquarters officer.

97 *Enhanced Cuban security rendered:* "Rebel-Harassed Castro Tightens Up on Island Security," *The Miami Herald,* February 21, 1963.

97 *In early 1963, Artime:* Rodriguez and Weisman, pp. 135–139. Al Burt, "The Mirage of Havana," *The Nation,* January 25, 1965. Enrique Encinosa, *Cuba: The Unfinished Revolution* (Austin: Eakin Press, 1988), pp. 164–165.

98 *The CIA budget:* Orville Bathe, "Manuel Artime," July 25, 1973. Bathe was an officer in the CIA's Western Hemisphere Division.

98 *"He couldn't stand it":* Clines, interview, January 14, 1992.

98 *When Artime visited:* Ramon F. Hart, "Manuel F. Artime Buesa," July 18, 1963. Hart was a CIA officer who worked on the Artime bugging project.

98 *CIA officers also worried:* M. K. Holbik, "Project [Deleted]," October 16, 1964. Holbik was an officer in the CIA's Office of Security.

98 *JMWAVE operatives ferried:* Ibid.

98 *Shackley's station also cheered: HSCA Volume X,* pp. 77, 137–139. Clines, interview, March 26, 1991.

99 *In April of 1963:* Sherman Kent, "Cuba a Year Hence," April 22, 1963.

99 *A report prepared:* Untitled, undated study. It was presented to the Secretary of the Army on May 10, 1963.

99 *At a May 28 gathering: Alleged Assassination Plots,* pp. 172–173.

100 *When Clines in Miami had:* Clines, interview, March 26, 1991.

100 *In the course of attempting:* The account of the Pawley mission is drawn from the following: Theodore Shackley, "Soviet Defectors," May 22, 1963. Theodore Shackley, "Pawley Soviet Defectors Operational Log," June 4, 1963. Both of the preceding were memorandums for the record. JMWAVE cable to headquarters, June 5, 1963. JMWAVE cable to headquarters, June 13, 1963. "Discussion [Deleted]," June 15, 1963; this memo was written by a JMWAVE employee who worked on the Pawley mission. JMWAVE cable to headquarters, June 28, 1963. Theodore Shackley, "Maritime After Action Report—Operation [De-

leted]," June 29, 1963. Theodore Shackley, "[Deleted] Operational Periodic Activities Report on JMWAVE's Relationship with [Pawley]," July 25, 1963. JMWAVE cable to headquarters, March 2, 1964. "Disastrous Mission: Miamian Pawley Tells of '63 Cuba Operation, Loss of 10 Exiles," *The Miami Herald,* January 8, 1975. Hinckle and Turner, pp. 170–173. Miguel Acoca and Robert K. Brown, "The Bayo-Pawley Affair: A Plot to Destroy J.F.K. and Invade Cuba," *Soldier of Fortune,* February 1976. (This hyperbolic and conspiratorial piece suggests the Pawley mission was designed to politically injure Kennedy by producing evidence that the Soviets still had offensive missiles in Cuba. The internal CIA records cited above show that was not the case.) Kappes, interview.

102 *A few months earlier, headquarters:* The account of the AMTRUNK operation is drawn from the following sources: Theodore Shackley, "Project AMTRUNK Operational Review," April 5, 1963. Theodore Shackley, "Operational Progress Report [Deleted]," September 19, 1963. Theodore Shackley, "Progress Report AMTRUNK Team, Period 1–30 September 1963," October 12, 1963. U.S. Central Intelligence Agency, "AMTRUNK Operation," February 14, 1977. U.S. Central Intelligence Agency, "Chronology of Significant Documents in AMTRUNK File," April 1977. U.S. Central Intelligence Agency, "AMTRUNK Operation," April 25, 1977. U.S. Central Intelligence Agency, "CIA Operations Against Cuba," May 10, 1977.

103 *On June 19, 1963: Alleged Assassination Plots,* pp. 173, 337.

103 *Five days earlier:* Director of Central Intelligence, "Situation and Prospects in Cuba," National Intelligence Estimate Number 85–63, June 14, 1963.

103 *He traveled to Shackley's station:* Confidential interview with senior JMWAVE officer.

103 *At station briefings:* Ayers, p. 101.

103 *One group of Shackley raiders:* U.S. Central Intelligence Agency, "CIA Operations Against Cuba Prior to the Assassination of President John Kennedy on 23 November 1963," undated. This memo, with its mistaken date in the title, was written sometime in the 1970s.

104 *With the clandestine war:* Ayers, pp. 102–103.

104 *On October 30, 1963:* "Castro Says CIA Uses Raider Ship," *The New York Times,* November 1, 1963.

104 *If any reporter:* Clines, interview, August 8, 1991.

104 *It recently had used:* Hinckle and Turner, pp. 137–142. Lynch, interview, March 5, 1991.

104 *Days afterward:* "Cuban Jets Attack and Damage U.S.-Owned Ship," *The New York Times,* October 23, 1963. "U.S. Says It Will Keep Up Policy of Economic Isolation of Cuba," *The New York Times,* October 24, 1963.

104 *Two weeks later, Cuba:* "Cuba Shoots 4 as Spies; Week's Total Reaches Thirteen," *The New York Times,* November 15, 1963.

105 *Following the episode:* JMWAVE cable to headquarters, December 11, 1963.

105 *And the CIA-backed JURE:* HSCA Volume X, p. 78.

105 *In early September:* "The Riddle of AMLASH," *The Washington Post,* May 2, 1976.

105 *The following month:* Schlesinger, pp. 576–578.

105 *In the fall of 1963, one of its:* The account of the AMLASH operation is drawn from the following: "The Riddle of AMLASH," *The Washington Post. Alleged Assassination Plots,* pp. 86–90. Headquarters cable to JMWAVE, August 4, 1962. J. S. Earman, "Report on Plots to Assassinate Fidel Castro." U.S. Senate, Select Committee to Study Governmental Operations with Respect to Intelligence Activities, *The Investigation of the Assassination of President John F. Kennedy: Performance of the Intelligence Agencies, Book V of the Final Report,* 1976, pp. 3, 17, 75. Hereinafter, *Book V.* Headquarters cable to JMWAVE, December 3, 1963. Nestor Sanchez, interview, January 23, 1992.

106 *A CIA internal report: Alleged Assassination Plots,* pp. 88–89. J. S. Earman, "Report on Plots to Assassinate Fidel Castro."

106 *In Cuba, Castro:* Jean Daniel, "When Castro Heard the News," *The New Republic,* December 7, 1963.

106 *The day after Kennedy's:* Headquarters cables to JMWAVE, November 23, 1963.

106 *In the months prior:* HSCA Final Report, pp. 139–147.

106 *The Agency even neglected:* Ibid., pp. 4–5.

107 *Two lawyers:* HSCA Volume X, pp. 5–6.

107 *After the assassination:* JMWAVE cable to headquarters, November 24, 1963. Evalena Vidal, "Possible Instructions from Headquarters to Miami Station Requesting Information on the Kennedy Assassination," June 8, 1977. Vidal was a JMWAVE case officer. JMWAVE cable to headquarters, December 7, 1963. "1963–1964 Miami Station Action to Aid U.S.G. Investigation of the Murder of John F. Kennedy," March 22, 1977. This memo was written by a JMWAVE case officer.

107 *But Shackley's station did not:* "Reaction in JMWAVE Station to Assassination of President John F. Kennedy," June 7, 1977. This memo was written by a JMWAVE case officer.

107 *Its effort:* Confidential interview with senior JMWAVE officer.

107 *Shackley believed that:* Book V, p. 58.

107 *"The conspiratorial atmosphere":* Book V, p. 59.

107 *In 1979, the House:* HSCA Final Report, p. 111.

108 *The House select committee concluded:* HSCA Final Report, pp. 1–2.

108 *In 1991, Shackley rejected:* Shackley, interview.

108 *When a cache:* Headquarters cable to JMWAVE, November 27, 1963. JMWAVE cable to headquarters, December 6, 1963. JMWAVE cable to headquarters, December 11, 1963. JMWAVE cable to headquarters, December 14, 1963.

108 *A Western diplomat who had:* JMWAVE cable to headquarters, December 1, 1963.

108 *More worrisome was:* JMWAVE cable to headquarters, November 21, 1963. JMWAVE cable to headquarters, November 23, 1963. JMWAVE cable to headquarters, November 24, 1963. JMWAVE cable to headquarters, December 3, 1963.

109 *Shackley also was weighing:* JMWAVE cable to headquarters, December 1, 1963.

109 *Stationed in East Germany:* JMWAVE cable to headquarters, December 6,

1963. JMWAVE cable to headquarters, December 11, 1963. JMWAVE cable to headquarters, December 14, 1963.

110   *But intelligence out of Cuba:* JMWAVE cable to headquarters, November 29, 1963. JMWAVE cable to headquarters, December 2, 1963. JMWAVE cables to headquarters, December 10, 1963.

110   *One program he supervised:* JMWAVE cable to headquarters, November 4, 1963. JMWAVE cable to headquarters, November 29, 1963.

110   *In early December, Shackley:* JMWAVE cable to headquarters, December 7, 1963. JMWAVE cable to headquarters, December 11, 1963.

111   *A weekly situation report:* JMWAVE cable to headquarters, December 7, 1963.

111   *As he oversaw:* Headquarters cable to JMWAVE cable, November 26, 1963. Headquarters cable to JMWAVE, November 22, 1963. Headquarters cable to JMWAVE, November 29, 1963.

111   *In mid-December, Shackley's own:* Lynch, interview, March 6, 1991. Theodore Shackley, "Sitrep 14 December 1963," December 15, 1963.

112   *In the past year, Shackley's station:* U.S. Central Intelligence Agency, "CIA Operations Against Cuba Prior to the Assassination of President John Kennedy on 23 November 1963."

112   *At the Miami station:* Ayers, pp. 182–183.

112   *Shackley, though, maintained:* Clines, interview, August 8, 1991.

112   *Some officers looked:* Ayers, p. 189.

112   *Losses at this stage:* Confidential interview with senior headquarters officer.

112   *In one disastrous episode:* U.S. Central Intelligence Agency, "CIA Operations Against Cuba Prior to the Assassination of President John Kennedy on 23 November 1963."

112   *Early in April of 1964: Alleged Assassination Plots,* p. 177.

112   *At an April 7 meeting:* Ibid.

113   *The next day, McCone:* Ibid.

113   *In March and June of 1964: Alleged Assassination Plots,* p. 89. J. S. Earman, "Report on Plots to Assassinate Fidel Castro."

113   *Questioned about these shipments: Book V,* p. 20.

113   *On April 2, 1964:* Theodore Shackley, "Special Activities Report on JMWAVE's Relationship with [Deleted]," April 2, 1964. See "Conspiracy in Cuba Awaits Outside Push," *The Miami Herald,* October 20, 1963; "Castro Could Have Been Saint But—," *The Miami Herald,* October 21, 1963; "The Mirage of Havana," *The Nation.* The two *Herald* stories, each written by Burt, are referred to in Shackley's dispatch as being penned by AMCARBON, who is not identified by name in Shackley's report.

114   *Years later, Burt:* Al Burt, interview, October 18, 1993.

115   *In the spring of 1964: HSCA Volume X,* pp. 78–79, 140. "Exiles Reported on Way to Cuba," *The New York Times,* May 18, 1964. "Cubans in Exile Remain Divided," *The New York Times,* May 21, 1964. *HSCA Volume X,* pp. 78–79, 140. "Ray, Exile Leader, Balked by Storms in 2nd Cuba Attempt," *The New York Times,* July 18, 1964.

115 *Artime's operation mounted:* Rodriguez and Weisman, pp. 139, 143. "Ex-iles Raid Port In Eastern Cuba," *The New York Times,* May 14, 1964. *HSCA Final Report,* p. 67.

115 *"I never saw such":* "The Mirage of Havana," *The Nation.*

115 *An MRR team seeking:* Rodriguez and Weisman, pp. 145–146. "Sea Raider Identity Unknown to U.S.," *The New York Times,* September 16, 1964. "U.S. Denies Blame in Attack on Ship," *The New York Times,* September 17, 1964.

115 *Months after the* Sierra Maestra: Rodriguez and Weisman, pp. 146–147. Orville Bathe, "Manuel Artime."

115 *But the station continued:* Orville Bathe, "Manuel Artime."

115 *"They never managed":* Clines, interview, August 8, 1991.

115 *Some of its boats and men:* Rodriguez and Weisman, pp. 146–147. Blum, *The CIA: A Forgotten History,* pp. 174–181.

116 *It covertly arranged: Alleged Assassination Plots,* pp. 89–90.

116 *In June of 1965:* Ibid., p. 90.

116 *Agency officers wondered: HSCA Volume X,* p. 163.

116 *Cubela was arrested: Book V,* p. 78. "The Riddle of AMLASH," *The Washington Post.*

116 *"I made myself damn unpopular":* Confidential interview with midlevel CIA officer who worked on Cuban matters.

116 *Shackley's days were consumed:* Confidential interview with senior JMWAVE officer.

116 *Shackley departed Miami:* Resume of Theodore G. Shackley.

116 *When John Dimmer replaced:* Yothers, interview. Yothers was a counterin-telligence officer for Dimmer.

117 *Months later, John Hart:* Agee, pp. 448–449.

117 *"That was not our problem":* Lynch, interview, March 12, 1991.

117 *In July of 1968:* "CIA Explosives Used to Bomb Officers Here, FBI Men Testify," *The Los Angeles Times,* December 31, 1968.

117 *Michael Townley, the assassin:* Hinckle and Turner, p. 316.

117 *Humberto Lopez:* Encinosa, pp. 167–170.

117 *Rolando Martinez:* Ranelagh, p. 521.

118 *Ramon Milian Rodriguez:* U.S. Senate, Subcommittee on Terrorism, Nar-cotics and International Communications of the Committee of Foreign Rela-tions, *Drugs, Law Enforcement, and Foreign Policy: Panama,* Hearings (Washington: U.S. Government Printing Office, 1988), pp. 219–266. Rodriguez testified on February 11, 1988.

118 *He received a Distinguished:* Huck, p. 62.

118 *Des FitzGerald was telling:* Parrott, interview. Jameson, interview, March 21, 1990. Bross, interview, December 14, 1989.

118 *As for the intelligence mission: Book V,* p. 58.

CHAPTER 5. LAOS: A SECRET WAR

Page

120 *It was late in the spring:* Confidential interview with the case officer.

121 *When Colby had needed:* William Colby, interview, June 25, 1991.

121 *About a year earlier:* John Rubel Mapother, interview, September 27, 1990. Resumé of Theodore G. Shackley. U.S. Department of State, *Biographic Register,* 1974, p. 310.

121 *The proprietor of West Berlin's:* "West Berliner Is Arrested on a Charge of Espionage," *The New York Times,* January 27, 1966.

121 *The Berlin base:* Confidential interview with Berlin base officer.

121 *At his first staff meeting:* Victor Marchetti, interview, October 10, 1991. Marchetti learned this when he passed through the Berlin base.

121 *Shackley's base managed:* Confidential interview with Berlin base officer.

121 *"Guys we hadn't seen":* Confidential interview with Berlin base officer.

121 *After the end:* "Spy Rings," *Newsday,* June 15, 1992.

122 *Shackley oversaw:* Confidential interview with Berlin base officer.

122 *"Probably the most":* Joseph Wechsberg, "Letter From Berlin," *The New Yorker,* October 15, 1966.

123 *Shackley possessed one agent:* Confidential interview with Berlin base officer. The base chief who replaced Shackley, and Richard Dane, who joined the base after Shackley left, confirmed that the base handled this spy. (Confidential interview; Dane, interview, February 25, 1992.)

123 *Many of Shackley's targets:* John A. Calhoun, interview, April 25, 1991. Calhoun was resident head of mission in Berlin.

123 *The base had agents:* Confidential interview with Berlin base officer.

123 *"We didn't like that":* Confidential interview with Berlin base officer.

123 *There was a long list:* Confidential interview with Berlin base officer.

123 *As student unrest flared:* Arthur Day, interview, April 23, 1991. Confidential interview with Berlin base officer.

124 *"One had a great feeling":* Day, interview.

124 *John Mapother, a reports:* Mapother, interview, September 27, 1990.

124 *Shackley's tendency toward quotas:* Dane, interview.

124 *"We went on":* Day, interview.

125 *In the modern era:* Roger Hilsman, *To Move a Nation* (New York: Dell Publishing, 1964), p. 94.

125 *"This is the end":* Charles Stevenson, *The End of Nowhere: American Policy Toward Laos Since 1954* (Boston: Beacon Press, 1972), frontispiece quotation.

125 *France could not hold:* Hilsman, pp. 97–98, 104–105. The summary of early Laos history is drawn from this work.

126 *"In this environment":* Douglas S. Blaufarb, *Organizing and Managing Unconventional War in Laos, 1962–1970* (Santa Monica, CA: Rand, 1972), pp. 2–3. This was a classified report Blaufarb wrote for the Advanced Research Projects Agency of the U.S. Department of Defense. Hereinafter, Blaufarb, *Organizing and Managing.*

126 *It provided the sole:* Hilsman, p. 114.

126 *An immense U.S.:* Blaufarb, *Organizing and Managing,* p. 3.

126 *CIA officers supported:* Hilsman, p. 114.

126 *When Washington held:* Ibid., pp. 117–124.

126 *Western journalists reported:* Douglas Blaufarb, *The Counterinsurgency*

Era: U.S. Doctrine and Performance, 1950 to the Present (New York: The Free Press, 1977), p. 137.

126   *As General Phoumi regrouped:* Bill Lair, interview, December 5, 1991.

127   *The Hmong were:* Christopher Robbins, *The Ravens* (New York: Crown Publishers, 1987), p. 31. Blaufarb, *The Counterinsurgency Era,* pp. 131–133.

127   *The tribe first earned:* Blaufarb, *The Counterinsurgency Era,* pp. 136–140.

127   *To pay the bills:* Alfred W. McCoy with Cathleen B. Read and Leonard P. Adams II, *The Politics of Heroin in Southeast Asia* (New York: Harper Colophon Books, 1973), pp. 92–96. Robbins, pp. 92–98.

127   *After the Geneva agreement:* Robbins, p. 99.

127   *In December of 1960:* Lair, interview, December 5, 1991.

127   *But the higher-ups:* Richard Bissell, interview, July 24, 1989.

128   *Come July of 1961: The Pentagon Papers: The Defense Department History of United States Decisionmaking on Vietnam,* the Senator Gravel Edition (Boston: Beacon Press, 1971), Volume II, pp. 646–647. Blaufarb, *The Counterinsurgency Era,* p. 140.

128   *Technically the unity government:* Blaufarb, *Organizing and Managing,* p. 8.

128   *The United States and the Soviet Union:* Ibid., pp. 8–9. Confidential interview with CIA officer who collected intelligence on the NVA in Laos.

128   *The Kennedy men needed:* Blaufarb, *Organizing and Managing,* p. 11.

128   *The United States also began:* U.S. Embassy, Vientiane, untitled memorandum, June 12, 1961.

128   *In July of 1963:* Historical Division, Joint Secretariat, Joint Chiefs of Staff, "Chairman's Historical Laos Update," October 7, 1969. This is a history of U.S. policy in Laos.

129   *The various Laotian:* Blaufarb, *Organizing and Managing,* pp. 22–24.

129   *But CIA intelligence showed:* Confidential interview with CIA officer in Laos.

129   *A pattern of warfare:* Blaufarb, *Organizing and Managing,* pp. vi–vii.

129   *The U.S. mission even:* Ibid., p. 29.

129   *A CIA report assessed:* U.S. Central Intelligence Agency, untitled memorandum, May 1961.

130   *Gradually the Agency:* Blaufarb, *Organizing and Managing,* p. vii.

130   *Chief of station Doug Blaufarb:* Blaufarb, *The Counterinsurgency Era,* p. 147.

130   *In the spring of 1966:* William Sullivan, interview, October 24, 1991.

130   *Vientiane in the mid-1960s:* "Visitor's View of Laos: Part State—And Part State Of Mind," *U.S. News & World Report,* June 17, 1968. "War's Signs Mark a Laos at 'Peace,' " *The New York Times,* June 13, 1966.

131   *"We described it":* Mark Pratt, interview, November 15, 1990.

131   *Their relaxed approach:* Robert Shaplen, "Letter from Laos," *The New Yorker,* May 4, 1968.

131   *A few miles outside:* "Americans Bringing a Touch of Suburbia to Laos," *The New York Times,* May 17, 1968.

131   *There were CIA bases:* Clines, interview, November 22, 1991.

131 *In the mountains south:* Blaufarb, *The Counterinsurgency Era,* p. 152. Robbins, pp. 35–37, 50–52. Confidential interview with CIA officer based in Long Tieng. Brenda Peters and Gary Peters, interviews, February 14 and 25, 1992. The Peterses worked for International Voluntary Services and often visited Long Tieng.

132 *Now a general:* U.S. Embassy, Vientiane, "Military Region Two and the Meo," August 30, 1971, p. 7. Clines, November 22, 1991.

132 *To his people:* "End of Laos War Has Brought No Peace to Thousands in Meo Clans," *The New York Times,* July 13, 1975. Pratt, interview, January 17, 1991.

132 *"As long as Vang Pao":* Confidential interview with CIA officer who worked with Vang Pao.

132 *At wild parties:* Brenda Peters, interview, February 14, 1992.

132 *Next to the tavern:* Robbins, pp. 35–40. Clines, interview, November 22, 1991.

132 *The other side:* "Laotian Hill Tribesmen, With American Help, Harass Pro-Reds," *The New York Times,* January 7, 1967.

132 *The master of Sam Thong:* Robbins, pp. 114–118.

132 *The logistical center:* Lair, interview, December 5, 1991. Clines, interview, November 22, 1991.

133 *Officially, Air America:* See Christopher Robbins, *Air America* (London: Corgi Books, 1988).

133 *As its number one:* Sullivan, interview.

133 *Continental Air:* Victor Marchetti and John D. Marks, *The CIA and the Cult of Intelligence* (New York: Dell Publishing, 1975), pp. 152–153.

133 *Ed Dearborn:* Ed Dearborn, interviews, February 27, 1992, March 12, 1992. For Dearborn in the Congo, see Robbins, *Air America,* pp. 100–103.

133 *The most notorious:* Robert Borosage and John Marks, eds., *The CIA File* (New York: Viking Press, 1976), pp. 56–57. This and subsequent citations to this work refer to an essay, "The President's Secret Army: A Case Study—The CIA in Laos, 1962–1972," by Fred Branfman, who spent four years in Laos. Robbins, *The Ravens,* pp. 125–127. Confidential interview with CIA officer who served with Poe.

134 *But one case officer:* Confidential interview with CIA officer who served with Poe.

134 *"Oh man, was Shackley":* Borosage and Marks, p. 51.

134 *One senior embassy officer:* Confidential interview with senior officer in Vientiane embassy.

134 *A graduate of:* Robbins, *The Ravens,* p. 123.

134 *He came into meetings:* Pratt, interview, November 15, 1990.

134 *"I wondered if":* Emory Swank, interview, October 7, 1991.

134 *Sullivan saw no:* Sullivan, interview.

134 *"One can only see":* Pratt, interview, January 17, 1991.

134 *The annual cost:* Marchetti and Marks, pp. 78, 132. One reasonably reliable estimate for 1970 put the combined tab of military, AID, and Agency programs contributing to the war in Laos at no more than $260 million—but this

number did not include the costs of the massive U.S. Air Force bombing campaign. (Blaufarb, *Organizing and Managing*, p. 55.)

135 *Sullivan was doing:* Sullivan, interview. Robbins, *The Ravens*, pp. 113–115. Blaufarb, *Organizing and Managing*, p. viii.

135 *"The situation in Laos":* Blaufarb, *Organizing and Managing*, p. 61.

135 *"It was great fun":* Confidential interview with senior officer in CIA Far East Division.

135 *A quarrel between:* "Laosing It Up," *Newsweek*, October 3, 1966.

135 *Then the commander:* "Laos: Gathering the Pieces," *Time*, November 4, 1966. "Laotian Says U.S. Aided His Ouster," *The New York Times*, November 22, 1966.

135 *In October, rebellious units:* "Some Laotian Officers Criticize the U.S. Over Air Force Revolt," *The New York Times*, October 26, 1966.

135 *A massive flood:* "3 Laotian Military Forces in a State of Ferment," *The New York Times*, October 28, 1966.

135 *He voiced support:* "Laos: Gathering The Pieces," *Time*, November 4, 1966.

135 *The economy was running:* Ibid.

135 *Nearly 200,000 refugees:* "Continuing Conflict in Laos Is Overshadowed by War in South Vietnam," *The New York Times*, February 13, 1967.

135 *"Often enough":* "Laotian Hill Tribesmen, With American Help, Harass Pro-Reds," *The New York Times*.

135 *Some military men:* "Economy of Laos Scarred By War," *The New York Times*, January 20, 1967.

136 *"Most of us in Laos":* Pratt, interview, November 15, 1990.

136 *"Shackley wanted more":* Almy, interview, April 6, 1992.

136 *"He was well prepared":* Pratt, interview, November 15, 1990.

136 *"All the attention":* Confidential interview with CIA officer who worked with Vang Pao.

136 *With Agency sanction and support:* Colby and Forbath, p. 200.

136 *"There was a very conscious":* Confidential interview with CIA officer who worked with the Hmong.

136 *"Up to then":* Lair, interview, December 5, 1991. Of all the CIA people interviewed for or mentioned in this book, none received as many tributes from his peers as did Lair. When asked about Lair, his former colleagues routinely praised him, his devotion to the tribespeople, and his expertise regarding Laos. Many said they would readily accept his judgments regarding the Agency program there.

137 *Shackley ordered the construction:* Richard Secord with Jay Wurts, *Honored and Betrayed: Irangate, Covert Affairs and the Secret War in Laos* (New York: John Wiley & Sons, 1992), p. 59. Lair, interview, December 5, 1991.

137 *After a few months in Laos:* Clines, interview, November 22, 1991.

137 *The team members:* Secord with Wurts, p. 60.

138 *Shackley would later install:* Robbins, *The Ravens*, p. 60. Clines, interview, November 22, 1991.

138 *For his deputy:* Clines, interview, November 22, 1991.

138 *Lair and Landry had not been:* Lair, interview, December 5, 1991.

138 *"Shackley didn't care whose":* William Young, interview, October 12, 1991.

138 *Agency men peeved:* Confidential interview with senior Vientiane embassy officer.

138 *Shackley adopted the same:* Lair, interview, December 5, 1991. Clines, interview, November 22, 1991.

138 *Shackley was not in Laos:* Sullivan, interview. U.S. Senate, Committee on Armed Services, *Hearings on FY72 Authorization for Military Procurement, Research and Development, Part 5-A* (Washington: U.S. Government Printing Office, 1971), p. 4272. Powers, p. 227.

139 *Prior to leaving:* W. W. Rostow, letter to Lyndon Johnson, November 28, 1966.

139 *After Symington arrived:* Pratt, interview, November 15, 1990.

139 *"At embassy staff meetings":* Ibid.

139 *After Shackley had been in Vientiane:* Charles W. Maynes, Jr., interview, November 7, 1990. Maynes was an economic officer in the Vientiane embassy.

139 *The chief of station escorted:* Sullivan, interview. Shackley, interview.

139 *In Langley, John Mapother:* Mapother, interview, September 27, 1990.

139 *Symington invited Shackley:* Shackley, interview. Powers, p. 227. Richard Helms, interview with Ted Gittinger, Lyndon Baines Johnson Library, September 16, 1981, p. 6. Confidential interview with senior CIA officer.

140 *Shackley's station ran agents:* Clines, interview, November 22, 1991.

140 *At the many fancy:* Pratt, interview, November 15, 1990.

140 *Senior embassy officers thought:* Pratt, January 17, 1991. Swank, interview. Confidential interview with senior Vientiane embassy officer.

140 *His station subsidized:* Pratt, January 17, 1991. Blaufarb, pp. 44–45.

140 *The Agency air-dropped:* Robbins, *Air America,* p. 135.

140 *"The whole thing":* Oliver Silsby, interview, February 3, 1992.

141 *In Laos, Shackley ordered:* Robbins, *Air America,* pp. 287–288. Soutchay Vongsavanh, *R.L.G. Military Operations and Activities in the Laotian Panhandle* (Washington: U.S. Army Center of Military History), 1981, p. 40. Secord with Wurts, pp. 60–61.

141 *Harry Aderholt:* Harry Aderholt, interview, December 13, 1991. William Colby, interview with Ted Gittinger, Lyndon Baines Johnson Library, June 2, 1981, p. 54.

141 *Every few weeks:* Lair, interview, December 5, 1991.

141 *Singlaub's outfit:* John K. Singlaub with Malcolm McConnell, *Hazardous Duty: An American Soldier in the Twentieth Century* (New York: Simon & Schuster, 1991), pp. 284–319.

141 *When Singlaub dealt:* Singlaub, interview, May 9, 1990.

141 *The high-level meetings:* Clines, interview, January 14, 1992.

142 *The station devised:* Theodore Shackley, *The Third Option: An American View of Counterinsurgency Operations* (New York: Dell Publishing, 1981), pp. 68–70.

142 *One day Carlton Swift:* Carlton Swift, Jr., interview, October 23, 1990.

142 *In 1970, tycoon:* H. Ross Perot, deposition, U.S. Senate Select Committee on POW/MIA Affairs, July 1, 1992.

143 *In the northwestern corner:* Robbins, *Air America,* pp. 138–139. McCoy with Read and Adams, pp. 266, 302–306.

143 *Young and the CIA had friends:* William Leary, *Perilous Missions: Civil Air Transport and CIA Covert Operations in Asia* (University, Alabama: University of Alabama Press, 1984), pp. 129–131, 195–196. Director of Central Intelligence, *Probable Developments in Burma,* National Intelligence Estimate Number 61-56, April 10, 1956. "War's Signs Mark a Laos at 'Peace,' " *The New York Times,* June 13, 1966.

143 *In the early 1960s:* Young, interview, October 12, 1991. McCoy with Read and Adams, pp. 265, 302.

143 *Young's cross-border project:* McCoy with Read and Adams, pp. 306–308. "CIA-Backed Laotians Said Entering China," *The Washington Post,* January 26, 1971. "CIA Patrols Into China Said Halted," *The Washington Post,* August 6, 1971.

143 *None of this:* McCoy with Read and Adams, p. 311.

144 *The high-risk cross-border:* Dyke, interview.

144 *Even Young conceded:* Young, interview.

144 *But "it sure was sexy":* Pratt, interview, November 15, 1990.

144 *Shackley delivered a message:* Ibid.

144 *"During my service":* Shackley, p. 55.

144 *In 1964, AID:* Blaufarb, *Organizing and Managing,* pp. 39–40.

145 *A 1966 AID report:* U.S. Agency for International Development, "Policy Problems and Prospects in Laos," 1967.

145 *Shackley inherited:* Blaufarb, *Organizing and Managing,* pp. 39–40. Clines, interview, November 22, 1991.

145 *AID personnel:* Blaufarb, *Organizing and Managing,* p. 99.

145 *"He would have defended":* Douglas Blaufarb, interview, October 7, 1991.

145 *"Villages in the area":* Blaufarb, *Organizing and Managing,* p. 40.

145 *In a U.S.-operated:* Ibid., pp. 47–51.

145 *Shackley and his subordinates:* Paul Pettigrew, interview, March 23, 1992. Pettigrew was the U.S. Air Force attaché at the Vientiane embassy.

145 *But the addition of airpower:* Blaufarb, *The Counterinsurgency Era,* p. 161.

146 *As the sorties:* Blaufarb, *Organizing and Managing,* p. 51.

146 *Decades later, Blaufarb:* Blaufarb, interview.

146 *"That assumption":* Blaufarb, *Organizing and Managing,* p. 51.

146 *Jerome Brown:* Seymour Hersh, "How We Ran the Secret Air War in Laos," *The New York Times,* October 29, 1972.

146 *Throughout 1967:* Borosage and Marks, p. 77. The bombing figures for 1967 and 1968 were derived by Senator Stuart Symington and placed into the *Congressional Record* on July 18, 1973.

146 *Sullivan assigned:* Sullivan, interview.

146 *But a United Nations adviser:* Fred Branfman, *Voices from the Plain of Jars: Life under an Air War* (New York: Harper Colophon, 1972), p. 19. Branfman quotes George Chapelier, "Plains of Jars: Social Change Under Five Years of Pathet Lao Administration," *Asia Quarterly,* 1971, number 1.

147   *War planes of the type:* Ibid., pp. 59–60.

147   *One evening, Frank McCulloch:* Frank McCulloch, interview, February 6, 1992.

147   *Northern Laos was part:* McCoy with Read and Adams, p. 379. These figures are based on a United Nations survey.

148   *And opium collection:* "Army Helps Laos Reap Her Crops," *The New York Times,* January 19, 1968.

148   *Air America planes:* Blaufarb, *The Counterinsurgency Era,* p. 151.

148   *The subsequent report:* U.S. Senate, Select Committee to Study Governmental Operations with Respect to Intelligence Activities, *Final Report,* Book 1 (Washington: U.S. Government Printing Office, 1976), pp. 227–230. Hereinafter, *Church Committee Final Report.* Shackley, interview.

148   *"We knew that we":* Robbins, *Air America,* pp. 246–247.

148   *The CIA did work with:* McCoy with Read and Adams, pp. 258–260. U.S. House of Representatives, Staff Survey Team of the Committee on Foreign Affairs, *The U.S. Heroin Problem and Southeast Asia* (Washington: U.S. Government Printing Office, 1973), pp. 27–28.

148   *One time, Eli Popovich:* Eli Popovich, interview, March 2, 1992.

149   *On a visit to Laos:* Almy, interview, April 6, 1992.

149   *During the so-called Opium War:* "Bombings By Laos End an Opium War," *The New York Times,* August 10, 1967. Robbins, *Air America,* p. 243, McCoy with Read and Adams, pp. 322–328. U.S. Embassy, Vientiane, "Lao Situation Report," October 11, 1967.

149   *"This was where":* Pratt, interview, November 15, 1990.

149   *"Yet their goodwill":* Church Committee Final Report, p. 232.

149   *In one case, the station:* Ibid., p. 232.

149   *"We found no evidence":* Shackley, interview.

149   *In 1968, John Everingham:* "Guns, Drugs and the CIA," *Frontline,* WGBH. This program was broadcast on the Public Broadcasting System on May 17, 1988.

149   *In 1971 Long Pot:* McCoy with Read and Adams, pp. 281–283, 289.

150   *During and after the war:* Ibid., pp. 244, 248–249. McCoy, quoting an unnamed U.S. federal drug agent, maintained that the U.S. Bureau of Narcotics had in its files reports that Vang Pao operated a heroin factory at Long Tieng. But this report has not been confirmed.

150   *Tony Poe, the irrepressible:* "Guns, Drugs and the CIA," *Frontline.*

150   *"He had to let":* Pratt, interview, January 17, 1991.

150   *Agency officers realized:* Confidential interview with CIA officer based in Long Tieng.

150   *The opium business in Laos:* Thomas McCoy, interview, March 13, 1990.

150   *As the I.G. report:* Church Committee Final Report, p. 229.

150   *CIA men occasionally warned:* Confidential interview with CIA officer based in Long Tieng.

150   *The Company-run radio station:* Almy, interview, April 6, 1992.

150   *One of Shackley's case officers:* Church Committee Final Report, p. 229.

150   *As Douglas Blaufarb noted:* Blaufarb, *The Counterinsurgency Era,* p. 152.

151   *"It's one of the things":* Richard Helms, interview with Ted Gittinger, Lyndon Baines Johnson Library, September 16, 1981, p. 20.

151   *Vang Pao's forces:* Blaufarb, *Organizing and Managing,* pp. viii, 35.

151   *His army:* U.S. Embassy, Vientiane, "Lao Situation Report," June 9, 1967.

151   *"I just didn't see":* Swank, interview.

151   *In May, CIA-backed irregulars:* Southchay Vongsavanh.

151   *In Luang Prabang:* Popovich, interview.

152   *The talk often was:* Jameson, interview, March 21, 1990.

153   *A detailed plan emerged:* Confidential interview with senior embassy officer.

153   *The point was:* Confidential interview with senior embassy officer.

153   *"I never thought":* Confidential interview with senior embassy officer.

153   *Shackley explained the scheme:* Lair, interview, December 5, 1991.

154   *"All the guys":* Clines, interview, November 22, 1991.

154   *One embassy officer who had listened:* Confidential interview with senior embassy officer.

154   *Shackley, as Sullivan put it:* Sullivan, interview.

154   *Over a course of months:* Carl Berger, ed., *The United States Air Force in Southeast Asia, 1961–1973: An Illustrated Account* (Washington: Office of Air Force History, U.S. Air Force, 1984), p. 126. U.S. Embassy, Vientiane, "Lao Situation Report," October 11, 1967.

154   *On December 22, 1967:* U.S. Embassy, Vientiane, cable, December 22, 1967.

154   *A few days later:* "Laotian Military Asserts Situation Is Normal," *The New York Times,* December 30, 1967.

154   *At a meeting of senior:* Confidential interview with senior embassy officer.

154   *The 4,500-man government force:* "Reds' Gains in Laos Discounted," *The Washington Post,* January 18, 1968. "Royal Troops Step Up Battle on North Vietnamese in Laos," *The New York Times,* January 9, 1968.

154   *Shackley looked for:* Lair, interview, December 5, 1991. Popovich, interview.

154   *He liberally interpreted:* Confidential interview with CIA officer in Laos. "Pirate Planes Raid Yunnan, China Says," *The New York Times,* January 13, 1968. Foreign Broadcast Information Service, Communist China, International Affairs, January 15, 1968, pp. BBB1-2.

155   *Less than a month:* "Laotians Report Loss of Key Town," *The Washington Post,* January 16, 1968. "Reds' Gains in Laos Discounted," *The Washington Post,* January 18, 1968. "2000 Laotian Troops Still Are Missing," *The Washington Post,* January 23, 1968. "Disaster at Nam Bac," *Newsweek,* January 29, 1968.

155   *Of the 3,278 men:* U.S. Central Intelligence Agency, "Appraisal of the Lao Armed Forces Defeat at Nam Bac and Repercussions From This Defeat as of 30 January 1968," January 30, 1968. This is a report Shackley's station sent to Washington.

155   *Most senior embassy officials:* Confidential interview with senior embassy officer. Pratt, interview, December 5, 1991.

155 *"Shackley wanted to be":* Pratt, interview, December 5, 1991.

156 *Lao commanders, who believed:* Ibid.

156 *"It was a terrible":* Confidential interview with senior embassy officer.

156 *The collapse of the royal:* U.S. Embassy, Vientiane, "Military Region Two and the Meo," August 30, 1971.

156 *One morning after the disaster:* Confidential interview with senior embassy officer. U.S. Central Intelligence Agency, "Appraisal of the Lao Armed Forces Defeat at Nam Bac and Repercussions From This Defeat as of 30 January 1968."

156 *In Washington, a staff member:* Marshall Wright, "Analysis of the Nam Bac Debacle in Laos," undated. This memo was sent to Rostow.

157 *After Nam Bac, Bill Lair:* Lair, interview, December 5, 1991.

157 *For weeks, Shackley periodically:* Clines, interview, November 22, 1991.

157 *When Poe returned:* Robbins, *The Ravens,* p. 127.

157 *"We all referred":* Confidential interview with CIA officer in Laos.

157 *In 1966, the mission:* Blaufarb, *Organizing and Managing,* p. 35. Robbins, *The Ravens,* pp. 41–42. Historical Division, Joint Secretariat, Joint Chiefs of Staff, "Chairman's Historical Laos Update."

157 *Surrounded by scarlet poppies:* Clines, interview, November 22, 1991.

158 *It was, as Blaufarb later noted:* Blaufarb, interview.

158 *After Tom Clines inspected:* Clines, interview, November 22, 1991.

158 *Shackley reported this:* Lair, interview, December 5, 1991. Clines, interview, November 22, 1991. Secord with Wurts, pp. 78–81. Hersh, "How We Ran the Secret Air War in Laos," *The New York Times.* Robert A. Lynn, "Caught in Harm's Way," *Vietnam,* December 1991.

158 *Secord was well versed:* See Secord with Wurts. Morgan Strong, "Playboy Interview: General Richard Secord," *Playboy,* October 1987.

158 *One time, the Agency ordered:* Robbins, *The Ravens,* p. 124.

158 *In late February:* "Caught in Harm's Way," *Vietnam.* Secord with Wurts, p. 81.

158 *The message came back:* Secord with Wurts, p. 82. Lair, interview, December 5, 1991. Clines, interview, November 22, 1991.

158 *Secord begged:* Secord with Wurts, p. 82.

158 *The Air Force even:* "Caught in Harm's Way," *Vietnam.*

158 *At three in the morning:* Robbins, *The Ravens,* pp. 42–45. "Caught in Harm's Way," *Vietnam.*

159 *In Udorn, Secord:* Clines, January 14, 1992. Secord with Wurts, pp. 84–85.

159 *Eleven of the seventeen:* "Caught in Harm's Way," *Vietnam.* Other accounts of the battle at Phou Pha Thi reported different casualty levels. Blaufarb noted thirteen Americans were killed. (Blaufarb, *The Counterinsurgency Era,* p. 162.) An official Air Force history maintained seven Americans were lost. (Berger, p. 126.) There are no good figures for losses experienced by the Hmong army.

159 *For a week afterward:* Robbins, *The Ravens,* p. 45.

159 *Not only was the loss:* Blaufarb, *The Counterinsurgency Era,* p. 162.

159 *The day Phou Pha Thi:* U.S. Embassy, Vientiane, cable, March 11, 1968.

159   *Life in Vientiane:* "Land of Make-Believe," *The New York Times,* January 27, 1968. "Hanoi Troops Set to Attack in Laos," *The New York Times,* February 19, 1968.

159   *Scores of American bohemians:* "Letter from Laos," *The New Yorker.*

159   *Annual casualty figures:* "Land of Make-Believe," *The New York Times,* January 27, 1968.

159   *If he had to join in:* Clines, interview, November 22, 1991.

160   *One night after the band:* Ibid.

160   *Throughout the first half:* John Prados, *The Presidents' Secret Wars* (New York: Quill, 1986), p. 282.

160   *"We are concerned":* "Reds Threatening South Laos Towns," *The New York Times,* April 14, 1968.

160   *North Vietnamese and Pathet Lao units:* Zalin Grant, "Report from Laos: The Hidden War," *The New Republic,* April 20, 1968. "Letter from Laos," *The New Yorker.*

160   *"We're bugging out":* "Report from Laos: The Hidden War," *The New Republic.*

160   *V.P. was losing:* "Letter from Laos," *The New Yorker.*

160   *The army of V.P.:* Clines, interview, January 14, 1992. Robbins, *The Ravens,* p. 46. Berger, p. 26.

161   *When the battle began:* Secord with Wurts, pp. 90–91.

161   *Na Khang would fall:* Robbins, *The Ravens,* pp. 152–153.

161   *"They were told":* Clines, interview, November 22, 1991.

161   *At other spots:* Ibid.

161   *"We got them into":* Lair, interview, December 5, 1991.

162   *Dr. Charles Weldon:* "Letter from Laos," *The New Yorker.*

162   *Buell unleashed:* Ibid.

162   *When in June the sky:* "Laotians Doubtful the Monsoon Will Curb Guerrilla's Attacks," *The New York Times,* May 12, 1968.

163   *At Shackley's insistence:* Secord with Wurts, p. 92.

163   *In the north:* U.S. Embassy, Vientiane, cable, June 21, 1968.

163   *Vang Pao was worried:* Clines, interview, November 22, 1991.

163   *"It was all slipping":* Jack Shirley, interview, February 5, 1992.

163   *And by the end:* Berger, p. 126.

163   *In July of 1968:* Lair, interview, December 5, 1991.

163   *His like-minded deputy:* Ibid.

163   *"I'm a do-gooder":* Lair, interview, December 19, 1991.

164   *"He was so closely":* Clines, interview, January 14, 1992.

164   *Nearly twenty-five years:* Shirley, interview.

164   *Before he left Udorn:* Lair, December 5, 1991.

164   *But he still wielded clout:* Colby, interview, June 25, 1991.

164   *But when he had recommended:* Halpern, interview, August 6, 1990.

165   *Shackley asked Clines:* Clines, interviews, November 22, 1991, January 14, 1992.

165   *Before leaving Vientiane:* Lou Connick, interview, October 10, 1991. Connick worked in Laos for the Asia Foundation.

165   *Not until 1970:* Robbins, *The Ravens,* pp. 236–238.

165   *A year after Shackley:* U.S. Senate, Committee on Foreign Relations, Subcommittee on United States Security Agreements and Commitments Abroad, *United States Security Agreements and Commitments Abroad: Kingdom of Laos* (Washington: Government Printing Office, 1970), pp. 365–366. Hereinafter, *Symington Hearings.* Prados, p. 285.

166   *In a memo to Helms:* Lawrence R. Houston, "Symington Subcommittee Hearings," October 30, 1969.

166   *"I couldn't figure out":* Shackley, interview.

166   *After Symington went public:* John Hart Ely, "The American War in Indochina, Part II: The Unconstitutionality of the War They Didn't Tell Us About," *Stanford Law Review,* May 1990, p. 1120.

166   *"I knew we were doing":* "Fulbright Attacks U.S. Role in Laos," *The Washington Post,* October 29, 1969.

166   *In late 1968, for instance: Symington Hearings,* pp. 544–547.

166   *"The Congress," Symington's:* Staff of Subcommittee on U.S. Security Agreements and Commitments Abroad, Senate Committee on Foreign Relations, *Security Arrangements and Commitments,* 1970, p. 5.

166   *Shackley and his colleagues:* See Ely, "The American War in Indochina, Part II: The Unconstitutionality of the War They Didn't Tell Us About." He presents a compelling case that Shackley and his patriotic comrades ran a decidedly unconstitutional operation.

167   *A month or so after:* "Laotian Forces Retake Posts Near Border of North Vietnam," *The New York Times,* November 13, 1968.

167   *In 1972, Douglas Blaufarb:* Blaufarb, *Organizing and Managing,* p. v, pp. 82–86.

167   *The U.S. operation:* Borosage and Marks, p. 47.

167   *Colby, in his memoirs:* Colby and Forbath, p. 198.

167   *"These grim statistics":* Blaufarb, *Organizing and Managing,* p. 86.

167   *But he defended:* Blaufarb, *The Counterinsurgency Era,* p. 166.

167   *"Arming the tribesmen":* Hilsman, pp. 115–116.

168   *When Jim Lilley's wife:* Confidential interview with a senior embassy officer.

168   *No matter what:* Jameson, interview, March 30, 1990.

168   *The United States, he noted:* Shackley, interview.

168   *"We had contingency plans":* Ibid.

168   *"The Hmong got shafted":* William Nelson, interview, August 13, 1990.

169   *In the early days of the secret war:* Ray Cline, interview, May 31, 1990.

169   *Years after his time:* Shackley, p. vii.

169   *"I had a lot":* Sullivan, interview.

169   *"He was an apparatchik":* Peter Lydon, interview, December 9, 1991.

169   *Another embassy man:* Confidential interview with senior embassy officer.

169   *In Langley, a sharp-tongued:* Confidential interview with staff aide to the Church Committee. Jerome Levinson, interview, October 25, 1991.

169   *After hearing Shackley was off:* Confidential interview with senior embassy officer.

CHAPTER 6. SAIGON: INTELLIGENCE AT WAR

Page

171   *Once a month:* Almy, interview, February 20, 1992. Roger McCarthy, interview, February 28, 1992.

172   *In the latter years:* Marilyn B. Young, *The Vietnam Wars 1945–1990* (New York: HarperPerennial, 1991), pp. 1–10. See also Archimedes Patti, *Why Vietnam? Prelude to America's Albatross* (Berkeley, California: University of California Press, 1980).

172   *After the French defeat:* Young, p. 41.

172   *It chose Ngo Dinh Diem:* Stanley Karnow, *Vietnam: A History* (New York: The Viking Press, 1983), p. 217.

172   *In 1954, Edward Lansdale:* Currey, pp. 137, 156–185.

173   *With help from Lansdale:* Young, p. 53.

173   *Months later, he initiated:* Ibid., p. 56.

173   *The Agency helped by:* Ibid., p. 61.

173   *One village chief:* Ibid., p. 62.

173   *In Saigon, CIA station chief:* William Colby with James McCargar, *Lost Victory: A Firsthand Account of America's Sixteen-Year Involvement in Vietnam* (Chicago: Contemporary Books, 1989), pp. 70, 83.

173   *He considered "pacification":* Zalin Grant, *Facing the Phoenix: The CIA and the Political Defeat of the United States in Vietnam* (New York: W. W. Norton & Company, 1991), p. 166.

173   *The Agency armed:* Colby with McCargar, pp. 89, 94.

173   *The CIA trained and paid:* Ibid., p. 92.

173   *The growing station:* Colby with McCargar, p. 109. Grant, p. 168.

173   *In September of 1960:* Young, pp. 68–71.

174   *After John Kennedy:* Ibid., p. 79.

174   *The resistance continued:* George McT. Kahin, *Intervention: How America Became Involved in Vietnam* (Garden City, N.Y.: Anchor Books, 1987), p. 133.

174   *In 1962, Saigon initiated:* Colby with McCargar, pp. 84–86. Neil Sheehan, *A Bright Shining Lie: John Paul Vann and America in Vietnam* (New York: Random House, 1988), pp. 309–310. Blaufarb, *The Counterinsurgency Era,* pp. 120–123.

174   *ARVN mounted division-sized:* Young, pp. 81–90.

174   *Diem continued his:* Ibid., pp. 95–96.

174   *Officials in Washington argued:* Ibid., pp. 96–98.

174   *Toward the end of October:* Grant, p. 201.

175   *As the United States increased:* Ibid., pp. 181–182.

175   *With few officers:* Ibid., p. 185.

175   *At a July 21, 1965:* Kahin, p. 374.

175   *In 1965, the CIA station:* Colby with McCargar, pp. 187–188. Blaufarb, *The Counterinsurgency Era,* p. 212.

175   *Another new CIA program was less warm:* Peer DeSilva, *Sub Rosa* (New York: New York Times Books, 1978), pp. 245–250.

175   *The Agency also built Provincial:* Ralph William Johnson, "Phoenix/Phung

Hoang: A Study of Wartime Intelligence Management," dissertation, School of International Affairs, American University, Washington, D.C., July 1982, p. 162. Johnson was a CIA officer. Blaufarb, *The Counterinsurgency Era,* p. 213.

175 *In the name of efficiency:* Blaufarb, *The Counterinsurgency Era,* pp. 245–247. Ralph William Johnson, pp. 156–199. Ranelagh, pp. 438–439.

176 *From 1966 to 1968:* Sherwood, interview, October 23, 1990.

176 *In 1964, a CIA special mission: Pentagon Papers,* Volume II, p. 194, Volume III, p. 33.

176 *A 1965 estimate:* Kahin, pp. 265–266.

176 *McCone irritated Johnson:* Powers, pp. 210–211.

176 *A March 1966 CIA report: Pentagon Papers,* Volume IV, p. 71.

176 *In 1967, a holy war:* Powers, pp. 235–248. Sam Adams, "Vietnam Cover-Up: Playing War With Numbers," *Harper's,* May 1975. Colby with McCargar, pp. 184–185. See Bob Brewin and Sydney Shaw, *Vietnam on Trial: Westmoreland vs. CBS* (New York: Atheneum, 1987).

177 *But a senior CIA official:* Confidential interview with senior CIA official.

177 *But as one report noted: Pentagon Papers,* Volume IV, pp. 551–552.

177 *"There was," he later said:* Shackley, interview.

177 *Saigon was an occupied city:* Frank Snepp, *Decent Interval: An Insider's Account of Saigon's Indecent End Told by the CIA's Chief Strategy Analyst in Vietnam* (New York: Vintage Books, 1978), pp. 3–10. Ralph McGehee, *Deadly Deceits: My 25 Years in the CIA* (New York: Sheridan Square Publications, 1983), pp. 125–127. Robert Sam Anson, *War News: A Young Reporter in Indochina* (New York: Simon & Schuster, 1989), pp. 29–33.

178 *He usually could be found:* Kevin Buckley, interview, September 19, 1990. Buckley was a correspondent for *Newsweek.*

178 *"There was such":* Michael Herr, *Dispatches* (New York: Avon, 1978), p. 44.

179 *The boss replied:* Phil Jones, interview, February 2, 1990.

179 *His secretary, Dana Meiggs:* Confidential interview with senior CIA officer in Vietnam.

179 *In his office:* Richard Dane, interview, February 25, 1992.

179 *Once the Nixon administration settled:* Eleazar Williams, interview, February 12, 1992.

179 *During a Kissinger visit:* Confidential interview with senior CIA officer in Vietnam.

179 *"On these occasions":* Joseph Lazarsky, January 15, 1992, interview.

180 *Shackley carefully cultivated:* Charles Hill, interview, March 5, 1992.

180 *One time in Vietnam:* Confidential interview with Shackley associate.

180 *Shortly after Shackley took over:* James Graham, interview, March 16, 1992. Russell Jack Smith, pp. 208–209.

180 *This issue was resolved:* Russell Jack Smith, pp. 210–211. Powers, pp. 276–279.

180 *Shackley nurtured good:* Snepp, p. 14. Lazarsky, interview.

181 *In 1971 Quang:* McCoy, p. 218.

181 *"Our reliance on these":* Snepp, p. 14.

181 *Shackley struck up friendships:* Grant, pp. 227–228.

181 *Shackley had little time:* Maynard Parker, interview, April 23, 1992. Alvin Shuster, interview, February 7, 1992. Both were war correspondents.

181 *Douglas Pike, an embassy:* Douglas Pike, interview. March 4, 1992.

181 *At the end of each week:* Frank Snepp, interview, March 21, 1992.

182 *Snepp was a native:* "Frank Snepp, Late of CIA, Exorcises the Ghosts," *The Washington Post,* December 2, 1977.

182 *Supposedly a woman analyst:* Snepp, interview, May 27, 1992.

182 *He was to extricate:* Lazarsky, interview.

182 *Orrin DeForest, a wiry:* Orrin DeForest, *Slow Burn: The Rise and Bitter Fall of American Intelligence in Vietnam* (New York: Simon & Schuster, 1990), pp. 27–28. DeForest's account is very critical of the CIA's overall program in Vietnam. But he celebrates the successes of operations he directed. Interviews with other Agency officers—including Daren Flitcroft, who for a time was De-Forest's boss—confirm the general thrust of his book, but a few of his former colleagues noted that DeForest had an understandable tendency to inflate his own achievements.

183 *"It became clear":* Douglas Valentine, *The Phoenix Program* (New York: William Morrow & Company, 1990), p. 277.

183 *Shackley began transferring:* Johnson, pp. 369–372. Evan Parker, Jr., interview, February 24, 1992.

183 *Before Shackley hit:* Lazarsky, interview, January 15, 1992.

184 *"Quite frankly":* Colby, interview, June 25, 1991.

184 *No one knew that:* George Allen, March 19, 1992.

184 *Four years later:* Ibid.

184 *"There were no real":* Jack Horgan, interview, February 20, 1992.

184 *"It was very frustrating":* Lewis Lapham, interview, May 18, 1992.

185 *In early 1969:* DeForest, pp. 31–34.

185 *"I'll tell you":* Ibid., p. 44.

185 *While visiting the Bien Hoa:* Ibid., pp. 54–55.

185 *For Shackley, the PICs:* Daren Flitcroft, interview, February 12, 1992.

186 *Between 1963 and 1973:* Dale Andradé, *Ashes to Ashes: The Phoenix Program and the Vietnam War* (Lexington, Massachusetts: Lexington Books, 1990), p. 4.

186 *"The problem was":* Flitcroft, interview.

186 *Dean Almy, ROIC for:* Almy, interview, February 20, 1992.

186 *Roger McCarthy, ROIC for:* McCarthy, interview, February 28, 1992.

186 *DeForest decided:* DeForest, pp. 77–87.

186 *When another officer asked:* Ibid., p. 82.

186 *Shortly after the system:* Ibid., pp. 90–91. Flitcroft, interview.

187 *But DeForest's operation:* DeForest, pp. 98–101.

187 *Flitcroft's Region III managed:* Flitcroft, interview.

187 *In the delta:* Dan Mudrinich, interview, March 3, 1992.

188 *By paying merchants:* For information on the drug smuggler: Snepp, interview, May 27, 1992.

188 *Among the many elusive:* Mudrinich, interview.

189   *Dean Almy, who trained:* Almy, interview, February 20, 1992.

189   *In Region I:* McCarthy, interview.

189   *But during Roger McCarthy's:* Yothers, interview.

189   *One of the better:* McCarthy, interview.

189   *He wooed:* Yothers, interview.

190   *The one singular success:* McCarthy, interview.

190   *He notified CIA people:* Almy, interview, February 20, 1992.

191   *"Shackley liked to keep":* Mudrinich, interview.

191   *Charles Yothers discovered:* Yothers, interview.

191   *Earlier one officer:* Halpern, interview, June 21, 1990.

192   *Charles Yothers, who worked:* Yothers, interview.

192   *Some Agency people shared:* Shatton, interview.

192   *"Every waking moment":* McGehee, p. 147.

192   *An officer who worked in Saigon:* Confidential interview with CIA officer.

192   *Shackley rarely left:* Almy, interviews, February 20, 1992, April 6, 1992.

192   *"Let me tell you":* DeForest, p. 60.

193   *In the spring of 1969:* George French, interview, March 2, 1992.

193   *The men who headed:* Chester McCoid, interview, February 26, 1992. McCoid was an assistant to Parker, Mason, and Tilton.

193   *"Shackley was happy":* McCarthy, interview.

194   *In late 1969 and early 1970:* Valentine, pp. 312–314. See "The CIA's Hired Killers," *True,* February 1970. "Training for Terror: A Deliberate Policy," *The Village Voice,* December 11, 1969. "The Mysterious Project Phoenix," *The Progressive,* February 1970.

194   *About this time, a DDI analyst:* Jones, interview.

194   *And Shackley retained control:* Colby, interview, July 15, 1991.

194   *Ever since the Phoenix program:* See Andradé.

194   *But the PRUs:* Flitcroft, interview. Lazarsky, interview.

194   *The Saigon station's bill:* Andradé, p. 179.

194   *The PRUs were a Nixon favorite:* Seymour Hersh, *The Price of Power: Kissinger in the Nixon White House* (New York: Summit Books, 1983), p. 135.

194   *In Saigon, Tucker:* Rodriguez and Weisman, p. 227.

194   *His deputy:* Mark Perry, "The Secret Life of an American Spy," *Regardie's,* February 1989.

195   *"But," Flitcroft admitted:* Flitcroft, interview.

195   *Mudrinich, the ROIC:* Mudrinich, interview.

195   *And Dean Almy:* Almy, interview, February 20, 1992.

195   *In December of 1969 in Quang Tri:* Andradé, p. 175. The source for this account was an end-of-tour report filed by Robert S. Hallock, a Phoenix adviser in Quang Tri.

195   *Years after the war:* Shackley, pp. 56–57.

195   *On the evening:* The account of this affair, which came to be known popularly as the Green Berets murder, is based on two prime sources: Jeff Stein, *A Murder in Wartime: The Untold Spy Story That Changed the Course of the Vietnam War* (New York: St. Martin's Press), 1992, and the main investigative file on the case compiled by the Criminal Investigations Detachment of the U.S.

Army. The army report covered the commission of the murder and the cover-up. *A Murder in Wartime* provided details on the legal proceedings, political machinations, and Agency activity (including Shackley's actions) that followed the murder. The author conducted interviews with several of Stein's sources, who attested to the accuracy of Stein's book. Another account of the case can be found in John Stevens Berry, *Those Gallant Men* (Novato, CA: Presidio Press, 1984). Any other sources are noted below.

197 *"Shackley surrounded":* Almy, interview, February 20, 1992.

199 *But it turned into front-page:* "Green Beret Case Stirs a Complaint," *The New York Times,* August 7, 1969.

199 *This term:* "Beret Case Details Reported in Saigon," *The New York Times,* August 14, 1969.

201 *Despite the distraction:* Charles Stainbach, interview, March 11, 1992. Wall, interview, March 11, 1992. DeForest, p. 34. Interviews with other CIA officers in Vietnam confirmed HACKLE's significance and the material he produced.

202 *"This was as close":* Snepp, interview, March 11, 1992.

202 *His confirmation:* Ibid.

203 *"We have not yet":* COSVN Resolution No. 9, July 1969. This copy was translated by the CIA.

203 *Shackley informed:* Snepp, interview, March 11, 1992.

203 *But they also reinforced:* Stainbach, interview.

203 *One paper produced:* U.S. Central Intelligence Agency, "Vietnamization: Progress, Problems, and Prospects," December 27, 1969.

203 *Near this time:* Mudrinich, interview, April 9, 1992.

204 *Yet Shackley insisted:* Snepp, interview, February 3, 1992. C. Philip Liechty, interview, February 3, 1992. Liechty was an officer in the Far East Division.

204 *The use of polygraphs:* Snepp, interview, February 3, 1992. DeForest, p. 230.

204 *By the summer of 1970:* Mudrinich, interview, April 9, 1992. Snepp, interview, May 27, 1992.

204 *Not too long afterward:* Ibid.

204 *"Shackley had distinguished":* Robert Simmons, interview, April 2, 1992. Simmons was a case officer in Tuy Hoa province.

204 *In the middle of 1969:* "Vietnam Cover-Up: Playing War With Numbers," *Harper's.*

204 *Counterintelligence was the:* Cord Meyer, interview, April 1, 1992. Meyer was the associate deputy director for plans.

205 *Ralph McGehee learned:* McGehee, pp. 150–151.

205 *At this time, the ROIC:* Confidential interview with ROIC for Region V.

206 *Shackley's station conducted:* Ibid.

206 *The ROIC, a tall:* Ibid.

207 *In search of the hard:* McGehee, pp. 152–155.

207 *News of the arrests:* "Assistant to Thieu Is Accused as a Spy," *The New York Times,* August 3, 1969.

207 *"While our Projectile":* McGehee, p. 155.

208 *Months after the roundup:* Confidential interview with ROIC for Region V.

208   *On May 11, 1970:* Laurence E. Lynn, Jr., "Viet Cong Military Proselyting," May 11, 1970. Henry A. Kissinger, "Viet Cong Military Proselyting," undated memorandum for the President.

208   *Nine months later, Nixon mounted:* Hersh, pp. 307–313.

208   *In September of 1970:* U.S. Central Intelligence Agency, "Communist Subversion in the South Vietnamese Army and Security Apparatus," September 1970.

208   *The analyst sent:* Snepp, interview, January 16, 1990.

208   *In October of 1970:* "CIA Says Enemy Spies Hold Vital Posts in Saigon," *The New York Times,* October 19, 1970.

209   *Adams scored:* "Vietnam Cover-Up: Playing War With Numbers," *Harper's.* Snepp, interview, January 16, 1990.

209   *Adams left the Agency:* Samuel A. Adams, interview with Ted Gittinger, Lyndon Baines Johnson Library, September 20, 1984, p. 2.

209   *"We never developed":* Graham, interview.

209   *In headquarters, James Angleton:* Meyer, interview.

209   *"It was a blindspot":* Halpern, interview, June 21, 1990. Cord Meyer, Karamessines's deputy, confirmed that Angleton wanted more CI in Vietnam.

209   *"We had quite":* Lapham, interview.

209   *Before Shackley was appointed:* John Stockwell, *In Search of Enemies* (New York: W.W. Norton & Company, 1978), p. 107. Lapham, interview. "Thieu Was Tapped by CIA," *The Washington Post,* June 11, 1976.

210   *Several Shackley subordinates:* Valentine, p. 295.

210   *"I had some problems":* Tran Van Don, interview, March 20, 1992.

210   *On the political front:* Williams, interview. Williams was the chief of Shackley's political unit in 1969. William Kohlmann, interview, June 6, 1992.

210   *Shackley's political officers funneled:* Snepp, p. 15. For information on the National Social Democratic Front, see Eleazer Williams, "The Election Process in Vietnam: The Road to a Functioning Policy," National War College, March 1971. This study was written by Williams after he returned to the States from Vietnam. In the paper, he noted that NSDF was a failure, but he does not mention any CIA support for the coalition. In an interview, Williams acknowledged that within the station, "there was talk of [building] a political party—it never amounted to much."

210   *Station personnel helped:* Snepp, p. 15.

210   *One of Shackley's men:* Kohlmann, interview.

210   *Shackley had handed:* French, interview. French returned to Vietnam in 1971 and worked on propaganda matters.

211   *Station officers aired:* Confidential interview with CIA officer involved in the radio operation.

211   *During the 1970 Tet:* See Grant.

211   *The opportunity came:* Confidential interview with ROIC for Region V. Grant, pp. 21–27.

212   *In 1965 and afterward:* Grant, pp. 60–61, 233–234. Tran Ngoc Chau, interview, April 27, 1992.

212   *Chau's American friends:* Grant, p. 61.

212 *When Richard Moose:* Richard Moose, interview, April 1, 1992. James Lowenstein, interview, May 6, 1992.

212 *In late December of 1969:* Grant, pp. 317–318.

213 *Keyes Beech, the conservative:* Grant, pp. 230–231, 318. George McArthur, interview, February 10, 1992.

213 *In February of 1970:* Grant, pp. 231, 302–303.

213 *After Jean Sauvageot:* Ibid., pp. 301–303.

213 *John Paul Vann told:* Daniel Ellsberg, interview, March 8, 1991.

213 *According to Ellsberg:* Ellsberg, interview, March 12, 1992.

213 *At one point during the Chau:* Lowenstein, interview.

214 *In mid-February:* Grant, pp. 321–323.

214 *In one exchange:* U.S. Senate, Committee on Foreign Relations, *Vietnam Policy and Prospects, 1970: Hearings Before the Committee on Foreign Relations* (Washington: General Printing Office, 1970), p. 327.

214 *"Something happened":* Moose, interview, May 6, 1992.

214 *On February 23, 1970:* Grant, p. 324.

214 *On March 6:* "Officials Say Bunker Delayed Chau Plea," *The New York Times,* March 27, 1970.

214 *Bunker's nonchalant attitude:* Grant, pp. 324–325.

214 *A few weeks later, Senator:* U.S. Congress, *Congressional Record,* April 3, 1970, pp. 10283–10284.

214 *Decades afterward, Chau:* Chau, interview.

214 *In early May of 1970:* U.S. Central Intelligence Agency, Saigon station, "An Appraisal of the Internal Unrest in Vietnam as of 7 May 1970," May 7, 1970.

215 *In March of 1970:* Rodriguez and Weisman, pp. 221–239. For Rodriguez's account of his role in the Guevara operation, see pp. 185–201.

215 *Despite Shackley's emphasis:* Valentine, pp. 369–370.

216 *One PRU raid conducted:* Ibid., p. 370.

216 *A Viet Cong village secretary:* DeForest, pp. 122–129.

216 *Using information:* Ibid., p. 126.

216 *"I visited":* Jones, interview.

216 *"We never came up":* Dane, interview.

217 *As part of this brief:* Confidential interview with CIA case officer who handled Thanh.

217 *A member of a notable:* "Saigon Refuses to Free War Foe," *The New York Times,* September 6, 1971.

217 *Some considered her:* Dane, interview.

217 *In the summer of 1971:* "Trial of Ailing Critic of Saigon Regime Put Off Indefinitely," *The New York Times,* March 23, 1972.

217 *In an episode reminiscent:* Confidential interview with CIA case officer who handled Thanh.

218 *Thanh was released:* "Saigon Frees One of Its Sharp Critics," *The New York Times,* September 22, 1973.

218 *A presidential election was:* Hersh, pp. 423–443.

218 *In a December 22, 1970, dispatch:* U.S. Central Intelligence Agency, Sai-

gon station, "Outlook for the 1971 Presidential Election in South Vietnam," December 22, 1970.

218   *Then, in concert with Shackley's:* Kohlmann, interview.

218   *Shackley, according to Frank Snepp:* Snepp, p. 436.

218   *"You're a damn fool":* McArthur, interview.

218   *In a June 12 cable:* U.S. Central Intelligence Agency, Saigon station, "Outlook for the 1971 Presidential Election in South Vietnam," June 12, 1971.

219   *A Shackleygram the next month:* U.S. Central Intelligence Agency, Saigon station, "Outlook for the 1971 Presidential Election in South Vietnam," July 1971. The precise date of the report is deleted.

219   *Shortly afterward, General Minh:* Hersh, pp. 437–438. Snepp, p. 11.

219   *A report filed by Shackley:* U.S. Central Intelligence Agency, Saigon station, "Outlook for the 1971 Presidential Election in South Vietnam," September 13, 1971.

219   *The ambassador visited:* Snepp, p. 11.

219   *Confirmation of the attempted:* Deposition of Norman Jones, *United States of America vs. Frank W. Snepp III,* Case No. 78–92-A, U.S. District Court for the Eastern District of Virginia, pp. 12–13. This deposition was taken by lawyers for Frank Snepp in the case the United States brought against Snepp for publishing his book *Decent Interval.*

219   *In September of 1971:* Bill White, interview, September 26, 1990.

220   *The number of reports:* Ralph McGehee, interview, August 17, 1989. Snepp, p. 13.

220   *"Most of it was":* McGehee, interview.

220   *The chief of station in Thailand:* Confidential interview with chief of station in Thailand.

221   *Joe Lazarsky, the deputy:* Lazarsky, interview.

221   *"As for learning":* Hill, interview.

221   *"The CIA put a lot":* Fred Z. Brown, interview, March 16, 1992.

222   *In Washington, Lou Sarris:* Lou Sarris, interview, March 23, 1992.

222   *"You knew it wouldn't":* Wall, interview, February 27, 1992.

222   *By the time his tour:* Yothers, interview.

223   *Bill Kohlmann, a case officer:* Kohlmann, interview.

224   *In headquarters, Shackley's tour:* William Johnson, interview, February 10, 1992.

224   *"His tenure was seen":* Polgar, interview, February 8, 1992.

224   *"He anticipated going":* McArthur, interview.

224   *"I presume that":* Jameson, interview, March 30, 1990.

224   *During one celebration:* Confidential interview with senior CIA officer.

224   *"It was a pretty":* McArthur, interview.

224   *The atmosphere of the station:* Polgar, interview, February 8, 1992. Confidential interview with senior CIA officer in Vietnam. Kohlmann, interview.

224   *"There were burn":* Snepp, interview, March 2, 1992.

225   *Polgar's after-the-fact:* Polgar, interview, February 8, 1992.

225   *"We didn't understand":* Hill, interview.

225   *After the war, Richard Helms:* Helms, L.B.J. Library interview, p. 25.

225   *Shortly after Shackley returned:* Snepp, interview, March 2, 1992.

CHAPTER 7. WASHINGTON: THE ENEMY WITHIN

Page

227   *The problem apparently:* Philip Agee, *On the Run* (Secaucus, N.J.: Lyle Stuart, 1987), pp. 11–38

228   *Years later, CIA people:* "CIA Turncoat Philip Agee Got Cuban, Soviet Funds," *Periscope: Newsletter of the Association of Former Intelligence Officers,* September 1992. Confidential interview with Western Hemisphere Division operations chief.

228   *"There was bewilderment":* Keith Gardiner, interview, September 25, 1992.

229   *In 1964, Random House:* David Wise and Thomas Ross, *The Invisible Government* (New York: Random House, 1964).

229   *Three years later, a series:* Ranelagh, p. 471.

229   *When William Colby returned:* Ibid., p. 475.

230   *Shackley inherited as his deputy:* James Flannery, interview, May 21, 1992. David Atlee Phillips, *The Night Watch* (New York: Atheneum, 1977), p. 89. In his memoirs, Phillips refers to Flannery as "Abe."

230   *His detractors in the division:* Gardiner, interview.

230   *As his deputy chief explained:* Flannery, interview.

230   *He placed his favorites:* Flannery, interview.

230   *Morales had a story:* Clines, interview, January 14, 1992.

230   *When Agee was based:* Joseph Burkholder Smith, interview, February 18, 1992.

231   *"If I had the slightest":* Philip Agee, interview, February 11, 1992.

231   *In headquarters, Shackley's chief:* Confidential interview with Western Hemisphere Division operations chief.

231   *"Not a single person":* Ibid.

231   *An Agency shrink:* Agee, *On the Run,* pp. 43–44.

232   *"When he was in Mexico City":* Confidential interview with Western Hemisphere Division operations chief.

232   *The officers of the Western Hemisphere:* Ibid.

233   *"I was disturbed":* Joseph B. Smith, pp. 11–13.

233   *According to hallway gossip:* Joseph Burkholder Smith, interview, July 5, 1990.

233   *Tom Gilligan, another:* Tom Gilligan, *CIA Life: 10,000 Days with the Agency* (Guilford, Conn.: Foreign Intelligence Press, 1991), pp. 141–146.

234   *In Paris, Agee continued:* Agee, *On the Run,* pp. 41–47.

234   *Along the way:* Confidential interview with Western Hemisphere Division operations chief.

234   *In 1977, a* New York Times: "Varying Ties to CIA Confirmed in Inquiry," *The New York Times,* December 27, 1977.

234   *That year, John Foster Berlet:* John Foster Berlet, interview, February 27, 1992. Theodore G. Shackley, letter to John Foster Berlet, September 21, 1977.

234 *"Of course, there was talk"*: Confidential interview with Western Hemisphere Division operations chief.

235 *"I prayed Agee wouldn't"*: Flannery, interview.

235 *Years afterward, Agee claimed*: Agee, interview.

235 *The interviews with Ferrera*: Agee, *On the Run*, pp. 49–51.

235 *The day after the break-in: The Senate Watergate Report* (New York: Dell, 1974), pp. 733–756. This volume contains both the final report of the Senate Select Committee on Presidential Campaign Activities, better known as the Senate Watergate Committee, and a report on CIA involvement in Watergate— dubbed the Baker Report, after Senator Howard Baker, Jr.—written by the committee's minority staff. The Baker Report is the source for the Martinez information. Powers, p. 328.

237 *Days following the Watergate*: Agee, *On the Run*, pp. 51–53. Confidential interview with Western Hemisphere Division operations chief.

237 *"Once in your lifetime"*: Confidential interview with Western Hemisphere Division operations chief.

237 *Her name was*: Ibid.

237 *As soon as she had*: Confidential interview with Western Hemisphere Division operations chief. Flannery, interview.

238 *Many officers still carried*: Clines, interview, January 14, 1992.

238 *Leslie Donegan left Paris*: Agee, *On the Run*, pp. 53–57.

238 *Shackley and his operations chief*: Confidential interview with the Western Hemisphere Division operations chief.

238 *Agee was dependent*: Agee, *On the Run*, pp. 58–59.

238 *Sal Ferrera was another concern*: Agee, *On the Run*, p. 59.

238 *At a café*: Agee, *On the Run*, pp. 60–64. Confidential interview with the Western Hemisphere Division operations chief. Flannery, interview.

239 *Yet the operations chief*: Confidential interview with the Western Hemisphere Division operations chief.

239 *"The irony was"*: Agee, interview.

239 *Agee did not confront*: Agee, *On the Run*, pp. 64–69.

239 *One document observed*: A. E. Marum, undated memorandum to Robert Keuch.

239 *The British secret service*: Flannery, interview.

240 *In 1976, Agee learned*: Agee, *On the Run*, pp. 127, 147–148, 163–165.

240 *After the Agee operation*: Confidential interview with Western Hemisphere Division operations chief.

240 *On March 21, 1972*: "Memos Bare ITT Try for Chile Coup," *The Washington Post*, March 21, 1972. "ITT Pledged Millions to Stop Allende," *The Washington Post*, March 22, 1973.

241 *Acquiescing to the Nixon*: U.S. Senate, Committee on Foreign Relations, Subcommittee on Multinational Corporations, *The International Telephone and Telegraph Company and Chile, 1970–1971* (Washington, D.C.: U.S. Government Printing Office, 1973), p. 1. Hereinafter, *The International Telephone and Telegraph Company and Chile, 1970–1971*.

241 *Helms, whom Nixon had*: Powers, p. 11.

241   *Helms was fired:* "Transcripts of Excerpts from the C.I.A. Memorandums About the Watergate Case," *The New York Times,* June 4, 1973. Ranelagh, pp. 521–530.

241   *About this time, John Maury:* John M. Maury, "Briefing of Chairman Lucien Nedzi, Intelligence Operations Subcommittee, House Armed Services Committee, Re Agency Connection with Watergate Affair and ITT Involvement in Chile," February 23, 1972.

241   *On February 9, 1973:* "Transcripts of Excerpts from the CIA Memorandums About the Watergate Case," *The New York Times,* June 4, 1973.

242   *Church requested Helms's presence:* Levinson, interview.

242   *On February 23:* Theodore Shackley, "Meeting with Senator Jackson to Discuss How CIA Should Handle Inquiries From Senator Church's Subcommittee on Multinational Corporations in Regard to CIA Involvement with ITT in Chile in 1970," February 23, 1973. This memo was included as a footnote in the Pike Committee report leaked to the press in 1976. Shackley's name was deleted as author of the memo, but he was identified by position.

243   *Adopting Shackley's advice:* James R. Schlesinger, undated letter to Senator Frank Church.

243   *"We heard that Jackson":* Jack Blum, interview, September 26, 1991.

243   *Then McClellan called:* Levinson, interview.

243   *His subcommittee called:* Ibid.

244   *On a winter's day:* Levinson, interview. Blum, interview.

244   *The subcommittee was interested:* The International Telephone and Telegraph Company and Chile, 1970–1971, p. 6.

245   *As Jack Anderson had reported:* "CIA Knew of False Testimony," *The Washington Post,* December 23, 1976.

245   *Shackley assigned the case:* Flannery, interview. Motion to Replace Pages Four Through Seven of the Information With Amended Pages Four Through Seven, *United States of America v. Robert Berrellez,* U.S. District Court for the District of Columbia, Criminal Case No. 78–120, November 8, 1978. Hereinafter, *Berrellez* Motion.

245   *Hendrix told Shackley's:* "2 ITT Aides Charged in Chile Probe," *The Washington Post,* October 21, 1978. "Trial Could Shed Light on CIA Activity in Chile," *The Washington Post,* October 23, 1978. *Berrellez* Motion.

245   *Hanke held a meeting:* [Author Deleted], "Meeting with Hal Hendrix, 11 May 1972," May 15, 1972. Though the author's name was deleted, the document contained his bureaucratic designation, "C/WH/CA," which corresponded to Hanke's position.

245   *In early February of 1973:* Berrellez Motion.

245   *To protect his small:* Transcript of October 23, 1978, confidential conference, *The United States of America v. Robert Berrellez,* U.S. District Court for the District of Columbia, Criminal Case No. 78–120, pp. 14–15. Hereinafter, Transcript of October 23, 1978, confidential conference. *Berrellez* Motion.

246   *On March 20, 1973:* U.S. Senate, Committee on Foreign Relations, Subcommittee on Multinational Corporations, *Multinational Corporations and*

United States Foreign Policy (Washington, D.C.: U.S. Government Printing Office, 1973), pp. 1–3.

246 *When Hendrix appeared before:* "CIA Knew of False Testimony," *The Washington Post,* December 23, 1976.

246 *After Berrellez testified, Hanke:* "ITT Aide's Perjury Trial Could Disclose Data on Ties Among Firm, CIA, Chileans," *The Wall Street Journal,* October 23, 1978.

246 *On March 27: Multinational Corporations and United States Policy,* pp. 243–261.

246 *"Someone is lying":* "Senate ITT Inquiry to Consider Possibility of Perjury Action," *The Washington Post,* March 30, 1973.

246 *Moreover, Charles Meyer:* Ibid.

247 *Ten years earlier:* U.S. Senate, Select Committee to Study Governmental Operations with Respect to Intelligence Activities, *Covert Action in Chile, 1963–1973* (Washington, D.C.: U.S. Government Printing Office, 1976), pp. 9–11, 15–17. Hereinafter *Covert Action in Chile, 1963–1973.*

247 *"If the Reds win":* Blum, p. 223.

248 *In the five years following: Covert Action in Chile, 1963–1973,* pp. 7–9, 17–19.

248 *Come 1970:* Ibid., pp. 19–22.

248 *"The CIA had had":* Hersh, p. 269.

248 *Days after the election: Covert Action in Chile, 1963–1973,* pp. 47–48.

248 *On September 15:* Ibid., pp. 10–11. Richard Helms, "Meeting with President on Chile," September 15, 1970.

249 *Of the thirty-three: Covert Action in Chile, 1963–1973,* p. 49.

249 *At first the Agency hoped:* Ibid., pp. 23–25.

249 *As part of Track II:* Ibid., pp 10–11, 25–26. Hersh, pp. 276, 288–293. Ranelagh, pp. 518–519. Powers, p. 298. U.S. Central Intelligence Agency. cable (title deleted), October 16, 1970.

249 *After Allende became: Covert Action in Chile, 1963–1973,* pp. 8, 59–60.

250 *In June of 1972:* Ibid., pp. 45–47.

250 *Once Shackley was running:* Ibid., p. 8.

250 *One agent's report:* U.S. Central Intelligence Agency, "Subject: [Deleted]," May 30, 1972.

250 *The Santiago station produced: Covert Action in Chile, 1963–1973,* pp. 29–30. Blum, p. 240.

250 *Overall, the CIA dumped: Covert Action in Chile, 1963–1973,* pp. 1, 10.

250 *A summary of CIA:* U.S. Central Intelligence Agency, "DCI Briefing Notes for Chairman Mahon," July 27, 1972.

251 *They compiled lists: Covert Action in Chile, 1963–1973,* pp. 1, 38–39.

251 *In October—as Allende: Covert Action in Chile, 1963–1973,* pp. 31, 60. Nathaniel Davis, *The Last Two Years of Salvador Allende* (Ithaca, N.Y.: Cornell University Press, 1985), pp. 309–310.

251 *As part of his usual:* Clines, interviews, January 14, 1992, April 14, 1992.

252 *In the months before:* U.S. Central Intelligence Agency, "CIA Involvement in Chilean Elections," March 7, 1973. *Covert Action in Chile, 1963–1973,* p. 30.

252 *Around this time:* David Wise, *The American Police State* (New York: Random House, 1976), p. 181.

252 *In February, the White House: Covert Action in Chile, 1963–1973,* p. 60. Davis, p. 308.

252 *In Washington, Nixon: Covert Action in Chile, 1963–1973,* p. 30.

252 *"Ted Shackley and other people":* Flannery, interview.

253 *Shackley's insistence:* Confidential interview with Western Hemisphere Division operations chief.

253 *Maybe Shackley took:* Ibid.

253 *"This was typical":* Clines, interview, April 14, 1992.

253 *Jim Adkins was one:* Jim Adkins, interview, December 20, 1991.

254 *On February 4, 1973:* U.S. Foreign Broadcast Information Service, Caribbean, February 5, 1973. "Leader in '65 Dominican Revolt Is Reported Killed as Guerrilla," *The New York Times,* February 17, 1973.

254 *Reports of Caamano's:* U.S. Foreign Broadcast Information Service, Santo Domingo Service, "Official Communique from the Public Relations Office," February 6, 1973. U.S. Foreign Broadcast Information Service, Agence France Presse, "Bosch Statement," February 6, 1973.

254 *No one in Langley:* Flannery, interview.

254 *Every day, Adkins:* Adkins, interview. Flannery, interview.

254 *"If they captured him":* Flannery, interview.

254 *On February 17:* U.S. Foreign Broadcast Information Service, Santo Domingo Domestic Service, "Government Reports Caamano Deno Killed in Clash," February 17, 1973.

255 *Bosch's party later:* U.S. Foreign Broadcast Information Service, Santo Domingo Radio, "P.R.D. Statement Studies Implications of Caamano's Death," February 20, 1973. See also "Dominican Episode," *The Washington Post,* March 17, 1973.

255 *Shackley and others in Washington:* Adkins, interview.

255 *Occasionally the Agency:* John Murray, notes, undated.

255 *In the fall of 1972:* Rodriguez and Weisman, pp. 245–249.

255 *He feared he was targeted:* Wall, interview, February 22, 1992.

255 *A 1973 cable:* U.S. Embassy, Buenos Aires, "Summary of Extremist Activity, January 1–April 30, 1973," May 14, 1973.

255 *In the summer of 1972:* "Argentine Protests Countered by Army," *The Washington Post,* June 29, 1972.

255 *This CIA-aided general:* Rosendo Fraga, *Ejército: del escarnio al poder, 1973–1976* (Buenos Aires: Grupo Editorial Planeta, 1988), pp. 15–43.

256 *One bright prospect:* John Dinges, *Our Man in Panama* (New York: Random House, 1990), pp. 34–49. "Section 5 Classified Information Procedures Act Submission," *United States of America vs. General Manuel A. Noriega,* U.S. District Court, Southern District of Florida, Case No. 89–79, pp. 27–30. This is a submission filed by Noriega's defense team that outlined Noriega's relationship with U.S. agencies.

256 *During one of Noriega's trips:* Jacob Esterline, interview, April 30, 1992.

256 *Washington fretted:* "Panama's Leader Hits U.S. on Canal," *The Washington Post,* March 16, 1973.

256 *On Shackley's watch:* "Bush Is Disputed on U.S.-Noriega Tie," *The New York Times,* October 2, 1988.

256 *The money was officially justified:* "Section 5 Classified Information Procedures Act Submission," p. 36. Dinges, pp. 51–52.

257 *According to evidence collected by:* Dinges, pp. 53–72.

257 *While Noriega was providing:* Joe Conason and John Kelly, "Bush and the Secret Noriega Report," *The Village Voice,* October 11, 1988. Michael A. DeFeo, Thomas H. Henderson, and Arthur Norton, "Report of June 18, 1975, to the Attorney General," p. 11. This report, produced within the Justice Department, is known as the DeFeo Report and was prepared in response to an order to investigate misconduct within the Drug Enforcement Administration.

257 *When Torrijos visited:* Dinges, p. 78. "Section 5 Classified Information Procedures Act Submission," p. 70.

257 *President Nixon had declared:* Edward Jay Epstein, *The Agency of Fear* (New York: G. P. Putnam's Sons, 1977), p. 242.

258 *As the sophisticates:* Flannery, interview.

258 *"Surveillance should":* Ibid.

258 *In October of 1972:* Chief of Station, Miami, "[Deleted] . . . ," October 26, 1972. Chief of Station, Miami, "[Deleted] . . . ," October 31, 1972.

258 *The feeling was:* Gerry Strickler, interview, March 10, 1992. "Bush and the Secret Noriega Report," *The Village Voice,* October 11, 1988.

258 *Shortly after Shackley entered:* Strickler, interview. The quotes from Strickler in this section are all from this interview.

260 *At William Colby's urging:* Colby and Forbath, pp. 337–338.

260 *Murray became a Company:* John C. Murray, "Refusal to Accept Assignment as COS, Haiti," January 11, 1973.

260 *In December of 1972:* Ibid. John C. Murray, "Foreign Assignment—John C. Murray," January 29, 1973. Theodore G. Shackley, "Comments of Reviewing Officer," undated.

261 *He was also suspicious:* John Murray, notes, undated.

261 *Two years earlier:* John Murray, "Memorandum of Conversation," February 17, 1971. John Murray, "Memorandum of Conversation—Events Pertaining to Mexico City Station," February 17, 1971. John Murray, "Conversation with Bruce MacMaster—Chile Operations." John Murray, "Sensitive Information on the Chilean Operation," April 16, 1974.

261 *Following the fistfight:* Angus J. Laverdure, "LITEMPO-12/Identity A," undated. Laverdure was the code name for Juan Noriega, a Mexican station official.

262 *In May of 1973:* John Murray, "Sensitive Information on the Chilean Operation," April 16, 1974.

262 *Moreover, Sforza was:* Confidential interview with senior CIA official.

262 *Murray was to serve:* John C. Murray, "John C. Murray, C/WH/1," May 23, 1973.

262   *In Jamaica, Murray:* Dolores Murray, interview, January 31, 1993. She was John Murray's wife. Clines, interview, April 14, 1992. David A. Phillips, "Mr. John C. Murray," October 15, 1973.

262   *He came to believe:* John Murray, notes, undated. John Murray, "Discussions between Chief, CMG and C/SOG/GB," March 6, 1974. See Theodore G. Shackley, "Comments of Reviewing Officer," undated.

263   *In 1974, Inspector General:* U.S. Central Intelligence Agency, "Watergate —Guidelines for Agency File Review," March 22, 1974. Murray's notes are written on the last page.

263   *Much to Murray's:* John Murray, notes, June 12, 1973. Resumé of Theodore G. Shackley.

263   *A week earlier, the President:* Ranelagh, pp. 547–552. Colby and Forbath, pp. 331–332.

263   *Shackley was promoted:* Resumé of Theodore G. Shackley.

263   *His division had achieved no:* Flannery, interview.

263   *"I think he was tired":* Ibid.

264   *"The CIA is":* Agee, *Inside the Company: CIA Diary,* p. 617.

264   *When Agee exposed:* Agee, *On the Run,* pp. 130–134. Ranelagh, pp. 472–473. "CIA Critic Agee Reportedly Paid by Cuba," *The Los Angeles Times,* August 10, 1992. Philip Agee, Letter to *The Los Angeles Times,* August 10, 1992.

264   *The covert program against Allende: Covert Action in Chile, 1963–1973,* pp. 30–31, 61.

264   *CIA officers maintained: Covert Action in Chile, 1963–1973,* pp. 11, 39.

265   *A group of striking:* "The Bloody End of a Marxist Dream," *Time,* September 24, 1973.

265   *One congressional report: Covert Action in Chile, 1963–1973,* p. 31.

265   *The U.S. military was reportedly:* Hortensia Bussa De Allende, "Chile Made in U.S.A." This was a speech delivered by Allende's widow at a conference on "The CIA and World Peace" at Yale University on April 5, 1975. The transcript was published in *Counterspy,* Spring/Summer 1975.

265   *A young American:* See Thomas Hauser, *The Execution of Charles Horman* (New York: Harcourt Brace Jovanovich, 1978).

265   *In his memoirs, Colby:* Colby and Forbath, p. 305.

265   *Following the coup:* "Probe of U.S. Role in Chile Coup Asked," *The Washington Post,* September 22, 1973.

265   *On April 22, 1974:* Davis, pp. 316–317. "CIA Role in Chile Revealed," *The Washington Post,* September 8, 1974. "CIA Chief Tells House of $8-Million Campaign Against Allende in '70–'73," *The New York Times,* September 8, 1974. "Revealed Chile Data, Harrington Admits," *The Washington Post,* June 20, 1975.

266   *The revelations caused:* "U.S. Again Denies Anti-Allende Policy," *The Washington Post,* September 10, 1974. "Disclosure of CIA Chile Role 'Surprises' Overseers on Hill," *The Washington Post,* September 13, 1974. "CIA Chief Colby Facing Confrontation on Chile Operations," *The Washington Post,* September 12, 1974.

266   *Senator Frank Church was:* Levinson, interview.

266   *On January 27, 1975: Church Committee Final Report,* p. 2.

267   *"All that really did":* Clines, interview, April 14, 1992.

267   *After Colby's secret testimony:* "Perjury Inquiry Urged on Chile Data," *The Washington Post,* September 17, 1974.

267   *Helms was already in trouble:* Powers, pp. 14, 383–384. Colby and Forbath, pp. 337–340. Ranelagh, pp. 556–557.

267   *David Phillips, Shackley's:* Phillips, p. 236.

268   *When Shackley left:* McGehee, interview, August 17, 1989.

CHAPTER 8. THE WAR AT HOME

Page

269   *On April 30, 1975:* Confidential interview.

270   *With this defeat in mind:* Shackley, *The Third Option,* p. 110.

270   *When Shackley took over:* Young, pp. 267–280.

270   *"A grim, sad mood":* DeForest, p. 204.

270   *DeForest and other case officers:* Ibid., pp. 204–213.

271   *In the summer of 1973:* Stockwell, p. 201. Stockwell, interview, November 4, 1989.

271   *In the base headquarters:* Stockwell, interview.

272   *One of the best intelligence sources:* Confidential interviews with two senior CIA officials.

272   *Asked about the bugging:* Williams, interview.

272   *In Saigon, Polgar won:* Polgar, interview, February 8, 1992. Snepp, interview, January 16, 1990.

273   *"He saw his job":* Snepp, p. 88.

273   *"Polgar would say":* White, interview.

273   *When Shackley came through:* Snepp, pp. 89–90. Snepp, interview, January 16, 1990.

273   *In a later series of cables:* "Recommendation for Quality Step Increase," undated. This memo was prepared by a Saigon station officer. Thomas Polgar, "Promotion Recommendation for Mr. Frank Snepp," February 1, 1974. Thomas Polgar, "Mr. Frank W. Snepp—Commendation for Intelligence Briefings," June 12, 1974.

274   *Shackley the organization man:* Snepp, interviews, January 16, 1990, May 27, 1992. Gilligan, p. 175.

274   *"The priority it received":* Confidential interview with East Asia Division officer.

274   *His division secretly slipped: Church Committee Final Report,* pp. 200, 454, 568.

274   *On the afternoon of August 8:* Robert Boettcher with Gordon L. Freedman, *Gifts of Deceit: Sun Myung Moon, Tongsun Park and the Korean Scandal* (New York: Holt, Rinehart & Winston, 1980), pp. 225–226. Boettcher was staff director of the House Subcommittee on International Relations, which investigated the Korean scandal of the mid-1970s.

275 *When the CIA station in Seoul:* Liechty, interview, January 7, 1993.

275 *A day or two after he was seized:* Boettcher, p. 226. Lee Keun Pal, interview, January 7, 1973. Lee was a senior aide to Kim Dae Jung.

276 *After the Kim Dae Jung episode:* Liechty, interview, January 7, 1993.

276 *In the years that followed:* Blaufarb, *Organizing and Managing,* p. vii.

276 *"The principal effect":* Blaufarb, *The Counterinsurgency Era,* p. 164.

276 *As Pop Buell lamented:* W. E. Garrett, "No Place to Run," *National Geographic,* January 1974.

276 *Thirty thousand Hmong:* Ibid.

276 *Unhappy with the cease-fire:* "End of Laos War Has Brought No Peace to Thousands in Meo Clans," *The New York Times,* July 13, 1975.

276 *In the northwest of Laos:* Garry Parrott, interview, July 20, 1989.

277 *"We were not really able":* McCarthy, interview.

277 *Richard Helms, when he was:* Confidential interview with senior CIA official.

277 *In the late 1960s, Ralph McGehee:* McGehee, p. 118.

277 *Jim Lilley, Shackley's:* U.S. State Department, *Biographic Register* (Washington: Government Printing Office, 1974).

278 *As one senior CIA officer:* Halpern, interview, August 6, 1990.

278 *"We had," one of Shackley's superiors:* Confidential interview with senior CIA officer.

278 *In one instance, the Hong Kong station:* Confidential interview with senior CIA officer.

278 *"But these did not provide much":* Confidential interview with senior CIA officer.

278 *In the fall of 1973, the station: Nest of Spies,* Volume 38, pp. 91–100. This is a collection of documents and cables found in the CIA station in Tehran by the student radicals who stormed the U.S. embassy in 1979 and took hostages. Scores of volumes were produced and disseminated by the Iranian government. The Mourad episode is based on a series of shredded CIA cables painstakingly reassembled by Iranians.

279 *He and the Agency eventually received:* Confidential interview with senior CIA official.

279 *He tried to set quotas:* Jones, interview.

279 *"As always, Shackley ran":* Kohlmann, interview.

279 *Afterward there would be:* "CIA Plans to Reduce Thai Operations," *The New York Times,* January 19, 1974. Confidential interview with senior CIA officer.

279 *The communist rebellion:* "CIA Plans to Reduce Thai Operations," *The New York Times,* January 19, 1974. "U.S.-Thai Relations Expected to Survive CIA Blow," *The New York Times,* January 21, 1974.

280 *In December of 1973:* U.S. Foreign Broadcast Information Service, "Bangkok Paper Says Communists Propose Cease-Fire," December 10, 1973, Thailand, p. J3. The item refers to a story in *Prachathipatai,* December 9, 1973. U.S. Foreign Information Broadcast Service, "C.S.O.C. Investigates Proposal," December 10, 1973, Thailand, p. J4. The item refers to a story in *The Nation*

of Bangkok, December 10, 1973. U.S. Foreign Broadcast Information Service, "Prachathipatai Details," January 7, 1974, Thailand, p. J1. This item refers to a story in *Prachathipatai,* January 6, 1974. "U.S. Regrets CIA Agent's False Letter," *The Washington Post,* January 6, 1974. "Strain May Develop," *The New York Times,* January 10, 1974.

280 *Shackley's base chief had committed:* "U.S. Regrets CIA Agent's False Letter," *The Washington Post,* January 6, 1974.

280 *Industrious Thai reporters:* U.S. Foreign Broadcast Information Service, "Prachathipatai Details," January 7, 1974, Thailand, p. J1. This item refers to a story in *Prachathipatai,* January 6, 1974.

280 *The Thai government protested:* "Thai Consider Ban or Curb on the CIA," *The New York Times,* January 16, 1974. "Thailand Officially Chides U.S. Over CIA Interference There," *The New York Times,* January 18, 1974.

280 *Editorials and columnists:* U.S. Foreign Broadcast Information Service, "*Siam Rat* Writer Wants More Than U.S. Apology," January 9, 1974, Thailand, p. J3. This item refers to a story in *Siam Rat,* January 8, 1974.

281 *"Because he previously worked":* U.S. Foreign Broadcast Information Service, "Quotes from Chula Group's Anti-Kintner Statement," *Thai Rath,* November 21, 1973. U.S. Foreign Broadcast Information Service, Thailand, November 21, 1973, p. J8.

281 *After the Thai press revealed:* "Protesting Thai Demand American Envoy's Ouster," *The New York Times,* January 20, 1974.

281 *The U.S. embassy took:* "Thai Consider Ban or Curb on the CIA," *The New York Times,* January 16, 1974. "Thailand Officially Chides U.S. Over CIA Interference There," *The New York Times,* January 18, 1974.

281 *In Washington, a disgusted:* Confidential interview with senior CIA official. "CIA Plans to Reduce Thai Operations," *The New York Times,* January 19, 1974.

281 *Months after the episode:* "The Spies Who Came in From Sakhon Nakhon," *The Washington Post,* April 7, 1974.

282 *In January of 1975, Shackley:* Snepp, p. 147.

282 *When Polgar visited the Bien Hoa:* DeForest, p. 249.

282 *Reports from the agent code-named:* U.S. Central Intelligence Agency, "Effectiveness of U.S. Intelligence Analysis on Vietnam, December 1974–April 1975," October 22, 1975.

282 *Throughout 1974, the general:* Frank Snepp, Letter to William F. Buckley, Jr., March 10, 1978.

282 *He did allow his regional officers:* Thomas Polgar, Letter to William F. Buckley, Jr., February 7, 1978.

282 *In headquarters, Ralph McGehee:* McGehee, pp. 175–189. McGehee, interview, August 17, 1989.

283 *As Snepp viewed it:* Snepp, pp. 151–153.

283 *DeForest's intelligence operation:* DeForest, pp. 251–252.

283 *"By the third week of March":* Ibid., pp. 214–215.

284 *In defense of his actions:* Thomas Polgar, Letter to William F. Buckley, Jr., February 7, 1978.

284   *A national intelligence estimate:* Snepp, pp. 226–227, 233–234.

284   *Shackley went to witness:* Snepp, pp. 235–237.

284   *During the long flight:* David Hume Kennerly, interview, July 7, 1990.

285   *Less than half:* Snepp, p. 261.

285   *"It was sadly ironic":* Ibid., pp. 279–280.

285   *Shackley, once the prime briefer:* Ibid., pp. 280–281.

285   *But on April 1, in a safe house:* Ibid., pp. 287–288.

285   *The station began compiling lists:* Ibid., pp. 293–294.

285   *"This was a pressure-packed":* Theodore G. Shackley, Deposition, *United States of America vs. Frank W. Snepp III,* U.S. District Court for the Eastern District of Virginia, Case No. 78–92-A, May 3, 1978, p. 25. Hereinafter, Shackley deposition, Snepp case.

286   *He was a different man:* Snepp, interview, January 16, 1990.

286   *At one CIA base outside:* Confidential interview with CIA officer.

286   *On April 3—a day:* Nguyen Tien Hung and Jerrold L. Schecter, *The Palace File* (New York: Harper & Row, 1986), pp. 298–300.

287   *On April 5, the U.S. military aircraft:* Kennerly, interview.

287   *As soon as they were off:* Shackley, interview. Hung and Schecter, pp. 307, 468–476.

287   *In Palm Springs, official:* "Ford Gets Pessimistic Report," *The Washington Post,* April 6, 1975.

287   *Now the Saigon station was flooded:* Snepp, pp. 309–313.

288   *For months, he had socialized:* See Snepp. Polgar's relationship with the Hungarians is described throughout the book.

288   *He cabled Shackley:* Thomas Polgar, Letter to William F. Buckley, Jr., February 7, 1978.

288   *One of the station's better agents:* Snepp, pp. 326–328. U.S. Central Intelligence Agency, "Effectiveness of U.S. Intelligence Analysis on Vietnam, December 1974–April 1975."

288   *DeForest's agents were:* DeForest, pp. 253–254.

289   *In Tay Ninh, John Stockwell:* Ibid., pp. 255–258.

289   *On April 17, Snepp:* Ibid., pp. 366–368.

289   *Polgar took issue with:* Thomas Polgar, Letter to *The Washington Star,* December 10, 1977.

289   *Martin, though, at the time:* Snepp, interview, March 11, 1992.

289   *A postwar CIA memo:* U.S. Central Intelligence Agency, "Effectiveness of U.S. Intelligence Analysis on Vietnam, December 1974–April 1975."

289   *On April 19, Polgar:* Snepp, pp. 380–384.

290   *After the Pentagon withdrew:* Ibid., p. 408.

290   *On April 27—after the:* Ibid., p. 448.

291   *In Bien Hoa, the National Police:* DeForest, p. 261.

291   *HACKLE, the CIA's only:* Snepp, interview, March 11, 1992.

291   *In the last days:* "The Secret Life of An American Spy," *Regardie's.*

291   *One of the thousands:* Grant, pp. 341–348. Snepp, p. 15.

291   *Years after the Vietnam War:* Grant, p. 341.

291   *"They tried to destroy me":* Chau, interview.

292   *The fall of Saigon:* Snepp, pp. 495–548. DeForest, p. 274.

292   *Prior to hustling onto:* Thomas Polgar, cable, April 30, 1975.

292   *In Washington, Colby:* Snepp, p. 557.

293   *Afterward, Colby conceded:* Colby, interview, July 15, 1991.

293   *After escaping Saigon, Snepp:* U.S. Central Intelligence Agency, untitled cable, June 12, 1975. Snepp, interview, January 16, 1990.

293   *He arranged to see Shackley:* Snepp, interview, January 16, 1990.

293   *"We recognize," it read:* U.S. Central Intelligence Agency, "Vietnam Evacuation Questionnaire," undated. Snepp, interview, January 16, 1990.

294   *Shackley did have loose ends:* Shackley deposition, Snepp case, pp. 17–18, 23.

294   *Shackley's chief of Vietnam operations:* Confidential interview with VNO chief.

294   *In Langley, CIA people:* Dolores Murray, interview, January 31, 1993.

294   *One day Snepp came:* Confidential interview with VNO chief.

295   *Lieutenant General Dang Van Quang:* Confidential interview with VNO chief. "CIA Reported to Aid Viet Emigre's Exit," *The Washington Post,* May 24, 1975.

295   *Shackley directed the VNO chief:* Confidential interview with VNO chief.

295   *Despite their difference:* Snepp, p. 573.

295   *In mid-August, Snepp:* Ibid.

295   *In October, Colby told:* William Colby, "Allegation Concerning Reporting of the Strength of the South Vietnamese Regime," October 24, 1975.

296   *The paper evaluated reporting:* U.S. Central Intelligence Agency, "Effectiveness of U.S. Intelligence Analysis on Vietnam, December 1974–April 1975."

296   *Responding to Colby's request:* Norman A. Jones, "Interview with Frank Snepp—Vietnam Investigation," November 10, 1975.

296   *Snepp asked to write:* Snepp, p. 574.

297   *Norman Jones in 1978:* Norman Jones, untitled cable, March 14, 1978.

297   *In November of 1975, he met:* Shackley deposition, Snepp case, pp. 68–70. "Frank W. Snepp III," December 7, 1976. The author of this memo, an officer in the CIA Operations Support branch, is deleted.

297   *The I.G.'s office produced:* Donald Chamberlain, "Investigation of Allegation Concerning Reporting of the Strength of the South Vietnamese Regime," November 28, 1975. Shackley deposition, Snepp case, p. 28.

297   *After attending a December awards:* Snepp, pp. 573–575.

297   *Shackley's officers in Laos:* Robbins, *The Ravens,* p. 333.

297   *On May 18, 1975:* "End of Laos War Has Brought No Peace to Thousands in Meo Clans," *The New York Times,* July 13, 1975. Charles E. Hood, "Vang Pao: Guerrilla General," *The Sunday Missoulian,* November 21, 1976.

298   *But many tribespeople:* McCarthy, interview.

298   *"We bore a great deal":* Ibid.

298   *"Those of us who had worked":* Confidential interview with senior CIA official.

299   *In June, the Rockefeller Commission:* "Panel Finds CIA Illegality But Backs Record," *The Washington Post,* June 11, 1975.

299 *On Capitol Hill, the Church Committee:* "Senate Panel Accelerates CIA Probe," *The Washington Post,* June 12, 1975. "Senate Panel Probes CIA Role in Chile," *The Washington Post,* July 15, 1975.

299 *"But once the decisions":* Shackley, interview.

299 *Sam Halpern, a former:* Halpern, interview, August 6, 1990.

299 *When Congress demanded:* Richard Fuller, interview, February 4, 1993.

299 *In July of 1975, Shackley had:* Carl Duckett, Letter to Charles H. Percy, June 26, 1975. Duckett was Acting Director of the CIA when he wrote Percy. "Drug Suspect Spied for CIA, It Admits," *The Washington Post,* July 1, 1975. "House Papers Allege CIA Drug Role," *The Washington Post,* October 3, 1977. U.S. House of Representatives, Committee on Government Operations, Subcommittee on Government Information and Individual Rights, *Justice Department Treatment of Criminal Cases Involving CIA Personnel and Claims of National Security* (Washington: Government Printing Office, 1975). This is the compilation of five days of hearings.

301 *At a public hearing in September:* "Deadly Toxins Cached by CIA, Church Says," *The Washington Post,* September 10, 1975.

301 *Another hearing disclosed:* "CIA Opened Mail of Humphrey, Nixon, Kennedy," *The Washington Post,* September 25, 1975.

301 *In Langley, morale:* Colby and Forbath, p. 13.

301 *Several times in 1975:* Frederick Baron, interview, March 6, 1992. William Miller, interview, February 11, 1992. Miller was staff director for the Church Committee. Patrick Shea, interview, December 14, 1993. Shea was a staff member of the Church Committee. Confidential interview with investigator for the Church Committee.

302 *"He felt he was a":* Jameson, interview, April 3, 1990.

302 *One time Shackley briefed:* Gregory Treverton, interview, February 18, 1992. Treverton was a staff member of the Church Committee.

302 *To push this process along:* Dolores Murray, letter, May 1, 1975. Dolores Murray, letter, July 2, 1975. Dolores Murray, letter, September 5, 1975. The recipient of all three was a journalist.

302 *He covertly contacted William Miller:* John Murray, untitled notes, December 5, 1975.

303 *On November 2, 1975:* U.S. Embassy, Canberra, "Prime Minister Whitlam Accuses National Country Party Doug Anthony of Receiving CIA Money," November 2, 1975. Brian Toohey and William Pinwill, *Oyster: The Story of the Australian Secret Intelligence Service* (Port Melbourne, Victoria: Mandarin Australia, 1989), p. 179.

303 *At the time, Colby:* Colby and Forbath, p. 368.

303 *Whitlam's party was not:* Toohey and Pinwill, pp. 138–141.

303 *The Agency, according to Colby:* Colby, interview, July 15, 1991.

303 *In the desolate center:* Jonathan Kwitny, *The Crimes of Patriots: A True Tale of Dope, Dirty Money, and the CIA* (New York: W. W. Norton & Company, 1987), p. 126.

303 *The CIA, the Navy:* Colby, interview, July 15, 1991.

304 *"We had a lot riding":* Ibid.

304 *Early in his administration:* Toohey and Pinwill, p. 144. The authors cite an official Department of Foreign Affairs record of this conversation.

304 *The raid, recalled Jim Angleton:* Ibid., pp. 144–145. The Angleton quote comes from the transcript of a 1977 interview conducted for an Australian television show.

304 *Within his own party:* U.S. Embassy, Canberra, "Prime Minister Defends U.S. Bases," March 26, 1973.

304 *The Australian intelligence service continued:* Toohey and Pinwill, p. 152.

304 *The Australian press reported:* John Pilger, *A Secret Country: The Hidden Australia* (New York: Alfred A. Knopf, 1991), p. 158.

304 *The* Financial Review *reported:* U.S. Embassy, Canberra, "Alleged CIA Involvement in Australian Politics," November 5, 1975.

304 *During a November 6, 1975:* U.S. Embassy, Canberra, "Alleged CIA Involvement in Domestic Australian Politics," November 6, 1975.

305 *Press accounts in Australia were:* Toohey and Pinwill, pp. 175–176.

305 *On November 8, Shackley:* Kwitny, pp. 137–138.

305 *A year before Whitlam had raised:* Robert Lindsey, *The Falcon and the Snowman: A True Story of Friendship and Espionage* (New York: Pocket Books, 1979), pp. 61–63, 81–83, 92–93, 145. "CIA Infiltrated Aussie Unions, Spy Trial Told," *The Los Angeles Times,* April 27, 1977.

306 *He proposed to confirm:* Toohey and Pinwill, p. 180.

306 *More alarming to Shackley:* Pilger, pp. 167–168.

306 *The Queen's representative:* Kwitny, pp. 140–141.

306 *He sacked Whitlam:* Toohey and Pinwill, pp. 180–181. U.S. Embassy, Canberra, "Australian Political Crisis," November 12, 1975.

306 *Australian and British press accounts:* Pilger, pp. 168–171.

307 *He later asserted to an American:* Kwitny, p. 134.

307 *Years following the affair:* James A. Nathan, "Dateline Australia: America's Foreign Watergate?" *Foreign Policy,* Winter 1982.

307 *After the Christopher Boyce trial:* Gough Whitlam, *The Whitlam Government, 1972–75* (London: Viking, 1985), p. 52.

307 *On February 6, 1976:* Thomas Polgar, cable, February 6, 1976.

307 *He asked the Agency's:* Shackley deposition, Snepp case, p. 37.

307 *Ten days earlier:* U.S. House of Representatives, Special Subcommittee on Investigations, Committee on International Relations, *The Vietnam-Cambodia Emergency, 1975, Part III—Vietnam Evacuation: Testimony of Ambassador Graham A. Martin* (Washington, D.C.: Government Printing Office, 1976).

308 *Shackley's division quickly reviewed:* U.S. Central Intelligence Agency, untitled cable, February 11, 1976. The author of the memo is deleted.

308 *Shackley decided not to respond:* U.S. Central Intelligence Agency, untitled cable, February 11, 1976. Thomas Polgar, untitled cable, June 1, 1976. Shackley deposition, Snepp case, pp. 45–46.

308 *Shackley was hearing from:* Leo J. Dunn, "Frank Warren Snepp," March 22, 1976. Dunn was chief of operations for the security office. "Conversation with Frank Snepp Evening of 25 March at the Holiday Inn Coffee Shop at Tysons Corner," March 30, 1976. The author of this memo is deleted. S. D.

Breckinridge, "Frank Snepp and Vietnam," April 1, 1976. Breckinridge worked in the inspector general's office.

308   *The Pike Committee report:* Pike Committee Report, *The Village Voice,* undated supplement.

309   *In April of 1976: Church Committee Final Report.*

309   *The introduction quoted:* Ibid., p. 2.

309   *The report was harsh:* Ibid., p. 10.

310   *In a statement attached:* Ibid., p. 565.

310   *Amidst all the fuss:* "Writer Refuses Offer to Spy on Palauans," *The Sunday News* (of Guam), March 7, 1976.

311   *During the JMWAVE days:* Confidential interview with senior officer in JMWAVE station.

311   *Shackley approved extensive training:* Confidential interviews with CIA official in Taiwan.

312   *The intelligence reports on Taiwan's:* "Taiwan Seen Reprocessing Nuclear Fuel," *The Washington Post,* August 29, 1976. "Taiwan to Curb A-Role," *The Washington Post,* September 23, 1976. Also see, "Taiwan's Nuclear Plans Concern U.S. Officials," *The Washington Post,* December 20, 1978.

312   *But the Taipei station managed:* Bob Woodward, *Veil: The Secret Wars of the CIA, 1981–1987* (New York: Simon & Schuster, 1987), p. 170.

312   *By the spring of 1976:* Confidential interview with senior CIA official. "CIA Losing Chief for Covert Actions," *The New York Times,* April 28, 1976.

313   *The previous November:* Colby and Forbath, pp. 8–17.

313   *To fill the slot:* Resumé of Theodore G. Shackley.

CHAPTER 9. THE END OF THE CLIMB

Page

314   *On the morning of April 12:* Stansfield Turner, interview, December 23, 1992. Stansfield Turner, *Secrecy and Democracy: The CIA in Transition* (New York: Perennial Library, 1986), pp. 57–59. Maas, pp. 4–5. "Ex-CIA Aide, 3 Cuban Exiles Focus of Letelier Inquiry," *The Washington Post,* April 12, 1977.

315   *Much of Bush's time:* George Bush with Victor Gold, *Looking Forward* (New York: Doubleday, 1987), p. 169.

315   *Bush won significant:* "At CIA, a Rebuilder 'Goes With the Flow,' " *The Washington Post,* August 10, 1988.

315   *When the Defense Intelligence Agency discovered:* Mark Perry, *Eclipse: The Last Days of the CIA* (New York: William Morrow & Company, 1992), pp. 110–111.

315   *As Tom Clines put it:* Clines, interview, April 14, 1992.

315   *Shackley's immediate boss:* Confidential interviews with senior CIA officials.

316   *While Wells juggled:* Shackley, interview.

316   *'You couldn't see Wells":* Clines, interview, April 14, 1992.

316   *He once called in a division:* Confidential interview with senior CIA official.

317   *Harold Fiedler, a personnel officer:* Harold Fiedler, interview, February 1, 1992.

317   *Murray and his wife, Dolores:* Dolores Murray, letter to Senator Thomas McIntyre, March 22, 1976. John Murray, "Meeting with Senator," May 18, 1976. John Murray, "Quick Note," March 31, 1976. John Murray, "Memorandum of Conversation," April 6, 1976.

318   *Wilson embodied everything:* For Wilson's general background, see Maas, pp. 14–57. Joseph Goulden with Alexander W. Raffio, *The Death Merchant: The Rise and Fall of Edwin P. Wilson* (New York: Bantam Books, 1985), pp. 3–72.

319   *The Agency man in charge of Maritime:* Clines, interview, May 7, 1992.

319   *Clines relied on Wilson:* U.S. Federal Bureau of Investigation, "Clines Interview," undated. See *Iran-Contra Final Report,* Appendix A, Volume 2, p. 181. Clines, interviews, April 14, 1992, January 14, 1992.

319   *Years later, Shackley could only:* Shackley, interview.

320   *One account of Wilson's departure:* Goulden with Raffio, p. 23.

320   *Richard Secord, introduced to Wilson:* U.S. Federal Bureau of Investigation, "Secord Interviews," undated. See *Iran-Contra Final Report,* Appendix A, Volume 2, p. 172. Secord, p. 185.

320   *The two became reacquainted:* Shackley, interview.

321   *"He was on the fringes":* Ibid.

321   *Suzanne Shackley befriended:* Confidential interview.

321   *The families shared:* Confidential interview.

321   *Suzanne loved to ride:* Maas, p. 53. Shackley deposition, p. 314.

321   *One time Wilson told Shackley:* Kappes, interview.

321   *Shackley later declared:* Shackley, interview.

321   *Wilson was all over the map:* Kwitny, pp. 114–119.

321   *A 1981 report:* "CIA Fears Former Agent Will Spill Secrets to Block Probe," *Wilmington News Journal,* September 13, 1981.

321   *In another scheme, Wilson recruited:* Rodriguez and Weisman, pp. 251–254.

322   *Shortly after the Lebanon mission:* Ibid., p. 254.

322   *Eventually Donald Nielsen:* Maas, pp. 55–56.

322   *At a February lunch:* Goulden with Raffio, pp. 63–66.

322   *Then Inman heard from Shackley:* "CIA Fears Former Agent Will Spill Secrets to Block Probe," *Wilmington News Journal,* September 13, 1981.

322   *Before the task force was disbanded:* Jack L. Bowers, "Navy Program for Clandestine Intelligence Collection; disestablishment of," July 20, 1976. Bowers was Acting Secretary of the Navy.

322   *On August 4, 1976:* Shackley deposition, pp. 55, 166–167, 282. Theodore G. Shackley, "Mr. Albert Hakim, Iranian National and Import/Exporter Dealing Primarily in Security Systems and Technology of Interest to Military Establishments and Intelligence Services," August 5, 1976. See *Iran-Contra Final Report,* Appendix A, Volume 2, p. 168.

323   *The CIA cooperated with SAVAK:* William Sullivan, "General Nassiri Re-

lieved as Head of SAVAK," June 6, 1978. This is a cable Ambassador Sullivan sent to State Department headquarters. Confidential interview with a Deputy Director for Operations.

323 *The CIA was failing in Iran:* U.S. House of Representatives, Permanent Select Committee on Intelligence, *A Staff Report: Iran: Evaluation of U.S. Intelligence Performance Prior to November 1978* (Washington, D.C.: Government Printing Office, 1979).

323 *A 1976 review of reporting:* David Blee, "Part I, Reporting Assessment—FOCUS Iran," November 4, 1976.

323 *In 1977, Agency analysts: A Staff Report: Iran: Evaluation of U.S. Intelligence Performance Prior to November 1978.*

323 *He saw a chance:* Clines, interview, April 14, 1992.

323 *In his August 5 memo:* Theodore G. Shackley, "Mr. Albert Hakim, Iranian National and Import/Exporter Dealing Primarily in Security Systems and Technology of Interest to Military Establishments and Intelligence Services."

324 *At the same time, Hakim was developing: Iran-Contra Final Report,* p. 329. Shackley deposition, pp. 59–60. Maas, pp. 58–59.

324 *Shackley, as ADDO, usually:* Shackley deposition, p. 295.

324 *In an August 16 memo:* Theodore G. Shackley, "Mr. Albert Hakim, Iranian National and Import/Exporter," August 16, 1976. See *Iran-Contra Final Report,* Appendix A, Volume 2, p. 165.

324 *Von Marbod was not in a:* "IBEX: Deadly Symbol of U.S. Arms Sales Problems," *The Washington Post,* January 2, 1977.

324 *Shackley, Clines, Secord, and von Marbod:* U.S. Federal Bureau of Investigation, "Clines Interview."

325 *Whether Shackley knew it: Iran-Contra Final Report,* p. 329.

325 *By this time, Wilson and Terpil:* Maas, pp. 61–62.

325 *The man Wilson had in mind:* Maas, pp. 64–68. Thomas Clines, "Rafael Quintero—Activities re Libya," September 20, 1976.

325 *Clines sometimes took Quintero:* Affidavit of Shirley A. Brill, July 15, 1988.

325 *In 1987, Shackley told congressional:* Shackley deposition, p. 130.

325 *In a brief reply:* U.S. Central Intelligence Agency, untitled cable, August 18, 1976. See *Iran-Contra Final Report,* Appendix A, Volume 2, p. 159.

326 *Eleven years after these events:* Shackley deposition, pp. 57–58, 280–282.

326 *Kevin Mulcahy spent:* Maas, pp. 69–74. "The Qaddafi Connection," *The New York Times,* June 14, 1981. "Exposing the Libyan Link," *The New York Times,* June 21, 1981.

327 *A month earlier, John Harper:* Goulden with Raffio, p. 102.

327 *Meanwhile, Quintero and two Cubans:* Maas, pp. 69–81. Goulden with Raffio, pp. 102–110.

327 *Clines had no choice:* Thomas Clines, "Rafael Quintero—Activities re Libya," September 20, 1976.

328 *In a separate report:* Thomas Clines, "Rafael Quintero—Activities re Libya," a memorandum to the Inspector General, September 20, 1976.

328 *Its officers spoke:* Clines, interview, April 14, 1992.

328 *When questioned by the I.G.:* Goulden with Raffio, p. 116.

328 *"We didn't want to muddy":* John Waller, interview, February 4, 1993.

328 *"It's hard to dignify":* Goulden with Raffio, p. 116. See "Rooting Out Abuse at the CIA: A Clash Over Means, Not Ends," *The New York Times,* September 30, 1978.

328 *The Agency was struggling:* Theodore Shackley, "Policy Issues Concerning Appearance of Agency Personnel as Witnesses for Department of Justice," August 27, 1976. Anthony A. Lapham, August 27, 1976, "Policy Issue Concerning Appearance of Agency Personnel as Witnesses for Department of Justice," August 27, 1976.

329 *Shackley was overseeing Agency endeavors:* Theodore G. Shackley, "Offer of Alleged Uranium Sample," July 21, 1976.

329 *In October and November:* John Dinges and Saul Landau, *Assassination on Embassy Row* (New York: Pantheon Books, 1980), pp. 243–244. "No New Leads Uncovered in Letelier Probe," *The Washington Post,* November 1, 1976.

329 *At the same time, the CIA station:* Confidential interview with CIA officer in Chile.

329 *While the misleading leaks poured:* Jack Murray, untitled memorandum, October 29, 1976. The memo recorded Murray's discussion with Larry Laser, a DDO officer.

329 *A subsequent investigation uncovered:* Dinges and Landau, pp. 382–388. Taylor Branch and Eugene M. Propper, *Labyrinth* (New York: The Viking Press, 1982), pp. 1–14.

329 *In 1989, Robert Scherrer:* Saul Landau, untitled notes of interview with Robert Scherrer, March 21, 1989.

329 *The CIA "has weathered":* "Bush Says the CIA 'Weathered Storm,'" *The Washington Post,* September 17, 1976.

329 *Jack Anderson revealed:* "CIA Trained Iranian Secret Police," *The Washington Post,* November 4, 1976.

329 *One news account declared:* "CIA Linked to 1971 Swine Virus in Cuba," *The Washington Post,* January 9, 1977.

329 *The socialist Ethiopian:* "Ethiopia Denounces CIA," *The Washington Post,* October 8, 1976.

330 *In Jamaica, Prime Minister:* "Jamaica's Emergency Rule Reduces Political Violence," *The New York Times,* July 16, 1976.

330 *In 1977, Penthouse magazine:* Ernest Volkman and John Cummings, "Murder As Usual," *Penthouse,* December 1977.

330 *Years later, Tom Clines:* Clines, interview, April 14, 1992.

330 *Prior to the election:* Hamer, interview, March 13, 1991.

330 *On the hustings:* Ranelagh, p. 632.

330 *A year ago, in December of 1975:* "U.S. Probes ITT-CIA Testimony," *The Washington Post,* January 29, 1976.

330 *A federal grand jury began:* Powers, p. 385.

330 *In July, he ordered:* William W. Wells, "The ITT/Chile Investigation," July 13, 1976.

330 *Bush was trying to protect:* "As CIA Director, Bush Sought to Restrict Probe of Agency Officials by Justice Dept.," *The Los Angeles Times,* September

30, 1988. Robert L. Keuch, "Criminal Investigation—Richard Helms," October 14, 1976. Keuch was the deputy attorney general for the criminal division.

331 *Bush managed to defend:* George Bush, letter to Edward H. Levi, October 14, 1976. Levi was the Attorney General of the United States.

331 *Subpoenas arrived:* John Murray, untitled notes, October 29, 1976.

331 *He was called before:* G. Allen Carver, Jr., "Richard M. Helms et al.," November 3, 1976. Carver was a Justice Department lawyer.

331 *He borrowed money:* John Murray, untitled notes, October 29, 1976.

331 *A bad sign arrived:* "ITT Ex-Official Charged With Holding Back Data," *The Washington Post,* November 6, 1976. "CIA Knew of False Testimony," *The Washington Post,* December 23, 1976. "CIA-ITT Conspiracy Charged at Hearing," *The New York Times,* December 23, 1976.

331 *As Justice attorneys dissected:* Dolores Murray, "Memorandum to Hamilton Jordan," December 17, 1976. "CIA Bugging Micronesian Negotiators," *The Washington Post,* December 12, 1976. "Justice Dept. Studies Surveillance by CIA on Micronesia Talks," *The New York Times,* December 12, 1976. "Micronesia Aide Bids Ford Halt CIA's Surveillance," *The New York Times,* December 15, 1976. "Inouye Panel Will Probe CIA Role in Micronesia," *The Washington Post,* December 21, 1976. "Kissinger Tied to CIA Surveillance," *The Washington Post,* May 4, 1977.

332 *After Wiecha botched:* William W. Wells, "Personnel Announcement, International Activities Staff," September 29, 1976.

332 *On December 17, she sent:* Dolores Murray, "Memorandum to Hamilton Jordan." Dolores Murray, interview.

333 *On May 31, 1976:* "Saigon's Secrets Seized," *The Washington Post,* May 31, 1976.

333 *Shackley was to be a point:* Leo J. Dunn, "Destruction of CIA Documents in Saigon," June 3, 1976. Robert W. Gambino, "Frank Warren Snepp III," June 22, 1976.

333 *At a Washington-area restaurant:* Thomas Polgar, untitled cable, June 21, 1976. Snepp, pp. 576–577.

334 *On June 30, Shackley:* Theodore G. Shackley, "Mr. Frank Snepp and His Plans to Write a Book on Vietnam," July 1, 1976.

334 *Throughout the summer, Layton:* B. E. Layton, "Frank Snepp," August 5, 1976. B. E. Layton, "Meeting with Mr. Frank Snepp," September 3, 1976. B. E. Layton, "A Personal Appreciation of Mr. Frank Snepp," September 7, 1976. B. E. Layton, "Conversation with Mr. Frank Snepp," November 3, 1976.

334 *But at a September 28 meeting:* Robert W. Gambino, "Frank W. Snepp, III," October 4, 1976.

334 *Smith's book:* Joseph Burkholder Smith, pp. 11–13.

335 *In late December, Layton:* B. E. Layton, "Conversation with Frank Snepp," December 23, 1976.

335 *At a January 3, 1977, meeting:* Robert W. Gambino, "Frank W. Snepp, III," January 4, 1977.

335 *In March of 1977:* McArthur, interview. Theodore G. Shackley, "Frank Snepp," March 14, 1977.

336 *On March 9, 1977:* Turner, pp. 9–20.

336 *In the years after his rocky tenure:* Turner, interview.

336 *"I came in naive":* Ibid.

336 *"It was very unsettling":* Ibid.

336 *His apprehensions were:* Turner, pp. 43–45. Turner, interview.

337 *"The message of the case":* Turner, interview.

337 *CIA people immediately:* Ranelagh, p. 636. Confidential interviews with senior CIA officials.

337 *One time he visited a station:* Confidential interview with senior CIA official.

337 *Williams complained to:* Confidential interview with senior CIA official.

337 *When in mid-April the admiral:* Turner, pp. 55–57. Turner, interview. "CIA Director Fires 2 for Aiding Ex-Agents," *The Washington Post,* April 27, 1977.

338 *Most startling to Turner:* Turner, interview.

338 *Clines hurried to:* Turner, interview. Clines, interview, April 14, 1992.

338 *"It was beyond":* Turner, interview.

338 *Turner called Shackley:* Turner, p. 58. Turner, interview.

339 *The CIA learned from:* W. R. Johnson and P. L. Johnson, "Frank Snepp," March 15, 1977. The Johnsons, William and Pat, were a husband-wife pair of retired CIA officers.

339 *And on April 10, 1977:* Stockwell, pp. 269–275.

339 *Days after Stockwell's letter:* B. E. Layton, "Conversation with Mr. Frank Snepp Concerning Mr. John Stockwell," April 15, 1977.

339 *Stockwell soon learned:* W. R. Johnson, "Snepp/Stockwell," April 30, 1977.

339 *But even as Snepp claimed:* William Parmenter, "Conversation with Frank Snepp," April 15, 1977.

340 *In a memo to Turner:* Frank Snepp, "Memorandum to the Director," undated.

340 *In a subsequent memo, Shackley:* Theodore G. Shackley, "Mr. Frank Snepp," May 9, 1977.

340 *Knoche reported to Turner:* E. H. Knoche, "Frank Snepp," May 10, 1977.

340 *The two met:* John D. Morrison Jr., "Director's Meeting with Frank Snepp," May 17, 1977.

340 *Turner wanted an abridged:* Turner, interview.

341 *Turner kept over a dozen:* McMahon, interview.

341 *"The covert action cupboard":* Turner, p. 84.

341 *"They never left my office":* Turner, interview.

341 *The admiral was skeptical:* Turner, p. 176. Turner, interview.

341 *Shackley, though, viewed Turner:* Shackley, p. 125.

342 *Turner also saw a cautiousness:* Turner, interview.

342 *The DCI, Shackley later griped:* Shackley, interview.

342 *Turner did believe that:* Ranelagh, pp. 636–637. Turner, interview.

342 *While Turner was out of town:* Turner, interview. "Knoche Is Resigning CIA's No. 2 Post," *The Washington Post,* July 14, 1977.

343 *Just what Langley needed:* Shackley, p. 123.

343 *Since moving into Langley:* Turner, interview.

343 *On August 7, 1977:* Ibid.

343 *Shackley thought Turner:* Shackley, p. 121.

343 *"Had they put up":* Turner, interview.

343 *"This made his burden":* Jameson, interview, April 3, 1990.

344 *The pink slips:* " 'Dear John' Letters at the CIA," *The Washington Post,* November 26, 1977. "In a Way, the End of an Era," *The Washington Post,* December 4, 1977. "CIA Shaken by Job Cutbacks," *The Washington Post,* December 4, 1977. "CIA Author of 212 Dismissal Notes Is Ousted as Operations Branch Chief," *The Washington Post,* December 29, 1978. Confidential interviews with senior CIA officials.

344 *Station chiefs in:* "Cutbacks by CIA's New Director Creating Turmoil Within Agency," *The New York Times,* December 10, 1977.

344 *But, as Turner later claimed:* Turner, interview.

344 *Shackley, who had drawn:* Shackley, pp. 122–123.

344 *The staff reductions did not:* McMahon, interview.

344 *Richard Helms, the former Director:* "Helms Fined $2,000, Term Suspended," *The Washington Post,* November 5, 1977.

345 *Finally, the Agency took:* "Defense for Ex-CIA Agent Snepp to Focus on 1st Amendment Issue," *The Washington Post,* March 9, 1978. "High Court Backs CIA on Curb on Articles Its Employees Write," *The Washington Post,* February 20, 1980.

346 *After the Halloween Massacre:* Turner, interview.

346 *When he asked a group:* Ibid.

347 *"Ted Shackley should've":* McMahon, interview.

347 *Turner had to do something:* Turner, interview.

347 *Shortly after Christmas:* Confidential interview with senior CIA official.

347 *After the session:* Confidential interview with senior CIA official.

347 *Turner's decision to replace:* "CIA Author of 212 Dismissal Notes Is Ousted as Operations Branch Chief," *The Washington Post,* December 29, 1977.

348 *The assignment, recalled a Shackley colleague:* Lapham, interview.

348 *The NITC was:* Turner, pp. 260–262. Turner, interview.

348 *Shackley's new home:* Fred Feer, interview, April 7, 1992.

348 *On the wall of Shackley's office:* Baron, interview.

348 *Shackley told people:* Confidential interview with senior CIA official.

348 *His friend Tom Clines:* Clines, interview, April 14, 1992.

349 *Clines sat down:* Ibid.

349 *While still a Company man:* Clines, interview, April 14, 1992. Federal Bureau of Investigation, interviews with Douglas Schlachter, December 11, 1981, December 29, 1981. "Proposal to the Government of Nicaragua," undated.

349 *Since Wilson's brush:* Maas, pp. 85–101.

350 *Clines later said:* Clines, interview, April 14, 1992. Deed of Bargain and Sale, August 2, 1978. Deed of Gift, August 29, 1983.

350 *After the Nicaraguan plan:* Clines, interview, April 14, 1992. Goulden with Raffio, pp. 155–156.

350   *To hundreds of Company people:* "Carter Seeks to Boost CIA's Morale, Delivers Pep Talks at Langley," *The Washington Post,* August 17, 1978.

350   *Three months later, Carter:* "Carter Criticizes Quality of U.S. Intelligence Abroad," *The Washington Post,* November 25, 1978.

351   *In March of 1978, the Justice Department:* "2 ITT Aides Charged in Chile Probe," *The Washington Post,* March 21, 1978. *Berrellez* motion. U.S. Central Intelligence Agency, untitled cable, March 21, 1978. Transcript of October 23, 1978, confidential conference, p. 19.

351   *In the summer of 1978:* U.S. Marshal Service, "Instruction and Process Record," August 14, 1978.

351   *Justice considered putting:* Subpoena Duces Tecum, *United States of America v. Robert Berrellez,* Case No. 78–00120, October 11, 1978. "ITT Indictment Is Cut Back," *The Washington Post,* August 19, 1978.

351   *The morning of October 23:* "Trial Could Shed Light on CIA Activity in Chile," *The Washington Post,* October 23, 1978.

351   *The trial began with:* Transcript of October 23, 1978, confidential conference, pp. 4–20, 83, 97.

352   *At a bench conference:* "ITT Jury Dismissed, Deadline Set," *The Washington Post,* October 25, 1978. "Bring Out CIA Data or Drop Case, US Told," *The Baltimore Sun,* October 25, 1978.

352   The Washington Post *editorialized:* "Countering 'Graymail,' " *The Washington Post,* November 1, 1978.

352   *In February of 1979:* "U.S. Drops Case Against ITT Aide to Protect Data," *The Washington Post,* February 9, 1979.

352   *Several times Shackley approached:* Confidential interview with senior CIA official. "Tinker, Turner, Sailor, Spy," *New York,* March 3, 1980. This article was written by Michael Ledeen, a future business associate of Shackley.

353   *After twenty-eight years:* Resumé of Theodore G. Shackley.

353   *During his final days:* Turner, interview.

353   *Turner in his memoirs:* Turner, p. 217.

CHAPTER 10. IN THE COLD

Page

354   *In a suburban:* Clines, interview, April 14, 1992.

355   *But he needed the help:* U.S. Federal Bureau of Investigation, "Clines Interview," March 23, 1982. See *Iran-Contra Final Report,* Appendix A, Volume 2, p. 178. Edward Coughlin, "Arcadia Loan to International Research & Trade Ltd.," August 24, 1981. Clines, interview, April 14, 1992. Maas, pp. 138–139. Edward Coughlin, untitled memorandum, undated.

355   *In the spring of 1979:* U.S. Federal Bureau of Investigation, "Clines Interview," March 23, 1982. "Ex-CIA Agent's Associates Run Arms Export Concerns," *The New York Times,* September 6, 1981.

355   *Clines invited Shackley:* Shackley deposition, pp. 12, 27–28, 213–218, 226. Clines, interview, April 14, 1992. U.S. Central Intelligence Agency, "Interview Luncheon with Thomas G. Clines at Casa Maria Restaurant," February 10, 1982. This memo was written by two Inspector General officers.

356 *Shackley was aware:* Shackley deposition, p. 225.

356 *He chatted several times:* Kwitny, p. 312.

356 *When Michael Hand:* Shackley deposition, pp. 322–323.

356 *There was no clear link:* Kwitny, pp. 315–318.

357 *Shackley complained to Agency:* Goulden with Raffio, p. 156.

357 *Shackley left Clines:* Shackley deposition, pp. 17–18, 23–24, 27.

357 *"Political risk assessment":* Theodore G. Shackley, "Using Political Risk Analysis to Aid Decisionmaking," *Chief Executive,* Summer 1983. This magazine was started and owned by John Deuss, a Shackley client.

357 *Around the time Shackley:* Peter Karlow, interview, May 28, 1992.

357 *But Shackley and his associates worried:* Confidential interview with RAI employee.

357 *Shackley also established:* Shackley deposition, pp. 36–40. Donald "Jamie" Jameson, interview with David MacMichael, May 5, 1988. This is a transcript of a taped conversation between Jameson and MacMichael, an investigator for the Christic Institute. Hereinafter, Jameson-MacMichael interview. Johnny V. Carter, interview with David MacMichael, April 1, 1988. This is a transcript of a taped conversation between Carter, a former TGS employee, and MacMichael. Hereinafter, Carter-MacMichael interview.

358 *Though he threw:* Jameson, interview, March 30, 1990.

358 *In the early phases:* "Coming in From the Cold, Going Out to the Bush Campaign," *The Washington Post,* March 1, 1980. See U.S. House of Representatives, Committee on Post Office and Civil Service, Subcommittee on Human Resources, *Unauthorized Transfers of Nonpublic Information During the 1980 Presidential Campaign* (Washington: Government Printing Office, 1984), pp. 1112–1114.

358 *Hazel Shackley worked:* Jameson-MacMichael interview.

358 *Shortly after Bush was named:* Jameson, interview, March 30, 1990. Jameson-MacMichael interview. Shackley, interview.

358 *Rafael Quintero was saying:* Kenneth Conklin, undated notes of discussion with Quintero. The notes were written shortly after August 4, 1980.

358 *Ledeen, a bearded forty-year-old:* "Ledeen Seems to Relish Iran Insider's Role," *The Washington Post,* February 2, 1987. "A Mole in our Midst?" *New York,* October 2, 1978.

359 *In a March 3, 1980:* "Tinker, Turner, Sailor, Spy," *New York,* March 3, 1980.

359 *General Giuseppe Santovito:* Michael Ledeen, interview, April 6, 1993. Deposition of Michael Ledeen, *Iran-Contra Affair,* Appendix B, Volume 15, pp. 1316–1318. Shackley deposition, pp. 196–197, 472–473.

359 *But near the time of this exercise:* "Why an Italian Spy Got Closely Involved In the Billygate Affair," *The Wall Street Journal,* August 8, 1985. "Qaddafi, Arafat, and Billy Carter," *The New Republic,* November 1, 1980.

360 *Using Felix Rodriguez:* Shackley deposition, pp. 132, 425–427.

360 *The Iranian-American contacted:* Shackley deposition, pp. 63–88, 364. Jameson-MacMichael interview.

360 *On December 5 and 6, 1980:* Roy Godson, ed., *Intelligence Requirements*

for the 1980s: Covert Action (Washington: National Strategy Information Center, 1981), pp. 135–165.

362 *Shackley's presentation to the:* Theodore G. Shackley, *The Third Option: An American View of Counterinsurgency Operations* (New York: Dell, 1988). This is the paperback version.

363 *His friend and Agency colleague:* Rodriguez and Weisman, pp. 1–10.

363 *In* The Washington Post, *reviewer:* "Using Our Intelligence to Beat Them at Their Own Game," *The Washington Post,* June 28, 1981.

363 *For years, federal officers:* Maas, pp. 102–136.

364 *He took his story:* Maas, p. 183.

364 *Hersh produced a two-part:* "The Qaddafi Connection," *The New York Times,* June 14, 1981. "Exposing the Libyan Link," *The New York Times,* June 21, 1981.

364 *A few weeks after the Hersh:* U.S. Federal Bureau of Investigation, untitled report of Wilson meeting, July 22, 1981. Richard Pedersen, "Wilson/Terpil et al.," July 20, 1981. This is a report of the Rome meeting written by a BATF agent who attended the session.

364 *A September 6, 1981:* "Ex-CIA Agent's Associates Run Arms Export Concerns," *The New York Times,* September 6, 1981.

364 *Four days later, a front-page:* "Relationship With CIA Aide Gave Credibility to Arms Seller," *The Washington Post,* September 10, 1981.

365 *Clines showed up:* Edward Coughlin, "Arcadia Loan to International Research & Trade," August 24, 1981.

365 *Salem eventually provided:* U.S. Federal Bureau of Investigation, "Clines Interview," March 23, 1982. Maas, p. 224.

365 *"If there's an 'old-boy'":* "Panel in House Will Investigate Ex-CIA Agent," *The New York Times,* September 19, 1981.

365 *The Senate intelligence committee:* Simmons, interview, April 10, 1992.

365 *He questioned the former ADDO:* Maas, pp. 233–234.

365 *Years later, he acknowledged:* Shackley deposition, p. 228.

366 *In October of 1981:* Maas, pp. 234–235.

366 *On November 9, 1981:* Secord with Wurts, pp. 183–197.

366 *With Barcella interested in him:* Maas, p. 235.

366 *Doug Schlachter had told Barcella:* Ibid., p. 231.

366 *Then in December of 1981:* Ibid., p. 278.

366 *Barcella concentrated on capturing:* Ibid., pp. 235–268.

366 *Meanwhile, Clines's EATSCO:* Ibid., pp. 247–248.

367 *In suburban Virginia:* Excerpt of Quintero Interview. This is a document that surfaced in the course of the Wilson cases; its author is unidentified.

367 *Wilson also discussed:* Goulden with Raffio, p. 388.

367 *"The Ed Wilson I knew":* Shackley, interview.

367 *In a sharp, defensive tone:* Ibid.

368 *On March 21, 1983:* [Deleted author], "Meeting at the White House, 21 March 1983," March 21, 1983. Declaration of Katherine M. Stricker, *Edwin P. Wilson v. Department of Justice, et al.,* U.S. District Court for the District of Columbia, Case No. 87–2415, November 8, 1990. This is a Freedom of Informa-

tion Act lawsuit brought by Wilson for EATSCO records. Stricker is the Information Review Officer of the CIA's Directorate of Operations.

369 *A month after the White House:* Stanley Sporkin, "Note for DCI, DDCI, ExDir," April 26, 1983. Edwin P. Wilson, "Edwin P. Wilson Operations in Morocco & Egypt," May 12, 1981.

370 *In the case of Tom Clines:* Transcript of guilty plea conference, *United States of America vs. Systems Services International,* January 16, 1984.

370 *The Justice Department continued: Iran-Contra Final Report,* p. 328. *Iran-Contra Final Report,* Appendix A, Volume 2, pp. 188–189.

370 *He advised Hakim:* Shackley deposition, pp. 70–78, 440–443. Theodore G. Shackley, letter to Albert Hakim, March 1, 1983.

370 *He and Secord:* Shackley deposition, p. 109.

371 *William Friedman, a Washington consultant:* William Friedman, interview, June 7, 1992. D. C. MacMichael, "Meeting with William J. Friedman," March 18, 1988.

371 *Shackley hoped that TGS:* Jameson-MacMichael interview.

371 *Due to political considerations:* The report was untitled and unsigned but marked "Secret-Proprietary" and dated March 8, 1984. Correspondence between William Friedman and Daniel Arnold indicate that Arnold wrote the report.

371 *Joe Clark, the company's president:* Joe R. Clark, letter to William Friedman, March 16, 1984.

371 *Friedman ended the company's:* Friedman, interview.

372 *Much of Shackley's professional attention:* Shackley deposition, p. 20.

372 *Johannes Christiaan Martinus Augustinus Deuss:* "Feasting on the Oil Glut," *Texas Monthly,* October 1984. "The Mystery Man Who Is Buying Arco's Refinery," *The Philadelphia Inquirer,* June 30, 1985. "The High-Octane World of John Deuss," *Business Week,* June 30, 1986.

372 *But Deuss privately negotiated:* "Top Oilman Fuels Apartheid," *The Observer,* October 26, 1986.

372 *Between 1979 and 1983:* Shipping Research Bureau, "South Africa's Lifeline: Violations of the Oil Embargo, 1983–1984," September 1986.

372 *Much of the oil came:* Shipping Research Bureau, *Newsletter on the Oil Embargo Against South Africa,* June 1985.

372 *Shackley advised Deuss's operations:* Shackley deposition, pp. 98–99.

372 *Once Shackley attempted:* Ibid., pp. 377–385.

373 *It advertised its:* See *Journal of Defense and Diplomacy,* January 1985.

373 *Associates familiar with RAI:* Confidential interviews.

373 *For his own company:* Shackley deposition, pp. 450–451.

373 *TGS International did obtain: Robert J. Springer and RJS Custom Builders, Inc. vs. TGS International, Ltd., Theodore G. Shackley and Vernon W. Gillespie,* U.S. District Court, Eastern District of Virginia, Case No. 84–0052-A. Springer's complaint was filed on January 17, 1984.

373 *Gillespie, a three-tour:* Deposition of Vernon Gillespie, *Appeal of TGS International, Ltd., Before Armed Services Board of Contract Appeals,* June 2, 1988.

374 *"The CIA can be bad boys":* Robert Springer, interview, November 30, 1992.

374 *Shackley viewed Kuwait:* Testimony of Vernon Gillespie, *Appeal of TGS International, Ltd., Before Armed Services Board of Contract Appeals.* Gillespie testified over the course of several days in July of 1988.

374 *Toward the end of 1983:* Opinion by Administrative Judge Paul, *Appeal of TGS International, Ltd., Before Armed Services Board of Contract Appeals,* March 29, 1990.

374 *"It appeared that TGS":* Deposition of Charles R. Kubic, *Appeal of TGS International, Ltd., Before Armed Services Board of Contract Appeals,* June 3, 1988.

374 *At a hearing of the case, Shackley:* Testimony of Theodore Shackley, *Appeal of TGS International, Ltd., Before Armed Services Board of Contract Appeals.* Shackley testified on July 26, 1988.

374 *He tried putting:* Shackley deposition, pp. 359, 373.

374 *Jamie Jameson, his partner:* Shackley deposition, pp. 435–437. Jameson-MacMichael interview. Jameson, interview, April 3, 1990.

375 *In 1983, Jameson and Gillespie met:* Kevin Kattke, interview, October 23, 1992. Jameson, interview, September 28, 1992. Clifford Kiracofe, interview, December 16, 1992. Kiracofe was an aide to Senator Jesse Helms. "Ollie's Army," *New York,* December 7, 1987. "The K-team," *Washington CityPaper,* December 4, 1992.

375 *In 1984, he was approached:* Shackley deposition, pp. 429–433. See House Select Committee to Investigate Covert Arms Transactions with Iran and the Senate Select Committee on Secret Military Assistance to Iran and the Nicaraguan Opposition, *Testimony of Adolfo P. Calero, John K. Singlaub, Ellen C. Garwood, William B. O'Boyle, Joseph Coors, Robert C. Dutton, Felix I. Rodriguez, and Lewis A. Tambs* (Washington: Government Printing Office, 1988), pp. 88–89, 462–465. Singlaub testified on May 20, 1987.

375 *In mid-1984, Shackley flew:* "Explanation of General Hashemi," *Kayhan,* April 23, 1987. This is a letter to the editor written by Hashemi and published in a Farsi language newspaper in London. Amir Taheri, *Nest of Spies* (New York: Pantheon, 1988), p. 166. Shackley deposition, pp. 142–143, 157.

376 *Razmara had come:* Shackley deposition, pp. 65–70.

376 *On the night of November 19:* The account of Shackley's meeting with Ghorbanifar is drawn from the following: *Tower Report,* p. B3, *Iran-Contra Final Report,* pp. 163–164. Shackley deposition, pp. 5–6, 143–157, 262, 324–326, 391–400. Theodore Shackley, "American Hostages in Lebanon," November 22, 1984. Taheri, p. 166. "Explanation of General Hashemi," *Kayhan.*

377 *With a thick file on Ghorbanifar:* Iran-Contra Final Report, pp. 163–164.

378 *Ghorbanifar did not give up:* Ibid., pp. 164–165.

378 *About then, Michael Ledeen:* Ibid., p. 165.

379 *But in May of 1985, Shackley:* Tower Report, pp. B12–13. *Iran-Contra Final Report,* p. 172. Shackley deposition, pp. 202–204. Ledeen deposition, pp. 970–972, 1078, 1454–1455. Ledeen, interview.

380 *While Secord and Hakim were busy:* Shackley deposition, p. 92.

380 *His main pursuer was Daniel Sheehan:* Affidavit of Daniel P. Sheehan, *Tony Avirgan and Martha Honey v. John Hull, et al.,* December 12, 1986. "Law and the Prophet," *Mother Jones,* February/March 1988.

381 *Throughout 1985, Paul Hoven:* Paul Hoven, interview, March 17, 1992.

381 *As Wheaton has related:* Deposition of Gene Wheaton, *Tony Avirgan and Martha Honey v. John Hull, et al.,* U.S. District Court, Southern District of Florida, Case No. 86–1146, March 1–3, 7–8, 1988. "In Search of the Secret Team," *The Village Voice,* May 24, 1988.

381 *When he met Hoven:* Deposition of Carl Jenkins, *Tony Avirgan and Martha Honey v. John Hull, et al.,* March 15, 1988. Wheaton deposition. Carl Jenkins, interview, March 3, 1988. Dearborn, interview.

381 *They had even complained:* Deposition of Cresencio Arcos, *Iran-Contra Final Report,* Appendix B, Volume 1, pp. 1306–1307, 1311, 1313.

381 *Jenkins had occupied space:* Shackley deposition, p. 345.

381 *Hoven set up a meeting:* Hoven, interview.

381 *Rafael Quintero, a key player:* Jenkins, interview. Wheaton deposition.

382 *Sheehan already had developed:* Sheehan affidavit. Daniel Sheehan, interview, May 7, 1993.

382 *Sheehan and Wheaton sat down:* Hoven, interview.

382 *Sheehan spoke a few times:* Jenkins, interview. Hoven, interview.

383 *Throughout the winter and spring:* Martha Honey, interviews, February 8, 1992, May 12, 1993. Brian Barger, interview, May 21, 1993. Barger was an AP reporter in contact with Avirgan and Honey. See Tony Avirgan and Martha Honey, *La Penca: Report of an Investigation* (San José, Costa Rica: Editorial Porvenir, 1985).

383 *It was not until 1993:* "Who Bombed in La Penca," *Washington CityPaper,* August 6, 1993. Tony Avirgan, "Unmasking the La Penca Bomber," *The Nation,* September 6/13, 1993.

384 *The imprisoned rogue officer:* Sheehan, interview, April 13, 1993.

384 *Avirgan and Honey shared:* Tony Avirgan, interview, May 27, 1993. Honey, interview, January 29, 1992

385 *He started telling Jenkins:* Jenkins deposition.

385 *In a Miami federal court:* Civil Complaint, Motion to Amend Civil Complaint, *Tony Avirgan and Martha Honey v. John Hull et al.* The complaint was filed May 29, 1986. The motion was filed July 9, 1986.

385 *"I had been left with":* Hoven, interview.

386 *Shackley learned about:* Shackley deposition, pp. 85–86, 111.

386 *Days later, Shackley and his attorney:* Ibid., pp. 125, 175–176.

386 *Shackley also chatted with Singlaub:* Ibid., pp. 422–423.

386 *In September, federal Judge:* Order Dismissing Complaint Without Prejudice, *Tony Avirgan and Martha Honey v. John Hull et al.,* September 5, 1986.

386 *The White House declared:* "Bay of Pigs Survivors Find Common Cause With Contras," *The Washington Post,* October 26, 1986.

386 *On December 12, 1986:* Sheehan affidavit.

387 *Rob Hager, a lawyer:* Rob Hager, interview, February 24, 1992.

388 *"Shackley is like a black":* Transcript of meeting of board of Fund for Constitutional Government, December 9, 1986.

388 *On January 30, 1987:* Order Denying Motions to Dismiss and Dismissing Count VI with Prejudice, *Tony Avirgan and Martha Honey v. John Hull et al.,* January 30, 1987.

388 *Shackley's role in the Iran initiative:* "The Arms Trafficking Connection," *The Washington Post,* January 18, 1987.

388 *In* The New York Times Magazine: "Oliver North's Strange Recruits," *The New York Times,* January 18, 1987.

389 *The study, parts of which were still secret:* "North's Aides Linked to Australia Study," *The New York Times,* March 8, 1987.

389 *But Shackley kept maintaining:* "Link to Iran Arms Deal and Nugan Bank Denied," *The New York Times,* March 30, 1987.

389 *A Miami Herald investigation:* "Bush Sent Doctor to North Network," *The Miami Herald,* March 15, 1987.

390 *A year after the story:* Jameson-MacMichael interview.

390 *They sent him a subpoena:* "Investigators Issue Subpoenas in Hunt for Money Trail," *The Miami Herald,* March 26, 1987.

390 *The deposition covered:* See Shackley deposition.

390 *Cameron Holmes, the lead interrogator:* Holmes, interview.

390 *In a 1992 interview, Clines:* Clines, interview, April 14, 1992.

391 *On February 7, 1984:* Oliver North, untitled diary, February 7, 1984.

391 *Rodriguez claimed in his memoirs:* Rodriguez and Weisman, p. 264.

391 *North, on December 20, 1984:* Oliver North, untitled diary, December 20, 1984.

391 *But in a 1991 interview, Shackley:* Shackley, interview.

391 *And Clarridge, in April of 1984: Iran-Contra Final Report,* p. 38.

392 *"Ted is hypersensitive":* Jameson, interview, April 3, 1990.

392 *But in 1983, Bill Kohlmann:* Kohlmann, interview.

392 *After talking to Ledeen:* Oliver North, untitled diary, June 3, 1985.

392 *And on April 17, 1986:* Oliver North, untitled diary, April 17, 1986.

392 *The Christics were still:* The author was in contact with several Christic employees and Sheehan throughout this period, and he received most of their public materials.

392 *At one of Sheehan's speeches:* "The Law and the Prophet," *Mother Jones.*

393 *Shortly before Christmas of 1987:* Deposition of Edwin Wilson, *Tony Avirgan and Martha Honey v. John Hull et al.,* December 17–18, 1987.

393 *"You and I," read one:* Christic Institute, solicitation letter, January 1, 1988.

394 *The political cult of:* "Long Hot Summer for Irangate's 'Invisible Men'?" *Executive Intelligence Review,* June 24, 1988. *E.I.R.* is published by the LaRouche operation. See also in the same issue "'Theodore Shackley's 'Third Option,'" "Behind Irangate: the Lonrho Link," and "John Deuss, Shackley's Piggybank." "Drugs, Banks and Money Laundering: The Sordid Side of the Story That the News Media Isn't Telling You," *The Spotlight,* 1989. This is a report published by the Liberty Lobby.

394 *During the Iran-Contra investigation:* "North Riddle Over London Arms Link," *The Observer,* July 26, 1987. "Fictitious Oliver North Role," *The London Times,* July 25, 1988.

394 *In early March of 1988:* Deposition of Gene Wheaton, *Tony Avirgan and Martha Honey v. John Hull, et al.,* March 1–3, 7–8, 1988. The author attended this deposition.

395 *One day Shackley and Vernon Gillespie:* Hoven, interview. Affidavit of Paul Hoven, February 20, 1988.

395 *Shackley gathered affidavits:* Affidavit of Douglas Schlachter (December 3, 1987), Affidavit of John H. Harper (November 24, 1987), Affidavit of William Hamilton (January 25, 1988), Affidavit of Paul Hoven (February 20, 1988), Affidavit of Robert Owen (February 24, 1988), Affidavit of Richard V. Secord (September 30, 1987), Affidavit of John K. Singlaub (October 2, 1987), Affidavit of Adolfo Calero (February 25, 1988), Affidavit of Carl Jenkins (November 21, 1987), *Tony Avirgan and Martha Honey v. John Hull et al.*

395 *He considered suing Shackley:* Affidavit of Paul S. Blumenthal, *Edwin Paul Wilson vs. United States of America,* U.S. District Court, Eastern District of Virginia, Case No. 87–009-M, February 29, 1988. Associated Press, June 19, 1987.

395 *Wilson's lawyer acquired:* Affidavit of Lloyd D. Jones, February 22, 1988.

396 *Even more fascinating:* Affidavit of Shirley A. Brill, July 15, 1988.

396 *When called before the Iran-Contra:* Senate Select Committee on Secret Military Assistance to Iran and the Nicaraguan Opposition and House Select Committee to Investigate Covert Arms Transactions with Iran, *Testimony of Adolfo P. Calero, John K. Singlaub, Ellen C. Garwood, William B. O'Boyle, Joseph Coors, Robert C. Dutton, Felix I. Rodriguez, and Lewis A. Tambs,* pp. 331–332, 337. Rodriguez testified on May 27 and 28, 1987.

396 *According to Rodriguez's own:* Rodriguez and Weisman, pp. 251–253.

397 *King declared Sheehan's:* "Supreme Court Leaves $1 Million Sanction Intact in Nicaraguan Bombing Case," *The New York Times,* January 14, 1992.

397 *Sheehan and his followers:* Sheehan interview, May 7, 1993.

397 *Shackley took his wife:* "Letters to the Editor," *Periscope,* Summer 1988. *Periscope* is the newsletter of the Association of Former Intelligence Officers.

397 *His friends estimated:* McArthur, interview.

397 *He appealed to his fellow:* "Letters to the Editor," *Periscope.*

397 *"This attack," Shackley wrote:* Ibid.

397 The Journal of Defense and Diplomacy—*a publication:* "The Christic Institute: Enforcing the Brezhnev Doctrine in Central America," *The Journal of Defense and Diplomacy,* Study Series No. 3.

397 *In a media interview, Secord:* "The Christic Institute's Legal Terrorism," *Human Events,* November 25, 1987.

397 *In his memoirs, Secord:* Secord with Wurts, p. 278.

398 *In 1989, Susan Huck:* Huck, pp. 145–152.

398 *In February of 1989, Judge King:* "Defendants Win Fees in Suit on Contra Aid," *The New York Times,* February 6, 1989.

398 *From the Christic payment:* Shackley, interview.

398 *According to Wheaton:* Wheaton, interview, April 7, 1993.

399 *During the two-week Clines trial:* The author attended the trial.

400 *Shackley wrote another book:* Theodore G. Shackley, Robert L. Oatman, Richard A. Finney, *You're the Target: Coping with Terror and Crime* (McLean, VA: New World Publishing, 1989), pp. 9, 15, 18, 27, 37, 97, 127.

400 *He delivered a lecture:* The author attended the lecture.

400 *He gave a talk:* The author attended the event.

401 *He was active:* See *Periscope,* the newsletter of the association for 1991 to 1994.

401 *Shackley even participated:* Charlie Hoots, letter to author, October 17, 1990.

EPILOGUE

Page

402 *"I have great respect":* Oleg Kalugin, interview, September 4, 1992.

404 *"It's hard for people":* Confidential interview with former senior CIA official, June 3, 1993.

405 *"Tell [Corn] thanks":* Huck, p. 66.

405 *In his reply to me:* Theodore G. Shackley, letter to author, June 13, 1989.

405 *Finally, in June of 1991:* Jack McKay, letter to author, June 10, 1991. McKay was an attorney representing Shackley.

INDEX